Classical conditioning and instrumental learning

John F. Hall
The Pennsylvania State University

Classical conditioning and instrumental learning:

a contemporary approach

J. B. Lippincott Company
Philadelphia
New York   San Jose   Toronto

ISBN 0-397-47346-X

Library of Congress Catalog Card
Number 75-32539
Printed in the United States of America

135798642

Library of Congress Cataloging in Publication Data

Hall, John Fry
    Classical conditioning and instru-
    mental learning.

    Bibliography: p.
    Includes index.
        1. Learning, Psychology of. 2. Con-
    ditioned response. 3. Motivation in edu-
    cation. I. Title. [DNLM: 1. Conditioning,
    Classical. 2. Conditioning, Operant.
    BF319 H117c]
    LB1051.H226   370.15'2   75-32539
    ISBN 0-397-47346-X

Contents

v

Preface

Although learning has often been thought of as a general process, I am now convinced that the examination of learning principles, independent of the kind of task which is used, is not a profitable venture. Accordingly, I have written a text organized around two frequently delineated learning paradigms—classical conditioning and instrumental learning. As with earlier texts which I have written, my approach has been an empirical one; within each paradigm, the material has been organized around an examination of those variables which have occupied the attention of the contemporary investigators. The text should be appropriate for advanced undergraduate students.

I should like to convey my appreciation to Russell M. Church, Isidore Gormezano, and Delos D. Wickens, who read portions of the text, for their many helpful suggestions. I am indebted to Esther Beittel for typing the bulk of the manuscript and to Elaine Terranova of J. B. Lippincott for making the text a much more readable one. Finally, I am particularly grateful to my wife, Jean, not only for her help with the myriad tasks that are involved in writing a text but also for her understanding and patience during the research and writing.

I should like to express my thanks to the following organizations who gave me permission to use the figures and tables obtained from their publications: Academic Press, Inc., American Association for the Advancement of Science, The American Psychological Association, Grason-Stadler, Irvington Publishers, Inc., The Journal Press, Lafayette Instrument Company, Perceptual and Motor Skills, Prentice-

Hall, Inc., The Psychonomic Society, Scott, Foresman and Company, the Society for the Experimental Analysis of Behavior, the Society for Psychophysiological Research, the University of California Press, and the University of Illinois Press.

I should like also to thank the many authors, who in cooperation with the publishers, permitted publication of their materials. Acknowledgment of their contribution has been provided in the specific figures and tables located throughout the text.

John F. Hall

University Park, Pa.

1
An Introduction to Conditioning and Learning

There is little subject matter in psychology that has generated as much interest as the topics of conditioning and learning. It is not difficult to account for this preoccupation since most individuals, at least those living in North America and Europe, spend a considerable portion of their lives in educational institutions where learning is their major activity. But, obviously, learning is not confined to such institutions. We learn to ride bicycles, drive automobiles, pilot airplanes, adjust carburetors, repair watches, smoke cigarettes, and play golf. Moreover, it is likely that the learning process helps to shape many of the behavior patterns which society has labeled as normal or abnormal, and which contribute to the uniqueness of one's personality. The pervasiveness of the learning process, then, is undoubtedly one of the primary reasons why psychologists have been interested in its analysis.

The reasons why we learn are not always clear. This obscurity is a product of a number of factors. An important one, certainly, is that in most learning situations, the environment is poorly controlled; therefore, it becomes difficult to determine those variables which have (or have not) contributed to the process. As a result, psychologists have taken learning into the laboratory in an effort to control the learner's environment and thus to better determine how learning takes place.

How Shall Learning Be Defined?

What do we mean by the term learning? Although most of us would be unable to provide a precise definition of the term, in general, we associate learning with instruction, teaching, and training; frequently, we think of it as a process whereby we gain information or acquire skills.

If we seek a psychological definition, we can find a variety of them. Some of them are:

> Learning is a process by which the behavior of an organism is modified by experience. . . . In other words, learning is a process inferred from examination of differences in some overt performance by an organism at two or more points in time (Jung, 1968, p. 6).
> Learning is a relatively enduring change in behavior which is a function of prior behavior (usually called practice) (Marx, 1969a, p. 5).
> Learning is a relatively permanent process resulting from practice and reflected in a change in performance (Logan, 1970, p. 2).
> Learning is a relatively permanent change in behavior resulting from conditions of practice (Kling, 1971, p. 551).
> Learning may be defined as a relatively permanent change in behavior which occurs as a result of experience (Tarpy, 1975, p. 4).

The definitions provided have much in common. There is a consensus that learning is a process taking place within the organism, inferred from changes in performance, and arising as a result of experience or practice.

There is less agreement with regard to the permanence of the process. Some authors have indicated that the change must be relatively enduring in order for the learning process to be inferred. The reason for this qualification is that many believe it necessary to distinguish those behavior changes which take place as a result of learning from those which may be attributed to fatigue. A typist who begins typing at 80 words per minute but at the conclusion of a sustained period of work is typing only 60 words per minute satisfies the definition of learning as a change in behavior that grows out of practice or experience. It is assumed, however, that this kind of change does not arise from a learning process but rather results from tiredness or fatigue. Those psychologists who consider learning to be "relatively permanent" would eliminate the possibility that this behavior change would be used as a basis for inferring a "learning" process since the reduction in performance level to 60 words per minute would not be "relatively permanent." It would be anticipated that the typist would regain her usual speed when properly rested.

Other psychologists, however, have not included the "relatively permanent" phrase in their definition of learning. Some years ago, Woodworth and Schlosberg (1954), in their discussion of the "relatively permanent" aspects of the definition of learning, wrote that the term "relatively" spoils such a definition for "some things, like telephone numbers, are learned well enough for immediate use but are soon forgotten" (p. 530). The experimental work originating in the late fifties that has been done in the area of short-term memory has also raised a question concerning the "permanent" part of the definition.[1] We shall take the position, however, that for the kinds of learning situations which will be dealt with in this text, it makes most sense to consider learning as a relatively permanent process.

The Construct of Memory

Learning frequently has been related to the construct of memory or to the behavior which we term remembering. Remembering generally refers to the persistence of learning over time. The individual who is able to reproduce or recall in considerable detail material learned some time ago is said to have a good "memory"; the many "memory" systems which have been written about in current magazines and newspapers testify to the importance that is placed on having a good memory.

When we attempt to distinguish the construct of learning from memory, however, we may note some problems. For example, if we present a subject with a task, with instructions to learn or remember, we can note that greater and greater amounts of material are acquired as additional trials are provided. It is obvious that with multiple presentations of the material, or trials, each trial after the first reflects the retention (or memory) of material presented earlier. Thus, any so-called learning trial reflects some contemporary process which has been designated as learning in addition to the remembering (or a memory process) of material learned earlier.

The intertwining of learning and memory, at least in typical multiple-trial psychological experiments, has long been recognized. As Marx (1969a) has written, "It is apparent upon reflection that without retention there could be no learning; that is to say, unless the effects of one trial or response persist until the next trial or response, over a period of time, they cannot have the effect upon subsequent behavior that we have identified as learning" (p. 13).

What we must recognize, at least with our current state of knowledge, is the impossibility of determining whether a particular experimental situation reflects the operation of a learning or memory process. It would appear that performance on most tasks reflects both of these.[2]

[1] A typical short term memory experiment consists of presenting a trigram (three unrelated letters) to a subject for a very brief period of time, e.g., one second, following which the subject is asked to engage in some type of mental activity, such as counting backwards by threes for 30 seconds. The subject is then asked to recall the trigram. Findings have indicated very poor recall for the experimental material. It has been assumed that the trigram was originally learned, but that such learning was not very permanent.

[2] In some situations, a subject may have acquired material at a given point in

It must be acknowledged, however, that tradition has designated certain experimental areas as related to learning, while other areas have been presumed to deal with retention or memory. Many investigators have adopted the position of Melton (1963) who wrote that a change from trial N to N + 1 should be used to infer a learning process when the variable of interest was the ordinal number of trial N and not the temporal interval between trial N and N + 1. When the variable of interest was the interval and/or the events which filled the interval between trial N and N + 1, the process of retention was being examined.

This distinction provided a convenient organization for those studies which used a multiple trial presentation of material, in contrast to those studies in which an interval of time, frequently measured in hours, was interpolated between the last "learning" trial and a test for retention. The utilization of multiple trials almost invariably meant that the investigator was interested in the operation of a particular variable that manifested itself over trials, thus permitting an examination of the influence of that variable on the learning process. When the experimenter permitted a lengthy time period to elapse between the presentation of the material and a subsequent test for recall, the process measured on the recall test was presumed to be memory (or retention).

This distinction continues to be a viable one for most of the learning situations which we shall discuss in this text, although Melton's position does have difficulty accommodating short term memory tasks which we described earlier.[3]

A Learning Taxonomy

Although there are some problems in defining learning as well as differentiating it from memory, we can point to situations or use tasks which virtually all experimenters would agree involve the learning or memory process. Our approach to the study of learning and memory, then, is one which will con-

---

time; a considerable period of time later the subject is provided a single trial to "remember" this material. It may be that such a task clearly reveals the operation of memory. Such experiments, however, are only infrequently performed, and have not as yet provided us with any general guidelines which are relevant in distinguishing between the two processes.

[3] From the time of Ebbinghaus until Watson, the concepts of learning, memory, and retention were used almost interchangeably. Ebbinghaus (1885) conducting human learning experiments entitled his classic monograph, *Memory: A Contribution to Experimental Psychology*. With the founding of behaviorism, Watson (1924) substituted the construct of retention for memory. Watson wrote, "Instead of speaking of memory, the behaviorist speaks of the retention of a given habit in terms of how much skill has been retained and how much has been lost in the period of no practice. We do not need the term 'memory,' shot through as it is with all kinds of philosophical and subjective connotations" (p. 179). In another section of his text, he wrote, "By 'memory,' then, we mean nothing except the fact that when we meet a stimulus again after an absence, we do the old habitual thing . . . that we learned to do when we were in the presence of that stimulus in the first place" (p. 190). In brief, the construct of retention replaced memory although a distinction was made between learning and retention.

A number of contemporary investigators have suggested that the construct of retention or memory be used in place of learning. Tulving (1968) has posited sider relatively permanent changes in behavior arising from multiple trials provided in a number of specific kinds of tasks. However, the kinds of tasks which reflect learning and memory processes are exceedingly diverse—there is an almost infinite variety of them.

When such a situation exists in a scientific discipline, the first task is to provide a "natural grouping" or ordering so that the study of the underlying processes and/or products can take place with maximum efficiency. It becomes necessary to provide some classificatory scheme or taxonomy.

The early naturalists could identify thousands of plants and animals, but their inability to provide a universally accepted classificatory system led to considerable confusion. Since the naturalists of each country used their own system, effective communication among them was impossible. It was not until the middle of the eighteenth century that a Swedish naturalist, Linnaeus, introduced the binomial method of scientific nomenclature which has become the basis of the classification system used today.[4]

In chemistry, it was the Russian Mendeleev who, in the middle of the nineteenth century, classified the chemical elements which had been discovered up to that time in an arrangement which we know today as the periodic table. In doing so, he was able to predict elements which were yet to be discovered.

Unfortunately, psychology has not had its Linnaeus or Mendeleev. No single individual has been able to provide a learning (or memory) taxonomy which has had universal acceptance by experimental investigators.

It is necessary, however, to establish some kind of classificatory system if we are to present something more than a confusing array of experimental studies. It should be acknowledged that one of the most widely adopted classifications has been proposed by Hilgard and Marquis (1940), who divided learning tasks into two general types: (1) classical conditioning and (2) instrumental learning. The logic as well as the popularity of this taxonomy virtually demands that we use it in our examination of the learning process.

---

that in the typical multiple item, multitrial type of experiment, learning refers to the more or less systematic increase in the number of items retained over successive trials and can be described as the slope of the function relating the number of items recalled to the ordinal number of the trial.

Tulving has written that, "when learning is used as a descriptive term in multitrial experiments, it serves as a shorthand expression for the fact that recall increases over trials. To ask why learning occurs, or to ask what processes are involved in learning . . . means to ask why recall scores increase from trial to trial, or what processes are involved in such an increase" (p. 7).

Murdock (1960) has similarly suggested that learning be considered the slope of the curve showing the number of correct responses as a function of the number of trials. Such a distinction between learning and retention is analogous, he wrote, to the distinction between velocity and position in mechanics. Just as velocity is the rate of change of position with respect to time, so learning is the rate of change of retention with respect to the number of presentations.

[4] Linnaeus's system consisted of assigning each species of plant or animal a name consisting of two words, the combination of the two being exclusive to that species. The first word, the generic name, is shared by all species sufficiently allied to be included in the same genus. The second word is an adjective or modifying noun and is applied to a single species within any one genus.

Classical conditioning refers to a set of experimental operations that involve an unconditioned stimulus (UCS) having the capacity to elicit a response (UCR), and a conditioned stimulus (CS) which at the beginning of the experiment has been shown not capable of evoking the UCR. The repeated presentation of the CS and UCS in a specified temporal patterning results in the CS eliciting a conditioned response (CR)—a response which is markedly different from any response which was made to the CS prior to the pairing and which bears some similarity to the UCR. Instrumental learning refers to learning situations in which the response which is learned is instrumental in securing reward or escaping from or avoiding punishment.

The Stimulus-Response Analysis of Behavior

Psychologists most frequently describe learning tasks in terms of stimulus and response, a position arising from the work of John B. Watson and the early behaviorists who held that it was possible to analyze behavior in terms of stimulus-response relationships. A stimulus was defined as an environmental event or an energy change in the physical environment which excited a sense organ and initiated a response. A response was defined as a muscular contraction or a glandular secretion occasioned by the presentation of a stimulus.

The stimulus-response approach to the study of behavior has not had the enthusiastic endorsement of all psychologists, and over the years a variety of objections have been raised. The more important of these follow.

Some critics have pointed out that the definition of a stimulus as well as a response is circular; that is, a stimulus must be defined with reference to the response that it presumably elicits, while the presence of a response assumes that a stimulus has been responsible for its elicitation. Moreover, it is not always possible to determine the stimulus in a variety of learning tasks. Skinner (1938), for example, has argued that when a rat learns to press a lever in a Skinner box, it is impossible to discover the stimulus which elicits the bar pressing response.

Other critics have indicated that the formulation of behavior in terms of stimulus and response does not permit the utilization of such constructs as "intention" which they believe play important roles in determining behavior. As Taylor (1964) has written, stimulus-response theorists wish to do away with all notions which involve the "intentionality" of the subject; however, it is the "intention" of the organism which in many instances determines the individual's behavior.

Finally, critics have likened the stimulus-response position to the operation of a telephone switchboard but have argued that behavior, certainly human behavior, can be neither described nor explained in such simplistic terms. Miller (1965), for example, has written that any attempt to understand how a language is learned based upon stimulus-response relationships is doomed to failure.

There is little doubt that many of the objections that have been raised have merit, although it should be noted that the stimulus-response approach is only a first step in the study of behavior, rather than a "basic truth." Perhaps more important is that critics of the stimulus-response position have almost invariably failed to provide an alternative method of analyzing behavior.

Contemporary psychologists who have continued to examine the study of behavior within a stimulus-response framework have been aware of the criticisms raised and have attempted to answer many of them. For example, there has been a general recognition of the need to distinguish different usages of the term stimulus.

Spence (1956) has pointed out that the concept of the stimulus has had at least three different referents. The first—situational stimuli—are physical objects or events in the environment that may be specified by the experimenter and are under his direct control. A second class of stimuli—intraorganic stimuli—are specified on the basis of known physiological laws or specific hypothesized internal relations. The third class—effective stimuli—refer to those energy changes which actually excite a receptor and produce a response.

Gibson (1960) and Underwood (1963) have posited somewhat similar classifications based upon the situational vs. effective distinction. Gibson has suggested that stimuli which are capable of exciting receptors be classified as potential stimuli while stimuli which actually do result in receptor activity, neural impulses, sense organ adjustment, and overt responses, be given the term effective stimuli.

Underwood (1963) has proposed that the stimulus situation, which is presented to the subject and defined by the experimenter, be known as the nominal stimulus while the characteristics to which the subject actually responds be called the functional stimulus. The identification of the effective or functional stimulus is not an easy task in many learning experiments, particularly when animals are used as experimental subjects.

Changes in usage of the term response must also be noted. Responses have been defined, not only as muscular contractions or glandular secretions, but also as acts of the organism which are directed toward producing some change in the environment. Thus, two ends of the response continuum have been acknowledged as (1) molecular and (2) molar.

The molecular position describes responses in terms of specific qualitative or quantitative variations of muscular contractions or glandular secretion. For example, in classical conditioning, the amount of salivation or the closing of an eyelid is clearly a molecular response.

The molar approach describes responses in terms of changes that the organism produces in the immediate environment and ignores differences in the detailed movement or patterns of muscular or glandular activity. The pressing of a bar or lever by a rat in a Skinner box is treated as a molar response—a single response class regardless of the specific muscular movements which are involved. One lever press is treated like any other, although the animal may have used his right paw to depress the lever on one occasion and his left paw to depress it on another.[5]

[5] A position which is orthogonal to the molecular-molar dimension has been taken by Logan (1956, 1960) who has proposed a micromolar theory of behavior. Logan has posited that responses that differ in any way whatsoever differ in that they may be placed in separate response classes so that varying response tendencies can be calculated for them. Such an approach parallels the traditional analysis of the stimulus. It makes the response side of the stimulus-response rela-

A contemporary stimulus-response position has also recognized the importance of mediating responses in order to provide an adequate understanding of behavior. The mediating response is hypothesized to act as a bridge between an external stimulus situation and the overt observable response. Mediating responses are postulated to have stimulus characteristics which elicit other responses. This point of view assumes that in certain situations, the organism may make an internal or unobservable response which produces a characteristic stimulus which in turn serves as a cue for another response. Using the S-R analysis, one can provide the following diagram:

$$S—r—s—R$$

Here, the S is an observable stimulus while the r is a mediating response which has stimulus characteristics, s, which elicit the observable response, R.

Mediating responses play an obvious role in the examination of human behavior since these responses can be conceptualized as thoughts or ideas which are produced by certain stimulus events. At the same time, these responses become stimuli for other responses.

For example, assume that a child is asked to learn a simple perceptual-motor task: when a red light is illuminated, a button on the righthand side of the response panel should be pressed; when a green light is illuminated, a button on the left side should be pressed. Pressing the correct button will turn off the stimulus light. The child in learning this task may learn to verbalize the response "right" with the appearance of the red light, and "left" with the appearance of the green; thus, these verbal responses can be conceptualized as mediating responses to the observable, visual stimuli. At the same time, these mediating responses can serve as stimuli for the overt motor response which the child makes. This can be diagrammed as follows:

Overt Stimulus	Mediating Stimulus and Response	Overt Response
Red light	Verbal response: "right"	Manual responding of right hand
Green light	Verbal response: "left"	Manual responding of left hand

In the chapters that follow it will be possible to cite many other examples of the stimulus-response position which can be described as more sophisticated (or

tionship similar to the stimulus side in having a number of dimensions along which generalization takes place and discriminations are formed.

Logan (1960) has experimentally demonstrated that a rat can learn to traverse a runway at a speed determined by the experimenter in order to maximize reinforcement. To achieve this result, a running speed which is more rapid or slower than that prescribed by the experimenter results in delayed reward. Contemporary investigators have acknowledged the validity of these findings, that is, that rats can learn to adjust their running speed in order to obtain immediate reward. Nonetheless, it has generally been held that different rates of responding in the same task do not indicate different responses but only different strengths of the same response.

enlightened). To defend the assertion that there are no problems or that a stimulus-response analysis of learning has complete applicability to all of the situations which have been investigated would be foolish. Our approach would be that, in many instances, such an analysis does have utility and that, whenever it does, it makes sense to adopt it.

The Distinction Between Learning and Performance

We have stated that learning represents a physiological process and/or product that is inferred from changes in an organism's behavior. But everyday observation reveals the inappropriateness of assuming that this process is always mirrored by performance. The distinction between how an individual performs and what he has learned has motivated a number of investigators to attempt to distinguish between the two constructs.

Although Lashley (1929) had written earlier about differentiating between learning and performance, it was the experimental work of Tolman (1932) and his associates in their examination of a kind of learning situation termed latent learning, which was primarily responsible for calling psychologists' attention to this distinction.

In an early study by Blodgett (1929), a Tolman associate, three groups of rats were given 1 trial a day on a six unit multiple T-maze. The control group was provided 7 trials with each animal permitted to eat for 3 minutes in the goal box. Experimental group 1 was also given 7 trials. For the first 2 trials this group did not find food in the goal box, but was retained there for 2 minutes. They were then placed in a cage and an hour later were given food. Reward was introduced on the third trial, and it continued to be present for the remaining trials. Experimental group 2 was treated similarly to experimental group 1 except that reward was omitted for the first 6 trials and introduced on the seventh. These experimental group 2 animals were then run two additional trials. The results are illustrated in Fig. 1-1. It may be noted that the discovery of food by experimental group 1 at the end of the third trial resulted in an error score on trial 4 not unlike that found by the control group on trial 4. This change in performance taking place as a function of finding reward on a single trial is even more dramatically revealed by the error scores made by experimental group 2. As a result of finding food in the goal box on trial 7, performance for this group on trial 8 was not significantly different from the performance on trial 7 of the control group.

The control group's continuous rather than abrupt change in performance gives rise to the inference that the learning process does not take place rapidly, but rather on a gradual or incremental basis. The observation of relatively rapid reduction in errors following the introduction of a single reward in experimental groups 1 and 2 has thus been used to make the distinction between learning and performance. Learning was taking place in all groups; reward was contributing only to the animal's performance. As Tolman (1932) has written:

> The latent learning, which takes place without any strong differential effects [introduction of food], does not, to be sure, manifest itself until

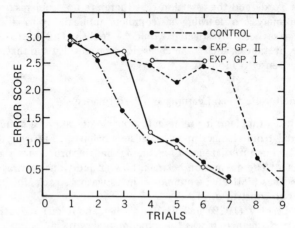

Fig. 1-1. The influence of reward on maze learning. The Control Group has been reinforced on
every trial. Experimental Group I had reward introduced on Trial 3, while Experimental Group II had
reward introduced on Trial 7. *Adapted from Blodgett (1929)*

after such effects have been introduced. But, once these latter have been
provided, then the sizes of the immediate drops in the performance
curves, which appear, indicate that the learning has been just as great as
it would have been, if strong effects had been present throughout. Differential effects are, that is, necessary for *selective performance*, but they
are not necessary, or at the most in only a very minor degree, for the mere
learning *qua* learning which underlies such performance. (p. 364)

A more contemporary example is found in a study by Hillman, Hunter, and
Kimble (1953) who placed rats under 2 or 22 hours of water deprivation and
had them run a multiple T-maze for 10 trials. On trial 11, the group of animals
on 22 hours of deprivation was subdivided, with half of them serving as a control
and remaining on 22 hours, while the other half was shifted to 2 hours of deprivation. Similarly, the original 2-hour deprivation group was subdivided with half
of the group remaining on 2 hours and thus serving as a control group, while
the other half was shifted to 22 hours of deprivation. In summary, four groups
of subjects were provided additional training on trials 11 through 15. Two of
these groups served as controls, 2-2 and 22-22; the two others were experimental groups, 2-22, 22-2. The findings, as indicated in Fig. 1-2, reveal that the
2-hour group which was switched to 22 hours of deprivation had a performance
increment on a single trial which made it comparable with the 22-hour control
group; on the other hand, the 22-hour deprivation group which was switched to
2 hours had a performance decrement which made its performance similar to
the 2-hour control group. Thus, the immediate change in performance for the
two experimental groups would indicate that deprivation was influencing performance and not learning—certainly, the group which was changed from a

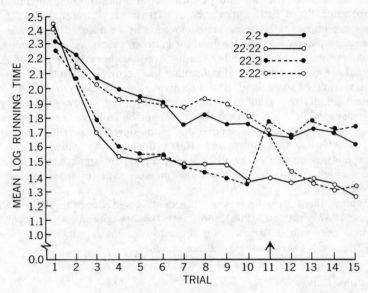

Fig. 1-2. Learning curves showing time scores for each experimental group as a function of trials. The arrow indicates the point at which the drive was changed for the two groups. *Adapted from Hillman, Hunter, and Kimble (1953)*

deprivation period of 22 to 2 hours did not *unlearn* their rate of responding; similarly, the rapidity with which the 2-22-hour group increased its rate of responding would indicate that performance rather than learning was being influenced by the deprivation variable.

The validity of the distinction between learning and performance has been acknowledged by almost all experimenters. Hull (1943, 1951) and Spence (1956) have provided the most definitive programmatic attempts to make a distinction between learning and performance. Hull's (1943) formula:

$$\text{Habit strength [learning]} \times \text{motivation} = \text{performance}$$

illustrates this position. Many of the early experiments, including those of Perin (1942), Koch and Daniel (1945), as well as a number which followed (Saltzman and Koch, 1948; Strassburger, 1950; Teel, 1952; Barry, 1958), were designed to determine how motivation, measured by hours of deprivation, contributed to learning as distinct from performance.

A basic assumption made by Hull as well as these other investigators was that the performance measure, resistance to extinction, could be used to distinguish between learning and performance. There is considerable question concerning the validity of this assumption. Moreover, the experimental findings obtained in these investigations have been controversial and of little value in helping to provide an operational (as well as generally accepted) distinction between the two constructs.

McGeoch (1942) writing at about the same time as Hull (1943) stated, "the distinction between learning and performance is logically valid, but practically and operationally of little importance in a treatment of learning. . . . The only way we can know that learning has occurred is by an observation of successive performances, since *learning is a relation between successive performances. . . .* This does not mean that learning cannot occur without being measured, but only that we can never know that learning has occurred without measurement or observation of some kind. The statement that it can occur without being measured admits the validity of the logical distinction between learning and performance, while the statement that it cannot be known as a scientific datum without being observed or measured denies the operational validity of the distinction. Assertions that motive and effect influence performance but not learning become meaningless in the absence of quantitative demonstration, a demonstration which cannot be made without measurements of performance" (pp. 598-599).

Although there have been some dissidents to McGeoch's (1942) position (Adams, 1967; Postman, 1968), most investigators appear to agree that until such time that valid criteria can be obtained it seems appropriate to disregard the distinction between learning and performance.

Learning Curves

Frequently, investigators are interested in determining how behavior changes throughout a series of learning trials, and one of the most effective techniques for obtaining this information is the learning curve. Such curves are plotted by placing trials or the independent variable along the abscissa while performance measures are placed along the ordinate. Although it would be possible to plot individual learning curves in a given experiment, such a project would not only be laborious but the individual curves would be quite irregular as well, and the assumed orderliness of the learning process would be obscured. As a result, group curves are used.

The simplest way to construct a learning curve is to average the scores made by all the subjects on the first trial, then on the second trial, and so forth. These scores are then plotted as a function of trials to reveal the course of learning. When an experimenter provides a fixed number of trials to his subjects, this procedure is most satisfactory. On some occasions, the experimenter may have his subjects learn to a criterion—that is, reach some arbitrary level of performance, usually set by the experimenter. When this is done, the number of trials that each individual takes to reach the criterion will vary. Thus, one subject may reach the criterion in 10 trials, another in 13 or a third in 22. If scores are averaged across trials, it is obvious that many points on the learning curve will reflect differing numbers of subjects since once a subject has reached the criterion, his scores will no longer be used in obtaining an average value. It is possible, of course, to assume that once the subject has reached the criterion, his performance will continue to reflect criterion performance thereafter. Here, the individual's hypothesized criterion score would be averaged along with the other scores provided on a given trial. If the experimenter sets a very rigorous criterion, such an assumption is reasonable; on the other hand, when a lenient criterion is used, individual subjects on postcriterion trials frequently regress to a perfor-

Table 1-1   Records for Three Subjects (A, B, and C) Learning a List of
            Eight Adjectives

	Trials									
	1	2	3	4	5	6	7	8	9	10
Subject A:										
No. Correct Responses	1	3	4	4	6	6	7	8		
Subject B:										
No. Correct Responses	2	4	3	4	5	5	6	6	6	8
Subject C:										
No. Correct Responses	1	4	5	7	8					

Adapted from Hall (1966)

mance level lower than that obtained on the criterion trial, and the basic assumption is obviously erroneous. Few experimenters use this procedure.

The most frequently used method for constructing a group learning curve when a learning criterion has been used was devised by Melton (1936) and is called a successive criterion curve or a trials-to-criteria curve. With this method, the average number of trials to reach successive criteria, that is, succeeding numbers of correct responses, is plotted. As an example, we may hypothesize that three subjects, A, B, and C, are asked to learn a serial list of eight words to a criterion of one perfect trial. The protocols are illustrated in Table 1-1. In order to convert a subject's specific learning score into data that can be used to construct the successive criterion curve, we should note the following: Subject A obtained one correct response on Trial 1; as a result, it took him one trial to reach the criterion of one correct—the first of the successive criteria. Two correct responses were obtained on trial 2 for subject A so that the second successive criterion was obtained with a value of 2. Note that three correct responses were also achieved on trial 2. Four correct responses were obtained on Trial 3, while five and six correct responses were obtained on trial 5. Seven correct responses took place on trial 7 and eight correct responses on trial 8—the last of the criteria used. When such a conversion is made for all subjects, the mean trials to reach each successive criterion are obtained, and the data are then plotted by placing the criterion score on the abscissa and the mean trials to criterion on the ordinate. Table 1-2 illustrates the data that are used to construct the successive criterion curve, while the curve itself can be noted in Fig. 1-3.

A less frequently used method for constructing a group learning curve has been devised by Vincent (1912) and modified by Kjerstad (1919) and Hunter (1929). Here, each individual's learning curve or trials to mastery is divided into equal fractions; performance at these varying fractional intervals is summated, averaged, and then plotted. On the abscissa, equal fractions of learning are used rather than trials, while the performance measured is plotted on the ordinate.[6]

The use of a learning curve is an exceedingly helpful device for depicting dif-

[6] For an example of the actual plotting of such a curve, the reader can refer to Hall (1971).

Table 1-2 Data Used to Construct the Successive Criterion Curve

| Subject | The Learning Trial on Which Each Successive Criterion Was Achieved | | | | | | | |
	1	2	3	4	5	6	7	8
A	1	2	2	3	5	5	7	8
B	1	1	2	2	5	7	10	10
C	1	2	2	2	3	4	4	5
Total	3	5	6	7	13	16	21	23
Mean	1.0	1.7	2.0	2.3	4.3	5.3	7.0	7.7

Adapted from Hall (1966)

ferences among the various groups that are employed in an experiment. Too much dependence should not be placed on the reliability of these curves, however, as indications of individual behavior. Over the years a number of serious questions have been raised concerning the use of the group learning curve. Spence (1956) has written that the averaging of individual data often produces considerable distortion with the consequence that the group curve does not accurately reflect the individual curves. He has proposed that an alternative procedure for treating data from a group of subjects would be to construct a curve based upon the mean of all "like" or homogeneous subjects. There is a problem of determining the criteria to be used in deciding whether a subject should be included in the group from which the learning curve was derived. Hilgard and Campbell (1936) classified subjects into subgroups on the basis of the shapes of their individual conditioning curves, while Spence (1952) selected subjects on the basis of the similarity of their response measures for the total learning period.

There is no question that group learning curves perform a very useful func-

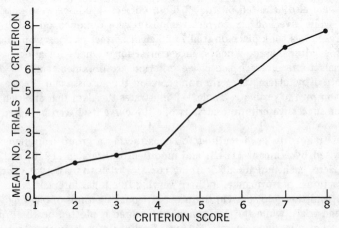

Fig. 1-3. Successive criteria curve derived from data in Table 1-2. *Adapted from Hall (1966)*

tion for the experimenter; however, a sampling of individual learning curves should be plotted as well. The smoothing of such individual curves may be accomplished by averaging measures over blocks of trials, provided such blocks each contain only a relatively small number of trials. It is then possible to see if individual curves mirror the performance of the group curve. If serious discrepancies are revealed, considerable doubt must be raised concerning the value of the group curve.

Summary

A logical approach to the topic of learning must begin with an appropriate definition. There is reasonable agreement that learning should be defined as a relatively permanent process taking place within the organism, inferred from changes in performance, and arising as a result of experience or practice. Although some investigators have attempted to distinguish the learning process from the memory process, this cannot be accomplished at this time. Every behavior change from which we infer a learning process reflects a memory process as well. As Marx (1969a) has written, ". . . without retention or memory there could be no learning."

A basic problem in the study of learning has to do with the establishment of a learning taxonomy—a classification or ordering which makes possible an examination of the process with maximum efficiency. Psychologists have not established any completely acceptable classification of learning tasks, although a (1) classical conditioning, (2) instrumental learning distinction has proved to be the most popular and viable classification of the many that have been proposed. Classical conditioning refers to a set of experimental operations which involve the presentation of an unconditioned stimulus (UCS) which has the capacity to elicit an unconditioned response (UCR), and a conditioned stimulus (CS) which has been shown to be incapable of evoking the unconditioned response at the beginning of the experiment. The repeated presentation of the CS and the UCS in a specified temporal patterning results in the capability of the CS to elicit a response designated as the conditioned response (CR). The CR is markedly different from any response which was made to the CS prior to the pairing, and usually, the CR bears some similarity to the UCR. Instrumental learning refers to learning situations in which the response which is learned is instrumental in securing reward or escaping from or avoiding punishment.

We are aware of the many instances in which individuals have been unable to recall the name of an acquaintance at the time of meeting, only to be able to recall it at a later time. This illustrates the difference between what has been learned and appropriate performance. Many investigators have attempted to demonstrate experimentally the validity of this distinction; unfortunately, it has not been possible to set up criteria which would solve the problem.

Most experimenters are interested in determining how learning takes place over the acquisition trials that are provided. One technique for obtaining this information is to plot a learning curve, placing trials or the independent variable along the abscissa while placing performance measures along the ordinate. When a learning criterion is used which precludes a simple averaging of performance over trials, it is most appropriate to use a successive criterion curve. With this method, the average number of trials to reach successive criteria, that is, successive numbers of correct responses, are plotted.

2
Classical Conditioning:
Introduction

Historically, some early investigators, among them, Pavlov (1927) and Watson (1924), believed that the conditioned response was the basic unit of learning and that more complex kinds of behavior were merely concatenations of conditioned responses—one conditioned response added to another in order to obtain the desired complexity of behavior. Pavlov (1927) wrote, "It is obvious that the different kinds of habits based on training, education, and discipline of any sort are nothing but a long chain of conditioned reflexes" (p. 395).

Although contemporary psychologists do not accept this point of view, classical conditioning does represent a viable area of experimental inquiry, and a number of reasons can be cited for the enthusiasm of experimenters working in this area. Classical conditioning has been considered one of the simplest forms of learning, and many believe that it is necessary to first understand the processes involved in simple learning tasks before moving on to more complex ones.[1]

[1] Although a number of investigators have considered

A related position is that classical conditioning experiments have often been regarded as a source of deductive principles. Hull (1935), one of the early advocates of this position, adopted the working hypothesis ". . . that the principles of action discovered in conditioned reaction experiments are also operative in the higher behavioral processes" (p. 227). It should not be assumed that the principles discovered in conditioning experiments are directly applicable to complex learning tasks; rather, the conditioning experiment is a useful paradigm from which one can deduce many of the laws of learning.

The Pavlovian Procedure

It will be recalled that Pavlov was a Russian physiologist who was interested in examining glandular secretions which were involved in digestive processes. During the course of his experimental studies with dogs, he noted that the smell, sight, or other more general stimuli which were related to the presentation of food came to elicit salivation. Physiologists who worked in this area during Pavlov's era were familiar with this kind of response but they were inclined to ignore it. Such a response was presumed to be related to the animal's thoughts and not, therefore, subject to physiological laws. Pavlov, on the other hand, was sufficiently intrigued with his findings to investigate this phenomenon in depth. He believed that these "psychic" secretions indicated an animal's adaptive behavior to its external and internal environments. Perhaps most important was Pavlov's belief that his method provided an objective way of investigating the nature of brain processes.

In order to examine the salivary response of the dog, it was necessary to provide a means whereby such a response could be measured. Pavlov has described how this was done. "For the purpose of registering the intensity of the salivary reflex all the dogs employed in the experiments are subjected to a preliminary minor operation, which consists in the transplantation of the opening of the salivary duct from its natural place on the mucous membrane of the mouth to the outside of the skin. For this purpose the terminal portion of the salivary duct is dissected and freed from the surrounding tissue, and the duct, together with a small portion of the mucous membrane surrounding

---

classical conditioning to be the most elementary form of learning, others have given that distinction to the process of habituation. Habituation has been defined as a response decrement that occurs as a result of repeated stimulation—an operation identical to that used in producing experimental extinction. Thorpe (1956) has written that habituation is probably the simplest as well as the oldest form of behavior modification. Many ethologists, among them, Lorenz (1965), believe that the functional significance of habituation lies in "the elimination of the organism's responses to often recurring, biologically irrelevant stimuli without impairment of its reaction to others" (p. 50).

The question has arisen as to whether a learning process should be inferred from this type of behavioral change since at the end of a series of trials, there is no obviously overt response attached to the presented stimulus. One answer that has been put forth is that the disappearance of the habituated response may arise from the learning of some overt competing response (not measured) to the presented stimulus. In such a case, some associative or learning process would appear to be present.

its natural opening, is carried through a suitable incision, to the outside of the cheek in the case of the parotid gland, or under the chin in the case of the submaxillary gland. In this new position the duct is fixed by a few stitches which are removed when the wound has healed. As a result of the operation the saliva now flows to the outside, on to the cheek or chin of the animal, instead of into the mouth, so that the measurement of the secretory activity of the gland is greatly facilitated. It is only necessary for this purpose to adjust a small glass funnel over the opening of the duct on to the skin" (p. 18).

The general experimental procedure which Pavlov used was as follows: The dog was trained to stand quietly in a loose harness on a table in a room which was sound deadened to prevent distracting noises or vibrations. A metronome or tuning fork was sounded and 7 or 8 seconds after the onset of the sound, a small quantity of powdered food was moved within reach of the animal's mouth. On the first trial, the sound did not elicit salivation although eating the dry food did so. After a number of pairings of the sound and the meat powder, it was observed that when the sound was presented alone, it elicited salivation in the animal. A conditioned response had been established.

Conditioned Response Terminology

Pavlov's experimental procedure has resulted in a number of specific terms being used to describe the classical conditioning paradigm. In the experiment cited, the meat powder has been designated as the unconditioned stimulus (UCS); the response which is elicited by the meat powder is called the unconditioned response (UCR). The sound arising from the metronome or tuning fork is referred to as the conditioned stimulus (CS). On early trials, responses of the animal to the conditioned stimulus have been called orienting responses (OR). Following a number of paired presentations of the CS and UCS, a response to the CS is known as the conditioned response (CR).[2]

More general definitions of these terms are as follows:

Unconditioned stimulus—any stimulus which will evoke a regular and measurable response in the subject for an extended period of time. The characteristics of the UCS determine whether or not the conditioning situation shall be termed appetitional or aversive. If the UCS is shock or some other stimulus which is noxious to the subject, the conditioning situation is classified as aversive; on the other hand, if the UCS is food, or an object related to satisfying some need of the organism, the situation is termed appetitive. Other investigators (including

[2] Conditioned and unconditioned responses are the terms now used to describe the conditioning procedure. It is a matter of interest, however, that they were originally translated from Russian as conditional and unconditional reflexes. Some writers have pointed out that the term "conditional" rather than "conditioned" makes more sense since at the beginning of the experiment, the neutral stimulus is not a conditioned one but is conditional. Woodworth and Schlosberg (1954) state, "Consider the bell which will be experimentally associated with food; at the outset it is a to-be-conditioned stimulus but not yet a conditioned stimulus, though it is often so called" (p. 542).

Gormezano and Moore, 1969) have designated these situations as classical defense and classical reward conditioning.

Unconditioned response—the response which is elicited by the unconditioned stimulus.

Conditioned stimulus—a stimulus which does not have the capacity at the beginning of the training session to elicit the unconditioned response.

Conditioned response—a response elicited by the conditioned stimulus. This response may be a component of the UCR; some investigators have also pointed out that the conditioned response appears to prepare the organism for the occurrence of the UCS.

Orienting response—skeletal (looking, listening) as well as autonomic responses which are originally elicited by the CS or by other changes which take place in the conditioning situation. Pavlov (1927) designated this response as the investigatory reflex. Hartman (1965) has written that contemporary Russian investigators have hypothesized that the orienting reflex is a simpler, more primary way, of evaluating sensory analysis, and is considerably more direct than the use of classical conditioning since the orienting reflex precedes the information of the CR in the typical conditioning experiment.[3]

Classical Conditioning Defined

The procedure utilized by Pavlov has been designated as classical conditioning and its essential features are as follows: (1) a conditioned stimulus (CS) which originally does not elicit the to-be-conditioned response; (2) an unconditioned stimulus (UCS) which evokes a regular and measurable unconditioned response (UCR); (3) the repeated presentation of the CS and the UCS in a controlled and specified manner and independent of the behavior of the subject. Any new or altered response to the CS which depends upon CS-UCS pairings is defined as a conditioned response.

For some years following Pavlov's discovery, a number of variations of the Pavlovian procedure were employed, virtually all of them described as conditioning. In an effort to provide some order to the area, Hilgard and Marquis (1940) suggested that the basic distinction between Pavlov's procedure and these variations could be made by examining the consequences of the conditioned response. In Pavlovian or classical conditioning operations, the occurrence of the conditioned response does not result in any change in the CS-UCS

[3] Sokolov (1960), who has extensively examined the nature of the orienting reflex, has attributed to this response system two general properties. The first is that it is an unspecific reflex and is initiated by an increase, decrease, or qualitative change of a stimulus; the second property is that it is subject to habituation arising from repeated stimulus presentations.

To illustrate the operation of the orienting reflex, we can cite Voronin and Sokolov's (1960) description of a study by U-Boa-Hua. One hundred subjects were presented with a single 1000 Hertz (Hz) tone of 50 decibels (db). With these 100 subjects, the tone elicited 95 shifts in the electrodermal response (EDR), 85 blockings of the alpha rhythm, 63 alterations in breathing, 53 cases of blocking of the motor region rhythm, and 42 eye movements.

pairings. Although the organism responds to the CS, the UCS continues to be presented. Thus, the operational definition of a classically conditioned response is the UCS being presented at a fixed interval following the presentation of the CS, regardless of the nature of the subject's response. In utilizing Pavlov's procedure, it is not the experimenter's intent to change behavior in some predetermined fashion but only to study the way in which the functional property of the CS is changed by virtue of its contiguity with the UCS.

In other situations, which Hilgard and Marquis (1940) termed instrumental conditioning, the learned response is instrumental in the organism securing reward or escaping and/or avoiding punishment. Thus, instrumental learning is defined by a contingency between the response demanded by the investigator and the presentation of reward or an aversive stimulus.[4]

Origins of the Conditioned Response

Franks (1970) has written that the basic techniques of conditioning, if not the terminology, predate Pavlov by countless centuries; in fact, the literature of the world has countless illustrations of such mechanisms at work. Cellini, a sixteenth century author, described the process of conditioning in some detail, while in more recent times a number of eminent scientists have made reference to the various phenomena of conditioning in language similar to that of Pavlov. The distinguished British psychologist, James Ward, writing in the ninth edition (1878) of the *Encyclopedia Britannica* gave this example: "The dog's mouth waters only at the *sight* of food, but the gourmand's mouth will also water at the *thought* of it." As a part of his lecture series in Paris, circa 1855, Claude Bernard described the experimental demonstration of salivary conditioning in the horse under controlled conditions (Rosenzweig, 1959). There is a critical difference, however, between the reports of Pavlov and those of his predecessors. Whereas virtually all early investigators confined themselves to the sporadic demonstration of already established conditioned responses, Pavlov was one of the first to initiate a program of investigation that included the systematic study of the formation and extinction of new and deliberately induced conditioned reflexes.

Pavlov's contemporary Bekhterev must also be singled out for his contribution to the area of conditioning. In contrast with the writings of Pavlov, which were then virtually unknown, Bekhterev's work was translated into French and German by the early part of the twentieth century. It was not until several decades later that Pavlov achieved distinction. Both Pavlov and Bekhterev were intimately involved in the attempt to transform psychology—in particular,

---

[4] Bitterman (1966) has suggested that tasks in which the subject must learn to avoid the presentation of a noxious stimulus should merit a separate classification of its own. The reason is that early in the learning trials, a CS and a UCS are presented in a fixed temporal relationship, fitting the definition of a classical conditioning procedure. In subsequent learning trials, the subject learns to respond to the CS; thus, its response is instrumental in avoiding the presentation of the aversive stimulus (UCS). This aspect of the task places it in the instrumental category.

animal psychology—from a mentalistic series of speculations into a biologically rooted science. But it was Pavlov who did most to bring about the substitution of quantitative, objective, and permanent records of muscular and glandular activity for the introspective reporting of sensations, ideas, and images espoused by the structuralists, the dominant school of psychology of the time. It is not surprising that Pavlov eventually became a dominant figure in psychology.

Unfortunately, Pavlov's name is associated almost exclusively with the conditioned response. Pavlov's real concern, however, was an attempt to understand the principles of brain function or higher nervous activity. While conditioning represented the basic mechanism in this inquiry, it was regarded neither as an end in itself nor as a basic unit of brain function. To Pavlov the two basic processes underlying brain function were excitation and inhibition; conditioning procedures were the means whereby these processes and their properties could be subjected to systematic study.

Secondary sources have frequently given credit for the discovery of the conditioned response to E. B. Twitmyer, a graduate student at the University of Pennsylvania. In Twitmyer's study, the knee jerk response was being investigated, using a bell to indicate to the subject that a hammer would strike the patellar tendon. On one occasion, the bell was accidentally rung, and although the hammer did not fall, Twitmyer noted that an anticipatory knee jerk was made. These findings were presented at the annual meeting of the American Psychological Association in 1904 but little interest was evinced in this phenomenon.

It would appear, however, that Pavlov had been working on "conditioning" experiments prior to Twitmyer's discovery. Pavlov's speech to the plenary session of the International Medical Congress in Madrid in April, 1903, was entitled, "The Problem of the Study of Higher Nervous Activity and the Ways of Its Experimental Solution." It is therefore evident that Pavlov and his associates had been interested in the stimulation of the salivary glands by conditioned stimuli for some time. Pavlov stated, "In the psychical experiments the salivary glands are stimulated not only by the properties of the objects essential for the work of the glands, but absolutely by all the conditions surrounding these objects, or with which they are connected one way or another—for example, the dish in which they are contained, the article on which they are placed, the room, the people who usually bring the objects, even the noises produced by these people. . ." (p. 157). It was in this address that Pavlov first used the terms, conditioned and unconditioned reflex, and also noted the phenomenon of experimental extinction, asking the question, "Why does a conditioned reflex, when repeated, invariably become ineffective?" (p. 164)

Classical Conditioning Procedures

CS-UCS Operations

A notable feature of the classical conditioning procedure is the experimenter's precise control over the onset and termination of both the CS and the UCS. With such control, it is possible to vary the presentation of these stimuli in a number of ways and these variations have been provided with different designations.

Delayed conditioning. The most frequently used operation found in classical conditioning experiments is known as delayed conditioning. This procedure involves the presentation of the CS some time prior to the onset of the UCS, with the CS continuing until the UCS is presented. Fig. 2-1 illustrates this operation.

Simultaneous conditioning. As Fig. 2-1 reveals, simultaneous conditioning consists of presenting the CS and the UCS so that their onsets occur at the same time.

Trace conditioning. With trace conditioning, the CS is presented and terminated prior to the onset of the UCS. This results in an interval of time coming between the termination of the CS and the onset of the UCS. The term arises from the assumption that the neural trace left by the presentation of the CS acts as the CS. If the interval of time is less than one minute the procedure is referred to as a short trace conditioning procedure, while if the interval is a minute or longer, it is known as a long trace. Fig. 2-1 illustrates this operation.

Temporal conditioning. The temporal conditioning procedure is one in which the UCS is presented at regular intervals, for example, once every 60 seconds. (See Fig. 2-1.) With such a procedure, a conditioned response may appear increasingly near the point in time at which the UCS is presented. Pavlov (1927) wrote that from the results of his experiments, it seemed that time had acquired the properties of a conditioned stimulus. Time, of course, is only a frame of reference within which events take place. Presumably, it is some neural or behavioral event which occurs during the time period and which

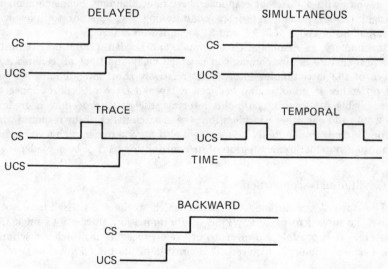

Fig. 2-1. Time relationships existing between the CS and UCS (except with temporal conditioning) in the various conditioning paradigms.

serves as the CS. This kind of situation has been used very little by American investigators, but as the review by Dmitriev and Kochigina (1959) reveals, it has been frequently employed by Russian experimenters.[5]

Backward conditioning. The last of these procedural operations is one in which the CS is presented following the UCS. This is illustrated in Fig. 2-1.

All classical conditioning procedures, with the exception of trace conditioning, have been defined in terms of CS and UCS *onset*; the termination of the CS and UCS is generally a matter of experimenter preference. The termination of the CS and UCS may be simultaneous, or one of these may continue after the other has terminated.

One question arising from our description of the varying classical conditioning procedures we have just described would be, is one procedure better than another? It has generally been found that the simultaneous, backward, and temporal paradigms are not very effective in establishing stable conditioned responses; as a result, delayed and trace procedures have been used most extensively. Ross and Ross (1971), and Ross, Ross, and Werden (1974), comparing the trace and delayed paradigms in human eyelid conditioning, and using either a simple or conditioned discrimination task, found no difference between these two procedures. Although a variety of interstimulus intervals were used in these studies, e.g., .25, .30, .35, .50, .80, 1.10, and 1.40 seconds, it must be noted that they were all relatively short, the longest being just 1.40 seconds.

Other investigators have found the delay procedure to be superior when longer interstimulus intervals are used. Ellison (1964) examining the conditioned salivary response in dogs found that the delay procedure was superior to the trace when the interstimulus interval was 16 seconds, although no difference was found when the interval was 8 seconds. Using a different organism, the rabbit, with a different response heart rate, Manning, Schneiderman, and Lordahl (1969) noted that delay conditioning was superior to trace when interstimulus intervals of 7, 14, and 21 seconds were utilized.

In summary, as Manning, Schneiderman, and Lordahl (1969) have indicated, a critical feature in any comparison between delay and trace procedures is the length of the interstimulus interval. At relatively short interstimulus intervals, the difference in conditioning between delay and trace procedures appears to be negligible. At long interstimulus intervals, the delay procedure is superior. We would add one other consideration—the characteristics of the response which is conditioned. Undoubtedly this variable also plays a role in such a comparison although a systematic examination of its contribution has not been made.

Conditioned Discrimination

The classical conditioning operations which we have discussed have not required the subject to make any kind of discrimination, since only a single CS is presented. It is possible, however, to utilize a procedure in which a discrimination between stimuli is required. This consists of the presentation of two CSs;

[5] Badia and Harley (1970) were unable to find evidence for the temporal conditioning of the EDR, although in an earlier study, Lockhart (1966) was presumably able to demonstrate this phenomenon. An unusual result, however, was that Lockhart was not able to extinguish the response.

one of these, designated as the positive stimulus or CS+, is followed by the UCS; the other, designated as the negative stimulus or CS-, is never followed by the UCS. This general procedure has been called differential conditioning or conditioned discrimination. Pavlov was the first investigator to employ this procedure which he termed the method of contrast.

Two different conditioned discrimination operations can be described. One has been to condition the response to the CS+, as would be done in a typical conditioning experiment. After the conditioned response has been established, the CS- is introduced by being randomly presented with the CS+. This procedure has been designated as separate phase differential conditioning. The more frequently used method is one in which both the CS+ and CS- are presented in random fashion from the beginning of the experiment. An experiment by Hartman and Grant (1962) illustrates this latter procedure. Two windows consisted of 10 cm. circular milk-glass discs with their centers approximately 15 cm apart. The illumination of one disc (either right or left) was always followed by the UCS—a puff of air to the cornea of the eye. The illumination of the adjacent disc was never followed by the UCS. Subjects were given 44 reinforced trials and 44 nonreinforced trials, with these trials being assigned randomly. CS-UCS intervals of .4, .6, .8, and 1.0 seconds were provided and conditioning to the positive and negative stimuli during six blocks of trials for each of these intervals is indicated in Fig. 2-2. The measurement of the CR to the CS+ and the CS- is plotted in terms of percent responding.

Rather than merely observing the differences as reflected in response frequency to the CS+ and CS-, many investigators have been interested in obtaining a single quantitative measure of conditioned discrimination. Most experimenters use some type of difference score expressed in terms of a percentage proportion, or ratio, but as Hilgard, Jones, and Kaplan (1951) noted some years ago, there is no single satisfactory way of measuring discrimination performance. One measure which has been used is the difference in percentage frequency of response to the positive and negative stimulus; an objection to this method is that the possible difference can never exceed the percentage frequency of response to the positive stimulus.

Another difference measure has been provided by Restle and Beecroft's (1955) index of relative differentiation (IRD). This measure, in its most general form, expresses the difference in response strength to the CS+ and CS- as a proportion of the sum of the response strengths. The formula is:

$$IRD = \frac{CR+ - CR-}{CR+ + CR-}$$

It may be noted that this measure can take any value from +1.00, which indicates perfect discrimination, through 0, which reflects no discrimination, to -1.00, which is perfect negative discrimination. In this latter, and completely improbable case, the subject is responding to each presentation of the CS- and not responding to the CS+.[6]

[6] Hilgard, Jones, and Kaplan (1951) have suggested that a measure which turns out to be in many respects the most satisfactory is not a difference score at all, but simply the percentage frequency of response to the negative stimulus. Thus, any subject who responds at a high frequency to the negative stimulus is

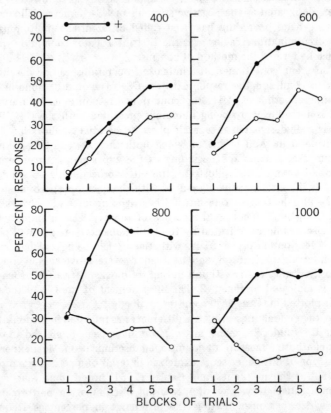

Fig. 2-2. Percentage frequency of anticipatory responses to the positive and negative stimuli during successive blocks of acquisition trials for the four CS–UCS intervals. The first block was four trials; subsequent blocks were eight trials each. *Adapted from Hartman and Grant (1962)*

Experimental Extinction and Postulated Inhibitory Processes

Following the establishment of a conditioned response, the repeated presentation of the CS without its being paired with the UCS will lead to a decrement or a decline in strength. Pavlov termed this decrement, experimental extinction, assuming that some internal inhibitory process was responsible for such a behavior change.

Response decrement could also arise from what Pavlov hypothesized to be

___

not discriminating very well. They further state, "Such a measure has the advantage of being derivable directly from the data, with conversion neither to a difference score nor to a ratio score; interpretation of the score is made easier by this lack of conversion" (p. 96).

(1) internal as well as (2) external inhibition. Internal inhibition arose from the introduction of a new conditioned stimulus. Operationally, this took the following form. Following the establishment of a conditioned response to one stimulus (CS_1), a new stimulus (CS_2) was occasionally presented with CS_1, although the combined stimuli were never accompanied by the UCS. As a result of these pairings, the combined stimulus (CS_1 + CS_2) gradually became ineffective, although CS_1, when presented alone, retained its capacity to elicit the conditioned response.

Pavlov found that the course of development of conditioned inhibition was not always the same. In some cases, the addition of a new stimulus (CS_2) to the conditioned stimulus (CS_1) resulted immediately in a diminution or even a complete disappearance of the conditioned response. With successive repetitions of the combination, the conditioned response returned almost to its original strength, and then declined. In other cases, the first few combinations of the new stimulus (CS_2) and the CS_1 resulted in an augmentation of the response as compared with the normal operation of the CS_1; only on subsequent trials did the response gradually diminish to zero.

External inhibition was posited to develop as a result of the introduction of the occurrence of an external stimulus, which was generally extraneous to the experimental environment. Pavlov has described the circumstances leading to the postulation of external inhibition as follows: "The dog and the experimenter would be isolated in the experimental room, all the conditions remaining for a while constant. Suddenly some disturbing factor would arise—a sound would penetrate into the room; some quick change in illumination would occur, the sun going behind a cloud; or a draught would get in underneath the door, and maybe bring some odour with it. If any one of these extra stimuli happened to be introduced just at the time of application of the conditioned stimulus, it would inevitably bring about a more or less pronounced weakening or even a complete disappearance of the reflex response, depending on the strength of the extra stimulus" (p. 44).

Of the varying operations described by Pavlov which have been posited to produce inhibition, experimental extinction has been of greatest interest to contemporary investigators. It is an easily reproducible or replicable phenomenon, and its similarity to habituation suggests that it is a basic type of behavior modification. Moreover, a number of experimenters have used experimental extinction as a response measure from which to infer the strength of the previously acquired conditioned response. Hull's (1943) *Principles of Behavior*, which posited experimental extinction as a basic measure of habit strength and performance, lent considerable support to this practice.

We should indicate that we are not in agreement with the use of experimental extinction as a measure from which to infer the strength of a conditioned response. If the experimental findings obtained during acquisition and extinction are similar, the extinction data are redundant; if they are different, considerable question must be raised in accepting extinction data as representing the strength of conditioning. The reason is that the elimination of the UCS may have changed the organism's motivation, attitude, expectancy, or some other related condition, with the result that responding during extinction is undoubtedly influenced by this changed organismic state. Consequently, extinction responses must be regarded as suspect when used to infer the strength of a conditioned response.[7]

Spontaneous Recovery

A phenomenon which Pavlov also called attention to was spontaneous recovery. If, following the experimental extinction of a response, the organism is provided with a rest period, and the CS is again presented, thus providing a second series of CS alone trials, the, conditioned response will again be elicited. The recovery of an extinguished response following an interval of rest is known as spontaneous recovery. Riess (1971) has written, "Of all the major phenomenon bequeathed by Pavlov to several generations of American psychologists interested in the conditioning process, spontaneous recovery has been by far the most unanimously ignored."[8] Riess has speculated that the reasons for this lack of interest have been the "atheoretical" nature of spontaneous recovery. As an experimental phenomenon it generated no differential predictions capable of testing the major learning theories which dominated conditioning research in America during the late forties and fifties—a period when there was interest on the part of many psychologists to establish a single, all-encompassing theory of learning. Riess has further pointed out that although these grand theoretical systems have passed into history, the hierarchy of experimental importance and investigative priorities assigned to various paradigms and variables during this period has continued to play an important role in experimental work so that spontaneous recovery continues to suffer its earlier neglect.

Higher Order Conditioning

The last classical conditioning procedure we would like to discuss is higher order conditioning. Following the establishment of a conditioned response, the experimenter may provide the subject with additional trials in which a new CS is paired with the previously utilized CS—in effect, the old CS serves as a UCS. After a number of pairings, the second CS becomes capable of eliciting the CR—a phenomenon known as higher order conditioning.

In an early experiment cited by Pavlov (1927) the ticking of a metronome (CS) followed by the presentation of meat powder (UCS) resulted in the metronome's eliciting salivation. Following such training, a visual stimulus in the form of a black square (CS_2) was paired with the metronome so that on the

---

[7] Bunch (1963) made a similar point some years ago when he wrote that the point of view which regards resistance to extinction as a measure of learning is one of the deepest blind alleys students have entered in quite a while. We would not want, however, to give the impression that experimental extinction should not be the subject of investigation. It is a most interesting type of behavior change but it should be investigated as a phenomenon in its own right rather than as a measure of learning.

[8] One exception to this is found in a series of studies by Grant and his associates (Grant, Hunter, and Patel 1958; Howat and Grant 1958; Beeman, Hartman, and Grant 1960).

tenth pairing, the black square was capable of eliciting salivation, although the response was about only half as strong.

The capacity of a second conditioned stimulus (CS_2) to elicit the conditioned response (the response having been conditioned to CS_1) has been specifically designated as second order conditioning. Third order conditioning procedures would involve the presentation of a third stimulus, CS_3, being paired with the CS_2 (the CS_2 serving as the UCS), while fourth order conditioning would consist of paired presentations of a fourth stimulus, CS_4 with CS_3 (CS_3 serving as the UCS). Early Russian investigators were interested in determining whether it was possible to set up conditioned responses above the second order. Pavlov's (1927) experimental studies led him to write that third order conditioning was possible if aversive stimulation such as shock was used as the UCS in the establishment of a defense response, such as, foot withdrawal. He indicated, however, that fourth order conditioning could not be established with his experimental subjects (dogs).

Russian experimenters have hypothesized that words (or language in general), by being paired with conditioned stimuli, may serve as second order conditioned stimuli in eliciting conditioned responses. When the human child is capable of using words to convey meaning, Soviet investigators have designated this as the second signalling system. Presumably, behavior comes under the control of this second signalling system in the same manner that higher order conditioned responses are established.

The use of words in the higher order conditioning experiment is illustrated by an experiment by Degtiar (1962, cited by Brackbill and Koltsova, 1967) who used children from 1-1/2 to 3 years of age as his subjects. The sound of a bell or the onset of a dim light served as conditioned stimuli in the development of a conditioned eyeblink response. Following such conditioning, the words "bell" and "lamp" were spoken by the experimenter prior to presenting either the auditory or visual stimulus. After a number of trials, the verbal stimuli alone were capable of eliciting the eyeblink. When older children were used as subjects, following the establishment of the bell or light as a conditioned stimulus, it was possible for the words to elicit the conditioned response without being previously paired with the sound or light. In summary, although the younger subjects had given evidence of knowing the meaning of these abstract words, it was necessary to establish a training procedure in order for these words to elicit the appropriate response. When older subjects were used, in whom the associative network among words and external stimuli had developed, the words themselves were effective.

An Analysis of the Conditioned Response

Many early experimenters believed that the CR was identical with the UCR and this hypothesized identity led to the use of the expression "substitution learning" as a synonym for classical conditioning. It was assumed that during the course of the conditioning trials, the CS came to substitute for the UCS in eliciting the UCR. In fact, a diagram, p. 30, which can be found in many introductory texts published during the past two or three decades and which indicates that the CS is connected to the UCR, has done much to encourage this point of view.

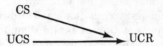

This position is contrary to the experimental evidence. Zener (1937) conditioned the dog's salivary response to a bell which served as a CS, and photographically recorded the whole conditioning procedure. His description of the animal's behavior during this period follows:

> Except for the component of salivary secretion the conditioned and unconditioned behavior is not identical. (a) During most of the time in which the bell is reinforced by the presence of food, chewing generally occurs with the head raised out of the food-pan but not directed either at the bell or into the food-pan, or at any definite environmental object. Yet this posture practically never, even chewing only occasionally, occurs to the conditioned stimulus alone. Despite Pavlov's assertions, the dog does not appear to be eating an imaginary food. (b) Nor is the behavior that does appear an arrested or partially unconditioned reaction consisting of those response elements not conflicting with other actions. It is a different reaction, anthropomorphically describable as a looking for, expecting, the fall of food with a readiness to perform the eating behavior which will occur when the food falls. The effector pattern is not identical with the unconditioned. (c) Movements frequently occur which do not appear as part of the unconditioned response to food: all the restless behavior of stamping, yawning, panting. (p. 393)

Most investigators following Zener (1937), if they had not before, recognized the impropriety of considering the conditioned response a replica of the unconditioned response. Shortly after Zener (1937), Hilgard and Marquis (1940) wrote that "conditioned and unconditioned responses are seldom, if ever, identical, and that the conditioned response is not simply a duplicate of the unconditioned response. . . . When attention is directed to the differences between conditioned and unconditioned behavior, as well as to similarities, the conditioned response is found to be very complex" (pp. 36–37). They went on to describe different kinds of conditioned responses, namely, (1) redintegrative, (2) fractional component, and (3) preparatory. Redintegrative responses were almost exact replicas of the unconditioned response, while the fractional component category represented a conditioned response which was merely one component of the unconditioned response. Finally, preparatory responses appeared to prepare the organism for the presentation of the UCS.

Having appropriately "defined" the nature of the conditioned response, experimenter interest turned toward theory testing and the analysis of variables which were believed to contribute to conditioned response learning. During the last decade, as Levey and Martin (1974) have indicated, there has been a renewed interest in the description and analysis of conditioned responses, as well as in how these responses change over a series of trials. We cannot at this time provide in any great detail the specifics of this work; however, a few examples will illustrate the approach.

The electrodermal response or GSR has frequently been used in classical conditioning, and traditional experiments have considered it to be only a single response. Recently, however, investigators have recognized that it consists of a number of components and that these components may vary differentially as traditional variables are manipulated. Undoubtedly, the results of many early experiments were specifically related to which component (or combinations of components) was being measured. Levey and Martin (1974) have similarly shown that in the human eyelid conditioning experiment, there is an orderly sequence of response development involving separate responses to the UCS, to the CS, a "double" CR/UCR, as well as final blending of the CR and UCR. This is obviously a far cry from conditioned eyeblink analysis which considered the conditioned eyeblink to have only a single form.

It has also been noted that the form as well as latency of the conditioned response may change as a function of the variable which is manipulated. For example, in a study by Wickens, Nield, Tuber, and Wickens (1969) cats were classically conditioned to respond with a paw movement and an electrodermal response at a variety of CS-UCS intervals. These investigators found that the responses which were acquired at longer CS-UCS intervals were different in both latency and form from responses acquired with the shorter CS-UCS intervals.

Methodology

Response Measurement

If the experimental procedure is such that the conditioned response can be made by the subject prior to the onset of the UCS, it is possible to secure a record of the growth of the conditioned response as a function of the number of CS-UCS presentations which are provided. On every trial it becomes possible to determine if a conditioned response has been made. Obtaining this kind of record demands that the conditioned response which is being examined have a short latency and/or the CS-UCS interval be of sufficient length to permit the conditioned response to be elicited without any interfering effects provided by the presentation of the UCS and its associated response. For example, the nictitating membrane response of the rabbit has a latency of 25 to 50 milliseconds; the use of a CS-UCS interval as short as 250 milliseconds will provide the experimenter with sufficient time to record a conditioned response on each trial.

In some instances, investigators may wish to examine the conditioning of responses which have long latencies, or desire to employ very short CS-UCS intervals. An experimenter may be interested in conditioning the nictitating membrane with a 25 millisecond CS-UCS interval. Under such circumstances, he may elect to use test trials to measure the conditioned response. The nature of these vary; in some instances, such trials consist of presenting only the CS on a fixed or random basis throughout the acquisition period while in other situations, the CS-UCS interval may be lengthened which permits the recording of a conditioned response clearly distinguishable from the unconditioned response. To illustrate, Bitterman (1964) provided goldfish with pairings of light (CS) and shock (UCS) which elicited generalized activity. In his investigation of the role of the CS-UCS interval which consisted of either 0, 3, or 9 seconds (Experiment 1) every tenth trial consisted of using a 10 second CS-UCS interval during which conditioned responses could be recorded. In Experiment 2, CS-UCS intervals consisting of 1, 9, or 27 secohds were used with a 40 second CS-UCS interval on every tenth trial.

A third procedure has been to use extinction trials. Inasmuch as the UCS is not presented, the response elicited by the CS is obviously independent of any unconditioned response. It has been recognized that in some instances, the absence of the UCS may cause the subject to realize that a "different" situation exists, with some change taking place in the characteristics of the extinction response.

The measurement of the specific characteristics of the conditioned response is of fundamental importance, and over the course of the acquisition and/or extinction trials, a variety of response measures may be obtained. These include: (1) frequency, (2) latency, (3) amplitude, and (4) magnitude.

Frequency, of course, refers to the number (or percentage) of times that the CS is able to elicit the response. Response latency is the length of time it takes the conditioned response to appear, as measured from the onset of the CS to the onset of the CR. Amplitude, as well as magnitude, refer to the amount or size of the conditioned response. When amplitude is obtained, trials in which no conditioned responses have been elicited are included in the averaging; magnitude measures, on the other hand, do not include these trials.

To make this distinction between amplitude and magnitude a little clearer, assume that the conditioned salivary response was obtained for ten dogs. If, on trial N, just eight dogs responded with salivation to the presentation of the CS, the mean magnitude response for that particular trial would be obtained by summing the varying amounts of salivation and dividing by 8. On the other hand, if an amplitude measure was desired, the divisor would be 10.[9]

The selection of the response measure in one sense may be regarded as an arbitrary decision, although most investigators are guided by those response measures which earlier experimenters have used, and which have shown an orderly relationship to the variable (or variables) under consideration.

The Interrelationship Among Response Measures

What is the relationship among the varying classical conditioning response measures? Table 2-1 presents a sampling of the correlation coefficients which

[9] Pennypacker (1964) has called attention to another definition of magnitude. Using the conditioned eyelid reflex, he has defined magnitude as the integral of the amplitude over the time course of the blink and has suggested that this measure provides a description of the physical properties of the response which is statistically superior to that provided by other measures. It has been used, however, only infrequently.

Table 2-1 Intercorrelations Among Various Classical Conditioning Measures

	Frequency and Amplitude	Frequency and Magnitude	Frequency and Latency	Latency and Amplitude	Latency and Magnitude	Magnitude and Amplitude
Campbell & Hilgard (1936) (Conditioned eyelid in the dog)	.63		-.54	-.15		
Campbell (1938) (Conditioned knee jerk in human)	.63		-.27	-.27		
Kellogg and Walker (1938) (Conditioned flexion in dog)	.94		-.18	.22		
Brogden (1949) (Conditioned forelimb flexion in dog)	r between number of trials to reach acquisition criterion and extinction criterion = .19					
Pennypacker (1964)* (Conditioned eyeblink in human)		.59			-.71	.86
Wittig and Wickens (1966) (Conditioned EDR in human)					-.68 to -.85	

*Magnitude measure is the integral of momentary amplitude with respect to time.

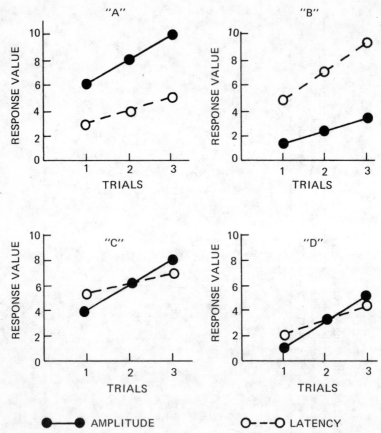

Fig. 2-3. Amplitude and reciprocal latency values plotted for three conditioning trials and for four subjects, A, B, C, and D.

have been obtained. It is obvious from the size of these correlations that it is difficult to predict one response measure from knowledge of another.

Most psychologists working in this area have been interested, however, not in the attempt to make predictions about one response measure from another; rather, their concern has been in determining whether the varying response measures reflect similar changes which occur as a result of the manipulation of basic conditioning variables. Thus, this specific question can be asked: if increasing the number of CS-UCS pairings results in decreasing the latency of the conditioned response, would response amplitude also change appropriately? In answering this question, the correlations among individual measures of response strength as presented in Table 2-1 are not appropriate. Such analyses introduce into the situation a number of sources of variance, for example, individual differences, which reduce the value of any correlation coefficient that is obtained.

Table 2-2   Computation of the Rank Order Correlation Between Amplitude
and Reciprocal Latency Values

Subjects	Mean Amplitude	Mean Latency	Rank Amplitude	Rank Latency	D	D^2
A	8	4	4	2	2	4
B	2	7	1	4	3	9
C	6	6	3	3	0	0
D	3	3	2	1	1	1
						14

$$\text{rho} = 1 - \frac{6 \cdot 14}{4\,(16 - 1)} = 1 - 1.4 = -.40$$

A hypothetical situation may make this a little clearer. Our procedure consists of conditioning the human eyeblink, with four college students, A, B, C, and D, serving as our experimental subjects. The response measures are (1) latency as well as (2) amplitude of the response. Each subject is provided 3 CS-UCS trials. For ease of understanding, we have used the reciprocal of latency, and converted these response measures into arbitrary values, placing them on the ordinate of Fig. 2-3.

Analysis of the data found in Table 2-2 reveals that the rank order correlation between the two response measures is -.40, so that accurate prediction of one response measure from the other cannot be made. On the other hand, both response measures increase as a function of CS-UCS presentations. It is this similarity of function which is most important at this stage of our development. Unfortunately, there has been little systematic investigation of this type of interrelationship among response measures.

Other Response Measurement Considerations

Two interesting developments may be noted in the response measurement area. One has been the concomitant measurement of several responses obtained during the same experiment. Such instances demand, of course, that the UCS be capable of eliciting several UCRs so that their accompanying CRs may be examined.

An excellent example of this type of measurement operation is found in a study by Yehle (1968) who examined differences in conditioned discrimination among the following responses in the rabbit: (1) nictitating membrane, (2) heart rate, and (3) respiration rate. Three tones, namely 350 (low), 1650 (medium) and 2950 (high) Hz served as conditioned stimuli, while the UCS was a 5 ma electric shock delivered near the subject's right eye. Six different groups of subjects were used, with each group receiving differing combinations of CS+ and CS-. Table 2-3 indicates the tone frequencies and reinforcement contingencies for each of these groups. Thus, for Group A, the CS+ was associated with the low frequency tone while the CS- was associated with the medium and high frequency tones.

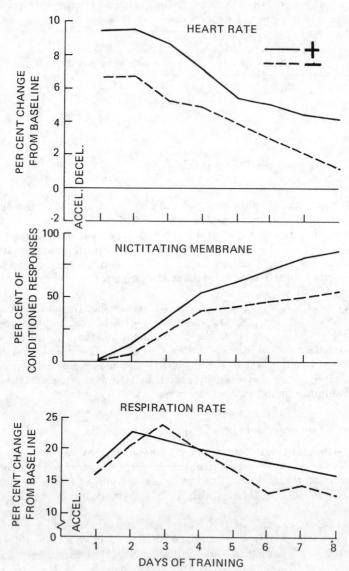

Fig. 2-4. Combined responses to the reinforced and to the nonreinforced tones for each of the three response systems. *Adapted from Yehle (1968)*

All of the groups received one day of adaptation and eight days of acquisition. During each acquisition day all subjects received 72 trials consisting of 24 presentations each of the three different CSs. It would serve no useful purpose to provide a detailed examination of the experimental findings; however, Fig.

Table 2-3   Tone Frequencies and Reinforcement Contingencies in Each
Group During Acquisition

	Low Frequency	Medium Frequency	High Frequency
Group A	+	–	–
Group B	–	–	+
Group C	+	+	–
Group D	–	+	+
Group E	–	+	–
Group F	+	–	+

Note.— + = reinforcement, – = nonreinforcement.
Adapted from Yehle (1968)

2-4 presents the combined responses to the reinforced and nonreinforced tones
for each of the three response systems over the eight acquisition days. It may
be noted that conditioned heart rate appears at full strength during the first
two days, followed by a gradual decline. A somewhat similar, though less pronounced function was found for respiration rate. On the other hand, the conditioned nictitating response increased gradually from 0 strength on the first day
to a high value on the last. When conditioned responding to the varying reinforcement contingencies was examined, Yehle (1968) found that heart rate
for all six groups revealed early and reliable evidence of discrimination; an examination of the conditioned nictitating membrane response revealed reliable
discriminations for just three of these groups, while only two groups showed
reliable evidence of respiration rate discrimination. As Schneiderman (1973)
has written, such findings suggest that general statements about classical conditioning based upon performance in which only a single response measure is
obtained must be made cautiously. If only the nictitating membrane response
had been examined, it would have been tempting to conclude that the conditioned response was acquired only gradually; an examination of just the heart
rate response would have led to the opposite conclusion. Where these kinds of
results will lead us in our examination of classical conditioning is difficult to
say. What is obvious, however, is that they cannot be ignored.

A second development is found in the use of mathematical models to describe
the classical conditioning process. Perhaps the most promising of these has been
provided by Prokasy (1972) who, in his investigations of human eyelid conditioning, has proposed a two-phase model. He has assumed a beginning or first
phase (starting with the first conditioning trial) in which response probability
remains constant. During this phase, learning does not take place. During the
second phase, there are increases in response strength—the outcome of each
trial contributing to subsequent response probability. (We may note that his
basic response measure is probability.) In summary, the subjects begin training
with one set of rules governing response probability but at some trial, there is
a switch to another set. In describing this two phase model, a number of param-

eters have been identified. One is the initial rate of the subject's responding, while a second is the parameter K, represented by the trial that separates the first, nonresponding phase from the second during which there are increases in response strength. The third parameter is theta, θ, or rate of growth of response strength, while the fourth is P ∞ which represents the conditioning asymptote.

Aside from those contributions that the model can make in describing as well as predicting the development of a conditioned response, the model becomes an excellent tool for the analysis of conditioning data. As Prokasy (1972) has written, where precedent has been that statistical analysis is made on such measures as overall response probability, the model provides four dependent variables (parameters) with which to analyze the effects of independent variable manipulation. In almost all conditioning experiments, the investigator provides some gross overall measure which frequently results in a statistically reliable treatment effect. The use of the model, however, shows precisely the locus of treatment effects and thus provides more information on the role that the independent variable plays in the development of the conditioned response.

The Use of Control Procedures

As we have already noted, a conditioning trial consists of the presentation of a CS followed by a UCS, and the appearance of the conditioned response is assumed to be a product of this double stimulation (CS-UCS) procedure. It is possible that the conditioned response may arise as a result of conditions other than the pairing of stimuli; in order to be sure that the double stimulation procedure is a necessary condition for the establishment of the conditioned response, control procedures must be employed.

It is a common practice for many investigators to provide separate presentations of the CS to all subjects prior to the introduction of the CS-UCS pairings. This is done in order to observe the characteristics of the response to the CS alone. This response can be compared subsequently with the response resulting from the CS-UCS pairing.

In addition, separate control groups employing specific control operations should be utilized. These are as follows:

1. Presentation of the conditioned stimulus alone. With this procedure, control subjects are provided the same number of CS presentations as the experimental subjects. The UCS is not administered.
2. Presentation of the unconditioned stimulus alone. Here, control subjects receive the same number of UCS presentations as the experimental subjects. The CS is not administered.
3. Random (or unpaired) presentation of the conditioned stimulus and the unconditioned stimulus. With this procedure, control subjects receive the same number of CS and UCS presentations as the experimental subjects; the difference, however, is that stimulus presentations are not paired. There are a variety of ways to program these presentations but the most typical has been to present the CS and the

UCS singly and in random order but subject to the restriction that they never appear in close temporal contiguity.

Many studies have indicated that some of these control procedures are capable of eliciting "conditioned" responses similar to those obtained with the paired presentation of the CS and UCS. These responses have been identified as alpha, beta, and/or pseudoconditioned responses, their classification depending upon the nature of the response as well as the preference of the investigator.

In the conditioning of some responses, for example, the eyeblink, experimenters have noted that the CS will elicit a reflex response which they have identified as an *alpha* response. This response bears a basic similarity to the response which is made to the CS after a number of CS-UCS pairings. It can be differentiated from the conditioned response only by a careful examination of its latency, duration and amplitude. For example, the experimental studies of Grant and Adams (1944) and Moore and Gormezano (1961) have demonstrated that when a change in illumination served as the CS in eyeblink conditioning, the CS would elicit a slight lid closure which had a much smaller amplitude than the unconditioned response, with a latency of 40 to 120 milliseconds. The criterion used for conditioning, however, was lid closure with a latency of 200 to 500 milliseconds after CS onset.

A frequently used procedure, as we have stated earlier, has been to provide CS presentations prior to conditioning trials until the alpha response habituates or adapts out. One problem, however, is that sometimes, a single CS-UCS pairing may be capable of reinstating the alpha response. This phenomenon is referred to as sensitization, an example of which is found in an early study by Prosser and Hunter (1936). The presentation of an auditory stimulus did not elicit a startle response in the rat. The occurrence of shock serving as the UCS, which did elicit the startle response, resulted in the previously ineffective auditory stimulus being capable of eliciting this response.

Beta responses have been identified in a series of studies by Grant and his associates (Grant, 1943a, 1943b, 1945; Grant and Norris, 1947) investigating the conditioned eyeblink. Like alpha, these responses are reflexive responses but are specifically elicited by visual stimuli. Moreover, beta responses have a longer latency than alpha responses—100 to 200 milliseconds. They were first observed as the CS was presented to subjects who were becoming more and more dark adapted under the low illumination conditions which early experimenters needed in order to photograph their subjects' responses.

Contemporary investigators, no longer dependent upon photography to record the eyeblink response, now use well-illuminated subject-cubicles, and as Moore and Gormezano (1961) have demonstrated, such illumination reduces the occurrence of beta responses to relatively low frequencies.

Pseudoconditioned responses, according to some investigators, among them, Kimble (1961) include alpha and beta responses; other experimenters like May (1948) and Gormezano (1966) prefer to consider pseudoconditioned responses as arising primarily from presentations of the UCS alone, most usually when an aversive UCS is used. As Wickens and Wickens (1942) have written, "if a series of fairly strong unconditioned stimuli is presented alone and that series is followed by a previously neutral stimulus, it is found that this previously neutral stimulus now produces a response similar to the one given to the unconditioned stimulus—this, although the two stimuli have never been paired" (p. 518).

Although classical conditioning procedures were not employed, a study by Wickens and Wickens (1942) does serve to illustrate the phenomenon. Their general procedure consisted of having white rats learn to escape from shock by running from one end to the other end of a partitioned box when the grid floor was electrified. Following 35 shocks, administered over a three day period, animals were placed in the compartment and a test trial consisted of the presentation of a light. Four groups of animals were used. For one group, the shock which was presented occurred suddenly and the test light occurred suddenly; for the second group, both shock and light increased gradually. For the third group, the shock was sudden and the test trial light was gradual, while for the fourth group, the shock was gradual and the light presentation was gradual. Results revealed that of 19 animals in the sudden–sudden, or gradual–gradual groups, 15 responded to the presentation of the light. Quite obviously, pseudoconditioning in these groups was quite marked. On the other hand, of 18 animals in the other two groups, only 3 responded to the light.

A number of studies examing a variety of responses in a number of different organisms have indicated that pseudoconditioning procedures are capable of eliciting responses similar to those found with normal conditioning operations. A sampling of these studies is found in Table 2-4.

Sheafor and Gormezano (1972) have recently called attention to the fact that little is known about the parametric determinants of pseudoconditioning. Similarly, explanations for the phenomenon have been few. Perhaps the most prevalent position has been to posit a classical conditioning process involved in UCS alone presentations. Wickens and Wickens (1942) have proposed that the organism responds to the CS after a series of UCS alone trials ". . . by virtue of the fact that the pseudoconditioned stimulus actually had some characteristics in common with the unconditioned stimulus." In their experiment, cited earlier, the common characteristics or conditioned stimulus, was the rate of change of the stimulus. Thus, "in groups where the rate of change of the pseudoconditioned stimulus and the unconditioned stimulus was similar, there was a high degree of conditioning, or, if you will, pseudoconditioning. In the groups in which there was a differing rate of the change for the pseudoconditioned and the unconditioned stimuli, the amount of conditioning was slight" (p. 524).

The Truly Random Control Group

In a series of papers, Rescorla (1967, 1968, 1969) has argued that the relevant dimension in conditioned response learning is the learning of a contingency between the CS and the UCS. The conditions for the establishment of a CR are met when there is a positive contingency between the CS and UCS, or when the probability of the occurrence of the UCS is higher during and just following the presentation of the CS than it is at any other time. Conversely, a CS which forecasts a reduction in the probability of the occurrence of the UCS

Table 2-4   Summaries of a Sampling of Studies Examining Pseudoconditioning

Investigators	Organism	CS	UCS	Response
Grether (1938)	Monkeys	Bell	Snake blow-out or exploding flash powder	Backward movement of head and torso
Harlow (1939)	Goldfish	Weak shock or vibration	Strong shock	Struggling or flight
Harlow and Toltzien (1940)	Cats	Buzzer	Shock	Variety of responses ranging from dilation of pupil and blinking of eye
Wickens and Wickens (1940)	Infants	Buzzer	Shock	Foot withdrawal
Grant and Hilgard (1940)	Humans	Tone or Light	Airpuff	Eyeblink
Harris (1941)	Humans	Tone	Shock	Finger movement
Grant and Meyer (1941)	Humans	Buzzer or Light	Shock	Hand withdrawal
Wickens and Wickens (1942)	Rats	Light or Tone	Shock	Running response
May (1948)	Rats	Buzzer	Shock	Running response
Champion and Jones (1961)	Humans	Tone	Shock	Electrodermal response
Mitchell and Gormezano (1970)	Rabbits	Tone	Water	Jaw movement
Sheafor and Gormezano (1972)	Rabbits	Tone	Water	Jaw movement

results in the development of an inhibitory process which effectively retards the subsequent establishment of a CR to that CS.

As a result of this position, Rescorla believes that all of the control groups which we have delineated are inadequate, arguing that each of the control procedures, although attempting to eliminate the CS-UCS contingency, can be shown to do considerably more. In the case of the control group which has the random presentation of the CS and the UCS—the group which is most frequently used as a control—Rescorla argues that the unpaired presentation of the CS and the UCS introduces a new contingency for the organism. This contingency is one in which the UCS cannot follow the CS for some minimum time interval, so that the CS acts as a signal for the absence of the UCS. Rescorla (1967) has written, "Although this is an interesting procedure in itself, it does not allow a comparison between two groups, one with a CS-US contingency and one without it. We are, instead, in the position of having two different CS-US contingencies which may yield different results" (p. 73).

Rescorla (1967) has suggested that a "truly random" control procedure would solve the problem which he has raised. With this procedure ". . . both the CS and US are presented to S but there is *no contingency whatsoever* between them. That is, the two events are programmed entirely randomly and independently in such a way that some 'pairings' of CS and US may occur by chance alone. All CS and US occurrences for the control group are the same as for the experimental group except that the regular temporal contingency between CS and UCS is eliminated. The occurrence of the CS provides *no information* about the subsequent occurrences of the US" (p. 74). Another way of looking at Rescorla's position has been to conceptualize the CS, as a result of being presented alone, as acquiring inhibitory properties. In consequence, the organism has difficulty in attaching any response to this stimulus.

A number of experimenters have obtained results which support Rescorla's assumption that the traditional control procedure results in behavior which is different from that obtained with the truly random control condition. In general, the kinds of experimental operations which have been supportive of Rescorla have been classical conditioning procedures used in conjunction with an instrumental learning task. The classical conditioned emotional response is one example. Briefly, this procedure consists of exposing a rat to the pairing of a CS (light or tone) with a UCS (shock) for a number of trials. Although it is assumed that the CS will elicit an emotional response, this response is not measured during the paired presentation of the stimuli. The animal is then returned to an instrumental learning task (Skinner box) where it had learned on a previous occasion to press a bar in order to obtain food. The presentation of the CS while the animal is bar pressing results in a suppression of this response. This finding is used to infer the presence of an emotional response which has been elicited by the CS and which interferes with the instrumental response of bar pressing. When the traditional control group is used in this experiment—the single and random presentation of the CS and UCS—Rescorla avers that the animal *learns* the CS is not followed by shock. The truly random control procedure, however, does not result in the animals learning this contingency. As a result, the traditional control group should reveal less suppression of bar pressing than subjects provided the truly random control procedure. The experiments of Rescorla (1968, 1969), and Hammond (1966, 1967, 1968) have been of this general type and have supported the position that the truly random procedure does produce a different level of instrumental responding than traditional control groups.

However, the issue of which control group is appropriate to use has not been completely resolved. First, some experimenters have found that when the truly random control procedure is used, there is the opportunity for CS-UCS pairings to take place, and the number of these pairings may contribute to the experimental findings. Kremer (1961) has shown that the outcome of a truly random control treatment may depend on what he has termed the "stimulus density" of the training schedule. He has found that if any experimental session contains a fairly large number of temporally contiguous CS-UCS presentations, excitatory properties are acquired by the CS. If the experimental sessions contain only a few of these, the CS appears to have neutral characteristics. Although Benedict and Ayres (1972) were unable to demonstrate that the absolute number of these CS-UCS pairings were of experimental importance, they did find that when a CS-UCS pairing took place early in the experimental session, the CS acquired excitatory properties. In summary, the truly random control procedure does not always result in a "neutral" CS. Whether it does or not appears to depend on the location and number of CS-UCS pairings that take place during the experimental session. Perhaps what this suggests is that the truly random control procedure should not be completely random; that an appropriate control procedure is to provide the organism with some CS-UCS pairings but that these pairings should not take place early in the training session and that they should be limited in number.

It should also be acknowledged that Rescorla's position has not had experimental validation when the conditioning of electrodermal responses has been undertaken. Studies by Furedy and Schiffmann (Furedy, 1971a; Furedy and Schiffmann, 1971; Schiffmann and Furedy, 1972; Furedy and Schiffmann, 1973) have provided little support for the position that the truly random control group produces different experimental results than traditional control groups. In summarizing their experimental findings, Furedy and Schiffmann (1973) have written that "when considered together, the data from these studies seem to strongly indicate that Rescorla's (1967) methodological criticism of the propriety of the traditional nCS- control has little empirical force, and that there is little evidence to suggest that, in human autonomic conditioning, the nCS- control develops any detectable conditioned inhibition, a process for which Rescorla (1969) has adduced considerable evidence from nonautonomic animal-conditioning studies" (p. 215).

Finally, Seligman (1969) has taken issue with Rescorla's position on the general grounds that one cannot always determine a priori what kinds of control groups should be used. He has written that one controls not only for the experimental operations which are used but also for the results that those operations are expected to produce.

For example, if a CS and UCS (shock) are presented in an unpredictable or truly random sequence, it is possible that such unpredictability may have consequences of its own which in turn lead to a confounding of the experimental findings. Seligman has experimentally demonstrated such to be the case. In his experiment, two groups of rats learned to press a bar for food. Following the establishment of a stable bar pressing response, a conditioning paradigm was instituted. Here, a tone served as a CS while shock was used as the UCS. For one group, a truly random control procedure was used in which the tone and shock were programmed independently of each other, thus making the onset of shock unpredictable. A second group was run in which they received the typical CS-UCS presentation.[10]

When the two groups were returned to the bar pressing task, the presentation

---

[10] With this kind of task, it is assumed that the contiguous presentation of the CS and UCS results in some emotional response being produced by the CS—a consequence of the fact that pain produced by the electric shock usually has an emotional component. Moreover, it has been observed that the presence of such an emotional state results in the secession or inhibition of appetitive activities. If the animal was pressing a bar for food, the presentation of the CS would elicit an emotional state which in turn would result in a secession or suppression of the bar pressing response.

of the tone for the predictable shock group resulted in reducing the bar pressing response for a short period of time, but, inasmuch as shock never followed the presentation of the CS, the animals' responding returned to normal. In contrast, the animals in the unpredictability group stopped bar pressing completely and did not recover.

In this situation the independence between the CS and the UCS while eliminating the CS-UCS contingency, also did considerably more. It introduced a new factor—that of unpredictability of shock—into the control group. As a result, bar pressing was not only completely disrupted, but a physiological examination of the control animals revealed the presence of ulcers. Seligman has argued that one could hardly view the unpredictable group as an appropriate control for this experiment. In summary, Seligman's position is that when a control group is used, the experimenter must be alert to the possibility that one operational difference may produce several effects and that appropriate controls should be exercised for all of these effects.

Summary

Discovered by Pavlov, the classically conditioned response is generally regarded as one of the simplest forms of learning and has served as a paradigm from which investigators could deduce basic learning principles. The experimental procedure consists of the pairing of a conditioned stimulus (CS) with an unconditioned stimulus (UCS). The CS has been defined as a neutral stimulus, while the UCS has the capacity to elicit a regular and measurable response known as the unconditioned response (UCR). The consistent presentation of these stimuli in close temporal contiguity results in the CS being capable of eliciting a response which generally has some of the characteristics of the UCR and is designated as a conditioned response (CR).

A variety of different conditioning procedures, such as delayed, simultaneous, trace, temporal, and backward conditioning, have been examined. The basic dimension manipulated in all of these situations except temporal conditioning is the temporal relationship existing between the CS and the UCS.

It is possible to use a classical conditioning procedure in which a discrimination between stimuli is demanded. This consists of randomly presenting two CSs, one positive, and always followed by the UCS, the other negative and never associated with the UCS.

The repeated presentation of the CS, not paired with the UCS, results in experimental extinction—a diminution and eventual cessation of the conditioned response. Pavlov assumed that an internal inhibitory process was responsible for this type of behavior change. In addition, Pavlov posited the existence of another inhibitory state, external inhibition, which would also produce conditioned response decrement. Here, an extraneous stimulus presented concurrently with the CS would result in response decrement or cessation.

If a rest period is interpolated between the last extinction trial and a subsequent presentation of the CS, there is the spontaneous recovery of the response, although the CR is not as strong as those obtained on early extinction trials. This phenomenon has been described as spontaneous recovery.

A final classical conditioning phenomenon is higher order conditioning. Following the establishment of a conditioned response, the association of a new CS (CS$_2$) with the old CS (CS$_1$) will result in the CS$_2$ being capable of eliciting the CR. CS$_1$ appears to assume a UCS function.

Early investigators believed that the CR was the same as the UCR and that the conditioning process was one of substituting the CS for the UCS. Contemporary experimenters, however, have pointed out that there are substantial differences between the two responses. The CR appears to prepare the organism for the presentation of the UCS, or else represents some fractional part of the unconditioned response.

An important consideration in the classical conditioning experiment is the use of a control group—a group which is not provided with the double stimulation procedure and against which the experimental group's performance is judged. It has been accepted that the presentation of (1) the CS alone, (2) the UCS alone, or (3) the random presentation of the CS and the UCS, are all appropriate control procedures. Recently, concern has been raised over the use of each of these methods; most criticism has been directed at the random presentation procedure since it is most frequently used. The argument has been that since the UCS never follows the CS in close temporal contiguity with the random method, the organism *learns* this contingency. An alternative procedure has been suggested—the use of a truly random control. This consists of presenting the CS and UCS in a truly random order—a procedure which on occasion does result in a close temporal pairing of the CS and UCS and which has the characteristics of a conditioning trial.

3

An Examination of a Variety of Classical Conditioned Responses

It is not surprising that a number of classical conditioned responses have been experimentally investigated. We cannot describe all of these, but we should like to discuss those which have been most frequently examined. In view of the variety, it seems appropriate to provide some classification of them. The taxonomy which we would propose is based upon whether the response is primarily related to the (1) autonomic or (2) skeletal system. Within each of these general categories it is also possible to classify a conditioned response in terms of whether the UCS is (a) aversive (shock, acid) or (b) appetitive or nonaversive (food).

It is of some historical interest that Watson (1916) originally proposed a classification based upon (a) conditioned motor reflexes and (b) conditioned secretion reflexes. He wrote, "whether there is any genuine distinction between the two types depends, I think, upon what ultimately will be found to be true about the *modus operandi* of the glands (i.e., whether under such conditions muscular activity is essential to glandular activity or whether control of the glands can be attained independently of the muscles through nervous mechanisms)" (p. 92).

The Conditioning of Responses Controlled by the Autonomic Nervous System

The Salivary Response

Pavlov's early work in conditioning the salivary response of dogs stimulated a number of American investigators to attempt to condition this response in humans. A basic difficulty was how to measure the response since the surgical procedures which were used with dogs could not be employed. One early attempt to solve this problem was provided by Lashley (1916) who used a small metal capsule which was placed over one of the salivary ducts in the mouth of his subjects. Attached to this capsule was a tube which conveyed the saliva out of the mouth. Drops of saliva were counted as they emerged from the end of the tube. After considerable experimentation, Lashley believed that this technique was not sufficiently promising to pursue and as a result, moved on to other areas of interest.[1]

General difficulties with the salivary capsule led Razran (1935) to devise a much more simple procedure for measuring salivation. This method consisted of placing a preweighed dental cotton roll under the subject's tongue for a given period of time. The cotton roll was subsequently removed and reweighed with the difference in weight being used to infer a corresponding salivary response. In salivary conditioning experiments, the eating of pretzels was used as the UCS, while tones or increases in illumination served as the CS.

Feather's (1967) review of early experimental work with human salivary conditioning has indicated that, although a variety of other procedures have been used to measure the response, only the two which we have discussed had sufficient numbers of subjects to enable him to evaluate their usefulness. Feather stated that with the cotton roll technique, considerable extraneous stimulation takes place as a result of inserting and removing the roll. As a result, it becomes difficult to separate this effect from that produced by the presentation of the conditioned stimulus. A second factor is that this procedure does not indicate how a single CR develops over time. The capsule technique, on the other hand, minimizes these difficulties and seems to be a superior method of measuring salivation.

It is obvious that the measurement problem which occurs with humans is easily solved when dogs are used as subjects. A surgical procedure is employed in which there is the insertion of a plastic tube into the parotid duct of the animal. The tube is then brought to the outside of the animal's jaw. Measurement of the response can be made on each CS-UCS presentation. The salivary

[1] The Russian investigator, Krasnagorsky (1926), independently devised a salivary capsule almost identical to that used by Lashley. He was considerably more successful than Lashley since by 1933 he had used this procedure in more than two dozen experiments (Razran, 1933).

secretion can be elicited in the dog by appetitive stimuli—meat powder—as well as by aversive stimuli—acid or alkaline solutions, so that comparisons can be made between the two experimental procedures. In spite of the obvious advantages in using dogs as experimental subjects, American investigators have used these animals infrequently. Russian experimenters, on the other hand, have made extensive use of them.[2]

Electrodermal Activity: The Galvanic Skin Response

Two different techniques have been involved in electrodermal measurement, namely, endosomatic and exosomatic methods. With endosomatic, no external electrical current is provided and the only source of electrical activity is the skin itself and its interaction with the electrode-electrolyte system which connects the surface of the skin with an appropriate measuring device. This procedure was discovered by Tarchanoff in 1890; the response measure obtained is generally acknowledged to be an increase in skin potential. This method is only infrequently used by classical conditioning investigators since there is considerable difficulty in obtaining reliable response measurement.

The second method of measurement, exosomatic, was discovered by Feré and presumably results from bioelectric changes attendant upon excitation of the eccritic sweat glands which is produced by an external source of electrical current.[3]

If two electrodes are placed on the surface of the skin, and a weak *direct* current is provided, the skin acts as a resistor. A voltage develops across these electrodes, and by the application of Ohm's law, it is possible to calculate the apparent resistance. If an appropriate stimulus is presented to the subject, there will be a decline in the measured voltage, the decline indicating a fall in the resistance provided by the skin. Measures of apparent resistance may also be expressed in terms of its reciprocal, conductance. If a weak *alternating* current is provided, impedance—a measure which is analogous to resistance—is used. The response which is measured as a function of stimulation has a characteristic waveform, with a latency of 1 to 4 seconds, while the waveform itself takes from 1 to 5 seconds to reach its peak.

The term galvanic skin response, or GSR, has been used to describe all of the various response measures which have been obtained from the electrical activity of the skin. Woodworth and Schlosberg (1954) suggested some time

---

[2] Razran's (1957) extensive bibliography indicates that there were 618 Russian experiments on salivary conditioning of dogs, with 334 of these published after 1927.

[3] We say "presumably" since it should be recognized that even now some controversy exists over the specific peripheral processes involved in this response. Edelberg (1972), writing of this continuing controversy, has stated, "It is of more than academic interest, for, until the basic nature of the peripheral events in this reflex has been elucidated, the absence of a rational basis for appropriate quantitative treatment of electrodermal measures and for the behavioral interpretation of this form of biological adaptation will continue to be a barrier to progress" (p. 368).

ago that electrodermal response (EDR) was the safest term to use, and recently, other investigators, e.g., Prokasy and Raskin (1973), have begun to accept this position. Edelberg (1972) has suggested that EDR deserves adoption and "that the terms GSR or PGR [psychogalvanic response] despite a long tradition, may have to be sacrificed in the interest of standardization" (p. 374). In view of the fact that most contemporary psychologists use the term GSR, there would appear to be no good reason why GSR and EDR could not be used interchangeably. Perhaps of greater importance and in keeping with recent suggestions, investigators should be more precise in describing their measurement operations, using such terms as skin conductance level (SCL), skin resistance level (SRL), etc.

The conditioning of the EDR in animals has been attempted only infrequently. Wickens, Meyer, and Sullivan (1961) were able to condition the EDR in cats; however, an extensive period of adaptation to the experimental room and apparatus was necessary prior to successful conditioning.

Response Measurement

The measurement of the "conditioned" EDR represents a problem with which many investigators have wrestled. One difficulty arises from the extreme sensitivity of the response. A variety of random external as well as internal stimuli may elicit responses which in turn contribute to the variability of the response measure. It has been frequently demonstrated that the EDR is made as an orienting response to the CS and this response continues to occur for a number of trials. A sufficient number of trials in which the CS is presented alone must be provided at the beginning of the experiment in order for this response to habituate.

The history of EDR conditioning begins with John B. Watson's (1916) early work, reported in his presidential address to the American Psychological Association. Using the sound of a bell as a CS combined with electric shock to the foot, he believed that if the double stimulation procedure was provided for a sufficient number of trials, the CS would produce body changes which could be recorded on the galvanometer. Much to his dismay, he was forced to write that the only fault to be found with such a train of reasoning is that it does not work out when put to practical test. Six years later, however, a study by Golla (1921), and subsequent experiments by Slight (1929), Jones (1930), and Freeman (1930) demonstrated that the EDR could be conditioned. Virtually thousands of EDR studies have been conducted since these early demonstrations.

The presentation of a tone or light typically serves as the CS, although a variety of other stimuli have been used, depending upon the nature of the experiment. Usually shock serves as the UCS, although a loud noise is sometimes used, Geer and his associates (Geer, 1968; Geer and Klein, 1969; Price and Geer, 1972) have employed slide photos of dead bodies as their unconditioned stimuli.

Young (1965) has suggested that a nonaversive UCS might be just as effective in eliciting the EDR as shock, and a few investigators have successfully demonstrated this. Furedy (1967) has reported that the use of a cool puff of air on the forehead of his subjects who had been placed in a very warm room was sufficient to elicit a regular EDR, while Corah and Tomkiewicz (1971) have shown that slides chosen on the basis of "novelty" may serve as appropriate unconditioned stimuli in a differential conditioning study. The pictures were not only "novel" but it appeared that a number of them would arouse some emotional response in their female subjects, so that many individuals would consider them to be aversive (e.g., a frog eating worms, a male auto accident victim, or a snake strangling a mouse).

The pairing of the CS and UCS for a number of trials will result in the CS's eliciting the EDR. But the UCS also elicits the EDR. As Badia and Defran (1970) have indicated, if a short CS-UCS interval is used (a frequently used procedure) there is the likelihood of a blending of the responses elicited by the CS and the UCS. If the experimenter attempts to avoid such response confounding by omitting the UCS and presenting the CS alone, thus obtaining a supposedly uncontaminated measure of the conditioned response, the omission of the UCS may again elicit the EDR in the form of an orienting response.

In order to help solve these problems, a common procedure has been to use CS-UCS intervals ranging from 6 to 10 seconds. When this has been done, three responses (or components) have frequently been identified. Using a 6.5 second CS, Stewart, Stern, Winokur, and Fredman (1961) identified the following: (1) an orienting response which was evoked by the CS and which had a mean latency of 2.5 seconds from the onset of the CS; (2) a conditioned anticipatory response which had a mean latency of 6.3 seconds from the onset of the CS; and (3) an UCR which was evoked by the UCS and which had a mean latency of 9.6 seconds from the onset of the CS.[4]

A subsequent study by Prokasy and Ebel (1967) has produced findings in general agreement with Stewart et al (1961). The general procedure used by Prokasy and Ebel was to employ either a 74 or a 100 decibel tone as the CS with an 8 second duration. This was followed by shock which served as the UCS. Thirty-two trials were provided, 8 of them test trials (UCS omitted) scattered throughout the series. Three response intervals were examined; the first interval was from 1.35 to 4.95 seconds after CS onset, the second, from 4.95 to 9.53 seconds after CS onset, while the third was from 9.53 to 14.55 seconds after CS onset.

The authors concluded from their findings that the first and second responses were distinct responses rather than integral parts of a single response. The evidence they used to support their position was the observation that (1) CS intensity influenced the first response but not the second, (2) the CS-UCS pairings resulted in an amplitude change in the first response but not in the second, and (3) the first response tended to decrease in frequency over trials while the second response increased with CS-UCS pairings.

It should be noted that the third response could be measured only on test

[4] Lockhart and Grings (1964) and Kimmel (1964) have criticized these findings because of the absence of appropriate pseudoconditioning control subjects. This criticism was answered by Leonard and Winokur (1963), and McDonald and Johnson (1965) who used adequate control groups and replicated the results.

trials since it occupied a position in time normally associated with the onset of the unconditioned response. The authors observed that the third response bore a marked resemblance to the second; the authors believed that, although it was not statistically independent of the second, it was sufficiently distinct to merit further study.

With the delineation of three presumably different components of the EDR, there has been interest in attempting to relate each of these to specific events which take place in the conditioning experiment. The first component has frequently been described as an orienting response which is made to the presentation of the CS, while the second component has been designated as a conditioned response—one anticipating the presentation of the UCS. The third component, arising from the omission of the UCS, has been classified by Grings (1960) as a response which may be likened to an orienting response and is assumed to arise from the disparity existing between what the subject expects (the presentation of the UCS), and what is received (omission of the UCS). Grings (1960) has labeled this as a perceptual disparity response.

Cardiac Conditioning

As virtually everyone is aware, the heart is a muscular organ and its rhythmic contractions can be recorded with an electrocardiograph. An early observation of heart rate conditioning was made by Sherrington (1900) who reported a drop from 180 to 54 beats per minute in the heart rate of a dog hearing the sound of the vibrator of an inductorium which had previously been used to apply shock. Liddell (1908) remarked that this finding "is of equal importance with Pavlov's first experimental studies of psychical secretion," but Sherrington "neither extended . . . nor discussed it in relation to Pavlov's work."

It was Watson (1916) however, who was one of the first investigators to actually attempt heart rate conditioning; this effort, however, was not successful. As he wrote, "We have also made one brief attempt to establish the reflex on the heart beat, but on account of the fact that the respiratory changes show markedly on the tracing of the heart, we have been unable to convince ourselves that we have produced a genuine conditioned reflex" (p. 99).

Heart rate conditioning did not interest a great many investigators during the next three decades. Virtually all of the work was exploratory in nature, using animals as subjects and demonstrating that heart rate conditioning was possible.[5]

Undoubtedly, the reluctance of early investigators to examine heart rate conditioning could be attributed, in a large part, to methodological problems. The heart is continuously active and the conditioned response must be denoted as either acceleration or deceleration of the beating, with beats per minute being used as the response measure. As a result, the experimental procedure must include an adaptation period in order to permit the subject's heart rate

_____

[5] Representative of these studies were investigations by Gantt (1942), Kosupkin and Olmstead (1943), Moore and Marcuse (1945), and Robinson and Gantt (1946).

to reflect a normal rate of responding prior to the presentation of the CS-UCS pairings.

A second methodological problem is that the orienting response—the original response to the CS—may include changes in the organism's heart rate. Although this response may be adapted out by presenting the CS prior to introducing the CS-UCS sequence, the first presentation of the paired stimuli may reinstate it. The presentation of the UCS (frequently shock) over successive training trials may also produce unusual modifications of heart rate.

Finally, it has been noted that a variety of events, some of which the subject can voluntarily control, may influence heart rate. We have already noted that Watson (1916) recognized the contribution of respiratory changes on changes in heart rate. It has now been routinely acknowledged that the subject's respiration rate—his pattern of inhalation and exhalation—may reflexively control heart rate, in turn producing heart rate changes. Hastings and Obrist (1967), for example, have found that sustained breath holding produces heart rate acceleration. Moreover, even the subject's expectation may produce a modification of the heart rate. Westcott and Huttenlocher (1961) have observed that the mere warning that shock will be presented will produce respiratory changes which in turn influence heart rate.

Contemporary interest in human heart rate conditioning began with a study by Notterman, Schoenfeld, and Bersh (1952), who used Columbia Universiity students as subjects. The CS was a 750 Hz tone of 1000 milliseconds in duration. Six seconds later a shock serving as the UCS was administered to the subject's left hand. Results indicated that after 11 reinforced trials, the CR took the form of deceleration or a reduction in beats per minute. These investigators also demonstrated experimental extinction of this response, as well as spontaneous recovery and reconditioning. A variety of subsequent investigators working with animals as well as humans have likewise found the CR to be one of deceleration; others, however, have reported that the CR is one of acceleration. Table 3-1 provides a sampling of these controversial findings. Perhaps such differences are not surprising since heart rate, as we have noted earlier, is so easily influenced by a number of variables that investigators have had difficulty in controlling.

We are of the opinion that the conditioned heart rate is one of deceleration. The extensive work of Schneiderman and his associates (Schneiderman, Smith, Smith, and Gormezano, 1966; VanDercar and Schneiderman, 1967; Yehle, Dauth, and Schneiderman, 1967; Manning, Schneiderman, and Lordahl, 1969; Schneiderman, VanDercar, Yehle, Manning, Golden, and Schneiderman, 1969; Schneiderman, 1970), using rabbits as subjects, as well as Wilson's (1969) careful investigation with humans, supports such a position. Wilson has provided a very thoughtful appraisal of what appears to be happening in the typical cardiac conditioning experiment when humans are used as subjects. He has proposed that the CS as well as the UCS, when presented alone, evokes appropriate cardiac responses—the CS eliciting an orienting response, and the UCS evoking the UCR.

When the CS and UCS are presented in sequence for the first time, each will

Table 3-1 Summaries of a Sampling of Heart Rate Conditioning Studies

Investigators	Organism	CS	UCS	Results (Characteristics of HR)
Notterman, Schoenfeld, and Bersh (1952)	Humans	Tone	Shock	Deceleration
Church and Black (1958)	Dogs	Tone	Shock	Acceleration
Westcott and Huttenlocher (1961)	Humans	Buzzer	Shock	Acceleration
De Leon (1964)	Humans	Light	Noise	Deceleration
Geer (1964)	Humans	Light	Shock and/ or Tone	Deceleration
Holdstock and Schwartzbaum (1965)	Rats	Click	Shock	Deceleration
Obrist, Wood, and Perez-Reyes (1965)	Humans	Light	Shock	Deceleration
Fitzgerald (1966)	Dogs	Tone	Shock	Acceleration
Fitzgerald, Vardaris, and Brown (1966)	Rats	Tone	Shock	Deceleration
Fitzgerald, Vardaris, and Teyler (1966)	Dogs	Tone	Shock	Acceleration
Schneiderman, Smith, Smith, and Gormezano (1966)	Rabbits	Tone	Shock	Deceleration
Yehle, Dauth, and Schneiderman (1967)	Rabbits	Tone	Shock	Deceleration
Black and Black (1967)	Rats	Noise	Shock	Deceleration followed on later trials by acceleration
Hastings and Obrist (1967)	Humans	Lights	Shock	Deceleration
Schneiderman, VanDercar, Yehle, Manning, Golden, and Schneiderman (1968)	Rabbits	Tone	Shock	Deceleration
Manning, Schneiderman, and Lordahl (1969)	Rabbits	CS+ CS− Tones	Shock	Deceleration
Wilson (1969)	Humans	Tone	Shock or Noise	Deceleration
Cohen and Johnson (1971)	Humans	Tone	Shock	Deceleration
Cohen and MacDonald (1971)	Pigeons	Light	Shock	Acceleration
Laird and Fenz (1971)	Humans	Tone	Shock	Acceleration

elicit its characteristic cardiac response. If the temporal arrangement of the two stimuli is within certain limits, the two responses may occur in phase and in effect reinforce each other. With other arrangements, the responses may be out of phase and, as a consequence, be partially depressed. Wilson points out that the response at the start of training is principally a composite of the responses to the CS and the UCS superimposed one upon the other. The resultant curve, however, is not a simple additive combination inasmuch as the presentation of the CS undoubtedly reduces the potency of the UCS and thus limits the size of any response produced by the UCS.

As training continues, the composite response curve is influenced by the habituation of the responses as well as by a signalling function acquired by the CS. Here, repeated pairings of the CS and UCS result in the CS's initiating a preparatory set on the part of the subject—an expectancy of the UCS to follow the CS. This preparatory set focuses upon the occurrence of the UCS at a specific point in time. When administered, the presentation of the UCS terminates the trial exactly as the subject expects it, and it is this element of routine predictability that finally culminates in a decelerative response at UCS onset.

Wilson has suggested that the prominence of this decelerative response during training depends upon the original direction of the response to the UCS and the degree to which habituation and predictability play a part in the experiment. When shock is used as the UCS the initial response is acceleration. It requires repeated training trials for habituation and predictability to overcome such acceleration and produce the drop in rate which can be noted on later training trials. Thus, the response to shock is directionally opposed to the response being established by training, and a composite curve on any given trial is therefore a joint function of the declining potency of shock vs. the increasing predictability that shock will take place as indicated by the presentation of the CS.

When the predictable sequence of the CS-UCS is changed by omitting the UCS, as would be done with the presentation of test trials, the sudden change produces a disparity response which can be verbally described as, "What's going on?" This response also results in heart rate deceleration. It is superimposed upon the deceleration which is assignable to the expectancy that the UCS will follow the CS. These two factors combine to produce the conditioned cardiac response. Thus, Wilson points out that while the response may be modulated by a number of other factors, the decelerative component will be found whenever a well-established pair of stimuli are decoupled by omitting the UCS.

Cardiac Conditioning Using Electrical Stimulation of the Brain

Those experimental findings indicating cardiac deceleration when shock (UCS) has been applied to the body of the subject are in keeping with the results obtained when brain stimulation is used as the UCS. Malmo (1965), in an early study, used electrical stimulation to the lateral septal area of the brain as the UCS, while the CS was a tone. The general sequence was to present the tone alone for 3 seconds and follow it by tone and brain stimulation for ½ second.

(A year earlier, Malmo (1964) had demonstrated that electrical stimulation to this area of the brain elicited a relatively nonhabituating heart rate slowing response.) Following preliminary sessions to assess the influence of brain stimulation alone as well as tone alone, 10 paired tone and brain stimulations were presented each day for 12 successive days. Two days of rest separated the last acquisition trial and the first extinction trial. Results revealed that all 20 rats showed clear and consistent conditioned heart rate deceleration responses. Figure 3-1 presents these findings.

In a subsequent study by VanDercar, Elster, and Schneiderman (1970), a conditioned discrimination task was performed with rabbits used as subjects. In this study, electrodes implanted in the hypothalamic or septal area locations served as the site for the UCS while electrodes were also implanted bilaterally in the lateral geniculate nucleus for presentations of the CS. Following an adaptation period, seven days of discrimination training and three days of extinction were provided. During every training session, the animal received 30 stimulations of each geniculate nucleus. The classical discrimination conditioning procedure consisted of stimulating one geniculate and following this by presentation of the UCS, while stimulation in the other geniculate was not followed by the UCS.

Of the 60 trials per day provided in acquisition training, 26 were actually paired with hypothalamic or septal stimulation, while 4 were CS+ alone presentations which served as test trials for the reinforced geniculate stimulation. Of the 30 CS- presentations, 4 served as test trials for the nonreinforced geniculate stimulation. The findings as revealed in Fig. 3-2 demonstrate the development of a conditioned discrimination, a finding in keeping with the earlier study by Malmo (1965).

Finally, a study by Sideroff, Schneiderman, and Powell (1971) using either high, medium, or low intensity UCS stimulation has also been in keeping with the general finding that the classically conditioned heart rate response to septal stimulation consists of a decrease in heart rate.

In summary, there is little doubt that cardiac conditioning can take place. Whether deceleration or acceleration is the response conditioned is open to some question, although we believe the bulk of the experimental evidence as well as Wilson's theoretical position lends support to the position that deceleration is the direction of the change.

Conditioned Emotional Response (CER)

Emotional responses have been of interest to psychologists for a long time, and it has generally been believed that learning plays an important role in determining the stimulus situations which elicit such responses. It is not surprising, therefore, that classical conditioning procedures have been used as the vehicle for the experimental validation of this belief.

The use of the classical conditioning paradigm to examine how neutral stimuli can elicit an emotional response is found in an early study by Watson and Rayner (1920). Their single subject, Albert, was an 11-month-old child

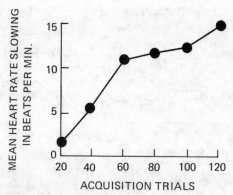

Fig. 3-1.   Acquisition curves for classically conditioned heart rate slowing. *Adapted from Malmo (1965)*

who was not afraid of animals but revealed a distinct fear of loud noises. The experimenters attempted to condition a fear of animals in Albert by presenting a white rat which served as a CS, along with a loud sound (UCS) produced by the striking of a steel bar. After five paired presentations of the white rat and the loud sound, the sight of the rat resulted in Albert's withdrawing and beginning to whimper. After two additional paired presentations of the sound and rat, the authors report, "the instant the rat was shown alone the baby began to cry. Almost instantly he turned sharply to the left, fell over on his left side, raised himself on all fours and began to crawl away so rapidly that he was caught with difficulty before reaching the edge of the table" (p. 5). Thus, it was evident that a conditioned emotional response had been established.

There are obvious difficulties in using human infants to explore the conditioning of emotional responses. One alternative has been to use animals, and the early work of Estes and Skinner (1941) and Hunt and Brady (1951) represent a contemporary approach to this problem. Estes and Skinner (1941) first trained rats to press a lever in a Skinner box on a reinforcement schedule in which they received a pellet of food for the first lever press after each four minute interval. Two weeks of daily training sessions resulted in the animal's responding at a fairly constant response rate. For the next six sessions, the experimenters presented a tone lasting for three minutes and terminated it with a brief shock. (This double stimulation procedure took place regardless of what the animal was doing.) Although the early tone-shock pairings produced little change in the animals' rate of lever pressing, gradually there was a decrement in their rate of responding when the tone was presented. Subsequent presentations of tone and shock eventually resulted in complete suppression of the lever pressing response.

Studies by Hunt and Brady (Hunt and Brady, 1951; Brady and Hunt, 1951) which followed the Estes and Skinner (1941) experiment, were similar in procedure; for some emotional conditioning trials, however, the pairing of the CS (clicking noise) with the UCS (shock) took place in a grill box—an apparatus

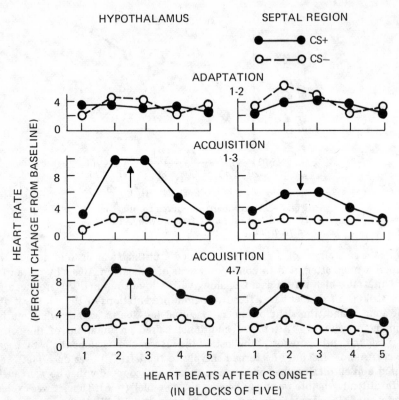

Fig. 3-2. Conditioned heart-rate response topographies obtained during test trials in the hypothalamic and septal region unconditioned-stimulus groups. (Mean heart-rate percentage changes from base line are plotted separately for responses to stimulations of the reinforced [CS+] and nonreinforced [CS−] lateral geniculates for five successive blocks of five beats occurring after conditioned-stimulus onset. The arrow indicates where the unconditioned-stimulus onset would normally occur during nontest trials. In all cases the heart-rate responses consisted of decreases in rate [shown as upwards deflections].) *Adapted from Vandercar, Elster, and Schneiderman (1970)*

distinctly different from the Skinner box in which the animals had learned their lever pressing response.[6] Moreover, the shock was presented just before and just after the auditory stimulus. When the animals were returned to the Skinner box, the suppression of lever pressing which occurred as a function of the presentation of the CS, noted by Estes and Skinner (1941), was also observed by Hunt and Brady. (Their procedure included the presentation of the UCS.)

[6] Hunt and Brady (1951) pointed out that the emotional conditioning trials were provided in the grill box in order to avoid depressing the output of the lever response in general, "a rather common secondary complication of this conditioning procedure when carried out in the lever apparatus."

The general rationale for this type of experiment has been the assumption that shock, which serves as the UCS, elicits an emotional response in the animal and that pairing this aversive stimulus with a conditioned stimulus will result in the eliciting of the emotional response by the CS. The presence of this response is inferred from the decline or suppression of the earlier learned bar pressing response.

It would be possible to assess the interfering effect of the emotional response by simply examining the decline in the number of responses made while the emotional eliciting CS was being presented (treatment session). Individual differences in rate of responding, however, have usually dictated that a relative measure of strength of emotional response be employed. This measure has been designated as a suppression ratio and it compares (1) the number of responses made during a period prior to the introduction of the emotional eliciting stimulus (A), with (2) the number of responses made during the treatment session (B).

The suppression ratio has been computed in a variety of ways. Stein, Sidman, and Brady (1958) have used the simple ratio, B/A. Here, a value of 0 reveals complete suppression; a value of 1 indicates no suppression since response frequency during the treatment session is as large as that obtained during pretreatment. Hoffman and Fleshler (1961) have used the suppression ratio, $A-B/A$ which also provides a 0 to 1 range but reverses the interpretation. A value of 1 indicates complete suppression and 0 no suppression. Finally, Annau and Kamin (1961) have used a $B/A + B$ ratio which means that a value of 0 indicates complete suppression while .5 represents no suppression. Each ratio measure has its advantages and disadvantages. Most important is that the reader be aware of which ratio is being employed.

Pupillary Response

It is well known that decreases in the ambient illumination level result in pupillary dilation, while increases in illumination result in pupillary constriction. A number of investigators have been interested in determining whether it is possible to condition such pupillary changes when an illumination change serves as the UCS. Early studies by Watson (1916), Cason (1922), Hudgins (1933), and Baker (1938) were all apparently successful; however, the attempted replication of these findings by many other investigators have been unsuccessful (Steckle and Renshaw, 1934; Hilgard and Ohlson, 1939; Wedell, Taylor and Skolnick, 1940; Hilgard, Miller, and Ohlson, 1941; Young, 1954, 1958; Hilgard, Dutton, and Helmick, 1949; and Crasilneck and McCranie, 1956).

Contemporary experiments have continued to reflect this difference of experimental results. Fitzgerald, Lintz, Brackbill, and Adams (1967), and Brackbill, Lintz, and Fitzgerald (1968) have reported the successful conditioning of both the light and darkness reflexes of the pupil using light intensity as the UCS. Goldwater's (1972) review of these studies suggests that the findings be accepted with caution since two aspects of the studies are somewhat unusual: the first, that they were conducted with infants and the second, that conditioning was successful with a temporal conditioning paradigm but not with delayed conditioning. This latter finding is most unusual since there is little evidence in the literature of successful temporal conditioning. Moreover, later studies by Kugelmass, Hakerem, and Mantgiaris (1969) and Voigt (1968) have been unable to replicate these results.

It should be acknowledged that the pupillary reflex can be conditioned when shock is used as the unconditioned stimulus. Harlow and Stagner (1933), and Harlow (1940) have reported the conditioning of pupillary dilation to a bell in both cats and dogs with shock used as the UCS; the more recent experiments of Gerall and Woodward (1958) using cats, and Gerall and Obrist (1962) with humans, have confirmed these findings.

Young's (1965) careful examination of the status of pupillary conditioning deserves consideration. He has suggested that an essential component of any conditioning procedure is the necessity for the UCS to elicit sensory impulses which have strong attention value or which elicit orientation responses in the organism. When pupillary constriction is elicited by an increase in the intensity of a light (which the experimenter designates as the UCS), sensory impulses arising from the pupil are not elicited, so that the conditioning of pupillary constriction to the CS cannot take place. Young has acknowledged, however, that when shock is used as the UCS, such conditioning can take place; however, pupillary dilation is only a part of a generalized response to noxious stimuli. Thus, Young (1965) writes, "... it is far more likely that the generalized response is conditioned to the CS than that the pupil itself is conditioned. The nature of the generalized response in terms of latency and magnitude is modified during the course of conditioning in the expected direction, so that comparable changes in the behavior of the pupil probably represent the changes occuring in the generalized response. This hypothesis may be checked through the use of some other measure of the generalized response such as the galvanic skin response or vasodilation response. If both measures, GSR and pupil, show the same changes in the same time relationships, it is far more likely that they represent the generalized response rather than specific conditioned responses" (pp. 372-373).

Interoceptive Conditioning

An unusual kind of classical conditioning situation is interoceptive conditioning. This can be defined as classical conditioning in which either the conditioned stimulus or the unconditioned stimulus or both are delivered directly to the mucous membrane or to one of the internal organs of the body. An example of an interoceptive conditioning experiment would be one in which an animal is first prepared with a gastric fistula so that there are inflow and outflow tubes into the stomach. These tubes enable the experimenter to provide a CS in the form of a flow of water over the receptors of the lining of the stomach. Paired with the CS would be a UCS such as shock which would elicit leg flexion or food, eliciting salivation. Following a number of CS-UCS presentations, the internal flow of water will elicit the appropriate response.

Experimental work on interoceptive conditioning has been virtually limited to Russian laboratories. Razran's (1961) examination of the Russian literature on this topic has resulted in his concluding that interoceptive conditioning, whether involving conditioned or unconditioned interoceptive stimuli is, a bona fide phenomenon.

The Classical Conditioning of Other Autonomic Nervous System Responses

A review of the literature reveals that a number of autonomic nervous system responses other than those which we have delineated can be conditioned.

A series of studies by Woods and his associates (Woods, Makous, and Hutton, 1968, 1969; Hutton, Woods, and Makous, 1970) have demonstrated that hypoglycemia—a deficiency of sugar in the blood—can be conditioned. In the Woods, Makous, and Hutton (1968) experiment, rats were used as subjects and a small portion of the animal's tail was cut off so that blood samples could be drawn whenever desired. Following five days during which one blood sample per day was taken from each of the subjects, permitting them to become accustomed to the blood-drawing apparatus and procedure, the animals were randomly divided into two groups. Four experimental animals received insulin injection, which produces hypoglycemia, while three control subjects received a saline solution.

The general experimental procedure consisted of injecting the animal with insulin and placing it in an individual experimental chamber with 85 db of white noise. Exactly twenty minutes after the first blood sample was taken, a second sample was taken following which the subject was returned to its home cage. Fifteen conditioning days were distributed over a 33 day period in order to permit the physiological state of the subjects to return to normal following each trial. On the test day, (two days after the last conditioning day), the same procedure was followed, except that the experimental subjects were injected with saline instead of insulin. Control procedures insured that no experimenter had information on the type of injection which was associated with any particular subject or blood sample. The experimenters found that there were no differences in blood glucose levels between the two groups on the five preconditioning days or on the first blood samples taken on the conditioning and test days. On the 15 conditioning days, the injection of insulin was followed by a decrease in blood glucose of 14 to 50 mg. percent but injection of saline was followed by an increase in blood glucose on 41 out of 45 determinations, the magnitude of the changes ranging from –3 to +37 mg. percent. On the test day, the decrease in blood glucose level in the experimental group, which had been injected with saline and not insulin, was significantly different from the increase which occurred in the control group.

The classical conditioning paradigm as applied to these experimental findings would indicate that the UCS is represented by the insulin which elicits the UCR, a decrease in blood glucose level. In this situation, the CS was a complex one which included white noise and many, if not all, the components of the entire procedure beginning with the removal of the subject from its cage. This appeared to lead to the CR, a change in the blood glucose level in the same direction as the UCR but smaller.

In a second study by these authors (Woods, Makous, and Hutton, 1969), these findings were replicated. An added aspect of this second study was to vary the number of conditioning trials (Experiment 1) as well as to investigate the role of a distinctive CS (Experiment 2). In this latter experiment, the odor of menthol which served as the CS was introduced within the experimental chamber where the subjects were kept between blood drawings. The results of both studies (Woods, Makous, and Hutton, 1968, 1969) can be noted from Fig. 3-3, which indicates the change in blood glucose on the first test trial and is plotted against the number of conditioning trials provided the varying groups. The effect of a very distinctive CS (menthol) obviously plays an important role in the ease of conditioning.

A second example of the range of classically conditioned autonomic responses is found in the conditioning of bronchial asthma. Although allergic bronchial asthma rarely develops in infrahuman animals, it can be produced experimentally in the guinea pig. When sensitized by forced inhalation or systematic infusion of a foreign protean, the animal develops a bronchoconstrictive reaction that resembles the clinical attack. This response appears to be amenable to classical conditioning. Although Ottenberg, Stein, Lewis, and Hamilton (1958) classically conditioned this response in the guinea pig, they relied upon gross visual inspection to index attacks. More recently, Justesen, Braun, Garrison, and Pendleton (1971) used a superior response measure—one based on whole-body plethysmography—and also obtained positive findings.

The Conditioning of Skeletal Responses

It will be recalled that at the beginning of this chapter we indicated that classical conditioning procedures could be used with skeletal responses—responses controlled by the central nervous system.

Conditioned Sucking

The first classically conditioned skeletal response we should like to discuss is the sucking response in infants. It is one of the few well-defined responses in the infant's repertoire, although its measurement is somewhat more complex than might be anticipated. The sucking response is generally considered to be comprised of two components; the first is the amount of tongue squeezing pressure provided by the infant, while the second is the sucking response itself. An apparatus designed to measure these two sucking components has been designed by Sameroff (1968) and is illustrated in Fig. 3-4. Thus, it is possible to obtain a measure of the frequency and amplitude of the squeezing pressure, as well as the frequency and amplitude of sucking (defined as the negative pressure applied by the infant to the tip of the nipple).

Marquis (1931) was one of the early investigators, perhaps the first, to condition the sucking response. Her conditioning procedure consisted of presenting a buzzer for 5 seconds prior to giving the baby its bottle for its regular feeding. The buzzer was again sounded for the first 5 seconds of sucking. The bottle was removed and reintroduced from 2 to 5 times during each feeding, with the

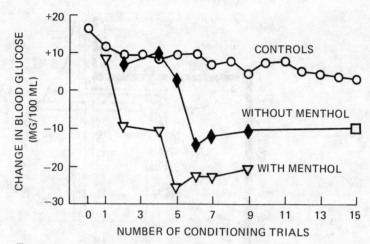

Fig. 3-3. A collation of the results of Experiments 1, 2, and Woods, et al (1968), indicated by □. The change in blood glucose on the first trial is plotted against the number of conditioning trials given to the various groups. *Adapted from Woods, Makous, and Hutton (1969)*

procedure the same each time. This procedure was repeated at every feeding during nine days of testing, for a total of over 50 experimental sessions per subject, with 100 to 250 trials being provided. Anticipatory sucking movements were recorded, and for 7 of the 8 babies on which complete data were available, increases in both sucking as well as general mouth movement over the experimental period were revealed. It should be indicated, however, that no statistical evaluations were made, although a control group run under a nonpaired buzzer and bottle presentation revealed no change in anticipatory sucking.

These early findings have been viewed with some caution since the temporal relationship between the CS and UCS was not clearly defined and there was no statistical evaluation of the experimental results. However, the more recent studies of Lipsitt and Kaye (1964), and Kaye (1966) (as reported by Kaye, 1967), have provided confirming evidence that the sucking response in the neonate can be classically conditioned. In the Lipsitt and Kaye (1964) experiment, 3-to 4-day old infants served as experimental subjects. These infants were given 20 pairings of a tone which served as the CS and a pacifier (UCS) which elicited the sucking response. On each trial, the CS was presented 1 second before the UCS, with both stimuli continuing to be presented for 15 seconds. Five test trials consisting of presenting the CS alone were provided— 1 after every fourth paired presentation. A group which received unpaired presentations of the CS and the UCS served as a control. Following 20 paired conditioning and 5 interspersed test trials, extinction trials were provided. Results indicated that the experimental group was significantly superior in the percentage of trials in which at least one conditioned response took place.

Kaye's (1966) subsequent study, similar in procedure to the Lipsitt and

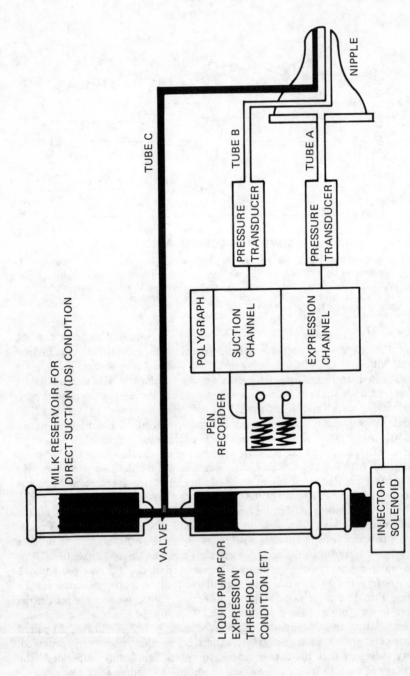

Fig. 3-4. Experimental nipple and milk delivery system. *Adapted from Sameroff (1968)*

64

Kaye (1964) experiment, confirmed their findings. Since Kaye (1966) used five control groups, the evidence appears to be unequivocal that the sucking response in the neonate can be conditioned. Additional support has also come from Stanley, Cornwell, Poggiani, and Trattner (1963) who conditioned the sucking response of newborn puppies.

Eyeblink Conditioning

A much more frequently investigated response is the eyeblink. Cason (1922) and Switzer (1930) were two early American experimenters working with this response. Both employed an auditory CS. For his UCS, Cason applied an electric shock to the orbital region of the eye, while Switzer used the blow of a padded hammer to the facial tissue below the subject's eye. Both of these stimuli, of course, produced regular blinking responses in the subject. Of prime importance at that time was the appropriate recording of the response. Cason accomplished this by attaching a coupling to the subject's eyelid so that lid closure would break an electrical contact; thus, the latency of the response could be measured. Switzer cemented a silk thread to the eyelid, in turn coupled to a writing lever which enabled him to obtain a continuous record of the eyelid movement.

A major improvement in response measurement was provided by Hilgard (1931) using the Dodge pendulum photochronograph which simultaneously controls the presentation of the CS and UCS and photographically records the movements of the eyelid. This procedure required that the experimental setup be only dimly illuminated since the photographic recording could not take place under the usual laboratory illumination. The photographic procedure has now been abandoned. Most contemporary investigators have converted eyelid movements into changes in resistance that use the technique of attaching a piano wire to the subject's eyelid which in turn rotates the shaft of a micro-torque potentiometer. The resistance changes from the potentiometer are amplified and recorded using an ink writing system. The conditioned stimulus is frequently an abrupt change in illumination whereas the UCS is typically a puff of compressed nitrogen delivered to the cornea. A detailed description of eyeblink conditioning apparatus may be found in Gormezano (1969).

An apparent taxonomic problem is that the response to the CS results in the air puff falling upon the closed lid which largely, if not totally, eliminates the aversive characteristics of the UCS. Under such circumstances, even though the UCS continues to be paired with the CS, the conditioned eyeblink would appear to take on the characteristics of an instrumental avoidance learning task. An alternative is to use shock (UCS) delivered to the paraorbital region of one eye which elicits lid closure. With such a procedure, the shock can be presented regardless of whether or not the subject closes his eye; moreover, the subject's response does not eliminate the aversive characteristics of the UCS, so that the procedure fulfills the requirements of a classical conditioning operation.

In a study examining human eyelid conditioning using paraorbital shock as the UCS, Gormezano and Fernald (1971) administered 60 CS-UCS trials to their experimental group and obtained an acquisition curve similar to that obtained by other eyelid conditioning investigators using a puff of air as their UCS, the aversiveness of which could be ameliorated by lid closure. Moreover, in a second experiment, Gormezano and Fernald found that the rate and asymptotic level of conditioning was a function of UCS intensity, a finding similar to that obtained by other experimenters who manipulated air puff intensity. It would appear that the similarity of experimental findings obtained when either an air puff or an electric shock is used as the UCS would lend support to the thesis that the conditioned eyeblink obtained with the air puff as UCS is a classically conditioned response.

Conditioning the Eyelid of Infrahumans

The number of eyelid conditioning studies employing infrahumans have been relatively few. Hilgard and Marquis (1935, 1936) conditioned dogs and monkeys; Hughes and Schlosberg (1938) and Biel and Wickens (1941) have used rats. The most interesting development in this area was recently undertaken by Gormezano and his associates who have used the albino rabbit. This animal, because of its docility, large eyelid, and low spontaneous blink rate appears to make an ideal subject.

In an early study Schneiderman, Fuentes, and Gormezano (1962), using an 800 Hz tone as a CS and compressed nitrogen delivered to the right cornea as a UCS, were able to demonstrate typical conditioning curves. In a second study, Gormezano, Schneiderman, Deaux, and Fuentes (1962) focused their attention on the nictitating membrane of this animal. This membrane consists of a curved plate of cartilage covered with glandular epithelium. It is drawn from the inner canthus of the eye laterally across the cornea. Observations which were made in their previous study indicated that activation of the membrane could be reliably elicited by the UCS. It was also observed that when the membrane was activated it rarely extended past the midline of the pupil, always leaving a portion of the cornea exposed. Thus, with the eyelid held open by the apparatus, it was not possible for the animal to eliminate the sensory consequences of the UCS by activation of the membrane; this procedure is similar to eyelid conditioning using shock as the UCS. The results of this experimental investigation revealed that, as with the conditioned eyelid response, it was possible to reliably condition the nictitating membrane of the rabbit.

Measurement

In the measurement of the human eyeblink, any response which occurs 150 milliseconds after the onset of the CS is classified as a conditioned response. One problem arises from the fact that subjects spontaneously blink their eyes at fairly regular intervals; in addition, other conditions may produce the blinking of the eye. The subject's cornea may become excessively dry from the presentation of the UCS which increases his blinking rate; or, tension arising from the experimental operations may increase which will also result in increased blinking. The problem, then, becomes one of differentiating these spontaneous eyeblinks from those which are presumed to be conditioned.

Frequently, experimenters instruct their subjects to blink prior to receiving the CS. The problem is not completely solved by using this procedure but it is considerably lessened.

A second problem is that when light has been used as the CS, a reflexive blink to the presentation of the CS has frequently been noted. Reflexive blinks to light (as well as sound and possibly other stimuli) have been designated as alpha responses. Generally, the experimenter can differentiate these responses from conditioned responses on the basis of magnitude, duration, and latency. Studies by Grant and Adams (1944), Hilgard (1931), and Moore and Gormezano (1961) would indicate that the alpha response to light is approximately 1/10th the amplitude of the UCR, has a latency of 40 to 120 milliseconds and a duration of 30 to 50 milliseconds. As might be anticipated, the frequency and magnitude of alpha responses decrease over conditioning trials.

A second reflexive response elicited only by light has been designated as the beta response, although modern recording techniques have virtually eliminated its occurrence in the conditioning experiment. Grant (1943a, 1943b, 1945), using the Dodge pendulum photochronograph, found that subjects frequently made a reflexive response to the CS and that this response increased in frequency as the subject became more dark adapted under the reduced illumination required by this procedure. Grant and Norris (1947) discovered that beta responses occurred with a latency of 120 to 240 milliseconds after CS onset and appeared comparable in magnitude and form to responses generally designated as CRs. With current recording devices, it is not necessary to reduce the illumination of the conditioning cubicle so that the presence of beta responses is not a problem.

The last measurement problem is that, inasmuch as the eyeblink is a skeletal response, it can be brought under the subject's voluntary control. The subject may "voluntarily" blink his eye rather than produce the eyeblink as a "conditioned" response.[7]

Some contemporary investigators have taken the position that these voluntary responders should be excluded from participating in conditioned eyeblink studies. The rationale for such a policy, as indicated by Spence and Ross (1959), is that voluntary responses appear to be "governed by different laws" than those responses which have been judged to be involuntary. The letter V has been used to designate "conditioned" responses which appear to resemble a voluntary instructed eyelid closure, e.g., the form or characteristics of the eyelid response in which the subject is simply instructed to blink his eye. In contrast, the letter C has been used to indicate those conditioned responses in which this voluntary component was presumably lacking. Hartman and Ross (1961) have indicated that the V form is a complete closure of the lid of long duration and rapid recruitment, whereas the C form is likely to be incomplete, have a gradual recruitment, and often terminating before the onset of the UCS.

Grant's (1972) extensive work with eyeblink conditioning has led him to

[7] Contemporary interest should not lead the reader to believe that this is a new problem. Concern over this issue can be noted in the early discussions of Peak (1933) and Wickens (1939).

conclude "it necessary and desirable to classify the subjects as V or C form responders . . . because there is convincing evidence that subjects showing these two response topographies react very differently to verbal conditioned stimuli and appear to process the verbal information differently" (pp. 30–31). Moreover, he has asserted that the V-C classification can be a nearly complete dichotomy, noting that Fleming (1968) found 80% or more of the responses from subjects classified as Vs by the Hartman-Ross criterion to be of the V form, and about 80% or more of the responses from Cs were of the C form.

The issue is far from settled, however, since other investigators, such as Prokasy and Kumpfer (1969) and Gormezano and Fernald (1971), have been unable to obtain support for the position that V and C form responders function according to different laws. For example, in the eyelid conditioning study of Gormezano and Fernald (1971) to which we referred earlier, paraorbital shock, it will be recalled, was used as the UCS. The use of unavoidable shock should have effectively eliminated those voluntary responders presumed to blink in order to reduce the noxiousness of the unconditioned stimulus. However, Gormezano and Fernald (1971) found that the proportion of subjects in their study (Experiment 2) who would be classified as voluntary responders was considerably larger than the proportion found in typical eyelid conditioning studies using an air puff as the UCS. Moreover, an examination of the topographical features of the conditioned responses revealed many responses which would be classified as voluntary; that is, responses which had short latency, sharp closure, and long duration.

Conditioned Jaw Movements

The use of rabbits as experimental subjects for the classical conditioning of the eyeblink and the nictitating membrane response has suggested to Gormezano and his associates the possibility of conditioning jaw movements in this animal. Their apparatus consists of a muzzle-like device which rests on the animal's head and is anchored by a brass ring around the base of the pinnae. A length of tubing, connected to a liquid reservoir, is anchored to the subject's head mount and terminates in a hypodermic needle which is inserted into a plug in the animal's right cheek. A solenoid valve interrupts the tube below the reservoir and when activated, delivers a liquid unconditioned stimulus to the subject's oral cavity. A potentiometer attached to the head mount and positioned on the right side of the subject's head just below eye level records jaw movements.

The conditioning procedure consists of providing a tone (CS) followed by a concentration of saccharine (UCS). The signal from the potentiometer generated by the jaw movement is amplified and provides a record of the response.

Smith, DiLollo, and Gormezano (1966) have demonstrated the successful conditioning and extinction of this response. Control groups which were provided the presentation of the CS alone, the presentation of the UCS alone, or a random pairing of the CS and UCS, exhibited virtually no responding. The authors have indicated that the exceedingly low base rate of spontaneous jaw movements has the methodological virtue of permitting an assessment of conditioning in terms of both response frequency and latency. Inasmuch as rabbits are used only infrequently as experimental subjects, investigations of the conditioned jaw movement have been few.

Conditioned Flexion

The early experimental work in conditioning flexion responses was performed by Bechterev (1928) who believed that Pavlov's experimental work with the salivary response could not be applied to humans. Bechterev's method consisted of using a bell as a CS and shock as the UCS in order to elicit foot withdrawal.

In his presidential address to the American Psychological Association, Watson (1916) indicated that the conditioning of foot withdrawal responses as reported by Bechterev was inconvenient for laboratory work and stated that the finger withdrawal reflex was just as satisfactory. The conditioning of this response could be undertaken with shock being used as the UCS and a tone serving as the CS.

Almost two decades after Watson's address, Liddell (1934) conditioned foreleg withdrawal in sheep. Here, a metronome set beating once per second for 5 seconds was used as a CS, and this was paired with a shock delivered through electrodes attached to the left foreleg of the animal. After four presentations of the metronome and shock in combination, the conditioned stimulus caused a definite change in breathing and skin resistance and on the sixth trial there was a slight movement of the leg. By the eleventh trial, the conditioned leg flexion was fully established and with further training was quite constant and stable.

Early conditioned finger withdrawal studies were undertaken by Wolfle (1930, 1932) and Gibson, Jack, and Raffel (1932). Although contemporary finger withdrawal conditioning procedures have been used to examine the same range of problems as the conditioned eyeblink, these procedures do have several deficiencies (Beecroft, 1966). Frequency and latency of the response can be measured, but measures of amplitude have not been promising. Moreover, acquisition levels are typically lower than those found for the conditioned eyeblink.

A basic problem with flexion conditioning is that frequently the operations that are used to examine it remove it from the classical conditioning category. The reason for this is that the apparatus is arranged so that the removal of the finger (or foot) from the electrode to the CS enables the subject to avoid the shock. Under such circumstances, conditioned flexion should be classified as an instrumental avoidance type of learning rather than as classical conditioning. In some instances, as Liddell (1934) has done, the experimenter may attach the electrodes to the subject to make receiving the UCS independent of the subject's response. When such a procedure is used, conditioned flexion responding can be properly classified as classical conditioning.

Instructed Responses

This classical conditioning procedure, originating with the work of the Russian investigator, Ivanov-Smolensky (1933), who first utilized it, consists of a CS, frequently a light or tone, which is paired with verbal instructions or a command which serves as the UCS. The UCR is the subject's response to the command. It is the occurrence of the instructed response to the CS which constitutes the CR. Berlyne's (1960) review of the Russian literature indicates that this procedure has been particularly successful and convenient to use with school children. American investigations, however, have met with only limited success.

One recent American investigation of the Ivanov-Smolensky procedure was conducted by Siebert, Nicholson, Carr-Harris, and Lubow (1969). Two experiments were run. In the first study, a buzzer of moderate intensity served as a CS while the UCS was the verbal command "close switch,"—an instruction which required the subject to close a microswitch by a downward pressure of his toe. Although the subject was led to believe that his toe pressing response was being recorded, the response which the experimenters measured was a change in pressure on the seat of the chair on which the subject sat caused by the initiation of the foot-lifting response. This change in pressure was measured by having a carbon-filled rubber catheter tube stretched across the chair and covered by a canvas cloth. Current from a battery flowed through the tube so that any change in pressure against the tube resulted in a change in electrical resistance. The experimental group received 30 paired trials while a random control group received 30 presentations of the CS and 30 presentations of the UCS in an alternating sequence. Although a statistically significant greater number of conditioned responses was provided by the experimental group, results revealed no significant change in performance across blocks of 5 trials. Moreover, only a 48% level of responding was achieved.

In a second study by these investigators, the procedure was one in which the subjects were commanded to squeeze a soft rubber bulb. The bulb was fastened to a rubber tube, both of which were filled with brake fluid, creating a hydraulic system capable of detecting depressions in the bulb of less than .5 mm. The conventional CS was a 2500 Hz tone but the experimenters also utilized a "subtle CS" which consisted of a click. Following the presentation of the CS, the subject was given the command "squeeze." Thirty acquisition trials as well as 5 extinction trials were provided. Again, the percentage of conditioned responses which were obtained was not high; the level of responding ranged from 46% to 52%.

The reasons for the relatively low levels of conditioning that American investigators have obtained with the Ivanov-Smolensky (1933) procedure may be attributable to suppression of the CR on the part of most subjects. Subjects regard anticipatory responses to the CS as "incorrect" and not in keeping with their original instructions which are to respond to the UCS. Presumably, children are not as likely to exhibit such an inhibition—a position supported by data provided by Dmitriev (1956), as reported by Hartman (1965), and found in Table 3-2.

Although it seems evident that the Ivanov-Smolensky (1933) procedure is difficult to use with adults, Hartman (1965) has pointed out that the method can be used if a physiological response is measured in addition to the motor response. A study by Solberg, Tyre, and Stinson (1970) has supported Hart-

Table 3-2   Percentage of Children of Different Age Groups that Formed
Conditioned Responses by Motor Method of Speech Reinforcement
with Subsequent Verbal Reinforcement

Age in Years	Percent Ss with Stable CRs	Percent Ss with Unstable CRs	Percent Ss with No CRs
7–8	73	23	4
9–11	64	29	7
12–13	63	20	17
14–15	41	34	25
16–18	20	50	30
19–22	16	25	59

Adapted from Hartman (1965) who obtained data from Dmitriev (1956)

man's position. In this study children obtained from the third and fourth grades
as well as adults (college students) were presented with the word "press" following which they were instructed to pull the trigger of a pistol grip apparatus.
A CS consisting of the illumination of a 40-watt electric light bulb mounted
at the base of the screen preceded the visual presentation of the UCS (the word
"press"). Three response measures were recorded. The trigger press was measured using an apparatus that was adapted so that any tension applied to the
trigger would be recorded. In addition, EMG (electromyogram) readings were
taken from an electrode attached to the outside surface of the arm in the region
of the ulnar nerve, just above the right elbow. (EDR recordings were also obtained, but could not be used.) Results indicated that during 40 acquisition
trials, neither the children nor the adults revealed much evidence of conditioning
in terms of overt anticipatory responding to the CS; both groups reached an
asymptote of only about 10% responding. The EMG measure, on the other
hand, revealed clear evidence of a rising function of conditioned responses for
all subjects, suggesting that the preparatory component of the UCR, an increase
in muscle tone or tension anticipating the UCS, can be readily conditioned.
The children revealed greater amounts of conditioning than the adults; the level
of conditioning for children approximating 50% - 60%, while that for adults
was 10% lower than this. An interesting finding was the fact that the children
failed to extinguish over 20 extinction trials while the adults extinguished almost
immediately.

The Conditioning of Blocking the Occipital Alpha Rhythm

We shall conclude this chapter by examining some of the experimental work
that investigates the conditioning of blocking the human occipital alpha rhythm.
We are discussing this response apart from the others which we have delineated
since there is some problem in its appropriate classification. An individual
who is awake but resting with his eyes closed will reveal in an EEG recording
a brain wave of about 8 to 10 cycles per second, which is particularly noticeable
in recordings from the occipital lobe. This is known as the alpha rhythm.

It has been known that this rhythm can be suppressed by illumination of the retina, by asking the subject to solve simple mental arithmetic problems, or in fact, by instructing him to attend to a particular stimulus. It is not surprising that some investigators have attempted to determine if such suppression could be conditioned. Shagrass and his associates (Jasper and Shagrass, 1941; Shagrass, 1942; Shagrass and Johnson, 1943) have reported positive findings. In these studies, the subjects were instructed to make some overt response such as pressing a key at the onset of the UCS (light). An interpretative problem in such studies is whether the suppression response is merely a concomitant of the overt response, or whether conditioning has actually taken place.

In experiments which do not demand that the subject make an overt response, but, rather, where the subject's instructions are to remain relaxed and passive, investigators frequently have been unable to obtain conditioning, or to differentiate conditioning from pseudoconditioned controls. For example, Stern, Das, Anderson, Biddy, and Surphlis (1961) were not able to demonstrate conditioning, while of three experiments conducted by Albino and Burnand (1964), two revealed no conditioning; in the third, although conditioning was demonstrated, the amount of suppression exhibited was minimal, with considerable individual variation revealed.

Putney, Erwin, and Smith (1972) have provided some recent support for the position that the blocking of the alpha rhythm can be conditioned. In this study, the CS was a 3 second, 400 Hz tone paired with a 3-second 150-watt light (UCS). Each trial was begun only when the subject's alpha reached a predetermined amplitude criterion. Three different sets of instruction were provided. The first two instructed the subject to press a lever to either light onset (Type 1), or light offset (Type 2), while the third set indicated that the subject was to make no response at all. Twelve subjects served in all three conditions, counterbalanced across three experimental sessions. Each session began with 20 tones and 20 lights being presented randomly, with these presentations serving as the pseudoconditioning control. Thirty conditioning trials followed. Extinction trials were also provided but were not reported.

Figure 3-5 presents the reduction of the alpha rhythm as a function of the tone alone as well as the kind of instructions provided. The authors concluded that conditioning was demonstrated under all response conditions because all had trends significantly different from the unpaired pseudoconditioning tone trend. Some question can be raised concerning the adequacy of the experimenters' control group since, typically, a separate group is used for this purpose. Moreover, a separate group's design should be used to test the generality of the findings. Before unequivocally accepting the position that the blocking of the alpha rhythm can be conditioned without an accompanying overt response, it seems wise to await confirmation by additional experiments.

Summary

A variety of responses have been classically conditioned; in view of their variety, it is appropriate to classify them in terms of whether the response is related to: (1) autonomic or (2) skeletal response system functioning.

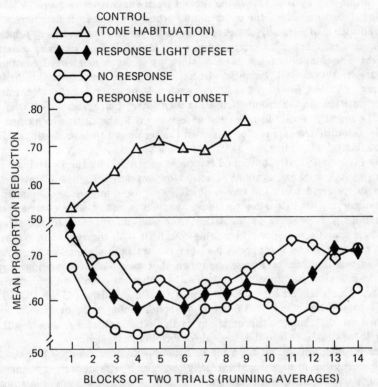

Fig. 3-5. Control (upper panel) and conditioning (lower panel) under the three response conditions, in blocks of two trials using running averages except for Trial Block 1. *Adapted from Putney, Erwin, and Smith (1972)*

Autonomic nervous system responses which have been conditioned include salivation, the electrodermal responses (EDR), heart rate, emotional responses, pupillary responses, as well as a number of others. Of these, the EDR is the response most frequently examined by American investigators.

There are a number of methodological problems involved in the conditioning of these responses. The EDR, for example, appears to consist of three different components, so that consideration of only a single one of these leads to difficulties. In heart rate conditioning, the response which is conditioned must take the form of either acceleration or deceleration; the heart rate of the subject just prior to receiving the CS-UCS presentation becomes an important determinant of whether acceleration or deceleration has been obtained as a function of the conditioning procedure. Although there is some controversy as to whether there is conditioned acceleration or deceleration when shock is used as the UCS, the use of electrical stimulation to the brain as a UCS does invariably produce conditioned deceleration.

The examination of conditioned emotional responses (CER) has generally been carried out by first having the subject learn some overt response, e.g., bar pressing, following which the conditioning procedure is undertaken. Here a CS is paired with a UCS, usually shock; the organism is unable to make any response which enables it either to escape or to avoid the UCS. It is generally assumed that the presentation of the aversive stimulus elicits a generalized emotional response in the subject which will interfere with the making of the original response. The test for such conditioning is made by returning the organism to the original learning situation. If there is such interference, the presentation of the CS generally results in a decline or cessation of the originally learned response. Conditioned suppression has been the term used to describe this decline or cessation of responding.

The examination of conditioned responses controlled by the central nervous system include sucking, eyeblink, and flexion responses. The use of instructed responses, referred to as the Ivanov-Smolensky procedure, are also included in this category. With this latter technique, the CS is paired with commands or instructions (which serve as the UCS) from the experimenter to the subject eliciting a specific response. The pairing of a light with the command, "Press," which results in the subjects pressing a lever, illustrates this general procedure.

Some question has been raised as to whether many of the conditioned eyeblink and flexion studies can be classified as "classical conditioning" since the response which is learned results in the successful avoidance of the UCS. The use of paraorbital shock in the eyeblink conditioning task, or an electrode attached to the limb of the organism in flexion conditioning, does result in fitting these situations into the classical conditioning paradigm.

Finally, mention should be made of attempts to condition the blocking of the alpha rhythm in man. Light typically serves as a UCS in such experiments. Although the evidence seems unequivocal that, when the subject is instructed to make an overt response to the UCS, conditioning can take place, the evidence is somewhat equivocal when instructions indicate that the subject should remain relaxed and passive.

4
Classical Conditioning:
Basic Considerations

As we noted, three variables may be considered basic to the classical conditioning paradigm, namely: (1) the conditioned stimulus, (2) the unconditioned stimulus, and (3) the temporal relationship related to their presentation—the CS-UCS interval. It is not surprising that many experimenters believe that an adequate understanding of classical conditioning must first begin with an examination of how these three variables contribute to the strength of the conditioned response.

The Conditioned Stimulus

Experiments examining the contribution of varied aspects of the conditioned stimulus to the classically conditioned response have been a diverse lot, and it is not within the scope of this text to examine all of them. Three areas, however, have generated a great deal of interest. These have been (1) the intensity of the conditioned stimulus, (2) the phenomenon of stimulus generalization, and finally, (3) compound conditioned stimuli.

Conditioned Stimulus Intensity

Razran's (1957) examination of a large number (more than 150) of Russian conditioning studies indicated that the intensity of the CS was a significant determiner of the ease of conditioning. Some of the early American investigations, Carter (1941), Grant and Schneider (1948, 1949), and Wilcott (1953), for example, were unable to demonstrate such an effect. Many subsequent studies, examining both skeletal and autonomic responses, have revealed the influence of the CS intensity variable, although it must be acknowledged that the effect in some instances has not been a robust one. To cite a few of these studies, Barnes (1956) demonstrated the effect of a CS intensity variable using a dog's flexion response. Walker (1960), Beck (1963), Grice and Hunter (1964), Mattson and Moore (1964), and Lipkin and Moore (1966) have all found that CS intensity influences the conditioned eyeblink response; Frey (1969), using the same response but another species (rabbit), has confirmed these findings. Kamin and Schaub (1963) found that CS intensity influenced the conditioned emotional response in the rat, while Woodard (1971) noted CS intensity effects with the respiratory response in fish, and Cohen (1974), with the heart rate in the pigeon. In summary, and in keeping with Gray's (1965) earlier conclusion, the effect of the influence of CS intensity is a real one, at least with many responses in a number of species.

It should be noted that in many of the studies in which either negative findings have been obtained or else only a relatively small positive effect has been found, the experimenter has used a between-subjects design—that is, different groups of subjects receive different intensities of the CS. The studies of Beck (1963) and Grice and Hunter (1964) are significant since they have used a within-subjects design and have obtained very robust effects. In the Grice and Hunter (1964) study, the eyeblink response was conditioned for 100 trials to only the loud tone; a second group was conditioned to only the soft tone. A third group received 50 trials with a soft tone and 50 trials with a loud one, the tones being presented in random order. The results of the last 60 trials to the loud and soft tones under the within- and between-stimulus conditions are presented in Fig. 4-1. Here it may be noted that exposing each of the subjects to two values of a CS intensity during conditioning substantially increases the effect of the intensity variable.

In a subsequent study by Frey (1969) the influence of CS intensity was examined with the conditioned eyeblink of the rabbit. The investigator's procedure differed from others in that he provided 100 conditioning trials per day for several days until a stable asymptotic level of performance was attained. Following the stabilization of each subject's performance, CS intensity effects were examined under the following 100 trials per session training sequences: (1) one session in which there was the alternation of a 75 db and 90 db tone, with each tone serving as the CS, (2) three sessions with the 75 db tone, (3)

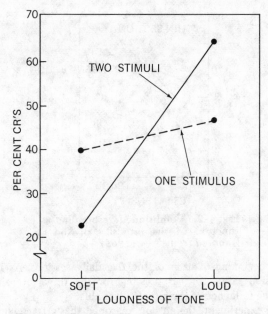

Fig. 4-1. Percent CRs during last sixty trials to the loud and soft tones under the one- and two-stimulus conditions. *Adapted from Grice and Hunter (1964)*

three sessions with the 90 db tone, (4) four sessions in which the 75 and 90 db tones were again alternated, and (5) a final session in which the 75 and 90 db tones were presented in 25 trial blocks. The schedule used permitted the experimenter to examine intensity effects both within and between sessions.

The findings as indicated in Fig. 4-2 reveal that conditioned responding changed as a function of the CS intensity and that these changes were primarily related to the intensity of the CSs used within a conditioning session. It may be noted that intensity differences obtained within and between sessions are similar to those obtained by Grice and Hunter (1964) using one and two stimuli with different groups of subjects. Frey's results suggest that the size of the CS intensity effect depends upon having both intensities presented within a single session, rather than having both intensities sampled by a single subject.

In a study investigating an autonomic response—the conditioned emotional response (CER) of rats—Kamin and Schaub (1963) also demonstrated CS intensity effects. In their first experiment, a bar pressing response was established initially. Conditioned emotional response training was then provided by placing the animals in the bar pressing apparatus and providing them with 4 trials per day in which either a weak (49 db), medium (62.5 db), or strong (81 db) sound served as the CS and was paired with a .5-second shock (UCS). The CS which was of 3 minutes' duration was presented 19, 55, 95, and 115 min-

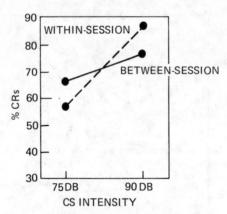

Fig. 4-2. Conditioned responding as a function of the intensity of the CS. *Adapted from Frey (1969)*

utes after the beginning of each of the five daily sessions. As Table 4-1 indicates, suppression ratios for bar pressing for the three intensities of the CS clearly reveal the influence of the intensity variable.

In a second experiment, the authors reasoned that a trace conditioning procedure (which involves the termination of the CS at some time prior to the presentation of the UCS) might be more sensitive to the influence of the intensity variable than the delayed conditioning procedure utilized in the first study. They reasoned that the intensity and duration of the neural trace of the CS, which presumably bridges the time interval between the termination of the CS and onset of the UCS, would be a function of CS intensity. Accordingly, the general procedure used in Experiment 1 was replicated except that only strong and weak intensity groups were used. The trace conditioning procedure consisted of the presentation of a two minute CS, followed after a 1-minute interval, by the UCS. Ten training trials were provided, with the results demonstrating that "the intensity of the CS has an overwhelming effect on acquisition of a trace CER" (p. 506).[1]

Some questions must be raised, however, as to whether an intensity effect which has been obtained in the studies cited, can be found with the conditioned EDR. An early study by Grant and Schneider (1949) did not provide positive findings. Similarly, studies by Kimmel (1959), Prokasy and Ebel (1967), and Orlebeke and VanOlst (1968) all have been unable to find CS intensity effects using this response.

In attempting to account for the difficulty of obtaining stimulus intensity

[1] There has been concern on the part of some experimenters as to whether CS intensity influences learning or performance. We do not believe that at the present time it is possible to provide an answer to this question. In any event, the conclusions drawn by different investigators vary, Cohen (1974) suggesting that the locus of the effect is upon performance, while Woodard (1971) has indicated that CS intensity influences both learning and performance.

Table 4-1   Mean Suppression Ratios, Days 1–5, as a Function of CS Intensity

| | CS Intensity | | |
	Strong	Medium	Weak
Mean	.09	.14	.26
Median	.08	.14	.26

Adapted from Kamin and Schaub (1963)

effects with the electrodermal response, experimenters have not used a within-subjects design—a design which we have noted to be quite sensitive in demonstrating these effects. Perhaps the use of such a design would provide positive findings.

A variety of theoretical explanations have been provided for the CS intensity effect. Hull (1951) simply asserted that CS intensity energized or facilitated the making of the conditioned response. That is, Hull assumed that there was a relationship between the strength of a conditioned response and the intensity of the stimulus to which it was attached, describing such an effect as "stimulus-intensity dynamism."

A second similar stimulus-intensity effect hypothesis was proposed independently by Perkins (1953) and Logan (1954). This theory has been expressed in terms of a differential conditioning situation. These investigators have assumed that when a particular response is elicited by a CS, other stimuli are capable of eliciting the response as a result of a stimulus generalization process. It is also assumed that the conditioned response is made to other stimuli; inasmuch as reinforcement is not provided, these other stimuli gain inhibitory properties which also generalize. Such stimuli have been assumed to be the absence of the CS (silence) or "background" cues which occur during the intertrial interval. This situation is indicated in Fig. 4–3, revealing generalization gradients

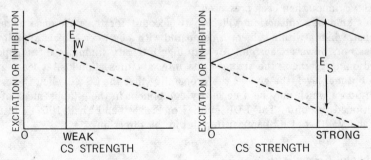

Fig. 4-3. Schematic diagram of the hypothetical gradients of excitation (continuous line) and inhibition (broken line) after reinforcement of responses to the onset of a weak CS (W) and a strong CS with nonreinforcement of responses to the intertrial stimulus of "silence" (O). (Net excitation is greater for the strong CS—E_s— than for the weak CS—E_w.) *Adapted from Champion (1962)*

for both excitation as well as inhibition. It should be noted that the response attached to the CS is presumed to acquire the same degree of gross excitatory strength, regardless of CS intensity. Such excitatory strength generalizes along the stimulus intensity dimension as indicated. Nonreinforced responses made during the intertrial interval result in the generalization of these inhibitory tendencies. It is further assumed that inhibition is subtracted from excitation to provide a net excitatory strength—thus, it may be noted that greater excitatory strength accrues to the more intense CS since less inhibitory strength is subtracted from the excitatory strength generated by it.

A variety of difficulties with both the Hull (1951), and Perkins (1953) and Logan (1954) positions have been found. Hull's specification of CS intensity in terms of absolute values has not been corroborated by the experiments of Grice and Hunter (1964) and others who have demonstrated relative intensity effects.

No useful purpose would be served in citing all of the experimental evidence which has provided problems for Perkins's (1953) and Logan's (1954) theoretical position. The interested reader can refer to the studies by Moore and Newman (1966) and Grice, Masters, and Kohfeld (1966). One obvious difficulty, however, is that the stimulus generalization gradients which have been obtained when conditioned stimulus intensity has been examined are much different from the symmetrical, linear slopes which Perkins and Logan have hypothesized.

In accounting for their experimental findings, Grice and Hunter (1964) proposed that conditioned stimulus intensity effects could be explained in terms of an organism's adaptation level. This position, based upon Helson's (1964) theory, states that the effect of any stimulus is related to the adaptation level of the organism, which in turn is determined by past as well as present stimulation. The influence of any stimulus, then, is not dependent upon its absolute characteristics but, rather, is related to a level which has been established by past as well as present stimulation. Presumably, the presentation of a low intensity CS along with a high intensity CS results in the latter appearing to the subject to be more intense, and the weak one even weaker than if only a single intensity stimulus had been presented.

This kind of explanation will help to account for the difference in results obtained when a within-subject is compared with a between-subject experiment; it does not, however, account for why high intensity stimuli result in superior conditioning. Perhaps the stronger the intensity of a stimulus, at least up to some optimal level, the greater the probability that the CS will elicit the orienting response which may be a necessary component in the establishment of any conditioned response. The EDR studies of Prokasy and Ebel (1967) and Orlebeke and VanOlst (1968) appear to point in this direction.

Stimulus Generalization

After a conditioned response has been established, the question may be raised whether stimuli other than the conditioned stimulus can elicit the conditioned response. Experimental findings obtained over the years have provided an affirmative answer to this question. The operation which has demonstrated this phenomenon, as well as the assumed process taking place in such an operation, has been termed stimulus generalization.

Pavlov's early experimental work provided a foundation upon which the concept of stimulus generalization rests. In writing about these early experiments, Pavlov (1927) stated, "... if a tone of 1000 d.v. [Hz] is established as a conditioned stimulus, many other tones spontaneously acquire similar properties, such properties diminishing proportionally to the intervals of these tones from the one of 1000 d.v. [Hz]" (p. 113). Although a second Russian investigator, Bechterev (1928) also called attention to this process, it was Pavlov's research which provided the impetus for inquiry by a number of American investigators.

Early studies were performed by Bass and Hull (1934), and Hovland (1937a, 1937b, 1937c, 1937d). In certainly a very unusual experiment, Bass and Hull placed four vibrators at roughly equal linear distances from the subject's shoulder to his calf, with tactual stimuli arising from the operation of the vibrators serving as conditioned and generalized stimuli. Shock served as the UCS. For half of the subjects, an electrodermal response was conditioned with stimulation on the shoulder serving as the CS; the other stimuli were used as generalized (or test) stimuli. For the other half of the subjects, tactual stimulation on the calf served as the CS, with the other three stimuli being used as generalized stimuli. Each subject received 14 CS-UCS pairings per day and 10 CS test trials with each stimulus. Generalization gradients revealed that the electrodermal response to the stimulus positioned next to the CS was almost as strong as the response to the CS itself. In brief, responses to the two closest points could not be differentiated although the responses to the other two points were reliably different from those elicited by the CS.

It is Hovland's (1937a, 1937b, 1937c, 1937d) studies, however, which have long been regarded as classic examples of the stimulus generalization experiment. In his first study (Hovland, 1937a), a psychophysical method was used to obtain 4 tones which were separated in pitch by 25 JNDs. The frequencies which were obtained using this scaling procedure were 153, 468, 1000, and 1967 Hz. A conditioning experiment was then undertaken in which either the highest or the lowest tone served as the CS, with shock used as a UCS in order to elicit the EDR. Following 16 conditioning trials, extinction trials were given in which each subject was presented with each of the 4 tones 4 times in a random order. The extinction trials were combined for both groups, and a single curve representing the generalization of tones separated by 25, 50, or 75 JNDs was plotted. Fig. 4-4 reveals this generalization curve.

Methodological Considerations

Before examining some of the variables which have influenced stimulus generalization, it is appropriate to consider methodology.

The basic operation in measuring stimulus generalization in classical conditioning has been to use a response measure obtained during extinction, although the specific extinction operations have varied from one experiment to another. As we have just noted, Hovland (1937a), presented all of the test stimuli to each subject, but some investigators have used only a single test stimulus. In a study by Wickens, Schroder, and Snide (1954), essentially replicating Hovland's procedure, 8 extinction trials were provided in which the test stimulus was a

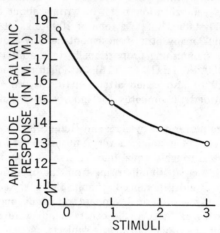

Fig. 4-4. Composite curve of generalization of conditioned excitatory tendencies. Electrodermal response to conditioned frequency of tone (0) and to other tones 25, 50, and 75 j.n.d.'s removed in frequency (1, 2, and 3 respectively). *Adapted from Hovland (1937a)*

tone of only a single frequency. Different test stimuli were used with different subjects. A variation of this method has been to provide only a single extinction trial following the conditioning trials, a method utilized by Grant and Schiller (1953) and Hall and Prokasy (1961). The position of these experimenters is that the first extinction trial represents the most appropriate measure of generalization, since subsequent extinction trial data may be influenced by the extinction process.

A second consideration is the selection of those stimulus values which are used to test for stimulus generalization. Such stimuli must be discriminable one from the other; otherwise, the critic can point out that the test or generalized stimulus was in fact perceived by the subject as the CS. Hovland (1937a) used JNDs to scale his stimuli—a procedure which was adopted by many subsequent investigators. However, the assumption that JNDs represent the appropriate scaling units for stimulus generalization studies can be questioned. There is no doubt that psychophysical scales can be established but such scales are invariably the product of extensive training of experienced observers. Although these scales may reveal the limits of sensory functions, they do not indicate anything about the discriminability of the stimuli which are perceived by the naive subject in the conditioning situation, or that equal numbers of JNDs represent equal intervals on the scale.

In fact, Slivinske and Hall (1960) obtained experimental evidence to indicate that the tones which Hovland had selected in one of his stimulus generalization studies were not absolutely identifiable by naive subjects participating in an experimental situation which paralleled the conditioning experiment. Razran (1949) has raised the question of whether or not a continuum, as indicated by the use of a JND scale, actually exists. He has hypothesized that in conditioning studies there is a crude qualitative categorizing of stimulus dimensions by the subject—one which consists of only a few steps.

On the other hand, the use of a physical scale, which many contemporary investigators have adopted, does not solve the problem. The arbitrary selection of units using a physical dimension provides no assurance that the generalized stimuli are discriminable or, if they are, whether they are equally so.

In summary, at least at present, there is no "answer" to the problem of what stimulus scale to use in stimulus generalization studies; the only admonition is that the experimenter be aware that his findings are relative to the scale that he has employed.

Stimuli Used as the CS

As might be anticipated, a variety of stimuli have been used by investigators examining the stimulus generalization process. Visual and auditory stimuli have been employed most frequently, although tactual stimulation, as we have noted in the early Bass and Hull (1934) experiment, has been used from time to time.

One interesting auditory effect—the octave effect—is obtained when pitch is used as the stimulus dimension. Humphreys (1939a), using college students, conditioned the EDR to a tone of 1967 Hz and then tested for generalization. The response to a test tone of 984 Hz—1 octave below the positive CS—was significantly greater than the response to a test tone of 1000 Hz, although in terms of frequency, the 1000 Hz tone is more similar to the 1967 Hz tone than is the 984 Hz tone.

When using human subjects, it is possible to condition a response to a conditioned stimulus consisting of a word or a sentence. Obtaining a response to the presentation of generalized stimuli consisting of semantically similar verbal items has been designated as *semantic* generalization. This designation is in recognition of the term *semantic* conditioning, first used by Razran (1939), to refer to those conditioning studies which used a verbal stimulus as the conditioned stimulus.

As Osgood (1953) has written, semantic generalization studies can be grouped into three categories: (1) sign-to-sign, (2) object-to-sign, and (3) sign-to-object. The sign-to-sign category refers to an experimental situation in which a response is conditioned to one word with the generalization test taking the form of presentation of another word—one which bears some relationship to the first, a synonym or an antonym, for example. The object-to-sign situation is one in which an object serves as a stimulus to which a response has been conditioned, and the generalization test consists of presenting a word which represents or is related to this object. Finally, the sign-to-object category is just the reverse of this.

Almost all semantic generalization studies have been of the sign-to-sign variety. In one of the early experiments, Razran (1939) utilized synonyms and homophones as his test material. A salivary CR was established by using words such as "style" and "urn" as conditioned stimuli, with pretzels, candy, etc., serving as unconditioned stimuli to elicit the salivary response. After the CR had been established, test stimuli consisted of presenting synonyms such as "fashion" and "vase" as well as homphones, e.g., "earn." The findings indicated that it was possible to obtain a CR to both synonyms and homophones, with the synonyms providing the greater amount of generalization.

It has been acknowledged that verbal stimuli may vary on a number of dimensions so that many of the investigators following Razran (1939) have been interested in examining semantic generalization as related to these attributes. Two examples will illustrate the type of study which has been conducted. Abbott and Price (1964) varied the formal similarity of a nonsense syllable (XUH) which was used as the CS. Following the establishment of a conditioned eyelid response to this syllable, a test for semantic generalization was provided in which generalized stimuli consisted of syllables which had either two, one, or no letters in common with the CS.

A similar type of study was conducted by Lang, Geer, and Hnatiow (1963) who examined semantic generalization by varying the emotional content of a word. An EDR was conditioned to the word "TORTURE" with subjects then tested with such words as "CONFLICT" or "DISPLEASURE." Perhaps not surprisingly, semantic generalization has invariably been reported, regardless of the verbal attribute which has been manipulated.

Stimulus Generalization and Stimulus Intensity

As we have noted earlier, it has been found that the strength of a CR is related to the intensity of the CS which elicits it. In Hull's (1943) early discussion of stimulus generalization, the role of stimulus intensity was not considered, but in a subsequent article (Hull, 1949), the contribution of an intensity dimension was recognized. Hull pointed out that the response strength associated with a generalized stimulus was related not only to the number of JNDs between the generalized stimulus and the CS but also to the intensity of the generalized stimulus. Generalized stimuli whose intensities were less than the intensity of the CS should produce weaker responses than the CS. On the other hand, generalized stimuli whose intensities were greater than the intensity of the CS should produce stronger responses. Since the intensity variable could provide differential contributions to response strength, it would follow that the stimulus generalization gradient would not be symmetrical. Hull wrote that when a response is conditioned to a weak stimulus and generalizes toward a fairly strong extreme of the stimulus-intensity continuum the resulting effective gradient is convex (rounded outward) upward, but when a response is conditioned to the strong extreme of the above stimulus-intensity continuum and generalizes toward the weak extreme, the resulting effective gradient is concave (rounded inward) downward. Fig. 4-5 provides an illustration of a stimulus generalization gradient in which the gradient has been influenced by the intensity variable.

Experimental support has come from both Russian as well as American laboratories. Razran (1949) has presented data obtained from 54 different experiments in Pavlov's laboratory examining the role of stimulus intensity and

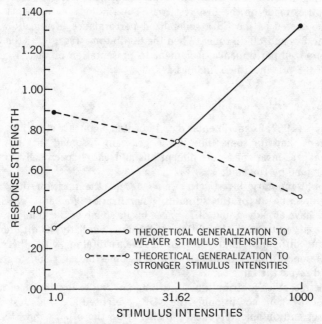

Fig. 4-5. Graphic representation of theoretical stimulus-intensity generalization as modified by stimulus intensity when extending from weak toward strong stimulus intensities and from strong toward weak intensities. The solid circles represent the origin of the respective gradients. *Adapted from Hull (1949)*

generalization effects of salivary conditioning in dogs. As Table 4-2 reveals, there is clearly an increase in response strength as higher intensity generalized stimuli are employed.

A study of Hall and Prokasy (1961) has also demonstrated the operation of an intensity dimension in a generalization study. Groups of subjects were given 16 EDR conditioning trials in which a 30- or 80-db 1000-Hz tone served as CS. Eight extinction trials followed with either a 30-, 54-, or 80-db 1000-Hz

Table 4-2 Stimulus Intensity Generalization of Salivary Conditioning in Dogs.
Data from 54 Different Experiments in Pavlov's Laboratory

Each entry is a mean percentage of conditioned salivation to the nonconditioned generalization stimuli. Figures in parentheses are numbers of determinations.

Conditioned Stimuli	Lower Intensity Steps			Higher Intensity Steps		
	I	II	III	I	II	III
Lights	79(14)	69(11)	58(8)	118(14)	128(9)	149(8)
Whistles	68(12)	58(11)	49(9)	137(13)	149(8)	165(8)
Bells	72(11)	64(9)	56(7)	124(10)	138(8)	149(6)

Adapted from Razran (1949)

tone being presented. The analysis of generalization effects was confined to EDR responses made on the first test trial. The findings revealed that when the 30 db tone served as the CS a generalized performance increment was noted to both the 54- and 80-db tones. When the 80-db tone was used as the CS, there was a generalized performance decrement to presentation of the 54- and 30-db tones. Fig. 4-6 presents these findings.

Stimulus Generalization Gradients

Hovland's (1937a) experimental data indicated a concave stimulus generalization gradient, and for some time it was generally assumed that the shape of the gradient was invariant across dimensions and, more specifically, was similar to that obtained by Hovland.

Most contemporary investigators now accept the position that no single form can describe all of the stimulus generalization gradients which are obtained. We have already noted differences in the shape of the gradient as a function of the intensity of the conditioned stimulus. Similarly, as different testing methods and different stimulus dimensions are used (along with other methodological differences), there is little reason to assume that all generalization gradients should reveal the same form.

To illustrate the contribution of testing methods, it will be recalled that Hovland (1937a), in conditioning the EDR, presented all of his test stimuli to each subject and obtained a concave gradient. On the other hand, the Wickens, Schroder, and Snide (1954) study, which we described earlier, replicated Hovland's experimental procedure except that Wickens et al presented their subjects with only one of the test stimuli. Their findings revealed a bell shaped generalization curve.[2]

The stimulus dimensions used also play an important role. A study by Vandament and Price (1964) has shown that the shape of the generalization gradient is related to the stimulus values placed on the abscissa. In this conditioned eyeblink study, subjects were trained to respond to a light of 3.20 apparent foot candles and then tested to lights of less intensity, e.g., 1.364, .4267, and .07459 apparent foot candles. When the physical values of the CS were plotted, the resultant generalization curve was concave; on the other hand, if the physical scale was converted into a log scale, which approximates a JND scale, the gradient was linear. Thus, the investigators have written that the shape of the gradi-

---

[2] It is quite possible that the failure of Wickens et al (1954) to obtain similar findings is not a function of the method of testing but rather related to problems of measuring the EDR. Littman (1949), Epstein and Burstein (1966), and Burstein, Epstein, and Smith (1967), all attempting to replicate Hovland's findings, have obtained still different gradients. Burstein, Epstein, and Smith (1967) have indicated that replication difficulties may be attributable to the use of the EDR, writing that " . . . the orienting component . . . may be so sensitive as to obscure those aspects of the response which are a product of conditioning" (p. 130). As we noted in Chapter 3, the EDR is now recognized as a multi-component response and it should be acknowledged that none of the experimenters cited have analyzed their findings in terms of the three component response model.

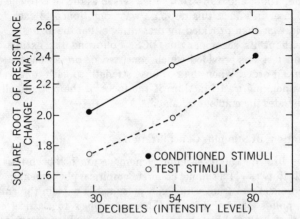

Fig. 4-6. Generalization gradients obtained as a function of the intensity of the CS. *Adapted from Hall and Prokasy (1961)*

ent varies considerably according to the scaling procedure employed; they have suggested that it might be parsimonious to disregard scaling procedures in generalization studies and concentrate on the parameters as they relate to some physical dimension.

Mednick and Freeman (1960), in their excellent review of stimulus generalization studies, have arrived at a similar conclusion, stating that without some specification of stimulus and response measurement scales, discussion of the shape of obtained gradients must proceed very cautiously.

One additional comment deserves mention. Stimulus generalization curves are similar to learning curves in that the average gradient is not necessarily representative of the generalization phenomenon for a single subject. The individual protocols found in many generalization studies provide ample testimony that the generalization gradients plotted differ markedly from the curve based on all of the subjects.

Generalization of Inhibition

Our examination of stimulus generalization has been limited to studies in which a CS has been associated with a UCS, with the test situation examining the strength of the organism's response to generalized stimuli. One can conceptualize these experiments as reflecting the generalization of habit strength or excitatory tendencies built up by the CS–UCS pairings.

A number of investigators have also demonstrated that generalization gradients can be obtained when the basic operation is one of nonreinforcement or extinction. In such instances, it has been assumed that there is a generalization of inhibitory tendencies or inhibition. An early study demonstrating such an effect was performed by Hovland (1937a). In this study, subjects received a number of CS–UCS pairings in which different auditory stimuli served as the

CS (153, 468, 1000, and 1967 Hz); shock served as the UCS to elicit an electro-dermal response. In effect, this response was conditioned to each tone. An extinction series was then provided by presenting either the highest or lowest tone 16 times without its accompanying UCS. Following the extinction series, a generalization test was provided which consisted of presenting the 4 tones in a counterbalanced order. When the response strength to each tone was examined, decreased responding as a function of the locus of the test stimuli was noted. Fig. 4-7 illustrates the gradient obtained.

Interpretations of Stimulus Generalization

Following Brown (1965), stimulus generalization has been looked upon by some investigators as (1) a simple, concrete empirical phenomenon, or by others as (2) a theoretical construct which can presumably explain the empirical findings. These points of view have not been confined to classical conditioning studies but have included instrumental and operant investigations as well. Thus, stimulus generalization, either as an empirical phenomenon or as a theoretical process, as conceptualized, has considerable generality. As a result, it seems appropriate to examine stimulus generalization in operant and instrumental learning tasks (Chapter 13) prior to considering an interpretation of the phenomenon.

Compound Stimuli

In his investigation of the conditioned response, Pavlov (1927) examined the contribution of compound conditioned stimuli, defined as a stimulus aggregate, consisting of more than one element, with each element subject to independent experimental manipulation. Some years later, Hull (1943) considered the examination of compound conditioned stimuli of fundamental importance, noting,

> some writers, in an attempt to simplify the account of the learning process, have left the erroneous impression that the conditioned stimulus . . .
> is a simple or singular energy operating on one receptor end organ or, at most, on a small number of such end organs of a single sense mode. In actual fact an immense number of receptor end organs are involved in every conditioning situation, however much it may have been simplified by experimental methodology. Each stimulus 'object' represents a very complex aggregate of more or less alternative potential stimulations, often extending into numerous receptor modes. (p. 221)

In spite of the importance Hull attached to this area, Razran's (1965) examination of stimulus compounding affirmed that for a long time it was almost exclusively the domain of Russian experimenters. Baker's (1968) recent review has indicated an awakening interest on the part of American investigators.

One American investigator interested in the role of compound conditioned stimuli has been Grings. In an early study by Grings and O'Donnell (1956), using human subjects, four CSs were used—red, green, blue, or yellow dots projected on a ground glass screen. The UCS was shock, which elicited an EDR.

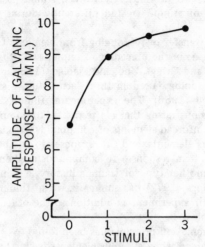

Fig. 4-7. Generalization of inhibition. All stimuli were provided reinforced trials, but only Stimulus 0 was given 16 extinction trials. The test for generalization of inhibition consisted of presenting the four tones in a counterbalanced order. *Adapted from Hovland (1937)*

The acquisition series consisted of each subject's receiving two CSs with each stimulus reinforced (CS+), along with a third CS which was presented without reinforcement, (CS-). A fourth CS was not presented (CSo). The assignment of colors to these varying conditions was rotated systematically from subject to subject. Four types of two element stimulus compounds were then presented during a series of test trials: (1) the two stimuli that were provided reinforcement (CS+, CS+); (2) one reinforced and one nonreinforced stimulus (CS+, CS-); (3) one reinforced stimulus along with the stimulus which had not been presented during training (CS+, CSo); and finally, (4) one nonreinforced stimulus along with the stimulus which was not presented (CS-, CSo). Results indicated that the largest EDR was elicited by the stimulus compound containing the two stimuli which had been reinforced during training. The next largest EDR was obtained by presenting a compound consisting of a reinforced stimulus element and a stimulus which had not been presented. Surprisingly, the nonreinforced stimulus and the stimulus element which had not been presented resulted in the next largest EDR, followed by the stimulus compound consisting of the reinforced and the nonreinforced stimulus.[3] As Grings and O'Donnell (1956) have written, "it appears safe to conclude that the magnitude of response

---

[3] It is not unusual for unexpected stimuli to elicit some type of surprise response on the part of the subject which in turn leads to the elicitation of an EDR. It is quite possible that this happened with the presentation of a stimulus that the subject had never previously experienced.

to a combination of two previously reinforced stimuli is significantly greater than to compounds of stimuli treated differently during the training series" (p. 357).

In examining the transfer of responding from elements to compounds made up of these elements, as in the preceding example, two other studies by Grings and Kimmel (1959), and Grings, Uno, and Fiebiger (1965) are relevant. We shall not detail the methodology used in these latter studies since it is similar to Grings and O'Donnell (1956). The experimental findings obtained, however, are consistent in demonstrating that (1) responses to compounds consisting of pairs of previously reinforced elements or compounds were larger than responses to the single stimulus elements, and (2) responses to compounds of reinforced elements were larger than responses to compounds containing elements which had been provided another type of training history, e.g., nonreinforcement or nonpresentation. Grings (1972) has summarized the findings from the Grings and O'Donnell (1956) experiment in addition to the other two we have cited; they are found in Table 4-3.

In summary, a summation principle has been found to operate, with an additive effect being obtained when stimulus elements having had separate histories of reinforcement are presented as a compound stimulus. On the other hand, the replacement of one of these stimulus elements with a stimulus element previously associated with nonreinforcement reduces the level of responding.

A study by Grings and Uno (1968) has provided an interesting extension of the summation principle. During training sessions, subjects were conditioned to respond with "fear" elicited by the presentation of shock (UCS) to a visual stimulus; they were also trained to relax to the visually presented word, "now." (It was acknowledged that this latter type of training was difficult to place within the classical conditioning paradigm since the UCS eliciting the relaxation was unknown.) When the compound stimulus, consisting of the two visual stimuli, was presented, a lesser fear response was hypothesized than would occur from the fear stimulus alone; results verified this prediction.

In the studies reviewed, the experimental design has been one in which stimulus elements have been provided a reinforcement or nonreinforcement history, followed by a compound stimulus made up of these elements being presented to the subject. Investigators have also used the reverse procedure: that is, a compound stimulus consisting of a number of elements is provided a reinforcement or nonreinforcement history, following which the stimulus elements are individually presented.

Table 4-3   Results of Element to Compound Transfer
(In Mean Magnitude EDR)

	Elements			Compounds			
	+	−	0	++	+−	+0	−−
1. Grings and O'Donnell (1956)	1.29	1.02	1.08	1.35	.75	.99	
2. Grings, Uno, and Fiebiger (1965)	.88	.63	.57	1.48	1.40	1.29	
3. Grings and Kimmel (1959)	1.30	.94		2.34	1.92		1.1

Studies by Grings (1969), and Grings and Zeiner (1969) have been conducted using this type of design. The general procedure consisted of providing discrimination conditioning with one compound CS (two colored dots) accompanied by shock, which elicited an EDR, while a second CS compound was presented without the UCS. Discriminatory responses to the two compound stimuli were obtained. Following this, test trials were introduced in which the stimulus elements making up the compound stimulus were individually presented. Surprisingly enough, both experiments indicated that compound stimulus training had virtually no influence when element or component testing was subsequently provided.[4]

Wickens (1965) is another American investigator to extensively examine conditioning with compound stimuli. His strategy has been to choose a variable known to influence the strength of a conditioned response when a single CS is used. A compound CS in which the elements differ from each other with respect to this variable is then provided. After the subject is trained to the compound CS, the elements are presented individually. The questions posed here are whether or not the individual elements will differ in their effectiveness of eliciting the CR, and if so, whether such a difference could be predicted from what is known of this variable's operations for a single conditioned stimulus?

Unlike Grings, who was interested in reinforcement, Wickens concentrated on the onset and offset times of the elements which make up the stimulus compound. Thus, an early problem was to examine differential offset times for elements of a stimulus compound when their onset times were simultaneous.

In an early experiment of this type by Wickens, Cross, and Morgan (1959), a tone and light served as conditioned stimuli while the UCS was a shock eliciting finger withdrawal as well as an EDR. A microswitch released by withdrawal of the subject's finger enabled the experimenter to obtain a latency measure as well as to terminate the CS.

Four groups of subjects were run: two with the single stimulus CS and two with a compound CS (light and tone). The single stimulus groups were conditioned to the tone whose onset was 450 milliseconds before the UCS. For one of these groups, the tone was terminated by the finger withdrawal response, while for the other group, it was terminated by a timer 450 milliseconds *after* shock onset. The total duration of the CS for this second group was 900 milliseconds. The compound CS groups were conditioned to the light and tone. The onset of these stimuli was simultaneous, 450 milliseconds before the UCS. As with the single stimulus groups, one stimulus of the compound was terminated by the response, whereas the other stimulus was terminated by the timer 450 milliseconds after shock onset. One compound CS group was tested on trial 8 (13 training trials were provided), and also on extinction trials 14 through

---

[4] The generality of Grings's findings can be questioned since Wagner, Saavedra, and Lehman (as reported by Wagner, 1969) have noted that stimulus elements making up a stimulus compound with a reinforcement or nonreinforcement history may differentially influence a response when presented individually. Inasmuch as these investigators used a more complex experimental design, as well as a different response (eyeblink), with another species (rabbits), differential findings are perhaps not surprising.

18, to the element terminated by the response. The second group was tested on the same trials to the element which had its termination delayed. (The groups were trained so that this element in each instance was the tone.) Fig. 4-8 and Fig. 4-9 present the findings, as measured by percentage of finger withdrawal CRs, for the groups trained to the single stimulus as well as for the groups trained to the compound CS. (Little difference was noted for EDR responding.) From these results, it would appear that at least in this particular experiment, a relationship which holds for stimulus elements also holds for the elements which make up the compound.

Wickens's second area of investigation has been the examination of differential onset times for the elements of a CS compound which terminate simultaneously. In studies of this kind, it should be acknowledged that the manipulated variable is the CS-UCS temporal interval. That is, when onset times are varied, the interstimulus interval (CS-UCS) will also vary so that, in effect, it is the influence of this variable which is being examined. It would be assumed that if one stimulus element of a compound has a more favorable interstimulus interval than a second, the testing of this first element should reveal superior conditioning.

Studies by Wickens, Gehman, and Sullivan (1959), Fletcher (1960), and Wickens, Born, and Wickens (1963) have examined differential onset times; the findings, however, are complex. The Wickens, Born, and Wickens (1963) study illustrates the general experimental design as well as the complexity of

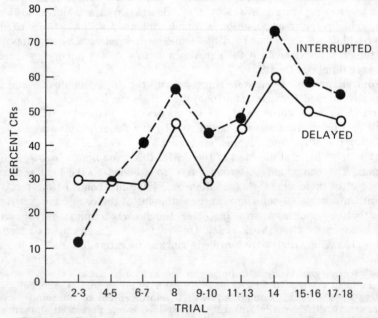

Fig. 4-8. Percent CRs across trials for groups trained to a single stimulus. *Adapted from data provided by Wickens, Cross, and Morgan (1959)*

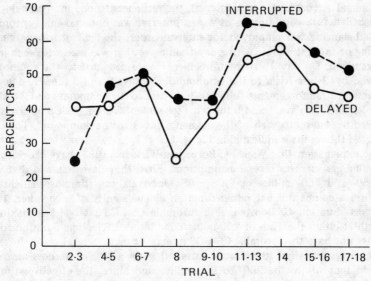

Fig. 4-9. Percent CRs for groups trained to a compound CS, with critical tests of the elements on Trial 8 and extinction trials, 14 through 18. *Adapted from data provided by Wickens, Cross, and Morgan (1959)*

the experimental results. In this study, the EDR of cats was conditioned to a compound stimulus in which the second and short stimulus element (light or tone) was 600 milliseconds in duration and always preceded the UCS (shock) by 550 milliseconds. The duration of first element (light or tone) was either 750, 1100, or 1300 milliseconds. The relationship between the elements making up the compound and the UCS is indicated in Fig. 4-10.

It may be observed that the conditioned stimulus elements overlapped each

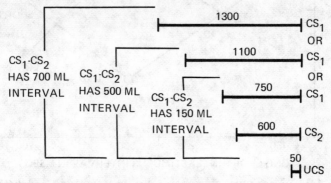

Fig. 4-10. The temporal relationship between the varying CSs which were used and the UCS.

other and all terminated simultaneously with shock. Six animals were used with each animal serving under each interval, the responses to one interval being extinguished before conditioning at a new interval was undertaken. Appropriate counterbalancing was employed for interval order, the light or tone serving as the long or short stimulus. A five day training session was used with each interval examined. On day 1, 10 reinforcements were provided to the compound, followed by 2 test trials to the compound. On days 2 and 3 the schedule was the same—10 reinforcements followed by 1 test to the compound and 2 tests to each element. On days 4 and 5 the same schedule was used: 1 UCS presentation followed by 4 tests to each of the elements and 4 to the compound. The complexity of the results is indicated in Fig. 4-11.

The explanation that Wickens, Born, and Wickens (1963) have provided for these findings involves several assumptions. First, they have assumed that with the 150- and 700- millisecond CS_1—CS_2 intervals, the stimulus elements do not form a compound but rather function independently of each other. Thus, the short duration CS located at a favorable CS-UCS interval has maximum strength at either the 150- or 700-millisecond interval. The long duration stimulus does not have the favorable CS-UCS interval at these two CS_1—CS_2 intervals and, as a result, is not as effective in eliciting the CR. The authors have also assumed that within the 200- to 600-millisecond range, the effective stimulus for the CR is some integrated effect of the two elements. In addition to the formation of a "true" compound at this interval, another process takes place—a type of sensory conditioning. Sensory conditioning results in the long duration element's acquiring the capacity to produce the effects of the compound itself, obeying the CS-UCS interval function (a 500-millisecond CS-UCS interval results in optimal conditioning) as has been found by experimenters such as Moeller

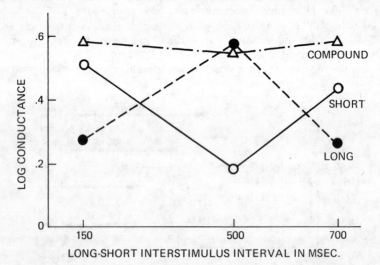

Fig. 4-11. Magnitude of response to the compound and both elements of the compound as a function of the interval between the long and short element. *Adapted from Wickens, Born, and Wickens (1963)*

(1954). As a result, the long duration stimulus becomes increasingly capable of eliciting the effective cue for the response as the interval between the long and short stimulus increases to approximately 500 milliseconds. The short stimulus, on the other hand, does not acquire the capacity to redintegrate the compound CS since it occurs after the onset of the long duration CS—an operation similar to backward conditioning. The complexity of these findings and the assumptions necessary to account for them suggest that other organisms as well as other response systems be used to further examine the role of stimulus onset in stimulus compounding.

The Unconditioned Stimulus

The second variable in the classical conditioning paradigm is the unconditioned stimulus. This stimulus plays a key role in the establishment of a conditioned response; as a result, the examination of its characteristics has generated a great deal of interest among experimenters.

The Nature of the Unconditioned Stimulus

Some investigators have assumed that the UCS must have some "motivational" significance for the organism. By motivational significance we mean that the stimulus must have reward or aversive characteristics. Certainly, the unconditioned stimuli which have been used in most classical conditioning experiments have been of this type: meat powder for a hungry dog to evoke salivation, shock to elicit the EDR, and so forth. In keeping with this point of view, classical conditioning experiments have frequently been defined in terms of classical reward or defense.

One approach to examining the motivational role of the UCS has been the attempt to condition "spinal" organisms—that is, first transecting the spinal cord and then attempting to condition responses below the transection. Stimulation received below the transection cannot be transmitted to the brain, so that shock which might be used to elicit a response could not be perceived as painful.

Shurrager and Culler (1940) reported that they were able to condition spinal animals, but a subsequent series of studies by Kellogg, Pronko, and Deese (1946), and Kellogg, Deese, Pronko, and Feinberg (1947) failed to provide confirmation. During the last decade, Forbes and Mahan (1963) and Lloyd, Wikler, and Whitehouse (1969) have been also unable to find evidences of conditioning; however, Buerger and Dawson (1968, 1969) did obtain spinal conditioning in two separate studies using spinal kittens. Patterson, Cegavske, and Thompson (1973) have confirmed these results.

The general procedure found in the three experiments of Patterson et al consisted of providing adult cats with a spinal transection following which they were injected with Flaxedil (a curare derivative which produces paralysis). Artificial respiration was instituted in order to keep the animals alive. The superficial sensory and deep peroneal motor nerves below the transection were dissected from each animal's lower left leg with electrodes being attached to each of these nerves. Experimental animals were classically conditioned by pairing

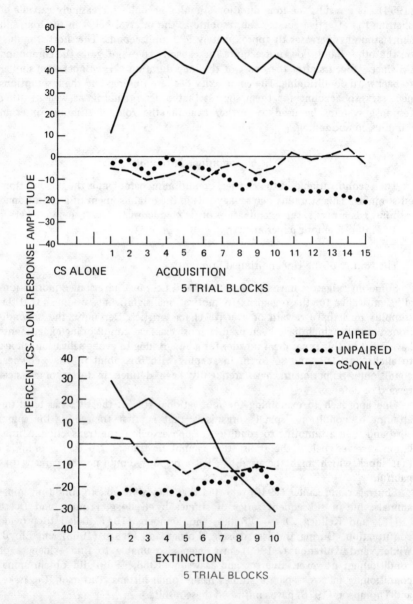

Fig. 4-12. Mean response amplitudes in acquisition and extinction over five-trial blocks as a percentage of CS-alone response amplitude for paired, unpaired, and CS-only groups in Experiment 2. *Adapted from Patterson, Cegavske, and Thompson (1973)*

stimulation of the exposed sensory nerve (CS), with cutaneous shock to the ankle of the same limb (UCS). The unconditioned response was a gross efferent volley from the motor nerve. Each of the three experiments revealed clear evidence of conditioning. In the investigators' second experiment, in addition to the experimental animals, one control group received unpaired presentations of the CS and UCS, while a second control group received only CS presentations during the experimental session. Seventy-five acquisition trials were provided in addition to 10 extinction trials. Results are presented in Fig. 4-12, which clearly reveals the development of the conditioned response.

The authors have concluded, "There is indeed no a priori reason why polysynaptic reflexes of the neurally isolated vertebrate spinal cord ought not to exhibit conditioning-like phenomena. Anatomically it is not a simple neuronal structure but contains a complex 'isodendritic core' of interneurons analogous to that of brain structures. The spinal flexion reflex is primitive, generalized, and defensive in character and might be expected to show some adaptive plasticity [learning] even in the absence of control from higher brain regions" (pp. 94-95).

In summary, the experimental investigations of Patterson et al. would indicate that the classical conditioning of a very simple response can take place without the UCS having "motivational" significance. On the other hand, it would not necessarily follow that the conditioning of more complex responses in the intact organism can be accomplished without the UCS serving as a motivator.

The Intensity of the Unconditioned Stimulus

If the UCS is considered a motivational variable, it is not surprising that increases in the intensity of the UCS should influence the strength of the conditioned response. Beginning with an early study by Passey (1948) a number of experimenters have demonstrated such to be the case.

To illustrate, the contribution of UCS intensity on the conditioning of a skeletal response, the eyeblink, was examined by Prokasy, Grant, and Myers (1958) who utilized four intensity levels of an air puff, as gauged by the fall of a column of mercury, e.g., 50, 120, 190, or 260 mm. A light served as the CS. Twenty acquisition trials were provided on day 1. On day 2, 20 additional trials were provided, followed by 20 extinction trials. Fig. 4-13 presents the acquisition data and reveals that the percentage of conditioned responses was a function of the intensity of the UCS for the first day's acquisition trials. On day 2, the 50-mm group continued to yield the smallest percentage of conditioned responses; there was no difference, however, among the other three groups.[5]

[5] One discordant note has been provided by Burstein (1965) who suggested that the variation in eyelid conditioning arising as a function of different UCS intensities can be attributed to the fact that a number of subjects provided the weaker intensity simply do not condition. He has written, "This view holds that with lower UCS intensities fewer Ss condition than is the case with higher intensities and that differences reported in previous studies are the artifactual

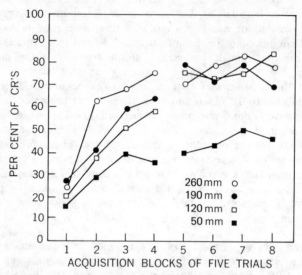

Fig. 4-13. Percentage frequency of CRs during acquisition with UCS intensity as the parameter. *Adapted from Prokasy, Grant, and Myers (1958)*

A variety of investigators have demonstrated that the intensity of the UCS also plays an important role in the conditioning of autonomic responses. For example, Wickens and Harding (1965) were able to show that the level of EDR conditioning was related to the amount of shock used as the UCS. In this study, 20 college students had one CS (a light or tone) associated with a strong UCS (2.5 ma shock) for 10 trials and a second CS (tone or light) associated with a weaker UCS (1.5 ma shock). Three test trials consisting of presenting the CS alone were introduced during the sequence of the 20 CS-UCS pairings. Finally, 6 extinction trials were provided, 3 with each CS. The results for both acquisition and extinction trials indicated that the CR established with the strong shock was significantly greater in magnitude than the CR associated with the weak UCS.[6]

result of averaging group data" (p. 303). Burstein's conclusions stemmed from a study of his own as well as the reanalysis of Passey's (1948) early study. In Passey's study, when the responses of the nonconditioners, defined as Ss who averaged less than 10% CRs, were removed from the data, the effect of UCS intensity was no longer significant. Spence and Platt's (1966) analysis of the UCS intensity studies performed in Spence's laboratory, using Burstein's criterion of eliminating subjects who averaged less than 10% CRs, continued to reveal significant differences as a function of the intensity of the UCS. Therefore, they have concluded that "the evidence . . . refutes the claim of Burstein that UCS intensity does not affect performance level in human eyelid conditioning, but determines only whether or not an S conditions" (p. 9).

[6] It should be noted that these findings were in contrast to those obtained in an earlier study by Wickens, Allen, and Hill (1963) who were unable to obtain statistical support for any relationship between conditioned response magnitude

In another example, Annau and Kamin (1961), using rats as subjects, found that shock intensity which served as the UCS was related to the strength of the conditioned emotional response (CER). In this study, a stable bar pressing response was first acquired. Following such training, 2-hour bar pressing sessions were provided each day for 10 days. During each of these daily sessions, 4 tone-shock pairings (CS-UCS) were provided. The intensity of the UCS was either .28, .49, 1.55, or 2.91 ma. The CS was presented for 3 minutes terminating simultaneously with the delivery of the UCS. Following these 10 days of CS-UCS presentation, extinction of the CER was carried out by presenting the CS four times daily without the UCS. The extinction training was continued for each subject until a day's suppression ratio reached a .50, a value which indicated that the response had not been suppressed.[7]

Acquisition findings are indicated in Fig. 4–14. Here it may be noted that the three highest shock intensities each resulted in almost complete suppression of the bar pressing response; the .49 ma level was only moderately successful in suppressing this response, whereas the .28 ma shock level was completely ineffective.

In the autonomic nervous system response studies cited, the UCS was aversive. Wagner, Siegel, Thomas, and Ellison (1964) examined the influence of UCS intensity with an appetitive UCS—food—on the conditioning of the salivary response. The manipulation of UCS intensity was accomplished by providing the experimental subjects (dogs) with either 6 pellets of food or just 1. The experimental findings, in keeping with the other studies cited, indicated that the 6-pellet group reached a higher level of anticipatory responding during the acquisition trials than the 1-pellet group.

Varied UCS Intensity

In examining the contribution of UCS intensity to the classical conditioned response, the most frequent procedure has been to utilize various groups of subjects who received different intensities of the UCS. Passey and his associates have been interested in examining the influence of variations in UCS intensity; more specifically, they have asked the question: will a subject given both weak and strong intensity UCS's condition more rapidly than a subject provided a constant intensity UCS the value of which is the same as the average value of the strong and weak intensities?

In an early study, Passey and Burns (1962), examining the conditioning of the eyeblink with varied UCS intensities, found that for those groups in which the air puff was most variable, poorest conditioning was obtained.

In a second study, Passey and Wood (1963) attempted to assess the effect

---

and UCS strength. These investigators used a between-subjects design, in general, less sensitive than the within-subjects design used by Wickens and Harding (1965).

[7] It will be recalled that the strength of the CER is generally reported in terms of a suppression ratio which compares the subject's response rate during the time that the CS is presented with the response rate during an immediately preceding (and equivalent) time period.

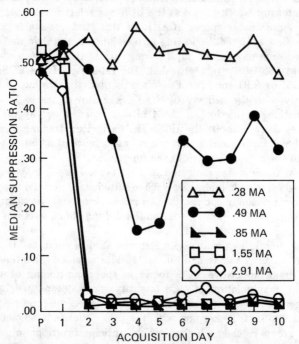

Fig. 4-14. Median suppression ratio as a function of day of acquisition training. Parameter is UCS intensity. *Adapted from Annau and Kamin (1961)*

of progressive incremental as well as progressive decremental UCS intensities. In this conditioned eyelid response study, for the ascending series group, the UCS was an initial pressure of 3.2 lbs per square inch (psi) during the first 10 trials; 4.4 psi for the second block of 10 trials; 5.5 for the third block; 6.8 psi for the fourth block; and, finally, 8.0 for the last 10 trials. A descending series group was provided with the first 10 trials, beginning with a UCS intensity of 8.0 psi; the second 10 trials, with 6.8 psi, and so on. In addition, a constant series group was provided with a UCS intensity of 5.5 psi while a random or variable series group was provided all five intensities, varied in a random manner, but also generating an overall mean of 5.5 psi.

The number of anticipatory responses during the 50-trial acquisition series was obtained for each group. It was noted that performance for all groups for the first 10 trials was quite variable; for the next 40 trials, the constant and ascending series groups were clearly superior to the descending and variable groups—a finding in keeping with the earlier Passey and Burns (1962) experiment. Thus, Passey and his associates have clearly demonstrated that the patterning of the intensity of the UCS can play an important role in the establishment of the conditioned response.

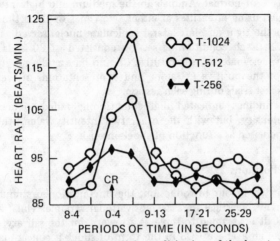

Fig. 4-15. Differential conditioning of the heart rate as a function of three intensities of shock, each associated with a different tone. *Adapted from Dykman and Gantt (1959)*

Differential Conditioning

In the studies reviewed, the task has been one of simple conditioning; an examination of differential conditioning tasks has revealed that the intensity of the UCS plays a similar role. Runquist, Spence, and Stubbs (1958) and Spence and Tandler (1963) have found that added UCS intensity results in increasing differential conditioning of the eyeblink.

Similarly, the differential conditioning of autonomic responses has been shown to be influenced by UCS intensity. Dykman and Gantt (1959) demonstrated this in the cardiac conditioning of the dog. In this study, a 256 Hz tone (CS) was paired with a UCS (shock) of low intensity; a tone of 512 Hz (CS) was paired with a UCS of intermediate intensity; and a 1024 Hz (CS) tone was associated with a high intensity UCS. Heart rate acceleration was observed when the UCS was presented. The mean heart rate for two subjects for an interval of time running from 8 seconds prior to the presentation of the CS to 32 seconds following the CS is shown in Fig. 4-15. Here, differential conditioning, established to each of the varying tones, is revealed to be a function of the intensity of the shock.

And in another cardiac conditioning study, Sideroff, Schneiderman, and Powell (1971) were able to demonstrate a UCS intensity effect when stimulation to varying sites of the brain served as the CS and UCS. In this experiment, a different intensity (high, medium, or low) of electrical stimulation to the septal area of a rabbit's brain served as the UCS. Such stimulation was found to produce a decrease in heart rate. Animals in the low intensity group were conditioned at an intensity of septal stimulation that elicited a heart rate deceleration of 15% of normal. Animals in the medium and high intensity groups were conditioned using intensities at either two times or three times this value. Stimulation to the right and left lateral geniculate nuclei served as the positive and negative CS. Each conditioning session consisted of 80 trials with half of these randomly designated as the positive CS and half as the negative CS. Four presentations of the positive CS alone and 4 presentations of the negative CS alone served as test trials during each session.

The major findings indicated that conditioning failed to occur with the lowest UCS intensity, but with the other two intensity values, the amount of conditioning increased as a function of shock intensity.[8]

Theoretical Positions

As we indicated in our introduction, the unconditioned stimulus has been regarded by many investigators as a motivational variable. Thus, when food is used as a UCS, it is assumed to serve as a reward for the salivary conditioning that takes place; an aversive UCS in the form of shock is conceptualized as having two roles—shock onset acts as an energizer or drive while its termination or offset serves as reward or drive reduction.[9] Such being the case, theoretical positions involving the role of UCS intensity in classical conditioning are generally subsumed under motivational theories—theories which include, but are not limited to, classical conditioning situations.

Probably the most pervasive of these has been provided by Hull (1943, 1951) and Spence (1956) who proposed that two motivational constructs, (a) drive and (b) reinforcement, contribute to the organism's learning or habit structure, as well as its performance.[10] Thus, Hull (1943) posited that an organism's performance in a learning task is a product of its drive as well as its habit strength, e.g., $D \times sHr = $ Performance.

As we have indicated earlier, when an aversive stimulus is used in a classical conditioning experiment, two events are assumed to take place. First, the onset of shock increases the organism's level of drive, while the termination of the shock serves as reinforcement, contributing to habit strength. (Any increase in habit strength on trial n, would not, however, increase performance until trial n + 1.) Inasmuch as aversive stimulation is thus presumed to have both a drive and a reinforcing function, Spence, Haggard, and Ross (1958) have attempted to separate these functions. Such a separation would provide a better understand-

[8] All investigators examining conditioned heart rate have not been able to obtain positive findings. Teyler (1971), examining cardiac conditioning in rats and varying the locus of the UCS (animal's chest or tail), degree of restraint, and intensity of the UCS (.8, 1.6, or 3.0 ma) was unable to find differences in the CR as a function of the intensity variable.

[9] All psychologists do not accept this position. Bitterman (1962), for example, has argued that "Pavlovian reinforcements cannot be treated as rewards or punishments in any meaningful manner, nor can rewards and punishments be distinguished in a Pavlovian experiment" (p. 88).

[10] This is only a brief introduction; a more extensive examination of the Hull-Spence motivational position will be provided in Chapters 8 and 9.

ing of whether the increased response strength which occurs as a function of UCS intensity could be attributed to the increase in the organism's drive level or to increased habit strength. The general procedure of these investigators was to equate the drive level for varying groups during the course of conditioning but, at the same time, provide for differences in reinforcement.

The position of Spence, Haggard, and Ross (1958) is that the basic mechanism in determining a given drive level is determined by the intensity of the UCS provided on earlier trials. (It would follow that a CR which occurs prior to the presentation of the UCS could not be influenced by the intensity of the UCS on that trial.) More specifically, they have assumed that an aversive UCS elicits an emotional response and that this response persists at least until the next trial. Thus, an organism's drive level is directly related to this emotional state which has been determined by the intensity of the aversive stimulus.

In the first experiment, two different intensities of the UCS (air puff) was employed with three groups of subjects. For the high drive–low reinforcement group, a weak puff always occurred with the CS—a conditioning trial—while a strong puff was always presented alone. Presumably, conditioning could not take place on these UCS alone presentations. For Group 2, the high drive–high reinforcement group, conditions were reversed so that the strong puff was presented with the CS, while the weak puff was presented alone. The authors assumed that since the two groups received the same average intensity of the noxious puff throughout the training period, drive level for each group would be the same. The intensity of the puff on the trials in which conditioning could occur, however, differed for the two groups. The group which had the strong puff on the CS-UCS trials should have developed a greater amount of habit strength (because of greater drive reduction) than the group that had the weak puff paired with the CS. In addition, a low drive–low reinforcement group was also run using a weak puff on both the conditioning trials and on the trials when the air puff was given alone.

The experimental procedure consisted of all subjects receiving 100 trials, 50 of these paired presentations of the CS and the UCS, with the other 50 involving the presentation of the UCS alone. The weak UCS consisted of an air puff of .33 psi, while the high intensity UCS consisted of 2 psi.

The results of the 50 conditioning trials are provided in Fig. 4–16. Here it is shown that of the two groups with high drive levels, the one which had the CS paired with the strong air puff revealed a greater amount of conditioning than the group which had the CS paired with the weak puff. Thus, with drive level equated, differential reinforcement resulted in different performance levels. The low drive–low reinforcement group (a weak puff provided on all trials) revealed poorest performance, the difference between this group and the high drive–low reinforcement group being attributed to a difference in drive level.

The results of a second experiment by these authors, as well as a subsequent one by Trapold and Spence (1960) have been in keeping with the same general findings—that both drive level and reinforcement, resulting from the onset and termination of an aversive UCS, contribute to the strength of a classically conditioned response.

The procedure used in the second Spence, Haggard, and Ross (1958) ex-

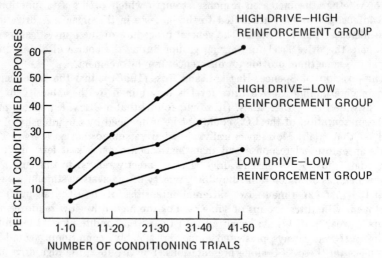

Fig. 4-16. Acquisition curves showing the percentage of CRs in successive blocks of 10 conditioning trials. *Adapted from Spence, Heggard, and Ross (1958)*

periment as well as the Trapold and Spence (1960) study consisted of the presentation of a CS and a UCS with a delay interval of 2600 milliseconds, in contrast to the procedure used in the first experiment which consisted of presentation of the UCS alone. The long delay between the CS and UCS presumably precludes the establishment of a conditioned response but, at the same time, provides the same number of CS-UCS presentations.

Spence and his associates' procedure for separating the drive and reinforcing function of an aversive stimulus is indeed an imaginative and ingenious one, although some question may be raised as to whether or not the procedure for equating drive level by providing the same average intensity of the UCS does result in equivalence between their experimental groups.

A different approach to the examination of the influence of UCS intensity on the conditioning of the eyeblink has been provided by Prokasy and Harsanyi (1968), based on Prokasy's (1972) two-phase model of classical conditioning which we described in Chapter 2. In the Prokasy and Harsanyi study, subjects received a series of 90 adaptation trials followed immediately by 280 CS-UCS pairings. The CS was an increase in the brightness of a small red light, while the UCS was a puff of nitrogen delivered to the subject's cornea of sufficient pressure to support either a 100-, 150-, or 200-mm column of mercury, thus providing three different UCS intensities.

In examining their experimental findings as a function of the 4 parameters which Prokasy has identified: (1) initial level of responding, (2) trial on which the shift from no learning to learning took place, (3) growth rate, and (4) asymptote or terminal level of responding, Prokasy and Harsanyi found that the three UCS intensities influenced these parameters in different ways. For example, the weak and medium UCS intensity groups differed in that the medium one shifted from no learning to learning on an earlier trial; moreover, this group had a higher terminal level of responding than the weak intensity group. On the other hand, the only difference between the medium and high UCS intensity groups was that the high UCS intensity group had a higher terminal level of responding. The results revealed that neither the initial level of responding nor the growth rate was related to UCS intensity differences. These findings are important in suggesting that UCS intensity, and quite possibly most independent variables, contribute to the varying classical conditioning parameters which Prokasy has identified in different ways.

The Duration of the Unconditioned Stimulus

The role of the duration of the unconditioned stimulus on conditioning has been examined only with aversive stimuli.[11] This variable has been of interest primarily because of its theoretical significance. Since the termination of an aversive UCS is conceptualized as providing the subject with reinforcement, any increase in the duration or length of the UCS presentation should increase the length of the temporal interval between the subject's making the conditioned response and the securing of reinforcement. According to drive reduction theory, this change should have a deleterious effect on the acquisition of a learned response.[12]

One of the early studies examining the conditioning of a skeletal response—the eyeblink—was conducted by Runquist and Spence (1959), who provided two groups of subjects in each of two experiments with either an air puff of 50 or 1000 milliseconds in duration. The primary difference between these experiments was that a 1-pound puff was utilized in Experiment 1, while an 8.3-pound puff was used in Experiment 2. Also, the 8.3-pound puff was delivered to the side of the subject's head, 2 cm. from the cornea of the eye—with the purpose of preventing the subject from reducing the noxiousness of the stimulus by closing his eye. All subjects were given 100 conditioning trials, the acquisition of the conditioned response being based on the percentage of CRs occurring in successive blocks of 10 trials. Results, as indicated in Fig. 4–17, revealed a slight and consistent superiority (but not a statistically significant one) in performance for the subjects conditioned with the shorter UCS.

In a more recent skeletal response conditioning study, in which the conditioned eyeblink of the rabbit was examined, Frey and Butler (1973) obtained

[11] One problem that arises in this area is that any increase in the length of the UCS presentation may be perceived by the subject as representing an increase in intensity—a variable which we have discussed in an earlier section. There is also the possibility that changes in the duration of the UCS produce transient changes in intensity. Ramsay, Knapp, and Zeiss (1970), for example, have reported that some types of apparatus may deliver large transient surges of current at shock onset and at termination. These perceptual and technical problems, however, have been largely ignored.

[12] The drive reduction theory of reinforcement states that reinforcement takes place as a result of the reduction of a primary drive, and that learning is a function of the time interval between the learned response and reduction of the drive state.

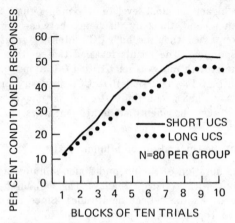

Fig. 4-17. Percentage of CRs in blocks
of 10 trials for all 50-msec. groups
combined and all 1000-msec. groups
combined. *Adapted from Runquist and
Spence (1959)*

different findings. Their UCS was an electric shock of either 50-, 100-, or 200-
milliseconds duration delivered to the rabbit's right cheek. In each case, the
CS was a 1500 Hz tone which overlapped and terminated with the UCS. Twenty
conditioning trials were provided each day for 6 days. The frequency of the
conditioned response as a function of the UCS duration is indicated in Fig. 4-18,
and reveals that the 100-millisecond UCS resulted in significantly more CRs
than UCSs of either 50 or 200 milliseconds.

An interesting undertaking of these authors in their study was to relate the
findings to the conditioning parameters which Prokasy (1972) identified and
which we discussed earlier. The authors noted that the 50-millisecond group
took significantly longer than either the 100- or 200-millisecond group to
shift from their operant level of responding to one of increased probability
of responding (K); on the other hand, asymptotic performance for the 200-milli-
second group was significantly lower than for either of the other groups.

An examination of differential conditioning reveals still different results.
Ashton, Bitgood, and Moore (1969) differentially conditioned the nictitating
membrane of the rabbit, using UCS durations of 50 and 350 milliseconds and
three UCS intensities, namely, .5, 2, and 4 ma shock. Five sessions of 100
differential conditioning trials per session were provided. A 400-Hz tone served
as the CS+, while a 1000-Hz tone was used as the CS−. The authors observed
that the 350-millisecond UCS provided superior conditioning, regardless of the
intensity which was used as the UCS.

In the conditioning of autonomic responses, the manipulation of the duration variable also appears to provide few stable findings. In an examination of
the differential conditioning of the EDR, Bitterman, Reed, and Krauskopf
(1952) examined two durations of shock, namely, .5 and 3 seconds. The proce-

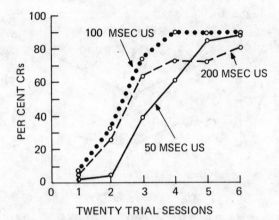

Fig. 4-18. Conditioned response frequency over sessions as a function of the duration of the unconditioned stimulus. *Adapted from Frey and Butler (1973)*

dure consisted of pairing one visual CS with one duration and a second visual stimulus with the other UCS duration. However, differences in conditioning as a function of the duration of the UCS were not obtained.

A failure to find performance differences as a function of UCS duration has also been reported by Wegner and Zeaman (1958) examining the conditioning of the heart rate in three separate experiments (Zeaman, Deane, and Wegner, 1954; Zeaman and Wegner 1954, 1957). These experiments were run using a trace conditioning procedure with different UCS (shock) durations, namely, .1, 2.0, 6.0, and 15 seconds. A 1-second, 60 db tone served as the CS. Inasmuch as individual differences in the form of the conditioned cardiac response were noted, these investigators used heart rate disturbance as their response measure. Fig. 4-19 presents the CR and UCR for four groups of experimental subjects receiving varying UCS durations. Although significant amounts of cardiac conditioning were obtained, conditioning did not vary as a function of the duration of the UCS.

A variable related to the duration of the UCS is its abruptness in termination. More specifically, it would be predicted from a drive reduction position that a UCS (shock) which undergoes abrupt diminution should result in more rapid conditioning than if the diminution of the shock is gradual. Mowrer and Solomon (1954) have examined the influence of this variable on the conditioned emotional response. Their procedure consisted of pairing a 3-second blinking light which served as a CS with a UCS (shock) under four different arrangements as indicated in Fig. 4-20. After appropriate training, the effect of the blinking light upon a previously established bar pressing response was examined. The typical conditioned emotional response paradigm was modified, however, so that the bar press, instead of providing food, resulted in the presentation of the blinking light—the stimulus which had been associated with shock. Although

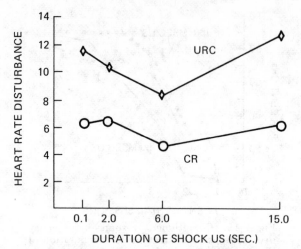

Fig. 4-19. Heart rate disturbance of the CR and UCR as a function of the duration of the UCS (shock). *Adapted from Wegner and Zeaman (1950)*

there was a marked decline in the rate of bar pressing, the characteristics of the UCS offset provided during the CS-UCS presentation did not influence performance.

In summary, it appears that in the classical conditioning of both skeletal and autonomic responses, the duration of the UCS, as well as the abruptness with which it is presented, is of little importance in the establishment of a conditioned response.

Temporal Relationships

The amount of time elapsing between the onset of the CS and the onset of the UCS has been denoted as the interstimulus interval (ISI). The ISI can vary from the simultaneous presentation of the CS and UCS to situations in which the onset of the CS precedes the onset of the UCS for seconds or even minutes.[13] It is also possible, of course, for the onset of the UCS to precede the onset of the CS, in which case we have backward conditioning.

Pavlov (1927) was aware of the importance of the interstimulus interval in the establishment of the conditioned response, writing, "We thus see that

[13] Some investigators have found that the learning of a taste aversion can take place when very long intervals of time, e.g., hours, are placed between an animal's drinking a flavored substance and receiving irradiation (x-rays) which produces nausea. The flavored substance has been identified as the CS and the presentation of the x-ray as the UCS, so that this type of task has been conceptualized by some investigators as classical conditioning with a long CS-UCS interval. We have preferred to consider such situations as instrumental avoidance; a discussion of these findings follows in Chapter 11.

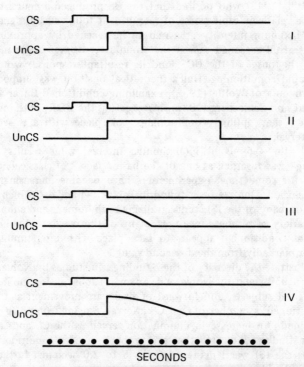

SECONDS

Fig. 4-20. SCHEMATIC REPRESENTATION OF THE DIFFERENT FORMS OF UNCONDITIONED STIMULUS (SHOCK). The signal, or conditioned stimulus, was a blinking light of three seconds duration, which was followed in each of the four groups of Ss by a shock of the duration and form shown. *Adapted from Mowrer and Solomon (1954)*

the first set of conditions required for the formation of a new conditioned reflex encompasses the time relation between the presentation of the unconditioned stimulus and the presentation of that agent which has to acquire the properties of a conditioned stimulus" (p. 28). Pavlov's concern, however, was in demonstrating that the temporal relationship between the presentation of the conditioned and unconditioned stimulus should be forward (CS-UCS) rather than backward (UCS-CS); of less consequence was the length of the interval between the onset of the CS and the UCS. The CS-UCS interval that Pavlov used was almost never shorter than five seconds and frequently longer, possibly because of the long latency of the salivary response.

With American investigators, the role of the CS-UCS interval has assumed greater importance; one reason is that they have employed many responses with much shorter latencies, e.g., eyeblink. One obvious problem arising from this experimental work deals with the determination of the particular interstimulus interval resulting in optimal conditioning. One theoretical solution was provided by Hull (1943) who posited that the CS produced a neural trace which underwent a relatively rapid phase of recruitment followed by a gradual fall in intensity. Maximum intensity appeared to be reached by approximately 450 milliseconds. Hull reasoned that if the stimulus trace was at its maximum at this point, the onset of the UCS (and its resultant response) would produce the most rapid conditioning. Hull's theoretical position was supported by the early experiments of Wolfle (1932), examining conditioned finger withdrawal, and Kappauf and Schlosberg (1937), investigating the EDR; both investigations demonstrated that optimal conditioning took place with a .5-second interstimulus interval.

Although the ".5-second interstimulus interval value results in optimal conditioning" was regarded as one of the basic "facts" of classical conditioning procedures for some time, experimenters have become increasingly skeptical of this conclusion. One reason is found in Tables 4-4 and 4-5 which summarize the results of many of the ISI studies utilizing both humans and animals and employing a variety of response measures. Many of the results noted here indicate that optimal conditioning appears to take place with interstimulus intervals which differ markedly from the .5-second value.

Let us illustrate the diversity of these findings. In studies by Noble, Gruender, and Meyer (1959), and by Noble and Adams (1963a), using mollienisia (fish) as experimental subjects, and forward or backward movement as the response to be conditioned, a number of CS-UCS intervals ranging from .5 to 4.0 seconds were examined. An increase in illumination served as the CS and shock as the UCS. Their findings indicated that the probability of a conditioned response increased as the ISI was lengthened from .5 to 2.0 seconds; further increases in the ISI resulted in a declining response probability.

In contrast is an experiment by Klinman and Bitterman (1963, Exp. I) also using mollienisia with general activity as the response to be conditioned and utilizing either a .5-, 2-, or 4-second ISI. These investigators found that the probability and magnitude of the conditioned response was optimal at the .5-second interval and then declined with the longer intervals of 2.0 and 4.0 seconds. In their second experiment, using the same design as the first but increasing the mean interval between trials from 1 to 4 minutes, the CS-UCS interval was not found to play a significant role in determining the course of conditioning. A third experiment, the procedure also mirroring the first but using goldfish as subjects, again resulted in the inability of the experimenters to find the CS-UCS interval contributing to the strength of the conditioned response.

It may be argued that the responses, e.g., forward and backward movement or general activity, used by these investigators was fairly gross, and that better results would be obtained if a simpler type of response was utilized. But this does not appear to be true.

Employing a variety of interstimulus intervals in their examination of the nictitating membrane of the rabbit, Schneiderman and Gormezano (1964), Schneiderman (1966), and Smith (1968) all used a tone as their CS, and provided substantial numbers of acquisition trials each day over a series of days. The findings obtained in these studies indicated that with interstimulus intervals

Table 4-4 Summaries of a Sampling of Studies Using Human Subjects Examining the Interstimulus Interval and Classified by Response Conditioned

Investigator	CS	UCS	CS–UCS Intervals Examined	Results
Response: Electrodermal				
White and Schlosberg (1952)	Light	Shock	0, .25, .50, 1.0, 2.0, 4.0 seconds	.5 second superior as measured by amplitude for 5 extinction trials.
Moeller (1954)	Noise	Shock	.25, .45, 1.0, 2.5 seconds	.45 seconds superior as measured by amplitude during 4 test trials interspersed among conditioning trials.
Prokasy, Fawcett, and Hall (1962)	Tone	Shock	0, .5, 1, 3, 5 seconds	Neither CR latency nor amplitude varied as a function of the interval employed; magnitude of CR revealed .5-second interval superior; all measures based upon the first extinction trial.
Wittig and Wickens (1966)	Tone	Shock	.15, .25, .35, .45, .60, .75, .95, 1.25, 1.55, 1.85, 2.15, 2.45 seconds	As measured on second extinction trial, following 10 acquisition trials, latency and magnitude showed greatest responding in the .45 to 1.25 ISI range.
Response: Eyeblink				
Bernstein (1934)	Click	Shock	−.90, −.50, .10, .20, .25, .30, .50, 1.0, 1.48 seconds	When CS precedes UCS by a range of .30 to 1.48 seconds, there is no variation in the amount of conditioning.
Reynolds (1945)	Click	Air Puff	.25, .45, 1.15, 2.25 seconds	Acquisition curves for 90 reinforced trials reveal that .45-second interval was superior as measured by percent responding.
Kimble (1947)	Light	Air Puff	.1, .2, .225, .250, .3, .4 seconds	For 6 test trials obtained within 60 reinforced acquisition trials, .4-second interval was superior as measured by percent responding.

Table 4–4 Continued

Investigator	Response: Eyeblink			
	CS	UCS	CS–UCS Intervals Examined	Results
Kimble, Mann, and Dufort (1955)	Light	Air Puff	.5, .8, 1.5 seconds	60 acquisition trials: analysis of trials 51–60 reveal .5 group superior as measured by percent responding.
McAllister (1953a)	Tone	Air Puff	.1, .25, .45, .70, 2.0 seconds	20 test trials interspersed among 80 reinforced trials indicated .25 group superior, although difference between .25- and .45-second intervals not significant, as measured by percent responding.
Ebel and Prokasy (1963)	Light	Air Puff	.2, .5, .8 seconds	.5-second group superior although not significantly so when frequency of responding over 400 acquisition trials was examined.
Lipkin and Moore (1966)	Tone	Air Puff	.5, 1.0, 2.0 seconds (trace)	Ss received 72 acquisition trials, with 75% partial reinforcement schedule; no difference in percent responding among groups.
Fishbein and LeBlanc (1967)	Light	Air Puff	.5, 1.5, 2.5, or 4.0 seconds	Ss received 100 acquisition trials with no reliable differences among .5-, 1.5-, or 2.5- second groups.
Fishbein, Jones, and Silverthorne (1969)	One of 2 tones (low or high intensity)	Air Puff	.5 and 2.0 seconds (Exp. 1); .3, .5, 1.0, 2.0 seconds (Exp. 2)	Both experiments revealed with high CS intensity, conditioning with a .5 ISI was superior; at low CS intensity, no significant differences among groups.
Ross and Ross (1971) (two studies combined)	Tone	Air Puff	.25, .30, .35, .50, .80, 1.10, 1.40 seconds	Highest level of both trace and delay conditioning appeared within .40 to .50 range with lower levels of performance at shorter ISIs, and little or no decline in performance at longer ISIs up to 1.40 seconds.

Response: Pupillary Dilation

	CS	UCS	Intervals	Results
Gerall and Woodward (1958)	Cessation of noise	Light offset, shock	.125, .50, 1.50, 2.50 seconds	1.5-second interval superior; no conditioning found with 2.50-second interval.

Response: Finger Withdrawal

	CS	UCS	Intervals	Results
Wolfle (1930)	Tone	Shock	-.50, -.25, 0, .25, .50, .75, 1.00, 1.25, 1.50 seconds	60 test trials interspersed among 280 CS–UCS presentations revealed .50 second-interval group superior as measured by percent responding.
Wolfle (1932)	Tone	Shock	-2.00, -1.00, -.6, -.2, 0, .2, .3, .4, .6, 1.00, 2.00, 3.00 seconds	Varying numbers of trials provided although all Ss had a minimum of 600 CS–UCS pairings; results indicated .2- and .3-second interval groups superior as measured by percent responding.
Spooner and Kellogg (1947)	Tone	Shock	.5, 1.0, 1.5 seconds	20 test trials interspersed amont 80 CS–UCS pairings; .5-second interval group superior as measured by percent responding.
Fitzwater and Reisman (1952)	Tone	Shock	-.5, 0, .5 seconds	20 test trials interspersed among 80 CS–UCS pairings; .5-second interval group superior as measured by percent responding.
Fitzwater and Thrush (1956)	Tone	Shock	0, .1, .2, .3, .4, .6 seconds	20 test trials interspersed among 80 CS–UCS pairings; .4-second interval group superior as measured by percent responding.

Table 4-5 Summaries of a Sampling of Studies Using Infrahuman Subjects Examining the Interstimulus Interval

Investigator	Experimental Subjects	CS	UCS	Conditioned Response	CS–UCS Intervals Examined	Results
Noble, Gruender, and Meyer (1959)	Mollienisia (Fish)	Increase in illumination	Shock	Vigorous forward and backward movement; also cessation of movement	.5, 1.0, 1.5, 2.0, 3.0, 4.0 seconds	Percent frequency of CR was maximum at 2.0 seconds.
Noble and Adams (1963a)	Mollienisia (Fish)	Increase in illumination	Shock	As above	.5, 2.0, 4.0 seconds	Percent frequency of CR was maximum at 2.0 seconds.
Noble and Adams (1963b) Exp. I	Pigs	Increase in illumination	Shock to rear leg	Leg flexion, head movements; bracing	.5, 1.0, 1.5, 2.0 seconds	2.0 provided reliably better conditioning than any other interval.
Exp. II	Pigs	Increase in illumination	Shock to rear leg	As above	1, 2, 4, 8 seconds	During early conditioning trials (1–15) conditioning was best for 1- and 2-second intervals; later trials (16–35) conditioning was best with 4- and 8-second intervals.
Noble and Harding (1963)	Rhesus monkey	Increase in illumination	Shock to waist	General bodily response	.5, 1, 2, 4 seconds	Only 2-second interval provided significantly more CRs than control.
Klinman and Bitterman (1963) Exp. I	Mollienisia (Fish)	Increase in illumination	Shock	General activity	.5, 2, 4 seconds	Probability and magnitude of CR declined from maximum at .5 seconds (1.5 min. between trials).
Exp. II	Mollienisia (Fish)	Increase in illumination	Shock	General activity	.5, 2, 4 seconds	Influence of CS–UCS interval not significant (4.0 minutes between trials).
Exp. III	Goldfish	Increase in illumination	Shock	General activity	.5, 2, 4 seconds	Influence of CS–UCS interval not significant.

Study	Subject	CS	UCS	Response	ISI	Results
Schneiderman and Gormezano (1964)	Rabbits	Tone	Air Puff	Nictitating membrane	.25, .50, 1.0, 2.0, 4.0 seconds	Conditioning was an inverse function of the CS–UCS interval.
Schneiderman (1966)	Rabbits	Tone	Air Puff	Nictitating membrane	.25, .50, 1.0, 2.0 seconds under delay and trace conditions	ISI functions differed in shape and slope for different delay and trace procedures.
Frey and Ross (1968)	Rabbits	Tone	Shock	Eyelid	.25, .40, .60, 1.0, or 2.0 seconds	Asymptotic response levels were similar from .25 to 1.0 second; rate of acquisition was a U-shaped function of the ISI with fastest conditioning at .40.
Smith, Coleman, and Gormezano (1969)	Rabbits	Tone	Shock	Nictitating membrane	-.05, 0, .05, .1, .2, .4, .8 seconds	Conditioning was superior for .2 and .4 groups; -.05, 0, and .05 groups revealed no conditioning.
Wickens, Nield, Tuber, and Wickens (1969)	Cats	Tone and Light	Shock	EDR, paw movements	.15, .30, .50, .75, 1.0, 1.5, 2.0 seconds	Latency of responding increased linearly as a function of the ISI interval.
Levinthal and Papsdorf (1970)	Rabbits	Tone	Shock	Nictitating membrane	.25, 1.25 seconds	1.25 CS–UCS interval was superior to .25 second.

of .25, .50, 1.00, 2.00, and 4.00 seconds, the .25 ISI resulted in optimal conditioning. However, Levinthal and Papsdorf (1970), examining the same response but providing only 1 trial per day, found that a 1.25-second ISI resulted in superior conditioning than a .25-second ISI.

Variability of optimal interstimulus intervals has also been found in classical conditioning discrimination studies. Hartman and Grant (1962), examining the conditioned eyelid response, employed CS-UCS intervals of .4, .6, .8, or 1.0 seconds; the CS+ and CS− were each presented 44 times, with the presentation of each stimulus assigned randomly but balanced within each block of 8 trials. Results revealed that the .8-second ISI resulted in the greatest percentage of responses to the positive stimulus. Kimmel and Pennypacker (1963), using the EDR and employing CS-UCS intervals of .25, .50, 1.0 and 2.0 seconds were unable to find any optimal interval. Finally, VanDercar and Schneiderman's (1967) study is most provocative since, in their differential conditioning experiment, three response measures were obtained from their experimental subjects (rabbits): (1) the nictitating membrane, (2) heart rate, and (3) respiration rate. The interstimulus intervals examined were .25, .75, 2.25, and 6.75 seconds. In this study, tones differing in frequency served as the CS+ and CS−, while shock to the lateral canthus of the right eye was the UCS. Seven days of 80 trials/day represented the training period. Results revealed that the highest level of nictitating membrane responding was obtained with an ISI of .25, but the greatest amount of differential responding was obtained with an ISI of .75. No conditioning took place with an ISI of 6.75. An examination of heart rate responding indicated that the highest level of responding as well as the greatest amount of differential responding was obtained with an ISI of 2.25. Conditioning was found, however, with an ISI of 6.75. Finally, none of the groups demonstrated reliable respiration rate conditioning.

There would be little value in further describing the conflicting findings obtained by other investigators who have used different responses with other species. The evidence seems clear that a single CS-UCS interval will not provide optimal conditioning for all responses with all species. As Bitterman (1965) wrote some years ago, the search for such an interval appears to be fruitless.

The inability to find a constant CS-UCS interval has encouraged some investigators to examine other approaches to determining the role of the CS-UCS interval in classical conditioning. One approach has been provided by Boneau (1958) and Prokasy and his associates who have proposed that the conditioned response examined by them—namely, the eyeblink—behaves as an instrumental response that can be altered or shaped by the reinforcing contingencies found in the experimental situation.

In an early study by Boneau (1958) a group of subjects received 50 conditioning trials with an ISI of .5 seconds. The group was then subdivided into (1) one subgroup which was shifted to a 1.0-second ISI for 100 additional trials and (2) a second subgroup which was shifted to a 1.5-second ISI for 100 additional trials. Two control groups were given 150 trials with either a 1.0- or a 1.5-second ISI. If a conditioned response is defined as a response appropriate to a short CS-UCS interval, i.e., lying in the latency range of .31 to .50 seconds the results are similar to those obtained in an earlier study by McAllister (1953b) where there was a *decline* in the percentage of conditioned responses for both the 1.0- and 1.5-shift groups. However, it must be kept in mind that a conditioned response, defined as a response found in the latency range of .31 to .50 seconds, is not appropriate for either the 1.0- or 1.5-ISI groups since the closing of the eyelid with this latency (.31 to .50 seconds) would necessitate the subject's keeping his eye closed for a rather long time to avoid receiving the UCS on the cornea. In many cases, for the subject to close his eye with this short latency would probably result in his opening the eye prior to the onset of the UCS. On the other hand, if the conditioned response is defined by a latency of .66 to 1.0 for the 1.0-second ISI group and 1.01 to 1.5 seconds for the 1.5-second ISI group, an increasing percentage of conditioned responses was noted as a function of trials with this new ISI. In these instances, the subject would be closing his eye just prior to UCS onset. This "different" definition of a conditioned response suggests that subjects were responding in a way which minimized the length of time that the eye remained closed as well as minimizing aversiveness of the UCS.

A study by Ebel and Prokasy (1963), also examining the shift of the ISI over 1200 training trials, has confirmed Boneau's finding that the latency of the response is related to changes in the length of the ISI. In this study, nine treatment groups were used and 3 ISIs were employed, e.g., .2, .5, and .8 seconds. Of the 9 treatment conditions, 3 involved only a single ISI value provided throughout training; the remaining 6 involved shifts from one ISI to another. Following 40 trials with a .2-second ISI, one group was shifted to a .5-second-ISI and a second group was shifted to a .8-second ISI for 400 trials. After these trials, the two groups were then shifted back to the original .2-second ISI. Two other groups, following 400 training trials with a .5-second ISI, were shifted to either a .2-second ISI or an .8-second ISI for 400 trials and then returned to .5 seconds. Finally, two additional groups, following 400 training trials on an .8-second ISI were shifted to either .2- or a .5-second ISI and then returned to an .8-second ISI. The investigators found that increases or decreases in the ISI produced correlated changes in latency means and standard deviations. Table 4-6 provides their findings. The .2-, .5-, and .2-second groups' mean latency of

Table 4-6   Latency Means and SDs (Msec.) over Three Blocks of Four Sessions

Group	Block 1		Block 2		Block 3	
	Mean	SD	Mean	SD	Mean	SD
222	268	67	245	65	231	57
252	342	137	425	163	302	97
282	306	135	465	199	286	129
555	527	128	413	82	305	69
525	499	153	314	131	469	153
585	393	87	575	158	420	107
888	760	193	773	145	693	171
828	623	213	308	116	515	224
858	647	172	508	106	558	181

Adapted from Ebel and Prokasy (1963)

responding, for example, was .342 for the first 400 trials (.2-second ISI), increased to .425 second for the second 400 trials (.5-second ISI), and then returned to a mean latency of .302 (.2-second ISI).

The experimenters, in complete agreement with Boneau's earlier findings, have supported the position that reinforcement in the conditioning of the eyeblink (relief from the aversiveness of the air puff) is contingent at least in part on the amount of time which separates the CR and UCS events. The fact that the CR eventually occurs just prior to the onset of the UCS strongly suggests some kind of instrumental shaping.

Ebel and Prokasy (1963) believe that the ISI function should reflect the efficiency with which the subject is able to maximize the CR-UCS reinforcement contingency. Thus, the optimal value of an ISI would be one in which it is possible for the subject to make a response just prior to UCS onset. Since subjects apparently are not able to make an eyelid response with a latency of much under .18 seconds, an ISI of less than this will result in reducing the effectiveness of the CR. As the ISIs increase beyond .5 seconds, the appearance of a CR (defined as response with a latency of .31 to .50 seconds) will reduce the effectiveness of reinforcement since, presumably, the individual will be opening his eye when the UCS is presented. This should result in a delayed latency of responding which will be related to the length of the ISI. The end result will be that the eyeblink should just precede the presentation of the UCS regardless of the length of the ISI.

An added consideration is the ability of the subjects to judge time. Ebel and Prokasy (1963) have suggested that the function relating the frequency of conditioned eyeblink responding to the ISI interval is also related to the relative difficulty of the temporal discrimination required for maximizing the CR-UCS reinforcement contingency. According to these investigators, the increase in CR latency which is usually observed with fixed ISI values reflects response shaping that maximizes the reinforcement through CR-UCS overlap, whereas the increase in variability of response latencies taking place as the ISI is lengthened reflects the increased difficulty of determining when to respond in order to avoid the UCS.

In a second study, Prokasy, Ebel, and Thompson (1963) have confirmed the position that the eyeblink can be shaped by appropriate training procedures. In this study, one group of subjects was given trials in which the subjects began their training with an ISI of .63 seconds, but the interval was then gradually shifted in six steps over a 60 trial/step period to a terminal ISI of 2.497 seconds. A second group received 300 trials with an ISI of .63 seconds and was then shifted for the last 60 trials to an ISI of 2.497 seconds. Finally, a third group received all 360 trials with an interstimulus interval of 2.497 seconds. Results revealed that for the last 60 trials the frequency of response was considerably greater for the gradually shifted group (approximately 60%) than for the other two groups (approximately 30%) which had identical ISIs but were either rapidly switched or started training at this interval.

Finally, we should like to call attention to a study by Wickens, Nield, Tuber, and Wickens (1969) who classically conditioned cats to respond with a paw movement and an EDR at a variety of CS-UCS intervals using a within-subjects design. Their procedure consisted of presenting a tone as a CS, and shock as a UCS eliciting the EDR, as well as movements of the left paw; the latter response was measured with a strain gauge. Subjects were successively conditioned (and extinguished) at CS-UCS intervals of .15, .30, .50, .75, 1.0, 1.5, and 2.0 seconds, in that order. Results indicated that mean latency of responding, whether for the paw response or for the EDR, increased as a function of the length of the interstimulus interval. It may be noted that these findings are similar to those reported by Ebel and Prokasy (1963) and Prokasy, Ebel, and Thompson (1963) who also found the length of response latency increasing as the ISI increased.

The Wickens et al (1969) finding is in keeping with Ebel and Prokasy's (1963) position that the subject learns to respond just prior to the presentation of the UCS. In the Ebel and Prokasy study using the conditioned eyeblink, such responding is adaptive since it insures that the airpuff will fall upon the closed lid, thus reducing the aversiveness of the puff. The adaptive characteristics of the subject's response in the Wickens et al study is not so obvious since aversiveness to the shock does not appear to be modified by the subject's delayed responding (increased latency).

One final aspect of this research should be noted. Wickens et al. (1969) have called attention to the fact that the response acquired with a longer CS-UCS interval is different in both latency and form from that acquired with the shorter CS-UCS interval CR. The significance of this finding remains to be explored.

We would reiterate that, in view of the variety of findings, any search for an optimal ISI in classical conditioning which disregards the kind of organism used, its response system, and the particular type of experimental procedure employed, will fail. What is needed is a more general approach, exemplified by the work of Boneau and Prokasy, which considers the ISI as a variable influenced by a variety of organismic conditions, only some of which have been identified.

Backward Conditioning

It will be recalled that backward conditioning involves the onset of the UCS prior to the onset of the CS. A problem of some interest has been to determine whether or not conditioning can take place with such an arrangement. Pavlov (1927) wrote, "it is ... necessary that the conditioned stimulus should begin to operate before the unconditioned stimulus comes into action. If this order is reversed ... the conditioned reflex cannot be established at all" (p. 27). Shortly thereafter, however, he revised his opinion, believing that backward conditioning was possible although the procedure did not result in a very strong response.

An unequivocal answer to the question of whether or not backward conditioning can be obtained remains to be provided. The early studies of Switzer (1930), Wolfle (1932), Bernstein (1934), Grether (1938), and Harlow (1939), in addition to the more recent investigations of Champion and Jones (1961), Champion (1962), and Trapold, Homzie, and Rutledge (1964) have supported Pavlov's revised position—that backward conditioning is possible. Moreover, after reviewing a number of Russian (as well as American) experiments, Razran (1956) concluded that there is no doubt backward conditioning is a genuine phenomenon obtainable under certain conditions. Razran indicated that in order to obtain a backward conditioned response, the UCS should not be too strong and the CS, not too weak. If shock is used as the UCS, backward conditioning appears to be possible only when the CS is applied after the shock has ceased, and not during presentation of the shock. If food is used as the UCS, backward conditioning is more readily obtained at the UCS-CS intervals of 15 seconds rather than 5 seconds, and at 5-second rather than 2-second intervals.

In contrast, Cason (1935), Porter (1938), Spooner, and Kellogg (1947), Fitzwater and Reisman (1952), and Kamin (1963) are only a few of the American investigators who have had difficulty in obtaining positive results. An observed difficulty with many of the studies purported to have obtained positive results is that pseudo-conditioning control groups have not been used; it is thus impossible to determine whether the behavior increment arising from the UCS-CS procedure is significantly greater than that obtainable by the random presentation of these stimuli. Cautela (1965) has called attention to this difficulty in many Russian experiments cited by Razran (1956).

In summary, backward conditioning using typical classical conditioning procedures with traditional responses remains to be unequivocally demonstrated.[14]

Summary

Experimenters have been concerned primarily with three basic classical conditioning variables, (1) the CS, (2) the UCS, and (3) the CS-UCS interval.

An examination of the first of these, the CS, reveals three areas of interest, namely, (a) the intensity of the CS, (b) stimulus generalization, and (c) stimulus compounding. Using a variety of responses and a number of species, it has been found that the strength of the CR is a function of CS intensity. One exception appears to be in the conditioning of the EDR, where a number of unsuccessful attempts to demonstrate the CS intensity effect have been noted. The CS intensity effect, when obtained, is much more pronounced in a within-subject than in a between-subject design. Stimulus generalization refers to the capacity of a stimulus, other than the CS, to elicit the CR. It has been noted that as the stimuli used to test for stimulus generalization differ from the CS, their capacity to elicit the CR declines. The characteristics of stimulus generalization were found to be a function of the kind of stimuli that are used, the sensory modality, and the testing methods. Stimulus compounding is another major area of interest to investigators. One procedure used has been to condition a response

---

[14] It should be acknowledged that Keith-Lucas and Guttman (1975) have obtained instances of backward conditioning; they have used these to attack Pavlov's early position which indicated that backward conditioning could not be obtained, or at best, was a very unstable phenomenon. An examination of this study suggests that the investigators have used what can be best described as a passive avoidance paradigm; thus, from our point of view, the study should not be included within the classical conditioning rubric.

to a number of stimulus elements (each element serves as a CS), and then test to a stimulus compound made up of the elements. Where this was done, a summation principle has frequently been found to operate—the response to the compound is larger than responses to the single elements. When the reverse of this experimental design is utilized—the response being conditioned to a stimulus compound and then tested to the specific elements making up the compound—inconclusive findings are reported.

In examining the UCS, a basic concern has been whether or not the UCS must have "motivational" significance for the organism. Although experimenters have found that classical conditioning of a very simple response can take place in "spinal" animals, it does not necessarily follow that the conditioning of complex responses in the intact organism can be accomplished unless the UCS serves as a motivator.

A variety of UCS parameters have been examined, perhaps the most important of these, intensity, having been found to play an important role in the conditioning of both skeletal and autonomic responses. The duration and abruptness of aversive unconditioned stimuli has also been examined but there has been little evidence to indicate that these parameters play very significant roles in conditioning.

The third variable, the amount of time elapsing between the onset of the CS and the onset of the UCS, has been denoted as the ISI. Beginning with the earliest investigators of classical conditioning, interest has been in determining the particular ISI which will provide optimal conditioning. Although early experimental evidence appeared to indicate that optimal conditioning took place with a .5-second ISI, contemporary experimenters agree that the optimal ISI is dependent upon the characteristics of the organism, the response which is conditioned, and other unspecified variables. Some investigators, rather than looking for an optimal interval, have considered the interval merely as a factor contributing to a shaping process.

Another CS-UCS issue is the question of whether it is possible to obtain backward conditioning. An unequivocal answer to this question has not been provided. Virtually all contemporary experimenters able to demonstrate backward conditioning have used the EDR as their conditioned response. Until it is possible to obtain backward conditioning with responses other than the EDR, and with appropriate pseudoconditioning controls, it is wise to hold in abeyance any firm conclusion that backward conditioning is a bona fide phenomenon. However, even if backward conditioning can be demonstrated, the conditioned responses it elicits are so weak and unstable that the procedure has little usefulness.

5
Classical Conditioning:
Partial Reinforcement and Experimental Extinction

In this chapter we will examine what the omission of the UCS means in terms of the classical conditioning paradigm, as viewed from two vantage points. First, investigators have studied the influence of the periodic omission of the UCS on the conditioned response— a procedure which is designated as partial or intermittent reinforcement. The second area of interest has been to determine how the elimination or nonpresentation of the UCS influences an already established conditioned response—an operation identified as experimental extinction.

Partial Reinforcement

Simple Conditioning

Humphreys (1939b), in examining the classical conditioning of the eyeblink, employed a procedure which at that time was most unusual—he did not present the UCS on every trial. Since Humphreys's early study, this type of operation has been identified as partial or intermittent reinforcement. Jenkins and Stanley (1950) have defined partial reinforcement as "reinforcement [or the UCS] given at least once but omitted on one or more of the trials or after one or more of the responses in a series" (p. 194).[1]

In Humphreys's (1939b) experiment, three groups of students were given the following training: (1) 96 trials with 100% reinforcement, (2) 96 trials with 50% reinforcement; here, of course only 48 UCS presentations were provided, and (3) 48 trials with 100% reinforcement, with rest intervals substituted for the nonrewarded trials. Humphreys reported no significant differences among the groups with regard to the number of conditioned responses or the magnitude of the response during acquisition, although the 50% reinforcement group was slightly lower than the other groups on both of these measures. An inspection of Humphreys's data reveals, however, that after the first few trials, the frequency of conditioned responses with the partial reinforcement group never attained the level of the 100% group at any point throughout the remainder of the 96 acquisition trials. Humphreys did not respond to this difference but rather remarked that "the lack of effect from non-reinforcement . . . is indeed paradoxical" (p. 146).

Although an occasional experimenter has found a partial reinforcement schedule to result in superior conditioning, for example, Grant, Riopelle, and Hake (1950), most experimenters using either humans or animals as their subjects, have found that the continuous reinforcement schedule results in more rapid acquisition. In a few cases, investigators have found no difference in performance between the two schedules. See Table 5-1 for a sampling of these studies.

It would be interesting to determine the locus of the effects produced by partial reinforcement, and Prokasy's (1972) identification of 4 conditioned response parameters, (1) the initial rate of the subject's responding, (2) when conditioned responding begins, (3) the rate of growth of conditioned response learning, and (4) performance asymptote, make logical candidates for such an analysis. As yet, however, little experimental evidence has been brought to bear on this issue.

A number of investigators have been interested in examining the role of partial reinforcement in the conditioning of the eyeblink. One of these has been Ross (1959) who was interested in determining how the switch from a continuous reinforcement schedule to one of partial reinforcement, or vice versa, would influence acquisition. In this experiment five groups of subjects were used: Group C received continuous reinforcement for 200 trials while Group P

[1] As might be anticipated, Pavlov (1927) was the first investigator to utilize a partial reinforcement regimen; it was Humphreys's study, however, which encouraged a whole host of subsequent investigators to further investigate this procedure. In Pavlov's study, a single dog received (at different times) three different patterns of partial reinforcement: the UCS being presented after every second, third, or fourth presentation of the CS. Presentations of the UCS on every second or third trial resulted in conditioning in almost as short a time as would be obtained with continuous reinforcement. On the other hand, presentation of the UCS after each fourth presentation of the CS did not result in conditioning.

Table 5-1   Summaries of a Sampling of Studies Examining the Effect of
Continuous and Partial Reinforcement Schedules on Acquisition

Investigator	Subject	Response	Results
Grant and Schipper (1952)	Humans	Eyeblink	Continuous reinforcement superior to partial.
Hartman and Grant (1960)	Humans	Eyeblink	Continuous reinforcement superior to partial.
Gonzalez, Longo, and Bitterman (1961)	Goldfish	Activity	Partial reinforcement superior to partial.
Longo, Milstein, and Bitterman (1962)	Pigeons	Movement	Partial reinforcement superior to continuous in Experiment I; continuous reinforcement superior to partial in Experiment 2.
Fitzgerald (1963)	Dogs	Salivation	Continuous reinforcement superior to partial.
Wagner, Siegel, Thomas, and Ellison (1964)	Dogs	Salivation	Continuous reinforcement superior to partial.
Thomas and Wagner (1964)	Rabbit	Eyeblink	No difference between continuous reinforcement and partial.
Berger, Yarczower, and Bitterman (1965)	Goldfish	Activity	Continuous reinforcement superior to partial.
Slivka and Bitterman (1966)	Pigeons	Movement	No difference between continuous reinforcement and partial.
Kimmel and Yaremko (1966)	Planaria	Turning or Contraction	Continuous reinforcement superior to partial.
Fitzgerald, Vardaris, and Teyler (1966)	Dogs	Heart rate	Continuous reinforcement superior to partial.
Wagner, Siegel, and Fein (1967)	Rats	CER	Continuous reinforcement superior to partial.
Holmes and Gormezano (1970)	Rabbits	Jaw Movement	Continuous reinforcement superior to partial.

received 50% partial reinforcement for 200 trials. As Fig. 5-1 demonstrates, both groups reached stable asymptotes with Group P's performance significantly below that of Group C. A third group, C20-P, and a fourth group, C100-P, given either 20 or 100 continuous reinforced trials, were then switched to a partial reinforcement schedule, with either 120 or 200 partial reinforcement trials provided. Both groups' performance declined to the performance level of Group P, which had received partial reinforcement throughout training. A fifth group, P40-C80, was given 50% reinforcement for 40 trials and then switched to continuous reinforcement for 80 additional trials. Following the switch, it may be noted that the acquisition curve for this group gradually approached that of Group C and was not significantly different from that group over the last block of 20 trials.

Another area of investigation has been the examination of differences in

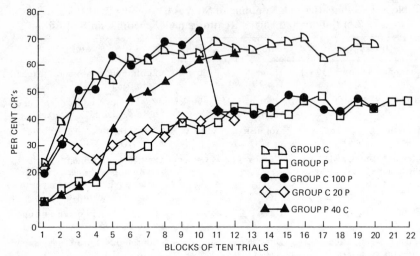

Fig. 5-1. Mean percentage of CR's in successive blocks of 10 trials. *Adapted from Ross (1959)*

partial reinforcement schedules; Grant and Schipper (1952) were early investigators to undertake this type of study. In their classically conditioned eyelid response experiment, the following percentages of UCS presentation were used: 0, 25, 50, 75, or 100 percent. A light served as the CS and an air puff as the UCS. Sixty training trials were given on day 1 and 32 training trials on day 2. Results revealed that the probability of response was an increasing function of UCS presentations, although there was a reversal of the 75% and 100% reinforcement conditions on day 2. Fig. 5-2 presents these findings.

In the Grant and Schipper (1952) study, 92 training trials were provided over their 2-day experimental period. With training trials held constant, it is obvious that the number of reinforced trials which were presented varied as a function of the percentage of reinforced trials used, that is, the 25% partial reinforcement group received only 24 reinforced trials, the 50% group, 48, and so forth. Hartman and Grant (1960) examined the same partial reinforcement schedules when the number of reinforced trials was held constant. In their eyelid conditioning study, all groups received 40 reinforced trials. However, the 25% partial reinforcement group received 160 acquisition trials; the 50% group, 80 trials; the 75% group, 54 trials; and the 100% group, just 40. The results mirrored those obtained by Grant and Schipper (1952): acquisition was an increasing function of the percentage of reinforced trials. The findings appear in Fig. 5-3.

In a subsequent eyelid conditioning experiment by Moore and Gormezano (1963), acquisition trials using either 25%, 50%, or 75% partial reinforcement schedules were also compared. An added interest on the part of these investigators was to examine performance when a "nonreinforced" trial consisted of the presentation of a CS and a UCS which was delayed for 2600 milliseconds—

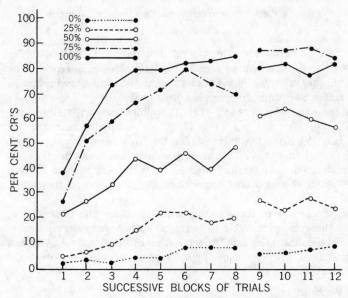

Fig. 5-2. The course of acquisition of the eyelid CR with varying percentages of reinforced trials during training. Percent frequency of CRs is plotted against successive blocks of trials. The size of the block during training (1-12) is eight trials except for Block 8 which is four trials. *Adapted from Grant and Schipper (1952)*

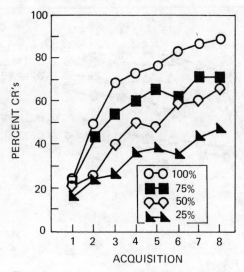

Fig. 5-3. Percentages of CRs plotted for successive eighths of acquisition with percentage of reinforcement as the parameter. *Adapted from Hartman and Grant (1960)*

127

a procedure which contrasts with the typical nonreinforced trial calling for the omission of the UCS. It will be recalled that the 2600-millisecond delay procedure, which does not result in the establishment of a conditioned response, had been used earlier by Spence, Haggard, and Ross (1958).

In brief, Moore and Gormezano's (1963) findings supported Grant and Schipper (1952), and Hartman and Grant (1960) in that performance over 80 training trials revealed highest acquisition for the 75% reinforcement group, followed by 50% and then 25%. This order was maintained whether the UCS was omitted or delayed; an interesting finding, however, was that the delayed procedure resulted in poorer overall acquisition. Fig. 5-4 presents these findings.

In summary, the results of those studies which we have just presented, as well as many of those found in Table 5-1 using animals as subjects, are reasonably consistent in demonstrating that the acquisition of a classically conditioned response is a function of the percentage of reinforced trials which are provided.

Differential Conditioning

The influence of partial reinforcement has also been examined when a differential conditioning situation was used. In an early study, Newman (1967) investigated a variety of reinforcement schedules using the conditioned eyeblink. The schedules are presented in Table 5-2. (In differential conditioning, the percentage of CS+ is designated as π_1, while the CS- is designated as π_2. Using such notation, Group 1 is described as $\pi_1 = 1.00$ with $\pi_2 = .00$.)

Using 600 and 1000 Hz tones as the CS+ and CS-, and an air puff as the

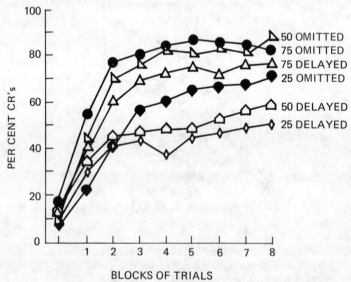

Fig. 5-4. The percentage of CRs plotted in 10-trial blocks during acquisition. *Adapted from Moore and Gormezano (1963)*

Table 5-2 Newman's Experimental Design Revealing
Varying Percentages of CS+ and CS–

Group	CS+	CS–
1	$\pi_1 = 1.00$	$\pi_2 = 0$
2	.75	0
3	.50	0
4	.25	0
5	1.00	.25
6	1.00	.50
7	1.00	.75
8	.75	.25
9	.75	.50
10	.50	.25
11 (Control)	.50	.50

UCS, 112 acquisition trials were provided with the CS+ and CS– each being presented an equal number of times. Acquisition trial performance is found in Fig. 5-5. As shown here, differential conditioning is maximized when $\pi_1 = 1.00$ and $\pi_2 = .00$; conditioning also takes place, however, with Groups 2 and 3 ($\pi_1 = 75\%$ or 50%, $\pi_2 = 0$). Newman's findings indicated, however, that when π_2 was greater than .00, differential conditioning did not take place.

There is some question of the validity of this last conclusion since a number of later investigators, e.g., Newman and Woodhouse (1969), Peterson and Newman (1970), and Allen and Branum (1971), have found differential conditioning with a CS– of greater than .00. In the Allen and Branum (1971) investigation, for example, differential eyelid conditioning was examined with four different reinforcement schedules, namely $\pi_1 = 1.00, \pi_2 = .00; \pi_1 = .80, \pi_2 = .00; \pi_1 = 1.00, \pi_2 = .20;$ and $\pi_1 = .80, \pi_2 = .20$. The CS+ and CS– were 2 lights, with each light being 1 inch in diameter and mounted 6 inches apart. One hundred conditioning trials were provided with each stimulus presented equally often and in random order. The percentage of conditioned responses to CS+ and CS– in blocks of 10 trials for each of the four experimental conditions is shown in Fig. 5-6. Unlike Newman's early study, it may be noted that differential conditioning was obtained when the CS– was reinforced 20% of the time. It is obvious that more research is needed in order to arrive at some firmer conclusions.

Partial Reinforcement and UCS Intensity

Inasmuch as both partial reinforcement and UCS intensity are variables that have generated considerable interest among experimenters involved in classical conditioning, it is not surprising that the influence of both of these variables has been investigated within the same experiment. Studies by Runquist (1963) and Boice and Boice (1966) have indicated that when a random 50% partial reinforcement schedule is used, eyeblink conditioning with a weak UCS intensity attains the same level or, in some cases, a higher level of asymp-

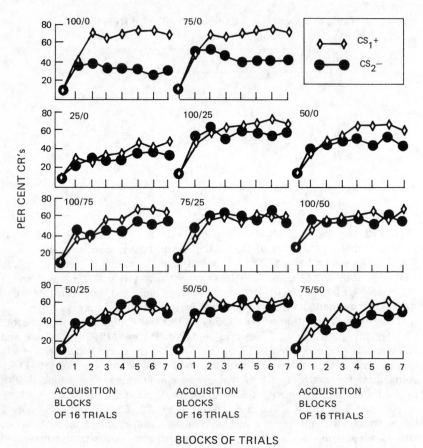

Fig. 5-5. Percentage of CRs to CS+ and CS- for each group over seven blocks of 16 acquisition trials. *Adapted from Newman (1967)*

totic performance if a stronger UCS intensity stimulus is used. This is indeed a surprising finding but it must be regarded as tenuous since Ross and Spence (1960), Fishbein (1967) and Furedy (1971b) have all been unable to confirm it.

Foth and Runquist (1970) have suggested that one variable which may interact with UCS intensity and partial reinforcement is the predictability of the occurrence of the UCS from the CS. In their eyelid conditioning study, two levels of air puff intensity were investigated along with three schedules of 50% partial reinforcement. The first schedule was double alternation (DA); the second, random (R); while the third schedule was described as run-bias (RB). This latter schedule consisted of 8 blocks of 20 trials in which the probability of a reinforced trial was .8 in blocks of 1, 3, 5, and 7 and .2 in blocks 2, 4, 6, and 8. The CS was a light, and the UCS, a puff of compressed nitrogen 75 milliseconds in duration and consisting of either high or low intensity.

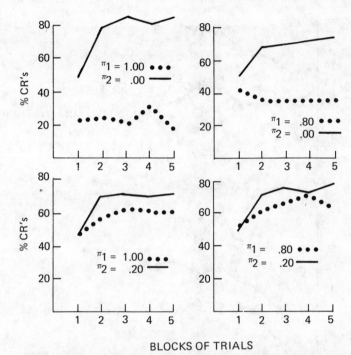

Fig. 5-6. Percentage of CRs to CS+ and CS- in blocks of 10 trials for the four reinforcement schedules. *Adapted from Allen and Branum (1971)*

Fig. 5-7 presents the percentage of CRs for the three schedules of partial reinforcement with weak and strong UCS intensities over blocks of 20 trials. It may be noted that while the randomly reinforced group was superior to the other two groups with weak UCS intensity, this effect was reversed with strong UCS intensity. An examination of the percent of CRs obtained by the random group with weak as well as strong UCS intensities supports the earlier findings of Runquist (1963). The authors have suggested that the degree to which the instrumental contingencies of UCS occurrence gain control over responding could depend on the degree UCS occurrence can be predicted from the occurrence of the CS. Thus, with a random partial reinforcement schedule, such control is low and UCS intensities should have little influence on performance. Further work, however, is necessary in order to confirm the validity of the authors' position.

Omission of the UCS: Experimental Extinction

As we noted in Chapter 2, if, following the establishment of a conditioned response, the UCS is omitted but the CS continues to be presented, a decline or decrement in responding will be noted. The operation of omitting the UCS has been termed experimental extinction.

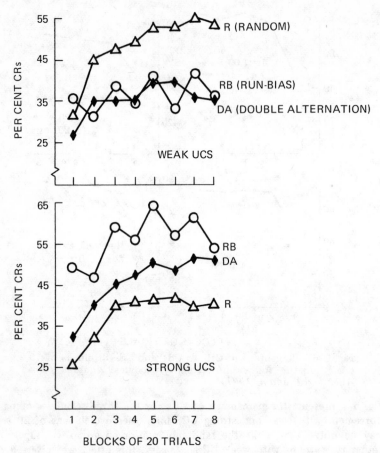

Fig. 5-7. Percentage of CRs for the Double alternation, Run-bias and Random schedules of partial reinforcement over blocks of 20 trials for each UCS intensity. *Adapted from Foth and Runquist (1970)*

We have already indicated that some investigators have used response measures obtained during experimental extinction to infer the strength of conditioning. In our discussion of the basic variables which contribute to classical conditioning, we presented these data only infrequently since, in many cases, extinction data mirrored the findings obtained during acquisition. In other experiments, where acquisition and extinction findings are not in agreement, our bias has been that results obtained during acquisition trials are the more valid measure of the "strength" of a conditioned response. Our reasoning is that the elimination of the UCS during extinction trials appears to change the motivation of the subject and in so doing, makes extinction a task which is "different" from acquisition. As a result, a performance measure obtained during extinction and used to infer acquisition performance is employed with considerable risk.

A great deal of interest has been generated, however, in the influence of partial reinforcement on extinction performance; as a result, we should like to discuss this topic briefly. Additional discussion will be found in Chapter 10, since instrumental learning tasks have more frequently been used to investigate this variable.

The Role of Partial Reinforcement

Although Humphreys (1939b) believed that a lack of difference in acquisition trials between his continuous and partial reinforcement groups was "paradoxical," the real surprise of the study was his extinction findings. Humphreys reported that Group 2, which was given 96 trials with 50%, reinforcement took significantly longer to extinguish than either of the two continuously reinforced groups, e.g., Group 1, 96 CS-UCS presentations; or Group 3, 48 CS-UCS presentations. Fig. 5-8 illustrates these findings. This superiority of a partial reinforcement schedule in producing superior resistance to extinction has frequently been designated as a partial reinforcement effect (PRE).

It is not surprising that Humphreys's findings were viewed by many psychologists with some concern, particularly theorists who assumed that learning was related to the number of reinforcements or CS-UCS pairings which were provided. (Presumably, each pairing should result in increasing the strength of the connection.) For if resistance to extinction was considered to be a bona fide response measure—an indicator of the strength of a stimulus response relationship—then Humphreys's findings indicated that just 48 CS-UCS pairing would result in conditioning which was superior to 96 pairings.

Humphreys's findings have been confirmed by a number of investigators using humans as experimental subjects and examining a variety of classical conditioned responses. And, as might be anticipated, a number of partial reinforcement schedules have been examined. Grant and Schipper (1952), it will be recalled, examined the influence of differing percentages of reinforced trials on acquisition; they also examined the influence of these schedules on extinction. Their findings can be found in Fig. 5-9, revealing that the 0%, 25%, and 100% reinforcement groups extinguished most rapidly, while the 50% and 75% groups extinguished least rapidly. A basic problem in the interpretation of these findings must be acknowledged: it is difficult to separate the influence of the terminal acquisition level from extinction performance.

One theoretical position which shows promise in explaining some of the classical conditioning findings is the discrimination hypothesis, originally proposed by Mowrer and Jones (1945). These investigators posited that resistance to extinction is a function of the difficulty of discriminating extinction trials from acquisition trials. Thus, when the acquisition and extinction trials bear some similarity to one another, as in partial reinforcement, the subject has difficulty in determining when acquisition trials end and extinction trials begin, so that acquisition behavior continues. On the other hand, if the subject is

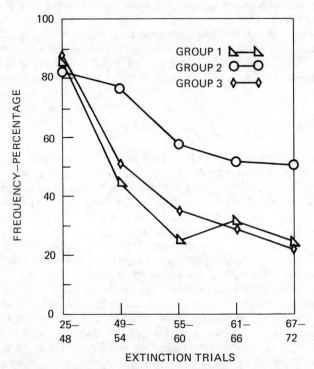

Fig. 5-8. Course of extinction-frequency. The 24 extinction trials are divided into 4 groups of 6 trials each. An average for the preceding 24 acquisition trials is plotted to serve as a reference point for the extinction results. The essential comparability of groups 1 and 3 (100 percent reinforcement) is easily apparent, while Group 2 (50 percent reinforcement) responds at a consistently higher level throughout than either of the others. *Adapted from Humphreys (1939b)*

provided with continuous reinforcement, the change to extinction trials in which reinforcement never takes place is quite marked. The result is that these trials are easily distinguished from acquisition trials, so that there is the cessation of responding.

The discrimination hypothesis predicts superior resistance to extinction for partial reinforcement groups when compared with continuous; it also predicts that if reinforcement in a partial reinforcement regimen was made predictable, this type of acquisition training would also result in poorer resistance to extinction than if the presentation of reinforcement was essentially unpredictable or random. In a test of this position, Longenecker, Krauskopf, and Bitterman (1952) conditioned the EDR to a random, partially reinforced group as well as

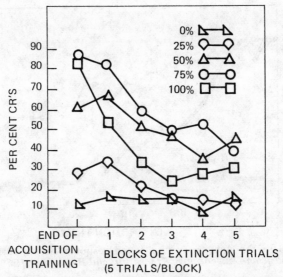

Fig. 5-9. The course of extinction of the eyelid CR with varying percentages of reinforced trials during training. *Adapted from Grant and Schipper (1952)*

a second group which received the UCS on odd numbered trials. Following 22 conditioning trials, 30 extinction trials were provided. Fig. 5-10 reveals the superior resistance to extinction of the randomly reinforced group.

Spence, Homzie, and Rutledge (1964) have provided a somewhat different version of the discrimination hypothesis. These investigators, examining the classically conditioned eyelid response, have hypothesized that discrimination of the change from conditioning to extinction trials leads the subject to adopt an inhibitory set not to blink. Extinction is extremely rapid since this inhibitory set interferes with the conditioned response. Partial reinforcement precludes or delays discrimination so that the decrement in the frequency of the conditioned response under such conditions is more gradual. Spence et al (1964) have acknowledged that their version of the discrimination hypothesis was put forward primarily to deal with the extremely rapid extinction effect (one or two nonreinforced trials) that occurs only with humans.

There is the problem, of course, of accounting for those experimental findings which reveal that partial reinforcement schedules employing small percentages of reinforcement result in poorer resistance to extinction than continuous reinforcement. For example, note that in the Grant and Schipper (1952) study, the 0% and 25% groups revealed less resistance to extinction than the 100% group. One explanation is that the amount of reinforcement provided either the 0% or 25% groups during acquisition trials does not result in sufficient conditioned response strength to support responding during extinction. This

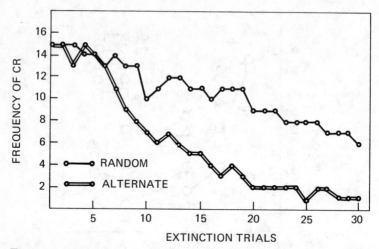

Fig. 5-10. Frequency of conditioned response during extinction.
Adapted from Longenecker, Krauskopf, and Bitterman (1952)

lack of response strength represents a second process (the discrimination process is the first), which Grant and Schipper (1952) have posited to account for their findings.

The evidence is almost unequivocal in demonstrating that extinction in normal humans is slower following a random partial reinforcement schedule than after continuous reinforcement; yet, findings obtained from classical conditioning experiments using animals are controversial. Gonzalez, Longo, and Bitterman (1961); Longo, Milstein, and Bitterman (1962); Thomas and Wagner (1964); and Wagner, Siegel, and Fein (Exp. 1, 1967), using fish, pigeons, rabbits, and rats, have failed to find a superiority for partial reinforcement groups during extinction.

However, a number of other investigators have obtained a partial reinforcement effect with animals, e.g., Fitzgerald (1963), Wyers, Peeke, and Herz (1964), Brimer and Dockrill (1966), Kimmel and Yaremko (1966), and Holmes and Gormezano (1970).[2] Table 5-3 provides a brief summary of many of these experiments. Studies by Thomas and Wagner (1964), and Fitzgerald (1963) illustrate the nature of these contradictory findings.

In the Thomas and Wagner (1964) study, two groups of rabbits received classical eyelid conditioning training. The CS was a 2000-Hz tone, with the UCS an air puff administered to the cornea of the right eye. The continuously reinforced group received 220 acquisition trials while the partially reinforced group received 440 acquisition trials with 50% reinforcement.

Following the last acquisition trial, 60 extinction trials were provided for

---

[2] When animals are used as subjects in instrumental learning tasks, the findings almost always reveal that a partial reinforcement schedule leads to greater resistance to extinction than does continuous reinforcement. (See Chapter 10.)

Table 5-3   Summaries of a Sampling of Studies Examining the Effect of Continuous and Partial Reinforcement Schedules on Resistance to Extinction

Investigator	Subject	Response	Results
Gonzalez, Longo, and Bitterman (1961)	Goldfish	Activity	No difference between groups (2 experiments)
Longo, Milstein, and Bitterman (1962)	Pigeon	Movement	No difference between groups
Fitzgerald (1963)	Dogs	Salivation	PRE obtained
Wyers, Peeke, and Herz (1964)	Earthworm	Withdrawal of anterior segments of the body	PRE obtained
Wagner, Siegel, Thomas, and Ellison (1964)	Dogs	Salivation	Findings were mixed: continuous reinforcement group was superior on first trial of each extinction day; partial reinforcement group revealed superior responding on late trials of each extinction day.
Thomas and Wagner (1964)	Rabbits	Eyelid	No difference between groups
Berger, Yarczower, and Bitterman (1965)	Goldfish	Activity	No difference between groups on any experiment (7 experiments)
Fitzgerald, Vardaris, and Teyler (1966)	Dogs	Heart Rate	PRE obtained
Brimer and Dockrill (1966)	Rats	CER	PRE obtained (2 experiments)
Slivka and Bitterman (1966)	Pigeons	Movement	No difference between groups
Kimmel and Yaremko (1966)	Planaria	Turning or Contraction	PRE obtained
Wagner, Siegel, and Fein (1967)	Rats	Startle	Continuous reinforcement superior to partial
Holmes and Gormezano (1970)	Rabbits	Jaw Movement	PRE obtained

both groups. Fig. 5-11 presents the mean percentage of CRs for the two groups on the last block of 10 acquisition trials and the 3 subsequent blocks of 20 extinction trials. As the authors have written, "the extinction data offer little suggestion that partial reinforcement leads to greater resistance to extinction than continuous reinforcement" (p. 158).

On the other hand, Fitzgerald (1963) was unable to obtain this result with the classically conditioned salivary response in dogs. The CS was a 400-Hz tone and the UCS, a dilute solution of acid delivered through a permanent fistula in the animal's cheek. Acquisition training consisted of providing each animal with 24 trials per day for 10 days. One group of animals was continuously rein-

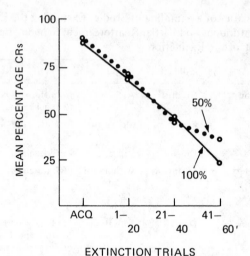

EXTINCTION TRIALS

Fig. 5-11. Mean percentage of CRs in two groups, on the last 10 trials of acquisition and subsequent blocks of 20 extinction trials. *Adapted from Thomas and Wagner (1964).*

forced; for the two other groups, the UCS occurred on either 50% or 25% of the trials. Although 10 days of extinction trials were provided (24 trials/day), the salivary fistulas of several subjects became unattached during extinction so that the examination of extinction responding was limited to the first day. Results indicated that the rate of decline in salivation during these extinction trials was greatest for the continuously reinforced group—88.5%. On the other hand, the group receiving 50% reinforcement declined just 26.8% while the 25% reinforcement declined 31.1%.[3]

It is difficult to account for the discrepant findings that have been obtained. Some of the variation in results may arise from methodological inadequacies— different terminal acquisition performance levels relating to partial and continuous reinforcement schedules have not always been taken into consideration when extinction performance between groups is compared. But, as Anderson (1963) has noted, there is no completely satisfactory way of equating different terminal levels of performance. One other suggestion arises from an examination of Table 5-3 in which, for most experiments, partial reinforcement effects are obtained with the conditioning of autonomic responses such as salivation and heart rate, but not with skeletal responses. The generality of this finding remains to be examined further since Holmes and Gormezano's (1970) recent findings are not in keeping with this hypothesis.

[3] Terminal acquisition levels for the 100% and 50% groups were quite similar, thus making a comparison between extinction performance for these groups appropriate.

Theoretical Explanations for Extinction

A number of investigators have been interested in "explaining" extinction effects found in classical conditioning, the earliest of whom is Pavlov (1927). Pavlov believed that extinction was one manifestation of a central inhibitory state built up by the presentation of the conditioned stimulus (without UCS pairings) and which, although dissipating rapidly, nonetheless accumulated sufficient strength to prevent the conditioned response from being made.

In contrast, Guthrie (1935) and Wendt (1936) assumed that the presentation of the CS without the UCS resulted in other responses being made by the organism in the experimental situation which interfered with the conditioned response. The strength or frequency of these interfering responses eventually precluded the appearance of the conditioned response and as a result, extinction was said to have taken place. This theory has been termed an interference theory in contrast to the inhibitory theory posited by Pavlov.

Early investigators found merit in both the inhibitory and interference theories of extinction. The interference theory had the obvious advantage of parsimony since it was not necessary to posit a second process (inhibition) in order to account for extinction phenomenon. In addition, the observation of subjects in the extinction situation frequently revealed that they were actually engaging in some other type of response.

On the other hand, many arguments were directed against the interference theory interpretation. Three of these, as indicated by Hilgard and Marquis (1940), were (1) the role of spontaneous recovery, (2) the effect of rate of elicitation of the extinguished response, and (3) the influence of drugs on the extinguished response. Spontaneous recovery, interpreted within an interference framework, could take place only to the extent that the interfering response which competed with the conditioned response was weakened during the interval between the last extinction trial and the test for spontaneous recovery. The experimental evidence indicated that spontaneous recovery could be obtained with very short durations; such time periods were generally acknowledged to be too short for the response to be forgotten. Moreover, if a conditioned response was "extinguished" by counter-conditioning—a procedure which clearly denotes the characteristics of the interfering response—there would be virtually no spontaneous recovery.

The second argument was derived from an examination of the effect of rate of elicitation of training and extinction trials. The massing of training trials frequently retards learning but the massing of extinction trials, according to the experimental evidence obtained by Pavlov (1927) and Hilgard and Marquis (1935) tends to hasten extinction. As Hilgard and Marquis (1940) subsequently wrote, "If the extinction process were essentially similar to the conditioning process, one would expect a positive correlation between the rates of acquisition and extinction, that is, rapid conditioning corresponding to rapid extinction, slow conditioning corresponding to slow extinction. The numerous correlations reported are, however, predominantly negative" (p. 119).

Finally, there was evidence to indicate that certain drugs could produce differential effects on conditioning and extinction. For example, caffeine and benzedrine were found to increase the rate of learning a conditioned response but to decrease the rate of extinction.

To these specific difficulties was added a very general one. The motivation for the interfering response could not be specified, nor was it possible to demonstrate how the interfering response grew in strength.

In contrast, the fact that the inhibitory process was tied to a physiological foundation appealed to many. Moreover, the findings from a number of classical conditioning studies were in keeping with the operation of an inhibitory process. The phenomenon of spontaneous recovery could be accounted for since inhibition was presumed to dissipate with time, permitting the reappearance of the conditioned response. In addition, the early studies of Pavlov (1927), and Hilgard and Marquis (1935) which revealed that distributed extinction trials produced superior resistance to extinction were also compatible with the postulation of an inhibitory process which dissipated with time.

Hull (1943) in his *Principles of Behavior*, utilized both points of view by positing a two-factor theory of inhibition. Hull hypothesized that inhibition was made up of (1) reactive inhibition as well as (2) conditioned inhibition.

Reactive inhibition was defined as follows: "Whenever any reaction is evoked in an organism there is left a condition or state which acts as a primary negative motivation in that it has an innate capacity to produce a cessation of the activity which produced the state" (p. 278). A basic corollary was that such an inhibitory state diminished progressively with the passage of time according to a simple decay or negative growth function.

The second inhibitory process—conditioned inhibition—was considered to be something similar to "conditioned resting." During continuous work, reactive inhibition accumulates, thus producing a negative drive state. When rest actually does occur, this drive is reduced by the reactive inhibition being dissipated. If a signal (CS) precedes the rest, it is possible for the resting response to become conditioned to the signal because the response is reinforced by the reduction of the drive state. Hull posited that the two inhibitory states combined to provide a total inhibitory potential or value which resulted in effectively reducing the organism's level of performance.

The reactive and conditioned inhibition constructs could readily account for experimental extinction and spontaneous recovery. It was assumed that extinction trials eventually produced an accumulation of both reactive and conditioned inhibition sufficient to prevent the occurrence of the learned response. Since reactive inhibition dissipated with time, the subsequent presentation of the conditioned stimulus resulted in a spontaneous recovering of the conditioned response. The lowered level of responding in this situation, however, presumably reflected a response decrement produced by conditioned inhibition—hypothesized not to dissipate with time.

Hull's conceptualization of inhibition did not go unchallenged and a number of investigators, e.g., Koch (1954), Gleitman, Nachmias, and Neisser (1954), Cotton (1955), and Jensen (1961) have pointed to empirical as well as conceptual difficulties.

When a conditioned response has been extinguished to the point that the organism no longer responds, further presentations of the CS will nevertheless serve to strengthen extinction, as measured by a decrease in spontaneous recovery. (This phenomenon has been termed silent extinction and is discussed more fully in Chapter 6). In another case, the presentation of the CS prior to the conditioning trials, an operation described as latent inhibition, will result in the development of an inhibitory state; this is inferred from the subject's increased difficulty in reaching the conditioning criterion when the CS-UCS pairings are provided. In both instances, the making of a response which must take place if reactive inhibition is to develop does not appear to be a necessary condition for the establishment of an inhibitory state.

There are also conceptual difficulties with Hull's theory of inhibition. Conditioned inhibition, or the habit of not responding, has been defined in a number of ways. Sometimes it has been identified with the absence of activity; at other times, with the cessation of activity; it also may appear to be reactive inhibition conditioned to the stimulus situation. The failure to specify the nature of conditioned inhibition leads to some obvious difficulties. Certain predictions which are generated from the operation of reactive and conditioned inhibition appear to be patently false. For example, it has been assumed that habit strength, as a result of continued reinforcement, will reach an asymptote so that further increments in habit cannot take place. However, it has been assumed that reactive and conditioned inhibition develop as a necessary consequence of the evocation of a response, regardless of the presence or absence of reinforcement. As a result, these inhibitory states would continue to increase, so that continued reinforcement should lead to a subsequent decrement in performance in turn resulting eventually in the total elimination of the response.

In summary, we do not have any general theory of extinction which can account for the variety of experimental findings which have been obtained. It would be surprising, indeed, if such a theory were found, considering the variety of organisms and experimental tasks which have been used. What appears to be needed are much more modest explanations, limited to perhaps a single species and a specific classically conditioned response situation. Only after a number of verifiable mini-theories have been established would there appear to be any hope of arriving at a more general theoretical position.

Summary

The omission of the UCS on some conditioning trials has been termed partial reinforcement. Humphreys's early eyelid conditioning experiment has resulted in continuing examination by others of the role of partial reinforcement in the classical conditioning of a variety of responses. Most investigators have found that acquisition when partial reinforcement schedules are used is poorer than with a continuous reinforcement schedule.

The continuous omission of the UCS is an operation which has been termed experimental extinction. The use of this operation results in a decline in the previously established CR. It is with experimental extinction that partial reinforcement schedules make their paradoxical contribution. Humphreys's early finding that a group of subjects provided 50% reinforcement required a signifi-

cantly longer time to reach the extinction criterion than a continuously reinforced group has been confirmed by many investigators examining a variety of
classically conditioned responses. Explanations of this finding have been provided by Mowrer, and Spence, Homzie, and Rutledge who have hypothesized that
the subject provided reinforcement during acquisition trials has difficulty in discriminating these trials from the extinction trials; as a result, he continues to respond longer during extinction than continuously reinforced groups of subjects
who are able to make this discrimination more readily. Although the evidence is
unequivocal in demonstrating that extinction in normal humans is slower following partial reinforcement, experiments using animals have not provided similar
findings. The difference in extinction findings between these two types of
subjects is interesting and further work is necessary in order to determine the
reason for it.

Theoretical explanations for experimental extinction have indicated that the
decrement in responding takes place as a result of (1) the development of an
inhibitory state in the organism, or (2) the organism's having learned not to
respond when the CS is presented. Hull has provided an explanation incorporat-
ing both of these constructs, identifying the inhibitory state as reactive inhibition and the learning factor as conditioned inhibition, with the two being
assumed to summate in order to account for the extinction of a response.

Experimental as well as conceptual difficulties with all these explanations
have been noted and, at the present time, there is no generally accepted theory
for the process(es) involved in experimental extinction.

6
Classical Conditioning:
Further Considerations

Traditionally, classical conditioning is assumed to be a simple and uncomplicated type of stimulus-response learning, consisting of the establishment of an association between a neutral [or conditioned] stimulus and a response which bears some resemblance or has some relevance to the response elicited by an unconditioned stimulus. This point of view has been adopted in our earlier chapters where we examined conditioning operations, the kinds of responses that have been conditioned, as well as the conditions contributing to the development of the conditioned response.

In the first three sections of this final chapter on conditioning, we should like to introduce some complexities to this traditional point of view; our concluding section will examine physiological contributions which should help provide a more adequate understanding of what is going on when conditioning takes place.

1. The Role of Responding

One basic assumption made by stimulus-response theorists has been that for an association to take place, it is necessary that the organism make some overt response during the conditioning trials. The experimental studies reviewed in our earlier chapters have, for the most part, been interpretable within a stimulus-response position.

During the past two decades or so, experimental evidence has been obtained which appears to necessitate some modification of this assumption. Such evidence has been related to the demonstration that presentation of a stimulus (or stimuli) without an apparent or observable response can influence the classical conditioning process. These varying procedures or processes have been identified as (1) sensory preconditioning, (2) latent inhibition, and (3) silent extinction.

Sensory Preconditioning

In 1939 Brogden asked the question, "If an organism be given successive experiences of two temporally simultaneous stimuli exciting two sense modalities without evoking any observable response, and if after this contiguous sensory experience, one stimulus be made a conditioned signal for the activity of a given behavior system by appropriate training, will the other elicit a similar conditioned response without the usual training?" (p. 323). Brogden's experiment, designed to answer his query, consisted of providing 8 dogs with 200 pairings of a light and a bell presented simultaneously. A conditioning experiment was then set up in which 1 of these stimuli served as the CS, and shock, which elicited foot withdrawal, served as the UCS. A criterion of 20 consecutive CRs was employed. Following such training, a transfer test was provided in which the other stimulus was then presented to the subjects. A control group of animals was given similar conditioning and transfer trials; however, the preconditioning sessions consisting of the pairings of light and bell were omitted. Animals in the experimental group produced 78 conditioned responses during the transfer test while in contrast, only 4 conditioned responses were made by the control group. These positive findings resulted in Brogden's conclusion that the results "must be due to an association found when the bell and light were presented contiguously, prior to the conditioning of flexion to one of them" (p. 330).

Almost ten years later, Brogden (1947) was also able to demonstrate sensory preconditioning with humans using the Ivanov-Smolensky procedure. Experimental subjects, following 10 simultaneous presentations of a light and tone, were instructed to depress a telegraph key when a light was presented. Following 30 such training trials, a transfer test revealed that the experimental subjects responded more frequently to the presentation of the tone than an appropriate control group.

Brogden's studies have illustrated the basic sensory preconditioning paradigm. More specifically, two "neutral" stimuli, e.g., light and tone, are presented simultaneously for a number of trials, following which one of them is used as the CS in a conditioning experiment. After the conditioned response has been established, the other neutral stimulus is presented in order to examine the probability that this second stimulus will elicit the conditioned response. The performance for the experimental group is compared with appropriate control groups. Fig. 6-1 illustrates the procedure used.

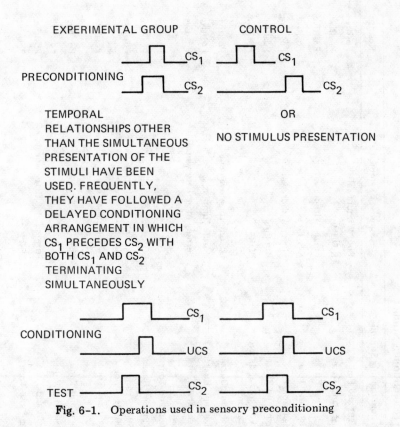

Fig. 6-1. Operations used in sensory preconditioning

Although Brogden's original investigation was designed to answer an empirical question, and was presumably devoid of any theoretical significance, sensory preconditioning has frequently been cited as an embarrassment to advocates of a stimulus-response position. The reason for this, as indicated earlier, is that these theorists assume learning is an association between a stimulus and a response, whereas the positive findings obtained from sensory preconditioning studies would indicate that what has been learned is an association between two stimuli.[1]

Since Brogden's early studies, positive findings have been obtained by virtually all investigators using a variety of organisms and employing both instrumental as well as classical conditioning tasks. Summaries of a sampling of these studies are provided in Table 6-1. Many of the experimenters have interpreted

---

[1] It is interesting to note that Brodgen (1947) concluded that sensory preconditioning is not necessarily critical to any learning theory. He explains that, "one must assume that any event which is a stimulus to an organism evokes a response of that organism . . . sensory conditioning, then, is no different from any other conditioning, except that the experimental operations do not permit specification of the responses involved" (p. 537).

Table 6–1 Summaries of a Sampling of Sensory Preconditioning Studies

Investigators	Subjects Used	Preconditioning Stimuli	Response Examined	Results
Brogden (1939)	Dogs	Light and Bell	Foot Withdrawal	Positive
Brogden (1947)	Humans	Light and Tone	Key Press	Positive
Karn (1947)	Humans	Light and Buzzer	Finger Withdrawal	Positive
Chernikoff and Brogden (1949)	Humans	Light and Tone	Key Press	Positive
Wickens and Briggs (1951)	Humans	Light and Tone	Finger Withdrawal	Positive
Bahrick (1953)	Rats	Light and Buzzer	Running	Positive
Bitterman, Reed, and Kubala (1953)	Humans	Two lights at different locations	EDR	Positive
Silver and Meyer (1954)	Rats	Light and Buzzer	Locomotor Movement	Positive
Seidel (1958)	Rats	Light and Buzzer	Hurdle Jumping	Positive
Hoffeld, Thompson, and Brogden (1958)	Cats	Light and Tone	Turning of activity wheel	Positive
Coppock (1958)	Humans	Light and Tone	EDR	Positive
Lovibond (1959)	Humans	Light and Buzzer	EDR	Positive
Kendall and Thompson (1960)	Cats	250 Hz Tone and 2000 Hz Tone	Turning of activity wheel	Positive
Hoffeld, Kendall, Thompson, and Brogden (1960)	Cats	Light and Tone	Turning of activity wheel	Positive
Prewitt (1967)	Rats	Light and Tone	CER	Positive
Parkinson (1968)	Rats	Light and Noise	CER	Positive
Parks (1968)	Rats	Light and Tone	Turning of activity wheel	Positive
Tait, Marquis, Williams, Weinstein and Suboski (1969)	Rats	Light and Tone	CER	Positive
Adamec and Melzack (1970)	Cats	Click and Flash	Licking	Positive

their findings within a stimulus-response, mediation framework, and although we cannot review all of these efforts, we should like to elaborate on the general nature of this explanation.

The mediation hypothesis assumes that each of the two stimuli used in the preconditioning phase of the sensory preconditioning experiment, for example, light and tone, elicits a common and unobservable response (or responses), perhaps of an attentional or perceptual nature. (As we discuss in Chapter 12, many investigators have conceptualized the attention process as consisting of specific overt responses.) These attentional responses also provide stimulation to the subject. During the conditioning phase of the experiment, when the light is conditioned to a new response, leg flexion, for example, the stimulation arising from the attentional response is conditioned to leg flexion as well. Subsequently, in the transfer test, the tone will elicit its attentional response and attendant stimulation, which in turn will elicit leg flexion. As Wickens and Briggs (1951) have written, "The transfer that occurs may be considered as arising not from the fact that the two stimuli had been associated together, but because a common and mediating response had been learned to both " (p. 197).

An obvious problem with this type of explanation is the necessity of accepting the central role of the mediating response and its resultant stimulation, both of which are unobservable to the experimenter. In an attempt to circumvent this difficulty, or at least demonstrate how an observable response may serve as mediator, Wickens and Briggs (1951) investigated the use of a verbal response which would act in this capacity. In their study, two stimuli, a tone and a light, were presented during preconditioning trials. Four groups of subjects were run. For Group 1, the stimuli were paired for 15 trials with the subjects being required to say the word "now" when the stimuli appeared. For Group 2, the two stimuli were presented independently with the same response ("now") to be given at the presentation of each stimulus. Fifteen presentations of each stimulus were provided. The procedure for groups 3 and 4 was similar to that utilized with Group 2 except that the subjects were required to say "now" when one stimulus was presented, but not the other. Following such training, a finger-withdrawal conditioning study was run in which the subject learned to avoid shock by lifting his finger when a tone was presented. The transfer test consisted of 10 presentations of the light following 30 conditioning trials.

Results revealed that Groups 1 and 2 showed a high frequency of response transfer or sensory preconditioning, but Groups 3 and 4 did not. The point critical to the authors' hypothesis is the fact that no significant difference in responding was found between Groups 1 and 2. Thus, although the tone and light were presented separately for Group 2 and together for Group 1, the subjects had to make a common response—"now"—to both stimuli which resulted in Group 2's performing as well as Group 1—the typical sensory preconditioning group.

Some investigators who have adopted the mediation response position, also have assumed that the presentation of the paired preconditioning stimuli may be likened to a classical conditioning operation. Silver and Meyer (1954) have written that "each stimulus is considered to be a UCS for a response that is not directly observed, and potentially a CS for a second response similar to the one elicited by the other stimulus. Prior to preconditioning, both responses occur only if both stimuli are present. After preconditioning, a response which resembles the entire complex follows presentation of either stimulus" (p. 57).

This hypothesis has led to a number of sensory preconditioning experiments examining the operation of traditional classical conditioning variables. An early study conducted by Silver and Meyer (1954) examined the temporal variable—the effectiveness of forward, simultaneous, or backward presentations of a buzzer and a light provided during the preconditioning trials. (It will be recalled from Chapter 2 that forward conditioning is superior to either simultaneous or backward conditioning.) Their experimental subjects were rats which, during the preconditioning trials, received a 1-second presentation of a buzzer and a light in either a forward, simultaneous, or backward order. One control group received no pretraining; a second control group was presented just the light, while the third control group was presented only the buzzer. Three thousand preconditioning trials were provided followed by the conditioning of movement of at least 6 inches prior to the onset of shock which was used as the UCS. When the criterion of 7 conditioned responses out of 10 trials was reached, a transfer test consisting of 100 presentations of the appropriate stimulus was provided. The authors found sensory preconditioning for all three experimental groups, but more important, forward conditioning yielded significantly more transfer than either the simultaneous or backward conditions.

Another sensory preconditioning study investigating the temporal interval separating the CS-UCS was conducted by Wickens and Cross (1963). Their procedure was to present their subjects (humans) with 10 preconditioning trials consisting of a light and a tone, using 1 of 4 different intervals between the two stimuli, namely, 0, 100, 400, or 600 milliseconds. Following these trials, the light was conditioned to the electrodermal response, with shock serving as the UCS. Following 10 conditioning trials, the tone was presented alone for 4 trials. Although no significant differences in responding were obtained on the first transfer trial, the subsequent 3 trials revealed that the greatest amount of sensory preconditioning was obtained with the 400 millisecond group, followed in order by the 100, 0, and 600 millisecond groups; a finding which the authors have pointed out is similar to what is found in ordinary conditioning studies investigating the interstimulus interval.

Within the context of investigating the operation of classical conditioning variables on the strength of sensory preconditioning, studies by Prewitt (1967) and Tait and his associates have all been supportive of the classical conditioning model. In Prewitt's (1967) study, rats were provided with either 0, 1, 4, 16, or 64 presentations of a tone and a light. Both stimuli were of 10 seconds' duration with the offset of one stimulus coinciding with the onset of the second. Control groups were run with the stimuli presented singly and in random order. Following preconditioning trials, conditioned emotional response (CER) training was provided which consisted of the presentation of 10 trials with a 10-second tone (or light) serving as the CS and a 1-second shock as the UCS. Transfer or test trials were then provided in which the suppressive influence of the light (or tone) was examined on the consummatory response of drinking. The author found that the amount of suppression was a monotonically increasing function

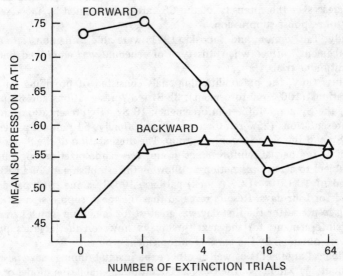

Fig. 6-2. Mean suppression ratios for groups given either forward or backward SPC as a function of the number of extinction trials given following SPC. (The abscissa scale is log N, base 4, except for the first point.) *Adapted from Tait, Marquis, Williams, Weinstein, and Suboski (1969)*

of the number of paired sensory preconditioning trials up to 16. The failure of the group provided 64 trials to differ significantly from the group given just 16 trials would suggest that the amount of conditioned suppression by sensory preconditioning training reaches asymptote by the sixteenth trial.

Using a procedure similar to that employed by Prewitt (1967), Tait, Marquis, Williams, Weinstein, and Suboski (1969) found that the strength of responding on transfer trials was related to the number of extinction trials provided following the preconditioning pairings. Thus, after 16 forward or backward preconditioning trials consisting of the presentation of a light and a tone, an extinction session was provided which consisted of presenting one of these stimuli alone for either 0, 1, 4, 16, or 64 trials. Ten CER training trials were then provided with either the light or the tone used as the CS and associated with shock as the UCS. In the transfer situation, the conditioned suppression of the drinking response was examined as a function of the number of extinction trials provided the stimulus not serving as the CS. As indicated in Fig. 6-2, response strength was a decreasing function of the number of extinction trials which followed the forward preconditioning trials. There is, however, little indication of suppression arising from the groups provided backward preconditioning trials at any of the extinction trial values.

Similar to results of traditional classical conditioning studies, the intensity of the stimuli used in the preconditioning trials has been found by Tait and Suboski (1972) to influence the amount of sensory preconditioning. Using the familiar conditioned emotional response paradigm, these investigators discovered that increases in the intensity of the CS_1 are accompanied by increases in the amount of response suppression.

Finally, Tait, Simon, and Suboski (1971) were able to demonstrate a partial "reinforcement" effect when this type of schedule was employed during the preconditioning trials.[2]

In this study, the preconditioning trials consisted of providing 64 S_1 - S_2 presentations (100% reinforcement); 32 S_1 - S_2 presentations and 32 presentations of the S_1 alone (50% reinforcement); 16 S_1 - S_2 presentations and 48 S_1 alone presentations (25% reinforcement); and, finally, 64 random presentations of the S_1 and the S_2 to a control group. The presentation of the S_1-alone trials for each of the partial reinforcement groups was randomized among the S_1 - S_2 trials subject to certain restrictions. Following the establishment of a CER which consisted of 10 CS_2 - UCS (shock) pairings, 10 CS_1 alone trials per day were provided for four days. Results revealed that the mean suppression ratio of the drinking response for the first day was greatest for the group which had received 100% reinforcement; for the next three days, however, the largest suppression ratios were obtained by the partial reinforcement groups.

But logical arguments as well as other experimental findings have raised questions about the validity of the classical conditioning-mediation model of sensory preconditioning. Certainly, the difficulty of identifying the UCS (or the source of reinforcement) as well as determining the nature of the conditioned and unconditioned responses should be sources of concern for all who have proposed such a theoretical explanation. Moreover, Hoffeld, Thompson, and Brogden (1958), examining the temporal interval between the CS_1 and the CS_2 have found that a greater amount of sensory preconditioning was obtained with an interval of 4 seconds than with 0, .5, 1, or 2 seconds—a result contrary to typical classical conditioning findings and in conflict with the experimental evidence provided by Wickens and Cross (1963).

In a second study, Hoffeld, Kendall, Thompson, and Brogden (1960) were unable to find any relationship between the number of preconditioning trials and the strength of the transferred response. It might be noted that in these studies, an instrumental avoidance task was used during the conditioning phase of the experiment. Following appropriate preconditioning trials of buzzer and light presentations, cats were trained to avoid shock by running in an activity wheel.

An attack on the mediation aspect of the model comes from the work of Cousins, Zamble, Tait, and Suboski (1971) who have reasoned that if the orga-

---

[2] It should be acknowledged that the placing of "reinforcement" in quotes stems from the lack of identification of the reinforcing stimulus in the preconditioning phase of sensory preconditioning experiments; for the most part, experimenters have not been concerned with the source of reinforcement for the "conditioning" that is presumed to take place. To illustrate, Wickens and Briggs (1951) in their early study indicated that their analysis of sensory preconditioning "although S-R in nature, did not necessarily assume reinforcement as essential for S-R formation" (p. 197).

nism was not capable of making a response during the preconditioning trials, and sensory conditioning continued to be obtained, there would be some difficulty in maintaining the mediation hypothesis.

These investigators carried out such a procedure by using curare—a drug which paralyzes the subject and presumably eliminates any overt response arising from the presentation of the stimuli during the preconditioning phase of the experiment.[3] In this study, two groups of curarized and two groups of control animals (rats) were given either 16 pairings of a light and a tone or 16 temporally separated presentations of these stimuli. Prior to such training all of the animals had learned to drink in a test chamber. Conditioned emotional response training for all animals was provided 24 hours after the preconditioning phase. Such training consisted of 10 pairings of one of the stimuli (light or sound) with unavoidable shock to the feet. The animals were then deprived of water for 48 hours and tested for drinking. The test began after each animal had begun to lick water from the spout and consisted of 10 10-second presentations of whichever stimulus had not been used in the conditioned emotional response training.

The ability of the unpaired stimulus to suppress drinking on the first trial is revealed in Fig. 6–3. Here it is shown that the presentation of the paired stimuli in the curarized rats resulted in almost as much suppression as that produced in the normal animals which also had paired presentation of the stimuli. In contrast, the temporal separation of the stimuli during the preconditioning trials resulted in significantly less suppression for both curarized and normal animals.

Some psychologists have assumed that associations can be formed between two stimuli as well as between a stimulus and a response. Birch and Bitterman (1949) hypothesized that when two afferent centers are continuously active, as found during the preconditioning phase of the experiment, a functional relation is established between them so that the subsequent eliciting of one will arouse the other. Since these authors have considered the establishment of stimulus-stimulus associations a basic aspect of learning, sensory preconditioning is nothing more to them than an example of this type of learning.

A contemporary analysis of sensory preconditioning has been provided by Thompson (1972) who believes that the learning process operating in typical classical conditioning experiments is fundamentally different from that operating in sensory preconditioning. Thompson has hypothesized that classical conditioning experiments utilize *effective reinforcing stimuli*—stimuli which result in increased probability of a response being made. Sensory preconditioning experiments, however, employ *effective stimuli*—stimuli which, with a limited number

[3] Curare is the generic term for a variety of poisons discovered in South America. (Primitive tribes used it on their arrows.) It appears to contain several alkaloids; the first of these to be successfully isolated and synthesized in the laboratory was D-tubocurarine. Grossman (1967) has observed that curariform drugs selectively block the transmission of nerve impulses at the neuromuscular junction and in autonomic ganglia, more specifically interfering with the nicotinic action of acetylcholine. As noted in Chapter 14, there is much still to be known about the action of curare-like drugs on the organism; as a result, findings obtained from experiments in which this drug has been used are not easy to interpret.

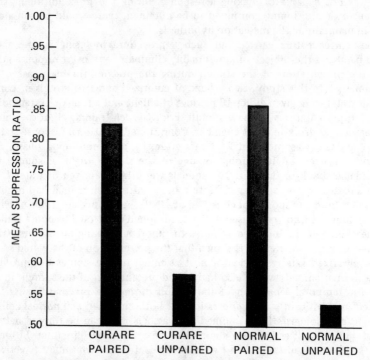

Fig. 6-3. Suppression ratios for the first test trial from rats given preconditioning in the curarized or normal state and paired or unpaired stimuli during preconditioning. (Larger ratios indicate greater suppression.) *Adapted from Cousins, Zamble, Tait and Suboski (1971)*

of presentations, will elicit an orienting response and result in only a temporary phase of increased responding.[4] Thompson has identified the nervous system process responsible for this type of responding as sensitization, a different process than that resulting from effective reinforcing stimuli.

Thompson has also assumed that contiguous experiences are to some degree retained. As he has written, "at least partial retention of contiguous experiences is a common fact in ordinary life and in the verbal learning laboratory for humans" (p. 122).

In "explaining" sensory preconditioning, Thompson has hypothesized that each of the preconditioning stimuli elicit an orienting response, all strengthened to some limited extent by presentations of each other, and that the mere contiguity of these stimuli result in their being retained and utilized during the transfer phase of the experiment. It is the sensitization process which is responsible

[4] The other side of the coin is that with continued presentation, the response which has been elicited by means of an effective stimulus declines in strength—the process underlying such response decrement has been identified as habituation.

for facilitating (or perhaps even making possible) the association of the two contiguous events.

Thompson has acknowledged that his postulation of an orienting response which is elicited by an effective stimulus could be taken as support for the mediation model. He has rejected this position, however, arguing that "the assumption that *behavioral* responses must occur to mediate learning . . . is an obsolete inheritance from early behaviorism. The evidence from many sources is now overwhelming that behavioral responses are not necessary for learning. Consequently, it is an unnecessary complication to postulate that behavioral orienting serves as a mediator for SPC [sensory preconditioning]" (p. 123). What "mediates" behavior from Thompson's point of view is the central nervous system.

Latent Inhibition

The difficulty of establishing a conditioned response that appears to result from presentation of the CS prior to the conditioning trials has led to the postulation of an inhibitory process, more specifically, latent inhibition. The presentation of the CS alone for a number of trials prior to the CS-UCS pairings is not unusual—in fact, a number of classical conditioning investigators have used this operation, known as preliminary adaptation, as a control procedure in order to be sure that the CS was not capable of eliciting the conditioned response prior to being paired with the UCS.

Two early studies by Grant and his associates (Grant, Hake, and Schneider 1948; Grant, Hake, Riopelle, and Kostlan 1951) examined the influence of these pretest trials on eyelid conditioning with humans. Findings from both experiments revealed that such trials did not effect either acquisition or extinction.

Some years later, Lubow and Moore (1959) again examined the role of pretest trials on conditioning. Goats served as subjects and received 10 nonreinforced presentations of one of two stimuli (flashing light or turning rotor) which would subsequently be used in the conditioning study. Following pretest trials, the classical conditioning procedure was instituted. Here, the animals were presented with either the pretest stimulus or a new stimulus as the CS on their first conditioning trial; a shock to the foreleg served as the UCS and elicited leg flexion. On the second trial, each subject received the signal which was not presented on the first trial. Thereafter, both signals continued to be alternated until a learning criterion of 10 CRs to each CS had been reached. The results revealed that the mean number of trials to reach the conditioning criteria for the preexposed light was 37.38; to the novel light it was just 19.75.

Unfortunately, the mean number of trials required to reach the criteria when the rotor was used as the CS (10 pretest trials vs. 0 pretest trials) was not statistically significant. Nonetheless, on the basis of their findings with the flashing light, the authors hypothesized that the pretesting or preexposure of the conditioned stimulus resulted in the establishment of an inhibitory state which interfered with subsequent conditioning. This state they identified as latent inhibition.

As Lubow's (1973) recent review has indicated, subsequent studies by him and his associates, as well as a number of other American investigators, have demonstrated the latent inhibition effect to be a reasonably robust one. It has been found using a variety of organisms, e.g., goldfish (Braud, 1971), sheep (Lubow 1965), rabbits (Lubow, Markman and Allen, 1968), and rats (Chacto and Lubow, 1967), and a number of different responses. Table 6-2 provides summaries of a sampling of these investigations.[5]

As might be anticipated, there has been interest in examining those variables which contribute to latent inhibition effects. Chief among these have been (1) the number of preexposures, (2) the time between the last nonreinforced preexposure and the beginning of acquisition, (3) the specificity of the to-be conditioned stimulus, and (4) the intensity of the preexposed stimulus.

When the influence of the number of nonreinforced preexposures on latent inhibition is examined, a fairly large number of preexposures are required to obtain the effect. Lubow's (1973) examination of many of the latent inhibition experiments has revealed only one which obtained a latent inhibition effect with less than 17 nonreinforced preexposures.

The contribution of the preexposures has been found to take place even when a fair amount of time elapses between the last nonreinforced preexposure and the beginning of the acquisition trials. Siegel (1970), for example, examining the conditioned eyelid response in the rabbit, found no significant differences in latent inhibition as a function of time of delay, namely, 0 or 24 hours. A subsequent study by James (1971), examining the CER with rats, using either a 0-, 30-, or 60-minute delay period, was also unable to find differences as a function of the temporal intervals he employed. In fact, using the same response, Carlton and Vogel (1967), and Lubow and Siebert (1969) employed a 48-hour delay between the last preexposure and the beginning of acquisition trials and continued to find the latent inhibition effect.

Some investigators have been interested in whether or not the presentation of the preexposed stimulus results in a general decrement in the subsequent conditioning trials, or whether the inhibition effect is limited only to the stimulus which has been preexposed. Experiments by Carlton and Vogel (1967), Lubow and Moore (1959), and Schnur and Ksir (1969) indicate that the inhibition is stimulus specific. For example, Schnur and Ksir (1969), in their eyelid conditioning study, preexposed subjects to a clicker prior to using a tone as a CS but did not obtain any inhibition effect.

Finally, Crowell and Anderson (1972) have demonstrated that latent inhibition is influenced by the intensity of the preexposed CS. In their study, experimental subjects, while drinking, received a preconditioning CS which consisted of white noise of either 70 or 100 db. A control group was not exposed to the noise. Following this pretest procedure, each group was subdivided into 3 groups in which they were conditioned using (1) the low or (2) the high intensity CS paired with shock, which elicited emotional responding (CER), or (3) provided

---

[5] The major discrepant note is found in a number of eyelid conditioning studies. We have already cited the early studies of Grant, Hake, and Schneider (1948) and Grant, Hake, Riopelle, and Kostlan (1951), who reported negative findings. Lubow (1973) has also reported unsuccessful eyelid conditioning experiments conducted by Allen (1967) and Schnur (1967). It should be acknowledged, however, that Schnur and Ksir (1969) have obtained positive findings.

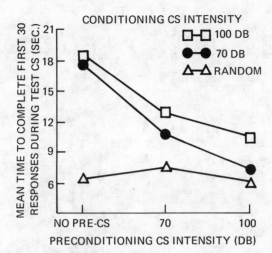

Fig. 6-4. Mean time to complete the first 30
responses as a function of preconditioning CS
intensity and conditioning CS intensity. *Adapted from Crowell and Anderson (1972)*

random presentation of the tone and shock. The following day they were returned to the operant chamber and the 70 or 100 db stimulus was presented in
order to examine its effect on suppression of the drinking response. The varying
experimental and control groups which comprised this study may be seen in
Fig. 6-4 which presents the mean time for these varying groups to complete the
first 30 responses as a function of preconditioning and conditioned intensity.
The latent inhibition effect, as influenced by the intensity of the preexposed
CS, can be readily noted.

A variety of explanations for latent inhibition have been provided. One of the
earliest was proposed by Lubow (1965) who hypothesized that the preexposed
stimulus becomes a CS for an undefined response during the preexposure period.
Presumably, the subject learns some response to the CS and it is this preexposed
stimulus-undefined response relationship which interferes with the establishment
of the to-be-learned CS-CR relationship. Lubow (1973), however, has reported
that a test using leg flexion and leg extension in sheep and goats has failed to
confirm this hypothesis.[6]

Other explanations for latent inhibition are related to the position that the
preexposure operation may (1) eliminate responses which are assumed necessary
for subsequent conditioning to take place or may (2) result in the development
of an inhibitory state. The eliminated response theory has frequently centered

[6] This position bears a marked similarity to the explanation of extinction proposed by Guthrie (1935) and Wendt (1936) which assumed that the presentation
of the CS without the UCS resulted in the elicitation of responses interfering
with the CR. In order for extinction to take place, these interfering responses
had to gain sufficient strength to preclude the appearance of the CR.

Table 6-2 Summaries of a Sampling of Latent Inhibition Studies

Investigators	Subjects Used	Characteristics of CS	Nature of UCS	Conditioned Response Examined	Results
Grant, Hake, and Schneider (1948)	Humans	Light	Air Puff	Eyeblink	Negative
Grant, Hake, Riopelle, and Kostlan (1951)	Humans	Light	Air Puff	Eyeblink	Negative
Lubow and Moore (1959)	Goats	Flashing Light, Turning Rotor	Shock	Leg flexion	Positive only when light was used as the preexposed stimulus
Suboski, DiLollo, and Gormezano (1964)	Rabbits	Tone	Air Puff	Nictitating membrane	Negative
Lubow (1965)	Goats and Sheep	Light	Shock	Leg flexion	Positive
Chacto and Lubow (1967)	Rats	Tone	Shock	Moving of tail	Positive
Carlton and Vogel (1967)	Rats	Tone	Shock	CER as measured by suppression of licking	Positive
May, Tolman, and Schoenfeldt (1967)	Rats	Tone	Shock	CER as measured by suppression of bar pressing	Positive
Lubow, Markman, and Allen (1968)	Rabbits	Exp. I: Single tone Exp. II: [Any one of 4 tones differing in db]	Shock	Pinna reflex	Positive

Study	Subjects	CS	US	Response	Outcome
Leaf, Kayser, et al (1968)	Rats	Click (Tone)	Shock	CER as measured by suppression of licking	Positive
Lubow and Siebert (1969)	Rats	Tones	Shock	CER as measured by suppression of licking	Positive
Anderson, Wolf, and Sullivan (1969)	Rats	Buzzer	Shock	CER as measured by suppression of bar pressing	Positive
Anderson, O'Farrell, Formica, and Caponigri (1969)	Rats	Buzzer	Shock	CER as measured by suppression of bar pressing	Positive
Schnur and Ksir (1969)	Humans	Tone	Air Puff	Eyeblink	Positive
Siegel (1970)	Rabbits	Tone	Shock	Eyeblink	Positive
Cohen and MacDonald (1971)	Pigeons	Light	Shock	Heart rate	Negative
Surwit and Poser (1974)	Humans	Tone	Shock	EDR	Positive (when short latency responses were used)

on the orienting response (OR) which many investigators believe is essential if conditioning is to take place. The additional conditioning trials following a pre-exposure period are necessary in order to reestablish the organism's orienting response. If the orienting response is conceptualized as a part of the attention process, this explanation is similar to a second point of view which assumes that during the preexposure period, the subject habituates or simply fails to attend to the presented stimulus. A basic tenet of this second explanation is that some inhibitory state arises as a function of the presentation of the preexposed CS.

One experimental procedure believed to throw some light on the nature of latent inhibition has been the manipulation of the preexposed stimulus in a stimulus compound which is then used in a learning task following the preexposure period. For example, in a study by Reiss and Wagner (1972) the classical conditioning of the rabbit's eyelid was undertaken with two stimuli, A and B (tone and vibration), being differentially preexposed. Cue A was presented 1380 times, cue B was presented just 12. One hundred and twenty CS-UCS trials were then presented in which a third stimulus (C) served as the CS. In a subsequent test situation, the effectiveness of cues A and B in eliciting the CR was examined by pairing each with the CS (cue C), e.g., AC or BC.

Reiss and Wagner have hypothesized that if the preexposed CS results in the learning of a new response, a response which would undoubtedly be antagonistic to any CR subsequently established, the more frequently exposed stimulus (cue A) should result in poorer conditioning when combined with cue C than a combination of the less frequently exposed stimulus (cue B) with cue C. On the other hand, if the large number of preexposures of cue A resulted in a decrease of the orienting response, or lack of attention to cue A, this cue should be less detectable than cue B, permitting cue C to exert the major influence in subsequent AC test trials. As noted in Fig. 6-5, this result was obtained. The findings indicated that conditioning was greater in the case of the more frequently preexposed A cue than in the case of the less frequently preexposed B cue.

In a subsequent study, Halgren (1974) has varied the role of the preexposed stimulus as either an S+ or an S- in a discriminated operant task. More specifically, following either 0 or 200 preexposures to a 1000 Hz tone, rats were trained on a successive discrimination task in which the tone was used as either the CS+ or CS-. Results indicated that when the tone was used as the S+, responding to the S- was poorest for the group given the 200 preexposed trials. On the other hand, when the tone was used as the S-, lack of responding to the S- was superior for the group provided the 200 preexposure trials.

Both Reiss and Wagner (1972) and Halgren (1974) have indicated that their findings are consistent with the explanation of latent inhibition in terms of attentional deficit or stimulus habituation. But if one assumes that such habituation recovers its effectiveness over time, it may be noted that fairly long time intervals have been interpolated between the last preexposure trial and the beginning of the acquisition trials with little loss in latent inhibition—a finding difficult to reconcile with an habituation explanation.

Another difficulty with the attention process position is suggested by the findings of Siegel (1969) who demonstrated the generalization of latent inhibi-

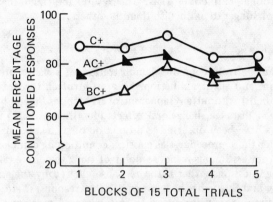

Fig. 6-5. Mean percentage conditioned eyelid responses to CS *C* and to the compounds *AC* and *BC*. *Adapted from Reiss and Wagner (1972)*

tion. Inasmuch as this construct indicates the operation of a learning process, it may be as Lubow (1973) suggests, that there is a need for a model that combines both attentional and learning constructs.

Silent Extinction

One final procedure of stimulus presentation without apparent overt responding that has been found to influence experimental extinction is termed silent extinction. Investigators are indebted to Pavlov (1927) for the discovery of this phenomenon. Pavlov found that when a conditioned response had been extinguished so that a response could no longer be elicited by the conditioned stimulus, further nonreinforced presentations of the conditioned stimulus would nonetheless serve to strengthen the extinction effect as measured by a decrement in spontaneous recovery.

Additional experimental support is found in a study by Brogden, Lipman, and Culler (1938). In this study, four dogs were conditioned to flex their right forelimb when a 1000 Hz tone which served as a CS was presented. Shock was used as the UCS. Following acquisition training, extinction trials were provided until the conditioned response could not be elicited by the presentation of the CS. Two dogs were then reconditioned, but 400 additional extinction trials were provided the other two animals prior to their being reconditioned. Reconditioning was much more readily obtained with the two animals not receiving the additional 400 extinction trials. Both groups of animals, however, were then given a sufficient number of training trials to be brought to the same acquisition criterion and then again extinguished. The two animals that had previously received 400 extra extinction trials were reconditioned immediately after they reached the extinction criterion, whereas the other two subjects were provided with 400 additional extinction trials. The results indicated that these latter two animals took longer to extinguish than the others.[7]

A Point of View

The procedures involved in the demonstration of sensory preconditioning, latent inhibition, and silent extinction, have all involved the presentation of a stimulus (or stimuli) without any apparent overt response made by the subject. And yet, in each instance, behavioral effects identified as being related to the learning process have been observed as a function of such stimulus presentation. We may consider these procedures as classical conditioning complexities, at least when viewed from a stimulus-response point of view; they have raised a number of embarrassing questions—What is the response elicited by the stimulus? What role does it play in influencing the learning of other responses? etc.

As noted, stimulus-response theorists have directed most of their attention to explanations for the sensory preconditioning findings, although the phenomena of latent inhibition and silent extinction deserve consideration as well. In any event, it may be time to acknowledge the position put forward by Thompson (1972) that the assumption that behavioral responses must occur to mediate learning is an obsolete inheritance from the early behaviorists. This does not mean that a stimulus-response analysis of behavior should not be undertaken wherever it seems efficient and useful to do so; it only means that we should stop our struggle to provide such an analysis for behavioral situations in which it is obviously not appropriate.

II. Cognitive Considerations

In 1965, Grings (1965) wrote, "It is well known that during conditioning experiments with humans Ss the S is usually trying to figure out what is going on, so that he can feel the master of the situation in which he finds himself" (p. 72). Grings's comment recognizes the position that the subject's expectancies, hypotheses, or ideas of what is taking place (or about to take place, in the experimental situation)—in brief, his cognitive structure—can play an important role in classical conditioning. The present section considers this complex variable.

The role of cognition in classical conditioning has been investigated within two contexts. The first we would like to discuss posits that classical conditioning is a type of learning situation defined only by the operations involved, for example, a behavior change arising from a CS-UCS operation. Here, cognitive variables are given the same status as other conditioning variables and are investigated in the same way. Grant's (1973) recent paper is an excellent example of this point of view.

The Role of Instructions

One way to manipulate a subject's idea about what is going on in a conditioning experiment is by means of the instructions which the experimenter

[7] The experimenters have suggested that this effect took place only for the first

provides. Thus, instructions designed to facilitate or inhibit conditioning have had a long history of experimental investigation.[8]

Early studies by Miller (1939) and Norris and Grant (1948) demonstrated that eyelid conditioning could be facilitated or inhibited by providing the subject with appropriate instructions. The more recent studies of Nicholls and Kimble (1964) and Fishbein and Gormezano (1960), using the same response, have confirmed the findings of these earlier investigators.

To illustrate the type of instructions as well as the experimental results, Nicholls and Kimble (1964) provided two groups of subjects with 40 conditioning trials, one group receiving facilitative and the other group, inhibitory instructions. The facilitative instructions were, "Relax and let your eye reactions take care of themselves. If you feel your eye close, do nothing to stop it." The inhibitory instructions indicated that the subject should "concentrate on not blinking until you feel the puff of air. That is, try not to blink after the light comes on until you feel the air puff." Fig. 6-6 reveals the percentage of conditioned responses for the two groups, clearly indicating the role of instructions in facilitating or inhibiting responding.

As might be expected, appropriate instructions can also influence experimental extinction. A study by Lindley and Moyer (1961) that examines the conditioning of finger withdrawal provides evidence of such influence. In this experiment, after reaching a conditioning criterion, four groups of subjects received different instructions just prior to extinction trials. Group 1 served as a control group and received no instructions. For Group 2, neutral instructions were provided. These merely reiterated some instructions which were provided prior to the conditioning trials, e.g., "Remember to let your finger move automatically. Whenever your finger feels like jumping up, just let it jump up." The subjects in Group 3 were told that there would be no more shock delivered on any future trials. However, they were instructed to let their finger move automatically and if it felt like jumping up, they were to let it jump up. Finally, the subjects in Group 4 were also told that there would be no more shock delivered on any of the trials. They received added instructions that they should try to prevent their finger from moving when the tone was presented. Twenty-five extinction trials were provided. Results indicated that Groups 3 and 4 had fewer conditioned responses during these trials than Groups 1 and 2. Group 4, in which subjects had instructions to try to prevent their finger from moving when the tone was presented, extinguished more rapidly than Group 3, although the difference was not statistically significant.

---

two conditioning and extinction cycles; subsequent cycles did not reveal any differential effect as a function of additional extinction trials.

[8] Experimenters not interested in examining "cognitive" variables, typically provide the subject with "neutral" instructions—instructions which are designed neither to facilitate nor inhibit the acquisition of the conditioned response. To illustrate, Gormezano and Moore (1962) in examining the conditioned eyelid response, instructed their subjects as follows: "You will see and feel a series of stimuli during the experimental session. The stimuli will consist of a light and a puff of air. Be careful not to control voluntarily your natural reactions to the stimuli. Do not try to figure out the experiment. Keep as detached an attitude as possible and simply let your reactions take care of themselves" (p. 488).

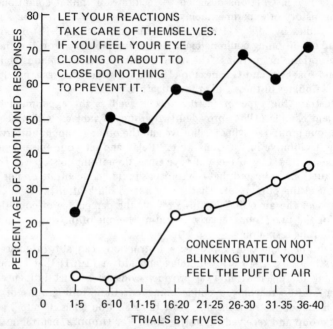

Fig. 6-6. Mean percentage of CR's for subjects conditioned with facilitative and inhibitory instructions. *Adapted from Nicholls and Kimble (1964)*

It might appear that one way to circumvent the problem of having instructions influence the course of conditioning would be to use involuntary or autonomic responses; unfortunately, this is not a viable solution since involuntary responses may be controlled or at least influenced by voluntary ones.

In one of the early experimental studies, Cook and Harris (1937) demonstrated that a "conditioned" EDR could be obtained merely by instructing the subject that electric shock (UCS) would follow a green light (CS). Their experimental findings revealed that following such instructions, the presentation of 15 or 30 conditioning trials did not increase the strength of the conditioned response beyond the strength obtained when only a single conditioning trial plus instructions were used. In a second part of this study, these investigators found that when the subjects were instructed that the shock would no longer follow the light (extinction trials), there was a marked decline of conditioning.

The contribution of facilitory and inhibitory instructions on autonomic responding has been more recently confirmed by a variety of experimenters, e.g., Wickens, Allen, and Hill (1963), Grings and Lockhart (1963), Hill (1967), Dawson and Reardon (1969) Swenson and Hill (1970), and Harvey and Wickens (1971, 1973).

Dawson and Reardon's study using the EDR illustrates the nature of these findings. Three experimental groups, (1) facilitory, (2) inhibitory, and (3) neutral, were all first given a detailed review of classical conditioning as well as a description of the CS and UCS which were to be used. In addition, the facilitory group was told that the most adaptive, sensible, and intelligent thing to do was to become conditioned, while the inhibitory group was told that the most adaptive, sensible, and intelligent thing to do was to not become conditioned. The neutral instruction group was not given a second set of the instructions. Finally, a pseudoconditioning group was merely told that a tone and a shock would be presented randomly. The experimental procedure consisted of providing the four groups of subjects with 24 acquisition trials, omitting the UCS on 8 trials (3, 5, 9, 10, 13, 15, 16, and 21). It was on these trials that response measurement was obtained. Five extinction trials immediately followed the acquisition series. Fig. 6-7 presents both the acquisition and extinction performance for the varying groups of subjects; it may be noted that the results support the general position that instructions can play an important role in the acquisition of a conditioned response.

Studies by Harvey and Wickens (1971, 1973) were undertaken in order to determine why the characteristics of the instructions should influence responding. In two experiments by Harvey and Wickens (1973), EDR conditioning was undertaken using a 1000 Hz tone as the CS and shock as the UCS. Preliminary instructions to the subjects suggested that they could control their EDR through their attitudes and, as a result, they should try to facilitate or inhibit their responses according to a visual signal the experimenters would provide on each trial. Acquisition trials, with the facilitory and inhibitory signals, were presented in a counterbalanced order. One atypical procedure which the experimenters employed was to present the UCS alone on some of the trials. Results revealed that the facilitating and inhibiting instructions influenced the magnitude of the UCR, with the facilitating instructions resulting in a higher level of responding. The authors have suggested that since the CR is a positive function of the UCS and its resulting UCR magnitude, some of the differential effects of instructions in conditioning could be understood vis-à-vis this mechanism. Precisely how UCR magnitude is influenced by instructional set, however, is not immediately obvious, although it has tentatively been proposed that instructions affect the subject's perception of the intensity of the UCS which in turn is reflected in higher responding.

Inhibitory Set

Spence (1966), in his study of eyeblink conditioning, believed that a major problem was to control, with a view toward eliminating, the influence of cognitive processes on this simple learned response. To the extent that such processes were operating in these experiments, any general finding and any principle derived therefrom was being contaminated by unknown as well as unwanted variables. In support of his point of view, Spence found that during the acquisition of the conditioned eyeblink, only 5% to 20% of his subjects were able to identify the procedure as one of conditioning. On the other hand, when extinction trials were provided, more than half of the subjects were able to recognize that this procedure was concerned with conditioning. Moreover, extinction took place very rapidly, suggesting that the subjects had instructed themselves not to

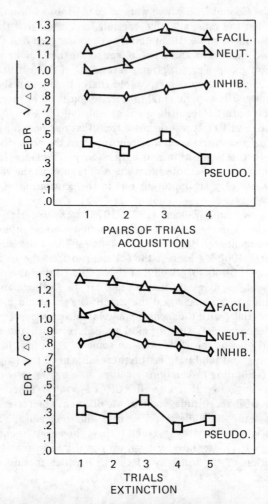

Fig. 6-7. Mean EDR magnitude on pairs
of acquisition test trials and on extinction
trials. *Adapted from Dawson and Reardon
(1969)*

respond after noting that the UCS was no longer being presented. Such findings
were in contrast to those obtained with animals, in which the extinction rate
was about the same as the rate of conditioning.

In order to reduce the subject's awareness of the conditioning procedure,
Spence, Homzie, and Rutledge (1964) used a masking task. This consisted of
instructing the experimental group that the investigator was interested in examining the effects of distraction on performance in a problem solving task. Subjects were told that following the onset of a center signal light, one of two small

lamps located on the right and left of the center light would go on. They were to indicate which lamp would be lit by pressing a button located on the right and left arms of their chairs. They were also told that distracting stimuli in the form of a tone and a puff of air would be administered between their response of pressing the button and the lighting of one of the small lamps. The onset of the tone (in reality, the CS) coincided with the turning off of the signal light. The puff of air (UCS) was presented 500 milliseconds after onset of the CS on conditioning trials and 2500 milliseconds after CS onset on extinction trials.[9] Fifty acquisition and 30 extinction trials were provided. Fig. 6-8 presents the extinction data for the experimental group and a control group which was obtained in another experiment. It may be noted that there is a relatively slow extinction rate for the experimental group; thus, responding during extinction was similar to that in conditioning trials, replicating the findings obtained with animals.

The authors have proposed that the subjects in the control condition were able to discriminate the change from acquisition to extinction which in turn led to the adoption of an inhibitory set, or more generally, a cognitive process, not to blink. This inhibitory set interfered with the conditioned response, in turn resulting in rapid extinction. When conditions were so arranged to preclude or delay the discrimination, the inhibitory set was not formed and extinction took place much more slowly.[10]

The Contribution of Awareness

The second context within which cognitive processes have been examined is the position some investigators take that in order for classical conditioning to occur, the subject must be aware of the CS-UCS contingency. From this point of view, awareness is not simply another independent variable to be manipulated; it is a condition that is necessary in order for classical conditioning to take place.

Fuhrer and Baer (1965), Baer and Fuhrer (1968), Dawson and Grings (1968), Fuhrer and Baer (1969), and Dawson (1970) are some investigators who have found that the acquisition (or nonacquisition) of a classically conditioned autonomic response is determined by whether or not the subject is aware of the CS-UCS contingency.

To illustrate the nature of these findings, Dawson and Grings (1968) informed a "classical conditioning" group of subjects that they were interested in determining the effects of distracting stimuli on a paper and pencil "speed

[9] In order to reduce the discriminability between acquisition trials and extinction trials, the procedure of these investigators was to continue presenting the UCS during extinction trials but to lengthen the CS-UCS interval to 2500 milliseconds or more. As we pointed out earlier, when the CS-UCS interval is of this length, conditioning does not take place; however, the presence of the UCS makes it more difficult for the subject to discriminate extinction trials from conditioning trials, since the presentation of the UCS is provided during both procedures.

[10] The authors (1964) have stated that the inhibitory set adopted by humans which results in rapid extinction is presumed not to apply to animals.

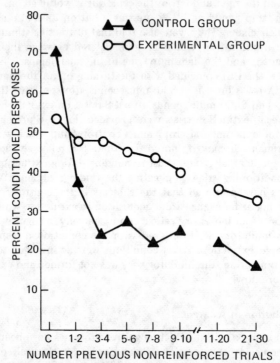

Fig. 6-8. Percentage of CRs during extinction as a function of number of previous nonreinforced trials. *Adapted from Spence, Homzie, and Rutledge (1964)*

mental test." Two tones and a shock were used as the distractors; in reality, the tones served as the CS+ and CS− in a conditioned discrimination of the EDR. A second group of "relational learning" subjects was provided the same instructions except that a pseudoconditioning procedure was used. This consisted of the single presentation of the CSs and the UCS in a random order. Following a series of acquisition trials, the relational learning group was then told to pay attention to the distractors and that, in this second series of acquisition trials, shock would sometimes, although not always, follow the positive CS. The classical conditioning group was told only to pay attention to the distractors. The additional trials were then provided. At the conclusion of the experiment, the subjects were asked to complete a questionnaire concerning their awareness of the relationship between the CS and the UCS.

For the first series of trials, the effect of the masking procedure was to produce responding in which there was no difference between the groups—conditioning was not obtained. For the second acquisition series, the relational group which was given instructions regarding the relationship between the CS and UCS revealed clear evidence of discriminative conditioned response learning, while again the classical conditioning group did not reveal conditioning. Thus, the mere pairing of CS-UCS, masked as it was by the distraction task, was not sufficient to establish differential responding in the classical conditioning group, whereas the instructions provided the relational learning group did produce such an effect.

One problem with this study was that conditioned EDRs may have been precluded in the classical conditioning group because the distracting task could have reduced the subject's awareness of the CSs. Dawson (1970) attempted to remedy this difficulty. His experimental procedure (Experiment 2) consisted of presenting 60 trials with 6 tones provided on each trial. The first tone on each trial was either 950-, 1000-, or 1050-Hz. The last 5 tones on each trial were 800-, 950-, 1000-, 1050-, and 1200-Hz presented in a random order. Subjects were instructed to perform three tasks following each trial: (1) determine which of the last 5 tones had the same pitch as the first tone, (2) determine which of the last 5 tones had the highest pitch, and finally, (3) determine which of the last 5 tones had the lowest pitch. Actually, the 1200- and 800-Hz tones served as the CS+ and CS-, with 75% reinforcement of the CS+. An aware group was told that shock would usually, but not always, follow the highest (or lowest) tone but would never follow any other tone. In contrast, an unaware group was told that shock would be presented periodically; the reason given was that the experimenter was interested in determining whether such stimulation would facilitate the subject's performance. At the end of the experiment, all subjects were administered a questionnaire which included the multiple choice question, "Shock usually followed (a) the highest tone, (b) the middle tone, (c) the lowest tone, (d) it wasn't systematic, (e) I couldn't tell."

The mean EDR discrimination scores for the aware and unaware groups are presented in Fig. 6-9. It should be noted that the measurement of the CS+ was for those trials in which the UCS did not follow the CS. These findings confirmed the earlier Dawson and Grings (1968) study in that repetitive CS-UCS pairings embedded in a masking task (which presumably reduced the occurrence of contingency learning to a chance level) were not sufficient to establish EDR conditioning. However, the same pairings embedded in the same masking task but with a single exception of providing appropriate instructions were sufficient to establish classical conditioning.

In almost all the studies conducted in this area, it has been customary for the experimenter to use some type of postexperimental questionnaire designed to ascertain whether or not the subjects were aware of any CS-UCS contingency present during the experiment. In some studies, e.g., Fuhrer and Baer (1969), the questionnaire has been used to identify subjects who became aware as well as those who were unaware of the contingency, following which the course of conditioning was noted for each of these groups. Significant differences in conditioning have been noted between subjects who can accurately verbalize the contingency and those who cannot.

In other experiments, as in the Dawson (1970) study, subjects in the unaware group who indicated an awareness as revealed by the questionnaire, have been typically omitted from the experimental analysis.

The use of a questionnaire in order to assess the amount of subject awareness

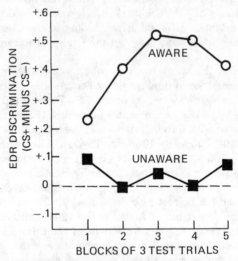

Fig. 6-9. Mean discrimination scores on blocks of test trials. *Adapted from Dawson (1970)*

has invariably aroused a certain suspicion on the part of many experimenters, as there is no assurance that the subject's report after the experiment has been concluded is a valid indicator of his cognitive behavior during the conditioning trials. Creelman (1966), summarizing a number of experimental findings in which postexperimental interviewing was provided, has reported that the more intensive the interview, the more awareness is noted on the part of the subject.

A conditioned EDR study by Dawson and Biferno (1973) is interesting because it measured awareness during the experiment in addition to using the postexperimental questionnaire. The conditioning task was identical to that used by Dawson (1970) which we have previously described. Prior to each trial, the subjects were instructed to predict the occurrence of shock by pressing one of 5 buttons positioned on a panel. The buttons were labeled from left to right: (1) certain of no shock, (2) uncertain no shock, (3) completely uncertain, (4) uncertain shock, and (5) certain shock.

Three experimental groups were used, (1) a contingent, instructed group which was informed that shock was predictable with respect to tone quality, (2) a contingent, noninstructed group which was told that shock was predictable, and (3) a noncontingent, noninstructed group which was administered shock in the same sequential order as the first two groups—however, the presentation order of the last tone was such that the highest and lowest tones were paired with shock equally often. Sixteen presentations of the CS+ and 16 presentations of the CS- were provided. Following the conditioning trials, all subjects were administered a short questionnaire which also measured awareness of the contingency.

Three major experimental findings were obtained: "First, conditioning occurred among groups of aware Ss (where awareness was defined by a concurrent measure and a postconditioning questionnaire measure) but not among groups of unaware Ss. . . . Second, conditioning failed to occur when the probability of awareness was experimentally attenuated (as indicated in the contingent-noninstructed and noncontingent-noninstructed groups) but did occur when the probability of awareness was experimentally facilitated. . . . Third, conditioning occurred only at the point in time that awareness was expressed" (pp. 60–61). Thus, the experimental evidence was clearly in keeping with the position that awareness is necessary if conditioning is to take place.[11]

Other experimenters, however, have indicated that the role of awareness is not so easily resolved. Fuhrer and Baer (1969), although they found a positive relationship between awareness and conditioning, also found that some subjects who were unable to verbalize the CS-UCS contingency revealed differential EDR conditioning.

Grant's (1973) examination of the role of awareness in eyelid conditioning resulted in his concluding that the relationship between awareness and conditioning is tenuous at best. He has called attention to the results of an early study by Hilgard and Humphreys (1938) who, in testing their subjects for retention of a conditioned discrimination many months after initial conditioning trials, found an inability on the part of these subjects to report the appropriate contingencies, although their conditioning performance was quite good. Grant's own research has been in keeping with these findings. He has written, "The poor correlation between reported awareness of CS-UCS contingencies and conditioning performance strongly suggests that this cognitive activity, at least as presently assessed, is not sufficient and may not be necessary to produce eyelid conditioning or differential eyelid conditioning" (p. 80).

Nelson and Ross's (1974) differential eyelid conditioning findings have been supportive of Grant's position. We shall not describe their procedure in detail but only point out that they were interested in examining the effects of two

[11] A reader might argue that many lower organisms that presumably have a very limited cognitive structure can be conditioned; thus, it does not seem reasonable to assume, as many of the cited studies suggest, that the presence of an awareness or cognitive attribute, is necessary for conditioning to take place. Razran (1955) made essentially this same point, writing that "primary or first-order classical conditioning . . . need not invoke cognition for its initiation and maintenance. . . . The basis for such a contention is plain. Classical conditioning is quite effective in a variety of instances in which the assumption of cognition would be patently gratuitous. Consider, for instance, the conditioning of decorticated and curarized animals, of paramaecia, of coelenterates. . ." (p. 330). Dawson (1973) has argued that neither the presence nor the absence of contingency learning can be adequately determined with animals. That is, to the extent that the existence of a contingency can be ascertained only by language, the argument is irrelevant, or as Dawson has stated, beyond the boundary conditions of the issue. He has also called attention to an interesting position of Hebb (1958), "Because a simple task could, theoretically, be handled by a simple mechanism does not mean in fact that the brain handles it that way. In an uncomplicated nervous system, yes; but in the complex brain of a higher animal other mechanisms may insist on getting into the act and turn the simple task into a complex one" (p. 453).

types of masking tasks: (1) the estimation of 2- and 5-second intervals after a tone had been presented, and (2) the viewing of a silent motion picture. They also provided their subjects with differential conditioning instructions—some subjects were told that one tone would be followed by an air puff while a second tone would not; other subjects were not given these instructions. A postexperimental questionnaire was also provided which attempted to assess the subject's awareness of the CS-UCS contingencies. Although Nelson and Ross found that subjects who were unaware of the stimulus contingencies performed more poorly than those who were aware; they also found that some subjects who were told of the contingencies prior to the beginning of the experiment revealed little differential responding. Thus, they have pointed out that an awareness of the appropriate stimulus contingencies did not contribute to a level of conditioned responding which would be expected if awareness were the only contributing variable. In this regard, their findings are in keeping with those obtained by Dawson and Biferno (1973) who concluded that human autonomic classical conditioning is not determined solely by awareness, since not all of their aware subjects exhibited EDR conditioning.

In summary, the bulk of experimental findings supports the position that awareness plays an important role in conditioning; however, further research is necessary to identify its appropriate contribution.

III. Autoshaping

This third section concerns the learning of a type of responding which utilizes classical conditioning procedures, and yet, is difficult to incorporate within a conditioned response framework. In an early series of experiments, Brown and Jenkins (1968) noted that the repeated pairings of an 8-second white keylight with the presentation of food, a Pavlovian procedure, resulted in the reliable emergence of a key peck in their experimental subjects (pigeons). Although the availability of the food was contingent upon the presentation of the lighted key, no response to the key was required in order for the food to be presented. The authors terms the emergence of this key pecking response "autoshaping."

A host of experiments have attested to the reliability of the Brown and Jenkins's (1968) findings, as well as to the generality of the process. Although pigeons have remained the favorite subject for most experimenters, autoshaping has been obtained with fish (Squier, 1969), rats (Peterson, Ackil, Frommer, and Hearst, 1972), quail (Gardner, 1969), dogs (Smith and Smith, 1971), and monkeys (Sidman and Fletcher, 1968). And in a recent experiment, Wilcove and Miller (1974) have obtained findings which suggest that a somewhat similar process can operate with humans. These latter investigators have noted an increase in the tendency of their subjects to make a lever pressing response as a function of a neutral cue temporally contiguous with the presentation of monetary reinforcement.

In view of the spontaneous emergence of the autoshaping response, it is not surprising that most experimenters have introduced controls to insure that the response arises only from an appropriate pairing of the two stimuli. In their original study, Brown and Jenkins (1968) noted that the forward presentation of light and food was necessary for the emergence of the response, and that the continued presentation of the lighted key throughout the session, in contrast with its intermittent presentation, resulted in very little responding. Moreover, they found that the location of the key near the food tray was not a critical feature, although it hastened the autoshaping process.

In a series of experiments also using pigeons as subjects, Bilbrey and Winokur (1973) utilized a number of variations of Rescorla's truly random control procedures in which the key light and the food were independently and randomly presented. Their findings, in support of Brown and Jenkins's results, revealed that the temporal pairing of the stimuli was necessary and that random presentation did not lead to the establishment of the response. They concluded that autoshaping "appears to be specific to a set of operations, namely presentation of food contingent upon the presentation of a visual stimulus" (p. 330). Gamzu and Schwam (1974), using monkeys as subjects, have also noted that when the delivery of food pellets was not paired with the presentation of a lighted key, but, rather, was equally probable during each second of the trial as well as during the intertrial interval, the key press response was not acquired.

Considerable interest has arisen as to whether autoshaping should be assumed to fit in a classical or an instrumental conditioning paradigm. It is obvious that the operation of the pairing of two stimuli one of which can be considered a UCS, is an example of Pavlov's procedure. Moreover, the pecking response of the pigeon at the key bears a marked similarity to the consummatory response of pecking at the grain, a second point which has been used to argue that autoshaping arises as a result of the temporal pairing of the two stimuli.

But an argument has also been made for considering autoshaping an instrumental or operant procedure, since the characteristics of the response change as trials continue. As Moore (1973) has written, ". . . autoshaped pecks look identical to those seen in operant conditioning experiments and arise through a similar progression of stages" (p. 160). These stages have been noted by Brown and Jenkins (1968) who, using direct observation and motion pictures, have noted the existence of three stages in the emergence of the key peck; first, a general increase in the pigeon's activity, particularly when the key is lighted; second, a progressive centering of movements around the area of the key when lighted, and finally, pecking movements in the direction of the key.

Moore (1973) has recently argued for the Pavlovian interpretation of autoshaping. He has reasoned that if water rather than food were used as reinforcement, according to a Pavlovian interpretation, the subject's response to the key should mirror the drinking rather than the eating response, and this is what has been found. Using films of key responses autoshaped with food and also water, Jenkins and Moore found that (as reported by Moore, 1973) judges were able to identify those key responses which were made when water was used as reinforcement in contrast to those responses made when food was used as reward. In commenting on this study, Moore (1973) wrote, "The judges characterized the food responses as sharp, vigorous pecks, whereas the birds auto-shaped with water were said to make slower, more sustained contact with the key, of ten accompanied by swallowing movements" (p. 161). Moreover, it was found that when birds were run under both food and water deprivation, and autoshaped with two stimuli, one stimulus paired with food and the other paired with water, responding to each stimulus mirrored the response to the type of reinforcement with which the stimulus had been paired.

Other support for the Pavlovian interpretation is found in a study by Williams and Williams (1969). In their experiment, the presentation of an illuminated key for 6 seconds was followed by the presentation of food for 4 seconds. Instead of the pigeon's key peck turning off the light and being followed by reinforcement, a negative response contingency was introduced. Here, when the lighted key was pecked, the peck turned off the key light and food was not presented. The authors report that substantial responding took place despite the negative correlation between pecking and reinforcement. If the key pecking response was controlled by its consequences—the omission of food—it might be assumed that the pigeon would soon stop pecking, which, of course, was not the case. On the other hand, if the autoshaping phenomenon was Pavlovian, omission-type training should merely weaken the tendency to respond by introducing a kind of partial reinforcement procedure. The authors report that substantial responding took place despite the negative correlation between pecking and reinforcement.

But there is some experimental evidence that is difficult to assimilate within the Pavlovian interpretation. Although Williams and Williams (1969) were able to show that negative contingencies did not eliminate their subjects' key pecking response, Gamzu and Schwam (1974) were unable to confirm this finding when squirrel monkeys were used as subjects. That is, the introduction of a negative response dependency resulted in a very rapid reduction of key pressing. Moreover, as Sidman and Fletcher (1968) demonstrated, the topography of the monkey's key pressing response, obtained by the repeated pairing of a lighted key and the presentation of a food pellet, is much different from its consummatory response, a finding which would be expected with instrumental learning.

Finally, Bilbrey and Winokur (1973) were unable to obtain autoshaping in the pigeon when a 1000 Hz tone was used as the stimulus which preceded the presentation of food. As they have stated, ". . . we do know that various investigators have been able to use stimuli such as hissing noises, electric fans, metronomes, bells, buzzers, lights, colored paper, and geometrical forms as conditioned stimuli, and that according to the traditional accounts of respondent conditioning, most organisms seem indifferent as to which stimuli are used" (p. 331). Thus, the failure of the tone to serve as a conditioned stimulus seemed most unusual, and not in keeping with traditional Pavlovian findings.

It does not seem possible, at least at this time, to state whether autoshaping can be considered an example of either classical or instrumental (operant) conditioning. Possibly, it should be identified as different from either of these; additional research is obviously needed before an appropriate classification can be made.

Physiological Factors

In an effort to understand more fully the nature of classical conditioning, thus providing additional information on the characteristics of the events that can serve as conditioned and unconditioned stimuli, the final section of this chapter examines the role of the central nervous system. A simplified version of the physiological components involved in classical conditioned responses is illustrated in Fig. 6-10. Here it may be noted that both the CS and UCS involve (1) a sensory component which includes the sense organ and afferent nerve fibers, (2) motor components of the CR and UCR which include the efferent nerve fibers as well as specific effectors, and (3) spinal and cortical components which connect the afferent and efferent pathways.

Three questions related to our overall concern have been asked most frequently. The first is whether or not stimulation directly applied to the cortex, and in turn eliciting a response, can serve as an effective UCS. In such an instance, the UCS afferent and spinal pathways (B and B') are effectively eliminated.

The second question is whether or not stimulation directly applied to the cortex can serve as an effective CS. In such a case, the CS afferent and spinal pathways (A and A') are eliminated.

The third question is, will CS-UCS presentations result in conditioning even though the muscle involved in making the response (UCR) is immobilized either by means of drugs or by damaging the efferent nerve fibers. In such a case, when the effects of the drug wear off or when the nerve fibers have been regenerated, the conditioned response should be elicited by the CS.

Electrical Stimulation Used as the UCS

Can conditioning take place when stimulation of the cortex serves as the UCS? One of the earliest investigators examining this question was Loucks (1933), who was able to produce a leg flexion response (UCR) by directly stimulating the sigmoid gyrus of the dog (UCS). Conditioning was attempted by pairing a 1.0-second buzzer (CS) with such electrical stimulation (UCS) that the .1-second UCS terminated simultaneously with the CS. Twenty conditioning trials were provided each day for a period of approximately two months. In spite of this prolonged training, Loucks was unable to obtain any indication of conditioning and concluded that direct electrical stimulation of the motor cortex could not serve as the UCS.

The subsequent studies of Gantt and Loucks (1938), Loucks and Gantt (1938), and Brogden and Gantt (1942) did indicate that successful conditioning with central nervous system stimulation serving as the UCS could take place. Considerable doubt was raised concerning these positive findings, however; they were attributed to the fact that the electrical stimulation used was quite intense and there was the suspicion that such stimulation spread to sensory pathways. Moreover, as Grossman (1967) has written, a large number of studies undertaken during this period confirmed the earlier findings of Loucks.

Doty (1961) has, however, reported that Giurgea was successful in demonstrating conditioning when direct electrical stimulation to the brain served as the UCS. Doty and Giurgea (1961) using dogs, cats, and monkeys as subjects have confirmed Giurgea's previous findings.

In Giurgea's experiments (as reported by Doty, 1961) both the CS and UCS

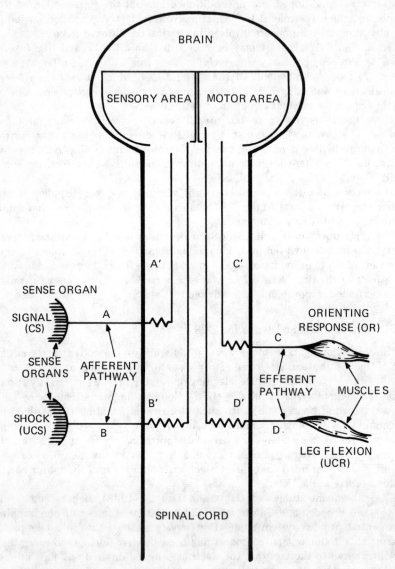

Fig. 6-10. Schematic diagram revealing afferent and efferent pathways involved in conditioning.

were applied directly to the cortex. The CS was electrical stimulation applied to the occipital area while the UCS was electrical stimulation to the sigmoid gyrus. Dogs, used in all experiments, were given 6 to 10 CS-UCS pairings each day at 3- to 5-minute intervals. Results with the first dog are typical of those obtained with the 30 animals which served as subjects. The cortical UCS produced an abrupt inclination of the head down 90°, then a slower rotation up to the right, with the right cheek up and a turning of the forequarters to the right. For the first 18 presentations of the CS, there was no response. However, by trials 35 to 42, the CS elicited a definite movement of the head to the right in 7 of the 8 presentations. The following day this CR of turning the head to the right took place in 18 of 21 trials.[12]

Another successful demonstration of the use of electrical stimulation as a UCS was reported by Segundo et al (1959), using cats as subjects. Electrical stimulation of the rostral or midbrain reticular formation was used as the UCS. The UCR was a stereotyped head-turning or cowering response. A tone served as the CS. The CS was first presented alone until all of the orienting responses and EEG arousal reactions had become habituated. CS-UCS pairings were then provided until the CS elicited a clear motor response 100% of the time—a result which required from 60 to 600 trials.

Aside from the empirical demonstration that it is possible to establish a conditioned response in which brain stimulation is used as the UCS, one might ask if such a finding has any theoretical significance. Doty (1961) has hypothesized that the establishment of a conditioned response based only upon a temporal association between the CS and the UCS suggests that learning can take place without motivation.

A basic objection to this point of view, however, has arisen from the experimental studies of Wagner, Thomas, and Norton (1967) and Thomas (1971). Wagner et al have pointed out that in a study by Doty and Giurgea (1961), also reporting successful conditioning, several subjects were trained to press a lever for continuous food reinforcement so that motivational effects of the cortical UCS might be examined. It was on the basis of Doty and Giurgea's failure to observe any subsequent increment or decrement in the rate of lever pressing when the cortical UCS was made contingent upon each press, that Doty and Giurgea concluded there was no motivation involved in the formation of conditioned responses by cortical stimulation.

In the Wagner, Thomas, and Norton (1967) study, dogs were used as subjects with a CS of a 1000 Hz tone and a 5 per second train of clicks. The UCS was electrical stimulation to the sigmoid gyrus. Conditioning sessions involved 20 to 30 training trials with an intertrial interval of 3, 4, or 5 minutes. CS duration was 2 seconds and when paired with the UCS, preceded the latter by 1 second, with the two sources of stimulation terminating together. Two test trials which consisted of presentation of only the CS were included in all conditioning sessions.

Stimulation through one pair of electrodes produced a lifting of the right hind leg while similar stimulation through another pair produced a discrete flexion of the right foreleg.

The results revealed that the percentage of anticipatory foreleg flexions to the CS increased from 0% to almost 100% over 25 daily training sessions. However, more compelling evidence of conditioning was provided by differentiation training in which the subject was taught to make a particular response to one CS and a different response to the other CS when both CSs were presented within

[12] Loucks's (1933) inability to obtain positive findings has been accounted for by the fact that he used intertrial intervals ranging from 30 to 120 seconds; Giurgea found that if the CS were applied at intervals of 2 minutes or less the CR disappeared in most, although not all, of his subjects.

the same acquisition session. Thus the authors confirmed the general principle that skeletal behavior could be modified as a consequence of a classical conditioning regimen in which a cortical UCS was employed. They noted, however, that an outstanding feature of the findings was the variability in the behavioral changes observed.

The experimenters noted that on several occasions during advanced stages of training, the subject was exposed to a UCS which was not paired with a CS. In such instances, two of the three subjects gave responses which appeared markedly more abrupt and vigorous than usual and less well integrated into their ongoing behavior. In fact, one subject occasionally lost its balance and fell against its restraint when presented with such UCSs. On the basis of such observations it appeared reasonable to assume that a particular kind of "motivation" was involved. More specifically, Wagner et al (1967) believed that some instrumental contingency might have a role in the conditioning situation. Thus it seemed possible that the subject, upon receiving the CS, could adopt a postural adjustment which served to minimize the abruptness or forcefulness of the UCR and partially, to mitigate any noxiousness that might be associated with this response. The authors did not think that the UCS was itself noxious nor that the UCR was grossly aversive. They suggested only that when the subject was faced, on trial after trial of conditioning, with making either a UCR or a CR-modified UCR, he "chooses to make the latter and that it is the acquisition of such instrumental behavior that have been previously interpreted as simple contiguous conditioning."[13]

In an effort to demonstrate the "motivating" characteristics of the response, Wagner, Thomas, and Norton (1967) conducted a second experiment. Here, the subject was allowed to press either of two panels which were reinforced by the receipt of food. On a relatively unpredictable schedule, the pressing of one panel resulted in the presentation of only the UCS, whereas the pressing of the second panel was followed by the CS-UCS relationship. Thus the subjects working for food were permitted to choose, according to which panel was pressed, to receive the UCS in isolation or to have its occurrence announced by the CS. Inasmuch as the receipt of the CS presumably permitted the subject to make a preparatory response, the subject was essentially allowed to choose between making a UCR or a CR-modified UCR. Results revealed that the animals chose to respond to the panel in which the CS-UCS pairing was provided. The authors have posited that the systematic adjustment of panel preferences to the prevailing UCS or CS-UCS contingencies implies a source of motivation which is manipulable through the auditory CS and the cortical UCS. If such motivation is sufficient

[13] Doty (1961) and Doty and Giurgea (1961) have considered the possibility that CRs in this situation might be motivated or instrumentally rewarded. Doty (1961) has written, "It could be argued that the CR's were a postural preparation to lessen the forcefulness of the UR" (p. 411). He has rejected this possibility by pointing out that ". . . in the great majority of cases the leg was lifted several centimeters in the CR, then returned to the floor and in no way appeared to alter the course of the UR" (p. 411). In some cases it was found that the CR occurred in the 'wrong' limb. The abrupt postural reversal necessitated by the occurrence of the 'wrong' limb CR, Doty has indicated, provided "further evidence that 'purposiveness' and 'preparation' are not adequate explanations for the CR's observed" (p. 411).

to exercise the observed control over panel pressing behavior, it is also reasonable to assume that it may influence the modification of skeletal behavior resulting from a classical conditioning regimen with the same CS and UCS. Thus these results are consistent with the proposition that the UCR is at least mildly aversive and that subjects will prefer to make a CR-modified UCR as compared to a UCR alone. On the basis of these findings the authors have suggested that the inability of Loucks to obtain conditioning was a result of his suspending his subjects in a hammock, thus reducing the utility of a preparatory response.

Thomas (1971) attempted to provide a further test of the hypothesis that the postural adjustments serve as a source of motivation. More specifically, manipulation of the posture of subjects was performed during a conditioning experiment.

This experimental manipulation was based on a premise regarding the value of a postural preparatory response under different required postures. When a dog is standing on all four limbs and one limb is lifted, in order to remain upright, the animal must shift its center of gravity toward th remaining sources of support—the remaining limbs. If the limbs are widely separated, a grosser weight shift is required than if the limbs are narrowly spaced. It is reasonable to assume that the grosser the shift required, the greater the utility of or incentive for a preparatory postural adjustment. Thus, it might be expected that subjects required to adopt the stance in which the limbs are widely separated would show greater conditioning than subjects required to adopt a narrow stance. The results of Thomas's study revealed that dogs required to make a large postural adjustment to the UCS evidenced greater conditioning than dogs not required to make large postural adjustments. Such data were at least consistent with the hypothesis that anticipatory CRs have a preparatory function, serving to modify the UCR in a manner that allows the subject to maintain balance when forced to make a leg flexion by the UCS.

Electrical Stimulation Used as the CS

It will be recalled that our second question dealt with whether or not stimulation to the brain could act as a CS. Unlike the controversy that surrounds the use of electrical stimulation as the UCS, most investigators have agreed that electrical stimulation can serve as a CS in the classical conditioning experiment. Early studies by Loucks (1933, 1935, 1938) revealed that stimulation in a variety of cortical areas could serve as a CS for the conditioning of limb flexion as well as salivation.

A series of investigations by Doty and his collaborators (Doty, Rutledge, and Larsen, 1956 and Doty and Giurgea, 1961) have verified Loucks's findings. In brief, the available experimental evidence unequivocally supports the position that the afferent circuit of the conditioned stimulus can be eliminated provided that comparable cortical effects can be substituted.

Is the UCR Necessary for Conditioning?

The third question to be examined is whether or not a conditioned response can be established even though training may prevent the response from actually being made. Typically, such response prevention takes place through the action of a drug or calculated damage to the appropriate nerve fibers.

The most frequently used drug in this area of research has been curare or one of its substitutes, D-tubocurarine or flaxedil.

The history of investigative work with curare began with an experiment by Harlow and Stagner (1933) studying pupillary conditioning and instrumental avoidance learning in curarized cats and dogs. Unfortunately, contradictory or controversial results at best were obtained. Presumably one of the problems in this study, as well as in others, arose from the fact that the curare utilized by early investigators produced dissociative or amnesic effects.

By using the curare substitutes of flaxedil and D-tubocurarine, it is possible to produce a complete flaccid skeletal paralysis without the dissociative or amnesic effects. Thus, the more recent studies by Gerall and Obrist (1962), Solomon and Turner (1962), and Leaf (1964) using these drugs all have indicated that, although the response may be prevented during the CS-UCS presentation, conditioning can take place.

In the Solomon and Turner (1962) study, dogs were first trained to avoid shock in response to the offset of a light. The avoidance response was the pressing of a panel while the shock was 4 ma in intensity and applied to the animal's foot pads. The time interval between signal onset and shock onset was 10 seconds. If the correct response occurred during this time interval, no shock was given and the signal was terminated. Following the period in which the animals were reliably pressing the panel in response to the signal with response latencies of 3 seconds or less, they were totally paralyzed by injections of D-tubocurarine. While the animals were completely immobilized, a Pavlovian discriminative conditioning session was carried out.

Two stimuli were used, a CS+ in which one tone was paired with shock and a CS- in which a second tone was never paired with shock. The positive (or negative) tone was 160 Hz while the other tone was 1200 Hz. Subjects were given 99 conditioning trials.

Following this conditioning session, the animals were given 48 hours in which to recover from the various physiological side effects of the drug. They were then returned to the training situation in a normal, undrugged state and the previously used stimuli were presented. The latency of panel pressing responses was recorded during these tests of the efficacy of the three stimuli. The dogs responded in a way consistent with their discriminative Pavlovian conditioning experience under curare. There were frequent panel presses in response to the first stimulus used in the original conditioning as well as in response to the positive stimulus in the discriminative conditioning situation. Very few responses were made to the negative stimulus.

A subsequent study by Leaf (1964) has confirmed the Solomon and Turner (1962) results. Leaf believed that, as a result of the curare, discriminative pairing of the CSs with shock may have elicited covert discriminative tendencies on the part of the dogs, causing them to perform the motor pattern learned previously for shock escape, and that such discriminative tendencies may have contributed to the transfer results obtained. To eliminate this possibility, Leaf's experiment carried out discriminative fear conditioning under D-tubocurarine paralysis prior to avoidance training.

The instrumental avoidance training which followed the Pavlovian conditioning session consisted of a visual stimulus produced by the darkening of two
40-watt bulbs that illuminated the side of the box in which the subjects stood at
the onset of the trial. A two-compartment shuttle box was used in the avoidance
training situation—it was necessary for the animal to jump to the next compartment in order to avoid shock. Following training, extinction transfer tests were
provided in which subjects were given test presentations of the tonal CSs used in
the Pavlovian conditioning procedure. Results revealed that all subjects responded
more quickly to the C+ (the CS that had been paired with shock during curarization) than to the C– (the discriminative contrasting stimulus that had not been
paired with shock). These results demonstrated that avoidance responding could
be discriminatively evoked by classically conditioned fear when (1) this fear was
conditioned prior to the acquisition of an instrumental avoidance habit, (2) this
fear was conditioned during complete skeletal paralysis, and (3) the conditioning
took place in an environmental background different from that in which avoidance responding took place.

Another procedure used in examining the role of overt responding in classical
conditioning has been to prevent the motor response by damaging the efferent
nerve which conducts impulses to the muscle. In an early study, Light and Gantt
(1936) crushed the motor nerves of the rear leg of a dog, following which they
"conditioned" the animal by using a buzzer as the CS and administering shock
(UCS) to the foot of the same leg. It was observed that the UCR could not be
made. After recovery of the damaged motor nerve, the animals were tested with
the CS and the conditioned response of leg lifting took place.

More than 20 years later, Beck and Doty (1957) trained cats by providing
550 to 750 trials in which a 2-second tone was paired with a .2-second shock
which elicited a flexion of the cat's right forelimb. During such training, the
animals were completely immobilized with bulbocapnine which resulted in
complete elimination of flexion in response to the shock. This drug produces
a cataleptic state so that movements to the UCS or other moderately noxious
stimuli are entirely lacking for several hours. When the animals were tested 5
days after completion of training, they were found to be thoroughly conditioned.

Although no perceptible limb movements occurred during training, according
to the authors, the objection could still be raised that even undetected movement
might have contributed significantly to the conditioning process. In order to
counter this criticism and to eliminate unequivocally the possibility of imper-
ceptible limb movements during training, a hind limb on the animals was de-
efferented by crushing the central roots controlling limb movement. Seven
hundred fifty trials were then provided the animal placed in the bulbocapnine
cataleptic state. When tested in the normal state following recovery, the subjects
again revealed conditioning.

Summary

A basic assumption made by stimulus-response theorists is that, in order for
classical conditioning to take place, the organism must make an overt response
during the conditioning trials. A number of different experimental situations
have demonstrated, however, that the presentation of the stimulus without overt

responding can influence conditioning. These situations have been designated as (1) sensory conditioning, (2) latent inhibition, and (3) silent extinction. With sensory preconditioning, a pair of stimuli, for example, light and tone, are presented to the subject, with one of these, e.g., light, serving as the CS in a subsequent conditioning experiment. It has been consistently shown that after such conditioning, the second stimulus, e.g., tone, is capable of eliciting the conditioned response.

A frequently noted explanation is found in terms of a mediated response hypothesis. The stimuli used in the preconditioning phase elicit a common (and unobservable) response which has stimulus characteristics; it is this response which mediates the connection between the stimulus not used in the conditioning phase of the study and the CR. There have been problems in identifying the nature of this mediating response and other explanations for sensory preconditioning have been sought. The second situation, latent inhibition, refers to a process inferred from a procedure in which the CS is preexposed—presented to the subject on a number of occasions prior to use in the conditioning experiment. Such preexposure results in a slower occurrence of conditioning. A number of variables have been demonstrated to influence this latent inhibition effect, including intensity of the CS, number of presentations, etc. Habituation of the preexposed CS has been posited to explain this phenomenon and some experimental findings have been obtained which are compatible with this explanation. One difficulty is that, if the preexposed stimulus does habituate, it should recover its effectiveness over time; yet this finding has not been obtained. Long intervals of time interpolated between the exposure of the stimulus and the conditioning trials have not resulted in diminishing the latent inhibition effect.

The third classification of experimental situations is silent extinction. Pavlov, as well as contemporary experimenters, has found that when a CR is extinguished so that additional responses could not be elicited by the presentation of the CS, additional nonreinforced presentations of the CS would, nonetheless, serve to strengthen the extinction effect as measured by a decrement in spontaneous recovery.

The effect of cognition on classical conditioning has also interested investigators. They have approached this problem area in two ways. One has been to examine cognitive variables in the same way as other conditioning variables. Within such a framework, the role of instructions has been investigated, with experimental evidence indicating that instructions designed to facilitate or inhibit conditioning result in such an effect during the conditioning sessions.

The second approach used to study cognition has been to assume that the human organism must be aware of the CS-UCS contingency if conditioning is to take place. Experimental studies in this area have been concerned with providing the subject instructions which do or do not indicate the nature of the contingency, and noting if conditioning can take place. Contemporary studies have indicated that the knowledge of the CS-UCS contingency appears to be a basic factor in the establishment of EDR conditioning with human subjects, although it has been found that merely because he is aware of the contingency, does not necessarily mean that the subject will be conditioned.

Our last topic centers around the role of physiological components in classical conditioning. Three questions have been raised: (1) Can stimulation which is directly applied to the cortex and which in turn elicits a response serve as an effective UCS? (2) Can stimulation which is directly applied to the cortex serve as an effective CS? (3) Will CS-UCS presentations result in conditioning even though the muscle involved in making the response (UCR) is immobilized either by using drugs or by damaging the efferent nerve fibers? The answer to all of these questions has been "yes." That is, experimenters have demonstrated that electrical stimulation applied to the brain can serve either as an effective CS or UCS (depending upon the locus of stimulation), while it has also been shown that CS-UCS presentations made when the organism has been immobilized by curare do result in conditioning after recovery.

7
Instrumental Learning:
Introduction

About the time that Pavlov was investigating the conditioned response, Thorndike (1898) undertook a series of experiments in which cats and dogs learned to escape from a puzzle box in order to obtain food which was visible but had been placed on the outside of the apparatus. The box was so constructed that it was necessary for the animal to press a latch or pull a looped string which would open the door and permit access to the reward. After obtaining the reward, the animal would be returned to the apparatus for another trial. Examination revealed that when the animal was placed in the box for the first time, it displayed much trial and error behavior. Eventually, it made a response which opened the door, enabling it to secure the reward. On subsequent trials, it was observed that the animal's activity was usually centered around that part of the box where the successful response was made. With continued trials, the irrelevant and erroneous responses dropped out so that the animal performed the correct response almost as soon as it was placed in the box.

A second kind of learning task employed by psychologists around the turn of the century was the maze, first utilized by Small (1899, 1900) who built a 6′ × 8′ reproduction of the famous maze at Hampton Court in England. The maze was constructed of wire mesh placed on a wooden floor. Like Thorndike, Small found that the amount of time it took his subjects (rats) to go from the entrance to the middle of the maze where they found food decreased as a function of the number of trials which were given.[1] Early investigators were interested only in describing the behavior that took place in these situations; eventually description was replaced with an interest in the "why" of the behavior. That is, experimenters became interested in how specific responses could be strengthened as a function of the manipulation of environmental variables. Concomitant with this approach was the assumption that a task in which the organism had only to make a relatively simple response such as traversing a runway or pressing a lever was the most effective means of pursuing this interest, since the strengthening of such responses could be readily measured.

In 1940, Hilgard and Marquis (1940) characterized the kinds of learning situations we have described as instrumental conditioning. The distinguishing feature of these tasks was that the organism received reward (or escape from noxious stimuli) only after a "correct" response had been made. As Hilgard and Marquis (1940) have written, "When the occurrence of the reinforcement [reward] is contingent upon the organism's behavior the procedure may be termed *instrumental conditioning*. . ." (p. 51).

The instrumental learning task has been also designated as operant conditioning—a term originally used by Skinner (1938). Skinner believed that many responses made by organisms were not elicited by identifiable stimuli and he designated such responses as operant. These responses, Skinner stated, operated on the environment. For instance, if a rat is placed in a Skinner box for the first time and the experimenter notes that it presses the bar during its confinement, such a response would be designated as operant, since no stimulus in the box could be identified as responsible for eliciting the bar press. The major feature related to the strengthening of an operant response, Skinner posited, was the contingency between making such a response and securing reinforcement.

It should not be assumed, however, that operant responses cannot acquire relationships to prior stimulation. The presentation of a tone in the Skinner box could be used as a signal or cue to the animal that the pressing of the bar would result in reinforcement. In this case, we have a discriminated operant, since the tone becomes an *occasion* for the bar pressing response; however, the tone does not elicit the response in the sense that the UCS elicits the UCR in the case of classical conditioning.

Inasmuch as reward is contingent upon the organism's response in both instrumental and operant tasks, some experimenters have used the terms interchangeably; others have not. Some investigators, like Ferster (1953a) have indicated that the operant should be defined as a response which takes only a short time to occur and leaves the animal in the same place ready to respond

---

[1] It is interesting to note that the use of the white rat as a subject for psychological experiments began with the experiments of Small (1899).

again. According to Dinsmoor (1966), the term operant has been almost exclusively restricted to work making use of the techniques that Skinner developed for investigating this type of behavior.

Instrumental Learning Tasks

We should like to describe briefly some of the more frequently used instrumental learning tasks. We can classify them primarily on the basis of (1) whether or not some discriminative response must be made by the organism, although (2) the kind of response must also be considered.

Nondiscriminative Tasks—the Runway and the Skinner Box

The task required of the organism in the runway (usually the white rat) is to leave a starting box, locomote down a straight (sometimes L-shaped) alley or runway, and enter a goal box in order to secure reward or escape from shock. The basic datum is time, as measured by (1) the animal's latency of leaving the starting box, or (2) the time required to traverse the length of the entire runway or some part of it.

A second type of nondiscriminative task is the Skinner box illustrated in Fig. 7-1 and Fig. 7-2. When rats are used as subjects, the task generally consists of the animal's learning to press a bar resulting in delivery of the reward to a receptacle placed near the manipulandum. A similar type of apparatus has been used with pigeons; however, plastic discs are placed on one wall of the apparatus

Fig. 7-1. A close-up of the experimental chamber used with the rat or small squirrel monkey. *Courtesy of the Grason-Stadler Company, Inc.*

Fig. 7-2. The operant conditioning apparatus used with the pigeon programming and recording equipment are not shown. *Courtesy of the Grason-Stadler Company, Inc.*

and the pigeon must learn to peck at these in order to obtain reward. The Skinner box differs from many other learning tasks in that, after the subject has made a response, the subject remains in essentially the same place ready to respond again. As we have described them, the runway and the Skinner box can be categorized as nondiscriminative tasks, since the organism is not presented with two (or more) stimuli and required to discriminate, with a response to just one being followed by reward. (This does not mean that these pieces of apparatus cannot be converted into a discriminative task for the organism. We shall note such a conversion in the next section.) With these nondiscriminative tasks, the experimenter is interested in examining the "strengthening" of a particular response, e.g., locomotion, bar pressing, or pecking, as measured by decreased latency or increased frequency of responding.

Discrimination Tasks

The discrimination task requires that the organism make a choice between two (or more) stimuli in order to secure reward or to escape or avoid aversive stimulation. A variety of discrimination tasks have been used. With rats, simple T-mazes, discrimination boxes, or jumping stands are most frequently employed. Usually these types of apparatus provide the animal with two discriminanda, e.g., a black and a white card, with a response to one of them being associated with reward and response to the other stimulus associated with no reward or with noxious stimulation.

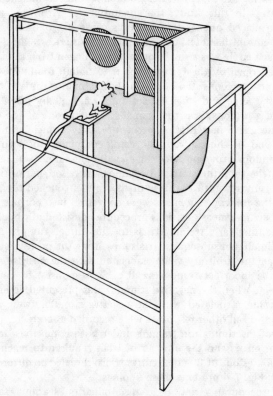

Fig. 7-3. One model of the Lashley jumping stand. The positive card falls over when the rat jumps against it, giving access to the food table. The negative card is locked and after jumping to it the animal falls into the net.

With discrimination tasks, it is possible for the discriminanda to be presented successively or simultaneously. With the simultaneous procedure two (or more) stimuli are presented at the same time and the subject must choose between (or among) them. Thus, the simultaneous presentation of a black and white stimulus card to a rat in a jumping stand would illustrate this procedure. Fig. 7-3 presents a Lashley jumping stand which has been used to study discrimination problems. Here, jumping to the correct stimulus would result in reinforcement; a response to the incorrect stimulus would not. The successive presentation procedure consists of presenting only a single stimulus on each trial; here, there is the presentation of the correct stimulus on some trials and the incorrect stimulus on others. The animal learns to respond with a very short latency when the correct stimulus is presented; latencies are much longer with the presentation of the incorrect stimulus card. If the animal's latency exceeds some arbitrary time period which has been designated by the experimenter, the trial is terminated.

A study by Grice (1949) illustrates both simultaneous and successive presentation procedures. In this study, the apparatus was a runway, at the end of which could be placed one or two stimulus cards. On one card a white circle was painted, 5 cm. in diameter; on the other card there was an 8-cm. circle. In the center of each circle was a small square door, hinged from the top. This door could be pushed open by the rat enabling it to obtain food. The simultaneous presentation procedure consisted of placing both stimulus cards at the end of the runway, with the large and small circles appearing equally often on each side. The criterion of a response was the animal's touching one of the doors with its nose. In the successive presentation procedure, only a single stimulus card was placed at the end of the runway, the cards containing the two circles being presented in random order on successive trials. The latency of responding was measured from the time the starting box door was raised, permitting the animal to traverse the runway, until the nose of the animal touched the goal box door at the end of the runway. Latencies were converted into correct and incorrect responses (probability) measures. This procedure consisted of obtaining arbitrary latency values during early training trials for the animals running to the positive and negative stimuli. On subsequent trials presenting the positive stimulus, latencies greater than the arbitrary value associated with the positive stimulus were considered to be incorrect responses—all other responses, of course, were recorded as correct. When the negative stimulus was presented, latencies less than the arbitrary value associated with the negative stimulus, were considered as incorrect responses—all other responses were recorded as correct.

The results of discrimination training under both conditions, in terms of the total number of errors and the number of trials required to reach a criterion of 18 correct responses out of 20 consecutive trials, revealed no differences between the two groups. Fig. 7-4 presents these findings.[2]

A second procedural variation in discrimination learning tasks concerns whether a correction or noncorrection procedure be used. With the noncorrection procedure, when the organism makes an incorrect response, it is confined in the goal box (which does not contain reinforcement) for a specified period of time. When the correction procedure is employed, although the animal may make an incorrect response (the error is recorded), the incorrect goal box door is locked, resulting in the animal's return to the choice point and selecting the other stimulus. The trial ends when the animal makes a correct response and secures reward in the positive goal box.

Discrimination learning in monkeys has been studied most extensively with the Wisconsin General Test Apparatus illustrated in Fig. 7-5. The animal responds by displacing one of the two stimulus-objects covering the food wells in the tray before him. An opaque screen separates the monkey and the stimulus situation between trials, and there is a one-way vision screen between the monkey and the

[2] Although Grice's (1949) results revealed no difference in learning between the two procedures, such findings appear to be specific to the particular experimental procedures used. Erickson and Lipsitt (1960) had children learn a three-stimulus discrimination problem using the successive and simultaneous procedures. In contrast to Grice, they found that the simultaneous procedure resulted in superior learning.

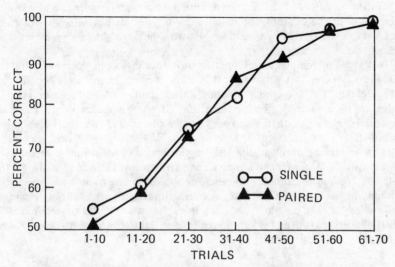

Fig. 7-4. Group learning curves for the two experimental conditions. *Adapted from Grice (1949)*

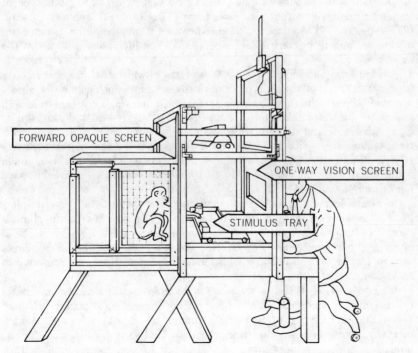

Fig. 7-5. Wisconsin General Test Apparatus. *Adapted from Harlow (1949)*

experimenter during trials. Simple discrimination tasks require the monkey to choose one of the two objects, which differ in multiple characteristics (a green square vs. a red triangle) and which shift from left to right in a predetermined order.

Two types of complex discrimination problems have been examined using the Wisconsin General Test Apparatus; they have been designated as (1) oddity and (2) matching. With the oddity problem, three stimulus objects are used, two of which are identical, along with a third, and differing, stimulus object. These are presented together, with the subject's choice of the odd stimulus object being rewarded.

In the matching problem, the test tray is divided into a sample compartment having a single food well and a choice compartment with two food wells. All the wells are covered by stimulus objects. The subject is first trained to displace the stimulus object found in the sample compartment, for which he is rewarded. The subject is then required to select from the two stimulus objects found in the choice compartment the one which is identical to the stimulus object found in the sample compartment.

Learning Taxonomies

The most frequently cited instrumental learning taxonomy is a classification provided by Hilgard and Marquis (1940) who suggested dividing this type of learning situation into four task categories: (1) reward, (2) secondary reward, (3) escape, and (4) avoidance. This classification, it may be noted, is based primarily on appetitive-aversive or motivational considerations utilized by the experimenter.

Reward training is illustrated by those tasks in which the organism receives food, water, or some other type of appetitive stimulus for making the correct response. The rat who finds food in a goal box after making a correct response in a T-maze illustrates this kind of training. Secondary reward tasks are similar except that a neutral stimulus which has previously acquired reward characteristics by association with a primary reward is used as the goal object. Saltzman (1949) found that following preliminary training in which rats obtained food in a white goal box, the white goal box without food would serve to reinforce a right turn in a simple U-maze.

In escape learning, a noxious stimulus is presented and the organism must learn to make a response which permits it to escape from the painful stimulation. To illustrate, in a study by Trapold and Fowler (1960), rats were placed in a straight runway where they received shock through the floor. The animals learned to escape from this aversive stimulus by running from the runway into an uncharged goal box.

It may be noted that the presentation of aversive stimuli which motivates the organism to respond is not unlike placing the organism in some state of deprivation; the removal of the aversive stimulus serves as a reward for an instrumental response in much the same way that food serves as a reward for the hungry animal. It is not surprising that many of the experimental findings which have been obtained with reward training have been replicated using escape learning tasks—which suggests that both of the types of training might be considered to fall under a single classification.

The last type of task suggested by Hilgard and Marquis (1940) is instrumental avoidance. Here, the instrumental response prevents the organism from receiving the aversive stimulus. Contemporary experimenters have broken down avoidance learning into two general types: (1) active and (2) passive.

With active avoidance, a stimulus or signal is presented and following some period of time, the aversive stimulus is presented. The organism must learn to make the appropriate instrumental response during this time interval in order to avoid receiving aversive stimulation. If the organism does not respond appropriately, the aversive stimulus is received and the situation becomes one of instrumental escape.

It should be recognized that during the early part of avoidance training, the procedure used mirrors a classical conditioning paradigm, since the organism has not learned to avoid the aversive stimulus (or UCS) and the UCS follows the signal (CS) in a fixed temporal relationship.[3] It is only after some training trials have been provided and the subject learns to respond to the CS (thus avoiding the presentation of the UCS) that the "instrumental" aspects of the avoidance task are apparent.

Another type of active avoidance task is known as nondiscriminated or Sidman (1953) avoidance. In this procedure, the signal or CS which predicts the onset of the aversive stimulation, e.g., shock, is not presented. Shock is provided on a regular interval, but the making of an instrumental response, e.g., bar pressing, will delay or postpone the shock for an arbitrary length of time. The interval between shock presentations is known as the shock–shock interval, while the amount of time that the instrumental response delays presentation of shock is known as the response–shock interval. It is possible for the organism to learn to respond in such a manner that the frequency of shock is greatly reduced.

With passive avoidance the subject is trained to make some instrumental response; following such training, it is provided with a noxious stimulus for continuing to respond in the same way. An illustration of this situation can be found in a study by Kamin (1959). Rats were first trained to avoid shock by running from one compartment to another. The cue was a buzzer, with shock to be administered 10 seconds following its presentation. After the animal had learned to avoid the shock by responding when the buzzer was presented, the task was changed. Now, upon reaching the second compartment, the animal received shock. (Shock was not presented in the first compartment during the second task trials.) As a result, the subjects had to learn to avoid this second shock by remaining in the first compartment and not responding when the buzzer was presented.

A second instrumental learning taxonomy which we would like to discuss has been proposed by Grant (1964) and recently modified by Cohen (1969) and

[3] Some investigators have subsumed avoidance learning tasks under the classical conditioning paradigm. It will be recalled that in our discussion of classical conditioning of flexion responses, Bechterev described a situation in which the organism, upon hearing a tone (CS), withdrew his limb from an electrode to avoid the UCS (shock).

also Woods (1974). Grant's classificatory system consists of delineating three basic dimensions found in instrumental learning tasks. The first dimension classified instrumental learning in terms of whether or not there is a cue or a stimulus to signal the presence of stimulus consequences, e.g., reward or punishment, while the second dimension dichotomizes the instrumental response in terms of its emission or omission. Finally, the last category is related to the experimenter's use of reward or punishment-stimulus consequences—which follows the response. Woods's (1974) modification of Grant's proposal has been to classify these stimuli, not as reward or punishment, but as desirable or undesirable, in addition to adding another dimension, namely whether such stimuli are (1) present or increased, or (2) removed or decreased.

The four combinations which arise from the desirable–undesirable, present (increased)–removed (decreased) categories are: (1) a desirable consequence which is present, (2) a desirable consequence which is removed, (3) an undesirable consequence which is present, and (4) an undesirable consequence which is removed. These four combinations have been identified by Woods as conditions of (1) reward, (2) penalty, (3) punishment, and (4) relief.

Woods' modification of Grant's taxonomy is illustrated in Table 7-1. Sixteen categories of instrumental learning can be derived from the permutation of the varying conditions which describe the nature of the stimulus–response–stimulus consequences relationship which is found in instrumental learning. Although we cannot describe each of these, we can indicate how the taxonomy handles some of the traditional laboratory tasks and introduces some novel ones. A runway at the end of which a rat finds food in a goal box, or a lever to be pressed for food in a Skinner box, would each be classed as an unsignalled stimulus with an emitted response followed by a desirable consequence which is present. However, if a stimulus light was used so that a food pellet was delivered in the Skinner box only when the light was lit, the classification described above would be modified to indicate a signalled rather than an unsignalled stimulus. Each of these learning situations would be classified as one of reward.

If an instrumental response was followed by the removal of a desirable consequence, we would have the postulation of a penalty—a concept not found in the instrumental learning literature; and yet, learning does take place as a result of penalties. They are used in everyday life: traffic fines, yardage loss in football, and imposed fines following the conviction for a crime are familiar ones.

A task in which an animal escapes from a grid providing shock to a safe compartment has been identified as an unsignalled stimulus; it results in an emitted response followed by an undesirable stimulus which is removed. Although this type of task has been traditionally identified as escape, Woods has changed the terminology to relief, thus providing a symmetry with reward tasks, that is, an animal obtains reward or secures relief.

If a signal informs the subject in advance of whether the instrumental response would result in successful relief (or escape), the above paradigm changes to one of signalled relief—a type of learning situation which has not received any laboratory study until recently. To illustrate its operation, Woods (1973) had rats swim in a cold water alley to a separate goal tank which, on "relief" trials, was warmer than the water in the alley, while on "nonrelief" trials, was the same temperature. At the beginning of each trial, a cue in the form of a light indicated

Table 7-1   A Taxonomy of Instrumental Learning

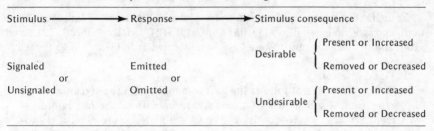

Adapted from Woods (1974)

to the animal whether the goal tank would be warmer. Woods found that animals did learn to swim with greater vigor on those trials in which relief was signalled.

Woods, examining the instrumental learning studies that have appeared in the literature for 1971 and for 5 and 10 years prior to that, has noted that only a few paradigms, specifically, reward training, avoidance conditioning, as well as the discriminated operant, have dominated the psychologists' research efforts in instrumental conditioning. He suggests that the proposed taxonomy expand our horizons to include the investigation of many other kinds of learning paradigms. It is too early to determine if this will take place. In any event, this taxonomy does represent the most systematic classification of instrumental learning tasks that we have at the present time.

We should like to conclude this section on taxonomy by referring to the instrumental–operant learning categories described earlier in this chapter. There we indicated that since the learned response in each situation was instrumental in securing reinforcement, these terms have been often used interchangeably. It must be acknowledged, however, that the procedures used with operant conditioning have been sufficiently different from those used with typical instrumental learning tasks to merit further consideration.

It will be recalled that the definition of an operant was a response made by the subject, after which it remained in the same place, ready to respond again. Investigators using this type of task typically do not use trials to measure learning but employ "sessions." That is, subjects are placed in the apparatus for a number of sessions with each session consisting of a specific interval of time, e.g., 30 minutes. The absence of trials in the free operant task and the rapidity with which the subject is able to make the response demand that provision of the reward be changed from the traditional approach, after each nth trial, to some other procedure. The result has been a scheduling of reinforcement in which the presentation of reward is determined by either the organism's rate of responding or the amount of time elapsing between reinforcements.[4]

---

[4] It is possible, of course, to program trials, and handle reinforcement in the traditional manner by introducing a retractable manipulandum at the beginning of a trial and removing it after each response. When pigeons are used, "trials" may be programmed by lighting the apparatus at the beginning of the trial and turning off the light following each response. Such a methodology makes the operant procedure similar to typical instrumental procedures.

Reinforcement Schedules

Four basic reinforcement schedules for instrumental learning tasks have been used and are designated as: (1) fixed interval, (2) variable interval, (3) fixed ratio, and (4) variable ratio. These have been defined as follows:

1. Fixed Interval
   Here, reinforcement follows the first response which the organism makes after some fixed period of time as measured from the last reinforcement. With a 30-second fixed interval schedule, reinforcement is provided for the first response which occurs 30 seconds or more following the previous reinforcement.
2. Variable Interval
   With this schedule, reinforcement is provided after a variable, rather than a fixed period of time separating one reinforcement from the next. Thus, a 30-second variable schedule consists of reinforcement administered for the first response which follows selected time intervals averaging 30 seconds.
3. Fixed Ratio
   Here, reinforcement is provided after every nth response. For example, a 20:1 fixed ratio schedule means that every twentieth response is followed by reinforcement.
4. Variable Ratio
   With this schedule, the number of responses which must be made in order to secure reinforcement varies, but the varying numbers of responses are averaged to provide a descriptive statement of the type of schedule employed. Thus, a 10:1 variable ratio schedule would be produced by the following: 4 responses (reinforcement); 14 responses (reinforcement); 10 responses (reinforcement); 6 responses (reinforcement); and 16 responses (reinforcement).[5]

The response measure which is used with these schedules is rate—the number of responses made by the organism in a fixed interval of time. This behavior is almost always plotted in terms of a cumulative curve obtained on a graph show-

[5] The reader may be curious as to how experimenters can cause organisms to acquire a new response, particularly when the reinforcement schedule provides reinforcement only infrequently. If, for example, a fixed ratio of 25:1 is used, how is it possible to get a rat to press a bar in a Skinner box 25 times before receiving reinforcement? The answer is that in such cases, the experimenter would "shape" the response. Shaping refers to the selective reinforcement of behavior—as the organism's response more closely approximates the type of response desired by the experimenter, reinforcement is provided. Thus, early in the training, the animal would be given reinforcement for approaching the bar, then for touching the bar, and then for each bar press. Later, the animal would be reinforced for every second response; still later, reinforcement would be provided for every sixth or seventh response, then after every fifteenth response, etc., until the animal would be responding at the rate which the experimenter desired.

ing the number of responses on the ordinate as plotted against time on the abscissa. Fig. 7-6 shows how a cumulative record is obtained. Each time the organism responds, the pen moves one step across the paper which is feeding the apparatus. Note that if the organism does not respond, a horizontal line is obtained in the direction of the paper feed. The more frequently the organism responds, the steeper the line. Although the rate of responding is directly proportional to the slope of the curve, at slopes above $80°$, small differences in the angle represent very large differences in rate. Fig. 7-7 reveals cumulative curves which illustrate responding as a function of the type of schedule used.

A few words may be said about the kinds of cumulative records which are provided by the varying reinforcement schedules described. The fixed and variable ratio schedules typically produce high rates of responding, providing the ratios are relatively small. What is relatively small for one organism and situation, however, may not be so for another; this becomes an empirical question that the experimenter must answer if the organism has not previously been used as an experimental subject or if he is employing a laboratory animal in a unique task. To illustrate, Fig. 7-8 presents the cumulative records obtained from a study by Sidman and Stebbins (1954) in which cats were placed on the FR of 20:1, while the FR for the monkeys was 25:1. Note the much higher level of responding for the monkeys even though their fixed ratio was the higher of the two used.

The fixed ratio schedule may also produce a pattern of responding which reveals a response pause after each reinforcement, to be followed by steady responding until the next reinforcement is provided. Note such pauses in Fig. 7-7. As the FR increases, the postreinforcement pause may lengthen, with a concomitant decline in number of responses.

Fixed interval schedules typically result in the organism's ceasing to respond immediately after reinforcement; this type of responding shows a progressive increase in rate until a burst of responding terminates in reinforcement. The

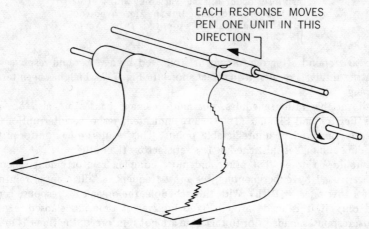

EACH RESPONSE MOVES PEN ONE UNIT IN THIS DIRECTION

Fig. 7-6. Diagram of a cumulative recorder. *Adapted from Ferster and Skinner (1957)*

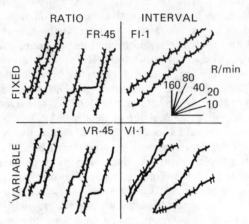

Fig. 7–7. Cumulative records of lever pressing by rats on the four basic reinforcement schedules. (Water was used as reinforcement, its presentation indicated by the diagonal marks.) With the FR schedule, water was presented after every 45th response (FR-45). Note the postreinforcement pauses found with this schedule. With the VR schedule, water was provided after a variable number of responses; however, they averaged to 45 (VR-45). With the FI schedule, water was provided for the first response occurring 1 minute after the previous reinforcement (FI-1). The familiar scalloping effect can be observed with this schedule. The VI schedule provided the animals with water for the first response occurring at variable times after the last reinforcement but the time averaged out to one minute. *Adapted from Nevin (1973a)*

failure to respond after reinforcement, followed by a very rapid response rate late in the interval, results in an effect shown in Fig. 7-7 which has been termed scalloping.

With variable ratio schedules, postreinforcement pauses are also observed but as Ferster and Skinner (1957) have indicated, response interruptions are frequently observed at unpredictable points. This results in less uniformity of responding and makes this schedule less satisfactory than others.

It should be noted that other and more complex reinforcement schedules have been used by experimenters, the most frequent, a "differential reinforcement for low rates " (DRL). With this schedule, the organism's response is reinforced only if it is made after a fixed interval of time has elapsed, e.g., 20 seconds; responses made prior to this time are not reinforced; the timer is merely reset for another 20-second interval. Obviously, this schedule results in a very low rate of responding, one which is related to the length of the interval set by the experimenter. It would appear that in order to maximize reinforcement, the

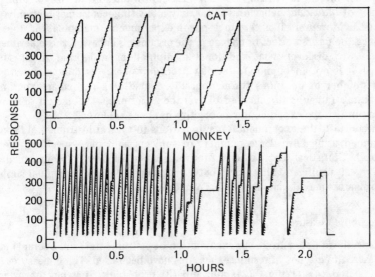

Fig. 7-8. Sample cumulative response records under FR schedules of reinforcement. The cat's schedule was FR-20; for the monkey the schedule was FR-25. *Adapted from Sidman and Stebbins (1954)*

animal must learn some type of temporal discrimination. It is sometimes observed, however, that the organism learns to make a stereotyped response (or responses) which appear to bridge the time interval that must elapse between the last reinforced response and the next response to result in reinforcement. We do not have to assume that the animal learns to discriminate time, but rather that it learns to make a series of responses which take the appropriate amount of time to complete.

Finally, three other types of schedules used with operant learning tasks should be described: (1) multiple, (2) chained, and (3) concurrent.

Multiple schedules consist of two or more schedules presented successively and correlated with external stimuli. Thus, a pigeon might be given 30-second presentations of a red, a yellow, and a green light. The presentation of the red light might be associated with a specific variable interval schedule, while the yellow light might be associated with a specific fixed ratio schedule. Finally, the green light might be associated with a variable ratio schedule.

Chained schedules also consist of two or more stimuli which are presented successively to the subjects; however, responding to the first stimulus merely results in the presentation of the second stimulus. Responding to the second stimulus then results in reinforcement.

Concurrent schedules involve two or more responses that are each reinforced by a separate schedule. For example, a pigeon may be reinforced for responding to a key placed on the right side of the box on a fixed interval schedule, while its response to a key placed on the left side of the box will result in a variable interval schedule.

Our last concern in this section on operant procedures is to acknowledge that most investigators using operant tasks are interested in the experimental analysis of *individual* behavior, so that only a few subjects (sometimes only one) are used. Moreover, if a certain type of experimental manipulation does not produce the desired effect or change in the organism's behavior, the experimenter attempts to discover what additional manipulations will bring about such a change. It is not uncommon to see new procedures being used by an investigator on a number of occasions throughout the course of a particular experiment. The basic strategy is to gain control over the experimental subject; if this can be accomplished, the experimenter's objective has been achieved.

In contrast, the experimental manipulations in typical instrumental tasks are performed using fairly large numbers of subjects and, once specified, are not changed. Statistical comparisons of average performances are provided and may reveal significant differences between groups although individual subjects' performances may deviate markedly from their group means.

Response Measures

As we have noted from our examination of instrumental (and operant) learning tasks, three types of response measures have been used. These measures have been related to (1) time, (2) rate, and (3) probability. Latency or speed of responding is recorded most frequently in runway situations; rate of responding in the Skinner box (or operant tasks); and probability of responding, e.g., number of correct or incorrect responses, in discrimination problems or tasks in which the organism is provided alternative ways or responding.

It must be acknowledged that these measures can be obtained during extinction as well as during acquisition or training trials (or sessions). As indicated earlier, our bias has been to stress response measures obtained with acquisition trials, and to place little emphasis upon extinction data. To reiterate our position, the removal of reward or noxious stimuli as required by the extinction procedure introduces an extraneous variable into the experimental situation, so that any inference made about the strength of the instrumental response becomes tenuous.

It will be recalled that when we examined the interrelationships existing among the varying classical conditioning response measures, we found correlations among these measures to be quite low, which suggests the difficulty of predicting one response measure from knowledge of another. A similar condition exists with instrumental learning tasks. For example, Hall and Kobrick (1952), correlating a number of response measures obtained when rats were trained to traverse a runway, found an r of .45 between latency and running time, an r of .15 between latency and trials to extinction, and an r of -.01 between running time and trials to extinction.

But few investigators have attempted to make predictions about one response measure from another; rather, they have been interested in determining whether the varying response measures reflect similar changes occurring as a result of the manipulation of a basic learning variable. But even here, there are problems involved in making such a prediction. Goodrich (1959), in training rats to run a straight alley, examined the contribution of partial and continuous reinforcement schedules. He found that partial reinforcement resulted in superior latency and speed of running the middle portion of the alley, but he also found that this type of schedule did not reveal such superiority when the speed of running the goal box section of the alley was obtained.[6]

In summary, there is no simple solution to the problem of what response measure should be used. Perhaps all the investigator can do is to use response measures demonstrated in earlier experiments to be reliable, and which reflect consistent differences as a function of basic learning variables that may be manipulated.

The Generality of Learning Principles

Most of the instrumental learning experiments reviewed in the following chapters have been conducted with animals using the simple kinds of learning tasks described. An immediate question arises concerning the generality of the learning principles which have been derived from these experiments. Can we generalize from the rat's learning to traverse a runway, for example, to a man's learning a much more complex type of task?[7]

An examination of the writings of early as well as contemporary psychologists reveal many who believe in the generality of learning principles. Thorndike (1911), for example, wrote that all animals were "systems of connections subject to change by the law of exercise and effect and they differ only in the particular connections formed as well as in the efficiency of the connection" (p. 280). Thorndike's working hypothesis became an article of faith for many experimenters who followed him. Perhaps its most important advocate was Clark Hull, who in his monumental text, *Principles of Behavior* (1943), and his revision, *Essentials of Behavior* (1951), proposed a series of learning principles (generated primarily from animals) which were purported to be basic behavioral laws having generality for all organisms.

More recently, Logan (1970) has written that ". . . man shares with many other animals some basic principles of behavior that are most easily isolated by studying simpler organisms such as rats, pigeons, and monkeys" (p. xvi); while Dinsmoor (1970) has been even more convinced of the generality position. He has written "the question remains, of course, whether experimental findings obtained with rats, pigeons, and monkeys can be applied to human beings. The

---

[6] The complexity of the response measurement problem is further revealed in a study by Edgington (1960) who used only a single response measure—speed of running—but expressed this measure in terms of either (1) feet per second, or (2) seconds per foot traveled. When the means of these two measures were examined for two animals, A and B, he found that one measure revealed rat A as superior, while the other measure indicated just the reverse.

[7] This question has relevance, of course, for those classical conditioning studies which have also used animals as experimental subjects. The nature and characteristics of the CS and UCS, the operations employed, as well as the response measures, are frequently similar if not identical in animal and human classical conditioning experiments, so that generalizing the findings of a classical conditioning experiment from animal to man is somewhat less tenuous than it is in instrumental learning situations.

similarities in anatomical structure and biological functioning would suggest that the fundamental principles should be much the same. The pigeon, to be sure, is not a mammal, and his physiology is somewhat different from that of man, but the correspondence between the behavioral processes observed with birds and with mammalian species adds to our confidence in the degree of biological continuity that prevails. The rat and the monkey might almost be considered to be smaller humans with fur and tails" (p. 3).

In recent years, considerable skepticism has arisen regarding this general assumption that learning principles discovered using animals as subjects have an automatic generality for man. Early European investigators, notably the ethologists, in contrast to their American counterparts, posited that the behavior of an animal in its natural setting was related to its sensory capacity and to its response capability, as well as to ethological factors. As a result, the ethologist never considered learning a general process that differed only in degree among species, but rather, believed it to be a more specific process interacting with the animal's adaptive characteristics in order to enable each species to survive in its particular enivornment. An example of this position is found in Tinbergen (1951), the noted European ethologist, who wrote, "The student of innate behavior, accustomed to studying a number of different species and the entire behavior pattern, is repeatedly confronted with the fact that an animal may learn some things much more readily than others. . . . In other words, there seem to be more or less strictly localized 'dispositions to learn.' Different species are predisposed to learn different parts of the pattern. So far as we know, these differences between species have adaptive significance" (p. 145).

An increasingly large number of current American investigators, e.g., Breland and Breland (1966), Bolles (1970), Lockard (1971), Rozen and Kalat (1971), Seligman (1970), and Warren (1972), have also come to question the generality position. The ethologist's position that the sensory capacity of the animal and its environmental demands play important roles in determining the nature of learning has been accepted. Warren (1972) made this point most succinctly, writing that

behavioral observations indicate that the learning abilities of animals are as specialized and as closely related to ecological factors as their sensory capacities are. Every species appears to have its own set of special learning abilities, each one evolved to facilitate adaptation to specific ecological and social requirements. Animals are now seen as 'intelligent' in distinctively different ways that are often more highly correlated with ecological than phyletic variables. Rhesus monkeys, for example, surpass cats and dolphins in the formation of visual discrimination learning sets, but are markedly inferior to dolphins in learning to emit vocal operants. Dolphins find their way about by echolocation, frequently under conditions of extremely limited visibility; their performance relative to monkeys on vocalization and visual discrimination tasks appears to reflect the importance of these processes in adaptation to their normal environment. (p. 582)

Considerable evidence has accumulated to support this point of view. For example, Rozen and Kalat (1971) found that some features of learning and memory as applied to food selection in the rat, more specifically, a wild rat's aversion to poisoned food, are strikingly different from features which characterize the laboratory rat's learning a traditional laboratory task. To Rozen and Kalat, these differences make sense in terms of evolutionary adaptation. An understanding of the role of learning and memory in food selection involves the discovery of specifically adapted learning mechanisms and the integration of these with genetically determined behavior patterns. Thus, these investigators conclude, there is no reason to assume that an extensive set of generally applicable laws of learning exist independent of the situation in which they are manifested.

Seligman (1970) made a somewhat similar point, stating that the organism brings into a given experimental situation a specialized sensory and receptor apparatus with a long evolutionary history, and that the organism may be *more or less* prepared to associate those events selected by the experimenter as an integral part of the task he desires the subject to learn. Seligman thus posits that there is a continuum of preparedness found in all organisms—the organism may be prepared to associate certain events, unprepared to associate some, and contraprepared to associate others. Such preparedness may be defined by the amount of input, e.g., numbers of trials, which must occur before output, e.g., responses, construed as evidence of learning reliably, takes place. In classical conditioning studies, all conditioned stimuli are not equally associable with a conditioned response; in instrumental learning tasks, the kind of response demanded by the experimenter plays an important role in determining if reinforcement will strengthen response. Seligman has argued that this point of view is contrary to the commonly held assumption about learning that all events are equally associable and that investigators must recognize the preparedness continuum in their delineation of learning principles.

An example of the incompleteness of laboratory learning principles is evident in the work of Breland and Breland (1966), who have been responsible for teaching animals a wide variety of "tricks." Their subjects have been exhibited at municipal zoos, department store displays, fair and trade conventions, and television shows. Overall, their training program has been successful with 38 species represented in 6,000 individual animals used, although they have reported some unusual failures and cite as one example, the attempt to teach a pig to pick up a large wooden coin and deposit it in a piggy bank. Several coins were placed a few feet from the bank and the pig was required to carry them to the bank and then deposit them, receiving a reward for every four or five coins deposited.

Inasmuch as pigs learn quite rapidly and are very tractable animals, problems were not anticipated. Problem behavior did develop, however, usually after a period of weeks or months and increased in severity. Although the animal would learn the task quite rapidly, over a period of weeks the behavior of depositing the coins in the bank became progressively slower. The animal might run eagerly to get the coin, but on its way to deposit it would repeatedly drop it, root it, drop it again, root it, pick it up, toss it in the air, drop it, and root it some more. This type of behavior, the authors point out, is not what would normally be expected on the basis of learning principles generated in the laboratory. In short, they observed, these animals, after having learned a specific behavior pattern gradually drifted into behaviors which were entirely different from those originally learned. They have termed this phenomenon "instinctive drift," and the general principle appears to be that wherever an animal has strong instinctive behaviors in the area of the learned response, after a number of trials, the animal will drift toward the instinctive behavior to the detriment of the learned behavior, and even to the delay or preclusion of reinforcement.

The role of innate responses in avoidance situations, described as defensive reactions, has been emphasized by Bolles (1970) who determined that animals come into the world with defensive reactions already a prominent part of their response repertoire. These defense reactions generally take one of three forms: (1) running or flying away, (2) freezing, or (3) the adoption of some type of pseudoaggressive response.

Thus, the gazelle does not flee from an approaching lion because it has been bitten by lions—it runs away from any large object that approaches it because this response is innate, one of its species' specific defense reactions. The gazelle cannot afford the luxury of *learning* to avoid the lion; survival is too urgent, the opportunity to learn is too limited, and the parameters of the situation make the necessary learning impossible. The animal which survives is one that comes into its environment with defensive reactions already a prominent part of its repertoire.

When avoidance learning tasks are utilized in the laboratory, it is noted that some responses cannot be learned at all or are learned only after very extensive training, even though all of the appropriate learning conditions are present. Bolles's position is that failure to learn in situations where contemporary learning theories predict subjects will learn is a result of the fact that some responses in the subjects' repertoire are not acquirable as avoidance responses.

It would be foolish not to acknowledge the arguments which have been marshalled against the generality of learning principles position. At the same time, it would be equally foolish to adopt the position that each learning situation with each different organism is separate and distinct, and that generalization to any other organism or any other task is impossible.

The experimental work conducted with animals using even simple learning situations has from time to time resulted in the identification of variables similar in effects to other types of organisms, including humans, who operate in more complex learning environments. The Brelands (1966), in spite of the difficulties which we have enumerated, were able to utilize basic learning principles in teaching a variety of species a number of different tasks.

It is obvious also that many experimental operations which can be carried out with animals cannot be duplicated with man. A number of physiological studies, for example, in which the investigator attempts to examine the relationship between the functioning of the brain and learned behavior cannot be conducted with human subjects. At the same time, the findings from such experiments can provide the experimenter with valuable insights and hypotheses concerning the way the brain functions in humans and the role it plays in learning. In fact it seems most likely that the neurological correlate of learning which experimenters have been seeking for such a long time will be identified first in animals.

Finally, it should also be noted that the use of animals as experimental subjects has frequently given rise to the postulation of a number of theoretical constructs or models which, although inferred from relatively simple situations with infrahumans, nonetheless are useful in helping to understand the more complex behavior of man.

In the last analysis, as Harlow, Gluck, and Suomi (1972) have written, a definite answer for the justification of generalizing nonhuman behavioral data to humans has never existed and the only way to test the limits of interspecies generalization is by experimentation. Positive findings presumably indicate the existence of generality; negative results perhaps prove nothing other than the limitations of the method or of the mind of the experimenter.[8]

As interesting example of the limitation of method is provided in studies of whether human language data generalize to chimpanzees. If one is concerned with vocal language, the experimental evidence avows that chimpanzees cannot acquire vocal language. Moreover, because of the mouth and the throat structure of these animals, they could not conceivably be able to effectively evoke human language sound. Can we conclude, then, that the chimpanzee cannot acquire language?

Such a conclusion would be premature, since experimental work by Gardner and Gardner (1969, 1975), as well as Premack (1970), has indicated that chimpanzees can acquire a sign language. The Gardners, instead of attempting to teach their female chimpanzee subject, Washoe, an inappropriate vocal language, trained her in the use of the American Sign Language. Beginning when she was approximately 11 months old, within 51 months she had acquired 132 signs. As humans do using words, Washoe employed her signs for classes of referents rather than for particular objects or events and also combined the signs in proper serial order to form simple sentences. In brief, Washoe's acquisition of the sign language appeared to parallel the acquisition of spoken language by children.

In summary, as noted by Harlow, et al (1972), it is obvious that some animal data generalize to man and some data do not. The basic problem is to select between or among the data that generalize and those that do not. Unfortunately, there is no completely logical or absolutely objective way to determine if the

---

[8] Harlow, Gluck, and Suomi (1972) suggest that the criterion for making the best guess as to the degree or amount of behavioral generalization that can be applied from one organism to another is related to anatomical similarity, although all analogous anatomical structures should not be given equal consideration. They have pointed out that the most highly sophisticated anatomical criterion for assessing complex behavioral capability is the cytoarchitectonic structure of the neocortex—not the mass of the brain but the delicately organized cells in or near the cortical outer fringe. Although this criterion appears to work well with many laboratory organisms, it comes apart when birds are considered. Birds have little or no cortex and yet are successful in solving problems at a performance level equal to or beyond representative carnivores and at a level approaching the performance of the higher primates. At the present time, there is no single or simple anatomical measure to account for the generalization (or lack of generalization) between animals in relatively disparate orders.

experimental findings obtained with animals will generalize. As these authors have pointed out, however, it is important to make such a decision; if competent scientists do not, incompetent ones will.

The Interest of Instrumental Learning Tasks for Psychologists

Psychologists have been interested in instrumental learning tasks for a variety of reasons and the material we shall present in the second section of this text traces the reasons for this interest, some of which are briefly noted here. First, the use of rewards and aversive or noxious stimuli has played such an important role in instrumental learning tasks that a number of investigators have tried to learn more about the characteristics or attributes of these motivational constructs. For example, in a learning task, a number of conditions may serve as reward for a human (or a rat) while many others will not. What is the nature of those events that have reward value for the organism?

A second area of interest has been to examine how instrumental learning takes place as a function of a variety of experimental or empirical variables. How does the learning of a particular task vary as a function of the amount of reward or the discriminability of the stimuli employed? Is punishment effective in eliminating an undesirable response? It may be noted that these aspects parallel some of the work that has been accomplished with classical conditioning.

Finally, experimenters have been concerned with the instrumental learning of autonomic responses. We are aware that these responses can be changed by using a classical conditioning procedure, but is it possible to modify them using the instrumental learning paradigm? It is this question which many contemporary experimenters have been trying to answer.

Summary

Instrumental learning tasks are so defined because the occurrence of reinforcement is contingent upon the organism's response—in other words, the response is instrumental in securing reward. The diversity of instrumental learning tasks has resulted in attempts by experimenters to provide some classificatory system, the most frequently cited of which was proposed by Hilgard and Marquis (1940) who divided instrumental learning tasks into (1) reward, (2) secondary reward, (3) escape, and (4) avoidance tasks. A more recent taxonomy has been proposed by Grant (1964) and later modified by Woods (1974). This system classifies tasks in terms of three basic decisions: (a) whether or not a cue or stimulus signals the presence of stimulus consequences, (b) whether the response learned by the subject is one of emission or omission, and (c) whether reward or punishment follows the response.

A type of instrumental learning task suggested by Skinner is the operant task. This type of procedure typically employs an experimental situation in which the organism remains in the same place after a response has been made, ready to respond again. The Skinner box, in which the animal must press a bar to obtain food, is an example of an operant task.

These tasks differ from other instrumental learning situations in that the reinforcement procedure utilizes sessions, or period of time, instead of trials. The absence of trials and the rapidity with which the subject is able to make the response demand that the provision of reward be changed from the traditional procedure, e.g., after the nth trial, to some other procedure. The result has been the use of reinforcement schedules which are determined by the organism's rate of responding, or the amount of time which must elapse between responses that secure reward. These schedules have been identified as (1) fixed ratio, (2) variable ratio, (3) fixed interval, and (4) variable interval.

A recent concern of many psychologists has been the generality of learning principles generated from experiments using animal subjects. Although early psychologists believed that basic behavioral laws could be generated from virtually any type of organism, many contemporary psychologists are questioning this generality principle. They are pointing out that the sensory capacity of the organism, the kinds of responses which it has available to it, and the demands of its environment play important roles in determining experimental outcomes. Thus, a principle generated from one experimental situation may not generalize to other organisms or other tasks. In the last analysis, however, a definite answer for the justification of generalizing nonhuman behavioral data to humans has never existed and as Harlow, Gluck, and Suomi (1972) have written, the only way to test the limits of interspecies generalization is by experimentation.

8
Instrumental Learning:
Motivational Considerations, I.

It has been generally accepted that appetitive and aversive stimuli, e.g., food deprivation, shock, and accompanying rewards, e.g., food and shock reduction, play important roles in learning. As a result, many investigators have been interested in examining the nature and operation of these motivational variables, using instrumental learning tasks as a means for doing this. The next two chapters will be concerned with this examination.

Hullian Theory

We shall start with a short description of the motivational system proposed by Hull (1943, 1951), since much contemporary experimental work has been related to his theoretical analysis. In brief, four motivational constructs: (1) primary drives, (2) secondary drives, (3) primary reinforcement, and (4) secondary reinforcement, form the foundation of his system.

Hull (1943) assumed that primary or bodily-need

states are responsible for motivation, that is, states based on needs arising from excesses or deficiencies within the body. To Hull, the satisfaction of these needs seemed necessary to the general health and well-being of the organism, as well as to the survival of the species. These need states were represented in his system by the concept of drive. He conceptualized a drive as an intervening variable which could be inferred from an examination of specific antecedent conditions, e.g., amount of deprivation, with the consequent condition being the behavior energized by the drive state. One basic behavioral attribute was general or spontaneous activity, measured traditionally with an activity or exercise wheel. Thus, the hunger drive could be assessed by relating the number of hours of food deprivation, on the one hand, to the amount of activity exhibited by the organism, on the other. The general finding of a positive relationship between the number of hours of deprivation and the amount of activity received experimental support in a number of early studies, e.g., Richter (1927), Hitchcock (1927).

In summary, it was assumed that the origins of motivation are to be found in the biological needs of the organism and that the role of such needs is to arouse activity. The resultant activity was hypothesized to stem from the metabolic processes in the organism and was characterized as unlearned or "spontaneous."

A second motivational construct proposed by Hull (1943) was primary reinforcement, originally defined as the reduction of a primary need. Learning was intimately related to need reduction; thus, Hull (1943) stated that if a stimulus-response relationship was followed by a reduction in the organism's need state, the probability was increased that on subsequent occasions the stimulus would elicit the response. Presumably, such a principle was clearly demonstrated by the hungry rat learning to press a bar in a Skinner box or making an appropriate turn in a T-maze in order to secure food.

Hull (1943) recognized that the constructs of drive and primary reinforcement could not be used to account for all learning. It was clear to him as well as to other experimenters that primary drives like hunger and thirst and their satisfaction were not the immediate determinants of all behavior. Certainly, few adult humans appeared to be influenced by such considerations. Accordingly, two other motivational constructs were posited: (1) acquired or secondary drives and (2) secondary reinforcement.

An acquired drive was posited to develop as a result of repeated and consistent association of neutral stimuli with the evocation and diminution of a primary drive. Two examples, one employing an aversive drive state and the other an appetitive one, were used by Hull (1951) to support his position. In the aversive situation, Miller (1948) used a box-like apparatus consisting of two compartments, a white one which contained a grid floor and a black one. Rats were given a series of trials in which they were shocked in the white compartment and allowed to escape into the black. When they were then given a series of nonshock trials, the animals persisted in their behavior of running from the white compartment to the black one. Miller believed, however, that the most appropriate test for the existence of an acquired drive would be one in which the animals had to learn a new response. In order to demonstrate this, the door between the compartments was closed; the animals could open it by moving a wheel placed between the compartments. Results indicated that the speed with which the animals operated the wheel increased as a function of trials.

The explanation for this result was that fear became associated with the shock given in the training series. Fear was a learned response to painful stimulation. It was posited that neutral stimuli closely associated with painful stimulation, e.g., the white box, should come to elicit the fear response. However, the fear response also has stimulus characteristics which in this case functioned as a drive. Thus, fear becomes a learned "drive"—learned in that it is a response to a previously neutral cue, and a drive because it is a stimulus which can motivate the learning of a new response in the same way as thirst, hunger, and other drives.

Hull's (1951) example of an acquired drive based on an appetitive drive is found in studies conducted by Anderson (1941a, 1941b). Anderson, like Hull, believed that the association and satisfaction of a drive in a constant stimulus situation should result in that stimulus situation's being able to arouse the drive state. Anderson conducted a number of experiments but the one which has most relevance for demonstrating an acquired drive was a study (Anderson, 1941b) in which rats were made hungry and received a number of trials in a multiple T-maze where they received food in the goal box as reinforcement. The animals were then satiated and transferred to a different maze. Reward was not provided. The animals showed evidence of learning the second maze although findings were somewhat difficult to evaluate, as statistical tests of significance were not reported.

The second learned motivational construct which Hull (1943) posited was secondary reinforcement. Neutral stimuli, by being consistently associated with primary reinforcement, could acquire reinforcing characteristics. An early experiment by Cowles (1937) illustrates the operation of this construct.

Hungry chimpanzees were first trained to insert poker chips into a slot machine which delivered a raisin for each poker chip that was inserted. In this manner, an association was built up between the primary reward of raisins and a neutral stimulus, poker chips. Following such training, and as a way of further establishing reward value for the poker chips, Cowles required the chimpanzee to work for the chips by pulling a weighted handle; the animal was permitted to exchange the chip as soon as it was received for a raisin. Over a series of trials, Cowles was successful in getting his subjects to accumulate chips before they could make the exchange. Finally, in subsequent learning tasks, poker chips proved to be adequate rewards.

In another demonstration of secondary reinforcement, Hull (1943) cited an experiment by Bugelski (1938) in which two groups of rats were trained to press a bar for a food pellet in a Skinner box. At the completion of training, the bar pressing habits of both groups of animals were extinguished by so adjusting the apparatus that a bar press was no longer followed by the delivery of the food pellet. With one group, the depression of the bar was followed at once by the customary click of the food release mechanism but with the other group it was not. Bugelski found that the click-extinction group responded 30% more than the non-click group. As Hull (1943) has written, "This indicates in a convincing manner the power of a stimulus (the magazine click) closely associated with the receipt of food to contribute to the maintenance of a receptor-effector connection at a superthreshold level" (p. 88).

The four basic motivational considerations in Hull's system are summarized in Table 8-1.

A Contemporary Examination of the Hullian System and Current Theorizing

The past three decades have revealed many investigators' questioning the validity of Hull's motivational system. Their concern has been with all four components of his system; some experimenters have been interested only in demonstrating the system's deficiencies, while others have proposed new points of view.

The Role of Drive

Hull's postulation of basic needs from which drive states and the energizing function were derived did not go unchallenged. One objection arose from investigators who believed that drive states could arise from the organism's external as well as internal environments. Harlow (1953), for example, argued that there was no justification for the assumption that drives elicited by internal states were more basic or important than drives aroused by the organism's external environment. The result was that increasing emphasis was placed on a variety of different kinds of external stimulation from which many drive states were posited to arise. Some of the more prominent drive states hypothesized to arise from specific types of or changes in the subject's external environment were exploratory, curiosity, manipulatory, boredom, and activity drives.

To illustrate the nature of this evidence, both Berlyne (1950) and Montgomery (1951) posited a curiosity or exploratory drive which was aroused by novel (external) stimulation and which elicited "exploratory" behavior. About the same time, Harlow, Harlow, and Meyer (1950) hypothesized the existence of a manipulation drive in the monkey. Noting that their subjects would disassemble mechanical puzzles even though no basic need states were present, and rewards were not provided for such behavior, these authors wrote, "It is the opinion of the experimenters that a manipulation drive can best account for the behavior obtained in this investigation. The stimuli to the drive are external and, in conjunction with the animals' capacities, set the pattern of behavior" (p. 233). A few years later, Myers and Miller (1954) suggested that exposure to constant stimulation produced a drive which they termed "boredom," while Hill (1956) posited an "activity" drive which arose as a function of activity deprivation.

It would serve no useful purpose to review the many experiments conducted by early (as well as contemporary) investigators, all of which were designed to indicate the importance of external stimulation for any completely adequate motivational position. There are, however, difficulties with the postulation of the "drive" states typically posited by experimenters in order to "explain" their findings. One is that the mere positing of a drive state does nothing more than describe the behavior which the drive state is purported to explain.

Table 8-1 Hull's Four Motivational Constructs

	Drive	Reinforcement
	e.g.	e.g.
Primary	Food Deprivation	Food
	Water Deprivation	Water
	Aversive stimulation	Reduction of aversive stimulation
	e.g.	e.g.
Acquired or Secondary	Stimuli associated with deprivation states, or aversive stimulation	Stimuli associated with reinforcement or reduction of aversive stimulation

The hypothesizing of a manipulation drive, for example, states only that animals may engage in a type of behavior which the experimenter has labeled "manipulation"; there appears to be little difference between the positing of such drive states and the identification of instincts—a practice common in psychology a half a century ago. The parallel has been noted by a number of writers and dissatisfaction with such a state of affairs has frequently been voiced. Estes (1958), for example, wrote "In a few well-studied experimental situations, involving for the most part food deprivation, water deprivation, or electric shock as antecedent conditions, all of the ingredients of the operational definitions are present and 'drive' can at least be used without ambiguity as a descriptive, or summarizing, concept. Its usefulness in this role breaks down, of course, when enthusiastic proponents extend usage of the term to situations in which only one of the defining relations can be identified, thereby generating such ill-endowed mutants as 'exploratory drives' and even 'activity drives'" (p. 33–34).

Another difficulty with the positing of externally produced drive states has been the inadequacy of the response or criterion measure used by experimenters to determine the existence of a particular drive state. For example, deLorge and Bolles (1961) argued that the use of a single behavioral measure—locomotion, or the distance travelled by the animal—was inadequate to measure the exploratory or curiosity behavior (from which a drive state was inferred) of the rat. They pointed out that locomotion would appear to be just one expression of a more general tendency of the animal to expose itself to novel stimulation; if there are a variety of other behaviors such as sniffing or manipulation which serve this purpose (as there undoubtedly are) the measurement of these other behaviors is necessary, and in fact may provide a different view of the exploratory or curiosity drive than the behavioral measure of locomotion alone.

Finally, we should add that considerable experimental evidence has been obtained which casts doubt upon the validity as well as the generality of a number of the drive states posited. To illustrate, Charlesworth and Thompson (1957) investigated the existence of the boredom drive, confining their experimental rats for either 3, 6, or 9 days in a homogeneous (1) light or (2) dark environment. Control animals were permitted to live in the normal laboratory environment during these experimental periods. Following such experiences, the animals were permitted to explore a box which was adjacent to their home cage. Although it would appear that the experimental conditions of the homogeneous light or dark environment should produce boredom which in turn should result in increased exploration, the experimenters found no difference in such behavior among any of their groups.

Another question which has been raised with Hullian drive theory (and with other drive theories as well) concerns a drive's energizing function. It will be recalled that the basic function of a drive state was hypothesized to be its capacity to energize the organism—to make it active—and that spontaneous activity was a basic indicant of this function.

In an important experiment relating to this question, Strong (1957) examined amount of spontaneous activity as a function of food deprivation using two types of stabilimetric cages. One cage was designed to be more sensitive to the rats' activity than the other. The experiment consisted of dividing the subjects into varying groups matched on the basis of sex, age, and previous activity, and then placing them under either 0, 24, 48, or 72 hours of food deprivation. Each group was given a series of 30-minute trials extending over a period of 30 to 45 days. Results indicated that when the less sensitive stabilimeter was used, there was no significant difference between the activity of the hungry and that of the satiated animals. On the other hand, hungry animals were less active than satiated ones when activity was measured with the more sensitive instrument! Like Strong, many other experimenters, e.g., Montgomery (1953), DeVito and Smith (1959), Hall, Low and Hanford (1960), Bryan and Carlson (1962), Miles (1962) Treichler and Hall (1962), have been unable to find any relationship between number of hours of deprivation and activity.

Another kind of evidence used to question the energizing function comes from the results of studies which indicate that "spontaneous" activity measured in the activity wheel or the stabilimetric cage is influenced by learning. These studies have demonstrated that activity wheel behavior can be viewed as an instrumental response, the strength of which is increased by appropriate reinforcement. To illustrate, in a study by Hall (1958) two groups of rats were placed on 19 hours of food deprivation and their activity was measured during the last deprivation hour. For one group, reinforcement immediately followed the activity exhibited during the last deprivation hour; for the other group, the last deprivation hour was followed by being locked out of the activity wheel. The results indicated that the activity of the group which was fed following the last deprivation hour was significantly higher than the group which was locked out of the wheel. Presumably feeding the animal immediately after running reinforced this behavior.

A last bit of evidence which bears on the validity of the energizing function arises from the deprivation-activity relationship which has been examined in species other than the rat. Campbell, Smith, Misanin, and Jaynes (1966) have demonstrated dramatically different patterns of activity arising in the same activity measuring device as a function of deprivation. Chicks, for example, became active during both hunger and thirst, while rabbits revealed a progressive decrease in activity under the same deprivation conditions.

Bolles (1967), after carefully surveying much of the experimental evidence in this area, has concluded, "We can no longer accept general activity as a direct measure of drive strength. We have discovered that activity as measured by any device, but particularly by activity wheels, consists of certain specific responses which are reinforceable just like any instrumental response and that, in fact, much of the rise in activity which had traditionally been taken as evidence of drive now appears to be the result of a change in the animal's habit structure [learning] rather than an increased drive level" (p. 285).

Other investigators have not only accepted Bolles's (1967) conclusion but have called into question the whole construct of drive. For example, Campbell and Misanin (1969), after their extensive review of the literature in this area, concluded, "few, if any, psychologists now believe that those conditions once labeled basic drives, such as hunger, thirst, sex, and maternal behavior, are predominately governed by some common underlying generalized drive state. Even if there is some activating or energizing state common to many basic drives, it is clear that the specific behaviors elicited by those drives are controlled by a complex of interactions among environmental stimuli, hormonal states, physiological imbalance, previous experience, etc., and that the basic drive concept is of little value in unraveling these complexities" (p. 77). A similar position had been taken earlier by Cofer and Appley (1964) who, after examining the experimental evidence in the area, wrote that the drive concept was not only "without utility" but actually, a "liability" that prevented investigators from arriving at new formulations.

Frustration

All investigators have not taken the position that the construct of drive is "without utility." In an early experiment by Rohrer (1949), frustration was conceptualized as producing a drive state that energized competing responses and resulted in experimental extinction. Brown and Farber (1951) have theorized that frustration is produced either by a conflict between responses or by some inhibitory state which varies as a function of (a) response blocking, (b) amount of work, or (c) nonreward. Like Rohrer, they posited that the primary consequence of frustration was that it energized behavior, functioning as any other drive state.

A contemporary analysis of frustration as a drive state has been provided by Amsel and his associates. In an early study which demonstrated the energizing properties of frustration, Amsel and Roussel (1952) deprived rats of food and trained them to traverse a runway into goal box 1. Following the eating of a pellet of food, the animals left this goal box and ran down a second runway into goal box 2 where they also found food. Eighty-four trials were spaced over 28 days at the end of which time the animals' speed over the second runway had reached a stable value. Thirty-six test trials were then provided in which, on 18 trials, the reward was absent in goal box 1, while on the remaining 18 trials it was present. The experimenters hypothesized that the omission of reward in goal box 1 was frustrating; such frustration, they posited, should energize the running response on runway 2, thus resulting in faster running speed. A comparison between running speeds on the second runway for the rewarded and nonrewarded trials supported the experimenters' position. This difference in vigor of performance following reward as compared with nonreward has been termed by Amsel, the frustration effect (FE). Fig. 8-1 provides a comparison of test trial performance under reward and nonreward conditions.

Amsel not only considered frustration to be a drive which energized subsequent responding, but placed the construct squarely within a Hullian framework. In order to adequately understand Amsel's theoretical position, the reader should first be introduced to the concept of the fractional anticipatory goal response. If a hungry rat traverses an alley and finds food in the goal box on each trial, there is obviously a goal response (Rg) which consists of eating the reward. Part of this response, however, is not directly related to the presence of food. The rat may lick, salivate, or make other food-related responses which do not depend on the actual presence of the food in order to be made. These responses can be conceptualized as being made prior to the Rg, as well as being a part or a fraction of the eating response itself. As such, they have been designated as rg—fractional anticipatory goal responses.

Since the fractional anticipatory goal responses can be considered as separate or detached from the goal response, it has been postulated that they can be classically conditioned to varying stimuli which are found in the experimental apparatus. Thus, we have a situation as shown in Fig. 8-2. Inasmuch as fractional anticipatory goal responses have a sensory component, it has been further posited that the rg will produce stimuli related to this response so that rg is invariably tied to its associated stimulus component, sg, thus providing an rg–sg mechanism.

By virtue of a stimulus generalization process, the rg–sg mechanism works backward so that eventually, stimuli at the beginning of the instrumental response sequence will elicit the fractional anticipatory goal response. The rg–sg mech-

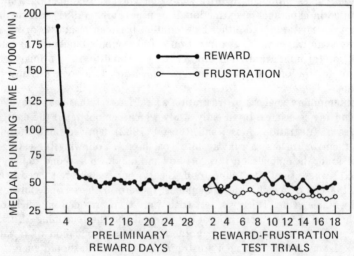

Fig. 8-1. Comparison of test-trial performance under reward and frustration conditions. *Adapted from Amsel and Roussel (1952)*

anism has been posited as the behavioral referent from which the organism's anticipation or expectancy that reward will be found at the end of the instrumental response sequence is inferred.

In his theoretical explanation of frustration, Amsel has posited a similar chain of events. The rat, running an alley and finding food in the goal box, develops an expectancy of food; when the animal does not find food in the goal box, a frustration response, Rf, is made. The Rf leads to an increase in the organism's generalized drive state which, it is posited, results in increasing the strength of the response immediately following the frustration. Thus, the more rapid running of Amsel and Roussel's rats on trials where the animals found no food in goal box 1 was attributed to the presence of a frustration drive which energized the response of running to goal box 2.

Amsel has assumed that a fractional anticipatory frustration response, rf, analogous to the rg mechanism, develops and is detachable from the frustration response, Rf, itself. Thus, these anticipatory responses can be conditioned to stimuli in the empty goal box and, through a process of stimulus generalization, can be elicited by stimuli found early in the instrumental response sequence. Presumably, the rf response has sensory consequences, so that the complete anticipatory frustration mechanism can be conceptualized as rf–sf.

During the past two decades, a number of experiments have been conducted in an attempt to obtain the frustration effect with subjects other than rats and with tasks other than the double runway. Many of these have indicated that such an effect can be demonstrated. Davenport and Thompson (1965), Carlson (1968), and others have been able to obtain the frustration effect using an operant procedure, with both rats and monkeys as experimental subjects. Davenport and Thompson's subjects were monkeys and their apparatus consisted of a box containing two retractable levers, the depression of which dispensed sucrose pellets. It was necessary for the subjects to complete a fixed number of responses on the left lever (first half of the trial) followed by an equal number of responses on the right (second half). The authors considered the period of responding to the left lever as analogous to trials provided on the first alley of the double runway trials, while right lever responding was similar to trials on the second runway. Following a training session, test trials consisted of omitting reinforcement on a random half of the left lever trials. This enabled the experimenters to compare right lever responding following an equal number of reinforced or nonreinforced left lever trials. A frustration effect, defined as faster right lever responding on nonreinforced trials than on reinforced trials, was obtained.

Frustration effects have been obtained using other types of response measures.

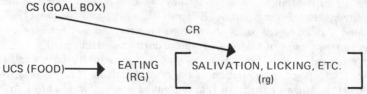

Fig. 8-2. Classical conditioning of the fractional anticipatory goal response.

Gallup and Altomari (1969), using rats as subjects, have found that locomotor activity in an open field increases as a result of the animals' finding no reward (after a series of rewarded trials on the runway), while Gallup (1965) has noted that significantly more aggression—fighting between two rats—takes place following nonrewarded trials. In such instances, it is assumed that the locomotor activity in the open field maze and aggression represent two kinds of responses which are energized by the frustration drive.

Finally, Penney (1960) and Berger (1969), among others, have obtained a frustration effect following nonrewarded trials when preschool children were used as experimental subjects.

Most investigators, however, have not been as concerned in demonstrating the generality of the frustration effect as they have been in determining how a number of empirical variables contribute to its strength. Reward variables have been investigated most frequently, since it is assumed that they contribute directly to the strength of the animal's anticipation of reward, which in turn has been recognized as a necessary condition for obtaining the frustration effect.

One reward variable investigated was the amount or magnitude of the reward used in the first goal box of the double runway apparatus. In a study by Peckham and Amsel (1964) this variable was examined using a within-subjects design. A double runway apparatus was employed; the first alley and goal box were black on some trials and white on others. The second alley and goal box were gray. Rats were given 4 trials per day, with 2 trials to the black alley and goal box where they obtained 8 pellets of food, while the other 2 trials were to the white alley and goal box which contained just 2 pellets. (A second group was given similar training with the alley and goal box conditions reversed). It was thus possible for the rats to learn a black-white discrimination problem on the basis of differential magnitude of reward. All animals ran the second gray alley and received the same reward in the gray goal box.

Following 64 days of training, 12 days of test trials were provided. Four trials per day were given to the animals—1 trial to the black goal box and 1 trial to the white, with no reward being present. On the other 2 trials, the customary 2 and 8 pellets of food were provided. Results revealed that the reduction from 8 pellets to 0 pellets in goal box 1 resulted in the animals' running faster on the second runway than when the reduction was from 2 pellets to 0. The findings are in keeping with Amsel's position which assumes that the frustration effect should be greater when there is a large reduction in the reward found in goal box 1 than when the reduction in reward is small—the greater expectancy of food produced by the large reward results in a greater frustration effect, in turn increasing drive strength. A second study by Peckham and Amsel (1967) has replicated these findings, while Krippner, Endsley, and Tacker (1967) have obtained similar results using a between-subjects design. This type of design employs two groups of subjects, of which, during the training trials, one receives a large reward in the first goal box, while the second receives a small reward.

Another type of manipulation of the reward variable is found in a study by McHose (1963) who has shown that continued nonreinforcement in goal box 1 will result in the diminution of the frustration effect. In this study, two groups of rats were trained to find 100% reinforcement in goal box 1 over a series of 72 training trials. Following such training, test trials were provided; here, group 1 found reinforcement in goal box 1 only 50% of the time, while group 2 never found reinforcement in goal box 1. An examination of the speed of running in the second runway after the switch in reward conditions revealed the usual frustration effect for these groups; however, after 16 trials, group 2's running grew progressively slower, from which the experimenter inferred that the frustration effect had dissipated. In keeping with Amsel's position, McHose hypothesized that frustrative effects of nonreward are dependent on the expectancy of reward in goal box 1 but with continued nonreward, the frustration extinguishes.

The frustration effect has also been investigated as a function of the type and number of training trials which precede the test or frustrative nonreward trials. In an early study, Wagner (1959) found that if a partial reinforcement schedule was used during the training trials, followed by nonrewarded test trials, the frustration effect could be obtained but that it was not nearly as abrupt or as large as if training trials had consisted of continuous reinforcement. This finding is, of course, in keeping with the theoretical position of Amsel, since expectancy of reward (strength of the rg–sg) should be greater with continuously reinforced trials than with a partial reinforcement regimen.

The number of training trials has also been found to contribute to the amount of the frustration effect. In a study by Yelen (1969), rats which were reduced to 85% of their normal body weight were provided either 12, 36, or 60 continuously reinforced trials in the double runway. Thirty test trials were then provided, using a partial reinforcement schedule which permitted the experimenter to examine the running speed for each animal following rewarded as well as nonrewarded trials. Findings indicated that the running speed on the second runway for the nonrewarded trials was related to the number of reinforced trials which had been provided—the animals with the greatest number of training trials revealing the largest frustration effect. An earlier study by Marzocco (1951) had resulted in a similar finding.

In a counterpart to the acquired drive of fear findings, Wagner (1963) has demonstrated that it is possible to produce an acquired drive based upon frustration. In one part of his study, rats were run in a U-shaped apparatus. On half of the trials, the animals found food in the goal box following the running response. On the other half of the trials, a CS (flashing light and intermittent noise) was presented, which was followed by the absence of food in the goal box. It was presumed that the pairing of the nonreinforcement (which was assumed to produce a frustration effect) with the CS would result in drive characteristics being acquired by the CS. Following such training, the animals were placed in a stabilimetric cage and the CS was presented along with a loud noise which produced startle. Twenty such test trials were provided. The amplitude of the startle response was measured on each trial. Findings indicated that the experimental subjects produced a more vigorous startle response than appropriate control animals that had never received the paired CS and nonreinforcement. The apparent energizing effect, inferred from the more vigorous startle response, was interpreted as support for the investigator's position that stimuli associated with a frustrative nonreward situation could come to elicit a conditioned frustration response.

Some interesting findings have been obtained by Bower (1962) which appear to demonstrate that frustration effects could be related to the amount of reward reduction found in goal box 1. In this study, 4 pellets of food were placed in the goal box during training trials; test trials consisted of reducing the number of pellets to 3, 2, 1, or 0. Goal box 2 contained the same number of pellets during both the training and test trials. Results indicated that running speed in the second alley increased, thus indicating larger frustration effects as the number of pellets found in the goal box were reduced. Thus, the frustration effect was found even in situations in which reward continued to be present in goal box 1. Unfortunately, the studies of McHose and Ludvigson (1965) and Barrett, Peyser, and McHose (1965) have indicated that Bower's results relating the frustration effect to graded reductions of reward found in goal box 1 are confounded by the depressive effect on running speed, which is related to the animal's having eaten more or less food in goal box 1. The frustration effect was found, however, when the reduction of reward went to 0.

A second experiment by Bower (1962) has indicated that frustration effects could summate. In this study, a third runway and goal box were added to the traditional runway apparatus. Following training trials in which the animals found 8 pellets in goal box 1, and 8 pellets in goal box 2, test trials consisted of varying the amount of reward found in both goal boxes, from 8 to 4, 1, or 0 pellets. In evaluating the speed of running the third alley as indicative of frustration, a summation effect was observed. When pellets were reduced in number in either the first or second or both goal boxes, running speed increased, with the most rapid running taking place when goal boxes 1 and 2 contained 0 pellets. Unfortunately, the role of depressive effects related to the amount of food consumed in either one or both goal boxes cannot be ruled out in this experiment; further study is needed to confirm these results.

In spite of the findings reviewed which have supported the postulation of a frustration effect, and indirectly, the rf-sf mechanism, all experimenters have not been able to obtain positive findings. We have already indicated the difficulty of McHose and Ludvigson (1965), and Barrett, Peyser, and McHose (1965) in obtaining a frustration effect when there is a reduction in reward in goal box 1 but the amount is still greater than 0. Levy and Seward's (1969) findings are of note since they determined that the frustration effect could not be obtained if water was used as a reward in goal box 1 and food as a reward in goal box 2. That is, the removal of water from the first goal box during the test trials had no influence on speed of running the second alley.

But, as noted, most experimenters have obtained evidence of a frustration effect, although not all have subscribed to Amsel's frustration drive hypothesis. One early alternative was proposed by Brown and Farber (1951) and Marx (1956) who emphasized the role of earlier learning. Marx has written, "This hypothesis is that the animal learns in previous situations to make more vigorous responses when frustrated. When the animal is frustrated in the experimental situation, he transfers, via frustration-produced cues, this earlier learning to a new situation, and we observe an increased vigor in responding" (p. 99). Although Marx (1956) found some experimental support for this hypothesis, it has generated little interest on the part of subsequent investigators.

Seward, Pereboom, Butler, and Jones (1957) proposed that the difference in running speed following reinforced and nonreinforced trials could be interpreted as a decrease on reinforced trials produced by eating in goal box 1, rather than an increase in running speed resulting from a frustration effect occasioned by a nonreinforced trial. This has been designated as a "demotivation" interpretation of the frustration effect. These investigators' interpretation of Amsel and Roussel's (1952) findings was supported by an experiment in which, in order to provide equivalent amounts of food consumed, they prefed their experimental group .5 or 1 gram of food in a special chamber prior to placing subjects in the starting box. Amsel (1958) agreed that prefeeding in the amounts provided by Seward et al does result in slower running times but noted that the amounts used in this study were considerably less than this.

Wagner (1959) attempted to evaluate the Seward et al position by using a control group which never received reinforcement in the first goal box. According to the frustration hypothesis, since these control animals were never rewarded in goal box 1, they should not have been frustrated by nonreinforcement and it could be expected that they would run slower on runway 2 than experimental subjects receiving a nonrewarded test trial. On the other hand, according to the demotivation hypothesis, the control subjects who were never rewarded in goal box 1 should not have their drive level reduced by feeding, and thus should run faster in the second runway than experimental subjects that received a rewarded trial. Wagner's results supported Amsel's position. Wagner found that his experimental group, provided continuous reinforcement in goal box 1 during the training trials and then shifted to partial reward during the test trials, ran significantly faster on nonrewarded trials than the control group that never received reinforcement in goal box 1. However, no difference in running speed was noted between the control group and the experimental group on trials where the experimental group received reward.

One interesting approach in the explanation of the frustration effect and the two-runway apparatus which has traditionally been used to demonstrate it was provided by Daly (1968) and McHose (1970) who considered this procedure representative of a differential conditioning task. As McHose (1970) has written, the two-runway or double alley experiment is a special instance of a situation 1, situation 2 ($S_1 - S_2$) discrimination training paradigm. The validity of this position is enhanced by the fact that the first and second alleys are typically of a different brightness and/or floor texture; in addition, the stimulus events which are associated with reward in goal box 1 differ from those associated with reward in goal box 2, e.g., handling and feeding events prior to locomotion. The discrimination task analog means that double runway subjects are trained under conditions of partial reward in goal box 1 (situation 1) and 100% reward in goal box 2 (situation 2).

McHose (1970) has suggested that the frustration effect may be explained on the basis of (1) the demotivational properties of reward, as well as (2) the effects of a generalization process obtained in differential conditioning tasks. When the frustration effect is obtained using subjects who experience both rewarded and nonrewarded trials in goal box 1, McHose argues that such an effect is due to demotivation. Experiencing reward (in contrast to nonreward) in goal box 1, slows down the subjects' running speed in the second alley. On the other hand, the between-subjects frustration effect, as obtained by Wagner (1959), arises because the lack of reward in goal box 1 (Wagner's control group) results in slower running in runway 2 than in the experimental group which receives partial or continuous reinforcement in goal box 1. The reason is that the faster running responses in the first alley (task 1) and arising from reward, generalizes to the second alley.

But as Scull (1973) has pointed out, the weakness of this two-factor analysis is that the demotivating effects of reward do not provide consistent results; moreover, there is a major difficulty in explaining the immediate occurrence of the frustration effect when a continuously nonrewarded animal is changed to a schedule of partial reward. Thus, in an experiment by McCain and McVean (1967), the difference between performance on nonrewarded and rewarded trials appeared almost immediately; in addition, this difference was represented by an increase in speed on nonrewarded trials rather than decreased speeds on rewarded trials.

Scull's (1973) careful examination of the research effort in this area has led him to conclude that "while early experiments on the frustration effect were taken as strong evidence for the existence of frustration drive, subsequent research and theorizing has shown that the double runway is such a complex situation that this basic conclusion may have been unwarranted" (p. 358). Unfortunately, investigators who have been critical of Amsel's position have not been able to provide a viable alternative.

Arousal

A second "drive" state which has interested investigators is related to the arousal or activation level of the organism. Behaviorally, arousal is defined by a continuum in which sleep represents one end, while the highly emotional and agitated states of excitement represent the other. It is generally accepted that autonomic as well as neural functions can be placed on the arousal continuum. A state of panic or high arousal is generally accompanied by increased autonomic nervous system activity as measured by heart rate, sweat gland activity, and blood pressure. The activity of the brain changes as a function of different arousal states. When the subject is awake but relaxed, an alpha rhythm with oscillations having a frequency of 8 to 12 cycles per second is observed; however, sudden changes in sensory stimulation or instructions to attend to or to think about something result in a disruption or "blocking" of these alpha waves. The "new" waves have a frequency of 20 to 40 cycles per second. A similar record is obtained if the subject is apprehensive, anxious, or excited in some way. At the other end of the continuum, during deep sleep, for example, delta waves are obtained, which have a frequency of approximately 3 cycles per second, with waves of extremely high amplitude.

A number of contemporary theorists have attempted to relate changes in the organism's arousal pattern to the concept of drive. For example, Hebb (1955) has written that any sensory event has, in addition to its cue function, an arousal or activating function. This state of arousal, Hebb suggests, is "synonymous with a general drive state—a state that is an energizer but not a guide; an engine but not a steering gear" (Hebb, 1955, p. 249). Malmo (1958) has also suggested that the arousal concept can be related to the notion of a generalized drive state, while Fiske and Maddi (1961), extending the position of Hebb (1955), have proposed that animals have a drive for an intermediate level of "overall stimulation." This level of activation which the organism seeks is varied and is assumed to depend on short term environmental conditions as well as the organism's characteristic sleep-wakefulness cycle.

A basic concern of experimenters is the problem of identifying a drive state with an arousal pattern; physiological evidence obtained during the past decade indicates that arousal cannot be considered a clear-cut unitary variable. Lacey (1967) has concluded, for example, that there are at least three different kinds of arousal: (1) autonomic, (2) electrocortical or neural, and (3) behavioral, which are functionally separable. In addition, correlations among these measures are particularly low, inasmuch as the relevant physiological processes differ in relative reactivity and combine to form different patterns from one individual to another.

In view of these problems, some question must be raised about the value of considering arousal states as reflections of the drive construct.

Acquired Drives

Hull (1943) hypothesized that drives could be learned or acquired and that this source of motivation plays an important role in accounting for human behavior.

The experimental evidence supporting the existence of acquired drives based upon aversive states is, for the most part, well accepted. It will be recalled that earlier in this chapter we pointed out Miller's (1948) experiment demonstrating that fear could serve as an acquired drive, a finding which has been replicated by other investigators, e.g., May (1948) and Brown and Jacobs (1949).[1]

---

[1] Not all investigators accept the position that the acquisition of a drive (fear) based upon aversive stimulation (shock) has been adequately demonstrated. Bolles (1967) has written, "Actually, it is difficult to show that fear can energize an arbitrary 'new response' because the predominant response to fear is freezing . . . in effect the case for fear as an acquired drive in the technical sense rests entirely on the supposition that the animal does learn a 'new response.'" It is Bolles's position that the "new" response learned by Miller's (1948) animals was not new at all but merely one of the unconditioned escape responses elicited by aversive stimulation. Rather than accepting the position that a wide variety of responses can be acquired by subjects learning to avoid an aversive stimulus, Bolles has suggested that only specific defense reactions are available to the organism.

An example of the experimental findings which, at least in part, support Bolles's position is an experiment by Allison, Larson, and Jensen (1967). Using an apparatus similar to that employed by Miller (1948) their experimental findings resulted in the conclusion that fear conditioning depresses initial performance in the shuttle box. Consequently, it was uncertain how much of the subsequent improvement in escape performance could be attributed to fear reduction. These experimenters also pointed out that fear conditioning operates upon an unlearned preference by rats for black over white. Consequently, if Miller's rats were reinforced by escape from the white to the black compartment, the reinforcing properties of the performance were probably not entirely acquired.

The evidence for an acquired drive based on appetitive states is much more tenuous. It will be recalled that Anderson's experiment (1941b) was one of the early studies Hull used to support his position that a drive could be acquired by associating a neutral stimulus with an appetitive state. A few other investigators have also reported positive findings. In a study by Calvin, Bicknell, and Sperling (1953), for example, two groups of rats were placed in triangular striped boxes 30 minutes a day for 24 consecutive days. One group received this daily experience under 22 hours of food deprivation; the other group received it under a 1-hour deprivation period. Following this experience, both groups were placed in the same box under 11½ hours of deprivation and food consumption was measured. The results revealed that the 22 hour group consumed more food than the 1-hour group. Studies by Wright (1965), Trost and Homzie (1966), Wike, Cour, and Mellgren (Experiment 1, 1967) have also reported positive findings.

However, Siegel's (1943) essential replication of Anderson's study (1941b), and Siegel and MacDonnell's replication of the Calvin, Bicknell, and Sperling (1953) experiment have failed to confirm the positive findings. As noted in Table 8-2, a variety of investigations have been unable to find experimental support for the existence of an acquired need based upon the primary needs of either food or water. Cravens and Renner's (1970) review of the appetitive acquired drive experiments has revealed that of 20 tests for the presence of an acquired drive obtained from 12 investigators, just 5 of these were successful in obtaining positive findings.[2,3]

Since Cravens and Renner's (1970) review, a series of studies were conducted by Seligman and his associates (Seligman, Ives, Ames, and Mineka, 1970; Seligman, Bravman, and Radford, 1970; and Seligman, Mineka, and Fillit, 1971) who have been able to condition a thirst drive in the rat.

[2] Inasmuch as it is a common practice of scientific journals not to report negative results, it is likely that many more negative findings have been obtained but not reported.

[3] Cravens and Renner (1970) have called attention to a number of methodological issues which must be considered by investigators interested in this problem area. First, the dependent variable, such as rate of eating or drinking, must be sufficiently sensitive to reflect the presence of the acquired drive. For example, longer periods of water deprivation in contrast to shorter periods do not clearly result in faster initial drinking rates, as demonstrated by Goodson, Hermann, and Morgan (1962). And, although the amount of food subjects will eat at two different levels of deprivation can be reliably differentiated if the animal is permitted to eat to satiation, Davis and Keehn (1959) and Moll (1959) have found that when a time limit is placed on eating, the amount eaten does not reliably differentiate between subjects with different levels of deprivation.

They have also concluded that experimenters must be sure the animal attends to the external stimulus which is associated with the drive state. If the subject does not recognize or attend to the stimuli paired with the drive state, then an association could not be expected to result even if it were potentially possible.

Finally, investigators must be sure that their subjects can discriminate among the varying levels of deprivation used. It is obvious that if a subject cannot discriminate between differences in drive level intensities, then these internal cues cannot be differentially associated with other stimuli which in turn could preclude the presence of a conditioned appetitive drive.

Table 8-2 Summaries of a Sampling of Studies Investigating Acquired Drives

Subject	Primary Drive State	Stimulus acquiring secondary drive characteristics	Response Measure	Results	Investigators
Rats	Hunger	Parts of the multiple T-maze	Instrumental Response: Errors on T-maze	Positive	Anderson (1941b)
Rats	Hunger	Striped Box	Consummatory Activity	Positive	Calvin, Bicknell, and Sperling (1953)
Rats	Hunger	Striped Box	Consummatory Activity	Negative	Siegel and MacDonnell (1954)
Rats	Hunger	White Box	Instrumental Response: Bar pressing	Negative	Myers and Miller (1954)
Goats	Thirst	Blinking Light	Consummatory Activity	Negative	Greenberg (1954)
	Thirst elicited by hypothalamic stimulation	Light or Tone	Consummatory Activity	Negative	Andersson and Larsson (1956)
Rats	Hunger	Striped Box	Consummatory Activity	Negative	Scarborough and Goodson (1957)
Monkeys	Hunger	Flashing Light	Instrumental Response: Placing coin in machine; bar pressing	Negative	Howard and Young (1962)
Rats	Thirst	"Distinctive" Cage	Consummatory Activity	Negative	Novin and Miller (1962)
Rats	Thirst	Light	Consummatory Activity	Negative	Pieper and Marx (1963)
Rats	Hunger	Black and White Boxes	Consummatory Activity	Positive	Wright (1965)
Rats	Hunger	Black Goal Boxes	Instrumental Response: Starting, running, and probability measures in a T-maze.	Four experiments conducted—all negative	Wike and Knutson (1966)
Rats	Hunger	Intermittent presentation of tone and light	Consummatory Activity	Positive	Trost and Homzie (1966)
Rats	Hunger	Striped Box	Consummatory Activity	First experiment positive; two others negative.	Wike, Cour, and Mellgren (1967)
Rats	Hunger	Alleyway or Chamber	Consummatory Activity or Hoarding	Two experiments conducted: both negative.	Cravens and Renner (1969)

223

In the first experiment of the Seligman, Ives, and Mineka (1970) study, following a six-day period which was used to permit the animals' water intake in a test cage to stabilize, two experimental groups received ten days of either one of two conditioning treatments: (1) rats in the hypertonic group were given 2 cc hypertonic (15%) NACL-2% procaine injected subcutaneously; (2) rats in the isotonic-procaine group were injected with 2 cc of procaine hydrochloride 2% made isotonic with NACL. Pilot work had indicated that hypertonic-procaine and, to a lesser extent, isotonic-procaine rapidly induced unconditioned drinking. A control group was injected with 2 cc of isotonic saline with no procaine.

Following the injection, all animals on 1 hour of water deprivation, were placed in a white experimental box where they remained for 60 minutes without access to water. Following 10 daily injections and placement in the experimental cage, 55 days of extinction training were provided. Here, all groups were placed in the white box, 1 hour deprived, and given free access to water during each 45-minute test session. Intake was recorded at the end of each session. No injections were given during extinction.

Results, as can be noted from Fig. 8-3, revealed conditioned increases in drinking for the experimental groups in contrast to the isotonic saline control. It is interesting to note also that no sign of extinction appears to be taking place in either of the experimental groups.

In a second experiment, the authors demonstrated that the 1 hour of water deprivation played an important role in preventing extinction since, when this period was eliminated as a part of the stimulus condition, extinction set in rapidly, however, at the end of 30 days of extinction trials, the animals were drinking about twice as much as they had during the pretest period. See Fig. 8-4.

In a subsequent experiment, Seligman, Mineka, and Fillit (1971) were able to demonstrate that the procaine, rather than the hypertonic saline, appeared to be the major active agent in conditioned drinking. The mechanism which they proposed to account for such an effect was clearly different from those proposed by other experimenters who were successful in demonstrating the acquisition of an acquired drive based upon food or water deprivation. Seligman et al (1971) proposed that isotonic procaine makes the animal sick and acts like a poison. They have assumed that this illness is relieved by drinking large quantities of water and that rats can learn this response. Here, the drinking response is reinforced by obtaining relief from the illness. During the extinction period in which the animals did not receive the procaine injection, it was proposed that the animals overdrank to prevent anticipated illness; they continued to overdrink because they never found out that the illness does not occur if they do not overdrink. In brief, overdrinking could be looked upon as an avoidance response.

The studies of Seligman and his associates place the conditioning of the thirst drive in the "acquired drive based upon noxious or aversive states" category. It is not surprising that positive findings have been obtained by these investigators since the acquisition of drive states based upon noxious stimulation have been almost uniformly successful. We have already discussed the early study by Miller (1948), as well as others who have confirmed his experimental results.

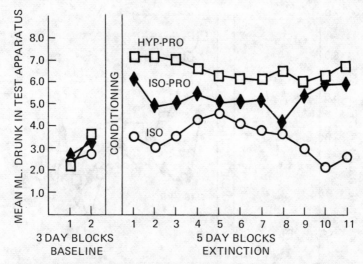

Fig. 8-3. Mean volume of water drunk in the test cage across 3-day blocks of baseline and 5-day blocks of extinction in Experiment 1. *Adapted from Seligman, Ives, Ames, and Mineka (1970)*

The question arises as to why drives are more successfully learned when learning is based on aversive stimulation rather than on appetitional states. Miller (1951) has suggested that the gradualness of the onset of hunger and thirst might be a contributing factor—a condition which contrasts markedly with the immediacy of shock or other aversive stimulation. An experiment by Fromer (1962) did demonstrate that an acquired drive based upon sudden onset of shock was superior in motivating a running response than an acquired drive based on gradual shock onset. Although this experiment does say something about the development of acquired drive based upon shock, the question must be raised as to whether one can generalize from shock to deprivation states.

Moreover, an unpublished study by Greenberg (1954) in which an almost immediate need for water was produced by injecting rats with a saline solution did not result in obtaining an acquired drive. In this experiment, the need for water was produced by injecting a saline solution in rats. A blinking light was then paired with the presence of this need in order to determine if the light could acquire drive characteristics. Measures of the frequency and amount of the drinking response during a test period in which the light was presented revealed no increase in drinking over frequency and amount obtained when the saline injection was not utilized.

It may be that the critical factor in producing an acquired drive is the concomitant arousal of an emotional response that can serve in turn as a stimulus upon which the acquired drive state is based. Inasmuch as emotional responses do not generally accompany food and/or water deprivation states, it is possible that acquired drives based upon such states are virtually impossible to obtain. In summary, the experimental evidence supporting the possibility of an acquired drive based upon appetitive states is weak, or as D'Amato (1974), after a recent

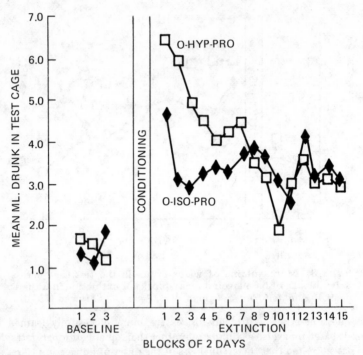

Fig. 8-4. Mean volume of water drunk in the test cage across 2-day blocks of base line and extinction in Experiment 3. *Adapted from Seligman, Mineka, and Fillit (1971).*

review of the experimental work conducted in this area, has stated, "The case for classically conditioned appetitive drive states is still unimpressive" (p. 86).

An Opponent-Process Theory of Acquired Motivation

We will conclude this section by briefly presenting a theoretical system of acquired motivation far removed from Hullian theory. This is Solomon and Corbit's (1974) opponent-process theory, which promises to generate considerable experimental interest. Solomon and Corbit's starting point is the behavioral phenomenon of addiction, resulting from the repeated use of drugs and manifested by the individual's craving a substance in which he had previously little interest. As the authors (1974) have written, addiction is the most vivid instance of acquired motivation because of its intensity and duration. They have regarded addiction as a fruitful, empirical model for analyzing many kinds of acquired motivation in the belief that addiction does not differ in principle from any other acquired motivational system.

The authors have proposed that a primary process, a, for a given emotional state, A, is aroused by an appropriate stimulus, after which there is a period of adaptation when the intensity of the affective state declines. As long as the stimulus intensity is maintained, the affective process maintains a steady level, but when it is terminated, there is an opponent process, b, which produces a second affective state, B, whose quality is different, in fact opposite, to that of state A. The opponent process b, when originally elicited is sluggish in its latency, recruitment, and decay. After the organism has been stimulated on a number of occasions, the characteristics of both emotional states change so that they can be characterized as A' and B'.

The authors have provided a variety of illustrations of the operation of these processes, only one of which we shall cite. A dog placed in a harness is stimulated by several 10-second shocks. During the first few shocks, the dog appears to be terrified—shrieking, urinating, placing its tail between its legs, etc. Following these shocks, the dog when freed from the harness shows a remarkable change in behavior. It moves slowly about the room, appears to be hesitant in its movements and unfriendly. The model would consider the emotional state elicited by the shock as A, and that after the dog was released from the harness, a second state, B, was elicited. However, state B gradually disappeared so that within a few minutes the dog appeared to be its normal, active, alert, and socially responsive self. After a few days of shock presentation a change in the animal's behavior took place. During shock the terror disappeared. The dog whined rather than shrieked, while struggling and urination did not take place. Unhappiness or anxiety (state A') replaced the terror. When the dog was released from the harness, an affective state, B', was elicited which might be called joy, since the dog rushed about, jumped up on people and wagged its tail. Finally, several minutes later, the dog was its normal self again, friendly, but not exuberant.

The authors' basic position is that process a is a relatively stable unconditioned reaction while its opponent process, b, is strengthened through use and weakened through disuse. The authors have provided three corollaries to their basic postulate. The first is that the peak of A' will be less intense because the b process increases in strength as the number of stimulations increase. Secondly, the steady level of A' during maintained stimulation will be close to the base line; while the third corollary is that the peak of B' should be intense and long-lasting in contrast to its intensity during early stimulation. Figure 8–5 graphically portrays the operation of this postulate and its corollaries, or what the authors have termed the manifest temporal dynamics generated by the opponent-process system.

An added feature of the model is that states A and B are conditionable. There is a major difference between the two cases, however, in that a CS which is capable of eliciting A will also elicit state B because of the coupling of the primary and opponent affective processes. If state A is a negative affective state, the conditioned elicitation of this state will be followed by a state of positive affect—thus, the elicitation of anxiety will be followed by "relief." The conditioning of affective state B, however, leads to no such reversal of affect.

At the beginning of this section, we indicated that the authors have used addiction as a model for their theoretical position. Their explanation for this behavior in terms of their model is as follows. First, the addictive substance must be capable of giving pleasure to the individual, at least sometime during its early use. When the dosage is repeated, the opponent-process will begin to

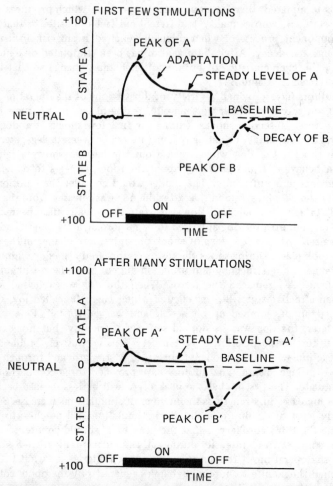

Fig. 8-5. The manifest temporal dynamics generated by the opponent process system during the first few stimulations and after many repeated stimulations. *Adapted from Solomon and Corbit (1974)*

strengthen, with withdrawal symptoms and craving for the substance intensifying and becoming longer lasting. These symptoms will be aversive and persistent enough so that the user will attempt to get rid of them. Inasmuch as the *b* process is the opponent of *a*, the quickest and most effective way of getting rid of this negative affective state is to use a substance which directly produces state A. The behavior resulting in obtaining and using the state A arousing substance will be strongly reinforced inasmuch as it produces A and simultaneously terminates B. This leads, however, to a further strengthening of the b process which will necessitate increasing amounts of the addictive substance in order to again elicit state A. An increase of dosage will then reinforce all the behavior upon which it was contingent, with the b process being further strengthened by more frequent use.

The authors have attempted to relate their model to a variety of behaviors; the relationship of these to states A and B, and A$'$ and B$'$ are indicated in Table 8–3.

There are some problems, however, with this model. The authors have indicated that in some instances, the b process is extremely weak or nonexistent, there being no appearance of a B state after stimulus termination. The example cited is the hedonic or affective state produced by marijuana, which results in a mildly pleasurable A state, but which does not result in the B state characterized by aversive withdrawal symptions or craving. The authors have speculated that some A states may not arouse B states; in addition, they have not provided any principles by which one could designate in advance whether or not a particular A state would be a part of an opponent-process. They look at this difficulty, however, not as a basic problem but only as an empirical one which needs experimental investigation.

There is also some question as to whether the model can handle all of the "facts" associated with addictive behavior. It will be recalled that one of the major assumptions is that the opponent-process is weakened by disuse. Thus, if a heroin addict could be prevented from taking heroin for an extended period of time, the craving for the drug should ultimately dissipate—the addiction would disappear. D'Amato (1974) has pointed out that this does not appear to be the case; it has been found that addicts who have been in prison for five years and totally abstinent are likely to become readdicted within the first month following their release.

In spite of these difficulties, the opponent-process model represents a "new" look in acquired motivational theory which holds promise for a better understanding of this area.

The Eliciting Function

One function of a motive, originally neglected by Hull (1943) but returning to current prominence, is the eliciting function. In a sense, the eliciting function is similar to the energizing function in that certain stimuli are able to produce activity; it differs in that the energizing function is purported to produce generalized activity while the eliciting function is usually related to a specific organismic response.

The role of aversive stimuli in eliciting behavior is well documented. With classical conditioning, an aversive UCS will elicit a UCR; in fact, most aversive stimuli will evoke "protective" responses from the organism. Note, however, that these responses are quite specific in their nature.

But rewarding stimuli also appear to have an eliciting function, with such

Table 8–3 Selected Examples of the Opponent-Process Model

Example	First few stimulations		After many stimulations	
	State A (input present)	State B (input gone)	State A' (input present)	State B' (input gone)
Dogs in Pavlov harness, 10-second shocks, gross behavior	terror, panic	stealth (subdued, cautious, inactive, hesitant)	unhappy (annoyed, anxious, afraid)	joy (euphoric, active, social), happy
Dogs in Pavlov harness, 10-second shocks, electrocardiograph responses	large cardiac acceleration	slow deceleration, small overshoot	small acceleration or none	quick deceleration, large overshoot
Behavior of parachutists, free fall, gross behavior, physiology	terror, autonomic nervous system arousal	stunned, stony-faced	tense, eager, expectant	exhilaration, jubilation
Opiate users, intravenous injection, moods and feelings	euphoria, rush, pleasure	craving, aversive withdrawal signs, short duration	loss of euphoria, normal feeling, relief	intense craving, abstinence agony, long duration
Dogs and M & Ms, gross behavior	pleasure, tail wagging, chewing	tenseness, motionless	—	—
Love, interpersonal stimulation, moods, feelings	ecstasy, excitement, happiness	loneliness	normal, comfortable, content	grief, separation syndrome, long duration
Imprinting, the attachment of creatures to their "mothers"	pleasure, cessation of fear, no distress	loneliness, distress cries, short duration	pleasure, no cries	loneliness, intense cries, long duration

Adapted from Solomon and Corbit (1974)

stimuli frequently being referred to as incentives. Incentives have been typically defined as goal objects which when anticipated, direct behavior toward them.[4]

The concept of an incentive was not included in Hull's *Principles of Behavior* (1943); an experiment by Crespi (1942), however, was largely responsible for Hull's (1951) revising his system to add the construct.

In Crespi's experiment, rats ran to a goal box which contained either 16, 64, or 256 pellets of food. Crespi noted that the 64- and 256-pellet groups were considerably more excited than the 16-pellet group when placed in the starting box. As a result, he posited that with different amounts of reward, varying amounts of anticipatory tension, excitement, or eagerness at the prospects of reward acquisition was generated. The differences he found among groups in their runway performance was attributed to this anticipatory tension or incentive function that developed with different reward amounts.

Spence (1956) has made the assumption that incentive is a motivational construct related to the amount of reward that is obtained by the organism. A problem exists, however, in accounting for the relationships between a reward provided at the end of the instrumental response sequence and the incentive's function of *eliciting* the instrumental response. Spence's (1956) explanation is based upon the operation of the fractional anticipatory goal response. As noted earlier in the chapter, it has been assumed that stimulus cues in the goal box and from the alley outside the goal box become conditioned to the goal response of eating, Rg. Through stimulus generalization, stimulus cues at earlier points in the runway are thought to acquire the capacity to elicit fractional conditioned responses which have been designated as rg. Through a process of stimulus generalization, they move forward to the beginning of the instrumental response sequence. Inasmuch as the fractional anticipatory goal responses produce interoceptive stimuli, sg, they also become a part of the stimulus complex and thus become conditioned to the instrumental locomotor responses. Spence has indicated that, in addition to this associative function, the rg-sg mechanism also has motivational properties, designated as the incentive function. The specific way in which the rg-sg mechanism operates to influence the organism's motivational level has not been spelled out. Spence (1956) has suggested that there may be some conflict when the tendency for the rg to occur at an early point in the instrumental response sequence is opposed by tendencies of the organism to make other responses. This conflict generates tension, which increases the organism's existing drive level, thus adding to the energizing function. It is interesting to note that stimulus-response theorists have consistently held that an incentive, rather than being conceptualized as a cognitive variable, e.g., thought or idea, should have a behavioral referent. The fractional anticipatory goal response operates in this capacity.

With the rg-sg mechanism playing such an important role in accounting for the incentive properties of reward, it is not surprising that some investigators

---

[4] A number of psychologists have accepted the thesis that the anticipation of a goal object can play an important role in facilitating learning. McClelland (1951), Tolman (1955), Woodworth (1958), and Mowrer (1960), as well as many others, have all acknowledged the role of anticipation of rewards as a motivational component of learning.

have attempted either to experimentally manipulate this reponse or to relate it to the instrumental response it presumably supports.

Many experimenters have considered salivation and/or licking to be fractional anticipatory goal responses associated with the rewards of food and water; consequently, Lewis and his associates (Lewis, Butler and Diamond, 1958; Lewis and McIntire, 1959; and Lewis and Kent, 1959) attempted to markedly reduce the amount of the salivary response by spraying into their experimental subjects' (rats) mouths, chlorbutanol plus benzocaine—a drug which partially anesthetizes the mouth, thus making the animal less sensitive to salivation. The authors assumed that the afferent consequences of the salivary response would thus be reduced or possibly eliminated. Three experiments were run using this procedure and then the animals were made to learn a maze or run in an activity wheel. Results revealed that the application of the drug had no influence on the instrumental behavior it was presumed to support.

Other investigators have attempted to examine only the relationship between the fractional anticipatory goal response, namely licking, and instrumental behavior. Patten and Deaux (1966) devised a type of harness for a rat which held a headset fastened to which was a small piece of tubing that entered the animal's mouth. It was possible to provide water through the tube. Using appropriately located electrical contacts, a measure of the licking response could be obtained whether or not water was presented. With a tone serving as the CS and water as the UCS, a conditioned licking response was obtained, with conditioning reaching an asymptote by the sixtieth trial. The authors noted, however, that extinction was very rapid, with practically no anticipatory licking taking place after 15 CS alone trials. Moreover, there was virtually no spontaneous recovery. The rapidity with which extinction took place indicated to the authors that there was some difficulty in using the rg-sg mechanism to account for the prolonged extinction behavior which frequently is noted in instrumental learning tasks.

Ellison and Konorski (1964, 1965), Miller and DeBold (1965), and Williams (1965) have all experimentally demonstrated the relative independence of salivation and acquired motor responses in both the rat and the dog—another piece of evidence which casts doubt upon the rg-sg mechanism as an explanation for the incentive function. To illustrate the nature of these findings, Williams (1965) examined the salivary response of dogs as they pressed a panel for food on various schedules of reinforcement.

Findings indicated that, although a high output of salivation generally occurred when the animal was pressing the panel or about to do so, salivation was frequently found at other times, so that there was little relationship between the instrumental response and salivation. Williams concluded that his results "cast doubt upon the possibility that incentive motivation is directly linked to the actual occurrence of classically conditioned responses" (p. 345). It is perhaps appropriate to conclude this discussion by quoting Bolles and Grossen (1970) who have written that "the attempts to anchor rg operationally, though admirable in their scope and persistence, no longer engender our enthusiasm. We really know little more today about what rg is or how it works than Hull did in 1952" (p. 152).

What must be regarded as a purely empirical examination of an incentive's function can be found in the studies of Marx and his associates (Marx, 1958, 1960; Marx and Murphy, 1961). In the Marx and Murphy study, rats were trained to make an instrumental response—poking their heads into a small compartment—in order to secure food. A discriminative cue (buzzer) was paired with the presentation of food pellets for the experimental animals. Control subjects also received buzzer and food but these stimuli were not temporally contiguous. Ninety trials were provided over a three day period during which the experimental subjects were required to make the learned response to the buzzer—poking their heads into the compartment—on at least 20 of the last 30 trials. The animals were then trained to traverse a runway and obtain food in a goal box. Following 20 training trials, the subjects were given massed extinction trials in which the buzzer or discriminative stimulus was introduced on the sixteenth trial and presented on every fifth trial thereafter. The buzzer was sounded just after the subject was placed in the starting box. When the door was raised, the buzzer stopped. The experimenters found that the experimental group took significantly longer to extinguish than the control (118.25 trials vs. 95.75), although latencies and running speeds for the first 15 extinction trials were similar. The effect of the buzzer was examined by comparing the first 7 buzzer presentation trials with the 7 trials immediately preceding these, on which, of course, the buzzer was not presented. Fig. 8-6 provides the appropriate comparisons. These findings clearly demonstrate the effect of the buzzer as an initiating or eliciting stimulus.

A somewhat similar outcome has been reported in a study by Longstreth (1962) using children as subjects. Preschool children were given preliminary training in which candy was associated with the presentation of a red light and no candy followed the presentation of a blue light. Following such an experience, the subjects were given test trials. When a light was activated, the children were instructed to run down a 12' runway in order to push a response button. Results revealed faster running to the red light—the stimulus which was associated with reward during the initial phase of training—but there was a decrement in the subjects' response to speed with the blue light. These findings clearly indicated that the stimulus associated with the reward had an incentive function in that it produced reliably faster speeds during test trials than stimuli not associated with reinforcement.

Summary

Many investigators have used instrumental learning tasks to examine the nature and operation of motivational variables. The motivational system most frequently cited has been that proposed by Hull. Here, motivational variables which have been postulated as playing a role in instrumental learning tasks have been: (1) primary drives and (2) primary reinforcement; and (3) secondary drives and (4) secondary reinforcement.

An organism's biological needs have assumed an important place in Hull's system, the role of such needs being to arouse activity. This activity is presumed to be unlearned or "spontaneous." Need states, however, are represented by the

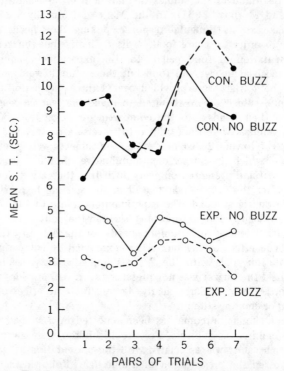

Fig. 8-6. Mean starting times for buzzer and no-buzzer conditions on seven critical pairs of trials in extinction. *Adapted from Marx and Murphy (1961)*

concept of drive—an intervening variable which can be inferred from an examination of specific antecedent conditions, e.g., hours of deprivation, and the measurement of consequent behavior, e.g., activity as measured in an activity wheel.

The second motivational construct is primary reinforcement, defined as the reduction of a primary need. Learning was thought to be intimately related to need reduction; thus, Hull postulated that if a stimulus-response relationship were followed by reduction in an organism's need state, the probability was increased that on subsequent occasions the stimulus would elicit the response.

Hull recognized that the constructs of primary drives and primary reinforcement could not be used to account for all learning that took place. Certainly, little adult human learning appeared to him to be influenced by these constructs. Accordingly, two additional motivational constructs were posited: (1) acquired or secondary drives and (2) secondary reinforcement.

Acquired drives were conceptualized as developing as a result of repeatedly and consistently associating neutral stimuli with the evocation and dimunition of primary drives; they could be based upon appetitive as well as aversive states.

To Hull, secondary reinforcing stimuli acquired their reinforcing power by being consistently associated with primary reinforcement.

A contemporary examination of Hull's motivational system has revealed many difficulties; in this chapter we have examined current conceptualizations of the drive and acquired drive constructs. The energizing function of primary drives has had little experimental support, and this has made many investigators conclude that the drive concept has been without utility. Perhaps one exception is the postulation of a "frustration" drive; the work of Amsel and his associates have demonstrated that nonreward which follows reward results in an aversive motivational state which does appear to energize the organism.

Acquired drives, at least those based on appetitive states, have been difficult to experimentally validate. One possible exception is found in the work of Seligman and his associates who found that stimuli associated with drugs used to stimulate drinking, were capable of eliciting the consummatory response from which an acquired drive was inferred. It has been proposed, however, that the drugs which were used to elicit drinking in this experiment made the animal sick and that the resultant illness was relieved by the animals' drinking large quantities of water. When placed in the same stimulus situation, the animals drank presumably to prevent anticipated illness. In brief, overdrinking could be viewed as an avoidance response in which the animals never learned that the aversive stimulus would not be presented. Viewed within this framework, such an acquired drive based on an appetitive state is similar to drives based on aversive states, e.g., pain.

One function of a motive, not found in Hull's original position, has been postulated as an eliciting function—that is, certain goal objects which, when anticipated, have the capacity to direct behavior. Anticipation represents a subjective variable and some investigators have attempted to obtain a behavioral referent for this construct. The fractional anticipatory goal response has been posited to serve this function. Other experimenters have been interested only in attempting to demonstrate that experience with goal objects can result in the anticipation of those goal objects and will elicit instrumental behavior; Marx and his associates have experimentally demonstrated such to be the case.

9
Instrumental Learning:
Motivational Considerations, II.

In this chapter we continue to provide a contemporary examination of Hullian theory and current theorizing.

The Nature of Primary Reinforcement

Contrary to the Hullian position, a variety of investigators have demonstrated that primary reinforcement is not necessary in order for learning to take place. In one of the early studies, Sheffield and Roby (1950) found that saccharine could serve as a reward for a rat learning a position habit in a T-maze—saccharine, however, contains no calories and does not reduce any of the rat's primary needs. Similarly, Sheffield, Wulff, and Backer (1951) found that naive male rats with no previous history of ejaculation would learn a simple habit with the only reward being an opportunity to copulate (but not ejaculate) with a receptive female.

The kind of studies just cited have been supplemented by a whole host of others (see Hall, 1961; Cofer and Appley, 1964), all demonstrating that stimuli in the form of light, sound, or even the presence of another animal may reinforce behavior. For example, in a study by Marx, Henderson, and Roberts (1955), five experiments were conducted in which the essential feature involved the opportunity for rats to make a bar pressing response in the dark for varying numbers of 30-minute pretest periods. These periods were followed by a number of 30-minute test periods during which a relatively weak light was presented following each bar press. In all five experiments, light was demonstrated to have a reinforcing effect. A subsequent study by Roberts, Marx, and Collier (1958) indicated that light offset, in addition to light onset, would increase the probability of a bar pressing response.

Butler (1957b), using monkeys as his experimental subjects, and Barnes and Kish (1961), using mice, have demonstrated that the onset of auditory stimulation may also serve to reinforce instrumental responses. In Butler's study, monkeys were placed in testing cages which in turn were placed inside experimental booths that prevented them from hearing outside auditory stimulation. Fastened to the interior of the cage were two levers (A and B); depression of one of the levers led to the presentation of a 15-second sound emitted by a monkey colony housed in another room. The pressing of the other lever did not produce such an effect. The subjects were given 4 blocks of test sessions with each block containing 4 30-minute tests. During blocks 1 and 3, the depression of lever A resulted in sound reinforcement, while responses to lever B were rewarded by sounds during blocks 2 and 4. Fig. 9-1 reveals the percentage of total responses to each of the levers throughout the 16 test sessions. We may note, then, that monkeys will learn a discrimination for the opportunity to hear sounds occurring outside the testing cage.

Other investigators have found that reinforcement could be defined in terms of the responses which the organism can make following an instrumental response. An early study by Montgomery and Segall (1955) demonstrated that rats could learn a simple black-white discrimination problem if the correct response were followed by the animals being permitted to explore a checkerboard maze, while Kagan and Berkun (1954) found that rats would learn to make a bar pressing response in a Skinner box if they were afterward permitted to run in an activity wheel.

The type of evidence just reviewed has resulted not only in a serious questioning of Hull's reinforcement position but, perhaps more important, has suggested new theoretical points of view regarding the nature of reinforcement. These positions can be described as emphasizing the role of the (1) stimulus, or the (2) response.

The Role of Stimulus Change

The experimental work demonstrating that visual and auditory stimuli may serve as reinforcers has led some investigators to posit that stimulus change may be the basic reinforcement ingredient. Thus, the presentation of some environmental change which follows the making of a correct instrumental

which would result in the strengthening of a secondary reinforcing stimulus. These have been: (1) the amount of primary reinforcement, (2) the frequency of primary reinforcement, (3) the schedules of primary reinforcement provided, and (4) the temporal relationships existing between the presentation of the neutral stimulus and the occurrence of primary reinforcement. The experimental work conducted has been so extensive that we can do little more than present a few of the basic studies in each area.

Amount of Primary Reinforcement. In the examination of this variable, it should be acknowledged that two different experimental methods, differential and absolute, have been used. The differential method is one in which each subject serves as its own control; here, the animal learns to associate one amount of reinforcement with one stimulus and a different amount with another. A test situation is then presented in which the subject must make a choice between the two stimuli.

Using the differential procedure, D'Amato (1955) was able to demonstrate that the strength of the secondary reinforcing stimulus varied as a function of the amount of primary reinforcement with which it had been paired. Rats first learned to associate 5 pellets of food with a goal box of one color and just 1 pellet with a goal box of another color. The test situation consisted of employing a T-maze with the 5-pellet box placed on one side and the 1-pellet box on the other. The animals were given 15 test trials in which primary reinforcement was never provided. Results indicated that the mean number of responses to the 5-pellet box was significantly greater than chance; 18 of the 20 rats used in the study made 8 or more responses to the goal box previously associated with the 5-pellet reward. A subsequent study by Lawson (1957) has confirmed D' Amato's findings.

The absolute method employs several groups of subjects, each having the opportunity to associate only one amount of reward with the secondary reinforcing stimulus. In a study by Butter and Thomas (1958) rats received 48 trials in which the click of the reinforcement mechanism was associated with the animal's running to one end of a box and receiving either an 8% or 24% sucrose solution. Following such training a bar was introduced into the apparatus and all bar presses were reinforced by the click which served as a secondary reinforcing stimulus. Experimental findings revealed that the 24% solution group made a significantly greater number of bar presses than the 8% group. In summary, then, most of the experimental evidence supports the position that the strength of a secondary reinforcing stimulus is a function of the amount of primary reinforcement provided during the training period.[2]

Frequency of Primary Reinforcement. A number of experimenters, e.g. Bersh (1951), Hall (1951a), and Miles (1956), have demonstrated that the strength of a secondary reinforcing stimulus is related to the frequency with which it has been paired with primary reinforcement. As an example of this general finding, Bersh (1951) provided 5 groups of rats with 10, 20, 40, 80, or 120 reinforcements for bar pressing. Each response produced a 3-second

---

[2] These findings are in contrast to earlier studies of Lawson (1953) and Hopkins (1955) who were unable to secure positive findings employing the absolute method.

light, with a food pellet provided after the light had been present for 1 second. A control group was given 120 reinforcements without the accompanying light. Following training with the appropriate numbers of reinforcements, all groups were then extinguished but the extinction situation did not include presentation of the light at any time. Presumably this procedure reduced the bar pressing response to the same level for all groups. Following this, a final testing session was provided in which each bar press resulted in the light's being presented for 1 second. Results, presented in Fig. 9-4, reveal a positive relationship between the number of times that light was paired with food and the median number of bar pressing responses for each of the groups.

Schedules of Reinforcement. A variable of considerable interest to a number of experimenters is the schedule of primary and secondary reinforcement provided the organism during the training and test situations. During the establishment of a secondary reinforcing stimulus or what we may designate as the training period, it is possible to provide the organism with either a continuous or an intermittent reinforcement schedule; here, primary reinforcement may be associated with the neutral stimulus on every trial (continuous); or the experimenter may provide an intermittent schedule in which primary reinforcement is not always provided when the secondary reinforcing stimulus is presented. During the testing period, primary reinforcement is, of course, not available. On the other hand, it is possible to provide the secondary reinforcing stimulus on either a continuous or intermittent schedule with the instrumental response. In summary, the primary reinforcing stimulus may be continuously or intermittently associated with the secondary reinforcing stimulus during the training procedure, while during the testing phase, the secondary reinforcing stimulus may continuously or intermittently be presented following the making of the instrumental response. Table 9-1 illustrates the varying combinations of continuous and intermittent schedules which may be used.

As we have noted when examining the amount of reinforcement variable, it is possible (1) to use a separate groups design or (2) to use subjects as their own control. With the separate groups design, during training, one group associates a secondary reinforcing stimulus with intermittently presented primary reinforcement, while a second group associates the secondary reinforcing stimulus with continuously presented primary reinforcement. A test situation which presents only the secondary reinforcing stimulus as a goal object provides a basis for the comparison between the groups. The second method is one in which subjects act as their own control. Here, subjects experience both continuous and partial reinforcement procedures during training, each reinforcement contingency associated with a different secondary reinforcing stimulus. A test situation is then used which places the secondary reinforcing stimuli in apposition.

In an early examination of continuous vs. intermittent primary reinforcement training procedure, using subjects as their own control, Mason (1957) trained rats to learn two discriminations. One consisted of black vs. gray with the black positive, while the other discrimination consisted of white vs. gray with the white positive. In one task, the positive stimulus was associated with primary reinforcement on only 50% of the trials; with the other task, the positive

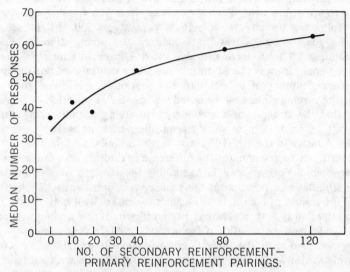

Fig. 9-4. Median number of bar-pressing responses made as a function of the number of secondary reinforcement–primary reinforcement pairings. *Adapted from Bersh (1951)*

stimulus was reinforced on 100% of the trials. Following training, the black and white stimuli were paired, thus forming a new discrimination task. The animals were then given 10 nonreinforced trials. Results revealed that 17 of the 20 animals made 6 or more choices to the stimulus which had been associated with continuous reinforcement during the original training. A subsequent study by D'Amato, Lachman, and Kivy (1958) has confirmed Mason's (1957) findings.

When the second experimental design, the separate groups design, is used, the experimental findings are just the reverse. Here, it has been found that the association of primary reinforcement with the secondary reinforcing stimulus on an intermittent basis results in superior performance. In a study by Klein

Table 9-1 Types of Training and Testing Sessions Using Continuous and Intermittent Primary and Secondary Reinforcement Schedules

		Testing Relationship Between the Response and the Presentation of Secondary Reinforcement	
	Training	Continuous	Intermittent
Relationship between the presentation of primary and secondary reinforcement	Continuous	a	b
	Intermittent	c	d

(1959) illustrating such an effect, six groups of rats were trained to traverse a runway for reinforcement. Each group was given 120 training trials with one of the following primary reinforcement percentages: 20, 40, 60, 80, 90, or 100. The goal box served as the secondary reinforcing stimulus. Following such training, 20 trials were provided on a T-maze in which the previously reinforced goal box was placed on one side and a neutral goal box on the other. The median number of entries into the previously reinforced goal box for each of the varying groups can be noted in Table 9-2. Inspection of these figures reveals that the strength of a secondary reinforcing stimulus increased as the percentage of reinforcement during acquisition trials decreased. A subsequent study by Armus and Garlich (1961) has provided similar findings.

It is difficult to account for the difference in findings between the two types of experimental designs used in examining the strength of a secondary reinforcing stimulus as a function of the primary reinforcement schedule. One procedural difference, of course, is that when subjects are used as their own control, a discrimination-type problem has been utilized during training in order to establish differential strengths of the secondary reinforcing stimulus, a kind of training not used with the separate groups design. It would also be interesting to provide subjects who are in the separate groups design with a discrimination training procedure in order to examine the influence of this type of training on the experimental findings.

In the studies examined, the secondary reinforcing stimulus has been continuously presented (always presented following the making of the appropriate response) during the testing period. A logical question which follows is: What is the influence on the strength of a secondary reinforcing stimulus if the stimulus is presented intermittently during the testing period? Studies by Zimmerman (1957, 1959), Myers (1960), and Fox and King (1961) have all been directed toward answering this question. In general, the findings of these investigators have been that the intermittent presentation of the secondary reinforcing stimulus during the test situation has resulted in increasing the probability of the response.

The Fox and King (1961) study is interesting inasmuch as these experimenters utilized an intermittent as well as a continuous presentation of primary reinforcement during the training trials and an intermittent and a continuous presentation of secondary reinforcement during the testing session. During training trials, a continuous reinforcement group received 100 presentations of a buzzer which was always paired with the presentation of water. An intermittent reinforcement group received 200 presentations of the buzzer, but only 100 reinforcements of water were provided. The ratio of buzzer-to-water presentations was not fixed but took place over 5 training sessions as follows: 50:50, 50:30, and 50:15, 50:5. Thus, the final ratio of buzzer-to-water presentations was 10:1. The test trials consisted of introducing a bar into the apparatus; when the animal pressed the bar, the sound of a buzzer followed. Subjects, from both the continuous and the intermittent primary reinforcement groups were randomly assigned to one of three testing groups: (1) those on a continuous schedule received the buzzer as a consequence of each bar depression; (2) those on a partial reinforcement schedule received the buzzer on a fixed interval

Table 9-2   Number of Entries into the Secondary
Reinforcing Goal Box during Testing

	Reinforcement Groups					
	100	90	80	60	40	20
Median Number Responses	11.5	12.5	14.5	16.0	18.0	18.5

Adapted from Klein (1959)

(1-minute) schedule; and, finally, (3) a control group never received the buzzer as consequence of bar pressing. Two 1-hour experimental sessions comprised the testing period. The mean number of bar presses for the first hour of each of the varying groups is indicated in Table 9-3 and reveals the clear superiority of using an intermittent primary reinforcement schedule during training as well as an intermittent secondary reinforcement schedule during testing.

Temporal Relationships. Both Jenkins (1950) and Bersh (1951) have demonstrated the strength of a secondary reinforcer as a function of the interval of time separating the presentation of the neutral stimulus and the occurrence of primary reinforcement. Using a Skinner box with the bar removed, Bersh (1951) first paired light with the presentation of food but varied the inter-stimulus interval. Light and food were presented simultaneously to one group; for five other groups, either .5, 1.0, 2.0, 4.0, or 10.0 seconds intervened between the onset of light and the receipt of reinforcement. Following training trials, the bar was introduced into the box and conditions were so arranged that a bar press resulted in the presentation of light. The number of responses taking place during the two 45-minute test sessions is shown in Fig. 9-5. It reveals that maximum secondary reinforcing strength appears to be present when a .5- or 1-second interval separates the presentation of the neutral stimulus and the occurrence of primary reinforcement.

Issues in Secondary Reinforcement

We have provided only a small sample of the many studies which have demonstrated that the strength of a secondary reinforcing stimulus is related to a variety of primary reinforcement variables. A frequent interpretation of these

Table 9-3   Mean Number of Bar Presses Obtained for the
Four Experimental Conditions

		Secondary Reinforcement Schedule	
		Continuous	Intermittent
Primary Reinforcement Schedule	Continuous	31.5	21.0
	Intermittent	23.6	70.6

Adapted from Fox and King (1961)

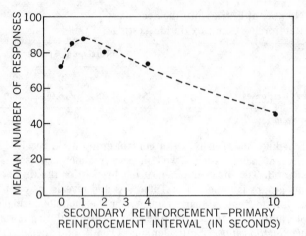

Fig. 9–5. Median number of bar-pressing responses made during two 45-minute test sessions combined. *Adapted from Bersh (1951)*

studies is that secondary reinforcing stimuli have a reinforcing function; that is, the capacity to strengthen old or establish new stimulus-response relationships. The mechanism by which such strengthening takes place has not been determined.

All investigators have not been convinced that secondary reinforcing stimuli have this function (see Myers, 1958; Bolles, 1967; Longstreth, 1971) and other explanations have been provided. The most viable of these appears to be that a secondary reinforcing stimulus serves as a discriminative stimulus which has the capacity to elicit responses previously learned. Thus, Bolles's (1967) critical examination of many of the secondary reinforcement studies has led him to conclude "that when the response-eliciting properties of the secondary reinforcer have been fully accounted for there may be nothing left over for the hypothetical secondary reinforcing property to explain" (p. 381).

We should like to indicate the general nature of the experimental evidence which has accumulated in support of the discriminative stimulus-eliciting function.

In an early study by Schoenfeld, Antonitis, and Bersh (1950) two groups of rats were trained to press a bar for food. For the experimental group, a light of 1-second duration came on when the animal began to eat. Thus, the light accompanied the consummatory response rather than preceding it as it does in most secondary reinforcement studies. A control group did not receive the presentation of the light. Following acquisition training, both groups were extinguished under conditions such that the bar press no longer produced food but did result in the presentation of the light. Results indicated that there was no difference in performance between the groups; although the light had accompanied the presentation of food, it did not acquire secondary reinforcing characteristics. Inasmuch as the light did not become a discriminative stimulus, it did not acquire secondary reinforcing strength.

Wyckoff, Sidowski, and Chambliss (1958) have argued that if the discriminative or cue function is removed from secondary reinforcing stimuli, secondary reinforcing effects cannot be demonstrated. In their experiment, they trained rats to approach and lick a water dipper in response to the sound of a buzzer. Such training was followed by a test period during which the pressing of the lever produced the sound of the buzzer but no water. Control subjects were given identical training during the test period, at which time the influence of the buzzer serving as a secondary reinforcing stimulus was examined. Each control animal was "yoked" to an experimental subject so that whenever the experimental animal received the presentation of the buzzer, control animals also received the buzzer (unless it had responded during the preceding ten seconds). This type of "yoked" control was necessary, the investigators argued, in order to control for the cue action of the buzzer. (In contrast to this type of control, a typical control group would have been one in which the buzzer was not presented during the lever pressing session.) The authors pointed out that having the buzzer serve as a cue for the subsequent presentation of water resulted in the subject's running vigorously to the water dipper, such activity tending to keep the animal awake and active and, accordingly, to increase the probability of additional lever pressing responses. Results indicated that the experimental group did not press the lever more than the controls, thus indicating that the buzzer had not acquired secondary reinforcing characteristics.

The cue function has been conceptualized by Miller (1961) in terms of an informational hypothesis. Miller suggests that the extent to which a stimulus acquires secondary reinforcing properties is the extent to which it provides the organism with information about the presentation of primary reinforcement. In brief, Miller has indicated that the stimulus must be informative or nonredundant in order for it to acquire secondary reinforcing power. In an examination of this position, Egger, and Miller (Experiment 2, 1963) trained rats to press a bar in a Skinner box for food. The bar was then removed and the following training procedures were instituted. A redundant group received at variable intervals 15 occurrences per session of a 2-second stimulus (either a flashing light or a tone) the last ½-second of which overlapped the delivery of 3 food pellets. Each of the 2-second stimulus–3-food pellet pairings, however, was preceded by ½-second with the delivery of a single food pellet. The 2-second light or tone stimulus in this case was redundant, since the single pellet of food indicated to the animals that 3 pellets would be forthcoming. An informative group received exactly the same food pellet—2-second stimulus—3 more pellet sequence as did the redundant group but 35 individual pellets were presented to the animals at random throughout each session. In this case, the 2-second stimulus became informative (and should have acquired secondary reinforcing characteristics), since the presentation of a single pellet did not always signal 3 additional pellets. Following nine 25-minute training sessions, the animals were given additional bar press training. Here, 30 pellets of food were provided with every third response rewarded. The bar was then disconnected from the feeder and subjects were given a 10-minute extinction session. (This was to reduce response variability.) The testing session then followed which consisted of 21 minutes of pressing for 1-second occurrences of the training stimulus without food; 48 hours later subjects were provided 25 minutes during which they were again permitted to press the bar for the light or tone stimulus without food being provided. Forty-eight hours later a third 25-minute test session was provided. The results for the two groups as measured by total presses during the first 10 minutes summated for the three test periods revealed that the informative group pressed the bar significantly more frequently than the redundant group, thus supporting Miller's position.

In summary, considering secondary reinforcing stimuli as discriminative stimuli which have an eliciting function appears to represent an appropriate way of looking at this construct. Obviously, more research is needed in order to further explicate this function.

Punishment

In our discussion of motivational constructs examined in instrumental learning tasks, it is interesting that the concept of punishment—long regarded as a basic motivational construct—has not been considered. The reason for this neglect is that Hull's (1943) system, around which we have organized much of our material, did not consider punishment as a motivational construct. Hull's neglect does not mean, however, that psychologists were not interested in this concept. Many of the early psychologists were actively engaged in punishment research; contemporary investigators have been similarly interested; in fact, Boe (1969) has noted that the frequency of articles on punishment during the last two decades has been increasing rapidly.

The Pioneer Work of Thorndike

One of the earliest investigators to consider punishment as a motivational construct was Thorndike (1913), who stated that responses closely followed by discomfort to the organism will have their connection with the situation weakened, thus, when the situation recurs, such responses will be less likely to take place. Viewed within a stimulus-response framework, the greater the discomfort, the greater the weakening of any bond existing between the stimulus and the response. In order to avoid circularity, Thorndike defined discomfort as a state of affairs which the organism commonly avoids and eventually abandons.

Almost twenty years later, Thorndike (1932b) revised his position. In *The Fundamentals of Learning*, he wrote, "In the early statements of the law of effect the influence of satisfying consequences of a connection in the way of strengthening it was paralleled by the influence of annoying consequences in the way of weakening it . . . . I now consider that there is no such complete and exact parallelism." This conclusion that punishment did not weaken an S-R connection was arrived at only after a number of animal and human studies had presumably indicated the inefficiency of punishment in weakening a stimulus-response relationship.

One of Thorndike's experiments examining the role of punishment can be described. College students were presented with 200 rare English words. For each word they had to choose the correct meaning from five alternatives provided. The sample below offers an example of the material:

dowlas: bowie/ /fabric/ /grief/ /Indian soldier/ /howls
edacious: daring/ /tractable/ /sober/ /devouring/ /polite
edolon: laziness/ /benefice/ /gift/ /duck/ /phantom
ern: long ago/ /foretaste/ /zeal/ /merit/ /eagle

On each trial the subject chose one of the alternatives and underlined it. If the chosen word was correct, the experimenter rewarded the subject by stating "right"; if the word was wrong, the experimenter "punished" the subject by saying "wrong." Twelve or more repetitions of the series were provided.

In the analysis of the results, Thorndike considered cases in which the response was right on the second trial but not on the first, and cases where the response was wrong on the second trial but was not the same wrong response that had been given on the first trial. The reason for not using cases where the same response had occurred on trial 1 and on trial 2 was that Thorndike wished to exclude from the experiment (a) all records with words whose meanings were known to the subject prior to the experiment and (b) records of words that may have had some strong connection with a particular response, right or wrong. The third trial represented the test trial in which the influence of the announcement of "right" or "wrong" was measured.

If the word "wrong" spoken by the experimenter acted as an immediate consequence to weaken the bond, the response that followed should have been weakened as evidenced by a shift to some other response on the next trial. On the other hand, if hearing "right" had a fixative effect, the response that followed should have been repeated on the next trial.

Thorndike's analysis revealed that although "right" strengthened the making of a response, "wrong" had little weakening influence. In fact, it was noted that a response gained more in strength from simply occurring than it lost from being followed by the word "wrong." As a result, Thorndike reasoned that an annoying aftereffect had no uniform weaking influence; if there was any effect, its method of action was indirect. That is, the subject was led by the annoying aftereffect to vary his response, which then increased the probability of the occurrence of the correct response.

Following these experiments with humans, Thorndike (1932a) carried out a series of discrimination learning experiments with chickens in which incorrect responses were "punished" by confinement to a small nonrewarded goal box. The results from these studies, confirming his earlier finding, led him to write: "The results of all comparisons by all methods tell the same story. Rewarding a connection always strengthened it substantially; punishing it weakened it little or not at all."

Contemporary Points of View

A contemporary analysis of the problem of punishment must begin with some consideration of an appropriate definition of the construct.

Most current investigators agree that punishment should be defined as the presentation of an aversive stimulus, contingent upon the execution of a specific response. Thus, if a pigeon which has learned to peck a key in order to secure food is then shocked for each key peck, a punishment situation is illustrated. Our definition of punishment acknowledges (1) the presentation of an aversive or noxious stimulus, (2) with such stimulation reducing the probability that a particular behavior will occur.

With regard to the first part of the definition—the presentation of a noxious stimulus—merely because an experimenter states that a stimulus is aversive does not necessarily mean that it is so perceived by the subject. Certainly, some question can be raised concerning Thorndike's assumption that the verbal statement of "wrong" constitutes an aversive stimulus. Frequently, the noxiousness of a stimulus is independently demonstrated by its capacity to serve as a UCS in classical aversive or defense experiments or by its ability to modify behavior in other types of learning situations, e.g., escape response in an instrumental learning task.

Secondly, most contemporary investigators have also assumed that the noxious stimulation must be presented upon the occurrence of moderately or highly motivated behavior; such stimulation reduces the probability that such behavior will reoccur. Here we are indicating the necessity of a contingency being established between the presentation of the aversive stimulus and the punished response which leads to decreased responding. Thus, the objective of punishment is not the acquisition of an instrumental response but rather the weakening or elimination of a response already in the organism's repertoire.

In summary, we may note that the concept of punishment is defined not only with respect to a particular type of motivating condition, but also in terms of a particular contingency relationship—one in which an aversive stimulus results in the cessation of a response. Following Mowrer (1960), punishment situations have been frequently classified as passive avoidance tasks, and can be contrasted with escape or active avoidance tasks which employ aversive stimuli to increase the probability that a response will take place.[3]

Early experiments which used the passive avoidance task were performed by Skinner (1938) and Estes (1944). Skinner's (1938) experiment consisted of conditioning two groups of rats to press a bar in the Skinner box. Following such training, the response was extinguished in both groups for 2 hours on each of two successive days. With the experimental group, all bar pressing responses were immediately followed by a slap to the paw during the first 10 minutes of the first day. An examination of the extinction curve revealed that although the re-

---

[3] All investigators do not restrict punishment to passive avoidance tasks only. Some, e.g., Solomon (1964) and Stevenson (1972), included in punishment aversive stimulation which by its termination or omission supports the growth of escape and avoidance responses.

sponse rate of the experimental group was depressed during the period when the slap was being administered, after the punishment period, the response rate rose more rapidly than the response rate of the control animals. By the end of the extinction period, there was no difference between the two groups of animals with regard to the total number of responses made during the two day extinction period.

Six years later, Estes (1944) made a much more extensive examination of the influence of punishment. Rats were first trained to depress a lever in the Skinner box in which these responses were reinforced every 4 minutes. Two or 3 hours of such periodic reinforcement, sufficiently long to produce a stable rate of responding, were provided. Extinction trials followed in which the influence of punishment was examined. Estes, in contrast to Skinner's use of a slap used shock as his aversive stimulus.[4] Typically, all responses were punished during the first extinction period, but during subsequent extinction periods, shock was omitted.

Results from Estes's first study supported the earlier findings of Skinner (1938). The effect of a short period of mild shock produced a temporary depression in rate of responding. This was followed later by a compensatory increase in rate, so that the total number of responses to reach the criterion was equal to the number which would have been required if no punishment had been administered. This phenomenon has been designated by Boe and Church (1967) as compensatory recovery. In a second study, Estes examined the influence of more severe punishment. Here, the immediate effect of punishment was a rapid decrease in the rate of responding until, at the end of the first 10 minutes of extinction, the animal stopped responding. For the next three extinction days, there was some responding on the part of the previously punished animals but the rate was markedly depressed. On the fourth extinction day and for the remaining three extinciton days, however, responding by the experimental subjects did not differ from that of the controls.

A basic conclusion which Estes came to was that the punished response was not eliminated from the organism's repertoire of responses but rather, continued to exist at a state of considerable latent strength. With punishment discontinued, the withdrawing response that the organism learns to make in the presence of

---

[4] As we shall note in the remainder of this section, electric shock has been used as the "punishing" stimulus in most experimental studies, since it is undoubtedly the simplest method of producing pain (and presumably fear) in animals. As Campbell and Masterson (1969) have indicated, however, shock is an inherently variable source of aversive stimulation when used to motivate free moving animals, e.g., animals placed on an electrified grid, primarily because the electrical resistance of the animal varies enormously as it moves about on the grid floor. This variation in resistance which can range from a few thousand ohms to several million, causes proportional variations in either current flow, power dissipation or voltage drop, depending upon the type of stimulator employed. Campbell and Masterson (1969) have provided the only thorough examination of the characteristics of electric shock as a behavioral stimulus, with variability in the aversiveness of shock stimulation being expressed in terms of "aversion difference limens," an obvious analogy to the traditional psychophysical estimate of sensation variability—the difference limen or JND (just noticeable difference).

the noxious stimulus is weakened and the original response recovers in strength. While the punished response is being suppressed, it is not only protected from extinction but may also become a source of conflict. As a result, Estes posited that the most effective way to "break a habit" or to prevent a response from taking place is to permit it to extinguish rather than to punish it.

Since the early studies of Skinner (1938) and Estes (1944) a variety of punishment parameters have been investigated and we shall examine these in a subsequent chapter. However, Estes's (1944) conclusion doubting the efficacy of punishment has been questioned by a number of experimenters. Masserman (1943) trained cats to feed in a particular experimental apparatus and then subjected them to a blast of air or shock at the moment of feeding. He noted that despite severe hunger, the animals inhibited their feeding response for long periods of time. Similarly, Lichtenstein (1950) observed that dogs which were shocked in the forepaw while eating refused to eat; this inhibitory state lasted for weeks and sometimes for months without further presentation of shock. The subsequent studies of Storms, Boroczi, and Broen (1962), Appel (1963), and Walters and Rogers (1963) using the free operant situation, have confirmed these findings. Both rats and monkeys have inhibited their bar pressing responses for food for durations of weeks and even months when severe shock has been associated with the bar pressing response.

Finally, Boe and Church (1967) have provided the most systematic examination of the Estes (1944) compensatory recovery phenomenon. Their procedure (Experiment 1) was designed to replicate as nearly as possible that of Estes (1944), but along with a control and a "mild" shock group, four additional groups were provided higher intensity shock levels. Following a number of sessions in which lever pressing was reinforced on a 4-minute fixed interval schedule, nine 1-hour extinction sessions were provided. For the experimental groups, shock, consisting of either 35, 50, 75, 120, or 220 volts, was contingent upon lever pressing during minutes 5 through 20 of the first extinction session only. During this 15-minute punishment phase, the stimulator was reset every 30 seconds and the next response was punished; thus a maximum of 30 shocks could be delivered to a particular subject if sufficient responding was maintained. The control group did not, of course, receive shock during this period.

Inasmuch as the varying groups of animals differed at the end of training with regard to response rate, the number of responses during the varying extinction sessions for each subject was divided by the number of responses that the subject made during the last session of reinforced training, and this ratio multiplied by 100. The resulting response measure was designated a response percentage.

The median response percentages for the control and five experimental groups are presented in cumulative form for the 9 extinction sessions in Fig. 9-6. As the authors report, it is obvious that there was both an immediate (i.e., during the 15-minute punishment period) and a permanent (i.e., during the 9 extinction sessions) decrease in responding with the amount of decrease dependent on punishment intensity. Although the response rate increased somewhat upon discontinuation of punishment in the three most intensely punished groups, there was no evidence of compensatory recovery.

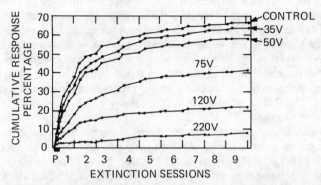

Fig. 9-6. Cumulative median response percentage during extinction. (Punishment, *P*, was contingent upon lever pressing during Minutes 5-20 of the first extinction session.) *Adapted from Boe and Church (1967)*

Punishment Theories

A variety of theoretical positions have been proposed to account for the fact that the presentation of an aversive stimulus changes the organism's behavior—in effect, suppresses the probability of previously learned responding. Thorndike (1913), for example, theorized that a punishing or aversive stimulus which was contingent upon a response simply decreased the strength of that stimulus-response connection. Contemporary theories, however, have emphasized (1) the contribution and importance of an emotional state or fear occasioned by the noxious stimulus as well as (2) the learning of avoidance responses which interfere with a previously learned response.

Estes (1944), in attempting to account for his experimental findings (reviewed earlier), posited that the noxious stimulus produced an emotional state within the organism and that, by means of classical conditioning, any stimulus which was presented simultaneously with the aversive stimulus became a conditioned stimulus capable of arousing this emotional state on subsequent occasions. Such conditioned stimuli could arise from the incipient movements of making the to-be punished response as well as external stimuli which were present when the punishment was administered. Thus, Estes (1944) wrote, "From the results of the present investigation, we may conclude that a great part of the initial effect of punishment is due to this sort of emotional conditioning" (p. 36).

A second theoretical position has assumed that punishment is a two-stage process. Mowrer (1947), an advocate of this position, hypothesized that the response followed by punishment produces certain internal and external stimuli which, by virtue of their contiguity with the aversive stimulus, acquire the capacity to arouse fear.[5] When the organism starts again to make the punished re-

---

[5] In an interesting series of papers, Dinsmoor (1954, 1955), from a strict behavioristic viewpoint, has stated that the inhibitory or suppressive reaction of punishment is due to the conditioning of avoidance responses which conflict

sponse, the resulting fear produces a conflict with the motivation originally un-derlying the response. If the fear is sufficiently strong, the original response will be inhibited or at least in some fashion modified; such inhibition or modification is learned as a result of fear reduction. Two learning processes are thus involved; first, there is fear conditioning, and secondly, the subject learns to make an instrumental response which eliminates or controls the fear.[6] It is this learned avoidance response which competes with the punished response and results in its suppression. Fig. 9-7 illustrates the two processes which presumably take place in punishment situations.

An important aspect of punishment theory concerns the roles of the external stimulus and the response, both of which may be associated with shock. It will be recalled that Estes (1944) took the position that the punishment stimulus, e.g., shock, was associated with two sets of stimuli: namely, (a) stimuli arising from the external situation, such as apparatus cues, etc. and (b) stimuli arising from the movements of initiating the punished response, and that both sets of stimuli were responsible for eliciting an emotional state in the animal. This emo-tional state was assumed to suppress the previously learned response.

Some theorists have asserted that the important contributor to response sup-pression is the association of shock with the punished response—a view which has been designated as the contingency position. On the other hand, others have indicated that this contingency is not necessary and that only an association need be established between the external stimuli and the shock in order for re-sponse suppression to take place—this latter point of view has been designated a noncontingency position.

An early study by Hunt and Brady (1955) attempted to examine these two positions. These authors investigated how the suppression of a previously learned response (lever pressing) was related to (1) the establishment of a contingency between making the response and receiving shock—a punishment procedure, as

---

with the original behavior being punished. Administering aversive stimuli for a given response provides the organism with cues or discriminative stimuli for this response which correspond to the warning signals typically used in avoidance training studies. Thus, the postulation of the construct of fear is unnecessary.

Mowrer (1960), commenting on Dinsmoor's position, has agreed that for some purposes it makes little difference whether one assumes that (1) a danger signal elicits an emotional state which acts to motivate and, through its reduc-tion, reward behavior or (2) the danger signal itself becomes aversive so that its presence is directly motivating and its removal rewarding. Mowrer believes, however, that the postulation of the emotional state provides greater flexibility in accounting for more complex situations. Moreover, Mowrer has questioned the fact that stimuli gain aversive properties in their own right, pointing out that aversiveness is a property of the effected organism and not of the stimulus itself.

[6] It should be noted that Mowrer considers both active and passive avoidance learning situations explainable by a common set of principles. The important distinction between the two tasks is related to the characteristics of the stimuli to which the fear becomes attached. With passive avoidance, or punishment situations, the stimuli are produced by the behavior for which the subject is being punished. With active avoidance, the fear arousing stimuli are not response produced but rather, arise from external sources usually provided by the ex-perimenter.

STAGE 1

STAGE 2

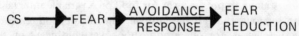

Fig. 9-7. The two stages involved in punishment. It should be noted that the presence of the avoidance response is inferred from the suppression of the punished response. This avoidance response may be some actual overt response or it may be the response of "not responding." In any event, it is presumed to interfere with the punished response.

well as (2) the establishment of a noncontingency between the response and shock. In this latter case, the procedure called only for the learning of an association between the external stimulus and shock—a procedure which would be identical to the establishment of a CER.

The authors reasoned that, in conditioned emotional responding, the CS acquires the capacity to elicit a generalized emotional response as indicated by defecation and freezing. If the suppressant effect of punishment depends primarily on the disruptive effects of fear elicited by the CS, both the punishment and CER groups should show an equal incidence of defecation and freezing. If, on the other hand, the punishment effect depends primarily on the development of more specific avoidance behavior, subjects in the punishment group should reveal a lower incidence of emotional disturbance but a higher incidence of avoidance behavior as reflected in decreased lever pressing.

The experimental procedure consisted of first training rats to press a lever in a Skinner box until a stable level of responding was obtained. Following such training, a noncontingent group received 9 conditioning trials in which the presentation of a CS during the fourth through the sixth minute of a 12-minute trial was associated with shock to the feet. Every effort was made to avoid providing shock when a lever pressing response was being made. The contingent group received a similar number of trials and presentations of the CS; however, each lever pressing response taking place during the 3-minute segment of the 12-minute trial was accompanied by shock.

The results were somewhat equivocal. The contingent group showed a lower incidence of general emotional disturbance; in the presence of the CS, the punished subjects tended to show abortive lever pressing activity, while no signs of such behavior appeared among the noncontingent group. No difference between the groups in the number of lever pressing responses (response suppression), however, was obtained. In spite of this similarity in the number of responses, the authors have interpreted their findings as consistent with the view that the effects of punishment depend heavily upon specific aversive conditioning. In such conditioning stimuli arising from the punished response itself became a critical and significant part of the compound conditioned aversive stimulus which governs suppression.

Subsequent studies by Azrin (1956), Camp, Raymond, and Church (1967), as well as an unpublished study by Church (1969) have been less equivocal in suggesting that the magnitude of suppression of an instrumental response is greater if the punishing stimulus is made contingent on the response than if it is not. This is clearly indicated by Church's (1969) study in which three groups of rats were trained to press a lever for food on a variable interval schedule. For the next ten sessions, the variable interval schedule of food reinforcement remained in effect; however, for one group, shock was contingent on the making of the response, while for the second group, there was no contingency between responding and shock. The third group was a control and received no shock. Results are shown in Fig. 9-8 and clearly reveal the role of response contingent shock on response suppression.

Support for the contingency position is also found in the delay of punishment gradient studies. That is, if the contiguity of response and punishment is critical, the longer the delay between making the punished response and securing punishment, the smaller the suppression effects should be. Studies by Warden and Diamond (1931), Sidman (1953), Kamin (1959), and Coons and Miller (1960) have all provided positive findings.

Kamin's study was most extensive. In two separate studies, rats were first trained to avoid shock by running from one compartment of a shuttlebox to another. The CS was a buzzer (Experiment 1) or a buzzer plus lifting of a gate separating the two compartments (Experiment 2). The UCS was a 1.1-ma shock administered through a grid floor with a CS-UCS interval of 10 seconds. After the animals had reached a criterion of 11 consecutive responses, punishment trials were instituted in which the animals received shock either 0, 10, 20, 30, or 40 seconds after making the avoidance response. Thus, punishment might occur immediately or as much as 40 seconds after the response. A control group which did not receive shock for responding was also used. The results of both studies, as indicated in Fig. 9-9, reveal similar findings and support the position that the time interval between response and presentation of the aversive stimulus is an important variable in punishment studies.

As can be observed in the Hunt and Brady (1955), and Church (1969) studies, as well as others, such as Camp, Raymond, and Church (1967), and Church, Raymond, and Beauchamp (1967), the emotionality occasioned by the aversive stimulus does play a role in response suppression even though the presentation of shock is not temporally contingent with the punished response. An examination of Church's (1969) findings, for example, clearly reveals a greater amount of response suppression for the noncontingent shock group than for the control group. Church (1969) has also reported that the amount of response suppression produced with noncontingent shock is a function of the intensity of the shock which is used.

An integral aspect of Mowrer's (1947) examination of the role of punish-

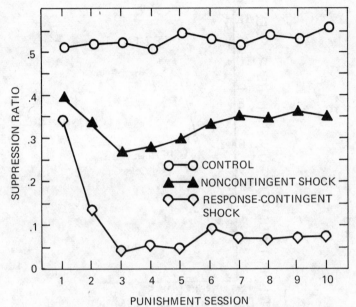

Fig. 9-8. Mean suppression ratio of subjects with response-contingent shock (punishment) and noncontingent shock, and of an unpunished control group. *Adapted from Church (1968)*

ment, it will be recalled, is his explanation that the eliciting of an avoidance response competes with the previously learned response. But one difficulty is that the presence of this avoidance response has never been found in direct observation. Moreover, the ease with which a response is suppressed by punishment does not agree with the extreme difficulty observed by many experimenters in their attempts to establish avoidance responses using the same intensity of the aversive stimulus. As a result, Estes (1969) has concluded that "the weight of the evidence seems to me to indicate that the conditioning of active avoidance responses cannot be a necessary condition for suppression of a response by punishment" (p. 64). He has not denied, however, that conditioned avoidance responses can be established in punishment studies. When they are so established, they should contribute to the suppressive effects noted. His basic position, however, is that the conditioned avoidance response should not be considered an integral part of punishment theory.

Estes (1969) has recently presented a revised single factor theory of punishment, the details of which, unfortunately, are too elaborate to provide in this text. Briefly, he has proposed, "The primary mechanism of punishment is not a competition of responses but rather a competition of motives" (p. 80). The establishment of a conditioned emotional response continues to be a major feature of his position; however, for Estes now it has its effect in suppressing behavior by weakening the motivational support for the punished response. As he has written, "Thus, a stimulus which has preceded a traumatic event, e.g., shock, as in the typical CER or punishment paradigm, acquires the capacity of

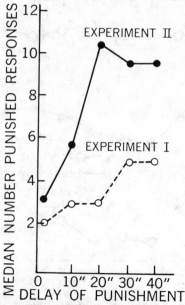

Fig. 9-9. Median number of extinction responses as a function of delay of punishment. *Adapted from Kamin (1959)*

inhibiting the input of amplifier elements from sources associated with hunger, thirst, and the like.[7] If, then, while the animal is performing an instrumental response for, say, food reward, this conditioned stimulus is presented, the facilitative drive will be reduced and so also the probability or rate of the instrumental response" (p. 80).

Physiological Mechanisms

We should like to conclude this chapter by examining some of the contemporary research which has explored motivation as related to physiological mechanisms, and more specifically, electrical and chemical stimulation of the brain. In organizing this material, we will consider two areas: (1) consummatory responses resulting from brain stimulation and (2) the reinforcing function of brain stimulation.

Consumatory Responses Resulting from Brain Stimulation

A number of experimenters using many organisms have found that chemical as well as electrical stimulation of the hypothalamus can produce a variety of consummatory responses.[8]

[7] An amplifier element is essentially a drive or motivational factor.

[8] We shall not describe in any detail the techniques for providing either electrical

Some of the early studies describing these effects are most interesting. A study by Andersson (1953) revealed that minute injections of hypertonic saline into the hypothalamus of goats would produce drinking. A few years later, Miller, Richter, Bailey, and Southwick (1955) implanted a hypodermic needle in the third and lateral ventricles of the brain of thirsty cats and found that .15 cc of a hypertonic solution (2%) reliably *increased*, while an injection of .15 cc of distilled water reliably *depressed*, the water consumption of the animals. Since these early studies, a number of experimenters, e.g., Fisher and Coury (1962), Levitt and Fisher (1966), have also demonstrated that chemical stimulation of certain areas in the brain will produce the drinking response.

In another study, Delgado and Anand (1953) observed that the electrical stimulation of certain points in the hypothalamus of cats would result in eating as well as the gnawing of inedible objects. A variety of subsequent investigations, e.g., Smith (1956), have indicated that this phenomenon can be reliably obtained. Moreover, it must be noted that this effect is not dependent on the subject's being deprived and that the amount of food eaten is not related to bodily requirements of the organism. In Delgado and Anand's (1953) experiment, for example, different parts of the cat's hypothalamus were stimulated for 1 hour daily over a five to ten day period. Their findings reveal that such stimulation resulted in as much as a 1000% increase in food intake when contrasted with subjects not provided such stimulation.

Sexual responses have also been produced by electrical stimulation of the hypothalamus. Vaughan and Fisher (1962) found that male rats which had permanently implanted electrodes in their lateral interior hypothalamus would engage in copulatory behavior with estrous females within seconds after the onset of stimulation.[9]

An important aspect of all of these hypothalamic stimulation studies is that the elicited consummatory responses are "stimulus bound." That is, unless appropriate goal objects, e.g., food, water, etc., are provided, the consummatory behavior will not be produced by such stimulation. This kind of evidence has been cited by many investigators to support the position that such behavior is not a stereotyped motor response on the part of the subject, but, rather, can be used to infer a specific drive or motivational state: hunger, thirst, etc. Stimulation at the particular hypothalamic site has been conceptualized as the physi-

---

or chemical stimulation to the brain. A number of sources, e.g., Delgado (1961), Spiegel, and Wycis (1961), and Sheatz (1961), may be consulted for such information. When chemical stimulation is provided, a thin polyethylene tube leads to a hypodermic needle which has been permanently implanted in the skull. Electrical stimulation, far more frequently used, involves the permanent implantation of electrodes which are insulated except at the tips. With bipolar electrodes, in which the tips are usually quite close together, the current flows from one tip to the other, restricting the stimulation to a very small area of the brain.

An atlas of the subject's brain is required so that the location of the electrodes which are to be implanted can be approximated. After the experiment has been completed, the animal is sacrificed, and the brain removed so that the exact location of the electrodes can be determined.

[9] We have provided only a few of the many studies in which a specific type of behavior has been elicited by electrical stimulation of the hypothalamus. See Valenstein, Cox, and Kakolewski (1969) for a more detailed listing.

ological correlate of the drive. Many experimenters have hypothesized that there are specific neural circuits controlling each of these consummatory activities, with the hypothalamus believed to consist of a number of centers, each located in a discrete anatomical region, and playing a major role in controlling a specific drive. But other points of view have been expressed. Valenstein and his associates have not only objected to the specific neural circuit hypothesis, but more important, have argued that "hypothalamic stimulation does not elicit hunger, thirst and other motivational states" (Valenstein, Cox, and Kakolewski, 1969, p. 276). Their point of view is that such stimulation is not motivating, at least as motivation is traditionally conceived. What is the nature of this evidence?

In an early study, Valenstein, Cox, and Kakolewski (1968a), found that the activation of the same neural substrate could elicit a number of behaviors rather than only one, as most earlier investigators had found. Their experimental procedure consisted of first making available to their subjects (rats), food, water, and a piece of wood (which could be gnawed). A test series of stimulating the lateral hypothalamus in the presence of these three goal objects elicited one of three behaviors, eating, drinking, or gnawing. Following the reliable demonstration of such stimulus-bound behavior, the animals were placed on a "night schedule." This consisted of stimulating the animal in the same hypothalamic site with the same intensity current for a 12-hour period with stimulation delivered for 30 seconds every 5 minutes. The two goal objects which were not related to the stimulus-bound behavior were available to the animal during this period. Thus, if eating was shown to be the stimulus-bound behavior elicited by the first test series stimulation, only the water and wood were placed in the goal box during the night schedule of stimulation.

Following such an experience a second series of test stimulations was provided. It will be recalled that in the first test series, the same behavior was elicited in each animal in almost all instances. The second series of tests which were provided following the night schedule, indicated that hypothalamic stimulation resulted in a different type of behavior when the appropriate goal object was provided. Moreover, such behavior was exhibited quite consistently. When stimulation was provided with all three goal objects present, approximately equal amounts of the two previously elicited behaviors were displayed. Additional tests resulted in the authors' concluding that once a second stimulus-bound behavior was established, the initial behavior elicited by stimulation could no longer be considered the dominant response.[10]

[10] Wise (1968) found that by increasing the intensity of the current in hypothalamic stimulation, more than one type of behavior could be elicited. He also observed that the threshold for eliciting a particular behavior tended to decline over time; his conclusion is that the second behavior which emerged in the Valenstein, et al (1968a) study, in which only one stimulus intensity was used, resulted from the gradual decline in the threshold of the neural circuits responsible for the original behavior. Wise has maintained that there are separate fixed neural circuits functionally isolated from one another and that it is the threshold changes in these circuits which create the impression of variability. Valenstein, Cox, and Kakolewski (1969) have not accepted Wise's explanation. In subsequent experiments, they have found that manipulation of the strength of the current did not result in obtaining the changes in behavior noted by Wise. In

The nature of these findings has led the authors to critically examine the "motivational" explanation for stimulus-bound behavior. In one experiment (Valenstein, Cox, and Kakolewski, 1968b), it was found that hypothalamic stimulation would result in the stimulus-bound eating of canned cat/dog food. When placed on a night schedule with Purina chow (a food with which the rats had previous experience) and water available, the animals would display stimulus-bound drinking. Or, in another experiment (Valenstein, Kakolewski, and Cox, 1968), it was observed that after stimulus-bound drinking from a water tube was obtained, providing a night schedule with food pellets and a dish of water available resulted in a switch in the animals' behavior to stimulus-bound eating. The failure of animals to exhibit behavior which generalized along a dimension appropriate to satisfy a particular need suggested that stimulus-bound behavior cannot be used to infer the presence of a motivational state, at least not as traditionally conceptualized.

Although the authors would accept the position that the hypothalamus is in some way involved in the expression of motivated behavior, it is their belief that the *biological consequences* of behavior elicited by hypothalamic stimulation is of little importance. Perhaps most significant is their conclusion that the usual conceptualization of the hypothalamus as comprising a number of centers, each playing a major role in controlling a specific motivational state, is much too simplistic an analysis, and that there is a basic need to revise this view of hypothalamic functioning.

The Reinforcing Function

Psychologists have been aware of the work of a number of experimenters who have demonstrated a relationship between certain sensory and/or motor events and the stimulation of specific parts of the brain. As early as 1932, Hess had reported that brain stimulation could elicit fear-like responses in the cat. And, as noted in the last section, the contribution of hypothalamic stimulation in eliciting specific consummatory responses had also been examined. However, for the psychologist working in the early fifties, the roles of brain stimulation and reinforcement remained a mystery. It was assumed that reinforcement had some neurological correlate yet to be discovered. If such a discovery could be made, perhaps many, if not all the questions related to reinforcement—the most important construct in learning theory—could be answered.

It was a most exciting event, then, when Olds and Milner (1954) reported the findings of a preliminary experiment which indicated that brain stimulation could serve as reinforcement for a bar pressing response. In this study, rats having electrodes implanted in the septal region of their rhinencephalon, when placed in Skinner Boxes in which brain stimulation was followed by the pressing of a bar, would continue to make the bar pressing response for long periods of time. Finally, the physiological correlate of reinforcement had been discovered.

A host of studies have been conducted since the publication of Olds and

---

fact, they have pointed out that once the second behavior is elicited, a decrease in stimulus intensity will continue to produce this type of behavior.

Milner's work, and as the earlier reviews of Zeigler (1957) and Gallistel (1964) indicate, many investigators have demonstrated the reliability of the brain stimulation or the intracranial stimulation (ICS) effect, as well as revealing its generality to guinea pigs, cats, dogs, goats, dolphins, monkeys, and man.

In addition to the Olds and Milner (1954) finding that the onset of stimulation could have reinforcing effects, it has been found by a number of investigators that it is possible to reinforce instrumental behavior also by terminating stimulation. In one of the early studies demonstrating such an effect, Delgado, Roberts, and Miller (1954) first trained cats to turn a wheel in order to terminate peripheral shock. Electrical stimulation was then provided in the tectal area, the lateral nuclear mass of the thalamus, and the hippocampus. After a number of trials, the animals learned to rotate the wheel in order to terminate such stimulation.

In a second study, the same procedure was employed, except that a tone was used as a conditioned stimulus and paired with brain stimulation (UCS). If the wheel was turned during CS presentation, it was possible to avoid the UCS. After a number of trials, it was observed that the animals would turn the wheel in order to avoid stimulation. The general explanation for these results is that such stimulation is aversive and its offset is reinforcing to the organism.

A most interesting finding is that both onset and termination of brain stimulation (at the same locus) have been shown to have rewarding characteristics. In an experiment (Experiment 2) by Roberts (1958), a symmetrical Y-maze was used in which entry into one arm turned stimulation on while entry into a second arm turned it off. A third arm was a "no change in stimulation" arm. Robert's found that cats learned to oscillate back and forth between the arm which turned the stimulation on and the arm which turned it off.

In a subsequent study by Bower and Miller (1958), a similar result was obtained with rats. In this study, rats were first provided with electrical stimulation as a reward for bar pressing. After learning this response, they were given escape training in a T-maze. Here, the animal was placed in the start box, the door opened, and electrical stimulation initiated. When the animal went to the side of the maze opposite its initial preference, stimulation was terminated. It was observed that the experimental subjects were able to learn this response, thus demonstrating the onset and offset reward characteristics of brain stimulation. It should be noted that the investigators were not successful in documenting this onset-offset effect with all their experimental subjects. Of 13 animals who learned to press the bar for electrical stimulation, just six of these also met the criterion for escape learning in the T-maze.

In this type of study, it would seem that the onset of stimulation is rewarding but that after continuing for a time, it becomes aversive which results in the animal's learning some instrumental response to terminate it.

A Comparison of ICS with Traditional Reinforcers

One area of experimental interest has been to compare the reinforcing effects provided by the ICS with traditional reinforcers. Virtually all experimenters recognize that the amount of traditional reward, e.g., food, that can be provided a subject during a single experimental session is limited, since satiation effects are soon obtained with a concommitant reduction in performance. The effects of ICS are in marked contrast to this finding. Olds (1958a) has reported that rats implanted with hypothalamic electrodes and provided stimulation for bar pressing, maintained a high level of responding for 48 consecutive hours—until they were physically exhausted. One animal maintained a rate of 2000 bar presses per hour for 26 consecutive hours, then slept, but upon waking went back to its 2000 per hour response rate. It must be noted that all electrode placements did not provide this kind of finding. Animals which had electrodes implanted in the telencephalon revealed rapid responding for the first 4 hours following which there was an abrupt slowing down in response rate.

But with subjects given a fixed amount of time for responding, thus negating any satiation effects, experimenters have been interested in examining the relative value of these two agents for reinforcing behavior. As we shall note, the evidence is mixed, although the reason for such a state of affairs is obvious. Any experiment which manipulates a traditional reward such as food or water must be concerned with the subject's hours of deprivation, as well as the quality and quantity of the reinforcing agent provided on each trial. Similarly, any experiment utilizing ICS must be concerned with the locus of stimulation, as well as the intensity and duration of the stimulation itself. Thus, when a comparison is made between these two "types" of reinforcement, the result will frequently depend on the specific parameters utilized.

One of the early studies by Burnsten and Delgado (1958) revealed the superiority of food in contrast to ICS. Here, monkeys were permitted to locomote over an entire table, receiving ICS just on one side of the table. In order to get the monkeys to the other side, a peanut was rolled across the table. Findings revealed that in no instance did the monkeys ever choose to remain on the side in which they were receiving stimulation to forego capturing the peanut. But one may wonder if the electrodes had been implanted in another site, or more intense stimulation provided, whether the results would have continued to demonstrate the superior reinforcing effects of the food.

The relativity of findings in this area is at least partially indicated in a study by Spies (1965). His subjects were rats and the apparatus used was a T-maze in which one arm led to food, the other to ICS. An extended period of training was provided in which two groups of animals, one with electrodes implanted in the lateral hypothalamus, the second with electrodes implanted at other loci, were trained to respond to one arm in order to receive ICS and to the other arm to receive food. Test sessions were then provided in which the animals' preference for food or ICS was examined by placing them under increasing levels of food deprivation. At the beginning of each session the animals were forced to run once to the right and once to the left arm as a "reminder" of the location in order to determine their reward preference. Subjects were tested at 2, 12, 24, 48, 72, 96, 120, 144, 168, 192, 216, and 240 hours of deprivation. Fig. 9–10 illustrates the difference between the two groups' average choice of ICS in preference to food during each 19-trial period at each level of deprivation. The partial relativity effect can readily be observed, since the group which had electrodes implanted at loci other than the hypothalamus consistently chose the ICS arm when food

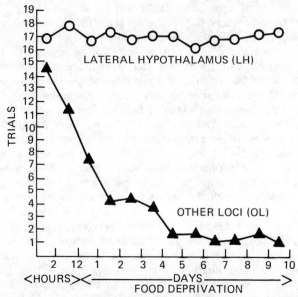

Fig. 9-10. Average number of trials (out of 19) ICS was chosen in preference to food by the LH and OL groups, at increasing levels of food deprivation. *Adapted from Spies (1965)*

deprivation was just 2 hours, but preference for this arm rapidly declined as the deprivation period was extended. At 48 hours of deprivation, this group averaged only four choices of ICS. On the other hand, the superiority of ICS over food as a reward preference was clearly demonstrated by the group which had electrodes implanted in the lateral hypothalamus.[11]

This latter finding of the superiority of ICS reinforcing effects over traditional rewards has been noted by a number of other investigators. Kling and Matsumiya (1961) implanted electrodes in rats' posterior hypothalamus and

[11] Spies's experimental procedure consisted of placing ICS animals under food deprivation in order to provide the appropriate test trials. One problem is that this procedure ignores any interaction effect that may exist between ICS and the deprivation state. Studies by Brady, Boren, Conrad, and Sidman (1957), Olds (1958b), as well as other experimenters, have indicated that deprivation states have an influence on behavior rewarded by brain stimulation. In the Brady et al study, following the establishment of a stable rate of lever pressing in which electrical stimulation was the only reward, cats were placed under food and water deprivation periods of 1, 4, 24, and 48 hours, and returned to the apparatus. A different group of subjects, rats, were provided a series of 1-hour sessions in which only 0 and 48 hours of food and water deprivation were alternated. Results indicated that with both species, lever pressing rates were significantly higher after 48 hours of deprivation than after 0 or 1 hour. The lever pressing rates for cats obtained after 4- and 24-hour deprivation periods tended to fall between the values obtained at the two extremes.

then used a bar pressing task in order to determine if ICS could serve as reinforcement in a subsequent task. Animals which failed to consistently respond were discarded. The animals were then pretrained to push open panels in a Y-shaped, two-choice discrimination apparatus; on some trials food was used as a reward, on other trials, ICS. Animals were then given training to learn the discrimination, half of the subjects learning the task with food as a reward, the other half with ICS. Following such learning, the task was reversed. Half of the group which was reinforced with food was switched to ICS while half of the group which was originally reinforced with ICS was switched to food. The other half of each group continued to be reinforced with the reward which was provided in the first task. Results in learning this first task indicated little difference between groups given ICS or food. The discrimination reversal, however, revealed that the group which was switched from ICS to food took significantly longer to learn the second task than the other three groups. The authors have noted that these findings support the position that ICS reinforcement results in learning which is more permanent than resulting from food reinforcement, the discrimination reversal task being a more sensitive measure of this effect than the original learning task.

Perhaps the most dramatic indication of the superiority of ICS as a reinforcer can be found in the studies of Routtenberg and Lindy (1965), and Eckert and Lewis (1967). In this first study, rats with electrodes implanted at either the medial forebrain bundle-posterior hypothalamus or the septal area, were trained to press a bar in a Skinner Box for food for 1 hour per day, the only time that food was made available to the animals. After the animals had learned to press the bar with sufficient frequency to maintain their weight, food—ICS competition tests were begun. Here, the pressing of one bar would result in ICS, the pressing of a second bar would result in food. Experimental sessions continued to consist of 1 hour per day. Results revealed that all the septal animals and 4 hypothalamic subjects pressed the food bar with sufficient frequency to maintain their weight; on the other hand, 6 hypothalamic animals ignored the food bar and spent most of the session pressing the ICS bar. Continuance of the program beyond the fourth day would have resulted in this latter group of animals starving to death.

Eckert and Lewis (1967) have demonstrated a somewhat similar phenomenon with adrenalectomized rats. They observed that some of their animals, when given a choice between pressing a bar for a sodium chloride solution which was necessary to maintain life, and pressing a bar which would provide ICS, chose the ICS bar with the result that death ensued after a number of experimental sessions.

On the other hand, there is some evidence which suggests that ICS, at least in certain situations, functions less effectively than traditional rewards. Some experimenters have had great difficulty in getting animals which were provided ICS as reinforcement to maintain a simple response, i.e., lever pressing, on anything other than small fixed interval or fixed ratio reinforcement schedules, and variable interval or variable ratio schedules typically result in much poorer performance than traditional rewards. Brady and Conrad (1960), for example, were barely able to keep their rats responding on a variable interval schedule with a mean interval of 60 seconds—an interval which compares poorly with variable interval schedules having means of 5 to 10 minutes which will maintain steady responding when traditional rewards are used.[12]

There is also some indication that experimental extinction takes place more rapidly when ICS has been used as reward. Olds and Milner (1954), Seward, Uyeda, and Olds (1959), as well as others, have noted this phenomenon. In the Seward et al study, rats had their bar pressing responses reinforced with ICS, with 2000 to 40,000 responses being made over a series of daily 15- or 30-minute sessions. Removal of the stimulation resulted in performance dropping very sharply, with steep extinction curves being observed.

More direct support for this position is found in a study by Culbertson, Kling, and Berkley (1966) who compared ICS and food rewarded animals using the traditional bar pressing response. All of their subjects (rats) had electrodes implanted in their hypothalamus and all were reduced to 80% of their ad lib body weight. During acquisition, two groups were provided continuous reinforcement of either ICS or food; two other groups were placed on a fixed ratio schedule in which every tenth response was reinforced (with ICS or food). After 10 sessions of 100 reinforcements per session, 4 daily 15-minute extinction periods were provided. Findings revealed that the animals reinforced with food were significantly more persistent in their bar pressing responses during these extinction sessions than animals which had received ICS regardless of the type of reinforcement schedule utilized. Fig. 9–11 illustrates these findings. It may be noted however, that the schedule of reinforcement appears to be a more effective variable in determining extinction responding than the type of reinforcement provided.

One interesting variable involved in extinction responding after ICS is related to the amount of time interpolated between the last acquisition trial and the beginning of the extinction session. In a study by Howarth and Deutsch (1962) in which rats were trained to press a bar in a Skinner box for an ICS reward, one group was given extinction trials immediately following the last reinforced bar press. A "delayed" group, on the other hand, after its last reinforced bar press, had the lever from the apparatus removed for 7 seconds, following which the lever was returned and extinction trials provided. Results indicated that the number of extinction responses for the "delayed" group approximated the number of responses made by the "immediate" group after 7 seconds of extinction responding. In summary, if the "immediate" group's responses made during the first 7 seconds of extinction were eliminated from consideration, the number of responses made by both groups for the remainder of the extinction session was quite similar. A second experiment in which the lever was removed for 2.5,

[12] It should be acknowledged that all investigators are not in agreement with these conclusions. Gibson, Reid, Sakai, and Porter (1965) as well as Pliskoff, Wright, and Hawkins (1965) have indicated that reinforcement with ICS results in findings not materially different from that provided by traditional reinforcers. After an examination of both fixed interval and fixed ratio schedules of ICS reinforcement, Pliskoff, Wright, and Hawkins concluded that ICS "is not markedly less potent than the more traditional reinforcers such as food, water, etc. Contrary to the commonly held view, BSR [brain stimulation reinforcement] can be used to maintain intermittent schedule performances in the range of parameter values often used with the conventional reinforcers" (p. 86).

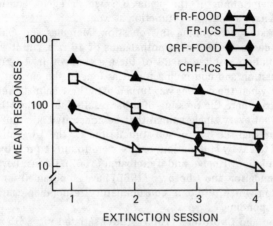

Fig. 9-11. Mean number of responses emitted during the four daily extinction sessions. *Adapted from Culbertson, Kling, and Berkley (1966)*

5.0, 7.5, or 10.0 seconds after the last reinforced trial, with extinction responses then examined, confirmed the findings of the first study. Thus, the amount of time elapsing between the end of the brain stimulation and the beginning of the extinction trials plays a critical role in determining the number of extinction responses emitted by the animal.

A somewhat similar effect has been noted when ICS is used to reinforce runway behavior and maze learning. Olds (1956) found that, although the use of the ICS resulted in the improvement of rats learning a complex maze, there was a spontaneous decrement in performance from the last trial of one day's session to the first trial on the next day. Similarly, Seward, Uyeda, and Olds (1960) have reported that runway performance as measured by running speed did not improve when 15 minutes was interpolated between trials; on the other hand, 15 seconds between trials resulted in performance increment. It should be noted that these kinds of findings are not typically obtained when traditional rewards are used.

This necessarily limited examination of the ICS studies provides some general understanding of the area; however, our introductory statement indicating how difficult it is to arrive at any general conclusions about the comparative reinforcing values of ICS and traditional rewards continues to hold. Early findings of the superiority of traditional rewards over ICS have given way to other results showing no difference or a superiority of ICS. But in the last analysis, the effectiveness of a traditional reward, or ICS, appears to depend on the specific parameters which are used in the experiment.

Consummatory Responding and the Reinforcing Function

As noted, brain stimulation which can elicit a consummatory response and that which can serve a reinforcing function have been thought of as two separate areas of experimental investigation. However, some experimenters have been interested in determining if the same ICS which elicits consummatory responding could have a reinforcing function as well.

In an early study examining this question, Margules and Olds (1962) implanted electrodes in the lateral hypothalamus of 46 rats, and it was found that electrical stimulation resulted in 28 of these eating within 2 seconds after the onset of stimulation and continuing to eat as long as the current remained on. Eating stopped when the current was turned off. These animals were then tested in a Skinner box where the pressing of a bar resulted in similar stimulation. Results revealed that every single animal that demonstrated stimulus-bound eating behavior also pressed the bar for self-stimulation. Of the 18 animals that could not be induced to eat by stimulation, only 4 were found to press the bar in order to receive stimulation. Hoebel and Teitelbaum (1962), Coons, Levak, and Miller (1965), and Mendelson and Chorover (1965) have all obtained similar findings— brain stimulation which results in consummatory responding can also reinforce instrumental responding.

In Mendelson and Chorover's (1965) study, satiated rats with electrodes implanted in the lateral hypothalamus were given T-maze training with food available in one of the goal boxes. Electrical stimulation provided at the beginning of each trial (resulting in eating when food was available) was terminated 10 seconds after the animal entered either goal box. These investigators found their animals were easily able to reach the criterion of 16 correct responses in two consecutive 10-trial sessions.

The importance of the reinforcing event—eating in the goal box—for the learning of an instrumental response was further demonstrated in a study by Mendelson (1966). He first found that satiated animals placed in a T-maze and provided brain stimulation (which would elicit the consummatory response) learned to go to a goal box containing food in preference to a goal box that did not. Since electrical stimulation was provided in both maze arms as well as in the goal boxes, it seems reasonable to assume that the consumption of food (while being stimulated) provided the differential reinforcement and accounted for the learning of the appropriate response. Mendelson then showed that his animals would continue to perform correctly even when brain stimulation was eliminated from the starting box and the arms of the maze. As long as the animals received stimulation in the goal box which contained food and resulted in eating, performance did not deteriorate. However, the elimination of stimulation from the rewarded end box, even when stimulation was present in the starting box and the rest of the maze quickly reduced choice point behavior to a random level and greatly increased running time. The facilitation of instrumental responding took place only when brain stimulation was accompanied by eating.

We should like to conclude this section with the description of a study by Mogenson and Stevenson (1966) who also examined consummatory responding and the reinforcing function. Their experimental apparatus contained a lever located approximately 3 centimeters below a water spout. It was found that the presentation of brain stimulation following a lever press would result in satiated animals' drinking and continuing to drink until the electrical stimulation was terminated. The termination of stimulation resulted in the animals' again pressing the lever in order to obtain stimulation. Lever pressing was reinforced by brain stimulation which in turn elicited the drinking response. The authors found that the duration of the electrical stimulation was a critical factor. Stimulation of less than one-half second resulted only in the bar pressing response, whereas stimulus durations greater than this resulted in bar pressing and drinking. A subsequent study by Mogenson and Kaplinsky (1970) has confirmed these findings. It was observed that when the duration of stimulation was 1.2 seconds, both bar pressing and drinking took place; with just .2 seconds of stimulation, the animals would continue to press the bar but would not drink.

It is obvious that these findings reveal brain stimulation to be a complex phenomenon. Certain types of stimulation will result only in consummatory responding while others are capable of reinforcing instrumental responding; still other types of stimulation may serve both functions. What is perhaps most interesting is that brain stimulation once looked upon as providing an answer in determining the nature of reinforcement, has succeeded only in raising more problems than it has solved.

Summary

The validity of Hull's concept of primary reinforcement has been examined over a wide range of experimental investigations, many of these have demonstrated that it is possible for learning to take place in the absence of primary reinforcement. Saccharine, for example, has been shown to reinforce maze learning in rats, although it does not reduce the organism's need for food; similarly, lights and sounds have been found to reinforce bar pressing, although again, it is difficult to determine how such stimulation is related to the satisfaction of the organism's need state. This type of evidence has resulted in the disavowal of Hull's position on reinforcement. A variety of other theoretical points of view regarding the nature of reinforcement have been proposed, some of these emphasizing the role of the stimulus or the response as basic mechanisms underlying reinforcement. Physiological mechanisms involved in reinforcement have been also investigated.

One theoretical position has proposed that reinforcement be conceptualized in terms of stimulus change; that is, stimulus response relationships followed by some stimulus change are thereby strengthened. Although a variety of experiments have demonstrated that learning can take place when responses are "reinforced" only by the onset (or termination) of light or sound, such reinforcing effects were found to be temporary, unstable, and often difficult to replicate.

A second position sees the consummatory response as the basic reinforcement mechanism. It has been proposed that the consummatory response provides the organism with a reinforcing state of affairs, as in the drinking of water sweetened by saccharine. The problem with this point of view is that learning has been shown to take place when the consummatory response is bypassed—food placed directly into the stomach can act as reinforcement.

Another response hypothesis was proposed by Premack who stated that reinforcement takes place when a response of a lower independent rate coincides with the stimuli governing the occurrence of a response of a higher independent rate. Thus, reinforcement involves a relationship between two responses, one of these serving as the instrumental response and being reinforced by the occurrence of the second. Of any two responses, the more probable will reinforce the less probable. Although a number of experiments have provided support for Premack's position, a number of others have not, so that the status of this concept of reinforcement is also questionable. Premack's contribution has been valuable, however, in emphasizing that reinforcement is relative, sometimes reinforcing a response while at other times not doing so. In summary, psychologists do not have any theory of reinforcement which has been demonstrated to hold over a wide variety of experimental situations.

An added construct, secondary reinforcement, was originally proposed to supplement the law of primary reinforcement. Secondary reinforcement was defined as a neutral stimulus which acquired reinforcing strength by association with primary reinforcement. Secondary reinforcement has been a more viable construct than primary reinforcement, and a number of studies have been conducted to examine how the strength of a secondary reinforcing stimulus varies as a function of a number of reinforcement variables, such as the amount of primary reinforcement associated with the secondary reinforcing stimulus. Many contemporary investigators consider secondary reinforcing stimuli only a discriminating stimulus which has the capacity to elicit previously learned responses.

The concept of punishment, although not a part of Hull's theoretical system, has interested investigators for some time. Most current experimenters define punishment as the presentation of an aversive stimulus, contingent upon the execution of a specific response. One of the most frequent explanations of how punishment operates is that the response followed by the aversive stimulus produces internal and external stimuli which, by virtue of their contiguity with the aversive stimulus, acquire the capacity to arouse fear. When the organism attempts to make the punished response, the fear which results produces a conflict with the motivation underlying the original response so that the original response is inhibited.

With regard to physiological mechanisms involved in reinforcement, a number of experimenters have demonstrated that either electrical or chemical stimulation of the brain or intracranial stimulation (ICS) will elicit a variety of consummatory responses, e.g., drinking, eating, although such studies have indicated that the appropriate goal object must be available if the response is to be made.

Olds and Milner were the first to show that ICS could reinforce behavior. Rats having electrodes implanted in the septal region of their rhinencephalon, when placed in Skinner boxes where brain stimulation followed bar pressing, would continue to make the bar pressing response for a long period of time. This effect has been confirmed by many subsequent investigators.

Although a number of experimenters have tried to determine if the reinforcing effect of brain stimulation is different from traditional rewards, there is some doubt as to whether or not this represents an answerable question. For the most part, the experimental findings can be related to the reward or ICS parameters manipulated.

10
Learning as a Function of Motivational Variables:
Deprivation and Reward

The two previous chapters were concerned with the nature of motivation. In the next two chapters we will examine how instrumental learning tasks are influenced by the manipulation of motivational variables. The experimental work that has been conducted in this area is quite extensive; consequently, we shall confine our attention to instrumental reward learning tasks here, and examine escape and avoidance tasks in Chapter 11.

Deprivation States

Although contemporary psychologists have not given the same prominence to the construct of drive and its contribution to learning as have earlier investigators, we should like to discuss briefly how deprivation states, from which the drive construct has frequently been inferred, influence performance.

Most instrumental reward experiments conducted support the position that performance, as measured by rate of responding, improves as a function of the intensity or length of the deprivation state. Table 10-1 summarizes only a few of these experiments. To illustrate the nature of these findings, Barry (1958) examined the speed of rats traversing a 4-foot runway, with the animals under either 2.5 or 26.5 hours of food deprivation. Fifty-two trials were provided over a 21-day testing period. Fig. 10-1 reveals running speed over the trials provided as a function of the level of deprivation.[1]

When probability of response measures are used, based on the number of errors or the frequency of correct responding, it is difficult to come to any general conclusion regarding the relationship between the length of the deprivation state and performance in the instrumental reward task. Table 10-2 provides a sampling of these studies. It seems obvious that we must search for the operation of other variables which presumably interact with the deprivation state in order to account for divergent findings.[2]

The Role of Reward

The role of reward in instrumental learning tasks has concerned a number of investigators during the past three decades and the experimental literature is voluminous. In general, interest has centered around three parameters: (1) the number and/or intermittency of the reward, (2) the amount of reward that is provided, and (3) the interval of time (or temporal delay) between the instrumental response and the securing of reward.

Number of Reinforcements

An examination of most instrumental reward learning studies in which the organism is presented with a series of continuously reinforced trials reveals that performance during these trials, as measured by either rate or probability of responding, is a function of the number of reinforcements which have been provided.

It would serve no useful purpose to detail the experimental evidence supporting this conclusion since an examination of most learning curves in which trials or number of reinforcements have been plotted on the abscissa indicate the basic truth of this position.

[1] There is, of course, a basic difficulty in assigning any change in performance to the deprivation state alone, perhaps because the reward used assumes new properties as a function of the length of deprivation. A single pellet of food used to reward a 2-hour deprived rate would not appear to have as much reward value as the same pellet of food given to a rat deprived for 24 hours. Thus, the value of a reward may be looked upon as being a function of the specific characteristics of the reward as well as of the physiological state of the organism.

[2] A decade after Hull's *Principles of Behavior* (1943) appeared, some investigators became interested in determining whether deprivation states influenced the organism's performance or habit strength (learning), a basic distinction in Hullian theory. This attempt was not successful since typical experiments conducted, e.g., Teel (1952), Hillman, Hunter, and Kimble (1953), Lewis and Cotton (1957), Barry (1958), yielded controversial findings. Readers interested in further examination of this area should consult Hall (1966).

others like her in urban Sri Lanka. For part of her life Somavati had lived among her kinsmen; then the vicissitudes of social change had pushed her family into other places of residence where they had few extended kin ties.

Meanwhile, the deity fixed a date for Somavati's induction as priestess about four months after her exorcism. Somavati went through a brief ceremonial in which she was elevated to the role of priestess, entitling her to have her own shrine and participate in some of the rituals of the cult. The principle involved here, often encountered in social life, is the role resolution of the psychological conflict or conflicts of the individual. The psychological problem of the individual is harnessed into social ends through a new role, which can utilize that problem in a new and positive direction; for example, when a homosexual is converted into a monk or berdache, or when Somavati's propensity for getting into a "trance" state is utilized for divine rather than demonic ends. Had it worked it would have elevated Somavati's social status and her own self-esteem; but Somavati simply could not take the role of priest, which was formally given to her in the ritual of investiture.

Her own reasons for her failure are partially satisfactory. If she were to become a priestess, she had to have a shrine in her own home, but this was not possible because of the crowded conditions in which she lived and her own poverty. Also I do not think she had the intelligence and resources required for the new role, as some others in the cult group had. Furthermore, she had a new but anticipated social problem: sex. The ritual had relaxed some of her sexual inhibitions: the new situation gave her freedom for "play." Within three months of the exorcism she had an "affair" with a young man who was a member of the cult group. In six months she had two other affairs, one with a priest of another shrine and a friend of the *Kapurāla*. She became pregnant and gave birth to a baby, but none of her lovers would acknowledge paternity. She now lives in her parents' house with her infant. It is interesting to note that the parents did not disown her or even reprimand her. They have recognized her right to "play." Moreover the *Kapurāla* interceded on her behalf, and met her parents about the possibility of getting her married to one of her lovers; the obstacle here was physiological paternity, which was very important to both lovers. The *Kapurāla* is optimistic that Somavati will eventually get married. What is important, however, is the *Kapurāla*'s fatherly role: the symbolic rebirth of Somavati as a child of the priests of the cult has a truly sociological dimension. The *Kapurāla* takes an interest in her future, and she finds comfort, security, and comradeship as a member of the cult group. Meanwhile the demons are quiet, perhaps waiting, as in all of us, ready to spring once again at an opportune moment.

POSTSCRIPT ON SOMAVATI: AUGUST 5, 1973

I interviewed Somavati once again in August 1973, when I visited Sri Lanka for summer research. She was more relaxed and communicative than I had ever known. She still lives with her parents, and her new child is well looked after and liked by them. Somavati has a new job: together with four other women, she cooks string hoppers (a noodle-like food) for the Vidyodaya University hostel nearby. The five women pool their resources and do the actual cooking at another woman's house. Although she works only four days a week, she earns about nine to ten rupees per working day, the largest income she has ever had. I was impressed by her enterpreneurial ingenuity. She gives most of this money to her mother for household expenses, but keeps some for her own use.

Somavati lights a lamp every evening for the goddess Pattini who, she says, is a mother to her. Pattini protects her, and she has had no demonic visitation. However, she has no intention of becoming a full time priestess, although she has the *ārude* (power) of the goddess Pattini. She visits the Nawala shrine often, and occasionally falls into a trance state in which she impersonates the goddess. Yet she still has no ability to utter prophecies. I saw her in one of these trance states during the annual celebrations of the shrine in August. Obviously her propensity for possession has been harnessed in a creative and meaningful way.

The *Kapurāla* told me that he is arranging a marriage for Somavati with one of his friends, a *Kapurāla* from another shrine.

NOTES

1. This research was a direct product of a larger project on healing rituals in Sri Lanka. The project was aided by a grant from the Foundations Fund for Research in Psychiatry (No. G. 67–363), for which I am immensely thankful. I am also indebted to my field assistants, Percy Livanage and Daya Jayasekera; and to Mr. Wijedasa of Wije-photo in Colombo, who took beautiful slides of the ritual. Above all my heartfelt gratitude goes to my friend, the *Kapurāla,* and to "Somavati" herself. (Somavati is a pseudonym used to maintain the informant's anonymity.)

2. Since this paper is not a comparative study, I have deliberately omitted reference to others who have written on "possession." The reader is requested to read the excellent works by Bourguignon (1965), Kennedy (1967), Messing (1959), Spiro (1967), Wallace (1959), and the book edited by Kiev (1964). My own views on the "idiom of possession" are spelled out in Obeyesekere (1970).

REFERENCES

ABERLE, DAVID

1952   "Arctic Hysteria and Latah in Mongolia." *Transactions,
                         New York Academy of Sciences* **5,** (14):291–297.

BOURGUIGNON, ERIKA

1965   "The Self, the Behavioral Environment, and the
                         Theory of Spirit Possession", In *Context and Meaning in
                         Cultural Anthropology,* Spiro, M. E. (Ed.), New York: The
                         Free Press, pp. 39–60.

CARSTAIRS, G. MORRIS

1967   *The Twice Born.* Bloomington: Indiana University Press.

DURKHEIM, EMILE

1915   *The Elementary Forms of the Religious Life* (trans. by J. W.
                         Swain). London: George Allen and Unwin.

FREUD, SIGMUND

1957   *Future of an Illusion* (trans. by W. D. Robson Scott). New
                         York: Doubleday Anchor.

KARDINER, ABRAM

1945   *The Psychological Frontiers of Society.* New York: Columbia University Press.

KENNEDY, JOHN G.

1967   "Nubian Zar Ceremonies as Psychotherapy." *Human Organization* **26,** (4) Winter: 185–194.

KIEV, ARI (ED.)

1964   *Magic Faith and Healing.* New York: the Free Press.

LAMBERT, W. W., TRIANDIS, L., and M. WOLF

1959   "Some Correlates of Beliefs in the Malevolence and Benevolence of Supernatural Beings: A Cross-Cultural
                         Study." *Journal of Abnormal and Social Psychology* **58:**2.

MESSING, SIMON D.

1959   "Group Therapy and Social Status in the Zar Cult of
                         Ethiopia." In *Culture and Mental Health,* M. K. Opler,
                         New York: Macmillan, pp. 319–332.

OBEYESEKERE, G.

1970   "The idiom of Demonic Possession: A Case Study." *Social Science and Medicine* **4:**97–111.

RENOU, LOUIS

1962   *The Nature of Hinduism.* New York: Walker and Company.

SPIRO, MELFORD E

1967   *Burmese Supernaturalism: A Study in the Explanation and Reduction of Suffering.* Englewood Cliffs, N. J.: Prentice-Hall.

SPIRO, M. E. and ROY D'ANDRADE

1958   "A Cross-Cultural Study of Some Supernatural Beliefs." *American Anthropologist* **60:**456–466.

TAMBIAH, S. J.

1969   "The Magical Power of Words." *Man, Journal of the Royal Anthropological Institute,* n.s., **3,** (2):175–208.

WALLACE, A. F. C.

1959   "The Institutionalization of Cathartic and Control Strategies in Iroquois Religious Psychotherapy." In *Culture and Mental Health,* M. K. Opler, (Ed.), New York: Macmillan, pp. 63–96.

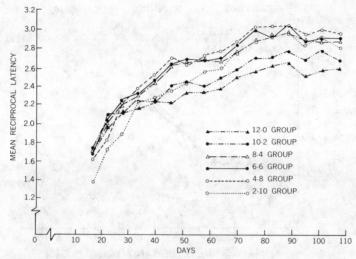

Fig. 10-2. Mean reciprocal latency as a function of trials by blocks of six for the acquisition series. *Adapted from Weinstock (1958)*

available for 30 seconds on all reinforced trials, while on nonreinforced trials, the subjects were left in the goal box for 30 seconds.

Following 108 acquisition trials, all animals were given 60 extinction trials. Response measures included both latency and speed of running, but inasmuch as these measures yielded the same findings, only latency measures were presented. Acquisition curves for the varying reinforcement groups are indicated in Fig. 10-2. It may be noted that many of the partially reinforced groups had the longest latencies early in the trials, while the continuously reinforced animals had very short latencies. By the fortieth trial, and continuing for the remainder of the acquisition series, the continuously reinforced animals had the longest latencies.

A second variable examined with runway studies of partial and continuous reinforcement regimens has been the magnitude of reward. Roberts (1969) compared one partial reinforcement schedule (50%) with a continuous schedule when either 1, 2, 5, 10, or 25 pellets served as the reward. Starting, running, and goal box speeds in the runway were recorded.[3] Forty-eight acquisition trials and 31 extinction trials were provided. The experimental findings for acquisition are indicated in Fig. 10-3 and reveal quite clearly that asymptotic responding for

[3] Many contemporary experimenters, in an effort to better understand the organism's behavior, have measured performance over different sections of the runway; hence, Roberts's use of these measures. In some experiments, when various measures have been used, the experimental findings obtained have differed, depending on which measure is used, e.g., Goodrich (1959). The relevance of these differential findings is seldom made clear and rarely have they added to a better understanding of the partial reinforcement mechanism.

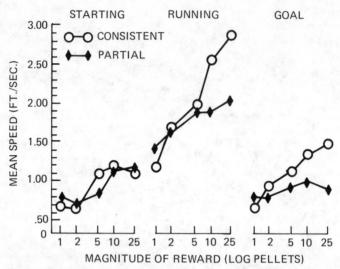

Fig. 10-3. Asymptotic response speed as a function of magnitude of reward for each section of the runway. *Adapted from Roberts (1969)*

both continuous and partial reinforcement, regardless of the response measure used, is a function of the magnitude of the reward. When continuous reinforcement is compared with partial reinforcement at a specific reward magnitude, the superiority of continuous reinforcement usually is revealed. It must be kept in mind, of course, that only a single partial reinforcement schedule was used in this study, and there is an obvious need to examine the magnitude of the reward variable using other partial reinforcement schedules.

Although other variables operating within the partial reinforcement regimen have been investigated, in general, acquisition performance has been of minimal interest to most investigators. One reason for this lack of interest is that relatively small differences are typically obtained; a second reason is that to some experimenters, "... extinction provides ... a better measure for determining what was learned in acquisition than the relatively insensitive acquisition measure itself" (Capaldi, 1970, p. 383).[4]

When the free operant task is used, as indicated earlier, the fixed interval, fixed ratio, variable interval, and variable ratio schedules represent the basic procedures for examining the role of partial reinforcement. However, experimental work with the free operant has resulted in such an extremely extensive literature

---

[4] Capaldi's point of view is contrary to the position expressed in Chapter 2 that we were not in agreement with the use of experimental extinction as a measure from which to infer the stength of a response. Inasmuch as the extinction operation removes the reward from the apparatus, extinction performance should be regarded as related to a reduction in the organism's motivational state. Under such circumstances, the strength of the organism's extinction responding could be used to infer persistence, a motivational construct rather than an associative one.

that we can do little more in this text than indicate some of the important relationships between response rate and the schedule of reinforcement provided.

One question asked from time to time has to do with how free operant performance differs under these varying intermittent schedules. Some of this material was previously discussed in Chapter 7. With fixed interval schedules, a relatively specific response pattern usually takes place during each reinforcement interval. At the beginning of the interval, relatively few responses are made; near the end of the interval, and just prior to reinforcement, the rate of responding increases markedly. This change in the rate of responding produces a scalloping effect similar to that indicated in Fig. 7-7.

The use of a variable interval schedule almost invariably eliminates the scalloping effect and produces a steady rate of responding. The rate of responding as a function of this type of schedule is inversely related to the length of the interval. That is, if on the average the interval is long, so that reinforcement is relatively infrequent, responding takes place at a slow rate. On the other hand, faster responding takes place when the interval is shorter and reinforcement is provided more frequently.

To illustrate, Clark (1958) examined the bar pressing response of rats on three variable interval schedules: VI 1, VI 2, and VI 3, along with seven deprivation levels. Fig. 10-4 indicates how response rate changes as a function of the schedule used. The fact that similar findings were obtained under a variety of deprivation conditions lends support to the generality of the phenomenon.

With fixed ratio (FR) schedules, the subject typically responds at a high rate, since reinforcement is provided only after a specific number of responses have been made. Moreover, as higher fixed ratios are employed, the rate of responding increases; thus, an animal on a FR 40 schedule responds more rapidly than an animal on a FR 10 schedule.

Empirical Findings: Extinction   The extinction findings obtained with partial reinforcement have piqued the interest of most investigators, and a number of variables have been manipulated in an attempt to discover their relationship to resistance to extinction as measured in the instrumental learning task.

Before proceeding, the reader should be aware that at times extinction data produce a basic interpretive problem. At the end of the acquisition trials, during which a particular variable has been manipulated, it is not uncommon to note that the varying experimental groups have different terminal levels of performance. Performance during extinction trials will obviously be influenced by the terminal level of acquisition, in addition to whatever role the manipulated variable might play. However, many experimenters have ignored terminal performance differences in their examination of extinction performance—a procedure which obviously confounds the experimental findings and makes interpretation of the data hazardous. As Anderson (1963) has written in his discussion of this difficulty, equating resistance to extinction measures when a correction for differences in terminal acquisition level is required presents a serious problem for which no single solution is appropriate.[5]

[5] Some investigators have assumed that providing a fixed number of reinforcements to all experimental groups during acquisition is an appropriate way of equalizing performance prior to extinction (see Culbertson, Kling, and Berkley,

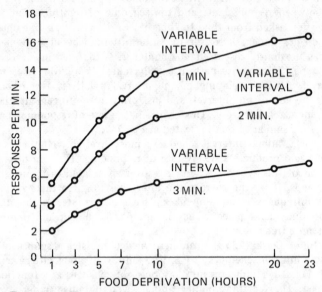

Fig. 10-4. Rate of bar pressing under three different schedules of reinforcement as a function of deprivation time. *Adapted from Clark (1958)*

In order to illustrate the relationship between the terminal level of acquisition and extinction performance, we can cite a study by Hill and Spear (1963) in which five groups of rats were given either 8, 16, 32, 64, or 128 trials on a runway with a 50% random reinforcement schedule. Twenty-eight extinction trials were provided the day following training, with an additional 12 trials provided the next day. Results are shown in Fig. 10-5 and, in general, indicate that resistance to extinction is related to the number of acquisition trials provided. Note, however, that this finding is confounded by the animals' level of response strength at the end of the training period.

Percentage of Reinforcement

The partial reinforcement schedule used by Humphreys (1939b) consisted of providing reinforcement on 50% of the trials. It is not surprising that his unusual extinction findings resulted in the percentage of reinforcement being manipulated by subsequent experimenters trying to further determine the influence of this variable on resistance to extinction.

In an earlier section, we referred to an experiment by Weinstock (1958) who provided either 16.7%, 33.3%, 50.0%, 66.7%, 83.3%, or 100% reinforcement to rats traversing a runway. It will be recalled that following 108 acquisition trials,

1966). The procedure seems questionable, however, if there are substantial differences in responding at the end of the acquisition period.

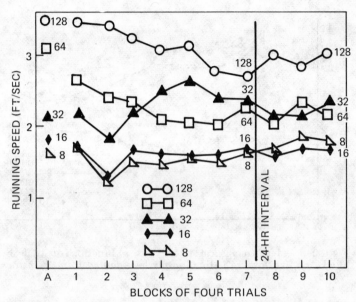

Fig. 10-5. Extinction curves for the five 50% groups. (A designates the final four trials of acquisition.) *Adapted from Hill and Spear (1963)*

all animals were given 60 extinction trials. When extinction findings were examined, as seen in Fig. 10-6, there was an inverse relationship between resistance to extinction and the percentage of reinforced trials provided during acquisition.

Bacon (1962) has also shown that rats traversing a runway and provided either 30%, 50%, 70%, or 100% reinforcement along with either 10, 30, 100 or 300 acquisition trials revealed extinction performance which was inversely related to the percentage of reinforcement received for each of the four levels of acquisition.

Similar findings have been obtained with college students playing a slot machine, as indicated in a series of studies by Lewis and Duncan (1956, 1957, 1958). In their first study, the acquisition series consisted of 8 plays or trials in which the following percentages were provided: 0, 12.5, 25, 37.5, 50, 75, 100. Reinforcement consisted of the subjects' receiving a disk which could be exchanged for 5 cents after each "correct" response. Extinction trials in which the subjects were permitted to play as long as they desired immediately followed the acquisition series. An examination of the number of pulls by each group revealed that resistance to extinction was an inverse function of the percentage of reinforcement obtained during the acquisition trials.

Both the 1957 and 1958 studies (Lewis and Duncan, 1957, 1958) in which the same apparatus and procedure were used confirmed these findings. Thus, in the 1957 study, 9 acquisition trials were provided with the following percentages

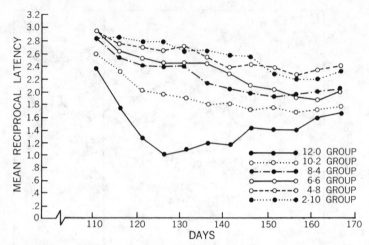

Fig. 10-6. Mean reciprocal latency as a function of trials by blocks of five for the extinction phase. *Adapted from Weinstock (1958)*

of reinforcement: 0%, 11%, 33%, 67%, and 100%. Results revealed that the smaller the percentage of reward, the more plays made during extinction trials with one exception—the 0% group played slightly fewer times than the 11% group. In the 1958 study, 3 percentages of reward were provided, 33%, 67%, and 100%, combined with 4 levels of acquisition trials, 3, 6, 12, or 21. Again the general trend was for the smallest percentages of reinforcement to produce the largest number of plays to extinction.

We can contrast these findings, however, with the studies of both Coughlin (1970) using 12.5%, 25%, 50%, 75%, and 100% reinforcement schedules for rats traversing a runway, and Lewis (1952) using children (6½-7½ years of age) and employing a task consisting of pressing buttons for toys. Like some of the classical conditioning studies, e.g., Grant and Schipper (1952), the experiments of Coughlin and Lewis revealed inverted U-shaped functions—that is, a continuous or 100% reinforcement schedule as well as 0 or very small reinforcement percentages resulted in less resistance to extinction than a range of reinforcement schedules which varied from 25% to 75%.

It seems reasonable to assume, as Lewis (1960) concluded some years ago, that the relationship between percentage of reinforcement and resistance to extinction can best be represented by a U-shaped function. It is obvious that very small percentages of reinforcement will result in the task being only minimally learned, so that extinction should take place very rapidly. On the other hand, continuous or very high percentage reinforcement levels should result in optimizing the acquisition process, at the same time maximizing other processes, e.g., frustration or discriminability between acquisition and extinction, which lead to declining extinction performance.

It should be noted that in the cases which have not supported a U-shaped function—small percentages of reinforcement resulting in superior extinction—considerable learning of the response by the experimental subjects had taken place prior to the introduction of the partial reinforcement schedule. It would be assumed that the lever pulling response made by college students in the Lewis and Duncan (1956, 1957, 1958) studies was well-learned even before the experiment began, while in Weinstock's (1958) study, all animals were first provided with 12 reinforced trials (1 per day) prior to being placed on one of the partially reinforced schedules.

Sequential or Patterning Effects

In addition to the possibility that an investigator may vary the percentage of reinforced trials, the sequence or pattern of reinforced (and nonreinforced) trials which make up the partial reinforcement schedule may also vary.

One of the early investigations of a patterning effect was the introduction of an acquisition schedule which provided alternating reinforced and nonreinforced trials. Tyler, Wortz, and Bitterman (1953), had rats traverse an alley for an extended series of acquisition trials followed by extinction. Results indicated that the alternating group extinguished much more rapidly than a second group which had been provided the same percentage of reinforced trials but in a random or irregular sequence. The alternating group appears to have learned the reinforcement pattern; an examination of the acquisition trials run by them indicates that they ran much faster on reinforced trials than on those which were nonreinforced. Since they could not see whether reward was in the goal box prior to running, they might be assumed to have learned that nonreward on one trial meant reward would be found on the next, and vice versa. A number of investigators, e.g., Capaldi (1958), Campbell, Knouse, and Wroten (1970) have obtained similar findings. That is, a series of alternating reinforced and nonreinforced trials will result not only in a characteristic fast-slow performance during acquisition, but also in more rapid extinction than will irregular reinforcement patterns.

In Capaldi's (1958) study, two groups of rats were provided alternating reinforced and nonreinforced trials for either (a) 7 days or (b) 14 days, while two other groups received random reinforced and nonreinforced trials for either (c) 7 days or (d) 14 days. Capaldi found that extinction was most rapid for the alternating 14 day group.

At about the same time that Tyler, Wortz, and Bitterman (1953) became interested in the effect of alternating patterns of reinforcement on resistance to extinction, Grosslight and his associates hypothesized that the pattern of reinforcement-nonreinforcement provided during acquisition trials was of singular importance in influencing extinction. It was assumed that a reinforcement-nonreinforcement (RN) pattern would not result in as much resistance to extinction as a nonreinforcement-reinforcement pattern (NR). In the latter case, the organism would learn that nonreward was followed by reward and this after-effect would result in maximizing resistance to extinction.

In a study by Grosslight, Hall, and Murnin (1953) employing college students, a Humphreys's light expectancy procedure was used with a pattern of training trials utilizing either an NR or an RN reinforcement schedule in addition to a continuous one. It should be noted that with the light expectancy procedure, the subject must determine whether or not a second light will go on after the first light has been presented. The presentation of the second light is considered to constitute a reinforced trial. Following five series of training trials in which RN, NR, or RR (continuously reinforced) sequences were found in each series, 10 extinction trials were provided. Results indicated that the mean number of extinction responses for the NR group was significantly larger than for either the RN or the RR group. Subsequent studies of Grosslight and Radlow (1956, 1957), using rats, have supported the position that a sequential effect in which a reinforced trial follows a nonreinforced trial, can significantly prolong resistance to extinction.

The fact that the sequence or pattern of reinforcement provided in the partial reinforcement regimen plays an important role in extinction has caused Capaldi (1966) to posit a theory of partial reinforcement based upon this process. We shall examine some of the more recent sequential studies within this context.

Partial Reinforcement Theory[6]

Humphreys's (1939b) finding of partial reinforcement effects stimulated a variety of theoretical positions, including his own, which has been described as the expectancy theory. Humphreys posited that responses were made to stimuli during acquisition because these stimuli led the subjects to "expect" the unconditioned stimulus. In extinction, after continuous reinforcement, the response dies out quickly because there has been a rapid and easy shift from a regular expectancy of 100% to one of 0%. Partial reinforcement, on the other hand, produces an irregular expectation of reinforcement and it becomes difficult for the subject during extinction trials to make the appropriate shift in expectancy. This interpretation has been criticized for its vagueness as well as its ad hoc nature. As Sheffield (1949) put it, subjects, after experiencing continuous reinforcement, could find it hard to believe that more reinforcement was not forthcoming during the extinction series. Lewis (1960), in reviewing partial reinforcement theory, has indicated that the expectancy hypothesis has been so discredited that it appears to have no remaining articulate supporter.

Another early theoretical position, proposed by Mowrer and Jones (1945), has been designated the discrimination hypothesis and has continued to generate interest over the years. The origins of this position can be found in a study (Mowrer and Jones, 1945) in which four groups of rats were trained in a Skinner box to make either 1, 2, 3, or 4 bar depressions before receiving food. A fifth

[6]Partial reinforcement theory has dealt exclusively with discrete trial learning situations. The fixed and variable ratio and interval reinforcement schedules which also represent types of partial reinforcement regimens, typically used with bar pressing or key pecking, have not been considered. Probably, most experimenters would agree with Amsel (1958) who wrote that "it is very likely that quite different principles and explanations may be required in the two cases, since the chained type of responding involves consideration of stimulus traces from previous responses and previous goal events, whereas the discrete, highly-spaced trial situation . . . involves primarily consideration of certain developing associative tendencies" (p. 113).

group received a food pellet after 1, 2, 3, or 4 presses; however, the presentation of food, although random, was provided on the average after 2.5 bar presses. Following extensive training, extinction sessions were provided on three successive days. Results indicated that resistance to extinction, as measured by the total number of bar presses, was a function of the number of bar presses required to obtain food during acquisition trials. The group which was required to press the bar four times in order to obtain a single food pellet took longest to extinguish, whereas the group which was required to press only once extinguished most rapidly. The experimenters proposed as one explanation for their findings that when the change from acquisition to extinction was difficult to discriminate, greater resistance to extinction would occur than when such a discrimination was easy.

One test of the discrimination hypothesis would be to provide a random versus a fixed pattern of partial reinforcement, keeping the percentage of reinforced trials the same in each group. The studies of Tyler, Wortz, and Bitterman (1953), Capaldi (1957, 1958) and Campbell, Knouse, and Wroten (1970), which we have already reviewed, demonstrate that a simple alternation pattern of reinforcement and nonreinforcement results in more rapid extinction than a random pattern—a finding which supports the discrimination hypothesis, assuming it is easy for the animal to discriminate alternating acquisition trials from extinction trials.

Since the extinction situation is one in which 0% reinforcement is provided, the discrimination hypothesis would predict that acquisition series containing a small percentage or 0% of reinforced trials should produce greater resistance to extinction than an acquisition series with a much larger percentage of reinforced trials; a number of investigators, however, have not found this to be true. Very small percentages of reinforcement produce rapid extinction. However, some question must be raised as to whether or not the frequency of reinforcement is sufficient to result in the organism's learning. Thus, the very low terminal level of acquisition resulting from a small percentage of reinforcement typically results in these responses being very easily extinguished.

Perhaps the major difficulty with the discrimination hypothesis has been the failure on the part of its supporters to provide a set of principles or conditions which experimenters could use in measuring the amount of discriminability between acquisition and extinction trials. Most frequently, judgments regarding the ease or difficulty of making the discrimination between acquisition and extinction are arrived at on an intuitive basis.

In recent years, primary interest in partial reinforcement theory has centered around the theoretical positions proposed by Amsel (1958) and Capaldi (1966, 1967, 1971).

Amsel has proposed that after some minimal number of reinforcements which are responsible for the establishment of the fractional anticipatory goal response (rg-sg), nonreinforcement (as part of a partial reinforcement regimen) will elicit a primary motivational response which he has termed frustration (Rf). As nonreinforced trials continue, an anticipatory or conditioned form of this emotional response (rf) develops and is assumed to generalize to stimuli which antedate the goal, providing an rf-sf mechanism. Thus, stimuli arising from the starting box and other parts of the apparatus become capable of eliciting anticipatory frustration. This frustration leads to responses which are antagonistic to the organism's response of running to the goal box, but at the same time, anticipatory goal responses (rg) are also elicited by the apparatus as a result of the reinforced trials. Presumably, some conflict arises between these two response tendencies. However, since reinforcement is provided on some trials, the running response continues to be made. The animal, although frustrated, continues to run and receive reinforcement; as a result, the frustration cues gradually become conditioned to the locomotor response itself. In short, the organism learns to accept nonreinforced trials and the resultant frustration as part of the stimulus situation and continues to respond.

In contrast, organisms which have been continuously reinforced are not frustrated, so that the anticipatory frustration response cannot be learned. Thus, there is no opportunity to learn the running response in the presence of frustration. It seems reasonable to assume, then, that animals trained to approach a goal object in the presence of frustration stimuli will be more resistant to extinction than will continuously reinforced subjects who become frustrated on extinction trials but have not learned to respond appropriately in the presence of frustration.

Capaldi (1966, 1967, 1971) has proposed a sequential hypothesis in order to account for partial reinforcement effects. Organisms which experience different sequences of reinforcement and nonreinforcement during acquisition literally learn different things—it is the type of sequence which is basic to an understanding of partial reinforcement effects.

The origin of Capaldi's position is found in an aftereffects hypothesis proposed some years earlier by Sheffield (1949). According to Sheffield, the stimulus aftereffect of a nonreinforced trial (Sn) becomes conditioned to the instrumental response. Such conditioning cannot take place with continuous reinforcement, since Sn is never present. Inasmuch as extinction trials involve the stimulus aftereffect, Sn, partially reinforced subjects have greater excitatory strength for the instrumental response of running to an empty goal box than subjects continuously reinforced during the acquisition trials.

Sheffield hypothesized that the stimulus aftereffect (trace) would dissipate with time, predicting that long temporal intervals between extinction trials would result in eliminating the partial reinforcement effect. A basic problem was that the experimental findings of a number of investigators, however, did not support this position; Weinstock (1954, 1958), for example, as well as many subsequent experimenters, have been able to obtain the partial reinforcement effect using 24-hour intertrial intervals, a time interval which should result in the dissipation of any stimulus trace effects.

Capaldi (1971) has suggested that the mechanism involved in his sequential hypothesis is a memorial process. Thus, he has written,

On a particular trial an animal is nonrewarded. Since the sequential hypothesis endows the animal with an impressive memory capacity, it is assumed that on the immediately subsequent trial the animal will remember being nonrewarded. That is, on the subsequent trial the animal's internal stimulus state will be that having the characteristics of nonreward rather than, let us say, reward. If on a given trial the animal remembers nonreward and is on that trial rewarded, then stimuli characteristic of nonreward will become conditioned to, and thus acquire control over, the instrumental reaction (p. 111).

Capaldi's sequential position emphasizes the memorial capacity of the organism. An animal receiving no reward on trial 1 will remember this experience when responding on the next trial. Such memories occur or take place from the beginning of the training trials and can be modified as a result of a single trial. In contrast, partial reinforcement mechanisms proposed by other investigators (such as anticipatory goal responses or anticipatory frustration responses) are presumed to be acquired as the result of at least a reasonable number of training trials.

In order to be more specific concerning the operation of the sequential hypothesis, let us assume that rats are provided the following 2-trial partial reinforcement schedules in traversing a runway:

Schedule 1	Schedule 2
1. N	1. R
2. R	2. N

In Schedule 1, with the second trial rewarded, the stimulus or memorial characteristics of nonreward received on the first trial and present during the second trial are conditioned to the instrumental response of running on trial 2— conditioning takes place because the running response is followed by reinforcement. In Schedule 2, the stimulus characteristics of nonreward are present on the second trial, but inasmuch as this trial is not followed by a reinforced trial, there is no opportunity for such stimulus aftereffects to be attached to the running response. Inasmuch as resistance to extinction is considered to be an index of the capacity of nonreward-related stimuli to elicit the instrumental response, it is obvious that the N-R sequence will be more successful than the R-N sequence in prolonging extinction.

Capaldi's theory of partial reinforcement effects has led him to reject the idea that percentage of reinforced trials is a viable variable in obtaining partial reinforcement effects. Rather, he has put his emphasis on the reinforcement and nonreinforcement transitions that are found in the partial reinforcement sequence. He terms himself a sequential theorist who directs attention to trial events, and in particular, to the variety of reinforcement and nonreinforcement transitions which are contained in the partial reinforcement sequence. As we have just noted, the partial reinforcement transitions, e.g., RN or NR, are posited as having different effects on the organism's resistance to extinction. Most acquisition sessions provide the organism with more than 2 trials, which means that a number of RN or NR sequences are found in the trial series. Capaldi's position is that the typical partial reinforcement effect takes place because the increasing effect of NR transitions on resistance to extinction exceeds the decreasing effect of RN transitions on resistance to extinction.[7]

Many of the experiments conducted during recent years have attempted to examine (and compare) salient aspects of Amsel's frustration hypothesis and Capaldi's sequential hypothesis. One important issue has been related to the number of acquisition trials provided partially reinforced subjects. Amsel (1958), in formulating his position, stated that "PRE will be evident only after some critical number of training trials. . ." (p. 114); as a result, the question arises as to whether, by limiting the number of acquisition trials, it would be possible to eliminate the partial reinforcement effect.

Although Surridge, Rashotte, and Amsel (1967) were unable to find differences in extinction between partially reinforced and continuously reinforced animals that had been provided relatively few acquisition trials, most of the experimental evidence appears to indicate that partial reinforcement effects can be obtained with limited acquisition training. Studies by McCain (1966), McCain and Brown (1967), Capaldi and Deutsch (1967), Godbout, Ziff, and Capaldi (1968), Capaldi, Lanier, and Godbout (1968), McCain (1968), Bowen and McCain (1967), and Padilla (1967) are representative of a large number of experiments, all of which indicate that the partial reinforcement effect can be found after as few as 2 to 5 training trials.

In fact, it has been demonstrated that the partial reinforcement effect can be produced in a runway apparatus without partially reinforcing the running response itself.

For example, in a study by Trapold and Holden (1966), following 36 continuously reinforced runway trials, the subjects were divided into four matched groups, each of which received a different experimental treatment during the next eight days. Group 8P received four direct placements into the goal box each day; one placement was reinforced, the other three nonreinforced. On these trials, the subjects were required to locomote about 8″ to the foodcup. Group 8C was treated exactly like Group 8P except that all of the direct placements into the goal box were reinforced. Two other groups were treated similarly to 8P and 8C except that these subjects were placed with their noses directly in the foodcup so that no overt locomotion was necessary.

Thirty-six extinction trials (6 per day) were then provided. Results revealed that only the 8P group displayed superior resistance to extinction, a finding in agreement with an earlier study by Trapold and Doren (1966). Thus, direct placement of the subjects in the goal box, after which they had the opportunity to locomote to the food cup, resulted in demonstrating the partial reinforcement effect.

As might be anticipated, frustration theorists have not regarded these findings as completely antithetical to their position. Amsel, Hug, and Surridge (1968)

---

[7] Capaldi holds that the nonsequential theorist—the experimenter who does not concern himself with the RN or NR pattern of reinforcement—produces an experimental design which is uninterpretable, since the number and characteristics of NR and RN transitions are ignored. Thus, the nonsequential experiment is not a well-controlled laboratory study but rather an irrelevant, misleading, concatenated task of infinite complexity.

note that, although few acquisition trials may be provided, the availability of a large number of pellets causes the rat to make multiple approaches to the food cup, and as a result, the partial reinforcement effect is obtained. Similarly, Trapold and Holden (1966) believe their findings can be reconciled with frustration theory if it is assumed that the feedback stimuli of the running response (to the food cup during the direct placement procedure) form a very important class of stimuli to which frustration is conditioned. The presence of running cues in both short run direct placement situations and running trial situations provides the most important basis for the generalization of frustration on which increased resistance to extinction rests.

Another type of evidence which appears to be damaging to Amsel's position is found in a study by Capaldi, Ziff, and Godbout (1970). In this study, two partial reinforcement groups were provided with one of the following patterns: NNRR, or NNNNNRR. Two continuous reinforcement groups received either 4 or 7 rewarded trials. Following these acquisition trials, 10 extinction trials were provided, with running speed measured over the three sections of the runway. Results revealed the existence of a partial reinforcement effect. And yet, as the authors have written, "Certainly, if reward were expected here, [a necessary feature for the development of the frustration effect] the source of that expectancy cannot be a prior rewarded trial, as Amsel, Hug, and Surridge (1968) have maintained, since, of course, reward did not precede nonreward in this investigation" (p. 62).

In an effort to accommodate some of the experimental findings, Amsel (1967) has suggested that there may be two partial reinforcement effects—one obtained with massed trials and dependent upon aftereffects, possibly of the type suggested by Capaldi (1971); the other obtained with long intertrial intervals and dependent on a frustration mechanism. Similarly, Black and Spence (1965) have suggested that

> when the number of acquisition trials is small, the opportunity for the instrumental response to become conditioned to the aftereffects of nonreinforcement may be a determinant of resistance to extinction. However, when acquisition training is sufficiently extended to insure, theoretically, the occurrence of frustration on nonreinforced trials, extinction performance is in accord with the implications of the frustration hypothesis. This suggests that, once conditioned frustration is developed, its influence on performance is sufficiently great that the role of differential stimulus aftereffects becomes negligible. (p. 562)

Capaldi's sequential hypothesis has generated a variety of experiments primarily designed to explore the role of the aftereffects, as well as to examine the particular pattern of rewarded and nonrewarded trials.

If aftereffects play a basic role in the determination of partial reinforcement effects, then events which take place during the intertrial interval could presumably modify the influence of such aftereffects.

In a study by Capaldi, Hart, and Stanley (1963) examining the role of aftereffects, two groups of rats were given 30 acquisition trials in running an alley under identical patterns of partial (50%) reinforcement. A third group received continuous reinforcement. Following such training, 20 extinction trials were provided. The salient feature of this experiment was the provision of seven inter-trial reinforcements to the two partial reinforcement groups. The intertrial rein-forcement procedure was as follows: the intertrial interval which subjects normally spend in a neutral waiting box was used to provide either reinforce-ment or nonreinforcement to the experimental animals. Thus, for one partial reinforcement group (PN), intertrial reinforcement was provided after runway trials which were not themselves reinforced but were followed by reinforced trials. (Thus, an N, N, R runway sequence would result in the animal's receiving intertrial reinforcement following the second N trial.) For a second partial rein-forcement group (PR), intertrial reinforcement was provided following those runway trials which were reinforced. The investigators reasoned that for the PN group, the intertrial reinforcement procedure prevented the stimulus charac-teristics (or aftereffects) of a nonreinforced runway trial from becoming condi-tioned to the response of running on the next, reinforced, trial. This, of course, was not true for the PR group, which, although given the same number of inter-trial reinforcements, did not receive reinforcement after any nonreinforced trial. With this group, it was possible for the stimulus aftereffects arising from non-reinforced runway trials to become conditioned to the running response. The results supported the researchers' hypothesis. Group PN was not more resistant to extinction than the consistently reinforced group; however, the PR group was significantly more resistant to extinction than either Group PN or the con-tinuously reinforced group.[8]

If it is assumed that the events which fill the intertrial interval are of primary importance, a basic consideration is the nature of the goal box in which inter-trial reinforcement is provided. The more dissimilar it is to the goal box which is used in training trials, the greater the probability that a portion of the nonrein-forced aftereffects will survive the intertrial reinforcement experience and be available for conditioning on a subsequent reinforced trial. In an examination of this position, using rats in a straight runway, Capaldi and Spivey (1963) found that as similarity between the goal box used in the acquisition series and that used in the intertrial interval decreased, resistance to extinction increased.

The number of reinforcement-nonreinforcement transitions found in the acquisition trials has also been of interest. In an early study by Capaldi and Hart (1962), two experiments were conducted in which rats were trained to traverse a runway under either continuous reinforcement, random reinforcement, or single alternation of reward. In their first study, 27 training trials were provided, with an intertrial interval of approximately 20 seconds. An important consideration between the two partial reinforcement groups was the number of nonreinforce-ment-reinforcement transitions provided each day. The single alternation group received four each day, while the random group received just one, although per-centage of reinforcement was the same. In a second experiment, a similar daily

---

[8] Black and Spence (1965), essentially replicating the Capaldi, Hart, and Stanley (1963) procedure were unable to obtain similar findings. These investigators found that both partial reinforcement groups were superior to the continuously reinforced group.

acquisition procedure was used, except that just 18 training trials were provided. Results from both experiments indicated that the single alternation group had greatest resistance to extinction, revealing the number of N-R transitions to be an important variable.

In a subsequent study by Capaldi and Wargo (1963), in which the intertrial interval was at least 20 minutes, it was noted that the single alternation group again took longer to extinguish than a random group. The authors have posited that the aftereffects of the N-R sequence remains functional for at least a 20-minute period.[9]

Capaldi's (1971) sequential position has appeared to fare reasonably well as a working hypothesis for partial reinforcement effects found with rats traversing the runway, and Robbins's (1971) careful review of this experimental area has led him to conclude that ". . . the sequential theory proposed by Capaldi appears to capture the major aspects of the extinction effect" (p. 426).[10]

Nonetheless, a number of investigators have expressed concern about work in this area. One problem has been the insistence of each investigator on the use of an experimental procedure which is idiosyncratic to each particular experiment. Jernstedt's (1971) comments are especially noteworthy:

A coherent picture of the nature of partial reinforcement can never emerge, unless by accident, if studies which are intended for comparison with other studies or for validation of theories are not carried out with very carefully selected values of pattern of reinforcement, intertrial interval, amount of reinforcement, and extinction criteria. By a less than careful choice of values for each of these parameters one can find nearly any difference between the resistance to extinction of experimental groups. Validating theories then becomes a dangerous proposition. (p. 428)

A second concern is the necessity of examining partial reinforcement effects (and hopefully providing theoretical interpretations) with organisms and tasks other than the rat traversing the runway.[11]

---

[9] According to Amsel's frustration theory, no differences should exist between the two partial reinforcement sequences, since the same number of reinforced and nonreinforced trials would result in the anticipatory goal and the frustration response mechanism being similar. In keeping with this prediction, Surridge and Amsel (1966) were unable to find differences in extinction when a single alternation pattern group was contrasted with a group provided random reinforcement.

[10] All experiments have not been supportive of Capaldi's position, e.g., Koteskey and Stettner (1968).

[11] Virtually all the experiments examining the partial reinforcement effect have used a between-subject design but it is possible to use a within-subjects design as well. The interesting finding has been that, with such designs, typical partial reinforcement effects are not usually obtained. To illustrate this type of experiment, Rashotte and Amsel (1968) had a group of subjects learn to traverse a black (or white) runway for continuous reinforcement, while 12 hours later, the same subjects were provided partial reinforcement (50%) for traversing a white (or black) runway. Separate continuous and partial reinforcement groups were also run under the same experimental conditions. Following 15 days of

Reward Amount

It is first appropriate to note that the concept of "amount" has certain attributes and it is important for experimenters to be aware that performance may be influenced by attribute differences.

For example, two amounts of food may weigh the same; however, one amount may consist of 20 small pellets while the other consists of only 1. There is some experimental evidence, as indicated in the early study of Wolfe and Kaplon (1941), as well as more recent ones by McCain (1969) and Traupmann (1971) to suggest that superior performance is obtained as a function of the number of items which make up the reward, although weight is held constant. In Wolfe and Kaplon's (1941) study, chickens were found to traverse a runway more rapidly for a grain of rice cut into 4 quarters than for the same amount presented in a single piece. More recently, McCain (1969) had rats running an alley, rewarding them with either a single 1000 mg pellet or 22 45-mg pellets.[12] Forty trials were provided with the results indicating that the multiple pellet group ran significantly more rapidly than the group given only a single pellet. After the 40 trials, the rewards were shifted so that the group which had received the single pellet now received 22 pellets, while the 22-pellet group received only 1. Subsequent trials indicated a shift in running speed with the performance of the two groups being reversed.

It has been recognized that differences in the amount of reward provided also result in (a) differing amounts of consummatory activity necessary to consume the reward, as well as (b) varying amounts of time spent in the goal box. Experiments by Czeh (as reported by Spence, 1956), as well as Wike and Barrientos (1957) have suggested that both of these variables result in differential performance.

These findings, which suggest that the attributes of reward may produce differential performance, have led a number of contemporary investigators to follow the lead of Guttman (1953) who manipulated the reward variable by varying the concentration of a sucrose solution, e.g., a 5% or a 25% solution. In so doing, it is possible to control the amount of time that the animal spends in the goal box as well as the amount of its consummatory activity. What has been neglected, however, is the recognition that the amount or quantity of reward attribute has been changed to one of quality. In essence, taste becomes the manipulated attribute.

---

acquisition training, seven days of extinction trials were provided. Results indicated that partial reinforcement effects were not found for the subjects provided training with both continuous and partial reinforcement; on the other hand, the between-groups design did reveal the superiority of the partial reinforcement group during extinction.

This failure to find partial reinforcement effects using a within-subjects design has been confirmed by a variety of investigators, e.g., Amsel (1964, 1967); Spear (1964); Brown and Logan (1965); Amsel, Rashotte, and Mackinnon (1965); Spear and Pavlik (1966); and Spear and Spitzner (1967).

[12] Although the 22 pellets totaled 990 mg, the author believed that the 10 mg difference was not discriminable to this subjects.

In examining the influence of amount of reward on performance as measured by rate or probability of responding, virtually all investigators have found that performance is some increasing function of the amount of reinforcement provided (see Tables 10-3 and 10-4).

An excellent study demonstrating the influence of taste on rate of responding was performed by Kraeling (1961). Nine groups of rats were given one trial per day for 99 days on a runway in which three concentrations of sucrose solution, 2.5%, 5.0%, and 10.0% were examined along with three exposure times to the sucrose—namely, 5, 25, or 125 seconds.

Curves for running speed over all blocks of trials for the three concentrations of sucrose are presented in Fig. 10-7, while running speed for the three drinking times are indicated in Fig. 10-8. It may be noted that running speed was primarily related to the concentration of the sucrose solution, while exposure time contributed little to performance. In summary, within the range of values used in this study, the characteristic of taste was the critical aspect of reward in relation to instrumental response strength.

One experimental variation in examining the amount of reward variable has been to provide the subject with a discrimination problem in which one cue leads to one amount, while a second cue leads to a different amount. A study by Davenport (1970) using this procedure is noteworthy, since he used a variety of organisms as his experimental subjects. Pigtail, stumptail, and squirrel monkeys, as well as albino rats, were given training in a 2-lever spatial discrimination task in which the left (or right) lever was associated with 5 sucrose pellets, while the right (or left) lever was associated with just 1. Thirty-six daily sessions were provided with 14 trials administered within each session. On trials 1 and 8, the animals were permitted to choose between the levers; trials 2 through 7 and 9 through 14 consisted of 6 left and 6 right lever trials being provided. Results indicated that all the subjects receiving choice trials developed a consistent preference (85-100%) for the 5-pellet lever early in acquisition and maintained this preference over the last ten days of acquisition.

In the studies listed in Tables 10-3 and 10-4, animals were used almost exclusively as the experimental subjects; there have been relatively few studies examining amount of reward with humans. In one such study, Siegel and Andrews (1962) found that the amount of reward does influence learning in the young child. Using children 4 to 5 years of age, these investigators utilized a task in which two identical containers were placed before the subject with the container in one position, e.g., left, containing the reward 75% of the time, whereas the other container held it just 25% of the time. In the low reinforcement condition, the reward was a button, selected to have minimum interest for the child. In the high reward condition, a small prize was provided which the child could keep. Knowledge of the results of each trial, that is, which container held the object, was also provided. One hundred trials were first given to the subject under one of the reward conditions. If the low reward condition was presented first, it was followed by 100 additional trials of high reward condition. On the other hand, if the high reward condition was presented first, only 12 additional trials of the low reward condition were given, since the child was usually reluctant to continue an activity unrewarded for which he had previously received a

Table 10-3 Summaries of a Sampling of Studies Examining the Relationship Between the Amount of Reinforcement and the Rate of Responding During Acquisition Trials

Type of Reinforcement	Amount	Task	Response Measure	Organism	Influence of Amount of Reinforcement on the Response Measure	Investigator
Food	0, 1, 2, 4, 6 grains	Runway	Running Time	Chicken	Positive	Grindley (1929)
Food	1, 4, 16, 64, 256 units	Runway	Running Time	Rat	Positive	Crespi (1942)
Food	2, 5 seconds of eating	Skinner Box	Rate of Pecking	Pigeon	Positive	Jenkins and Clayton (1949)
Food	.05, .20, .40, .60, .80, 1.60, 2.40 gm	Runway	Latency	Rat	Positive	Zeaman (1949)
Food	60, 120, 160 mg	Skinner Box	Time for 25 Bar Presses	Rat	Negative	Reynolds (1950)
Sucrose	4%, 8%, 16%, 32%	Skinner Box	Time for 500 Bar Presses	Rat	Positive	Guttman (1953)
Food	1, 5 pellets	Multiple T-maze	Running Time	Rat	Positive	Maher and Wickens (1954)
Food	1, 5 pellets	Runway	Running Time	Rat	Positive	D'Amato (1955)
Sucrose	2%, 6%, 18%, 54%	Skinner Box	Rate of Lever Pressing	Monkey	Positive	Conrad and Sidman (1956)
Sucrose	8%, 24%	Skinner Box	Speed of Approaching Bar	Rat	Positive	Butter and Thomas (1958)
Food	45, 450 mg	Runway	Starting and Running Times	Rat	Positive	Armus (1959)
Food	1, 3, 6, 12 pellets	Runway	Starting and Running Times	Rat	Negative	Weiss (1960)
Food	.1, 1.0, 2.0 gm	Runway	Running Time	Rat	Positive	Reynolds and Pavlik (1960)
Sucrose	3%, 12%, 24%, 48%	Runway	Running Time	Rat	Positive	Goodrich (1960)
Food	1 or 10 pellets	Runway	Running Time	Rat	Positive	Hill and Wallace (1967)
Food	1 or 3 pellets	Lever Press	Rate of Lever Pressing	Rat	Positive	Meltzer and Brahlek (1968)

Table 10-4 Summaries of a Sampling of Studies Examining the Relationship Between the Amount of Reinforcement and the Probability of Responding During Acquisition Trials

Type of Reinforcement	Amount	Task	Response Measureability	Organism	Influence of Amount of Reinforcement on the Response Measure	Investigator
Food	Small, large piece	Discrimination	Correct Response	Chimpanzee	Positive	Cowles and Nissen (1937)
Food	30, 160 mg	Discrimination	Trials to Criterion	Rat	Negative	Reynolds (1949)
Food	85, 271 mg	Discrimination	Errors	Rat	Positive	Greene (1953)
Food	20, 75, 250, 2500 mg	Multiple T-maze	Errors	Rat	Negative	Furchgott and Rubin (1953)
Food	1, 5 pellets	Multiple T-maze	Errors	Rat	Negative	Maher and Wickens (1954)
Food	.1, .7 gm	Multiple T-maze	Correct Response	Rat	Positive	Denny and King (1955)
Food	1, 2, 4 pellets	Discrimination	Correct Response	Monkey	Positive	Schrier and Harlow (1956)
Food	10, 150 seconds eating time	E-maze	Correct Response	Rat	Positive	Powell and Perkins (1957)
Food	.5, 2 peanuts	Discrimination	Errors	Monkey	Positive	Leary (1958)
Water	10, 40 seconds drinking time	U-maze	Errors	Rat	Negative	Fehrer (1956)
Food	Variety of comparisons 1-0, 2-0, 4-0, 1-1, 2-1, 4-1, 2-2, 4-2 pellets	T-maze with one Amount on One Side, Other Amount on Other	% to Larger Reward	Rat	Positive	Clayton (1964)
Sucrose pellets	1 or 5 pellets	2-Lever Bar Press	Probability of Response to Lever Associated with 5-Pellet Reward	Pigtail, Stumptail, Squirrel Monkeys and Rats	Positive	Davenport (1970)
Sucrose	8%, 16%, or 32%	2-Lever Bar Press	% Responding to Higher Sucrose % Bar	Rat	Positive	Collier and Rega (1971)

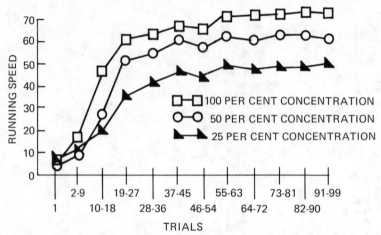

Fig. 10-7. Strength of instrumental response, broken down by concentration of sucrose solution.

prize. Findings revealed that children exhibited a greater tendency to maximize the probability of the correct response when the high reward was used.

Experimenters working with older children and adults frequently have difficulty in replicating the reward findings obtained with less complex organisms. For example. Miller and Estes (1961) had 9-year-old boys discriminate between drawings of faces which differed only in the heights and spacing of the eyebrows. Pictures were presented tachistoscopically for 2-second intervals with subjects receiving either 50 cents, 1 cent, or knowledge of results after each correct response. A subsequent study by Estes, Miller, and Curtin (1962) using the same experimental procedure was performed with college students as subjects. Here, a reward of 25 cents, 1 cent, or knowledge of results was provided for each correct response. In neither experiment did differences in performance accompany differences in the amount of reward received.

In another study, Cole, Gay, Glick, and Sharp (1970) examined the role of reward in a simple free recall learning task in which their subjects were a Liberian tribal group known as the Kpelle. In their first experiment, half of the subjects were told that they would receive at least 35 cents for their participation but they could earn up to 25 cents more if they performed well. The other half of the subjects were paid a flat 35 cents. Since 75 cents is considered a good wage for a full day's work in this community, and many workers receive only 50 cents a day, a promise of up to 60 cents for 20 minutes of the subject's time was thought to be an adequate reward. Although learning was observed in this situation, no difference was obtained between the two groups' performance. A second experiment by these investigators which replicated the first in all essential aspects also failed to reveal differences between the groups.

In attempting to account for these negative findings, it should come as no great surprise that the amount of reward used with college students had little influence on their performance. It is reasonable to assume that to the typical

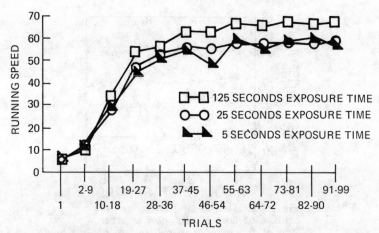

Fig. 10-8. Strength of instrumental response, broken down by time of exposure to the sucrose solution. *Adapted from Kraeling (1969)*

college student, the amount of monetary reward that can realistically be provided in an experiment means far less than certain intangible rewards such as the satisfaction of pleasing the experimenter or, simply, the student's desire to do well. The situation appears to be more complex with the Kpelle; it may be, however, that the payment of 35 cents resulted in optimizing human performance so that an additional 25 cents would have negligible incentive value. In any event, experimenters examining the amount of reward variable with adult humans must proceed cautiously; in general, it seems appropriate to determine first if differences in reward were actually perceived as such by the subjects prior to the learning experiment.

Intra-Subject Reward Variability

We have already noted that the within-subject design is a more sensitive procedure for examining the influence of certain variables in classical conditioning studies, e.g., CS intensity, so that it is not surprising to note a similar effect with the amount of reward variable. As Meyer (1951b) and Bower (1961) have both pointed out, amount of reward should not be considered a static parameter; its influence depends on the context in which a given amount of reward occurs.

In a demonstration of this effect by Schrier (1958) one group of monkeys received a 1-pellet reward for each correct response made throughout a series of discrimination problems. A second group received 2 pellets, while a third and fourth group received 4 and 8 pellets, respectively. All the groups were designated as nonshift groups, since the amount of reward remained constant throughout the entire experiment. A fifth group of subjects, designated as a shift group, experienced each of these rewards. That is, one amount would be used for correct responses on one problem, a different amount would be used for correct responses on a second problem, etc. Fig. 10-9 reveals the performance of

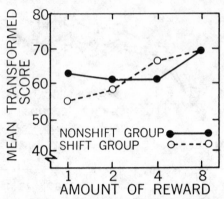

Fig. 10-9. Mean arcsin-transformed per-centage of correct responses as a function of the number of pellets provided as reward. Each point on the curve for the nonshift group represents a different subgroup, whereas each point on the curve for the shift group represents the same subjects. *Adapted from Schrier (1958)*

the varying groups as a function of the amount of reward received. It may be noted that for the nonshift group, rewards of 1 pellet, 2 pellets, or 4 pellets produced similar performance. It required 8 pellets to facilitate the organisms' learning. On the other hand, each variation in the amount produced an increasing percentage of correct responses for the shift group.

Shifts in Amount of Reward and Contrast Effects

One interesting aspect of the amount of reward studies has been the investigation of how shifts in amount influence performance. Crespi (1942) was one of the early experimenters to examine this variable, giving rats 19 acquisition trials, and providing either 16, 64, or 256 food pellets as the reward for traversing a runway. This was followed by a shift to 16 pellets for all animals. In a second experiment, subjects were given 19 trials with a 1- or 4-pellet reward followed by a shift to 16 pellets. In both studies, there were abrupt or sudden shifts in runway performance—the running speed for animals given the 16-pellet reward, after experiencing a larger reward, dramatically slowed down; however, when an animal was shifted to 16 pellets after having received a smaller number, running speed abruptly became more rapid.

Moreover, Crespi (1942) found that with animals shifted from 256 or 164 pellets to 16, the running speed was *slower* than that found with a constant 16-pellet group at its asymptote or limit of practice. On the other hand, with those animals shifted from 1 or 4 pellets to 16, performance rose above the level characteristic of a constant 16-pellet group which presumably had reached its asymptote of running speed. Increased performance as a result of going from a small to a large reward was termed a positive contrast or "elation" effect, whereas poorer performance associated with shifting from a larger to a smaller amount of reward was termed negative contrast or a "depression" effect. Fig. 10-10 presents the kinds of results which Crespi obtained.[13]

Many subsequent investigators have continued to support Crespi's (1942) early findings. Zeaman (1949); Ehrenfreund and Badia (1962); DiLollo (1964); Weinstein (1970); and Raymond, Aderman, and Wolach (1972) are only a few of the many investigators who have reported abrupt changes in rate of responding as a function of shifting rewards.[14]

Similarly, Blodgett (1929) and Dufort and Kimble (1956) have also found abrupt changes in probability of response measures. We examined Blodgett's (1929) findings earlier in our discussion of the distinction between learning and performance.

In summary, the experimental evidence supports the position that performance changes rapidly and in keeping with the amount of reward that is provided. Thus, when the amount of reward is shifted to a larger amount, the organism's level of performance increases abruptly; similarly, when the reward is shifted to a reduced amount, performance rapidly declines. Inasmuch as learning is not assumed to take place this rapidly (and certainly not in the case of response decrement), it has generally been assumed that it is the organism's performance which is changing, thus, supporting the frequently made distinction between learning and performance.

A basic question stemming from Crespi's (1942) study is whether the contribution of a current amount of reward to performance is related to earlier amounts received by the organism—in brief, if positive and negative contrast effects would be obtained.

A large number of studies, as attested by Black's (1968) theoretical paper and Dunham's (1968) review, have been conducted examining such effects. Following Dunham (1968), we can divide these into (1) nondifferential and (2) differential studies.

[13] It should be noted that the negative contrast effects were obtained after a single shift of reward; however, positive contrast effects were obtained only when Crespi's subjects had first been shifted to a smaller reward and then shifted to a larger one. Thus, the positive contrast effect was a double-shift phenomenon. Virtually all investigators of the contrast effect with the exception of Weinstock (1971) have used a single shift of reward in order to examine this phenomenon.

[14] The reader should be aware that all experimenters have not been able to replicate these findings. Homzie and Ross (1962), Rosen and Ison (1965), and Rosen (1966), for example, examining the influence of shifting different percentages of sucrose in running behavior of rats, noted gradual changes in performance rather than the abrupt shift which has characterized the more frequent finding. And Ison and Glass (1969) in one instance were not able to obtain any shift effect, gradual or otherwise. Here, a group of rats which was provided 400 licks of a 20% sucrose solution during a preshift period of 42 trials traversing a runway, continued to run as rapidly during the postshift trials although receiving only 20 licks of a 5% sucrose solution—a most unusual finding! A similar finding was reported by Lowes and Bitterman (1967) who noted that goldfish, following a shift from high to low reward, did not reduce their level of responding.

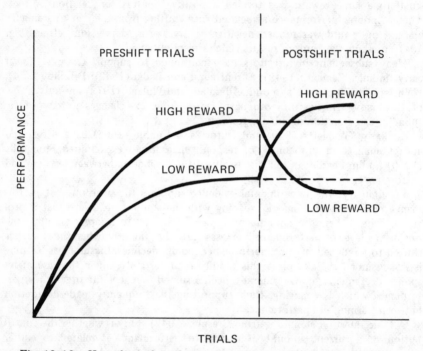

Fig. 10-10. Hypothetical performance curves arising from a shift in the amount of reward and demonstrating positive and negative contrast effects.

With the nondifferential task, two phases of training (preshift and postshift) are provided, while a single cue-response association is utilized in both phases. Crespi's (1942) experimental procedure illustrates this kind of paradigm, since the animals continued to traverse the runway under the same experimental conditions except for the shift in reward.

With the differential task, two distinct cue-response events are associated with different amounts of reinforcement. Training trials with tasks may be successive or random, thus providing a successive differential or random differential procedure.[15]

In a study illustrating successive differential conditioning, Collier and Marx (1959) provided eight days of consummatory training for rats in a Skinner box using either a 4%, 11.3%, or 32% concentration of sucrose solution. Training consisted of teaching the animals to *run* to the sucrose dispenser when they heard the characteristic click of the mechanism. Following such preshift training, all groups learned to *bar press* with an 11.3% solution as a reward during the postshift session.

[15] A simultaneous procedure has also been used, e.g., Spear and Hill (1965), but so infrequently that we have not presented its methodology.

The random differential procedure is indicated in a study by Bower (1961), who had his experimental animals receive a large reward of 8 pellets when run in a black (or white) alley and a small reward of 1 pellet when run in an alley of the opposite brightness. The performance of these experimental animals was compared to two groups of control animals who received a constant 1- or 8-pellet reward in both runways.

As Dunham's (1968) review of this area indicates, most investigators using either the nondifferential or differential paradigm have been unable to obtain positive contrast effects. On the other hand, negative contrast effects have been a common finding. Moreover, it has been shown (a) that such negative contrast effects can be made to disappear by gradually, rather than abruptly, reducing the size of the reward (Gonzalez, Gleitman, and Bitterman, 1962) and (b) that long intervals of time, e.g., 68 days, introduced between the preshift and post-shift phases of training will eliminate such effects (Gleitman and Steinman, 1964). Table 10-5 provides a summary of some of the studies conducted in this field of study.

Recent experimenters have pointed to what they consider several difficulties in many of the studies that failed to obtain positive contrast effects. When running speed is used as the response measure, a large reward may produce the fastest possible running speed, so that when the experimental group is shifted from low to high reward, an increase in running speed over that noted in the control animals is not physically possible.

One solution has been to use intermediate rather than maximum amounts of reward. The studies of Collier and Marx (1959), and Black, Adamson, and Bevan (1961) utilized medium levels of motivation in the postshift phase and it may be noted that positive contrast effects were obtained. One difficulty with this procedure, however, is that it reduces the amount of contrast provided. As a result, some investigators have proposed that a delay in reward, the lowering of deprivation states, or the use of an apparatus which requires some searching for the correct path be employed. All of these procedures result in reducing the running speed of the animals.

The studies of Shanab, Sanders, and Premack (1969) and Mellgren (1971), with both experiments utilizing a delay of reward procedure, and Shanab and Ferrell (1970), employing a complex maze and manipulating the deprivation level, have been able to demonstrate positive contrast effects. Positive contrast effects have also been obtained with what Shanab and Biller (1972) and Shanab and Cavallaro (1975) have described as double and triple shift procedures. Such shifts involve the manipulation of two or more reward variables. For example, in the Shanab and Biller (1972) double shift study, animals were provided with a small reward together with a long delay of reinforcement. The shift consisted of providing the animals with a large amount of reward together with a short delay. The triple shift procedure by Shanab and Cavallaro (1975) consisted of adding a partial reinforcement schedule to the small reward–long delay period, the shift consisting of a large reward provided on a continuous basis, along with a short delay. These procedures look promising in demonstrating the validity of positive contrast effects.

Explanations for the contrast effects depend on whether only negative con-

Table 10-5 Summaries of a Sampling of Studies Investigating Contrast Effects

Experimental Design	Task	Response Measure	Organism	Results	Investigators
Nondifferential	Runway	Running Speed	Rats	Positive and negative contrast effects obtained.	Crespi (1942)
Nondifferential	Runway	Running Speed	Rats	Positive and negative contrast effects obtained.	Zeaman (1949)
Nondifferential	Runway	Running Speed	Rats	Positive effects not obtained; negative effects obtained.	Spence (1956)
Nondifferential	Runway	Running Speed	Rats	Neither positive nor negative contrast effects obtained.	Metzger, Cotton, and Lewis (1957)
Nondifferential	Runway	Running Speed	Rats	Negative contrast effects obtained. Effect was shown to disappear if shift was gradual, experiment not designed to examine positive effects.	Gonzalez, Gleitman, and Bitterman (1962)
Nondifferential	Runway	Running Speed	Rats	Positive and negative effects obtained when animals were under 85% body weight, neither effect obtained when animals were under 95% body weight.	Ehrenfreund and Badia (1962)
Nondifferential	Drinking	Rate of Licking	Rats	Transient positive contrast effects obtained when Ss were shifted from 9% or 16% sucrose to 32%. Experiment not designed to examine negative effects.	Premack and Hillix (1962)
Nondifferential	Runway	Running Speed	Rats	Positive effects not obtained; negative effects found.	DiLollo (1964)

Nondifferential	Runway	Running Speed	Rats	Negative effects obtained when shift from high to low reward was immediate; not obtained when 68 days intervened between shift of high to low. Experiment not designed to examine positive effects.	Gleitman and Steinman (1964)
Nondifferential	Runway	Running Speed	Rats	Positive effects not obtained; experiment not designed to examine negative effects.	Ashida and Birch (1964)
Nondifferential	Bar Press	Bar Press Latency	Rats	Positive effects obtained when shift was from plain food pellet to 32% sucrose pellet. Rats shifted from 8% sucrose pellet to 32% sucrose pellet did not reveal positive effects. Experiment not designed to examine negative effects.	Marx (1969b)
Nondifferential	Runway	Running Speed	Rats	Positive contrast not obtained. Experiment not designed to examine negative effects.	Campbell, Crumbaugh, Knouse, and Snodgrass (1970)
Nondifferential	Bar Press	Rate of Bar Press	Rats	Negative effects obtained. Experiment not designed to examine positive effects.	Weinstein (1970)
Nondifferential	"Swimway"	Swimming Speed	Goldfish	Neither positive nor negative contrast obtained.	Raymond, Aderman, and Wolach (1972)
Nondifferential	Complex Maze	Running Speed	Rats	Positive contrast effects obtained. Experiment not designed to examine negative effects.	Shanab and Ferrell (1970)
Successive Differential	Bar Press	Rate of Bar Press	Rats	Positive and negative contrast effects obtained.	Collier and Marx (1959)
Successive Differential	Runway	Running Speed	Rats	Neither positive nor negative contrast effects obtained.	Goodrich and Zaretsky (1962)

309

Table 10-5 (continued)

Experimental Design	Task	Response Measure	Organism	Results	Investigators
Successive Differential	Black and White Runways	Running Speed	Rats	Neither positive nor negative contrast effects obtained.	Goldstein and Spence (1963)
Simultaneous Differential	T-maze: 1 pellet on one side, 1, 2, 10 pellets on other	Difference in running speed to arm with one pellet.	Rats	Negative contrast effects obtained.	Spear and Hill (1965)
Simultaneous Differential	T-maze	Difference in running speed	Rats	Negative contrast effects obtained.	Spear and Spitzner (1966)
Random Differential	Black and White Runways	Speed in Running	Rats	Positive contrast effects not obtained; negative contrast effects obtained.	Bower (1961)
Random Differential	Black and White Runways	Running Speed	Rats	Negative contrast effects obtained; experiment not designed to examine positive effects.	Ludvigson and Gay (1966)
Random Differential	Black and White Runways	Running Speed	Rats	Negative contrast effects obtained; experiment not designed to examine positive effects.	Ludvigson and Gay (1967)

trast effects are thought to be obtained or whether both positive and negative contrast effects can be considered bona fide phenomena.

If it is hypothesized that only negative contrast effects take place, poorer performance with a small amount of reward, following presentation of a larger one, may be assumed to result from emotional factors accompanying the downshift and disrupting performance. Thus, Spence (1956, p. 144) has stated that negative contrast is the result of disruptive emotional factors which accompany the downshift in the magnitude of reinforcement. A similar formulation has been provided by Amsel (1958, 1962) who has been somewhat more explicit in specifiying the emotional consequences of a reduction in reward. Amsel hypothesized that the occurrence of a nonreward or a reduction in reward elicits a primary frustration response which interferes with the animal's previous learning.

If it is assumed that both positive and negative contrast effects are obtainable, a different theory is needed to explain contrast effects; one can be found in Helson's (1964) adaptation level theory as applied to conditions of reinforcement, e.g., Bevan and Adamson (1960), Black, Adamson, and Bevan (1961). Here it is suggested that the organism averages a series of reinforcements over time or trials, with performance a joint function of the magnitude of the reinforcing agent and the difference between a previously established norm and such reinforcement. In accordance with such a theoretical position, both positive and negative contrast effects should be obtainable and the adaptation level position founders if positive contrast effects cannot be obtained.

Behavioral Contrast   As noted, the runway has been used almost exclusively to examine positive and negative contrast effects. Reynolds (1961a), using the free-operant situation, has demonstrated a somewhat similar phenomenon although he has termed it behavioral contrast. This effect can be illustrated as follows. A pigeon, placed in a Skinner box, is reinforced for pecking at a key which may be red, orange, or yellow. These colored keys are presented in succession a number of times throughout each of the bird's training sessions. Responding (defined in terms of pecks per minute) will be about the same to all three stimulus keys. If, however, reinforcement is now shifted so that reward is provided only when the red key is pecked and never when the orange or yellow keys are pecked, it will be noted that response to the red key will increase over the stable level of responding to red which took place during the earlier session. Positive behavioral contrasts have been obtained by a number of experimenters (e.g., Nevin and Shettleworth, 1966; Terrace, 1966; Bloomfield, 1967).

There has been little attempt on the part of investigators to relate the two types of contrast effects, probably because of the important procedural differences which must be considered. Thus, in most instrumental contrast studies, reinforcement manipulations involve magnitude of reinforcement, while behavioral contrast effects are related to reinforcement density, or the number of times the organism is reinforced during a fixed period. Typically, instrumental learning situations provide trials which are highly distributed, with a response measurement of latency or running speed; the operant procedure utilizes intertrial intervals of near 0, while response rate is the common measure.

Delay of Reward

As noted earlier in this chapter (see p. 278), the third motivational parameter has been concerned with the temporal interval or the delay between the instrumental response and the securing of reward.

In examining delay of reward in instrumental learning studies, it has been a common practice to discriminate between (1) response delay and (2) temporal delay. The response delay task is one in which the instrumental response chain, or the length of the behavior sequence, has been systematically varied. Thus, there are different distances between the first part of the sequence, or the initial portion of the chain, and the reinforcement received at the end of the behavior sequence. As an example, a T-maze may be used with the left arm 12' long and the right arm, 6' long. It is obvious that more time is required for the animal to move from the choice point of the T-maze to the goal box at the end of the left arm than from the choice point to the goal box located at the end of the right arm. Although response delay interested a number of early investigators, current concern has been primarily with the role of temporal delay.

Temporal delay involves the introduction of a period of time between the organism's response and the securing of reinforcement. It must be recognized that the temporal classification represents only a convenient way of describing a set of operations in which the experimenter does not require the subject to make any additional responses between the one required response and the securing of reward. It is obvious that responses of one type or another fill this delay interval, just as they filled the interval which is utilized in the response delay task.

Contemporary studies of temporal delay of reinforcement begin with Perin (1943), who found that when a delay of 30 seconds or more was introduced between the rat's making a bar pressing response and its receiving food, the animal was unable to learn this response. Subsequent studies by Perkins (1947), Grice (1948), and Smith (1951) indicate that this time interval should be further reduced. In Grice's (1948) study, groups of rats were required to learn a black-white discrimination problem with delays of 0, .5, 1.2, 2, 5 and 10 seconds introduced between the animal's making the correct choice and its securing of food. (It must be noted that the delay periods used in Grice's study were not all of the temporal variety. In some cases, a response delay was used.) The criterion of learning was 18 correct responses out of 20 trials. Learning curves for the varying groups revealed that the 0 delay group learned most rapidly, followed by the .5-, 1.2-, and 2.0-second delay groups. When a delay of 5 seconds was introduced, the animals in this group experienced great difficulty in learning; thus, the animals were responding at only 80% correct at the end of 700 trials. The group provided a delay of 10 seconds did not learn the discrimination task although in some cases the animals were given as many as 1400 trials. See Fig. 10-11 for these results.

Keesey (1964) has reported similar findings using a discriminative bar pressing response and intracranial self-stimulation (ICS). This study merits attention since the use of ICS permits the experimenter to exert precise control over the delay of reinforcement. Groups of rats who had electrodes implanted in their posterior hypothalamus were first trained to depress a single bar for stimulation

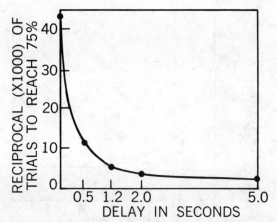

Fig. 10-11. Rate of learning as a function of delay of reward. The experimental values are represented by black dots, and the smooth curve is fitted to these data. *Adapted from Grice (1948)*

which was provided either 0, .5, 1.0, 2.0, 3.0, or 5.0 seconds after each bar press. Following such training, the subjects were placed in a two-bar discrimination situation. Over one bar had been placed a light. A response to the light bar, the position of which was randomly varied, resulted in the delivery of intracranial stimulation after the same temporal interval which animals had experienced in their first training session. A response to the non-lighted bar provided no stimulation. Following a response on either bar, the discriminative light as well as the lights which illuminated the apparatus were extinguished for 10 seconds. The reciprocal of the mean number of errors made by each group over 500 trials as a function of the delay interval is indicated in Fig. 10-12. The similarity between this function and that obtained by Grice (1948) can readily be noted. In a subsequent study, Hendricks and Gerall (1970), also using brain stimulation as reward, obtained similar findings.

Topping and Parker (1970) were interested in examining the delay variable with the probability learning task—a somewhat more complex task than had been used in the animal studies discussed. In this study, using pigeons as subjects, one key was designated as correct on 70% of the trials while another key was correct on the remaining 30%. If a correct response was made, reinforcement was presented after either a 0-, 8-, or 15-second delay. Results indicated that the delay of reinforcement had a decremental effect on the learning of this task. Thus, as the time interval between the making of the response and the securing of reinforcement increased, the animals revealed a slower rate of maximizing their correct response.[16]

[16] Maximizing the correct response means that the animals would peck the key which was reinforced 70% of the time, on all trials. In this way they would be sure that they would be receiving reinforcement 70% of the time.

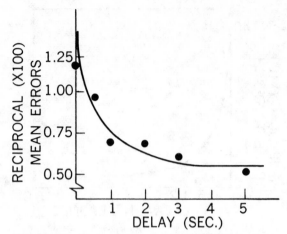

Fig. 10-12. Rate of learning as a function of the delay of reward. The curve has been visually fitted to the data points. *Adapted from Keesey (1964)*

Delay of Reward with Children

The delay of reward variable has stimulated a great deal of research using normal as well as retarded children. Table 10-6 summarizes a sampling of these studies. One conclusion which can be drawn is that delay plays an important role with retardates as well as with preschool and first-grade children.

For example, in a study by Terrell and Ware (1961) kindergarten and first-grade children were asked to solve concurrently two easy discrimination problems; with one problem there was an immediate reward (light flash) after the correct response; with the second problem, the reward was delayed for 7 seconds. Training was continued until the subject reached a criterion of 6 consecutive correct trials. In a second experiment, more difficult discrimination tasks were provided, although the same immediate and delayed reward conditions were examined. A criterion of 4 consecutive correct trials was utilized. Results from both experiments revealed that subjects learned significantly more quickly when rewarded immediately than when given a delayed reward. Thus, in Experiment 1, the mean number of trials to learn was 6.6 and 16.6 for the immediate and delayed conditions, respectively, while in Experiment 2, the means were 16.3 and 22.7 for the immediate and delayed conditions.

As children grow older, there appears to be some mitigation of the effect, perhaps because of verbal mediators; there does seem to be an interaction between the type of task and the subject's age. Hockman and Lipsitt (1961) examined the learning of an easy (two-stimulus) and a difficult (three-stimulus) discrimination problem with fourth-grade children. A successive procedure was used in which the presentation of a colored light was associated with a button pressing response. Correct responding was indicated by the presentation of a red light, while an incorrect response was accompanied by a buzzer. The delay in presentation of the red light or buzzer was varied—either 0, 10, or 30 seconds.

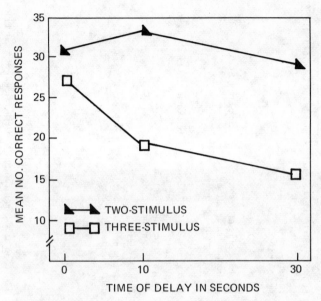

Fig. 10-13. The delay-of-reward gradients for the easy-and difficult-task groups. *Adapted from Hockman and Lipsitt (1961)*

All subjects were run to a criterion of 12 correct responses or a maximum of 36 trials. As Fig. 10-13 indicates, the learning of the easy discrimination task was not influenced by the delay interval—the delay did have an effect, however, on the learning of the difficult task.

Explanations for the Delay Effect

In attempting to explain the deleterious effects of delay, Spence (1956), as well as other investigators, have hypothesized that when a delay interval is introduced, the organism makes a variety of extraneous responses during the delay which compete with the to-be-learned response. It has been suggested that if the organism can maintain an orientation toward the response manipulandum, e.g., a bar in the Skinner box, or is so trained that specific responses can serve as cues, it is possible to reduce or even, perhaps, to eliminate any response decrement which might take place.

Spence (1956) has reported a study by Carlton, Harker, and Schilling which shows that the delay of reinforcement provides an opportunity for competing responses to occur. Rats were trained to leave a starting box and traverse a runway to a response bar which they had to press in order to secure a pellet of food. One group of animals received immediate reinforcement, whereas a second group was provided with a 10-second delay. Half of each of these groups used a runway just 2 inches wide and 3 inches high, while the other half used a runway which was much larger—17 inches wide and 11.5 inches high. It was assumed

Table 10-6   Summaries of a Sampling of Studies Investigating Delay of Reinforcement Using Normal and Retarded Children as Subjects

Subjects	Task	Delay Intervals	Response Measure	Results	Investigators
Preschool Children	Two-stimulus, one-choice apparatus, with reward delivered immediately to one stimulus, and after 7 seconds to the other.	0 and 7 seconds	Response speed and preference for one of the two stimuli.	Subjects preferred to respond to immediate rewarded stimulus; no difference in response speed.	Lipsitt and Castaneda (1958)
Fourth-Grade Children	Simultaneous and successive discrimination tasks.	0, 3, or 6 seconds	Number Correct	No delay of reinforcement gradient obtained, although 6-second group performed most poorly.	Erickson and Lipsitt (1960)
Fourth-Grade Children	Two-stimulus (easy) and 3-stimulus (difficult) successive discrimination problems.	0, 10, or 30 seconds	Number Correct	Increasing delay had progressively deleterious effect on difficult discrimination; no difference among groups with easy task.	Hockman and Lipsitt (1961)
Kindergarten and First-Grade Children	(a) Discrimination learning with Ss required to learn a size and form problem concurrently. (b) Three-stimulus size and form problem learned concurrently.	In both (a) and (b), one problem learned with 0-seconds delay, other problem with 7-seconds delay.	Number Correct	Both (a) and (b) revealed delay resulted in poorer learning.	Terrell and Ware (1961)
Moderately and severely retarded children; also normal first graders	Two-choice discrimination problem.	0, 1.5, 6, or 12 seconds	Errors and trials to criterion	12-second delay significantly increased errors and trials to criterion for all groups. No difference among other delay intervals.	Hetherington, Ross and Pick (1964)

Subjects	Task	Delay	Measure	Results	Reference
Mental Retardates	Discrimination of geometric forms; e.g. square, etc. Ss required to solve 10 problems (1 problem per day).	0 or 5 seconds	Errors	Delay increased difficulty of problem. Effect appeared to be limited to initial trials on each problem.	Schoelkopf and Orlando (1965)
Mental Retardates	Two-choice discrimination problem. Chosen stimulus was visible or not visible during delay.	0, 12, or 18 seconds	Errors and trials to criterion	0-second delay significantly superior to 12 or 18 second groups for both conditions.	Ross, Hetherington, and Wray (1965)
Normal and moderately retarded children	Simple discrimination	0 or 12 seconds	Errors and trials to criterion	12 second delay increased errors for retardates; no difference between 0- and 12-second delay for normals.	Hetherington and Ross (1967)
Mental Retardates	Two-choice discrimination problem.	0 or 15 seconds	Number of correct responses	0-second delay significantly superior to 15 seconds.	Keeley and Sprague (1969)

that the confining conditions of the small runway would discourage animals from turning away and losing their orientation to the food cup during any delays which were imposed. On the other hand, it was believed that the larger runway would encourage the occurrence of responses which were incompatible with the maintenance of orientation to the food cup and thus result in poorer learning. The results supported Spence's position. For the two groups given immediate reinforcement, no difference in bar pressing performance was obtained as a function of the size of the runway. However, the size of the runway did make a differential contribution in the learning of those groups which received the 10-second delay; the group running over the confined runway revealed superior performance.

If the delay of reinforcement is introduced gradually, it is possible that the organism can effectively learn to use responses during the delay to bridge the temporal interval. A study by Ferster (1953b), confirmed by Dews (1960), has demonstrated this effect. In Ferster's study, a stable pecking response was established with no delay of reinforcement. A 60-second delay was then introduced which resulted in a decline in the animal's rate of pecking to its operant level. This operant level of responding demonstrated that such a long temporal delay between response and reward prevented the animal from learning to associate the pecking response with the securing of food. Short reinforcement delays were then introduced and, as the pecking response became stable under each specific delay period, the delay interval was lengthened until the pecking response again stabilized. Ferster found that by using this graded delay technique it was possible to obtain a normal response rate with a 60-second delay period—a delay magnitude which had previously resulted in only operant level responding.

Champion and McBride (1962) have examined how the kind of activity which fills the delay interval may effect human subjects. A paired associate task was provided in which college students were required to read a list of words between the response and exposure of the work which would indicate whether or not a correct response had been made. For example, the word "needle" might be used as a stimulus word with the individual having to learn to respond with the word "thread." Between the subject's response and the exposure of the response word in the apparatus, the subject would have to read a list of words that were expected to interfere with the learning of the response word, e.g., sew, steel, thimble. Two- and 5-second delay periods were used, with half the subjects in each delay period required to read lists of interfering words during the delay, while the remaining subjects were instructed to fixate on the word appearing in the memory drum. Response latencies for the varying groups are indicated in Fig. 10–14; they confirmed the position that one important variable in delay of reward studies is the characteristics of the competing responses which fill the delay period.

Reinforcement, Free Loading, and Instrinsic Appeal

Much experimental work with animals is predicated on the theory that in order to get the animal to learn, some type of reinforcement, usually food or

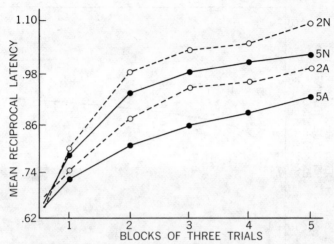

Fig. 10-14. Performance curves for groups learning with two- and five-second delay of reinforcement and with activity (A) or inactivity (N) during the delay period. *Adapted from Champion and McBride (1962)*

water, must be presented following the instrumental response. During the last decade, some interesting work has been done in which, after the reinforced response is learned, the animal is given the choice of continuing to respond for reward or receiving the reward without having to make the response. Contrary to the expectations of many, it has been observed that animals do not "free load" but continue to respond in order to "earn" their reward.

In one of the early studies by Jensen (1963), rats learned to press the bar in a Skinner box and were provided with either 40, 80, 160, 320, 640, or 1280 rewarded bar presses. The bar was then made inoperative and a small cup, identical to that found in the home cage, containing 250 pellets was placed in the corner of the test chamber furthermost from the bar. After two pellets had been eaten from the cup, the bar was again made operative and the animals had a choice of eating pellets from the cup or pressing the bar and receiving a pellet for each bar press. This period lasted 40 minutes. Fig. 10-15 shows the relationship between preference for bar pressing over free loading as a function of the number of rewarded presses made prior to the choice.

It may be noted that as the number of previously rewarded presses increased, the percentage of eaten pellets obtained by bar pressing increased also, so that with 1280 presses, almost 80% of the pellets that the animal ate had been obtained by pressing the bars. Jensen (1963) postulated that bar pressing held an intrinsic appeal for the rat—intrinsic appeal being defined as a pleasant emotional state experienced while performing the operant.

As Table 10-7 reveals, a number of investigators have obtained somewhat similar findings. Stolz and Lott (1964), for example, trained hungry rats to traverse an empty alley for a pellet of food in a goal box. They then found that their rats would persist in running down the alley and into the goal box even

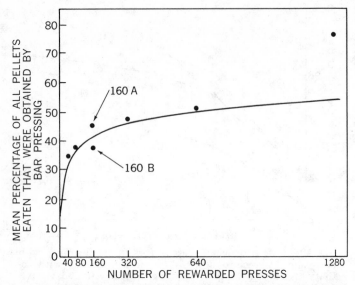

Fig. 10-15. Mean percentage of all pellets eaten during a 40-minute choice period where pellets were earned by bar pressing as a function of number of previous rewards. The A and B values plotted at 160 represent the performance of two groups given reinforcement under slightly different schedules. *Adapted from Jensen (1963)*

though a pile of pellets (6 inches long and ½ inch deep) was placed half way down the alley and it was necessary to run directly over the food.

The most frequently used procedure, however, has been to provide rats with a number of sessions of eating in the experimental apparatus, after which they are trained to press a bar for food, frequently on a continuous reinforcement schedule. Following such training, the animals are then given a choice of free loading—eating from a glass dish—or pressing the bar for each food pellet.

The preference for bar pressing has been found in a variety of situations. It has been demonstrated when water as well as sucrose solutions have been used as the reward; the effect has also been found to relate to the number of hours of deprivation. Moreover, it has been shown to be persistent over a number of preference test sessions.

But, as noted in Table 10-7, some experimenters have found a preference for free loading. One interpretation of the positive findings may be that since the rats are generally given fewer days of training in learning to eat food in the experimental apparatus than in learning to press the bar for food, the habit of eating in the experimental apparatus is not as strong as bar pressing, hence the preference for this latter activity. Or it may be that since the learning of the bar pressing response takes place closest in time to the preference test, there is a preference for the activity which has been learned last. It can be noted that in the studies by Taylor (1972) and Tarte and Snyder (1973), a preference for free loading was obtained when the habit of eating in the experimental apparatus was strengthened by additional days of training, or by having the animals learn to eat in the experimental apparatus just prior to the preference test.

It should be acknowledged that the results of some experimenters who have obtained a preference for bar pressing or pecking a disc for food have not supported this interpretation. In studies by both Neuringer (1969) and Carder and Berkowitz (1970), there appeared to be ample opportunity for experimental subjects to acquire a fairly strong habit of eating "free food" in the experimental apparatus. And a study by Singh (1970) was specifically designed to equate the habit of "eating" with bar pressing.

In this study, rats were trained to bar press in a "work" chamber on a FI schedule of either FI-1, FI-3, or FI-11, with 100 reinforcements provided each day. Training also consisted of permitting the animals to receive the same number of reinforcements in a "no-work" chamber. The rate of reinforcement delivery in the no-work chamber was determined on the basis of the animal's performance in the "work" chamber. If the subject received a pellet every 5 seconds by bar pressing, it received a free pellet every 10 seconds in the no-work chamber. Following five days of work and five days of no work, randomly presented, four days of preference testing was given. Here, animals had a choice of going to the work or the no-work chamber and obtaining pellets for behavior appropriate to the chamber they had chosen. Results revealed that each group of animals obtained significantly more reinforcement by working on each of the four preference test days. Moreover, there was a significant tendency for the FI-1 animals to obtain a higher percentage of reinforcement by working than either the FI-3 or the FI-11 animals.

It is possible that providing animals with food on a fixed interval schedule may have resulted in the establishment of certain superstitious behaviors; but the very regular contingency observed by the animal between bar pressing and the receipt of food may have resulted in the obtained preference for making this kind of response.

Singh (1970) and Singh and Query (1971) have presumably been able to demonstrate the preference for work phenomenon with both white and American Indian children. In the first study (Singh, 1970) the procedure consisted of having white children press a lever (work) for marbles on an FR-10 schedule, or having them receive the marbles without the necessity for lever pressing. In the latter case, the child was told to sit on a chair and wait for the marbles to be dispensed from a machine. Following such training, a preference test was provided with results revealing that significantly more marbles were obtained by working than by sitting. And in a subsequent experiment, Singh and Query (1971) used American Indian children as subjects. As they have written, if the responding of the white children "was due to certain attitudes prominent in Western cultures, especially white Protestant ethic, which stress that one should work to obtain rewards," they reasoned that American Indian children might reveal different experimental findings. Results with the Indian children replicated the findings with whites. Some question may be raised, however, regarding any explanation based on attitudes or intrinsic appeal. It is possible that sitting in a chair is slightly aversive for a young child, so that lever pressing represents a more desir-

Table 10-7 Summary of a Sampling of Studies Investigating Free Loading

Investigators	Subjects	Task	General Procedure	Results
Stoltz and Lott (1964)	Rats	Traversing Runway	Ss given opportunity to stop in middle of runway containing pile of pellets extending across the width of the alley only 1 or no pellets placed in goal box.	Nearly half of Ss with training ran over food in order to get to the goal box. Ss continued to run for 22 trials even after many trials in which the Ss had eaten from middle of runway.
Neuringer (1969)	Pigeons	Pecking at Disc	Two pigeons first trained to peck at disc for food. Training continued for 7 days. Next 15 days, food placed in cup. Pecking response also produced food.	Both pigeons and rats revealed preference for pecking at disc or bar pressing in order to obtain food.
	Rats	Bar Press	Two rats trained to press bar to obtain food. Each S lived in chamber for 15 days in which each response produced a pellet. Free food cup filled twice during this period. Then bar response produced no pellets for 10 days. Food was available in cup. Experimental condition of food in cup and bar press providing food reinstated for next 6 days.	
Carder and Berkowitz (1970)	Rats	Bar Press	Ss permitted to consume free food on each of 3 days; then Ss trained to bar press for 6 days on continuous reinforcement schedule. Then provided test with free food. Two additional sessions given on bar pressing with FR2 and tested with food. Two additional sessions given on bar pressing with FR10 and another testing provided.	Preference for bar pressing obtained with continuous and FR2 schedules. FR-10 resulted in preference for free food.
Singh (1970)	Rats	Bar Press	Two chambers used, one in which the Ss had to press a bar for food on an FR schedule. The other chamber provided free food on the same schedule.	Animals preferred to bar press for food.

Study	Subject	Response	Procedure	Results
	Children	Bar Press	Children could press bar for marbles (later exchanged for toy) or could receive them at same interval by sitting and waiting.	Children preferred to bar press for marbles.
Singh and Query (1971)	American Indian and White Children	Bar Press	Same procedure used as in Singh (1970).	Children preferred to bar press for marbles.
Taylor (1972)	Rats	Bar Press	(Exp. 1) Ss trained to bar press 20 min/day until a total of 1,000 pellets were earned. Following training, 300 pellets were provided free and Ss permitted to eat for 1 day. Fifteen 20 min/day sessions provided with Ss given a choice. (Exp. 2) Ss trained as above, but received water as a reward.	Mild preference for free food on early sessions; preference for free food continued so that at end of 15 days preference had increased to 80%. Ss revealed strong preference for free water.
Tarte and Synder (1972)	Rats	Bar Press	Ss permitted to consume pellets for 1 hr/day for 3 days, then trained to bar press for 6 days. Following such training 7 groups formed and food deprived for 0, 12, 24, 36, 48, 72 or 92 hours. Ss then given 1 hour-test session.	Results indicated percentage of bar pressing increased as a function of deprivation period.
Carder (1972)	Rats	Bar Press	(Exp. 1) Rats trained to press bar for 10% sucrose solution, with subsequent test provided giving Ss opportunity to obtain sucrose without bar press. Second group trained to press bar for water, with Ss having opportunity to obtain water without bar press. (Exp. 2) Similar procedure except that rats learned to press for increasing levels of quinine adulteration.	Sucrose Ss earned 83% of their total consumption. Water Ss earned a mean of only 26% of their total intake. Percentage of solution earned declined as a function of amount of quinine adulteration.
Tarte, Snyder (1973)	Rats	Bar Press	Five experiments conducted. Exps. 1–3 provided 3 days of free feeding and 6 days of bar pressing prior to 2, 3 or 10 days of choice. Exps. 4 and 5 equalized amount of time in bar pressing and eating prior to the choice.	Results for Exp. 1–3 revealed bar pressing for food was preferred to free loading. When eating and bar pressing time was equalized, animals preferred to free load.

able activity. Unfortunately, preference tests for these two activities were not provided prior to the experiment.

In summary, a variety of investigators have demonstrated that under particular circumstances, some organisms will reveal a preference to work for food rather than free load. The findings obtained from many of these studies can be explained, however, on the basis that instrumental responding represents a much stronger habit than eating in the experimental apparatus.

Summary

Studies examining the effect of deprivation and reward on instrumental learning have been quite extensive. When deprivation states are manipulated, most of the experimental findings support the position that performance, as measured by rate of responding, improves as a function of the length or intensity of the deprivation state. Probability of responding, however, does not show a similar function.

The role of reward as revealed by three conditions, (1) frequency, (2) amount, and (3) delay, has also been examined extensively. Most investigators have shown that performance measured by rate of response is a function of the frequency with which reinforcement is provided. One area related to frequency is partial reinforcement—providing and omitting reward on acquisition trials. Little interest has been shown in examining the effects of partial reinforcement on acquisition trials; performance on extinction trials has, however, generated considerable interest, since resistance to extinction is much superior for a partial reinforcement regimen than for a continuous one. One partial reinforcement variable which has been investigated is the percentage of reinforcement provided during acquisition trials. Perhaps the most acceptable conclusion arising from many studies is that the relationship between percentage of reinforcement and resistance to extinction is curvilinear, or more specifically, U-shaped. Either a small or a large percentage of reinforcement results in smaller amounts of extinction than does a medium percentage. A number of explanations have been provided—discrimination, frustration, and sequential effects; however, none of these seems able to explain all the experimental findings which have been obtained.

The second reward variable, amount, like frequency, has been demonstrated to influence performance—the larger the amount, the better the organism's performance. One area of interest has been in providing shifts in the amount of reward over acquisition trials in an effort to determine how performance changes. Generally if smaller rewards are provided following a large reward, or a large reward is provided following a small one, performance shifts to approximate the performance level which is characteristic of that amount of reward. However, some experimenters have found increased performance going from a small to a large reward, and also, decreased performance in going from a large to a small one. Increased or decreased performance in these instances is defined as performance different from that obtained with animals provided either the small or the large amount for the total training series. These effects have been labeled positive and negative contrast effects. Negative contrast effects have been obtained by many investigators, but positive contrast effects have been more difficult to obtain. It is possible that this inability to obtain positive contrast has been a result of a methodological problem. Animals running very rapidly for a large reward cannot run any more rapidly—a type of performance which would be required to demonstrate the positive contrast effect.

The third variable, delay of reinforcement, refers to the temporal interval introduced between the organism's making the correct response and its securing of reward. Studies with animals have demonstrated that delays of 5 or 10 seconds result in making a discrimination task very difficult, if not impossible, to learn. Preschool and first-grade children, as well as mentally retarded children, reveal a similar effect; however, older children are less influenced by the delay of reward since, presumably, they can span the delay with verbal mediators.

Finally, some experimental work has shown that animals and children will prefer to work for reward in contrast to accepting reward without work (or free loading). There are some methodological problems involved in many of the studies which have demonstrated this effect so that the validity of this conclusion must await further experimental work.

11
Learning as a Function of Motivational Variables:
Aversive Stimulation

Although Yerkes (1907) used shock to punish mice for incorrect responses in a learning task almost three quarters of a century ago, it is only during the past two decades that a substantial interest has been generated in the use of aversive stimulation and the instrumental learning tasks of escape and avoidance. As has been noted, with instrumental escape, the aversive stimulation is provided at the beginning of the learning sequence and the organism's instrumental response results in obtaining aversive stimulation termination. With active avoidance, a somewhat similar situation prevails, except that a stimulus is provided first which the organism can use as a warning or as a cue for making the instrumental response. If the response is not made, the aversive stimulation is presented, and the task becomes one of escape. With passive avoidance, or punishment training, the organism makes a response which is followed by the presentation of an aversive stimulus for a fixed period of time. The instrumental response learned in such tasks is to remain passive or to not make the punished response.

As might be anticipated, experimenters have frequently been guided by the work done with reinforcement, so that three conditions which influence aversive stimulation have been investigated: (1) frequency, (2) intensity, and (3) the temporal delay provided between the instrumental response and the presentation (or termination) of the aversive stimulus.

Frequency of Aversive Stimulation

Paralleling the work with reinforcement, a variety of experiments have been conducted in which performance in either escape or avoidance learning tasks have been examined as a function of the number of trials provided. In escape tasks, trials are perfectly correlated with the number of times the aversive stimulus is presented. With avoidance tasks, this is obviously not true since appropriate responding is the successful avoidance of the aversive stimulus. However, if it is assumed that, as a result of early learning trials, the stimulus which cues the response acquires the capacity to elicit an emotional response, e.g., fear, it may be hypothesized that fear serves as an aversive stimulus and presumably would be present on every trial.

In any event, an increasing percentage of avoidance responses as a function of trials provided has been noted in many studies. A good example is found in an experiment by Beecroft and Bouska (1967) in which rats could learn to avoid shock by leaving a starting box and running down a 6-foot alley into a goal box. If the subject had not entered the goal box within 3 seconds, shock was provided and continued until the animal escaped into the goal box. Fig. 11-1 reveals the percentage of avoidance responses as a function of trials.

The Intensity of Aversive Stimuli

A second area of research which has interested experimenters is the manipulation of the intensity of the aversive stimulus used in instrumental escape and avoidance tasks.

Shock Intensity and Escape and Passive Avoidance

With instrumental escape tasks, the rate of response reveals a positive relationship between shock intensity and performance. Amsel (1950), Campbell and Kraeling (1953), and Trapold and Fowler (1960) are among many investigators who have demonstrated that speed of learning is related to intensity of the shock utilized. Trapold and Fowler's (1960) study was a fairly extensive one in which 5 groups of rats were trained to escape a shock of either 120, 160, 240, 320, or 400 volts by running to an uncharged goal box. Twenty massed trials were provided all subjects. The results, as indicated in Fig. 11-2, show that running speed was a negatively accelerated function of the intensity of the shock; starting speed, on the other hand, was first faster and then slower with increasing shock intensity.

When passive avoidance or punishment tasks are used, a most frequent finding is that the degree of response suppression is a function of the intensity

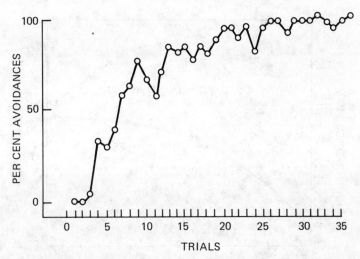

Fig. 11-1. Percent avoidances as a function of trials. *Adapted from Beecroft and Bouska (1967)*

of the shock. A study by Camp, Raymond, and Church (1967) illustrates the nature of these findings. Following eight sessions of training rats to press a lever for food on a 1-minute variable interval schedule, subjects were divided into 5 experimental groups that were given shock intensities of either .1, .2, .3, .5, or 2.0 ma. The shock was 2.0 seconds in duration and delivered according to a fixed-ratio schedule so calculated that each animal would receive an average of 1 shock per minute if its response rate remained unchanged. Finally, a control group did not receive shock. As Fig. 11-3 reveals, the amount of response suppression was a function of the intensity of the shock used.

Another way of manipulating intensity would be to increase the duration of the aversive stimulus; the influence of this variable on response suppression is quite similar to an increase in intensity. Seligman and Campbell (1965), Storms, Boroczi, and Boren (1962), and Church, Raymond, and Beauchamp (1967) have all demonstrated this effect. In the Church, Raymond, and Beauchamp (1967) study, following 5 sessions of training rats to press a lever for food on a 1-minute variable interval schedule, 42 rats were divided into 6 groups and given punishment for durations of 0, .15, .30, .50, 1.0, or 3.0 seconds. The punishment was a .16-ma shock delivered according to a 2-minute variable interval schedule. The mean suppression ratio as a function of the duration of the aversive stimulus is revealed in Fig. 11-4.

Shock Intensity and Escape Task Difficulty. There is the suggestion in an early study by Yerkes and Dodson (1908) that a very interesting relationship exists between intensity of the aversive stimulus and escape task difficulty. In this experiment, mice were used as experimental subjects in a visual discrimination task which involved three levels of difficulty. Three different shock intensities were manipulated. Results indicated that, with the easy discrimination problem, correct responses increased as a function of the strength of the shock.

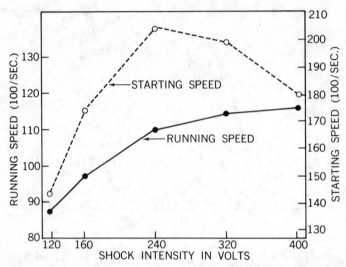

Fig. 11-2. Mean performance over the last eight trials as a function of shock intensity. *Adapted from Trapold and Fowler (1960)*

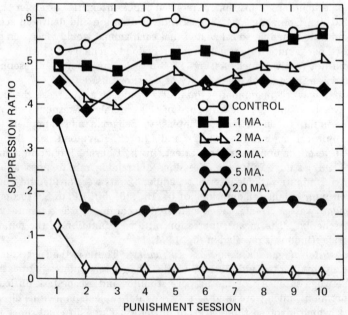

Fig. 11-3. Mean suppression ratio as a function of intensity of punishment. *Adapted from Camp, Raymond, and Church (1967)*

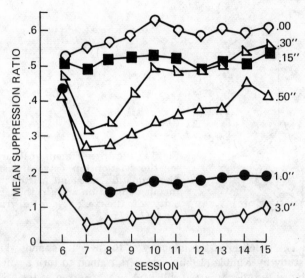

Fig. 11-4. Mean suppression ratio as a function of sessions of punishment training for groups with 0.0, 0.15, 0.30, 0.50, 1.0, and 3.0 sec. duration of punishment. *Adapted from Church, Raymond, and Beauchamp (1967)*

With the medium and difficult discrimination tasks, however, increases in shock intensity resulted in first increasing but then decreasing the number of correct responses. In summary, these findings, which provided the experimental basis for what has become known as the Yerkes-Dodson Law, indicated an optimum intensity of shock for a specific degree of task difficulty.

Subsequent studies by Hammes (1956) and Broadhurst (1957) have provided tentative confirmation of these early findings. In Broadhurst's study, the intensity of the aversive stimulus was manipulated by delaying the rat for either 0, 2, 4, or 8 seconds underwater, using three levels of difficulty in an underwater brightness discrimination task. As Fig. 11-5 reveals, increases in air deprivation resulted in increasing performance on the easy task; on the other hand, slight increases in air deprivation resulted in an increase in performance for the difficult task initially but as the time underwater increased, performance declined.

Active Avoidance and Shock Intensity

Intensity has been investigated with a variety of active avoidance tasks. For convenience, we shall divide these tasks into: (a) operant, (b) one-way, and (c) two-way.

The experimental findings obtained using active avoidance operant tasks agree with the findings obtained using passive avoidance tasks and indicate that

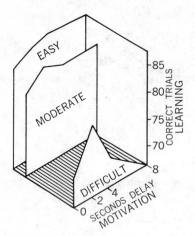

Fig. 11-5. A three-dimensional surface showing the relationship between learning in a
discrimination task and (a) the intensity of
the air deprivation and (b) the level of difficulty of the task. *Adapted from Broadhurst (1957)*

performance is a function of the intensity of the aversive stimuli which is used.
In an early study by Kimble (1955), rats were trained to turn a wheel within a
5-second interval in order to avoid shock. A buzzer served as the CS and 1 of 4
intensities of shock, either .2, .5, 1.0 or 2.0 ma, was used. The response measure
was the latency of responding. Results indicated that latency decreased as a
function of shock intensity, a finding supported in a subsequent study by
Boren, Sidman, and Herrnstein (1959) who determined that, as shock intensity
increased, the rate of a bar pressing response required to avoid shock also increased.

The one-way avoidance task differs from the two-way task according to the
spatial characteristics of the response demanded by the experimenter. In one-
way avoidance, the animal responds in only one direction, leaving a location
consistently associated with shock and entering a second location consistently
associated with safety. For example, the animal may be placed in a black box
where it receives shock. It learns to avoid shock by running to a white box which
is safe. The animal is placed in the black box at the beginning of each trial. On
the other hand, with two-way avoidance tasks, the animal must learn to respond
in two directions, leaving one compartment and entering a second on one trial,
and leaving the latter and entering the former on the next trial. Here, then, the
animal must learn to leave the black box and enter the white one on trial one,
but also learn to leave the white box and enter the black one on the second
trial. It now seems clear that the relationship between the intensity of an aversive stimulus and performance is dependent on whether a one-way or a two-way
response task is utilized.

The studies of Kurtz and Pearl (1960), Moyer and Korn (1966), Theios,
Lynch, and Lowe (1966), and McAllister, McAllister, and Douglass (1971) are
examples of investigations which determined that the learning of avoidance
responses is an increasing function of the intensity of shock when a one-way
task is used. For example, in a study by Moyer and Korn (1966), in which
animals were always shocked in the same compartment of a shuttle box and

using 4 shock intensities, e.g., .5, 1.5, 2.5, and 3.5 ma, rats received 50 acquisition trials on a single day. The task consisted of the animal's learning to avoid shock by running from the compartment where shock was presented to an adjacent one within 5 seconds. Results indicated that the longest latencies of responding were associated with the weakest intensity of shock.

On the other hand, using the two-way task, Moyer and Korn (1964), Johnson and Church (1965), Levine (1966), Theios, Lynch, and Lowe (1966), Cicala and Kremer (1969), and McAllister, McAllister, and Douglass (1971) have all found that performance declines as shock intensity is increased.

To illustrate the nature of this decline in performance as a function of the intensity presented, Moyer and Korn (1964) provided rats with 30 trials a day for 4 days, separating them into groups which received either .5, 1.0, 1.5, 2.5, 3.0, 3.5, or 4.5 ma of shock during training. A tone was used as the CS and the animals had to run to the other compartment within 5 seconds in order to avoid shock. Fig. 11-6 reveals the mean percentage of avoidance responses for all groups as a function of shock level.

A direct comparison of the differential effects of shock intensity on one-way and two-way avoidance tasks is found in a study by Theios, Lynch, and Lowe (1966). Three levels of shock intensity were used, namely, 1.0, 1.5, and 2.5 ma. All animals had to respond within 5 seconds in order to avoid shock; each subject was run to a criterion of 10 consecutive avoidance responses. With the one-way avoidance task, one of the compartments always served as the shock compartment while the other was always safe. Fifteen seconds after the end of each one-way training trial, the animal was picked up and placed again in the compartment where it had originally received shock, beginning a new trial. Subjects learning the two-way avoidance task, however, were never touched during the experiment.

As noted in Table 11-1, for subjects learning the two-way task, increasing shock intensity from 1.5 to 2.5 ma resulted in poorer performance. On the other hand, the high intensity shock did not depress subjects learning the one-way task, although superior performance as a function of shock intensity was not as evident here as in some other investigations.

As Olton (1973) has indicated, an appropriate post hoc explanation for the differences in performance between the two tasks appears to lie in the conflict characteristics of the two-way task. In order to avoid shock on any given trial, the animal must return to a location in which it was shocked on the preceding trial. The resulting outcome is an avoidance-avoidance conflict—a state of affairs which does not occur in the one-way task.

A somewhat more specific explanation for the difference in findings has been proposed by McAllister, McAllister, and Douglass (1971) who assert that the amount of effective reinforcement for an avoidance response is positively related to the amount of fear reduction occurring with CS termination, and negatively related to the amount of fear of the situational cues present following a response. Thus, it has been proposed that reinforcement in the two-way task is more effective under weak shock than under strong shock. Under strong shock, the greater fear reduction provided by CS termination is more than offset by increased fear of the situational cues present following the response.

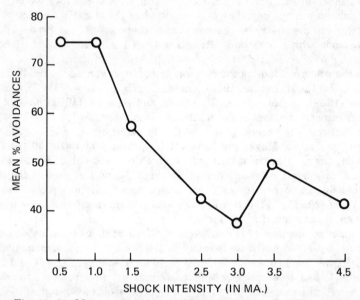

Fig. 11-6. Mean percentage avoidance responses for all groups as a function of shock level. *Adapted from Moyer and Korn (1964)*

A most interesting experiment has supported their position. In this study, the poorer performance of high shock level in contrast to low shock level was noted in a two-way avoidance task. Following the training trials, the experimenters provided their subjects with 25 trials in which a "safe" box was attached at right angles to the outside of one compartment wall of their two-way apparatus. A hurdle separated the compartment from the safe box and it was necessary for the animals, at the raising of a guillotine door, to jump the hurdle in order to obtain access to the safe compartment. Findings revealed that the strong shock subjects were superior to the weak shock subjects in learning to escape from the compartment by making the hurdle jumping response. During this latter task, neither shock nor the previously used CS (an increase in sound) was presented. Thus, the authors have reasoned that the learning of the hurdle jumping response had to be based only on fear of the situational cues condi-

Table 11-1   Amount of Shock

	1.0 ma		1.5 ma		2.5 ma	
	T	L	T	L	T	L
Two Way	32.3	54.2	47.8	63.6	100.3	127.3
One Way	5.0	8.2	5.4	10.3	4.7	5.4

T = mean total errors
L = trial of last error before reaching criterion
Adapted from Theios, Lynch, and Lowe (1966)

tioned during the prior two-way avoidance task, with the strong shock subjects having greater fear of the compartment in which shock was presented.

The Delay of Aversive Stimulation

Temporal delay is the third condition of aversive stimulation which has been investigated with instrumental escape and avoidance learning tasks. The operations used to examine delay have varied, however, depending on the task and the interest of the investigator.

Escape Tasks and Delay

With instrumental escape tasks, temporal delay refers to the time interval between the subject's making the escape response and obtaining relief from the aversive stimulus. Fowler and Trapold (1962) found that the speed of rats running down a charged runway was significantly slower when shock reduction was delayed following such running behavior. The delays used by these investigators were either 0, 1, 2, 4, 8, or 16 seconds. Fig. 11-7 presents these findings. Using a somewhat different source of aversive stimulation, Woods and Feldman (1966) had rats learn to escape from 15° C water in an alley tank into a goal box in which the temperature was either 0°, 5°, or 25° C warmer than the water in the alley. In this study, delays of either 0, 3, or 10 seconds were provided prior to the animal's being permitted to enter the goal box. As would be expected from the Fowler and Trapold (1962) experiment, findings were that a delay in relief from the cold water significantly retarded swimming speed.

Passive Avoidance and Delay

With passive avoidance learning tasks, the procedure calls for varying delay intervals to be placed between the response which will eventually be punished and the presentation of aversive stimulation. This has become known as the delay of punishment gradient.

We should like first to call attention to two experimental problems frequently involved in these aversive stimulation studies. The first is that the presentation of an aversive stimulus in the experimental situation may produce a generalized emotional state on the part of the subject which suppresses all responding, including the specific response to be punished. Some experimenters, although certainly not all, have attempted to control for such decremental responding by using a "noncontingent-shock" group. With this type of control, the organism receives the aversive stimulus, but its presentation is not contingent on the making of the to-be-punished response. If an experimenter has not used such a control group, it would be expected that response suppression coming about as a result of the punished response–shock contingency is probably overestimated.[1]

[1] It has frequently been observed that response suppression is more marked when such control groups are used than with control groups not receiving

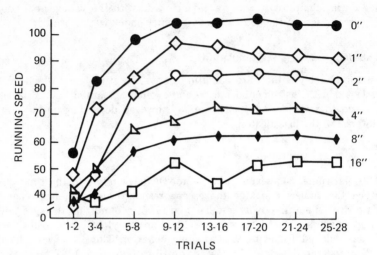

Fig. 11-7. Running speed (100/time in sec.) as a function of the delay (in sec.) of shock termination. *Adapted from Fowler and Trapold (1962)*

A second problem of investigation is that the aversive stimulus may be contiguous with the consummatory response rather than with the instrumental response which holds primary interest for the experimenter. Frequently, following the making of the instrumental response, the organism engages in consummatory activity. If the presentation of the aversive stimulus is delayed, it may be received while the consummatory response is being made. For example, in a study by Baron (1965), rats were trained to traverse a runway in order to secure water. They were shocked at varying intervals (0, 5, 10, 20, or 30 seconds) following their entrance into the goal box. For the 0 delay group, the animals were shocked immediately following their instrumental response of running; on the other hand, since water continued to be present in the goal box, the 10-, 20-, or 30-second delay groups were shocked while they were drinking. The experimental findings revealed that running speed was related to the temporal gradient; as Baron pointed out, however, the disruption of consummatory behavior (by the presentation of shock) could not be completely discounted as a factor contributing to observed differences in running speeds.

Although the early studies, e.g., Warden and Diamond (1931), Bevan and Dukes (1955), examining the delay of punishment and avoidance behavior did not lead to any clear picture regarding a functional relationship between these two variables, more recent studies have indicated the existence of a delay of punishment gradient.

Kamin's (1959) experiment was one of the first to demonstrate this gradient.

---

aversive stimulation; response suppression is considerably less for the non-contingent shock group, however, than for the experimental group whose aversive stimulation is contingent on making the punished response. An example of this finding can be noted in a study by Church (1969).

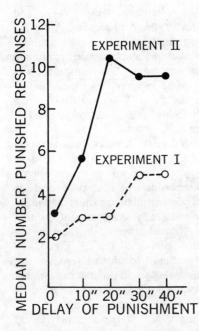

Fig. 11-8. Median number of extinction responses as a function
of delay of punishment. *Adapted
from Kamin (1959)*

In this investigation consisting of two separate experiments, rats were trained to avoid shock by running from one compartment of a shuttle box to another. The CS was a buzzer (Experiment 1) or a buzzer plus the lifting of a gate separating the two compartments (Experiment 2). The aversive stimulus (UCS) was a shock administered through a grid floor with the CS-UCS interval of 10 seconds. After the animals had reached a criterion of 11 consecutive avoidance responses, punishment trials were provided in which the animals received shock either 0, 10, 20, 30, or 40 seconds after making the avoidance response. Thus, punishment might occur immediately or as much as 40 seconds following the running response. A control group which did not receive punishment for responding was also used. The results of both studies are indicated in Fig. 11-8 and reveal similar delay of punishment gradients.

It may be noted that Kamin's (1959) study differs from many passive avoidance experiments in that the motivation for the original behavior was shock. Typically, punishment studies employ some prior form of positively reinforced behavior rather than providing aversive stimulation. One such study, conducted by Baron (1965), was described earlier. Baron obtained a delay of punishment gradient with performance as a function of the temporal interval between the instrumental response of traversing the runway in order to obtain water, and shock.

In a series of experiments, Camp, Raymond, and Church (1967) explored delay of punishment gradients along with variations in intensity using the free operant. We have discussed the results of their first experiment examining the suppression of bar pressing as a function of shock intensity in an earlier section.

In their second experiment, the contingency between lever pressing and punishment was manipulated, utilizing delays of 0, 2, or 30 seconds. Following five sessions of variable interval reinforcement training, subjects received punishment for the final 10 sessions. During these sessions, reinforcement continued to be available on a 2-minute variable interval schedule. When punishment was presented, the subjects in the 0-second delay group received shock immediately following their next response; a subject in the 2- or 30-second delay group received punishment either 2 or 30 seconds following its next response. Fig. 11-9 reveals the suppression ratio for the three delay groups.

In a third experiment, in order to work with discrete responses, animals were provided with discrimination training in which they learned to make a single lever pressing response whenever a clicking sound (S+) was presented. A response in the presence of the S+ resulted in the presentation of a food pellet and the termination of the stimulus. After 10 sessions of discrimination training, punishment training was provided. On 50% of the trials, shock was presented either 2.0, 7.5, or 30 seconds after the response. A noncontingent shock group received shock once every two minutes in the absence of the S+. Fig. 11-10 reveals the mean percentage of discriminative stimuli to which a response was made for the six groups. Although there is one inversion, in general, the findings support the position that the magnitude of suppression of an appetitive response is greater if punishment is contingent upon the response than if it is not.

Myer and Ricci (1968) have examined the delay of punishment gradient using goldfish as their experimental subjects. In their first experiment, they trained goldfish to eat in an experimental apparatus by presenting them with 20 clusters of worms each day. Punishment of the feeding response began on the day following original training and consisted of providing a 1-second shock either 0, 2.5, 5, 10, or 20 seconds following ingestion of food. Shock voltage was set at 0 on the first "punishment" day and was increased by 5 volts each day. This procedure continued for each subject until it reached a suppression criterion of 15 or more failures to feed on three successive days. As shown in Fig. 11-11, the delay of punishment gradient increased sharply as the delay of punishment increased from 0 to 10 seconds; further increases in the response-shock interval had no effect on suppression.

In a second experiment, a somewhat similar procedure was used except that shock was not increased over punishment trials; rather, two different shock intensities, 10 and 25 volts, were used along with three response-shock intervals of either 0, 5, or 10 seconds. Results indicated that the delay of punishment gradient obtained was significant both in the 10-volt and the 25 volt-conditions, although, as might be anticipated, differences among the groups were not as pronounced when a high shock level was utilized.

Active Avoidance and Delay

As noted, with both escape and passive avoidance tasks, the delay interval begins with the response and ends either with the cessation (escape) or the onset of an aversive stimulus (passive avoidance). In active avoidance tasks, the interval which has interested experimenters is that between the onset of the CS

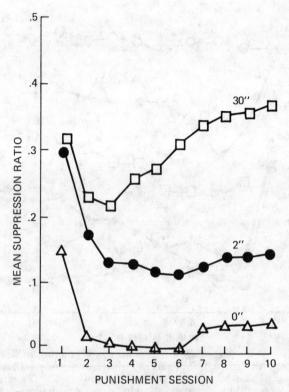

Fig. 11-9. Mean suppression ratio as a function
of sessions for groups with 0.0, 2.0, and 30.0-sec.
delay of punishment. *Adapted from Camp, Raymond, and Church (1967)*

and the presentation of the noxious stimulus. If this type of task is conceptualized as a classical conditioning paradigm, the noxious stimulus is regarded as the
UCS, so that investigation becomes an examination of the CS-UCS interval.[2]

In his examination of the role of this interval, Kamin (1954), with dogs
as subjects, employed a two-way task which required the animals to jump a
barrier in order to get from one side to the other. The CS was the sounding of
a buzzer for 2 seconds in the compartment where the animal was placed. Following an interval of either 5, 10, 20, or 40 seconds, as measured from the onset
of the CS, the UCS was presented. (The 2-second duration of the CS with the

[2] The appropriate classification of an active avoidance task is controversial.
Bitterman (1962) for example, has considered it distinct from instrumental
and classical conditioning situations, pointing out that early in learning, it fits
the classical conditioning paradigm—the CS and UCS are presented regardless
of the organism's response. After a number of trials, however, active avoidance
has instrumental characteristics, since the subject's response is instrumental in
avoiding the aversive stimulus.

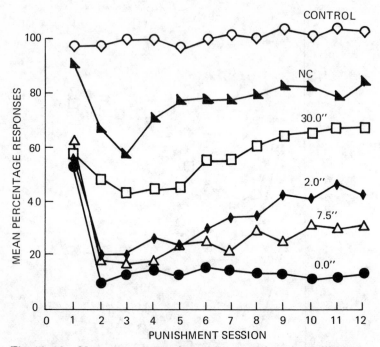

Fig. 11-10. Mean percentage of responses as a function of sessions for groups with 0.0, 2.0, 7.5, and 30.0 sec. delay of punishment, noncontingent shock, and unpunished control group. (Failure to press the lever within 10 sec. of stimulus onset was defined as non-response. *Adapted from Camp, Raymond, and Church (1967)*

long CS-UCS interval operationally defines this procedure as trace conditioning.) An acquisition criterion of five consecutive avoidance trials was employed. Once the criterion was reached, extinction trials were provided and continued until an extinction criterion of five consecutive failures to respond to the CS was observed. Results indicated that the briefer CS-UCS intervals led to most rapid acquisition of the avoidance response as well as to greater resistance to extinction. Fig. 11-12 reveals resistance to extinction as a function of the length of the CS-UCS interval. Davitz, Mason, Mowrer, and Viek (1957) have obtained similar findings when rats have been used as subjects.

A study by Brush, Brush, and Solomon (1955) examined the effect of the CS-UCS interval with a delayed conditioning procedure, in contrast to the trace procedure used by Kamin (1954). With the delayed conditioning procedure, the CS is presented until the onset of the UCS. In the avoidance learning situation, this requires that the CS be presented during the entire CS-UCS interval. In this study, the experimenters had considerable difficulty comparing their findings with those obtained by Kamin (1954), since there were a number of procedural differences which precluded a bona fide comparison. As a result,

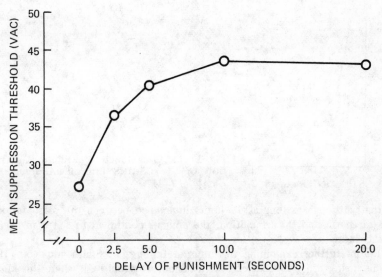

Fig. 11-11. Thresholds of suppression of feeding as a function of response-shock interval. *Adapted from Myer and Ricci (1968)*

a second study was undertaken by Church, Brush, and Solomon (1956) in which Kamin's methodology was duplicated, with the only procedural difference being the delayed conditioning technique. Results from the two studies for the comparable groups are presented in Fig. 11-13. Note that with the trace conditioning procedure, poorer learning results as a function of lengthening the CS-UCS interval—a finding previously reported by Kamin (1954) and Davitz, Mason, Mowrer, and Viek (1957). On the other hand, when delayed conditioning procedure is used, learning appears to be independent of the CS-UCS interval.

Taste Aversion

A study by Smith and Roll (1967) illustrates the nature of work in the area of taste aversion, as well as its relevance to avoidance learning. Rats were deprived of liquid for 24 hours and then given 20 minutes' access to saccharin. After one of the following time periods: 0, .5, 1, 2, 3, 6, 12, or 24 hours, the animals received either X-ray or sham exposure for 200 seconds. Twenty-four hours following such exposure, a 48-hour preference test was instituted. This consisted of providing each animal with a bottle of saccharin and a bottle of water and noting the amount consumed from each bottle during a 48-hour period.[3]

Results are indicated in Fig. 11-14. The provocative aspect of these findings

[3] It should be noted that a sucrose solution was also used in this experiment with fewer time intervals between its presentation and the X-ray exposure.

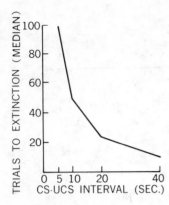

Fig. 11-12. Resistance to extinction as a function of the CS-UCS interval. *Adapted from Kamin (1954)*

is that, although as long as 12 hours intervened between the presentation of the saccharin and the irradiation, the animals continued to show an aversion to saccharin.

Before further examining the unusual findings of Smith and Roll (1967) or discussing other aspects of taste aversion, we should ask where this kind of task fits among the learning paradigms which we have delineated. Taste aversion studies have frequently been considered examples of classical conditioning, with the original substance, usually a liquid, being identified as the CS, the irradiation (or drug) as the UCS, and an inference of sickness or general discomfort as the UCR. However, the associative relationship acquired is based on the CS's eliciting a kind of passive avoidance response inferred from the cessation (or a decrement) in consummatory responding. Under such circumstances, we would prefer to conceptualize taste aversion studies as instrumental avoidance—since the organism's refusal to respond is instrumental in avoiding the consequences of an aversive stimulus.

Smith and Roll's (1967) finding, confirmed by many subsequent investigators, that an aversion to a particular taste can be learned even though hours may be interposed between the consumption of a liquid and the presentation of an

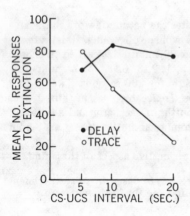

Fig. 11-13. Mean number of responses to extinction as a function of the CS-UCS interval in a delayed and trace conditioning procedure. *Adapted from Church, Brush, and Solomon (1956)*

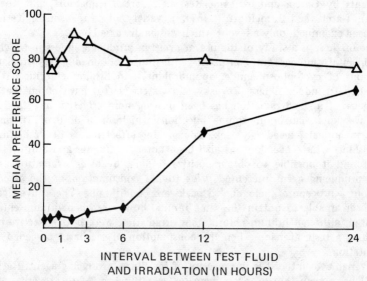

Fig. 11-14. The median preference score for each delay condition for the experimental and control subjects. *Adapted from
Smith and Roll (1967)*

illness-producing stimulus, is not in keeping with the findings obtained by experimenters examining other types of instrumental learning tasks where the
delay interval was measured in seconds, e.g., passive avoidance (Baron 1965),
escape (Fowler and Trapold, 1962), reward (Grice, 1949).[4]

It has been proposed that the difference in experimental findings between
traditional instrumental learning studies and taste aversion experiments does not
represent any fundamental difference between the two types of tasks; rather,
it is related to the relevance of the stimulus or the events to the organism. We
shall return to this issue in a subsequent section.

Since Smith and Roll's (1967) investigation, as well as studies by Smith and
Morris (1963), Smith, Morris, and Hendricks (1964) and a series of earlier ex-

---

[4] Two early explanations, both using a mediated response position, were provided for these findings. First, some have suggested the possibility of stimulus
after-effects which bridge the long delay from the consumption of the liquid to
the illness. Presumably, an after-taste arising from the mouth or stomach could
serve this function. One difficulty with this explanation is that a sucrose solution which is taken into the empty stomach is digested and absorbed into the
blood stream in far less than 6 hours, and yet it is possible to obtain an aversion
to sucrose when the delay interval is this long.

A related explanation has been that the organism vomits the consumed substance during the toxicosis, so that the aversion may be produced by the contiguity of vomited substances and the toxicosis. Such aversions are obtained,
however, when there is nothing in the stomach to be vomited. Equally important, when rats are used as subjects, they do not have sphincter control
that makes vomiting possible.

periments by Garcia and his associates, e.g., Garcia, Kimeldorf, and Koelling (1955), Garcia and Kimeldorf (1957), a variety of taste aversion variables have been examined, only a few of which will be discussed here.

One of these is a study of the use of drugs in producing illness in which the experimental findings are contrasted with those obtained using irradiation. Injections of cyclophosphamide, apomorphine, and lithium chloride have all been used to induce illness. Revusky and Garcia (1970) have noted that 100 roentgens of ionized radiation has been proven more effective in establishing taste aversions than apomorphine injections which, in a dose of 10 mg/kg, make an animal exceedingly sick. The greater effectiveness of irradiation in establishing a taste aversion has also been noted by Barker and Smith (1974) who found it possible to obtain positive findings by using irradiation as the illness-producing agent presented *prior* to the consumption of the saccharin solution—a procedure analogous to backward conditioning. These investigators have been unable to obtain the same results, however, when lithium chloride was used, although lithium chloride and irradiation were both effective in establishing a taste aversion when the consumption of saccharin preceded their presentation.

A variable of interest is the severity of the illness-producing agent. Revusky (1968) has shown that aversion increases as a function of the severity of the irradiation. In this study, all experimental animals (rats) were irradiated for 7 hours after they consumed a sucrose solution, with irradiation values of either 50, 150, or 250 roentgens. As Fig. 11-15 reveals, the preference for sucrose decreased as the radiation levels increased and was significantly lower than control values at every level except for the lowest value used. A similar decline in preference for saccharin was noted by Garcia, Ervin, and Koelling (1967) when varying dosages of illness-producing nitrogen mustard were injected intraperitoneally.

This relationship between response preferences and amount of sickness is intuitively reasonable—the sicker the animals become, the more they dislike those solutions with which they associate the illness. It is also similar to those passive avoidance studies which indicate that suppression of an instrumental response takes place as a function of the intensity of the shock administered.

A topic which we have not touched on is whether or not sickness must be induced for an aversion to be learned. As Garcia and Ervin (1968) point out, sickness arising from irradiation is inferred from experimental findings which indicate an aversion to the experimental substance. However, the symptomology of irradiated animals differs markedly from lithium chloride sickness; drug-injected animals revealing marked inactivity, diarrhea, and decreased fluid intake immediately following the drug injection period. Irradiated animals do not show these symptoms; moreover, there is no evidence of excessive urination, defecation, or squealing, as typically occurs when painful stimuli are applied. Berger (1972) has reported that an aversion to milk can be produced by injections of scopolamine, amphetamine, chlorpromazine, and benzodiazepine at moderate dosages. All of these drugs enjoy widespread use as therapeutic agents and do not cause *obvious* signs of illness or toxicity in animals at the dose levels which he used. He has concluded that "sickness is not a necessary

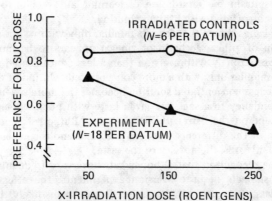

Fig. 11-15. Test preference for sucrose solution as a function of the level of irradiation received during training. *Adapted from Revusky and Garcia (1970)*

precondition for the development of conditioned food aversions" (p. 25). Although illness or discomfort may not be indicated behaviorally, or at least with the behavioral measures currently used, it is difficult to accept the hypothesis that irradiation or the drugs Berger employed did not cause some type of discomfort to the animals.

Another interesting facet of this experimental work concerns the ingestion of novel or familiar food stuffs. That is, since rats may consume a number of substances prior to receiving a drug or being irradiated and subsequent toxicosis, what can be determined regarding the mechanisms whereby they associate illness with one food stuff but not with others?

Revusky and Bedarf (1967) obtained some evidence related to this question. One group of hungry rats was made familiar with unsweetened grape juice over an 8-day period, while a second group of hungry animals was made familiar with a 50% solution of condensed milk. On the first experimental day, the two groups of animals were given 100 licks of each of these substances. An hour later, half of each group (experimental) was irradiated with 50 roentgens while the other half (control) was sham irradiated. Three days later, the rats were given 30 minutes of free access to both milk and grape juice. A substantial difference in consummatory responding was obtained, of course, between the control animals who did not receive the irradiation and the experimental rats which were irradiated. However, in examining the preferences of the experimental animals, it was noted that significantly less of the unfamiliar or novel substance was consumed than of the familiar one. Thus, novel foodstuffs were more strongly associated with toxicosis. Wittlin and Brookshire (1968) replicated the Revusky and Bedarf (1967) study, obtaining similar findings. Siegel (1974) has shown that familiarity with the substance need be no greater than a single preexposure in order for the aversion to be retarded. In a series of experiments, he demonstrated that one preexposure to a distinctive flavor (coffee or vinegar) results in the retardation of learning an aversion to this substance when it is later associated with lithium chloride.

Kalat (1974) has shown that for rats familiar only with water, a more concentrated solution of either saccharin or vinegar appears to be more salient or is associated more strongly with aversion than a less concentrated solution. However, for rats familiar only with a more concentrated solution of either saccharin or vinegar, the less concentrated solution becomes the more salient cue. Evidently, the rats' tendency to associate a given taste with poison does not depend to any great extent on the "strength" of the taste. Rather, it depends mainly on the magnitude of the difference between the taste and the tastes familiar to the animal—in other words, the novelty of the taste.

It should be recognized that although rats have very frequently been used as experimental subjects in taste aversion experiments, the effect has been obtained with cats, mice, and monkeys also. It also seems likely that an aversion to almost any kind of food or drink can be obtained using the procedures described. Aversion has been demonstrated for saccharin, sucrose, laboratory chow, chocolate-flavored milk, lavender- and citral-flavored glucose solution, coffee, vinegar, as well as a variety of other substances.

An interesting finding in this area, reported by Green and Garcia (1971), is that rats allowed access to a distinctive taste solution during recovery from an apomorphine injection would, following several such pairings, subsequently show an increased preference for the taste. They have suggested that the distinctive taste during the animals' recuperation endowed that taste with "medicinal" properties, i.e., the animal acted as if it were medicine during subsequent testing.

The Principle of Stimulus Relevance

Undoubtedly the most disturbing finding for many investigators working in this area has been the discovery that delay intervals could be measured in hours rather than in seconds, as earlier and more traditional instrumental learning studies had indicated.

One general explanation which has been proposed for this type of finding is the concept of stimulus relevance—a principle which states that the associative strength of a cue or stimulus with some consequence depends, at least in part, on the nature of the consequence (Dietz and Capretta, 1967). It is assumed that exteroceptive stimuli will be most likely to gain high associative strength with external consequences; on the other hand, interoceptive stimuli is likely to obtain high associative strengths with internal consequences.

With regard to the taste aversion studies, as Revusky and Garcia (1970) have written, "If an animal wants to decide what made it sick, it will tend to ignore external events and carefully consider the flavors of previously consumed substances; if it wants to decide what produced an external event, it will tend to ignore flavor and will carefully consider the preceding exteroceptive stimuli" (p. 22).

In the case of the experiments we have reviewed, the rats' aversion to saccharin was produced by drugs or irradiation; the discriminative stimulus here is the saccharin flavor, while the consequence is the discomfort produced by the illness-providing stimulus. The principle of stimulus relevance holds that it is the "relevance" of flavors to toxicosis which is responsible for this learning. However, if an irrelevant stimulus, an external one for instance, were substituted for the saccharin flavor in this learned aversion paradigm, learning should take place much less rapidly. Or, if the saccharin flavor stimulus was retained but a punishing event which emanated from the external environment were to be substituted for toxicosis, again, learning should not readily occur.

In order to examine the stimulus relevance principle, Garcia and Koelling (1966) conducted an experiment using the interoceptive stimulus, saccharin and an exteroceptive stimulus, shock, along with two types of consequences: toxicosis produced by irradiation and pain produced by the shock.

Their experiment consisted of using a drinkometer, a sensitive amplifying circuit that detects the contact of a rat's tongue with a water spout. Whenever the animal licked at the water, the drinkometer produced a flash of an incandescent bulb, as well as the click of a relay. In a sense, "bright noisy" water was produced by these stimuli. In contrast, "tasty" water was produced by adding saccharin.

When the audio-visual stimulus and flavored stimulus were each paired with electric shock, results revealed that the audio-visual stimulus would suppress drinking but the flavored stimulus would not. On the other hand, when each stimulus was paired with irradiation which produced toxicosis, avoidance responses were made to the flavored stimulus but not to the audio-visual stimulus.

As the authors have indicated, given reinforcers are not equally effective for all classes of discriminable stimuli. The cues which the animal selects from the welter of stimuli in the learning situation appear to be related to the consequences of the subsequent reinforcer.

The Concept of Learned Safety

Although stimulus salience undoubtedly plays a role in the learning of taste aversion, Rozen and Kalat (1971) proposed that the delay gradient found in taste aversion studies is actually a learning curve. As these authors have written, ". . . in the absence of unfavorable gastrointestinal events, as time passes following consumption of a novel solution, the animal *learns that the solution is safe*" (p. 477). The experimental work examining taste aversion as a function of the ingestion of novel and familiar food stuffs has been used to support this hypothesis. Thus, if a rat drinks both a novel and a familiar solution prior to being poisoned, it acquires a much stronger aversion to the novel than to the familiar solution. As a result of previous experience with the familiar substance, the animal learns of its "safety"; this experience will interfere with the animal's learning subsequently that the same substance has become toxic.

Additional evidence used to support this position is found in a study by these authors (Rozin and Kalat, 1973) who found that if rats were exposed to a novel substance (casein hydrolysate) 3 ½ hours before and again, ½ hour prior to, being poisoned, the animals developed a weaker aversion to this substance than if they had been exposed to the solution only ½ hour prior to poisoning.

Having had a previous experience in which the substance did not produce a toxic effect, they learned that it was safe, which in turn hindered subsequent learning that the substance was now toxic.

But the principle of "learned safety" does not account for why the ingestion of a solution, followed hours later by toxicosis, can still exert some influence on an animal's behavior. Although it would be assumed that the learned relationship between the ingested substance and "safety" would be near asymptote, experimental findings indicate that animals avoid, at least to some extent, the earlier ingested solution. An associative relationship must then have been established between the ingested solution and the illness.

It has been suggested that taste, unlike instrumental responses which have been investigated, remains in a transient associable state over considerable periods, of time, permitting the ingested solution-illness relationship to be formed. Such a transient associable state has adaptive significance for the organism. This explanation seems reasonable; on the other hand, it suggests that the mechanism which underlies the delay gradient found with instrumental learning studies is different than that operating in taste aversion experiments.

Summary

It is only recently that investigators have become interested in examining the role of aversive stimulation and its termination in learning the instrumental tasks of escape and active and passive avoidance. Because of the kind of experimental control that can be exercised over its presentation and termination, electric shock has been the most frequently used source of aversive stimulation. Guided by the work done with reward, investigators have examined three conditions affecting aversive stimulation: (1) frequency, (2) intensity, and (3) the temporal delay provided between the instrumental response and the presentation or termination of the aversive stimulation.

It has often been demonstrated that the learning of escape and avoidance tasks is a function of the frequency of aversive stimulation (and its termination). The intensity variable provides similar findings with easy escape tasks—increases in intensity result in increasing performance. One interesting aspect of this variable, however, is the finding that at high intensity levels, the learning of difficult tasks is poorer than it is at lower intensity level. Thus, in a study by Broadhurst, the intensity of the aversive stimulus was manipulated by delaying rats for either 0, 2, 4, or 8 seconds underwater, using three levels of difficulty in an underwater brightness discrimination task. Lengthening the air deprivation interval resulted in increasing performance on the easy task; on the other hand, increases in air deprivation with the difficult task resulted first in increases but then performance decreased.

Active avoidance as a function of aversive stimulation intensity has been examined with one- and two-way tasks. In one-way tasks, the animal responds by leaving one location consistently associated with shock and entering a second location consistently associated with safety. In two-way tasks, the animal must learn to respond in two directions, leaving compartment A and entering compartment B on one trial, but then leaving compartment B and entering compartment A on the next trial. When shock intensity is examined as a function of the task utilized, results reveal that performance in one-way tasks increases as a function of shock intensity; when two-way tasks are employed, performance declines as a function of shock intensity.

Learning has been proven a function of the length of the temporal delay between the making of an escape or active avoidance response and the securing of relief. A similar finding has been obtained with passive avoidance tasks. Here, we have a delay of punishment gradient which refers to the length of time between the punished response and the aversive stimulation. In all of these studies, in order for learning to take place, the delay period must be short and measured in seconds.

One exception to this general finding is in the area of taste aversion. Studies by a number of investigators have demonstrated that learning is possible even though the delay between the ingestion of a substance and the onset of illness is measure in hours. The general procedure is to make an animal thirsty and then provide it with a distinctively flavored substance to drink. Hours later, the animal is exposed to x-radiation or injected with a drug which produces toxicosis. Subsequently, when the animal is given the opportunity again to drink the distinctively flavored substance, and the amount of intake is compared with that consumed by control animals, intake is significantly smaller than that of the controls. The experimental work in this area has led to the formulation of the principle of stimulus relevance; this states that the strength of a stimulus which is associated with some consequence depends upon the nature of the consequence. Exteroceptive stimuli will most likely gain high associative strength with external consequences, while interoceptive stimuli will obtain high associative strength with internal consequences. As Revusky and Garcia (1970) have written, "If an animal wants to decide what made it sick, it will tend to ignore external events and carefully consider the flavors of previously consumed substances; if it wants to decide what produced an external event, it will tend to ignore flavor and carefully consider the preceding exteroceptive stimuli."

Rozin and Kalat (1971) have also proposed the principle of learned "safety" to account for such findings. In the absence of illness, as time passes following the consumption of a novel solution, the organism learns that the substance is safe. However, in order to account for the learning of an association between the ingested substance and illness, it has been necessary to assume that taste remains in a transient associable state over considerable periods of time, thus permitting the ingested solution–illness relationship to be formed.

12

The Role of the Stimulus:
I. Attention and Discrimination

In Chapter 7 we noted that one interest of psychologists has been to determine how instrumental learning is related to a number of experimental variables. In the two previous chapters, we have delineated how motivational variables affect learning; in these next two chapters we shall examine how learning is influenced by the contribution of the stimuli or cues which comprise the experimental task. Some contemporary investigators, particularly those interested in operant responding, have used the term "stimulus control" to describe this area. Traditionally, however, it has been subsumed under the categories of (1) attention, (2) discrimination, and (3) generalization, and we have chosen to use this kind of organization.[1]

[1] Terrace (1966) has raised the question, " Why . . . should a new term [stimulus control] be introduced into an area in which the terms generalization and discrimination have been traditionally used? . . . Briefly, the rational for favoring the concept of stimulus

Attention

It is generally recognized that organisms do not respond to, or are not controlled by, all of the stimuli that impinge on their receptors. Out of the welter of stimuli that strike the individuals' sense organs, only a few are selected for response—the others are ignored.

Early psychologists term this selection process "attention." William James (1890) writing in his *Principles* stated that attention "is the taking possession by the mind, in clear and vivid form, of one out of what seem several simultaneously possible objects or trains of thought. Focalization, concentration of consciousness are of its essence. It implies withdrawal from some things in order to deal effectively with others, and is a condition which has a real opposite in the confused, dazed, scatterbrained state which in French is called distraction . . ." (pp. 403–404).

Inasmuch as the status of attention rested primarily on introspective reports provided by the subject, it is not surprising that attention was one of the first mentalistic concepts to be discarded when Watson founded behaviorism. Attention was described as part and parcel of the homunculus view of behavior; by appealing to the operation of this inner-demon in order to explain behavior, it was argued that the problem was not solved, but merely translated "inward" and to the uncertain domain of unobservable events that could only hinder further investigation.

The analysis of animal discrimination learning during the late twenties and thirties indicated, however, the need for some type of attentional process; as a result, some investigators noted that preparatory responses, defined in terms of specific overt responses made by the organism, could serve this function. Spence (1937), for example, wrote that the animal learns many responses in the discrimination learning experiment. Prominent and important among these are "preparatory" responses—responses which lead to the reception of particular aspects of the total environmental complex, e.g., the orientation and fixation of the head and eyes toward the critical stimuli. That is, the animal learns to "look at" one aspect of the situation rather than another. In summary, and in keeping with a stimulus-response position, attention was conceptualized in terms of muscular responses made by the organism—in this case, specific responses which oriented the sensory apparatus of the animal so that he would be exposed, and respond, to certain experimental stimuli and not to others.

The Observing Response

Many contemporary investigators examining the instrumental learning of animals have continued to think of stimulus selection or attention in terms of

---

control over the traditional concepts of generalization and discrimination stems from the practice of using the terms generalization and discrimination to describe processes rather than empirical functions. It is one thing to say that an organism who has been conditioned to respond to a 1000 cps tone will respond, to a lesser extent, to tones of other frequencies, and another thing to state that response strength generalizes from the 1000 cps tone to receptor orienting responses. But the monitoring of eye movements or the measurement of a head turning response, to cite just two examples of receptor orienting responses, is difficult; their control even more so. One approach to this problem was proposed by Wyckoff (1952) who introduced the concept of an observing response. Wyckoff pointed out that in most discrimination learning experiments, it is seldom, if ever, possible to say with certainty that the subject has been exposed to the discriminative stimuli prior to the making of each response. He suggested that the organism be required to make some discrete, measurable response which in turn would expose a discriminative stimulus; following this, an appropriate response would lead to reinforcement. The making of this preliminary response, which he designated as an observing response, could be considered valid evidence of attention, since its presence would indicate that the animal perceived the discriminative stimuli.

An early study described by Wyckoff (1952) was designed to examine the operation of the observing response. In this study, pigeons were first trained to peck at a white key. Afterwards, the opportunity to make an observing response was provided. This response consisted of stepping on a pedal on the floor of the apparatus; when this response was made, the white key would change color to either red or green. If the red key appeared, a pecking response at the end of a 30-second interval resulted in food, if the key was green, no reward was provided. If the pedal pushing response was not made (thus, no observing response) the key remained white, and a pecking response which was made at the end of a 30-second interval resulted in food half of the time. In summary, both conditions resulted in the animal's being reinforced on just 50% of the trials. In the one case, reinforcement was unpredictable, while in the other case, it was correlated with the color of the key which the pedal pushing response produced. Results indicated that the pigeons learned the pedal pushing response, causing Wyckoff (1952) to conclude that "exposure to discriminative stimuli will have a reinforcing effect on the observing response to the extent that S has learned to respond differently to the two discriminative stimuli" (p. 435).

We may note then, that the observing response can be defined as "any response that results in exposure to a discriminative stimulus" (Stollnitz, 1965, p. 248), and it has been recognized by many as a valid indicator of attention. A number of investigators have examined the operation of the observing response under a variety of conditions, e.g., Prokasy (1956), Lutz and Perkins (1960), Wehling and Prokasy (1962), Mitchell, Perkins, and Perkins (1965).

Conceptually, the positing of an observing response has represented a way for many theorists to place the construct of attention within a stimulus-response framework, since an observing response must be made if the organism is subsequently to attend to the stimuli which make up the discrimination task. The observing response has the function of placing the organism in contact with a discriminative stimulus—a function which has been closely identified with the

---

other tones." Continuing, Terrace has suggested that "attention seems to be synonymous with stimulus control to the extent that failures to establish stimulus control are referred to as failures of attention" (p. 271).

attention process. Moreover, since the observing response is made early in a chain of responses which ends in reinforcement, the learning of this type of response can be readily accounted for.

There is no doubt that the orientation of the receptors (which may be inferred from the presence of an observing response) represents one aspect of the attention process. With humans, head and eye orientation have often been used as indicators that the individual is "paying attention." But many have objected to accounting for the total attention process in terms of only receptor oriented responses. An experiment by Reynolds (1961b) illustrates the nature of this objection.

In this study, two pigeons were given discrimination training in which the positive stimulus key was a white triangle on a red background (S+) while the negative stimulus key was a white circle on a green background (S-). Early training periods consisted of six daily, 3-hour sessions containing 30 cycles of a two-component multiple schedule. Each cycle had two 3-minute components; the first, in which the key was illuminated with a white triangle on a red background, reinforced responding on a VI 3-minute schedule. During the second component, the key was illuminated with a white circle on a green background and responding was not reinforced. At the end of the sixth session, several cycles with 1-minute components were provided. (Changing the component length did not alter rates of responding.)

Two subsequent test sessions (sessions 7 and 9) were provided in which the triangle, circle, and red or green light were presented separately for 1-minute sessions. A different order of stimulus presentation was used in each session with a total of 52 minutes' exposure to each separate stimulus being given to one pigeon and a total of 60 minutes to a second. Responses were not reinforced. (The procedure used during session 8 was the same as during the first 6 sessions.)

During training, both subjects came to respond predominantly in the presence of the white triangle on the red background. The discriminative control acquired by these stimuli is shown in Fig. 12-1. This presents the average rate of responding for 3 sessions in the presence of each of the two stimuli. The results of the test sessions in which each stimulus was presented separately are also indicated in Fig. 12-1. It may be noted that for one of the pigeons there was little responding to the red background, while for the other, there was little responding to the triangle. Inasmuch as both color and form were projected on the response key it is not very likely that a particular receptor orientation could be used to account for why the birds responded to only a single stimulus element. It must be assumed that the birds "saw" both attributes of the stimulus—color *and* form—but for some reason attended exclusively to only one of these.

It could be argued by those who maintain the response orientation position, however, that receptor oriented responses consist of more than those gross, observable responses which orient the organism to one discriminanda or another. Rather, such responses could be conceptualized as consisting of minute eye movements, or even changes in the ciliary muscles responsible for accommodation. In the case of Reynolds's (1961b) study which we have just cited, it could be hypothesized that one response might increase the sensitivity of the eye to color, and another to form. Thus, the procedure utilized by Reynolds, it could be maintained, did not effectively eliminate different orienting responses.

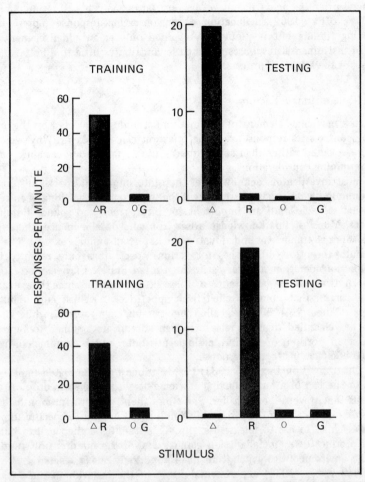

Fig. 12-1. The rate of responding of each pigeon in the presence of each of the key illuminations in the training and testing phases of the experiment. *Adapted from Reynolds (1961b)*

But such a receptor orientation position is nearly untestable, since it could always be argued that minute unmeasured muscular responses are responsible for any stimulus selection or attention process which might be inferred from experimental findings.[2]

Our bias is that the attention process must be considered central in nature—along with Trabasso and Bower (1968), we believe that the examination of

[2] We would not want to be too dogmatic about this and would at least admit the possibility that an appropriate test of the receptor oriented position might be made by using stabilized images or, perhaps, by constructing types of discriminanda consisting of two or more dimensions in which an observing or receptor oriented response designed to extract information about one dimension would also be oriented to the other.

peripheral orienting acts will not get us very far in analyzing attention phenomena. Wyckoff's (1952) delineation of an observing response represents an interesting finding but it should be regarded only as an added element in a chain of instrumental responses. As such it contributes little to a better understanding of the attention process.

The Role of Innate Factors

When a particular element of a compound stimulus is selected by the organism (or controls its response), a basic question can be asked, "Why was that attribute selected rather than some other?" Innate factors are certainly one of the determining considerations.

As most investigators acknowledge, there are important species differences in determining what types of stimuli will be important. It has long been recognized that visual stimuli are important for birds, smell and sound stimuli for dogs, etc. Much of this knowledge arises from anecdotal evidence—the experience of animal trainers or individuals who have had animals as pets. The role of stimulus-reception differences for various species has only recently been given the consideration it deserves in the United States. European ethologists have been aware of the importance of these differences for some time, examining the stimuli that come to elicit both appetitive as well as consummatory responses. Tinbergen (1951) has called such stimuli "sign" stimuli, while Thorpe (1956) has classified them as releasors. Sign stimuli are assumed to represent only a small portion, or possibly a single attribute, of the stimulus configuration that elicits an instinctive response.

To illustrate, Von Uexküll (1934) has described how the mated female tick climbs to the top of a bush, clinging at such a height that she can drop off onto mammals that traverse beneath her. She clings there, perhaps for months, without responding to any of the variety of stimuli about her until a specific stimulus acts as a signal for her to release her grip. This stimulus is the smell of butyric acid, a product of mammalian skin glands. Out of the hundreds of stimuli in the tick's environment to which it might respond, only one is selected.

In Tinbergen's (1951) experimental study of the behavior of male stickelback fish, he found that the "red belly" of the fish was the sign stimulus that elicited attacks from other fish, even if this red belly was painted on only a very crude model. Similarly, Lack (1943) found that the "red breast" of the male robin was the sign stimulus for attack by other male robins. Lack discovered that it was possible to elicit attack responses from male robins to a ball of cotton dabbed with red paint.

Many other studies could be cited in which investigators have made a detailed examination of the specificity of the stimulus which elicits an appetitive or consummatory response. A cataloging of these experiments would be of little value other than in demonstrating that the characteristics of the specific stimuli which elicit appetitive or consummatory responses are quite diverse, and are related to the kinds of organisms observed.

It appears that at least in some cases, however, an examination of the operation of these sign stimuli reveals a learning component. For example, ducklings will usually reveal an inborn or innate following response which appears to be released by rhythmical sounds and moving objects. The duckling will follow its mother, or as Lorenz (1935) has so aptly demonstrated, a human caretaker. Once the following response has been made, however, it appears that the animal *learns* the specific properties of the object it is following and stays attached to it. Thus, the releasing stimulus situation appears to become highly specific through a process which many investigators would consider to be learned.

The Role of Learning

It seems reasonable to assume that learning also contributes to selective attention and a number of investigators have demonstrated such to be the case. More than 25 years ago, Lawrence (1949) wrote, "If the S is trained to respond to some aspects of the situation other than the initially dominant one, then this new aspect will tend to become more distinctive and the other aspects relatively less distinctive. Consequently, when this same cue appears in another discrimination problem, it will be more readily associated with the instrumental behavior demanded by the new problem than it would be without the previous training" (p. 770).

Lawrence's hypothesis regarding the role of training in making cues more "distinctive" received partial experimental support in his study in which three apparatus characteristics: (1) brightness, (2) width of the goal compartment, and (3) texture or roughness of the apparatus floor, were used as discriminanda. Early training consisted of having rats first learn to make a simultaneous discrimination—that is, learn to differentiate either (1) black vs. white alleys, (2) wide vs. narrow alleys, or (3) rough vs. smooth floors. Following 90 trials (10 trials per day for nine days), a second task was provided. Here, the relevant cue was black vs. white alleys; the rough vs. smooth floor cue was made irrelevant by not correlating this discriminanda with reward. Lawrence's position predicted that the group which had learned the relevancy of the black and white alley cues on the first task should learn the second task very rapidly. On the other hand, the group which used the rough vs. smooth floor cue to learn the first task should have difficulty in learning the second task, since it would be presumed that the cues used in the first task would continue to be used in the second and thus result in negative transfer. Finally, the group which was trained with wide vs. narrow alleys as cues on the first task should show little positive or negative transfer, since this cue was not present during the second task. The results obtained from the second task did reveal the predicted beneficial effect of the original training on the black-white cues; negative transfer, however, was not obtained in the case of the rough vs. smooth floor cue group.

Lawrence's work made an early and important contribution to a better understanding of the effect of learning on selective attention. A number of contemporary investigations, many using the operant learning paradigm, have also contributed to this area. Johnson and Cumming's (1968) study is one of these.

In one experiment by these authors, pigeons were provided 10 sessions of single stimulus discrimination training in which either a green background *or* a vertical line served as the positive stimulus, while a horizontal line *or* a red background was the negative stimulus. Following such training, compound stimulus training sessions were provided; these consisted of reinforcing the two positive stimulus elements—a vertical line on a green background—and not reinforcing the two negative stimulus elements—a horizontal line on a red background. Finally, test sessions consisting of presenting each of the four single stimuli, e.g., horizontal line, vertical line, red background, and green background, were then provided. Results indicated that during these test sessions, more than 80% of all responding occurred to the single positive stimulus which was reinforced during the single stimulus discrimination training. In brief, these findings indicate that primary control by a single component of a compound stimulus may be produced by single stimulus training.

It is of some interest to note that in another part of their study, these experimenters found it possible to vary the amount of control exercised by the single stimulus element—the vertical line—by providing different intensities. Thus, if the line were made very bright, responding could be controlled almost exclusively by this stimulus element.

Another kind of evidence used to demonstrate the contribution of learning on selective attention has been termed "blocking," a term coined by Kamin (1968) and defined as a "reduced development of stimulus control by one of two covarying cues, resulting from prior learning to discriminate on the basis of the other cue" (Vom Saal and Jenkins, 1970).

The general design of experiments which have demonstrated this phenomenon follows: During stage 1 learning, an experimental group learns a discrimination task on the basis of cue A. In stage 2, the experimental group, as well as the control, are trained on a discrimination in which both cue A and a second cue—cue B—are provided, both cues being relevant to the solution of the problem. Finally, stage 3 consists of giving both groups test trials with only cue B present. The term blocking has arisen from the experimental findings, obtained by a variety of investigators, which indicate that the experimental group reveals poorer performance during stage 3 test trials than does the control. In effect, the earlier training with only cue A present has resulted in blocking any contribution that cue B might make during stage 2, an effect that can be observed during the test trials.

Although Kamin's (1968) study examined the conditioned emotional response (CER)—a task which we considered in our classical conditioning chapters—his procedures and experimental findings so clearly demonstrate this effect that we shall briefly describe his experiment. Two groups of rats were first trained to bar press for food. Afterward, stage 1 was initiated, which consisted of providing the experimental group with 16 training trials in which a white noise served as CS and was paired with shock. Within a relatively small number of trials, it was observed that the onset of the CS was sufficient to stop these animals from pressing the bar for food. In stage 2, the experimental group as well as a control group, received 8 training trials in which the white noise used in stage 1, as well as a visual stimulus—the turning on of an overhead 7.5-watt bulb—was presented along with the presentation of shock. Finally, stage 3 consisted of both groups of animals being presented with the visual stimulus.

Results indicated that the number of bar pressing responses for the experimental animals was much greater than for the control group. Thus, the control animals revealed almost complete suppression of the bar pressing response to the light during stage 3; on the other hand, the experimental animals revealed no indication of such suppression. In effect, the early learned association of noise and shock appeared to "block" the learning of the association between the visual stimulus and shock.

Experiments by Seraganian and Vom Saal (1969) and Vom Saal and Jenkins (1970) are just two of a number of subsequent studies which confirm that blocking can be demonstrated in instrumental learning tasks.

Discrimination

The discrimination process is inferred from the behavior of the organism making differential responses to unlike stimuli or, more specifically, a discrimination task. An examination of the learning literature reveals that a variety of theoretical issues have arisen concerning the nature of the discrimination process. In addition to examing some of these points of view, we should also like to look at some of the empirical findings related to discrimination learning.

The Nature of Discrimination Learning

In 1929, Lashley indicated that the rat, in learning a brightness discrimination task, attempts various solutions before he hits upon the correct one. Lashley wrote, ". . . in the discrimination box, responses to position, to alternation, or to cues from the experimenter's movements, usually precede the reactions to the light and represent attempted solution. The form of the learning curve is the more significant when considered in relation to such behavior. In many cases it strongly suggests that the actual association is formed very quickly and that both the practice preceding and the errors following are irrelevant to the actual formation of the association" (pp. 134-135).

A few years later, Krechevsky (1932a, 1932b, 1933), in a series of learning experiments, observed that his rats, prior to learning a discrimination task, appeared to engage in a number of systematic modes of responses. That is, the animal might first respond to position, e.g., left, and if such responding did not lead to consistent reinforcement, would adopt another type of response, e.g., brightness, in an apparent effort to solve the problem. From such behavior, Krechevsky was led to conclude that the animal selects, out of the many possible stimuli found in the learning task, only one to which it attends. While paying attention to such stimuli, the animal learns nothing about the correctness of the final discriminanda to be learned. These presolution responses were conceptualized by Krechevsky as hypotheses which the animal first adopts and then abandons until one leads to the solution of the problem.

In 1942, Lashley reaffirmed his position when he wrote, ". . . when any complex stimuli arouses nervous activity that activity is immediately organized and certain elements or components become dominant for reaction, while others become ineffective . . . In any trial of the training series, only those components of the stimulating situation which are dominant in the organization are associated. Other stimuli which excite the receptors are not associated because the animal is not set to react to them" (p. 242).

A few years later, Lashley and Wade (1946) outlined a perceptual dominance hypothesis which reiterated the position that in discrimination learning tasks, the organism responds only to the dominant cue while all other cues become irrelevant. Lashley and Wade (1946) stated, "... if a monkey is trained to choose a *large* red circle and avoid a *small* green one, he will usually choose any red object and avoid any green but will make chance scores when like colored large and small circles are presented" (p. 82). Under such circumstances, color is the dominant cue while size is irrelevant.

During this same period of time, other investigators adopted a different point of view regarding how the discrimination task was learned. Hull (1929) had written that "... all elements of a stimulus complex playing upon the sensorium of an organism at or near the time that a response is evoked, tend themselves independently and indiscriminately to acquire the capacity to evoke substantially the same response" (p. 498). Subsequently, both Spence (1936, 1937a, 1937b) and Hull (1939, 1943) proposed theories of discrimination learning which posited (1) every reinforced trial led to an increment of strength for a given stimulus and its response; (2) nonreinforced trials resulted in an inhibitory increment to a given stimulus and its response; (3) both excitatory and inhibitory tendencies generalized to stimuli along a stimulus continuum; and (4) the algebraic summations of excitatory and inhibitory increments result in a discriminatory response which is based on these algebraic summations.

The Continuity-Noncontinuity Issue

A number of theoretical issues have arisen from the Lashley–Krechevsky and Hull–Spence positions on discrimination learning. One issue has been whether all stimuli present at the time of the response become associated with that response or whether certain elements or components of the discriminanda become dominant for the organism while others are ignored and thus ineffective. It will be recalled that Hull and Spence held that all elements of the stimulus complex which reach the sensorium of the organism become effective stimuli, while Lashley and Krechevsky argued that some components of the discriminanda are dominant (selected by the organism) while others are not.

A second issue is whether learning takes place gradually and continuously—in increments of associative strength—or whether learning is noncontinuous, occurring very rapidly and perhaps in a single trial, with performance on earlier trials not contributing to the solution of the problem. These issues have coalesced into what is known as the continuity-noncontinuity controversy.

One experimental procedure believed to be of value in settling this controversy was the stimulus reversal task. This task consisted of providing a relatively small number of trials to experimental subjects in which two stimuli, e.g., black vs. white, were presented, with one of them being consistently reinforced. These trials were referred to as the presolution period, since, before the subject started to respond systematically to the positive stimulus, the cues were reversed. The learning of this stimulus reversal task was then carried out to some criterion set by the experimenter. The prediction of the continuity theorists was that the experimental group should learn the reversal more slowly than a group not given this kind of presolution training because the earlier training would be expected to interfere with the reversal task. The noncontinuity position predicted that the reinforced presolution trials should not provide interference because the subject was not responding to the relevant stimulus element and that practice prior to the time the association was established would be of no consequence in the subsequent solving of the problem.

An early study by Krechevsky (1938) illustrates the stimulus reversal task as well as the controversial findings obtained with it. In this experiment, rats were given discrimination training on a Lashley jumping stand in which difficult visual discriminanda were used. *Horizontal* rows of small black squares made up one stimulus card; *vertical* rows of small black squares made up the second. Experimental group 1 was given 20 presolution trials; Experimental group 2 was given 40. During these trials, one stimulus was positive and the other negative. Following the 20- or 40-trial session, the cues were reversed and training provided until the animals reached a criterion of 18 correct responses out of 20 trials. A control group was given training only on the second task. Krechevsky found that Experimental group 1 did not make any more errors than the control group, thus supporting the noncontinuity position; however, Experimental group 2 did reveal a significant amount of negative transfer, a finding in keeping with the continuity hypothesis. Krechevsky accounted for the negative transfer behavior of this second experimental group by suggesting that 40 trials was too long a presolution period. Subsequently, Spence (1940) argued that the subjects in Experimental group 1 did not "see" the rows of black squares because they were fixating on other aspects of the stimulus complex.[3]

It would serve no useful purpose to review the many studies which appeared during the late forties and early fifties examining the continuity-noncontinuity issue. Most experimenters, e.g., Ritchie, Ebeling, and Roth (1950), Gatling

---

[3] Spence's interpretation was supported by Ehrenfreund (1948) who, in two experiments, had rats learn to discriminate an upright from an inverted triangle in a Lashley jumping apparatus. During the second experiment, the jumping platform of the apparatus was raised above the level of the stimulus windows, enabling the subjects to fixate upon that area of the card which provided discriminable differences between the stimuli. This was in contrast to the first experiment in which, with the lowered jumping platform, the fixation habits of the rat (a tendency to fixate on the lower portion of the card) were likely to preclude discriminably different retinal excitations from the stimulus figures at the start of training. The results of the first experiment indicated that 40 presolution trials had no influence on the reversal learning situation; a similar amount of training during Experiment 2 did result in the experimental group's taking significantly longer to learn the reversal than the control group. Ehrenfreund, in agreement with Spence, has pointed out that it is possible for an animal not to learn anything about the differential cues at the beginning of the visual discrimination training period if the specific receptor exposure fixations are such that they do not provide discriminably different excitation of the retina necessary for discrimination learning.

(1951), obtained results supporting the continuity position. That is, the systematic reinforcement of a particular stimulus element during the presolution period retarded learning when the cues were reversed.

Contemporary Points of View

We have noted that, according to the noncontinuity position, animals in learning a discrimination task attend to, and thus learn about, only one cue at a time; conversely, the continuity position stated that animals learn equally about all cues which impinge on their receptors. Mackintosh (1965b) has indicated that there is a compromise or alternative position available—one which states that animals may attend to some cues more than to others, ". . . so that if the subject is attending predominantly to Cue A, it will learn more about Cue A than about Cue B . . . But there is no need to insist that the subject learns everything or learns nothing about a given cue" (p. 130).[4]

Certainly, some of the experimental evidence we have reviewed indicates the necessity for considering selective attention as a basic postulate in any theory of discrimination learning. As a result, Zeaman and House (1963), Lovejoy (1968), and Sutherland and Mackintosh (1971), among others, have all considered some selective attention process as a basic factor in their theories of discrimination learning. We shall provide a general discussion of these theories; the reader can refer to the referenced investigators for a more specific treatment.

All these theories may be described as two-process theories since it has been posited that the animal must learn to (1) attend to the relevant stimulus dimension and (2) attach the correct response to stimuli having different values on this dimension. To illustrate, rats in order to discriminate between a white and black stimulus card which make up the discriminanda on a Lashley jumping stand, must first learn that brightness is the relevant cue, and then learn to jump toward white and away from black.

It has been assumed that organisms, in order to learn a discrimination, must have a number of stimulus analyzers, each of which is sensitive to particular features and variations of the stimulation received. As we have indicated in the above illustration, an analyzer sensitive to brightness (black-white) must operate in order for the animal to learn that particular discrimination.

Rarely has there been any statement on the part of the theorists to indicate how many analyzers there are, how many are utilized in any discrimination problem, or in fact, anything about their operation. In any experiment, the dimensions of the discriminanda are noted by the experimenter and it is assumed that the subject has an analyzer for each dimension. The evidence that any animal has a particular analyzer is inferred from other investigations which have indicated that the species being used can solve a discrimination task on the basis of that particular stimulus dimension.

[4]Mackintosh (1965b) has further written, "Although in an empirical sense this may appear to be a compromise position between the two extreme poles of continuity and noncontinuity theories . . . the theoretical position that emerges clearly has more in common with noncontinuity theory than it has with continuity theory" (p. 130).

It has been assumed that not every analyzer is used or is active on a single trial but rather, that only a subset of the total number operate. Some difference of opinion, however, has been expressed about this conclusion. Zeaman and House (1963) for example, believed that only a single analyzer is selected on each trial; others, however, have hypothesized that more than a single analyzer may be active on any given trial. It must be acknowledged that subjects can attend to more than a single attribute or stimulus dimension on a single trial. For example, using a two-key Skinner box, a pigeon can be trained to peck the left key when both keys are illuminated with a green light, and to peck the right key when both keys are illuminated with a red light. Here, the pigeon must attend not only to color but also to position in order to respond correctly.

Moreover, it has been thought that analyzers may vary in strength. At the start of training, the varying analyzers have different base values; however, analyzers are strengthened or weakened by response outcomes. Some investigators have hypothesized that this strengthening of one analyzer is accompanied by the weakening of another. Thus, if a discrimination learning task contains two cues, the more an organism learns about one, the less it will learn about the other.

The second process, attaching the correct response to the appropriate stimulus, is presumably strengthened by reward and decreased by nonreward. However, the amount of change in response strength is related to the strength of the analyzer.

In summary, many of our current discrimination learning theories reveal a basic similarity to the early noncontinuity position, since such theories propose that a stimulus dimension that is not analyzed on any given trial will not influence the response made on that trial. Thus, the organism does not learn about stimulus attributes that it does not attend to, nor will this factor influence performance. However, by a trial and error process, the subject will try first one and then another analyzer with the analyzer appropriate to the relevant dimension gradually increasing in strength; similarly, the learning of the correct instrumental response to the output from this relevant analyzer will result.

Empirical Findings

A number of investigators have not been concerned with theoretical positions involved in discrimination learning. Instead, they have been primarily interested in examining how a variety of conditions related to the nature of the discriminanda have contributed to the ease or difficulty of learning the task.

Stimulus Salience

One variable related to the discriminanda has to do with the specific characteristics of the stimuli—what many have called stimulus salience. And one operation designed to manipulate salience has been to vary the physical difference that exists between the stimuli. It is well known that as the difference between the stimuli increases, the task becomes easier to learn. The experimental procedures used to vary these differences are diverse and are related to the type of discriminanda used. In the Broadhurst (1957) study which we cited in Chapter 11, it will be recalled that three difficulties of a discrimination task were produced by differentially illuminating the two alleys of a Y-maze. The difference in illumination between these alleys for each discrimination problem was represented by the ratios of 1:300, 1:60, or 1:15. Broadhurst found that the discrimination task which employed the largest difference in the illumination of the alleys, e.g., 1:300 yielded the most rapid learning, while the smallest difference, e.g., 1:15, resulted in the slowest. These findings were obtained regardless of the strength of the animal's motivation.

A second way of manipulating the physical difference between the stimuli has been to provide differences in cue area. Working with monkeys and using the Wisconsin General Test Apparatus, Warren (1953) used $3''$ squares of cardboard as discriminanda, and varied the amount of colored border on the cards. Four areas were used, specifically, 2.25, 4.50, 6.75, and 9.00 square inches, with these values representing 25%, 50%, 75%, or 100% of the total square. Each discrimination problem consisted of 10 trials. It should be emphasized that each pair of cards differed in color, e.g., color was the relevant cue, with the amount of colored border varying from one problem to another. Warren found that when the area of the colored figure was either 6.75 or 9.00 square inches, the color discrimination task was more readily learned than when the area was 4.50 square inches. This latter area, in turn, produced superior discrimination learning to discriminanda consisting of 2.25 square inches of colored area. Blazek and Harlow (1955) have confirmed Warren's (1953) findings.

A different procedure used to manipulate the physical differences between stimuli has been to employ differing numbers of stimulus elements which make up the discriminanda. In an early study by Harlow (1945) monkeys were given training in discriminating between three-dimensional stimuli, e.g., red pyramid vs. blue cube, and two-dimensional or patterned stimulus objects, e.g., a stimulus wedge with two wide magenta stripes painted across it vs. a stimulus wedge with just one wide magenta stripe. Monkeys were given a series of these problems, each one being presented until the animal attained 20 correct responses out of 25 trials or until 100 trials were provided. Findings revealed that three times as many errors were made when two-dimensional stimuli were used in contrast to three.

A similar finding has been reported more recently by House and Zeaman (1960) working with mentally retarded children. Discrimination problems were solved more readily if three-dimensional or object stimuli were used, e.g., a yellow "T" vs. a black square form cut from $1/4''$ masonite and mounted vertically on a base, than if patterned stimuli were employed, e.g., forms of the exact dimensions and colors of the object stimuli painted on $4'' \times 4''$ gray wedges.

The Role of Stimulus Elements

In the examination of three-dimensional stimuli (objects) in contrast to two dimensional stimuli (patterns), it is obvious that a greater number of stimulus elements make up the object discriminanda and it might be deduced that it is this factor which contributes to the ease of learning. The experimental manipulation of stimulus elements or cues which make up the discriminanda has been a problem of some interest.

In an early study by Eninger (1952), rats were placed in a simple T-maze with one group of animals having to choose the right arm of the maze after passing through a black stem pathway, and the left arm after going through a white stem pathway (visual group). A second group of subjects was required to choose the right arm of the maze when a tone was sounded and the left arm when no tone was presented (auditory group). A third group had these cues combined (auditory-visual group). The findings revealed that performance for the auditory-visual group was markedly superior to that of the other two experimental groups.

Warren's work (Warren, 1953, 1954; Hara and Warren, 1961) with monkeys and cats is particularly impressive in demonstrating that when discriminative stimulus elements are added to the discriminanda, the discrimination task becomes easier for the subject to learn. In his first study, Warren (1953) used 210 pairs of geometrical figures cut from colored paper. Each pair of figures which formed a discrimination problem varied in either (1) color, (2) form, or (3) size, or in combinations of these taken two or three at a time, e.g., (4) color and form, (5) color and size, (6) form and size, or (7) color, form, and size. Seven 10-trial discrimination problems, one taken from each of the cue categories, were provided each day for 30 days, which resulted in a total of 210 problems being presented to each monkey. Significant differences were obtained among the stimulus-cue categories; Table 12-1 provides an analysis of the role of the various cues in the discrimination learning task. It may be noted that size as a cue resulted in more errors than did the presentation of both form and size. The smallest number of errors took place when the discriminanda varied with regard to color, form, and size.

An important consideration in this study has to do with the discriminability of the cues themselves. The stimulus values which made up each stimulus dimension were chosen arbitrarily, with an implicit assumption that the difference between any two colors, e.g., red and green, was about the same as the difference between any two other dimensions, e.g., form, which consisted of a cross, square, circle, triangle, etc., as well as size, 1.8 square inches vs. 3.6 square inches.

In a subsequent study, Hara and Warren (1961) examined the contribution of stimulus cue additivity in the discrimination performance of cats when the differential limens (threshold) for visual form, size, and brightness discrimination were known. The experimental procedure consisted of first determining these limens by the method of constant stimuli. Psychophysical functions were thus obtained for individual cats on each of the three dimensions so that it was possible to specify for each subject which stimulus values were just below and just above the threshold, that is, which could be discriminated with approximately 70% and 80% success respectively. Fifty-five training trials were then presented each day for a period of 14 days. The first 15 trials of each day consisted of providing the animal with three 5-trial sets in which easily discriminated stimulus pairs involving each of the three dimensions were employed.

Table 12-1   An Analysis of the Role of
Various Cues in Discrimination
Learning

Stimulus Category	Percentage of Errors
Color, form, size	6.6
Color, form	7.6
Color, size	8.5
Color	8.9
Form, size	20.7
Form	22.7
Size	25.5

Adapted from Warren (1953)

This was done in order to maintain basic discrimination habits. These trials were then followed by four sets of 10 trials in which all 27 possible combinations of two and three subliminal (70% success) and supraliminal (80% success) cues, together with a control condition of no stimulus differences, were employed.

As Table 12-2 reveals, cats discriminate stimuli differing with three cues better than they discriminate on just two dimensions, while two-dimensional stimuli result in performance which is superior to that produced by stimuli differing on only a single dimension. McGonigle (1967) has repeated Hara and Warren's (1961) experiment using rats and obtained almost identical results.

Feature-Positive Effects

Sainsbury and Jenkins (Jenkins and Sainsbury, 1970; Sainsbury, 1971a, 1971b, 1973) obtained an interesting discrimination task finding which they termed a "feature-positive effect." They were able to show that if two stimulus displays which form the discriminanda are differentiated only by a single distinctive feature, locating the distinctive feature on the negative display results in poorer learning than locating it on the positive display. In an early study, Jenkins and Sainsbury (1970) found it impossible for pigeons to learn a discrimination task when the distinctive feature was on the negative display; a subsequent study (Sainsbury, 1971) has demonstrated that if the distinctive feature is placed close to the common element features rather than farther away, as was done in their earlier study, pigeons can learn a discrimination when the distinctive feature is placed on the negative stimulus.

Sainsbury (1973) has confirmed the findings of the Jenkins and Sainsbury (1970) study using 4- to 5-year-old children as subjects. Five of his 6 subjects were able to reach a criterion of 90% correct by the sixth session of training when the distinctive feature was located on the positive display; however, none of the 6 subjects who had the distinctive feature on the negative display were able to do so. It is interesting to note, however, that when 9-year-old children were used as subjects, 5 out of 6 could learn the problem when the distinctive

Table 12–2   Percentage of Correct
Responses to the Varying
Stimulus Compounds

Cues	Percentage Correct
None	53.5
c	71.8
C	82.2
cc	81.7
Cc	88.3
CC	90.0
ccc	87.5
Ccc	94.8
CCc	94.0
CCC	99.0

c = subthreshold stimulus difference
C = suprathreshold stimulus difference
Adapted from Hara and Warren (1961)

feature was located on the negative stimulus. All 6 were able to learn the task when the distinctive feature was on the positive stimulus.

In attempting to account for the experimental findings which indicate that animals and 4- and 5-year-old children have difficulty in learning a feature-negative problem in contrast to a feature-positive one, Sainsbury has hypothesized that the two different displays may be viewed as consisting of two parts, each part eliciting a separate response. The distinctive feature is one part while the common element of the two displays comprises the second part. On any distinctive feature trial, the subject may respond to either the distinctive feature or the common features, with the outcome of the trial influencing only the response probability of the feature responded to. In the feature positive case, the probability of reinforcement for a response to the distinctive feature is one; the probability of a reinforced response to the common element, however, is less than one. This difference in reinforcement probability facilitates a simultaneous discrimination between the two parts with the distinctive feature gaining control over the subject's responding. In the feature-negative case, the probability of reinforcement for the distinctive feature is zero, but the probability of reinforcement for a response to the common feature is greater than zero. Therefore, the common element gains control over the subject's responding even though responding to the common element does not lead to 100% reinforcement.

In accounting for those subjects who were able to learn the discrimination when the distinctive feature was on the negative display, it has been suggested that the discrimination was learned by using the distinctive feature as a "positive" cue. As Sainsbury (1973) has written, successful subjects appear to look for the distinctive feature and then respond to the other display. In a sense the distinctive feature assumes a role as part of a positive response chain.

There is some difficulty in accounting for why 4- and 5-year-olds fail to learn the feature-negative discrimination. One possibility may be that in order for the discrimination to be learned, the subject must look in one location and respond in a second.[5] Another possibility has been proposed by Sainsbury who suggests that perhaps 4- and 5-year-old children, given a choice between a partially correct simple response and a fully correct difficult response, may choose the simple response. This, of course, is no explanation, since it merely describes what has happened in the experiment. It is obvious that more research is needed in order to determine the factors which contribute to this finding.

The Contribution of Previous Learning

It would be most unusual if the organism's earlier or previous learning did not in some way contribute to the learning of a subsequent discrimination task. The most notable work in this area has been conducted by Harlow (1949) in his classic study of the formation of learning sets. The type of discrimination task used was one in which a monkey had to choose one of two objects, e.g., a small funnel vs. a wooden cube, both of which covered food wells, but only one of the wells containing food. The position of the objects was shifted from left to right in a balanced and predetermined order with the subject having to learn to choose one of the objects consistently in order to obtain reinforcement.

In an early study, a series of 344 problems was provided to a group of 8 monkeys. Every discrimination problem used a different pair of discriminanda. Each of the first 32 problems was run for 50 trials, but only 6 trials were provided for each of the next 200 problems. For the last 112 problems, an average of just 9 trials was provided. Fig. 12–2 represents learning curves which reveal the percentage of correct responses on the first 6 trials of these discrimination tasks, while Fig. 12–3 plots the percentage of correct responses on trials 2 to 6 as a function of the number of problems previously presented. As may be noted, both figures reveal an increase in learning efficiency as more and more problems are provided for the monkey to solve. Harlow has hypothesized that this increase in efficiency is based on a process which he has identified as "a learning set" or learning to learn. That is, the experience that the organism has had with this general type of problem has resulted in the animal's becoming much more efficient in its learning.

As might be anticipated, the formation of learning sets has been investigated and demonstrated with a variety or organisms, e.g. cats (Warren and Baron,

---

[5] In a subsequent section of this chapter, we note that some experimenters have found their subjects unable to learn a discrimination problem when they must look in one direction and respond in a different spatial location—there being, in effect, a separation of the discriminanda and the location of the response and reward. This finding is somewhat controversial, however, at least when applied to preschool children, since Compione and Beaton (1972) have indicated that separating the cue and response location does not appear to result in any learning difficulty for preschool children, while Sainsbury (1973) has also found that separating the cue and response location poses no learning difficulty for 5-year olds.

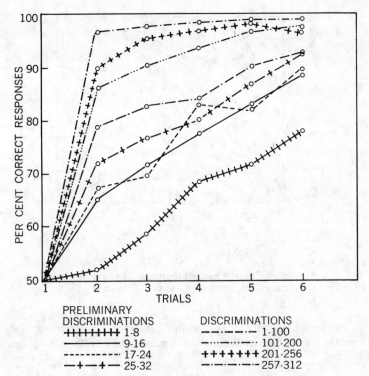

PRELIMINARY
DISCRIMINATIONS   DISCRIMINATIONS
+++++++++ 1-8   —·—·—·— 1-100
———————— 9-16   —·····—···· 101-200
---------- 17-24   +++++++ 201-256
—+—+— 25-32   —·—··—··— 257-312

Fig. 12-2. Discrimination learning curves obtained from successive blocks of problems. *Adapted from Harlow (1949)*

1956), rats (Koronakis and Arnold, 1957), pigeons (Zeiler and Price, 1965), infant monkeys (Harlow, Harlow, Rueping, and Mason, 1960), and normal and retarded children (Shepard, 1957; Kaufman and Peterson, 1958).

Learning set formation as been examined as a function of a number of variables. In general, those variables which contribute to the learning of a single discrimination problem have also been demonstrated to have an influence on learning set formation. The number of trials per problem, however, is a variable which is uniquely related to learning set formation. In an early study by Levine, Levinson, and Harlow (1959), two groups of monkeys were given either 3 trials per problem or 12 trials per problem. The 3 trials per problem group received 12 problems per day each for 3 trials. The 12 trials per problem group received 3 problems per day, but were given 12 trials with each problem. Thus, all subjects received 36 trials each day. The experiment was continued for 64 days at which time all subjects appeared to have reached a performance asymptote. No difference was obtained between the two groups when performance was measured over successsive blocks of trials. As a result, the investigators concluded that 3 to 12 trials per problem yielded equivalent learning set development. A second study by Levine and Harlow (1959) in which monkeys were given either 1 or

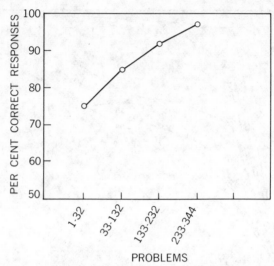

Fig. 12-3. Discrimination learning-set curve based on Trials 2-6 responses. *Adapted from Harlow (1949)*

12 trials per problem provided similar findings. That is, learning appeared to depend on the number of trials provided regardless of how they were organized into problems.

The Role of Overlearning

A continuation of looking at the role of learning set phenomenon leads to an examination of overlearning. Overlearning refers to the experimenter's providing his subjects with a specified number of additional learning trials after the learning criterion has been reached.

One basic problem with the concept of overlearning is that the designation of overlearning trials is always relative to the learning criterion which is adopted. If one experimenter decides that his learning criterion will be 9 correct responses out of 10 trials, trials provided after this criterion has been reached are considered overlearning trials. On the other hand, a second investigator may decide that his learning criterion will be 29 correct out of 30 trials. It is obvious that some of the learning trials provided in the second experiment would be considered overlearning trials in the first experiment if the investigator continued to run his animals.

The work of Reid (1953) illustrates the overlearning paradigm. In his study, three groups of rats were trained to make a simple visual (black-white) discrimination in a Y-alley apparatus. All groups learned the problem to a criterion of 9 out of 10 correct responses with the black card serving as the rewarded stimulus. Following this, one group learned the reversal task (white rewarded) immediately, a second group was given 50 overlearning trials, while the third

Table 12-3   Trials to Criterion in
Discrimination Reversal Learning

Group	Trials
Immediately reversed	138.3
50 overlearning trials	129.0
150 overlearning trials	70.0

Adapted from Reid (1953)

group was given 150 overlearning trials prior to learning the reversal. The number of trials to reach the same criterion with the white card as with the rewarded stimulus, for these three experimental groups is presented in Table 12-3. It may be noted that the group which was given 150 overlearning trials learned the reversal significantly more rapidly than the controls.

A few years later, Pubols (1956) demonstrated that overlearning would facilitate the learning of a spatial or a position reversal. In this study, groups of rats were trained to turn right (or left) in a Y-alley maze. Upon the attainment of a criterion of 18 out of 20 correct responses on two consecutive days, one group reversed immediately while the second group was given 150 overlearning trials, and then reversed. Pubols found that the overlearning group learned the reversal significantly faster than the group which had been reversed immediately after reaching the criterion.

This general finding is a most provocative one since it had generally been assumed that overlearning trials contributed to the strength of the original habit, and that poorer performance on the reversal of a discrimination task could be expected. Thus, subjects provided overlearning trials should have a more difficult time than their controls in learning the reversed task.

It is not surprising, therefore, that Reid and Pubol's experimental findings have resulted in a large number of investigators' attempting to replicate their findings, study the role of overlearning trials with other tasks and species, and provide theoretical accounts of the findings.

An examination of many of these overlearning studies, some of which we have summarized in Table 12-4, suggests a number of conclusions:

1. The overlearning effect is found more frequently with visual than spatial discrimination problems.
2. When visual discrimination problems are examined, the overlearning effect is more likely to be obtained with difficult than with easy problems.
3. When the overlearning effect is obtained, overtraining tends to increase the number of errors early in the reversal training but leads to more rapid learning in later trials.
4. The overlearning phenomenon is a relatively elusive one, with a large number of its investigators being unable to obtain positive findings.
5. The overlearning effect has been found almost exclusively with rats

Table 12-4   Summaries of A Sampling of Studies Investigating Overlearning

Subjects	Type of Task	Results	Investigators
Rats	Visual Discrimination	Facilitation	Reid (1953)
Rats	Visual Discrimination	Facilitation	Pubols (1956)
Rats	Visual Discrimination	Facilitation	Capaldi and Stevenson (1957)
Rats	Visual Discrimination	Facilitation	Brookshire, Warren, and Ball (1961)
Rats	Visual Discrimination	Facilitation	North and Clayton (1959)
Rats	Visual Discrimination	Facilitation	D'Amato and Jagoda (1961)
Rats	Visual Discrimination	Facilitation	Mackintosh (1962)
Rats	Visual Discrimination	Facilitation	Erlebacher (1963)
Rats	Visual Discrimination	Facilitation	Mackintosh (1963)
Rats	Visual Discrimination	Facilitation	Mackintosh (1965a)
Rats	Visual Discrimination	No Effect	D'Amato and Schiff (1965)
Rats	Visual Discrimination	Facilitation	Birnbaum (1967)
Rats	Visual Discrimination	Facilitation	Siegel (1967)
Rats	Visual Discrimination	Facilitation	Mandler (1968)
Rats	Visual Discrimination	Facilitation	Sperling (1970)
Octopuses	Visual Discrimination	Facilitation	Mackintosh and Mackintosh (1963)
Chicks	Visual Discrimination	Facilitation	Mackintosh (1965a)
Pigeons	Visual Discrimination	Facilitation	Williams (1967)
Monkeys	Visual Discrimination	No Effect	Boyer and Cross (1965)
Monkeys	Visual Discrimination	No Effect	Cross and Brown (1965)
Monkeys	Visual Discrimination	No Effect	Tighe (1965)
Monkeys	Visual Discrimination	No Effect	Beck, Warren, and Stebner (1966)
Rats	Spatial Discrimination	Facilitation	Pubols (1956)
Rats	Spatial Discrimination	Facilitation	Bruner, Mandler, etc. (1958)
Rats	Spatial Discrimination	No Effect	Galanter and Bush (1959)
Rats	Spatial Discrimination	Facilitation	Brookshire, Warren, and Ball (1961)
Rats	Spatial Discrimination	Facilitation	Ison and Birch (1961)
Rats	Spatial Discrimination	No Effect	Hill, et al (1962)
Rats	Spatial Discrimination	No Effect	D'Amato and Jagoda (1962)
Rats	Spatial Discrimination	No Effect	Clayton (1963a)
Rats	Spatial Discrimination	No Effect	Clayton (1963b)
Rats	Spatial Discrimination	No Effect	Paul and Kesner (1963)
Rats	Spatial Discrimination	No Effect	D'Amato and Schiff (1964)
Rats	Spatial Discrimination	Facilitation (large reward) No Effect (small reward)	Theios and Blosser (1965)

used as subjects, and consistently negative findings have been observed with monkeys, cats, and fish. This is perhaps the most important conclusion; one may certainly question the value of devoting so much time and effort in investigating an effect which appears to be found only with rats, and even here, is an elusive one.

The Location of the Cue and Response

Another empirical variable we should like to discuss is related to the location of the discriminanda, and the nature of the response which is demanded by the task. In almost all discrimination tasks, the location of the cue and the site of the organism's response are at the same physical location. In discrimination learning tasks with monkeys, for example, the animal displaces one of two discriminanda exposing a food well which may contain food. In this situation, the discriminanda, the response, and the reward are in the same location.

Murphy and Miller (1955) contrasted this situation with one in which the apparatus was modified by constructing a platform 6″ above the food wells. The objects to be discriminated were placed on this platform and above each well. The subject had to respond by displacing one of two identical wedges which covered the food wells. These investigators discovered that such apparatus modification resulted in the animals' inability to learn the discrimination. This confirmed a similar and earlier finding by McClearn and Harlow (1954), and was in marked contrast to the results obtained when the regular apparatus was used. In brief, a 6″ separation between the stimulus cue and the site of the rewarded response precluded successful solving of the problem.

Meyer, Polidora, and McConnell (1961), in a somewhat similar study, provided monkeys with a series of 8 daily sessions of a brightness discrimination learning task. With 4 randomly selected sessions, the required response of the monkey was to the stimulus itself—the normal procedure found with this type of task. With 4 other sessions, the required response was to a food receptacle located below the discriminanda. Fig. 12-4 reveals the performance of each of 12 monkeys under the stimulus-remote and stimulus-contiguous conditions, the investigators' findings being in keeping with earlier studies.

The generality of this finding has been extended to children, as the experiments of Murphy and Miller (1959) and Jeffrey and Cohen (1964) have demonstrated. As we indicated earlier in the chapter, however, Compione and Beaton (1972) and Sainsbury (1973) have been unable to replicate this finding.

The Role of the Negative Stimulus and Errorless Discrimination Learning

It has been accepted by a number of psychologists that, in discrimination learning tasks, it is necessary for the organism to respond to the negative stimulus, thus building up a hypothesized inhibitory state presumed to be an integral part of the discriminatory process. Although other investigators have not necessarily accepted the role of inhibition in discrimination learning, it has been acknowledged that the elimination of errors plays an important role in such

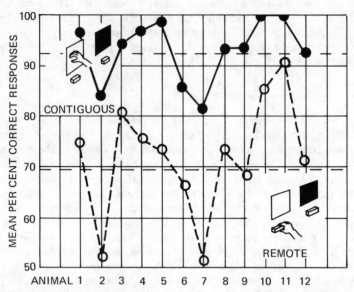

Fig. 12-4. Performances by individual monkeys under conditions of stimulus-remote and stimulus-contiguous responding. *Adapted from Myer, Polidora, and McConnell (1961)*

learning. It is not surprising, therefore, to find that the role of responding to the negative stimulus in discrimination learning has frequently been examined.

In an early study, Denny and Dunham (1951) had groups of rats learn a simple black-white discrimination task. Group I received 2 presentations of the positive stimulus and 1 presentation of the negative stimulus each day. Group II received 2 presentations of the positive stimulus and 4 presentations of the negative stimulus each day, thus running 6 trials/day in contrast to the 3 trials/day which group I received. Results, as measured by the first 2 free choice trials provided each day indicated that group II performed significantly better as measured by percentage of correct responses than did group I. Cantor and Spiker (1954), using children 3 to 5 years of age as subjects, performed a similar study, except that the presentation of positive and negative stimuli for their first group of subjects was 2:2; for their second group it was 2:1. Results, in agreement with Denny and Dunham (1951), revealed that the group which received 2 presentations of the negative stimulus each day made significantly more correct responses on free choice trials than the group which received just 1.

Both of these studies support the position that presentation of the negative stimulus and response to it, at least in the simple discrimination learning situation, is an important factor in learning the correct response. In both experiments, however, the two groups compared had unequal numbers of learning trials. Although it may be concluded that presentation of the negative stimulus provides greater learning than providing no trial at all, a basic condition to investigate would be keeping the number of trials constant, thus varying the ratio of positive to negative stimulus presentations.

Table 12-5   Discrimination Performance on the Test Trials

	One Training Trial Per Cent Correct			Two Training Trials Per Cent Correct		
	Test Trial 1	Test Trial 2	Test Trial 3	Test Trial 1	Test Trial 2	Test Trial 3
Test Stimulus Rewarded	74	95	96	79	93	96
Test Stimulus Nonrewarded	93	92	95	97	98	99

Adapted from Moss and Harlow (1947)

In an early study involving this procedure, Moss and Harlow (1947) trained 80 monkeys on 90 discrimination problems. The Wisconsin General Test Apparatus was used, providing either 1 or 2 training trials in which only a single stimulus was presented. With condition 1, the stimulus was always rewarded but with condition 2, the single stimulus was never rewarded. Following such training, two stimulus objects were presented in order to provide a typical discrimination problem to the subject. These stimuli consisted of a neutral stimulus and the stimulus object used in the training trials. Table 12-5 provides the percentage of correct responses on discrimination test trials 1, 2, and 3 as a function of whether or not the animals were presented with the positive or negative stimulus, and also as a function of whether 1 or 2 training trials were provided. As Table 12-5 reveals, performance on the first trial was clearly superior when the subject did not obtain reward during the training trials. Thus, presentation of the negative stimulus and its subsequent nonreward resulted in the monkeys' rapidly shifting to the other stimulus object during the discrimination test trials.

Perhaps an even clearer demonstration of the influence of the presentation of the negative stimulus is revealed in a subsequent study by Harlow and Hicks (1957). The same procedure as previously described was used on trial 1—only a single stimulus object was presented to the monkey. In one condition the stimulus object was never rewarded, whereas in the other condition it was always rewarded. On trials 2 through 6, the subject was given a discrimination problem in which the object presented on the first trial was used as one of the discriminanda. If this was the positive stimulus on trial 1, it continued to be positive on the following trials; if it was the negative stimulus on trial 1, it continued to be negative. Figure 12-5 presents the percentage of correct responses on trial 2 over the 90 problems provided the animals. It can be noted that presentation of the negative stimulus during the first trial, in contrast to presentation of the positive stimulus, resulted in superior learning.

It seems reasonable to ask if there is a specific ratio of positive to negative stimulus presentations which leads to optimal learning. Fitzwater (1952), Birch (1955), and Lachman (1961) have all conducted studies using rats as subjects, which, at least within certain limits, have attempted to answer this question. However, Fitzwater (1952) was unable to find any differences in learning using 1:7, 1:3, or 1:1 ratios of negative to positive stimulus presentations. Lachman

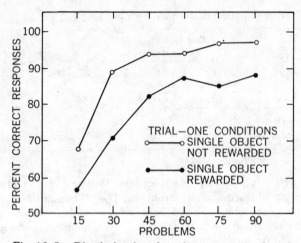

Fig. 12-5. Discrimination learning set curves based on Trial 2 responses following rewarded and unrewarded Trial 1 responses. *Adapted from Harlow and Hicks (1957)*

(1961) found that a 3:1 ratio was superior to that of a 1:1, which in turn was superior to a 1:3. On the other hand, Birch (1955) found that a 1:1 ratio was superior to either a 1:3 or a 3:1. At the present time, we must be content with the knowledge that some presentation of the negative stimulus in the discrimination of simultaneously presented discriminanda results in superior learning, with the specific ratio undoubtedly being a function of the experimental conditions which are used.

Errorless Discrimination Learning

The findings of the experimental studies cited in this last section of the chapter have provided support for the position that presentation of the negative stimulus plays an important role in the learning of a discrimination task.

It is of considerable interest, therefore, to note that some investigators have demonstrated that it is possible for an organism to learn a discrimination task without ever responding to the negative stimulus. In a very early study, Skinner (1938) determined that rats could acquire a brightness discrimination with virtually no responses to the negative stimulus (or S–) if discrimination training was started immediately after a bar pressing response had been conditioned. More recently, Terrace (1963a) has continued this work. Terrace's subjects were pigeons and the operant task he used was a successive discrimination problem in which the positive stimulus is presented for a fixed amount of time, followed by presentation of the negative stimulus for the same duration.

In Terrace's first study, two discrimination task variables were manipulated. The first was the way in which the negative stimulus was introduced; the second was at what time, or when, the presentation took place. Thus, the two negative stimulus presentation procedures consisted of either a (1) constant technique, in which case the negative stimulus (e.g., green key) was presented for the same length of time that the positive stimulus, (e.g., red key) was presented, with the brightness of the two keys being equated, or (2) a progressive technique which consisted of gradually changing the negative stimulus from a dark (nonilluminated) key of 5 seconds' duration to a fully illuminated green key of 3-minutes duration. These progressive changes in duration and intensity of the S– were made in three stages. During the first stage, the key was not illuminated (which did not elicit any responding in the subject), and the duration of the S– was gradually increased from 5 to 30 seconds. During the second stage, the duration of the S– was set back to 5 seconds; however, the intensity of the green key was gradually increased until the S– and S+ were equally bright. During the third stage, the brightness of the green key remained the same as the red, however, the duration of presentation was gradually increased from 5 seconds to 3 minutes.

The second variable Terrace investigated was when such training was instituted. For the early condition, discrimination training began during the first session and after 20 reinforcements had been made to the presentation of the positive stimulus (the negative stimulus was not presented). For the late condition, discrimination training was provided after 4 training sessions. In summary, then, 4 groups of subjects were used: progressive-early; progressive-late; constant-early; constant-late. Twenty-eight discrimination training sessions were provided and results are noted in Fig. 12-6. Here it can be observed that the 3 birds in the progressive-early group acquired the discrimination with virtually no responses being made to the negative stimulus. The range of responses to the negative stimulus for this group was 5 to 9. On the other hand, the range of errors for the progressive-late group was 36 to 760; for the constant-early, it was 191 to 210; and for the constant-late group it was 1922 to 4153. A second experiment in which Terrace made a slight modification in his procedure resulted in similar findings.

In summary, and as Terrace has written, "Both experiments provided clear evidence that an operant discrimination can be acquired with few or no responses to S–, and that the number of responses to S– that do occur during the formation of a discrimination depends upon the manner in which S– is introduced" (p. 23). The necessary conditions for the acquisition of such a discrimination without the occurrence of responses to S– seem to be (1) the introduction of S– immediately after conditioning the response to the stimulus correlated with reinforcement (S+) and (2) an initially large difference between S+ and S– that is progressively reduced to a smaller and constant S+, S– difference.[6]

---

[6] It should be acknowledged that all of Terrace's subjects did not achieve errorless discrimination, and that some of his subjects did respond to the S–. Terrace has indicated that the most commonly observed cause of responding to the S– was when too large a change in the value of the S– was provided. A second factor which encouraged responding to the S– was a sudden reduction in the number of reinforcements provided. Terrace has indicated that, when changing from a continuous reinforcement schedule to a variable interval, there were

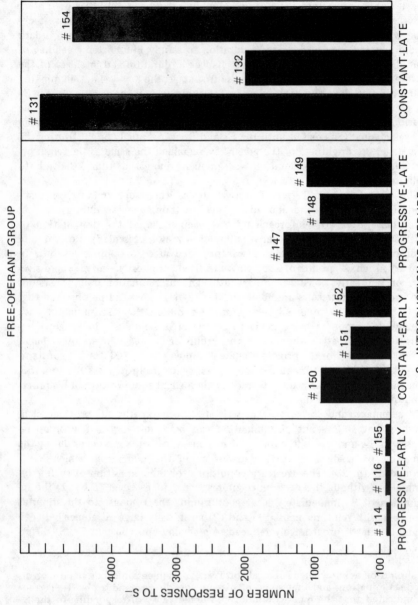

Fig. 12-6. The number of responses to S− made by each bird during all 28 S+ - S− sessions. *Adapted from Terrace (1963a)*

In a subsequent study, Terrace (1963b) showed that an errorless discrimination which was acquired with one pair of stimuli, in this instance, red and green keys, could be transferred to another pair of stimuli, namely, vertical and horizontal lines on the key. In this experiment, a white vertical line was superimposed on the positive green key and a white horizontal line was superimposed on the negative red key. After the pigeons had been given several successive exposures to the two compound stimuli, the intensities of the background stimuli, namely the green and red lights, were then gradually reduced. Eventually, the only difference between the two stimuli was the orientation of the line, with subjects revealing perfect transfer.

We should like to call particular attention to the procedure used by Terrace (1963a) which has been termed fading. It will be recalled that when the progressive procedure was used in presentation of the negative stimulus, only a darkened key was used; on subsequent trials, the brightness of the keys as well as its duration was increased in graduated steps so that, eventually, the brightness of the negative stimulus was the same as the brightness of the positive one. More generally, then, fading is a procedure used in getting the organism to learn a discrimination with early trials, maximizing the difference between (or among) stimuli; on subsequent trials, the stimulus is changed (in order to minimize the difference) but so gradually that the organism's behavior is not disrupted.[7]

In his first study, Terrace used a *fading in* procedure in which the negative stimulus became increasingly more discriminable from its background and less discriminable from the positive stimulus. It is possible, however, to use a *fading out* procedure, in which case the stimulus becomes less discriminable from its background. Thus, in Terrace's (1963b) second series of studies, the original positive stimulus, e.g., green key, gradually became less discriminable from its background, with the brightness of the key being gradually diminished; the other positive stimulus, e.g., vertical line, however, was faded in.

A basic question may be raised regarding the mechanism involved in the pigeon's not responding to the S-. Terrace has indicated that the most important factor appeared to be what the pigeon did following the first presenta-

---

times when the presentation of the S+ did not result in reinforcement. In such instances, the next presentation of the S- elicited a response. Once responding to the S- commenced, Terrace found that future presentations of the S- elicited responding, regardless of how brief the presentation was.

[7] The fading procedure may be looked upon as a kind of transfer of training task; as such, it has relevance to the early work of both Schlosberg and Solomon (1943) and Lawrence (1952). Schlosberg and Solomon (1943) found that rats could learn a simultaneous discrimination between two very similar grey cards with no errors if the discriminative stimuli were gradually changed from black and white cards to the final pair of grey cards. Lawrence suggested that a difficult discrimination may be learned more easily if the subjects are trained first on an easy discrimination and the transition to the difficult task takes place over a series of tasks which become progressively more difficult. In addition to Schlosberg and Solomon and Lawrence and other investigators, e.g., Baker and Osgood (1954), Restle (1955), and House and Zeaman (1960) have obtained findings in keeping with Lawrence's position.

tion of the S-. Terrace's training procedures utilized a dark key as the S-. The initial response to this stimulus was the bird's jerking back its head away from the key. Since the duration of the first S- was very short, with the S+ appearing soon after the pigeon's abrupt head withdrawal, it is possible that the reappearance of the S+ could have served as reinforcement for the withdrawing response made to the S-.

Summary

It is generally recognized that organisms do not respond to all the stimuli that impinge on their receptors. Only a few are selected by the organism for response, and this selection process has been labeled attention. Stimulus-response psychologists have attempted to obtain behavioral referents for this construct and as a result have looked at attention in terms of orienting or preparatory responses that the organism makes prior to responding to one of the cues which make up the discrimination task. One such response has been identified as an observing response and defined as a response that results in exposure to a discriminative stimulus.

There is some inadequacy, however, in assuming that the total attention process can be encompassed only in terms of receptor orientation and/or observing responses. Studies by Reynolds (1961b) and others have demonstrated that pigeons trained originally to respond to a compound stimulus consisting of a white vertical line on a red background, when presented with these stimuli separately, may respond only to the line, effectively ignoring the background (or vice versa). In these studies, it must be assumed that the orienting or preparatory response was the same when the pigeon responded to the background and the line, but for some reason, the bird attended exclusively to just one of these stimuli.

In the examination of attention, or why one attribute is selected rather than another, it has been experimentally demonstrated that innate as well as learning variables make a contribution to the selection process. The role of innate factors points to species differences which apparently result in the selection of some types of stimulation rather than others. The work of the European ethologist has been particularly noteworthy in indicating the nature of stimulus reception differences for different species. But it has been demonstrated that learning also plays a role, as Kamin's (1968) work with "blocking" reveals.

Discrimination learning tasks have been extensively investigated and from these experiments a number of hypotheses have arisen regarding how the discrimination task is learned. One point of view expressed early by Lashley and Krechevsky has been designated as the noncontinuity position, since these experimenters assumed that organisms, in learning discrimination tasks, respond only to the dominant cue with all other cues irrelevant. Moreover, these investigators have held that learning takes place rather rapidly, frequently in a single trial. In contrast to this position is the Hull and Spence continuity hypothesis which assumes that all perceived stimuli become associated with the particular response, and that learning takes place in incremental steps. Early studies using a discrimination reversal task were primarily supportive of the continuity position. Contemporary experiments have now indicated, however, that neither the Lashley-Krechevsky nor Hull-Spence positions can handle all the experimental findings and, as a result, a number of two-factor theories of discrimination learning have been proposed. In brief, these positions posit that in a discrimination learning experiment, the animal must learn to: (1) attend to the relevant stimulus dimension and (2) attach the correct response to stimuli having different values on this dimension. Thus, a rat learning a black-white discrimination problem must first learn that brightness is the relevant cue, and then learn to respond to white and away from black.

A number of investigators have not been concerned with theoretical explanations of discrimination learning but, rather, have directed their attention to an examination of empirical variables. The role of stimulus salience, feature-positive effects, learning to learn, and the relationship between location of the cue and the site of the organism's response, have been investigated.

The contribution that the negative stimulus makes in discrimination learning has also been examined. It has been accepted by most experimenters that, with discrimination learning tasks, it is necessary for the organism on some trials to respond to the negative stimulus, thus building up a hypothesized inhibitory state which is presumed to be an integral part of the discriminatory process. And in a number of experiments using simple discrimination tasks, it has been shown that both rats and monkeys learn a problem more efficiently if they learn something about the negative as well as the positive stimulus. Thus, the presentation to a monkey of a single stimulus, positive or negative, prior to the presentation of that stimulus and another which made up the discrimination task, resulted in superior performance when the single stimulus presented was negative.

Although this type of finding provides support for the position that the presentation of the negative stimulus, at least in the two-stimulus discrimination problem, plays an important role in learning, Terrace (1963a) has demonstrated that it is possible for an organism to learn a discrimination task without ever responding to the negative stimulus. In Terrace's study, two discrimination task variables were manipulated. The first was the way in which the negative stimulus was introduced, while the second was at what time, or when, the presentation of the negative stimulus was provided. Terrace found that when the negative (visual) stimulus was introduced early in the training series, for only a very short time and under very low intensity, but its duration and intensity were gradually increased until length and duration were the same for both negative and positive stimuli, it was possible for his subjects to learn the discrimination task without making errors.

13
The Role of the Stimulus:
II. Stimulus Generalization

The last topic we will consider in examining the role of
the stimulus is stimulus generalization. As noted in
Chapter 4, it was Pavlov's early experimental work from
which the stimulus generalization process was inferred.
The subsequent experiments of Hovland (1937a, 1937b,
1937c, 1937d) were long regarded as classic examples
of stimulus generalization.

Stimulus generalization studies using instrumental
learning tasks with animals as subjects were hindered for
some time since investigators believed that the appropriate selection of the test or generalized stimuli was
dependent on the use of a JND scale.

A break from this position was evident in the studies
of a few investigators such as Grice and Saltz (1950) and
Margolius (1955), who selected generalized stimuli in
terms of their physical characteristics, e.g., size. Grice
and Saltz (1950), for example, trained rats to traverse
a 2-foot runway in order to secure food. At the end of
the runway was a white disk which had a small square

door in its center. Attached to the back of the disk and just below the door was a food dish. One group of animals was first trained to run to a disk which was 20 square centimeters while a second group was trained to run to a 79-square centimeter disk. The training series consisted of providing each animal with 20 reinforced trials per day for three days. Five additional reinforced trials were presented just prior to the beginning of the test for stimulus generalization which consisted of 25 trials without reinforcement. For these test or extinction trials, the 79-square centimeter disk group was divided into five subgroups; the subgroups were extinguished on disks of 79, 63, 50, 32, or 20 square centimeters. The group trained on the 20-square centimeter disk was divided into four subgroups which were extinguished on disks of 20, 32, 50, or 79 square centimeters. The number of responses made during the extinction test series was recorded; a response failure was scored if an animal did not respond within 60 seconds. The mean number of responses made by each of the groups to the varying test stimuli can be observed in Fig. 13-1. It is interesting to note that these generalization curves not only differ from the classic concave gradient obtained by Hovland but differ also from each other.

Methodological Considerations

As we have just noted, one procedure in selecting stimulus values to test for stimulus generalization has been the use of a physical scale; visual and auditory stimuli have often been employed with frequency and intensity differences defining the training as well as test stimuli. The arbitrary selection of units using a physical scale provides no assurance that the stimulus which has been used in the training trials and the test stimuli are discriminable, one from the other, or if they are, whether they are equally so. On the other hand, the development of a psychophysical scale from which to select stimulus values is an extremely laborious task, particularly when animals are used as subjects; moreover, as we have noted in Chapter 4, there is no guarantee that stimuli which are discriminable in a psychophysical study are equally discriminable in a generalization experiment (see Slivinske and Hall, 1960).

As we pointed out in Chapter 4, in the selection of an appropriate response measure, the investigator meets with some difficulty. The choice of response measures obtained during extinction has been questioned since extinction data after the first trial may be influenced by the nonreinforcement procedure. On the other hand, the use of a single extinction trial, which some experimenters consider the most appropriate response measure, means that large numbers of subjects must be tested.

One relatively recent procedure has been to use the free operant with subjects placed on some type of partial reinforcement schedule. Here, the investigator is able to obtain large numbers of responses from each subject so that individual generalization gradients can be obtained. An example of this procedure was demonstrated by Guttman and Kalish (1956) who trained pigeons to peck at an illuminated key in order to receive food. Different groups of subjects were trained under a variable reinforcement schedule to respond to different hues, e.g., 530, 550, 580, and 600 nm (nanometers). Sixty-second-stimulus-on inter-

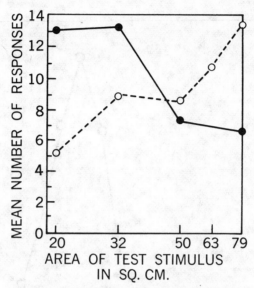

Fig. 13-1. Generalization functions showing mean number of extinction responses
for each test group. The solid line indicates
the group trained on the twenty centimeter
disc; the dotted line indicates the group
trained on the seventy-nine centimeter disc.
Adapted from Grice and Saltz (1950)

vals and 10-second-stimulus-off intervals alternated, with 30 stimulus presentations during each daily session. The stimulus-off or blackout condition was used
to enable the experimenter to change the color of the key from the subsequent
stimulus generalization test. Following training, generalization tests were carried
out using extinction trials. Eleven different hues ranging from 470 nm to 640
nm were randomized within a test series, and 12 different series presented to
each subject. An examination of the number of extinction responses made to
each stimulus presentation provided the basic data from which the stimulus
generalization gradient was plotted. With all CS groups combined, the generalization gradient obtained is indicated in Fig. 13-2. It may be noted that this
gradient bears some similarity to the concave gradient obtained by Hovland
(1937a), although the slope is considerably steeper.

A final methodological consideration has to do with the use of either absolute
or relative generalization measures. If an absolute measure is used, the gradient
is plotted as a function of the absolute number of responses made to the varying
test stimuli provided. Frequently, however, there may be considerable variability
of responding among subjects so that a relative measure is used. In such cases,
the response data are transformed to show the number of responses made to the
test stimuli as a proportion or percentage of the number of responses made to
the CS during the test series.

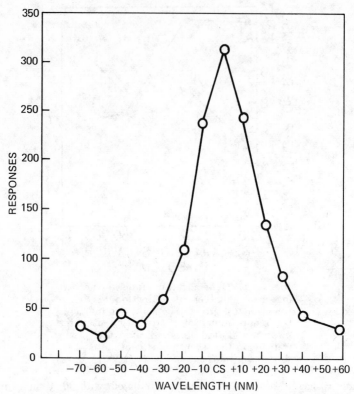

Fig. 13-2. The mean generalization gradient for all CS groups combined. *Adapted from Guttman and Kalish (1956)*

Absolute and relative measures do not necessarily provide the same kind of findings. To illustrate, Nevin (1973) has provided hypothetical stimulus generalization gradients as indicated in Fig. 13-3. Here it can be seen that when the absolute measures are transformed into relative ones, the characteristics of the slopes change markedly. As we have noted in dealing with many methodological problems, there is no correct answer to the problem of whether to use absolute or relative measures. Perhaps the major consideration is whether one of the measures leads to more reliable findings than the other. In this regard, and as Thomas (1970) has pointed out, the use of a relative measure permits the investigator to obtain a group average gradient to which each subject contributes equally. This relative average is perhaps more stable and more representative of individual performance than is an average based on absolute values.

Empirical Considerations

Considerable interest has been generated in theorizing about the nature of stimulus generalization. Many experimenters, however, have been content to

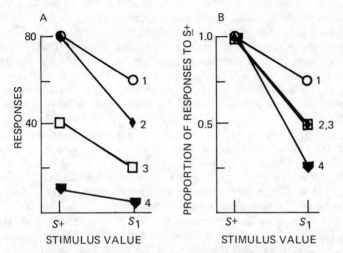

Fig. 13-3. Hypothetical gradients expressed as numbers of responses to $S+$ and a generalization stimulus, S_1, in panel A and transformed into relative gradients in panel B. Note that the transformation leads to quite different conclusions about slope comparisons. *Adapted from Nevin (1973b)*

consider stimulus generalization as an empirical demonstration of transfer of training. That is, a subject demonstrates stimulus generalization if, after he has learned to respond to one stimulus, he responds in a similar way to a second stimulus, the second stimulus bearing some relationship to the first. This approach had led investigators to examine the nature of stimulus generalization as related to (or as a function of) a variety of conditions. We should like to consider what we believe to be the most important of these.

Discriminability of the Stimuli and Discrimination Training

The relationship between generalization and discrimination has been acknowledged by a number of investigators, who have conceptualized discrimination as the reverse side of the generalization coin. If generalization represents responding to stimuli other than the original stimulus to which the subject learned to respond, discrimination, following training to respond to one stimulus, represents the failure to respond to other stimuli. As Brown (1965) has written, "Generalization and discrimination turn out to be nothing more than two different ways of reporting the same experimental results" (p. 11).

From this position, it would be assumed that if stimuli were difficult to discriminate, greater amounts of generalization, e.g., more responding, would take place than if the stimuli were easy to discriminate.

In an early study, Guttman and Kalish (1956) examined this assumption. These investigators noted that for the pigeon (and also for the human) the ease of discriminating two colors separated by a constant frequency is not constant over the spectrum. By an appropriate selection of frequencies (or colors)

Guttman and Kalish reasoned that it should be possible to produce a set of generalization curves in which slopes would reflect the ease or difficulty of the discrimination demanded of the subject. Thus, if two stimuli were difficult to discriminate, the generalization gradient should be relatively flat, but if two other stimuli were easy to discriminate, the gradient should be steep. The experimental procedure which these experimenters used has been described at the beginning of the chapter. Unfortunately, they were unable to find support for their hypothesis: there appeared to be no relationship between the discriminability function and the characteristics of the generalization gradient.

Kalish (1958), a few years later, was able to support the predicted relationship. This experiment was similar to that which has been used in the Guttman and Kalish (1956) study, except that college students rather than pigeons served as subjects. The procedure consisted of presenting one stimulus as a standard and instructing the subject to view it and to try to remember it; this differed from the procedure used with pigeons in that the tendency to respond to the standard stimulus was created by instructions rather than by reinforced trials. Hues of 500, 530, 560, and 580 nm were used as standards, while the test stimuli which were presented consisted of 4 hues above and below the standard, each hue separated by intervals of 10 nm. The test stimulus was presented for a period of 3 seconds followed by a blackout of 5 to 10 seconds which permitted the experimenter to record the response and change the stimulus. Subjects responded by lifting their hand from a telegraph key only if the test stimulus was the same as the standard. The findings revealed that the shape of the stimulus generalization gradients which were obtained conformed to the discriminability curves obtained for other human subjects. Kalish concluded that the findings provided "striking evidence for the supposition that the processes of generalization and discrimination, as generally defined, bear an inverse relationship to each other and that they are fundamentally dependent upon the characteristics of the underlying stimulus continuum" (p. 642). Thomas and Mitchell (1962) have replicated and confirmed Kalish's findings; Ganz (1962), using monkeys as subjects, has also obtained a stimulus generalizatiion gradient which conforms to the monkeys' discriminability function.

With the demonstration that the discriminability of the stimuli plays a basic role in stimulus generalization, it is not surprising that experimenters have been interested in examining how stimulus generalization is related to the type of discrimination training that is provided. In one of the early studies, Hanson (1959) provided 4 groups of pigeons with discrimination training in which a 550 nm hue served as the positive stimulus, with the negative stimulus being either 555, 560, 570, or 590 nm. Such discrimination training was not provided to a control group trained to respond only to the presentation of a 550 nm hue. All groups were trained under a variable interval reinforcement schedule. Following training the subjects were given tests for generalization which utilized 13 hues ranging from 480 nm to 620 nm. A basic finding was that the amount of training required to reach the discrimination criterion (no responding to 5 consecutive presentations of the negative stimulus, but continued responding to the positive stimulus) was related to the size of the difference between the positive and negative stimuli. As might be anticipated, as the difference between

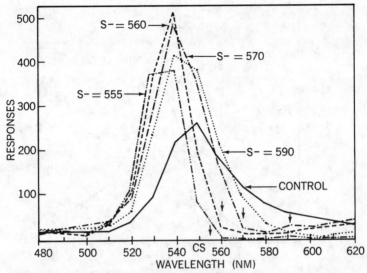

Fig. 13-4. Mean generalization gradients for the control and four discrimination groups, identified by the values of the negative stimulus. Arrows indicate the positions of the negative stimuli. *Adapted from Hanson (1959)*

the two stimuli grew smaller, the amount of training needed to reach the criterion grew larger. The generalization gradients for the varying groups are indicated in Fig. 13-4; it can be noted that the control group, which did not have the benefit of discrimination training, produced a much flatter gradient than the experimental groups.

The discrimination training which Hanson (1959) and other investigators utilized involved reinforcing one stimulus and not reinforcing a second. Hanson (1961) and Thomas and Williams (1963) have extended this area of inquiry by using a three-stimulus discrimination training situation. In Hanson's (1961) study, one group of pigeons was given discrimination training in which a 550 nm hue served as the rewarded stimulus but the presentations of 540 and 560 nm hues were not reinforced. Discrimination training continued until subjects met a criterion of complete suppression of the response to the two nonreinforced stimuli for three successive presentations of each negative stimulus. A control group trained to respond only to the 550 nm hue was not provided with discrimination training. Following training, 12 generalization test sessions were provided which consisted of the random presentation of stimuli ranging from 490 nm to 610 nm. The results, as Fig. 13-5 indicates, showed a relatively symmetrical gradient for both groups of subjects, although responding by the experimental group was essentially restricted to those stimuli bounded by the two nonreinforced stimuli. The use of two nonreinforced stimuli, it may be observed, resulted in a steeper gradient than that produced by a single nonreinforced stimulus.

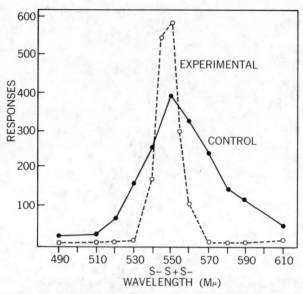

Fig. 13-5. Mean generalization gradients for a control group not given discrimination training and an experimental group trained on a discrimination with the 550 nm stimulus reinforced and the 540 and 560 nm stimuli not reinforced. *Adapted from Hanson (1961)*

What is obvious from these early studies, as well as from many others conducted subsequently, is that discrimination training results in steepening the generalization gradient. Moreover, such training produces what Reynolds (1961a) has called a "contrast" effect—the experimental group's responding to the CS is markedly increased over that of the control group.

Jenkins and Harrison (1960) have examined the influence of discrimination training on generalization gradients when auditory stimuli are employed. In their first experiment, control subjects (pigeons) learned to peck a key on a variable interval reinforcement schedule to the continuous presentation of a 1000 Hz tone. Experimental subjects received discrimination training consisting of some periods in which the 1000 Hz tone was presented and reinforced on a variable interval reinforcement schedule and other training periods during which no tone was presented with responses made at this time not reinforced. Reinforced and nonreinforced periods for the experimental group were presented in a random order; daily training sessions continued until the average rate of responding during the reinforced sessions was at least 4 times greater than that obtained during nonreinforced periods. In testing for generalization, eight test stimuli were presented which consisted of 7 tones approximately equally spaced along a logarithmic scale of frequency (300, 450, 670, 1000, 1500, 2250, 3500 Hz) and a nontone presentation. The percentage of responses made to each test stimulus for the control subjects is indicated in Fig. 13-6 and the generalization

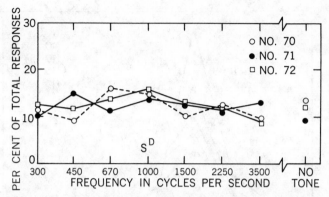

Fig. 13-6. Generalization gradients following nondifferential training with a 1,000 Hz tone as the reinforced stimulus. *Adapted from Jenkins and Harrison (1960)*

gradients for the 5 subjects who were given discrimination training are shown in Figure 13-7.

The flat gradient produced by the control subjects responding to auditory stimuli is in contrast to the gradients obtained by a nondiscrimination training procedure when visual stimuli are used. (To illustrate, note the generalization gradient for the control group in Fig. 13-6.) In attempting to account for variability in slopes, Jenkins and Harrison have written, "Since the training procedures appear to be the same in all important respects it may be concluded that the difference lies in the use of a visual—as compared with an auditory—stimulus. It does not appear that a lack of physiological capacity to detect or to make discriminations among auditory stimuli can account for the contrast in the results obtained with visual and with auditory stimuli" (p. 252).

A different explanation has been offered by Heinemann and Rudolph (1963), who propose that when the visual stimulus is presented on the response key, for pigeons trained in a Skinner box, ". . . so-called nondifferential training methods actually do involve some differential training, at least in the sense of training to discriminate between the presence and absence of the stimulus." They have assumed that ". . . such differential training could not occur if the visual stimulus completely surrounded the S . . . . Furthermore, it would seem that the smaller the area of the stimulus, the smaller would be the likelihood of its being present on the S's retinas during the occurrence of any given unreinforced sequence of behavior. Hence, the amount of differential training that occurs should be related to the geometric size of the stimulus" (p. 654).

Their experiment consisted of training pigeons to peck at a response key in the presence of a stimulus of 10.1 ft. L.[1] One stimulus area was quite large—a

[1] A ft. L. (foot Lambert) is a measure of luminance; brightness is its psychological counterpart, although it should be recognized that brightness is not directly related to or completely dependent upon the amount of luminance. (Brightness is influenced by contrast effects, exposure time, as well as other conditions, in addition to luminance.)

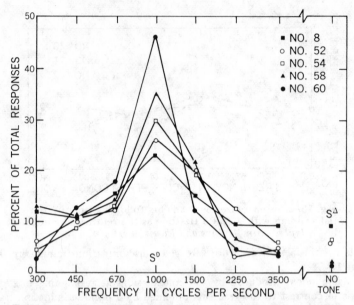

Fig. 13-7. Generalization gradients following discrimination training in which a 1,000 Hz tone served as the reinforced stimulus and no tone was nonreinforced. *Adapted from Jenkins and Harrison (1960)*

12″ x 16″ response panel that covered the entire end of the apparatus. This stimulus area, the authors believed, should result in nondifferential training. A middle-sized stimulus was circular with an outer diameter of 5¼″, while the smallest stimulus, also circular, had an outer diameter of 1¾″. When either the middle-sized stimulus or the small one was used, the remainder of the response panel was covered by black cardboard. Following training during which the subjects were placed on a variable interval schedule and had reached a stable level of responding, generalization tests using stimuli of 1.5, 10.1, or 15.4 ft. L. were provided. Fig. 13-8 reveals the percentage of responses made to each stimulus by each group of subjects. These findings clearly support the authors' position that the size of the stimulus is related to the type of generalization gradient obtained, and are in keeping with their hypothesis that differences in the slopes of the visual and auditory gradients arise from differences in the characteristics of the discriminative training provided during the training sessions.

Interdimensional, Intradimensional, and Extradimensional Discrimination Training

An analysis of studies which have examined the influence of discrimination training on stimulus generalization reveals that two types of training procedures have been used. The first has been to use no formal discrimination training—

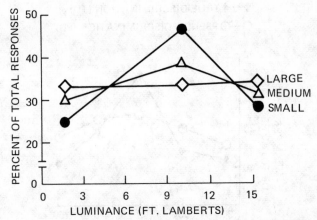

Fig. 13-8. Generalization gradients obtained after training with large, medium, and small stimuli of 10.1 ft.-L.
Adapted from Heinemann and Rudolph (1963)

an S– has not been employed. The second has been to use a discriminative
training procedure, with the S+ and S– represented by the same stimulus dimension. Switalski, Lyons, and Thomas (1966) and Thomas (1970) have described
these training procedures as (1) interdimensional and (2) intradimensional
training, respectively. These investigators have also identified a third type of
training procedure as extradimensional. Here, the S+ and S– are represented on
the same stimulus dimension but generalization testing is carried out along
another stimulus dimension present during the original training, or possibly,
introduced at a later time. An example would be a discrimination training
procedure in which the positive stimulus was a red key, the negative stimulus a
green key, and the extradimensional stimulus, an identical tone to be presented
with both the positive and negative stimuli. Subsequent testing for generalization
would take place along the tone dimension. The three types of discrimination
training and generalization testing are indicated in Table 13-1.

In keeping with the findings of interdimensional training procedures, the results of studies using an extradimensional training procedure support the posi-

Table 13-1   Types of Discrimination Training Used in Testing for
Stimulus Generalization

		Discrimination Training	Generalization Testing
Intradimensional	S+	Hue_1	Hue
	S–	Hue_2	
Interdimensional	S+	Tone	Tone
	S–	Silence	
Extradimensional	S+	$Hue_1 + Tone_1$	Tone
	S–	$Hue_2 + Tone_1$	

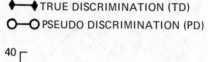

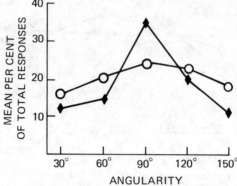

Fig. 13-9. Relative generalization gradients of true discrimination (TD) and pseudo discrimination (PD) groups trained along wavelength and tested along angularity dimensions. *Adapted from Thomas, Freeman, Svinicki, Burr, and Lyons (1970)*

tion that discrimination training results in sharpening the generalization gradient. To illustrate, we shall summarize the findings of two experiments, from a series of five, performed by Thomas, Freeman, Svinicki, Burr, and Lyons (1970). In one experiment (Experiment 3), pigeons maintained at 70 to 75 percent of their normal body weight were trained to respond to a key illuminated by a 90° white line on a 555 nm background, while the negative stimulus was the same line on a 538 nm background. Subjects in a true discrimination group were reinforced for responding to the positive stimulus and not reinforced for responding to the negative stimulus. A pseudodiscrimination group, however, was provided nondifferential reinforcement with the same two stimuli. Here, reinforcement was provided on a variable interval schedule for responses to either stimulus.

Following an extended training session, generalization tests along the angularity dimension were provided. The test stimuli were 5 different line angles, 30°, 60°, 90°, 120°, and 150°, all presented with the background removed. These stimuli were randomized within each series and 12 different series presented. The results are shown in Fig. 13-9 and reveal the flattened gradient for the pseudodiscrimination group—the group which did not receive discrimination training. A second experiment replicating the first, except that the training dimension was angularity and the test dimension wave length, again demonstrated that true discrimination training produced a sharper gradient, although as Fig. 13-10 reveals, the difference between the two groups is not as striking as that obtained in the first experiment. In summary, even though discrimination training is not provided on one stimulus dimension, such training provided on another dimension will result in superior discriminative control as indicated in the generalization test.

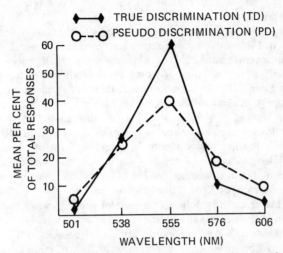

Fig. 13-10. Relative generalization gradients of true discrimination (TD) and pseudo discrimination (PD) groups trained along angularity and tested along wavelength dimensions. *Adapted from Thomas, Freeman, Svinicki, Burr, and Lyons (1970)*

The Phenomenon of Peak Shift

The discerning reader will note that in some generalization gradients obtained, and in particular where discrimination training has been provided, maximum responding during the generalization test is not to the S+. Rather, there is a shift in maximum responding from the S+ in a direction away from the S-. A good example is found in Hanson's (1959) experiment, described earlier, the results of which are found in Fig. 13-4. Here it may be noted that maximum responding during the generalization test is not to the 550 nm hue (S+), but is displaced to the 540 nm test stimulus.

A number of investigators have been interested in examining those variables which influence peak shift. The reader can refer to Purtle's (1973) review for a delineation of the conditions that were investigated. Briefly, it has been shown that the presence of peak shift is related to the kind of training procedure provided, the stimulus dimension utilized, the test stimulus separation, as well as the S+, S- separation. The peak shift can be eliminated by using an errorless discrimination training procedure, by providing extended discrimination training, and by administering certain drugs.

The Role of Extraexperimental Experience

A variable which appears to be related to discrimination training is the organism's extraexperimental experience. It is possible that the normal living experiences the organism is exposed to outside the experimental situation may provide some type of discrimination training which is reflected on tests for stimulus generalization.

Peterson's (1962) study was an early attempt to examine the contribution of this variable. In this study, 4 ducklings were raised in white-walled cages illuminated by a monochromatic light of 589 nm. As a result, these subjects were exposed to only a narrow range of visual stimulation. Two other ducklings were raised in a regular laboratory environment in which typical tungsten filament lamps were used to illuminate the cages. All ducklings were deprived of water for 22 hours and trained to peck at a single key illuminated by a 589 nm visual stimulus. Following 15 conditioning sessions in which a variable interval schedule was utilized, a test for stimulus generalization was conducted with 8 different wavelengths ranging from 490 nm to 650 nm illuminating the pecking key. Results for the test sessions in Fig. 13-11 show that for the 4 ducklings raised in monochromatic light a flat gradient best describes the findings. On the other hand, the frequently found decremental gradient was obtained for the 2 subjects raised in the normal environment.

Although Peterson's findings would appear to coincide with most intuitive predictions regarding the role of experience (or lack of it) in the discrimination process, a number of subsequent investigators have been unable to confirm his results. In one of these, Tracy (1970) also used ducklings as subjects and employed an experimental procedure similar to Peterson's (1962). In his first experiment, Tracy reported findings similar to those obtained by Peterson in that the generalization gradients of the subjects reared in normal white light were steeper than the gradients obtained with ducklings raised in monochromatic light. But there was also a basic difference in findings; in Tracy's experiment, nonzero sloped gradients with maximal responding at the value of the wavelength used in training (589 nm) were obtained for almost half of the experimental subjects. Of greater importance, however, was Tracy's discovery that ducklings preferred to peck at "green" wavelengths even though such responding was not reinforced (Experiment 2). Such preferential responding would, of course, seriously distort any generalization gradient obtained. As Tracy has written, "The demonstration of a 'green' preference in ducklings, strongly suggests the use of a different organism in investigations of the conditions necessary and sufficient for the development of stimulus control" (p. 178). It also suggests that experimenters must keep in mind the type of organism they are working with and be alert to the presence of innate behaviors which can seriously influence some of the learned responses they are examining.

Experimenters using organisms other than ducklings have also been unable to obtain a flat gradient for subjects raised in a restricted visual environment. Rudolph, Honig, and Gerry (1969), using quail and chickens as subjects, were unable to replicate Peterson's findings when these subjects were raised in either restricted spectral green, restricted spectral red, monochromatic sodium light, or darkness. During the test for generalization, experimental subjects raised with exposure to one of these very restricted types of visual stimulation revealed the largest amount of responding to the visual stimulus which had been used during the training period—flat gradients were not obtained.

Finally, in a study by Ganz and Riesen (1962), one group of infant monkeys

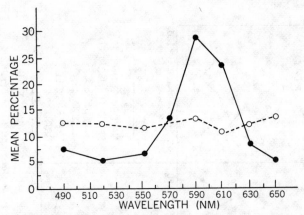

Fig. 13-11. Stimulus generalization gradients obtained for the birds raised in a monochromatic environment (broken line) and for the birds raised in an environment whose chromaticity was not controlled (solid line). *Adapted from Peterson (1962)*

was raised in total darkness while a second group was raised in a normally illuminated and visually patterned environment. At ten weeks of age, the experienced subjects joined the naive group in the darkroom environment. Both groups were then trained to make a key press response during the presentation of one monochromatic stimulus which was reinforced by a sucrose solution, and not to respond during a 15-second blackout interval. During such training, the left eye of each subject was covered by a black occluder so that the stimulus exposure was always monocular.

Following training, generalization tests were administered over seven days, with each test period consisting of the presentation of 7 monochromatic hues, one of which was the previously reinforced stimulus. Responses were not reinforced. The number of key presses made to the CS and generalized stimuli over the seven-day test period is noted in Fig. 13-12. The group reared in darkness provides a somewhat flatter gradient than the experienced group for the first day of testing—a finding in keeping with that obtained by Peterson (1962). However, the results for the next six days are in contrast to those of Peterson. Here it can be seen that the naive group's responses produce a typical decremental gradient while the experienced group's responses are almost flat—certainly less steep than that obtained by the naive group.

Equally important, however, is the wide diversity of generalization gradients obtained from individual subjects. See Fig. 13-13.

The influence of stimulus experience on the type of generalization gradient remains to be established. Flat gradients following the rearing of an organism in a restricted stimulus environment have not generally been obtained. Investigators may argue, as Heinemann and Rudolph (1963) have, that some type of discrimination learning takes place even though a nondifferential training procedure is

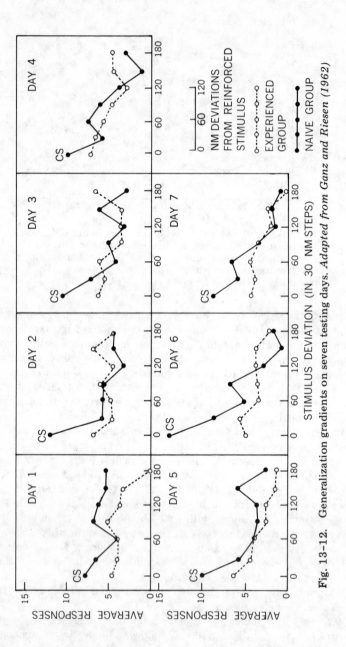

Fig. 13-12. Generalization gradients on seven testing days. *Adapted from Ganz and Riesen (1962)*

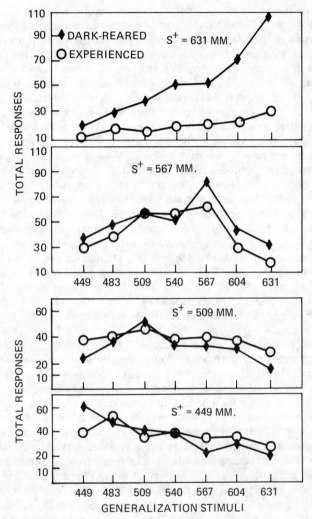

Fig. 13-13. Individual generalization gradients in hue-naive and hue-experienced *Ss. Adapted from Ganz and Riesen (1962)*

used; but more research in the area is needed. Any search for a general principle is discouraging, however, after noting the individual generalization gradients obtained by Ganz and Riesen (1962).

Time of Testing

Another variable which has interested investigators of stimulus generalization is the time of testing; more specifically, the amount of time which is placed between the training period and the test for stimulus generalization, or the amount of time interpolated between 2 stimulus generalization tests. In an early study by Perkins and Weyant (1958), four groups of rats were trained to traverse a black (or white) runway in order to secure food. Eighty-six trials spaced over a 12-day training session were provided, with intermittent reinforcement given during the latter stages of training. Following such training, all animals received a total of 18 test trials on two successive days. For two groups of subjects, 8 such trials were provided 60 seconds immediately following the last training trial; 10 additional trials were given 24 hours later. One of these groups was tested on the same runway over which the training trials had been run while the other group was administered test trials on a different runway. For the other two groups, 8 test trials were provided seven days following the end of training followed by 10 additional trials 24 hours later. As with the immediate testing situation, one group of subjects was tested on the same runway over which it had its training trials, while the second group was given test trials on a runway over which it had not received training. In brief, then, four experimental groups of subjects were used: same runway—immediate testing, different runway—immediate testing, same runway—delayed testing, different runway—delayed testing. Using running speed for the first 8 test trials as a response measure, results are indicated in Fig. 13-14. A much flatter gradient can be noted for the delayed testing group than for the groups provided immediate testing. McAllister and McAllister (1963), using an avoidance learning task, also found a flatter generalization gradient when a delayed testing procedure was used.

Finally, a similar result was obtained by Thomas and Lopez (1962) using pigeons in a free operant learning situation. In this study, three groups of pigeons were trained to peck a key illuminated by a 550 nm hue. After ten days of variable interval reinforcement training, the subjects were divided into three groups matched for rate of responding. Group 1 was tested for generalization 1 minute following the completion of training; group 2 was tested 1 day after the completion of training, while group 3 was tested one week later. Generalization testing consisted of presenting 11 different stimuli—500 nm to 600 nm in 10 nm steps—randomized within a series, with 8 different series provided each subject (the 550 nm training stimulus was not presented). A second generalization test was administered to each subject 24 hours after the first test with no training intervening between the two testing periods. The results indicated that a much flatter gradient was obtained for the groups tested either one day or one week following training, in contrast to the relatively steep gradient obtained for the group given the test immediately following training. Since there was no difference between the gradients obtained by the one-day and the one-week groups, the authors concluded that the process contributing to the flattening of the gradient appears to be complete within 24 hours.[2]

---

[2] All investigators have not been able to obtain flatter gradients as a result of delayed testing. Thomas, Ost, and Thomas (1960), using pigeons in a free operant learning task examined generalization gradients one, seven, or 21 days following training. No difference in the shape of the generalization gradient was obtained as a function of when the generalization test was made. The Thomas, Ost, and Thomas (1960) findings are in keeping with Thomas and Lopez's

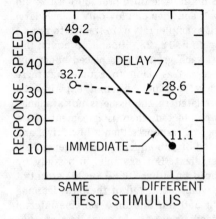

Fig. 13-14. Median response speed (100/response time in seconds) on the first eight test trials for each condition. *Adapted from Perkins and Weyant (1958)*

One explanation for the flatter generalization gradients obtained would be that the original as well as the generalized stimuli would be more discriminable immediately following the training session than after a delay. As a result, the delayed condition should produce less differential responding which in turn should result in a flatter gradient. As McAllister and McAllister (1963) have pointed out, however, this explanation is circular in the absence of independent evidence of a postulated difference in discriminability.

Motivational Variables

We should like to conclude this section by examining how motivational variables have been found to influence stimulus generalization. There has been a long tradition of examining the relationship of these variables to learning; the manipulation of drive and reward and their influence on generalized responding has interested a number of experimenters.

It is generally accepted that depriving an animal of food or water for a specified length of time or keeping it at a reduced percentage of its normal body weight are appropriate procedures for manipulating the organism's drive state. There is a methodological problem, however, concerned with how the drive should be manipulated in the actual experiment. A number of different procedures have been used, three of them employed most frequently. It is possible, as Thomas and King (1959) and Thomas (1962) have done, to provide subjects with different levels of drive at the beginning of training and maintain these differences throughout the training period as well as during the subsequent tests for generalization. A second often used procedure is to place all subjects on the same drive level during training and then vary drive level during testing. For example, Newman and Grice (1965) placed their subjects on an intermediate level of deprivation (23½ hours) during the training period. This group was then divided into two subgroups with one group given test trials under 12 hours of

_____

(1962) speculation that the process contributing to the flattening of the gradient is complete within 24 hours.

deprivation and the other group under 48 hours. The third procedure is to train subjects under a variety of deprivation levels and then employ only a single level for testing. In a study by Coate (1964), for example, rats were trained to press a bar under a variety of deprivation levels, e.g., 5, 12, 23, 40, and 48 hours; this group was then divided into 5 subgroups, each group being placed under one deprivation level and given test trials. It seems reasonable to assume that these varying methods of manipulating drive level produce different experimental findings, although experimental evidence related to this issue is not available.

However, with the many experiments conducted, there is agreement that a high drive level results in a greater number of responses than a low drive, and that this higher level of responding, reflected on subsequent tests for generalization, results in a steeper generalization gradient. For example, in a study by Kalish and Haber (1965) pigeons were placed on either 70, 80, or 90 percent of their normal weight.[3] Following training which consisted of the birds learning to peck at a plastic disk illuminated by a 550 nm hue on a variable interval schedule, generalization tests were provided using six different test stimuli: 550, 540, 530, 520, 510, and 490 nm. These stimuli were randomized within a series, with 12 different random series presented to each subject. The same drive conditions were maintained between training and testing. The generalization curves, as measured in terms of mean number of responses, an absolute measure of responding, are indicated in Fig. 13-15. Here it may be noted that the 70 percent group revealed many more responses than either the 80 percent or 90 percent groups. Newman and Grice (1965) have obtained similar findings when rats were used in an instrumental learning task.

As we pointed out earlier, it is also possible to obtain relative measures of generalized responding although in many instances, investigators have not analyzed their data this way. There is at least the suggestion from Coate (1964) that when relative measures are plotted, deprivation level does not have any influence on either the height or the slope of the gradient. In this study, rats learned to press a lever for water under a variable interval reinforcement schedule. Deprivation intervals of 5, 12, 23, 40, and 48 hours were used, each animal being trained under all deprivation levels but then provided the generalization test under only a single level. Thus, by the end of training, all subjects had had similar experience with the various deprivation levels. The stimulus consisted of a light display comprised of a horizontal array of 6 pairs of miniature lamps. The pair of stimulus lights used in training were placed immediately above the lever; the 5 other pairs were located progressively more distant from the training pair. Although results indicate that the mean number of total responses was highest for the groups under the two highest levels of deprivation, the generalization gradient using a relative measure revealed no differences among the groups. See Fig. 13-16.

The second motivational variable, reward, has been examined by manipulating the number of reinforcements and the number of training sessions. Since the strength of original responding has generally been found to be a function of

---

[3] The 80 percent group had been run in a previous study (Haber and Kalish, 1963).

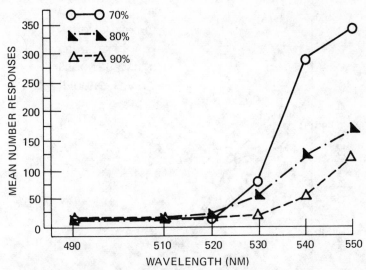

Fig. 13-15. Mean generalization gradients for three deprivation groups. *Adapted from Haber and Kalish (1963)*

these variables, generalization tests using absolute measures of responding invariably result in the finding that greater numbers of generalized responses occur when the reinforcement variable increases. For example, in an instrumental learning study by Margolius (1955), four groups of rats were trained to run down a 2-foot runway and open a door placed in the center of a white circle 79 square centimeters in area. These groups received either 4, 16, 64, or 104 reinforced trials to the training stimulus. Following training, each group was divided into five subgroups receiving 30 nonreinforced trials to either the 79 cm. training circle or to test circles of 63, 50, 32, or 20 square cm. Test performance was evaluated in terms of (1) the latency of responding over the first 3 trials, (2) the total number of responses made, and (3) the number of responses made within a 60-second period. (The latter measure was obtained by adding the latency of each succeeding response until a total of 60 seconds was reached.) Fig. 13-17 depicts a group of curves obtained when the median latency for the first 3 test trials was used as a response measure.

In an operant study, Hearst and Koresko (1968) trained pigeons on a variable interval schedule to peck the key when a vertical line was projected on it. One day of training consisted of a 50-minute session and subjects were provided either 2, 4, 7, or 14 days of training. Following training, tests for stimulus generalization were provided. Each of 8 orientations of the stimulus line, namely 0°, 22.5°, 45°, 67.5°, 90°, 112.5°, 135°, or 157.5°, were used. Ten blocks of stimulus presentation, each block consisting of the 8 different stimuli presented in a randomized order, were provided. Two experiments were run, one utilizing White Carneaux birds and the other, White King. Fig. 13-18 reveals the gradients of absolute generalization for the two different species of birds. In keeping with Margolius's (1955) finding, the number of responses is a function of the number

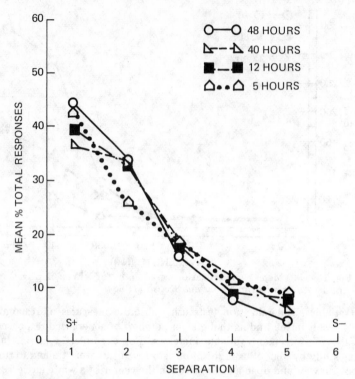

Fig. 13-16. Postdiscrimination relative stimulus generalization as a function of the water deprivation interval at the time of testing (Test II). *Adapted from Coate (1964)*

of training days; in addition, the generalization curve is much steeper for the 7- and 14-day groups.

Both of these investigators using relative measures of responding obtained similar findings; generalized responding was greater for the larger number of reinforcements or the greater number of training days.

Generalization of Inhibition

It will be recalled that in Chapter 4 we discussed the generalization of inhibition for classically conditioned responses. It is not surprising that a number of investigators have demonstrated this phenomenon with instrumental and operant learning tasks as well. In a study by Kling (1952), an instrumental response task similar to that employed by Grice and Saltz (1950) was used. In Kling's study, rats were trained to obtain food pellets by opening a small door placed in the center of a circle at the end of a runway. Each subject was given training on two circles of varying areas. Eight groups were used, each group trained on one of the following area combinations: 79-20, 79-32, 79-50, 79-79, 20-79, 20-50, 20-32, or 20-20. Each animal was provided 45 reinforced trials to each circle.

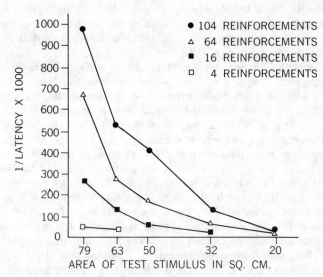

Fig. 13-17. Generalization gradients based upon the median latency of the first three test trials as a function of stimulus area and training trials. *Adapted from Margolius (1955)*

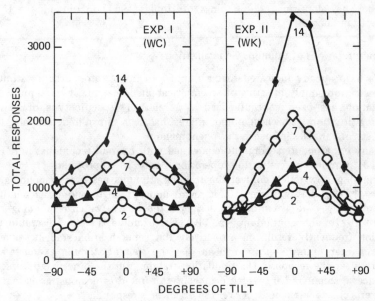

Fig. 13-18. Gradients of absolute generalization for groups receiving 2, 4, 7, or 14 days of VI training. The training stimulus for all *S*s was a vertical line [0°] on the response key. White Carneaux [WC] birds are shown on the left, White King [WK] on the right.) *Adapted from Hearst and Koresko (1968)*

The response to the first circle was then extinguished. Following this, generalization of extinction was examined by presenting the second circle of the training pair. Generalization gradients plotted in terms of median latencies of the first response are indicated in Fig. 13–19.

Honig (1961) has demonstrated a similar effect using the operant task. Three groups of pigeons, maintained at 80 percent of their free-feeding weight and placed on a variable interval reinforcement schedule, were trained to peck at a key containing 13 different-colored stimuli ranging from 510 nm to 630 nm. Following training in which all of the stimuli were equally reinforced, two experimental groups of subjects had their responses to the 570 nm stimulus extinguished; one group was given just 1 extinction session; the second group was given 2 such sessions. A control group was not provided extinction trials. Generalization testing was then instituted using a stimulus presentation procedure similar to that used in the original training, except that reinforcement was not provided. Results for the three groups, shown in Fig. 13–20, not only indicate the level of responding to each of the stimuli following training but also reveal generalization obtained during the first day of testing. It may be noted that for the two experimental groups, a reasonably orderly gradient was obtained with the smallest number of responses being made to the 570 nm stimulus, with increasing number of responses being made to stimuli as they became progressively more distant from the 570 nm stimulus. Dubin and Levis's (1973) recent examination of the generalization of extinction gradients using tones as the discriminative stimuli and a bar pressing response with rats as subjects, has confirmed the findings of Honig (1961) in obtaining a U- or V-shaped gradient.

Interpretations of Stimulus Generalization

We have already indicated that a number of investigators describe stimulus generalization simply in terms of an empirical phenomenon. Thus, stimulus generalization has been conceptualized as a relatively specific type of transfer training situation; as we have noted, interest has been shown in determining how a variety of variables influence this phenomenon.

Many experimenters primarily concerned with operant techniques have considered stimulus generalization operations only as a procedure to use for determining how much control the training stimulus has over responding. As Nevin (1973b) has written, "... it seems appropriate to adopt the relatively neutral term, *stimulus control*, to designate the way in which responding is related to a stimulus continuum" (p. 119). For example, a lack of discrimination training frequently results in a relatively flat generalization gradient; operant experimenters interpret this to mean that the training stimulus exercises little control over the response. Discrimination training, on the other hand, typically produces a steep gradient which has been interpreted as demonstrating that the S+ exerts considerable control over the organism's responding.

This point of view is held by Thomas (1970) who believes that responding in the stimulus generalization test can reveal information about the attentional process in the organism. He has proposed that discrimination training produces a

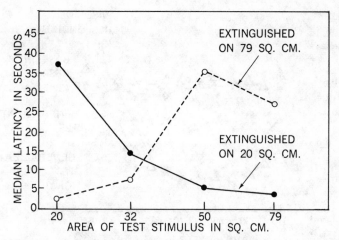

Fig. 13-19. Generalization functions, showing median latency to the first response for each group on the test trials. Note that the greater the latency, the weaker the response. *Adapted from Kling (1952)*

state of general attentiveness in the organism which is manifested when test stimuli are presented; the animal's increased sensitivity to stimulus differences results in a steep generalization gradient. On the other hand, when a nondifferential training procedure is utilized, such attentiveness is not present; control is split between or among a number of stimuli. This lack of control or decreased sensitivity results in a much flatter gradient during generalization tests.

One theoretical interpretation, proposed by Lashley and Wade (1946), has become known as a "failure of discrimination" hypothesis; a somewhat similar proposal being subsequently presented by Prokasy and Hall (1963). Lashley and Wade wrote that, "stimulus generalization is generalization only in the sense of failure to note distinguishing characteristics of the stimulus or to associate them with the conditioned reaction" (p. 81).

A further point these investigators have made is that the gradient of stimulus generalization is a product of the test period and develops as a result of directing the subject's attention to the relevant stimulus dimension. No decremental generalization gradient will be noted unless the CS is contrasted with a generalized stimulus so that the relevant stimulus dimension is made manifest to the subject.

Many investigators, however, have adopted the position of Hull (1943) who provided another explanation for stimulus generalization—that stimulus generalization is a basic organismic process arising from the reinforcement procedure. The generalization process was given particular prominence in resolving what Hull called the "stimulus learning" and "stimulus evocation" paradoxes.

A basic assumption of the Hullian system was the existence of a bond or association established between a very specific stimulus and a response. Hull (1943) commented, however, that the "flux of the world to which organisms must adapt has infinite variety, and therefore stimuli, especially conditioned stimuli,

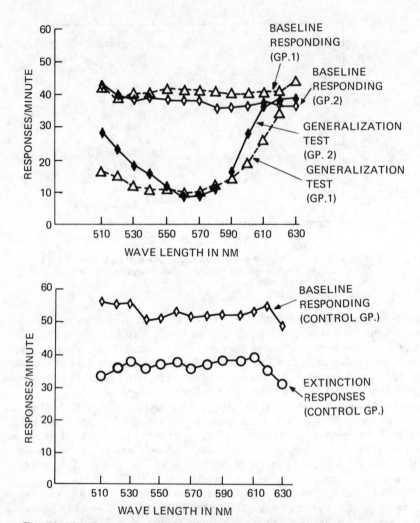

Fig. 13-20. Response rates for the two experimental and one control group at the end of training and for generalization or extinction. *Adapted from Figures 1, 2, and 3, Honing (1961)*

are never exactly repeated. . . . Since the stimuli are not exactly repeated, how can more than one reinforcement occur?" (p. 194-195). This, then, was the stimulus learning paradox. It might be assumed that it would be possible for a single reinforcement to produce an association of maximum strength, but the Hullian system considered associative strength a product of the number of reinforcements that the organism received. But even if such a possibility did exist, a second question could be raised, how could such a stimulus ever again evoke a response, since the exact stimulus to which the response had been condi-

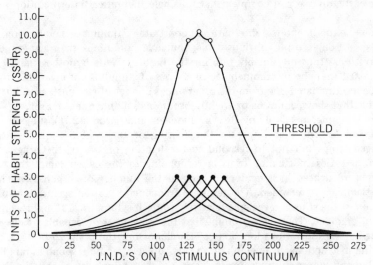

Fig. 13-21. Graph showing how the subthreshold primary stimulus generalization gradients from five distinct points on a stimulus continuum theoretically may summate to superthreshold values not only at the points of reinforcement but at neighboring points which have not been reinforced at all. Solid circles represent the results of single reinforcements; hollow circles represent the results of summation. The reaction threshold is arbitrarily taken at five. *Adapted from Hull (1943)*

tioned would never again be encountered? This was the stimulus evocation paradox.

By using the stimulus generalization process, Hull was able to answer both questions. A response involved in the original learning situation became attached to a considerable zone of stimuli other than, but adjacent to, the stimulus present in the original learning. Thus, learning or habit strength was built up between these generalized stimuli and the organism's response. Moreover, such habit strength summated on order to produce a response of greater than threshold value. Fig. 13-21 reveals how Hull (1943) conceptualized the summation of subthreshold primary stimulus generalization gradients in order to produce an overt response.

A second point of interest in the Hullian system was the distinction between primary and secondary stimulus generalization. In primary stimulus generalization, it was assumed that the similarity dimension of the stimulus was a product of the innate characteristics of the organism; in secondary generalization it was assumed that the similarity dimension had been acquired through previous learning.

Although controversy continues to arise from time to time concerning the relative merits of the Lashley–Wade and Hullian positions, as well as other theoretical interpretations of stimulus generalization, e.g., Razran (1949), Mednick, and Freedman (1960), the experimental findings obtained have been sufficiently diverse and complex that no single theoretical interpretation seems adequate.

Some experimenters who have demonstrated stimulus generalization gradients, although using obviously discriminable stimuli in their experimental observations (thus presumably refuting the Lashley–Wade hypothesis), have not recognized that the discriminability of a series of stimuli is not invariant; stimuli can be discriminated one from the other under one set of circumstances, but it is possible that they cannot be or are not discriminated under another set.

For example, in a study by Brown, Bilodeau, and Baron (1951), subjects were instructed to lift their finger to the lighting of the center 1 of 7 spatially arranged lamps but not to respond to the lighting of any of the others. Following a series of training trials in responding to the center lamp, the other lamps were lighted in a random order and the number of responses made to these lamps was recorded. The response frequencies plotted against the spatial position of the stimuli revealed a relatively smooth symmetrical stimulus generalization gradient. There is no doubt that the subjects were capable of discriminating among the various locations of the lamps but the point to be stressed is that the instructions given emphasized that subjects should respond as rapidly as possible and ignore false responses. Thus, the discriminability of the stimuli was a function of the experimental situation. Had the instructions emphasized accuracy, as well as unlimited time to respond, it is highly probable that no "gradient" would have been obtained. In fact, the investigators acknowledged such a position by stating, "If the subjects had been instructed to take plenty of time in responding . . . it is relatively certain that no false responses would have been observed" (p. 59).

At the same time, it is difficult to accept the position that the decremental stimulus generalization gradients obtained from organisms raised in restricted environments prior to training and testing, could have arisen from the subjects' observing the relevant dimension of the training stimulus and comparing it with the generalized stimuli presented during the subsequent testing period. In Ganz and Riesen's (1962) study in which infant monkeys were reared in darkness, following training with a single stimulus, decremental gradients were obtained on the second day of testing. (Responses were not reinforced during any of the testing periods.) They have concluded that it is not clear how the first testing session, in which flat gradients were obtained but no responses reinforced, could have shaped a decremental gradient, concluding that ". . . generalization in some cases simply follows automatically from the physiological properties of the receptor system involved and does not require previous experience" (p. 97).

Summary

Although Pavlov's experimental work with the classically conditioned response provided a foundation for further investigation of stimulus generalization, many contemporary investigators have used instrumental learning tasks to examine the construct. Perhaps the most frequently used of these is the operant task in which subjects are pigeons trained to peck an illuminated key for food, and following training, provided a stimulus generalization test.

The relationship between discrimination and generalization has been acknowledged by most investigators: discrimination is regarded as the reverse side of the generalization coin. Such a position leads to the assumption that if the S+ and the test stimuli (or two test stimuli) are difficult to discriminate, greater amounts of generalization will be obtained than if these stimuli are easy to discriminate. Kalish (1958), as well as other investigators, have experimentally demonstrated such to be the case.

Interest in the discrimination process has led a number of experimenters to examine the influence of discrimination training on generalization gradients. Following Switalski, Lyons, and Thomas (1966), three types of discrimination training have been designated: (1) intradimensional training, (2) interdimensional training, and (3) extradimensional training. With intradimensional training, the S+ and S- are on the same dimension which is also the dimension manipulated during the generalization test. In interdimensional training, the S+ lies along the generalization test dimension but the S- is the absence of a stimulus. Finally, with extradimensional training, the S+ and S- lie on the same dimension but generalization testing is carried out along another stimulus dimension which was present during the original training. The experimental findings obtained with all discrimination training procedures reveal that the generalization gradient is sharpened as a function of such training.

One question which arises is whether the organism's experience plays some role in the type of stimulus generalization gradient that is obtained. One way to manipulate that experience is to raise the experimental subjects in the dark, or to rear them in monochromatic light. Training is then provided followed by generalization tests. Peterson (1962) demonstrated a flat gradient for ducklings who were raised in monochromatic light; however subsequent investigators have been unable to obtain similar findings. Although the gradients obtained by subjects living in a restricted environment reveal somewhat different generalization gradients than normal subjects, they are not flat.

Stimulus generalization gradients have been investigated as a function of two other variables, namely (1) time of testing and (2) motivational level. There appears to be reasonable agreement that as the time increases between the end of the training period and the generalization test, the gradient becomes flatter. Increasing the motivation level of the organism results in many more responses being made to the S+, which in turns usually results in a steeper gradient.

Interpretations of stimulus generalization have been diverse. Investigators working within the operant paradigm generally conceptualize stimulus generalization as an empirical phenomenon—that is, as a procedure by which it is possible to examine how much control the training stimulus has over responding.

Theoretical interpretations have variously proposed that stimulus generalization is a failure of discrimination (Lashley and Wade, 1946), or a basic organismic process arising from the reinforcement procedure (Hull, 1943). At the present time, neither of these theoretical positions can explain all of the experimental findings which have been obtained.

14

The Instrumental Conditioning of Autonomic Nervous System Responses

In our examination of classical conditioning, we noted that autonomic as well as skeletal responses could be conditioned. In contrast, the history of instrumental learning reveals a general acceptance of the belief that the instrumental conditioning of autonomic responses is impossible. Both Konorski and Miller (1937) hypothesized that responses controlled by the autonomic nervous system could not be instrumentally conditioned. A year later, Skinner (1938) adopted a similar position, writing that "there is little reason to expect conditioning of Type R [instrumental conditioning] in an autonomic response, since it does not as a rule naturally act upon the environment in any way that will produce a reinforcement . . . ." (p. 112). Skinner's point of view was supported by his failure to operantly condition vasoconstriction in human subjects. He acknowledged, however, that this did not mean that voluntary control of some autonomic activities could not be established, citing those cases of children who have learned to cry "real tears." He accounted for such behavior by positing that a classically conditioned paradigm was primarily responsible for the effect. Thus, the autonomic response was elicited by an unconditioned stimulus but a voluntary response and its associated stimulation acquired "control" over the response by its association with the UCS. Skinner (1938) reported that vasoconstriction could be associated with a verbal report using this procedure. The subject was instructed to say "Contract," following which a gun was fired which produced strong vasoconstriction. After a few trials, the verbal report "Contract" was sufficient to elicit vasoconstriction. This possibility has concerned many contemporary investigators, since their objective has been to control autonomic responses directly, a point we shall return to later.[1]

The Use of Human Subjects

In the early sixties, interest in the problem of instrumentally conditioning autonomic responses was rekindled by Kimmel and his associates with a series of studies, as well as by Razran (1961), who reported that Lisina, a Russian investigator, was able to instrumentally condition the dilation of blood vessels.[2]

Reinforcement Paradigms

Although Kimmel and Hill (1960) were unable to increase or decrease the emission of EDR responses by reinforcing their subjects with pleasant or unpleasant odors, subsequent studies by Fowler and Kimmel (1962) and Kimmel and Kimmel (1963) were presumably successful. In this last study, the experimenters' procedure included providing subjects with a 10-minute rest period, the last 5 minutes of which were used to establish an operant level of EDR responding. Following this period, all EDRs which were emitted during a 16-minute test period were reinforced by the presentation of a white light. A control or noncontingent group received the light at random intervals but never when they were making an EDR. Kimmel and Kimmel (1963) obtained clear evidence for conditioning, with the experimental group revealing increases of up to 120 percent of their initial resting level, while the noncontingent group declined in their rate of emission to below 80 percent.

A number of investigators have reported the instrumental conditioning of other types of autonomic responses, e.g., vasoconstriction, heart rate, and saliva-

[1] In addition to Skinner (1938), Mowrer (1938) has also been cited as an early investigator who was able to operantly condition autonomic responses. Stern (1970) has called attention to the fact that a careful reading of Mowrer's paper reveals that he did not use a control group, which would have been necessary to determine whether instrumental conditioning had or had not taken place.

[2] It is interesting to note that when Lisina's (1965) work was published in English, it was evident that her experimental procedure differed from that reported by Razran (1961). Lisina demonstrated that a few of her subjects could gain control over vasodilation by relaxing the skeletal musculature and changing the depth of respiration. Visual feedback of the vasomotor behavior was also provided.

tion. Reinforcement has been typically a light or tone although monetary rewards have been used on a few occasions.

In a study by Snyder and Noble (1968), the instrumental conditioning of vasoconstriction was examined; here, the response was blood volume in the right index finger of the subject as recorded by a plethysmograph. Abdominal and thoracic respiration rate as well as muscle potential arising from the right fore-arm was recorded in an effort to control for the vasoconstrictive response being mediated by these skeletal response systems.

A 5-minute baseline period was first observed in order to obtain an operant level of responding for the four groups of subjects used in the experiment. During acquisition, subjects in two experimental groups received reinforcement (the presentation of a white light) at the peak amplitude of each vasomotor response which was not preceded by bodily movement. Subjects in one control group were provided noncontingent reinforcement, receiving the same number of reinforcements as the experimental subjects during each 5-minute session. A second control group (baseline) did not receive reinforcement throughout these periods. The two experimental groups were treated identically during the acquisition period; however, during 2 extinction periods, one group was countercondi-tioned—reinforcement was now provided for vasomotor stability, while the experimental group received normal extinction trials. Fig. 14-1 reveals the findings obtained for the conditioning as well as for the extinction sessions provided. The authors have concluded that their findings strongly support the position that vasoconstriction can be instrumentally conditioned and that such conditioning is independent of gross movement, muscle tension, respiratory irregularity, and minute finger movements.

Studies by a number of investigators have demonstrated the instrumental conditioning of the heart rate also using a reward procedure. Engel and Hanson (1966) were interested in conditioning heart rate decreases. Their subjects were first provided with a 30-minute adaptation period designed to permit the heart rate to stabilize. A second period, consisting of 5 to 8 minutes, was used to establish the subject's operant level of heart rate. Finally, the last phase was a 25-minute training period. During this period, the subject was told that a correct response, which was not identified by the experimenters, would turn on a light and a clock, both of which could be seen. The light served as the subject's cue for a correct response, while the clock, which accumulated time, was as an indicator of the amount of reinforcement the subject would receive. (Subjects were told that they would be paid at the rate of one-half cent per second.) Yoked control subjects received reinforcement which was identical in duration and pattern to the reinforcement received by the paired experimental subjects except that such reinforcement was not correlated with heart rate decreases. Breathing patterns were measured for all subjects.

Six experimental sessions were conducted; during the 25-minute training periods of sessions 1 and 2, an operant level of heart rate was used which would keep the subject's light on 80 percent of the time. That is, a particular heart rate base level was identified so that 80 percent of the subject's responses would be below this level. For each training period during the next 4 sessions, an

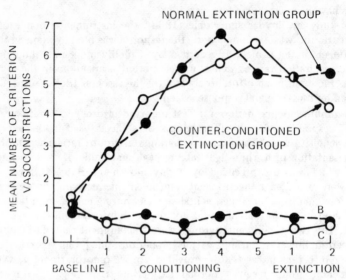

Fig. 14-1. Mean number of vasoconstrictions for successive 5-min. periods for experimental, matched control (C), and base-line control (B) conditions. *Adapted from Snyder and Noble (1968)*

operant level heart rate was chosen, so that the subject's heart rate would be below this level just 50 percent of the time. Heart rate responding was analyzed during these sessions in order to determine if learning took place.

Results indicated that 5 subjects were able to significantly reduce their heart rate over the 4 experimental sessions; 5 other subjects, however, could not be conditioned.

In a second study, Engel and Chism (1967) employed a similar procedure except that these investigators were interested in examining the conditioning of heart rate increases. Significant increases were obtained for all of their five experimental subjects.

One difficulty with Engel and Chism's (1967) findings was that 3 of the yoked control subjects also seem to have "learned," since they emitted faster heart rates during training than during the operant period. Engel and Chism have written, "It is possible that all Ss reacted to the experimental situation with a pattern of responses that included an increase in HR. If so there is a bias in the experimental design which favors significant results." However, the authors went on to point out, "The strongest arguments we can offer from our data in favor of HR learning . . . are: the differential effect, the total experimental situation had on the absolute level of HR—the experimental Ss' HRs were initially slower than the control Ss', however, by session 3 and thereafter the differences were reversed; and the differences between the experimental and control groups, both of which presumably were equally biased" (p. 425). Fig. 14-2 provides these findings.

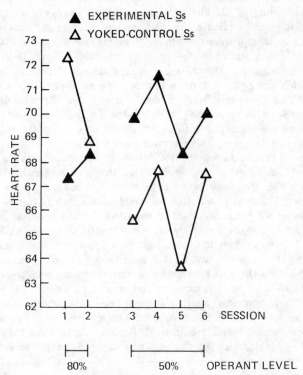

Fig. 14-2. Average heart rate during training. *Adapted from Engel and Chism (1967)*

In a more definitive heart rate conditioning study, Brener and Hothersall (1966) used 5 subjects who were placed in a small, dimly illuminated cubicle and presented with a green light and a red light during alternate periods. Between each presentation, there was a short period of darkness. During the presentation of a light, the subject received high-pitched tones upon the emission of fast heart beats, and low-pitched tones upon the emission of slow heart beats. Subjects were instructed that when the green light was presented, they should try to produce only high tones, and inhibit low tones, while when the red light was presented, they should try to produce only low tones and inhibit high ones. They were further instructed not to engage in any bodily movement during the presentation of either light and that control over the tones was to be exercised by mental processes only. Results supported the instrumental conditioning of both increases and decreases of heart rate since it was found that heart rate increased to the presentation of the green light and decreased to the red. Inasmuch as the experimenters did not control for respiratory activity, they replicated their study (Brener and Hothersall, 1967) with such a control, and obtained similar findings.

Finally, Frezza and Holland (1971) have been able to demonstrate instrumental conditioning of the human salivary response. Subjects were 4 students, with each individual serving as his own control. During the first two experimental sessions, stimuli were not presented and a base rate of salivation was obtained.[3] Swallowing was controlled by instructing the subjects to swallow only on signal. Beginning with the third session, the subject was reinforced for every response which was emitted in order to determine whether reinforcement would increase the rate above base level. When the subject reached a moderately high and constant level of responding, a discrimination task was introduced. Each discrimination session began with about 10 minutes of continuous reinforcement. Following this, periods of reinforcement for salivation were alternated with periods of reinforcement for not salivating. This discrimination took place by presenting a red light if reinforcement was going to be provided and a green light if it was not. Reinforcement was provided by a counter placed within view of the subject. The subject was told he would receive, in addition to a base pay, one cent for every point the counter recorded. Results revealed instrumental conditioning for 3 of the 4 subjects. Increases in salivation were made to the red light, and decreases when the green light was presented. Frezza and Holland (1971) observed, however, that their 3 conditioned subjects consciously began to suck and clench the jaws in order to increase salivation, even though instructed not to do so prior to each experimental session. As a result, the authors concluded that it is not clear whether an instrumentally conditioned increase in salivation can take place without concomitant muscular activity; on the other hand, they indicated that it would be difficult to account for the decreases in salivation they obtained using a similar explanation, e.g., muscular activity.

Escape and Avoidance Paradigms

All the studies we have examined used an instrumental reward procedure; a number of investigators, however, have used escape and avoidance paradigms. An example of the escape paradigm is found in a study by Johnson and Schwartz (1967). In this study, a 4-minute adaptation period was provided during which the base rate of unelicited EDRs was determined for each subject. The conditioning period consisted of presenting a loud noise to the experimental group each time a spontaneous EDR was recorded. A control group was given the same number of loud noises but the aversive stimulation was provided at times when there was no elevated EDR. In addition, half of the experimental and control groups received instructions which indicated that the presentation of the loud noise depended on what they were doing, while the other half received

[3] Saliva was collected from the parotid gland by a capsule similar in design to one used by Lashley (1916). The inner chamber of the capsule was placed directly over Stensen's duct and connected by tubing to a sialometer. This consisted of a dropper made from a hypodermic needle which was inserted through a rubber stopper placed in the neck of a Florence flask. A negative pressure of 15 mm HG was applied to the sialometer via another tube also inserted in the stopper of the flask. A drop of saliva entering the capsule would displace an equal volume of water from the tube and the dropper. As each drop of water fell past a photoelectric cell, it was recorded on a cumulative recorder.

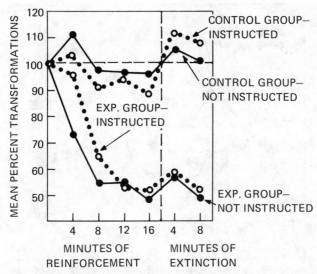

Fig. 14-3. Mean percentage transformations of spontaneous EDRs during reinforcement and extinction. *Adapted from Johnson and Schwartz (1967)*

no information regarding the response-aversive stimulation contingency. EMG recordings were obtained in order to examine any muscular activity which might mediate the EDR. Results are revealed in Fig. 14-3 and clearly indicate a substantial decline in spontaneous EDR activity for the experimental group over the 16-minute test period. An 8-minute extinction period which followed the acquisition session continued to reflect differences between the control and experimental groups. It may be noted that there was no difference between the two experimental groups, so that the different instructions provided did not have any influence on the findings.

An example of the use of the avoidance conditioning paradigm in the instrumental conditioning of the EDR is found in a series of studies by Kimmel and his associates. In the first study, using a trace conditioning procedure, Kimmel and Baxter (1964) provided subjects with 16 paired presentations of a 1-second, 1000 Hz tone, followed by a .1-second UCS 4 seconds after CS offset. Thus, the CS-UCS interval was 5.0 seconds. For the experimental group, the UCS (shock) was omitted if the subject made an EDR during the last 4 seconds of the CS-UCS interval that was equal to or larger than the smallest EDR made during the adaptation trials. In summary, shock omission was contingent upon the subject's response. Yoked control subjects were used; thus, shock was provided each control subject only when it had been received by the experimental subject. Results indicated a significant difference between the experimental and control groups, with the experimental group revealing superior conditioning. Fig. 14-4 shows the average EDR magnitude of the experimental and control groups over the 16 conditioning trials.

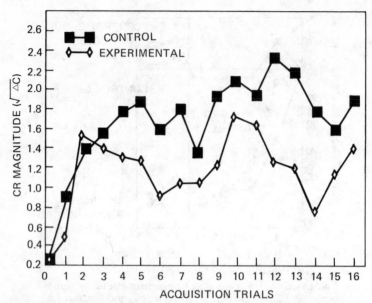

Fig. 14-4. Average EDR magnitude of experimental and control groups during 16 conditioning trials. *Adapted from Kimmel and Baxter (1964)*

Subsequent replications by Kimmel, Sternthal, and Strub (1966) and Kimmel and Sternthal (1967) have not provided statistically significant findings, although the fact that the experimental groups in these experiments consistently revealed superior conditioning has resulted in a common conclusion that the EDR can be conditioned using an instrumental avoidance procedure.

An interesting example of avoidance conditioning is found in a study by Lang and Melamed (1969). A nine-month-old male infant whose life was seriously endangered by persistent vomiting and chronic rumination was treated by the authors with an aversive conditioning paradigm. Electromyographic records were used in assessing the response characteristics of the emesis. The aversive conditioning paradigm called for brief and repeated shock to the leg (approximately 1 second long with a 1 second interpulse interval) as soon as vomiting occurred, and continuing until the response was terminated. An effort was made to initiate shock at the first sign of the reverse peristalsis. This contingency was determined by the nurse's observation of the patient and the concurrent EMG record. A 3000 Hz tone was temporarily coincident with each shock presentation. After 2 sessions, shock was rarely required; by the third session only 1 or 2 brief presentations of shock were necessary to cause cessation of any vomiting sequence.

Table 14-1 provides a summary of a sampling of instrumental conditioning studies which have been conducted with humans using autonomic responses. An examination of the results reveals that positive findings have been reported frequently, although a number of nonsignificant differences have also been found.

General Difficulties

One general difficulty of many of these studies is the possibility that the reinforcing stimulus may simply increase the subject's arousal or activation level which is reflected in turn in an elevation of the autonomic response being measured. As Mandler, et al (1962) have written, ". . . the reinforcement period as a whole apparently serves as a controlling stimulus for a state of the organism characterized by increased GSR rates. One possibility is that this state may be one of activation or arousal" (p. 320). It is noteworthy that the traditional incremental learning curve found with skeletal responses is frequently not found in these studies; rather there is an abrupt elevation of responding taking place very early on the conditioning trials, in some instances, even on the first trial. This kind of evidence provides some support for Mandler's, et al (1962) point of view.

Another frequently cited difficulty is the possibility that the reinforcing stimulus increases the probability of the occurrence of some voluntary muscular response or skeletal activity which is associated with the autonomic response being measured, an effect discussed early in the chapter. The experimenter who has not monitored respiration rate or who has not obtained EMG recordings during the instrumental conditioning of an autonomic response is open to the criticism that skeletal responses may have confounded his experimental findings.

Although many investigators have failed to monitor skeletal responses, it is now a fairly common practice to provide these controls. In Snyder and Noble's (1968) instrumental conditioning of a vasomotor response, a study which we described earlier, it will be recalled that a number of skeletal responses were monitored during the acquisition sessions. Similarly, Van Twyver and Kimmel (1966) carefully monitored respiration rate, respiration irregularity, and muscle potential for all experimental subjects in their instrumental conditioning of the EDR. In this study, light served to reinforce those EDRs which were equal or greater than 1 percent of the subject's basal skin resistance. Noncontingent subjects were matched with contingent subjects on the basis of the number of reinforcements provided each minute; reinforcement for the noncontingent group, however, was always received when no EDR was occurring. Following a 5-minute delay for adjustment of equipment and a 10-minute rest period, during which time the EDR criterion was determined, a 16-minute reinforcement period was provided, followed by 10 minutes of extinction. The results in Fig. 14-5, reveal the average percentage of transformed EDR frequency of contingent and noncontingent groups during reinforcement and extinction. Also shown in Fig. 14-6, 14-7, and 14-8 are indications of EMG and respiration activity. These findings would appear to eliminate muscle potential and respiration rate as skeletal mediators of the EDR.

One interesting attack on this problem can be found in a study by Birk, Crider, Shapiro, and Tursky (1966) who, in an effort to preclude gross motor responses as a contributory factor in the conditioning of the EDR, administered 1 subject an immobilizing but subparalytic dose of curare (d-tubocurarine). Their procedure consisted of first providing 6 control sessions, each of which in-

Table 14-1 Summaries of a Sampling of Studies Investigating the Conditioning of Autonomic Responses

Investigators	Response	Instrumental Reward Reinforcement	Results — Remarks
Kimmel and Hill (1960)	EDR	Pleasant and unpleasant smells	No evidence for conditioning. Some difficulty, however, in presenting odors.
Fowler and Kimmel (1962)	EDR	Presentation of light	Experimenters found evidence for conditioning. However, neither experimental nor control group showed higher rate of EDR emission than during base period. [No control for muscular mediation.]
Kimmel and Kimmel (1963)	EDR	Presentation of light	Clear evidence obtained for conditioning. Experimental group revealed increases up to 120% of initial resting level; control group declined in rate of emission to below 80%. [No control for muscular mediation.]
Mandler, Preven, and Kuhlman (1962)	EDR	Presentation of light; also small monetary (10–60¢) bonus given for improvement.	Larger number of EDRs emitted by experimental Ss over each of the 11 sessions, but each individual session reveals a declining function (unlike typical learning curve). Experimenters believe reinforcement period provided an arousal period which increased EDRs.
Van Twyver and Kimmel (1966)	EDR	Light	Positive findings obtained with reinforced responses revealing learning curve function. Noncontingent condition revealed decline in responding. Results indicate "that operant GSR conditioning occurred in the absence of identifiable mediation by somantic behavior."
Engel and Hansen (1966)	Slowing of heart rate	Light and time on clock; Ss paid .5 cents for each second.	5 of 10 Ss showed evidence of learning as revealed by increase in percentage times light on, decreases in average HR, shifts in frequency distribution.
Birk, Crider, Shapiro and Tursky (1966)	EDR	70 db tone	Positive findings obtained for both normal and drug condition, with drug condition resulting in consistently fewer number of EDRs. Major difficulty was that no noncontingent condition was run against which to compare experimental findings.

Study	Response	Reinforcement	Results
Crider, Shapiro, and Tursky (1966)	EDR	Tone, with each presentation worth 5¢	Positive findings obtained in 5 experiments.
Rice (1966)	EDR	Light	When EDR's were reinforced, regardless of preceding EMG changes, positive findings were obtained. When EDRs were reinforced only if there was an absence of EMG, no difference was obtained between contingent and noncontingent groups.
Engel and Chism (1967)	Speeding of heart rate	Light and time on clock; Ss paid .5 cents for each second.	All 5 experimental Ss learned; 2 of 5 control Ss revealed significant changes in HR.
Brown and Katz (1967)	Salivation	Illumination of sign indicating that a monetary bonus was to be paid.	Results indicated that experimental Ss rewarded for increases in salivary rate revealed significant increases. No changes occurred, however, for experimental group rewarded for decreases. Investigator noted that movements of tongue and mouth may have modified salivary flow.
Stern (1967)	EDR	Light	No differences between contingent and noncontingent groups.
Snyder and Noble (1968)	Vasoconstriction (Finger)	Light	Results revealed increase in number of vasoconstrictions for experimental group, a decrease for yoked controls, and no change for second control group which was provided no reinforcement throughout experimental period. Results were independent of bodily movement, muscle tension in forearm and finger, heart rate, and respiratory irregularities.
Frezza and Holland (1971)	Salivation	Counter which advanced with each drop of salivation. 1¢ was provided for each point.	Cumulative records revealed increase in responding under continuous reinforcement, and a decrease in responding under zero reinforcement for 3 of the 4 Ss. [No control for muscular mediation.]
Shapiro, Schwartz, and Tursky (1972)	Increasing and decreasing diastolic blood pressure.	Information indicating that blood pressure had increased or decreased. Rewards consisted of slides of landscapes and nudes.	Positive findings obtained with 7 of 10 Ss raising their pressure, 8 of 10 Ss lowered their pressure.

Table 14-1 Continued

Investigators	Response	Instrumental Escape Reinforcement	Results — Remarks
Senter and Hummel (1965)	EDR	Shock	Significant decline in number of unelicited EDRs for the experimental group. [No recording of muscular activity.]
Johnson and Schwartz (1967)	EDR	Loud Noise	Clear indication that experimental group revealed substantial decrease in spontaneous EDR activity.
		Instrumental Avoidance	
Kimmel and Baxter (1964)	EDR	Shock	Significant differences between groups with experimental group revealing superior avoidance conditioning. [No control for muscular activity.]
Kimmel, Sternthal, and Strub (1966)	EDR	Shock	Difference was not significant, although experimental group in two studies revealed superior conditioning. Authors concluded "that the GSR can be conditioned using an instrumental avoidance procedure." [No control for muscular activity.]
Kimmel and Sternthal (1967)	EDR	Shock	Difference was not statistically significant. Authors considered the results marginally successful

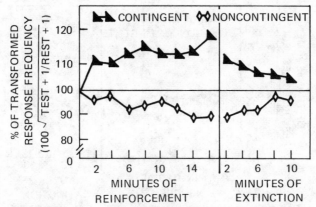

Fig. 14-5. Average percentage of transformed correct-ed EDR frequency of contingent and noncontingent groups during reinforcement and extinction, in 2-min. blocks. *Adapted from Van Twyver and Kimmel (1966)*

cluded the instrumental conditioning of the subject's EDR. Reinforcement, in this case, the presentation of a 70 db tone, was provided for any negative-going skin potential fluctuation of .1 mv. or greater. Recordings were also obtained of heart and respiratory rate. The experimental session took place 20 days after the last control session. The administration of the drug resulted in the subject's being unable to lift his head from the chair. It was also noted that he was unable to lift any extremity, open his eyes, swallow, or utter intelligible words, although lateral rolling of the head was possible with great effort. The subject was able to breath without marked distress. At this level of immobilization, a 4-minute operant level of EDR responding was obtained, followed by a 16-minute instrumental conditioning period similar to that used in the control sessions. Fig. 14-9 reveals the findings under the experimental and the fifth control session; it would appear that the amount of muscular immobilization provided had little influence on the conditioning.[4]

The Problem of Cognitive Mediators

Our discussion has centered around the role of skeletal mediators but it is possible to have cognitive mediators as well. Cognitive mediation refers to the subject thinking about some event or adopting some hypothesis which is respon-sible for mediating the autonomic response. Some early experimenters, e.g., Hudgins (1933), Menzies (1937), were able to show that instructing subjects to think about a specific item or event could serve as an effective stimulus for autonomic responding. A more recent study by Schwartz (1971) has also demonstrated this to be the case. Subjects were asked to generate, as well as to

[4] The fifth session was chosen for comparison because of its nearly equivalent operant level.

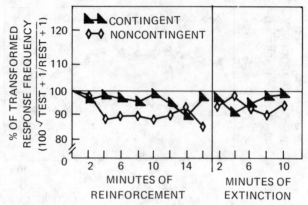

Fig. 14-6. Average percentage of transformed EMG frequency of contingent and noncontingent groups during reinforcement and extinction, in 2-min. blocks. *Adapted from Van Twyver and Kimmel (1966)*

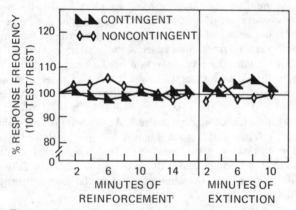

Fig. 14-7. Average percentage of respiration frequency (rate) of contingent and noncontingent groups during reinforcement and extinction, in 2-min. blocks. *Adapted from Van Twyver and Kimmel (1966)*

experience, thoughts which were aroused by a neutral sequence of items, e.g., the letters A, B, etc., as well as a sequence of words, e.g., sex, death, etc. Results revealed that the subject's heart rate, measured in beats per minute, was significantly greater to the affective words than to the neutral letters, thus providing support for the position that different thought sequences can produce differing autonomic responses.

A major difficulty, of course, is determining if cognitive mediators have been used. One "control" is to provide a postexperimental interview. Kimmel (1974)

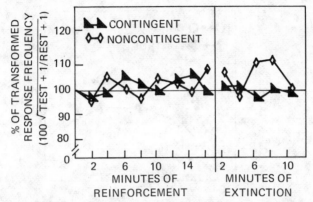

Fig. 14-8. Average percentage of transformed respiration irregularity frequency of contingent and noncontingent groups during reinforcement and extinction, in 2-min. blocks. *Adapted from Van Twyver and Kimmel (1966)*

has reported he is convinced that the extensive interviewing of his subjects following their participation in instrumental conditioning studies is of little value. He reports that "ninety-eight percent of the subjects interviewed in our laboratory report no awareness that *anything* they might have done during the conditioning session was correlated with the delivery of the reinforcement. These subjects typically respond with incredulity to our suggestion that something they were doing influenced the reinforcement" (p. 329).

On the other hand, Stern (1967) has obtained a different picture of the participating subject's cognitions. At the end of an instrumental conditioning EDR study, in which a light served as the reinforcing stimulus, subjects were asked to complete a postexperimental questionnaire which contained two items: (1) What do you think determined when the light went on?, and (2) If I told you it was something you were doing, then what do you think it might have been? Stern reported that the experimental group, in reply to his second question, stated that "muscular reactions," "slight movements," and "thinking about exciting things," were the kind of activities his subjects believed controlled the presentation of the light. On the other hand, "relaxing" represented the most frequent reply for the control group. The unusual aspect of Stern's findings was that in spite of many of his subjects' reporting the correct contingency, a significant difference in responding between the experimental and control group was not obtained.

A second type of cognitive control procedure has been to provide the subjects, prior to the experiment, with instructions which indicate (or do not indicate) that a response-reward contingency will be utilized. As noted in the discussion of the role of cognitive variables in classical conditioning of the EDR in Chapter 6, many investigators found that the subject had to be aware of the contingency between the CS and the UCS in order for learning to take place.

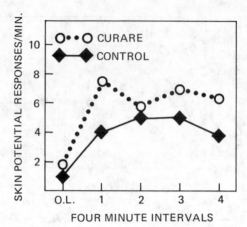

Fig. 14-9. Comparison of skin potential responses during curare and control sessions. *Adapted from Birk, Crider, Shapiro, and Tursky (1966)*

Shean (1970) has reported a similar finding in examining instrumental avoidance learning of the EDR. In his study, red and green lights were randomly presented to his subjects, with a red light indicating that shock could be avoided by making an EDR, while a green light indicated that shock could be avoided by inhibiting an EDR. One group of subjects was told of these contingencies at the beginning of the experiment, while a second group was not. Sixty discrimination trials were provided. Results indicated that those subjects who were aware of the contingencies revealed a large difference between the size of their EDRs on the very first red and green light presentations and that this difference increased over trials. The no-information group revealed no difference in the size of their EDRs during the presentation of the red and green lights and this did not change over trials. In commenting on these findings, Shean wrote that what has frequently been reported as evidence of instrumental autonomic conditioning is most often evidence of the already well-established fact that human Ss can and do exert voluntary control over their autonomic functions through a mediating voluntary operant.

Johnson and Schwartz (1970), on the other hand, were unable to obtain differences in their EDR conditioning study as a function of whether or not their subjects were aware of a response-aversive stimulation contingency. In this experiment, described earlier in this chapter, half of their experimental and control groups received instructions which indicated that the presentation of a loud noise was dependent upon what they were doing; the other half of each group received no information regarding the response-aversive stimulation contingency. Results indicated that such information had no influence on whether or not instrumental conditioning took place, as Fig. 14-3 reveals.

In summary, the experimental evidence regarding the role of skeletal and cognitive mediators in human instrumental conditioning is confusing and does not lend itself to any obvious interpretation.

The larger issue of whether or not autonomic responses of the human can be instrumentally conditioned without the contribution of mediators, in spite of assertions to the contrary, e.g., Kimmel (1974), remains questionable. A number of experimenters have been unable to obtain positive findings. In many of the successful studies, adequate controls have not been utilized; in other cases, only a part of the experimental subjects have been conditioned. In still other cases, the experimental findings have been "unusual." For example, Gavalas's (1967) study has frequently been cited as one of the successful attempts to condition the EDR; however, increased responding of the EDR as a function of trials was not obtained. Rather, Gavalas has reported that reinforcement (presentation of a light) appeared to prevent adaptation; thus, the experimental group revealed a relatively stable level of responding throughout the experiment, while decreasing activity was noted for the controls. Katkin and Murray's (1968) exhaustive survey of the literature led them to advise that "it is not safe to conclude that it [instrumental conditioning of autonomic responses] has been demonstrated in humans" (p. 66).

At this time, considerable doubt must be raised as to whether it will ever be possible to determine if the instrumental conditioning of autonomic responses can take place without cognitive mediation, since there is some problem in providing appropriate controls. We would conclude, however, that some type of human autonomic response modification frequently takes place as a result of the experimental procedures which are provided, although in some instances, the change that takes place suggests that something other than a learning process is involved. Moreover, the inability of many investigators to obtain positive findings, or their ability to secure them with only a fraction of their subjects would suggest that the effect is often a fragile one. It would seem axiomatic that attention should be directed toward an examination of the reason for this type of finding.[5]

But it must be recognized that any "explanation" of autonomic response conditioning based on the role of mediators is dangerous because it cannot be tested. The designation of skeletal or cognitive mediators can always be used as an ad hoc explanation for positive findings since, regardless of how careful the experimenter may be in controlling or eliminating these mediators, it can always be asserted that his controls were not adequate and that some unobserved response was responsible for the results.[6]

[5] It is of interest to note that Moeller (1954) and Smith (1954), sometime prior to this controversy argued that classical conditioning was dependent on reinforcement principles and that the conditioning of involuntary responses such as the EDR was in reality a conditioning of some unspecified skeletal response, in turn dependent on reinforcement. As Smith (1954) wrote, ". . . every 'conditioned visceral response' is in reality an artifact, an innate accompaniment of the skeletal responses inculcated by the conditioning process" (p. 217).

[6] An interesting attack on this problem is found in a study by Gavalas (1968) who noted that deep yawn-like inspiration elicited EDR deflections. By operantly conditioning this deep respiration response (skeletal), but at the same time observing the EDR, she felt it was possible to determine how this latter response was influenced by the conditioning procedure. She reasoned that if mediation theorists were correct, "conditioning" of the EDR should also take place. Her findings revealed that, although a classic instrumental learning curve

The Use of Curare and Animal Studies

Miller and his associates have suggested that one way to handle the general problem of eliminating muscular responses which might accompany autonomic responses would be to paralyze all skeletal responses using the drug curare. (It will be recalled that this drug was used in classical conditioning studies in which investigators were interested in determining if classical conditioning could take place without the unconditioned response actually being made during conditioning trials.) Food or water could not be used as reinforcement, since the organism is incapable of eating or drinking; however, the discovery of Olds and Milner (1954) that reinforcement could be provided by electrical stimulation of the brain would appear to solve this problem.

In an early study by Trowill (1967), curarized rats were first observed in order to obtain their average heart rate. Following this, one group of experimental animals received electrical stimulation of the brain only if their heart rate increased (over a base rate) while a second group of experimental animals received brain stimulation only if their heart rate decreased. Although rate changes were small, Trowill found that 15 of the 19 animals which were rewarded for increasing their heart rate actually increased their rate, while 15 of 17 animals rewarded for slow heart rate decreased their rate. Yoked control animals, on the other hand, failed to show changes observed in their experimental counterparts.

In another study, Miller and DiCara (1967) attempted to discover if the small (5 percent) heart rate changes achieved by Trowill (1967) could be obtained by shaping the response—that is by progressively shifting to a more difficult criterion after their subjects had learned to achieve an easier one. Trowill's experimental procedure was replicated except that the experimental apparatus was so programmed that once a 2 percent heart rate increment or decrement was achieved, this new level of responding was considered to be the base rate and an additional two percent change was required to receive reinforcement. Thus, each time the subject reached the criterion for reinforcement, the criterion was shifted another 2 percent.

The results are revealed in Fig. 14-10: 11 out of 12 rats rewarded for increasing heart rate showed significant increases; 10 out of 11 animals reinforced for decreasing their heart rate showed significant decreases. As the authors point out, since these changes were in opposite directions and were a function of the type of response rewarded, they cannot be accounted for by the unconditioned effects of brain stimulation. Moreover, movement of the animals could not be elicited by pinches or electric shock; no signs of recovery could be observed until at least 90 minutes after the end of the experiment and artificial respiration was necessary for a period considerably longer than 90 minutes. Thus, it would appear that mediation via feedback from skeletal movement was eliminated by using curare.

---

was obtained for the respiration response, there was an uncoupling of this response from the EDR and EDR conditioning was not obtained. Rather, she reports, the EDR revealed an orderly habituation to increasing repetitions of the skeletal response.

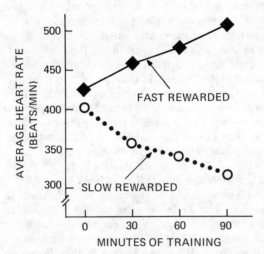

Fig. 14-10. Instrumental learning by heart in groups rewarded for fast or for slow rates. (Each point represents average of beats per minute during 5 min.) *Adapted from Miller and DiCara (1967)*

Miller and DiCara's (1967) findings have been confirmed by other experimenters, e.g., Hothersall and Brener (1969) and Slaughter, Hahn, and Rinaldi (1970). In general, however, these investigators have not been able to obtain heart rate changes as large as those reported by Miller and DiCara(1967).

Miller and Banuazizi (1968) pointed out the possibility that instrumental conditioning of autonomic responses might result from the general arousal of the organism produced by reinforcement, an argument made earlier by Mandler, et al (1962). As a result, Miller and Banuazizi (1968) attempted to determine if one autonomic response could be instrumentally conditioned, while a monitoring of the second would reveal only base rate responding. In addition to employing heart rate, intestinal motility was used as the second response system. The monitoring of this response was accomplished by placing a small balloon filled with water in the large intestine. Tied to the end of the balloon was a hypodermic needle which in turn was connected to a pressure transducer which yielded an electrical output in proportion to the pressure produced by the intestine. Brain stimulation was used to reward either intestinal contraction or relaxation and increasing or decreasing heart beat. The authors found that "intestinal contraction increased when rewarded, decreased when relaxation was rewarded, and remained virtually unchanged when either increased or decreased heart rate was rewarded. Similarly, heart rate increased when a fast rate was rewarded, decreased when a slow rate was rewarded, and remained virtually unchanged when either intestinal contraction or relaxation was rewarded" (p. 5).

In addition to demonstrating that heart rate and intestinal contractions are capable of being modified by an instrumental conditioning procedure, Miller and DiCara determined also that it was possible to condition peripheral vasomotor activity as well as rate of urine formation!

In the demonstration of vasomotor activity conditioning, DiCara and Miller (1968a) rewarded changes in peripheral blood flow in the tail of the curarized rat with brain stimulation, and found that the animal could learn either to constrict or to dilate its blood vessels in order to obtain reinforcement. Moreover, they demonstrated the specificity of such changes by providing brain stimulation when the blood flow in the ears (their second measuring site) revealed a relative imbalance. Here, 6 rats were rewarded for vasodilation of the left ear, while 6 other animals were rewarded for vasodilation of the right ear. Results revealed the unusual finding that, with appropriate reinforcement, a rat can learn to increase the rate of blood flow to one ear relative to the other.

In a second study, Miller and DiCara (1968) found that the rate of urine formation by the kidney could be instrumentally modified. In this study, rats that were rewarded with brain stimulation for decreased amounts of urine formation demonstrated significantly slower rates of urine formation, while a second group of animals reinforced for increasing the rate of urine formation revealed increased amounts. Miller and DiCara further discovered that it was the rate of renal blood flow which appeared to be responsible for the changes in kidney functioning.

In yet another study in their provocative series, DiCara and Miller (1968b) found that instrumental conditioning of autonomic responses could take place using the avoidance learning paradigm, and was not dependent on brain stimulation, which up to that time, had been used exclusively as the reinforcing stimulus with curarized animals.

In this experiment, on shock trials, two groups of curarized rats were presented with a flashing light (or tone) for 5 seconds and if they failed to increase or decrease, respectively, their heart rates, shock was administered with the animal receiving a .1-second pulse once every 2 seconds until the criterion was achieved. At this time, both the visual signal and the shock were turned off. On nonshock trials, a tone (or flashing light) was presented for 5 seconds and was never followed by shock. To compare the effects of training on heart rate when no signals were present, subjects also received "blank" trials, each lasting 5 seconds, during which time heart rate was recorded but nothing else happened. One hundred shock trials, 100 nonshock trials, and 100 blank trials were given in a counterbalanced sequence.

The results were in keeping with the findings obtained in earlier studies which had used brain stimulation to instrumentally condition heart rate increases or decreases. In brief, the two groups of animals learned to increase or decrease their heart rates in order to escape or avoid mild electric shock. Thus, the authors argued that the instrumental learning of a visceral response was not limited to any unique property of direct electrical stimulation of the brain.

We should like to conclude this section with a word of caution. Miller and his associates' work has been recognized as an event of major theoretical and practical significance, since his use of curarized animals presumably eliminates the possibility of skeletal mediators. But Miller and Dworkin (1974) have recently reported considerable difficulty in replicating the findings of those studies which provided the early experimental evidence that autonomic responses of curarized animals could be conditioned.

Most of these attempted replications have been concerned with the examination of the conditioned heart rate. A basic problem in this work has been the finding of increased and variable heart rate in curarized animals, a condition which effectively precludes the conditioning of the response. In an attempt to solve this difficulty, Miller has used other strains as well as other suppliers of animals; has hypophysectomized his subjects, examined a variety of respiration parameters, and analyzed the drug, d-tubocurarine—all to no avail. On the chance that the difficulties might be specific to the cardiovascular system, an attempt was made to replicate the avoidance conditioning of intestional motility, e.g., Miller and Banuazizi (1968), but positive results could not be obtained.

It has now belatedly been recognized that there are two general problems in using curare. First, there is the problem directly associated with producing and maintaining a paralyzed organism—the criteria of muscular blockage and artificial respiration. The second problem has to do with assessing the side effects produced by the drug—side effects which include the promotion of histamine release, altered sensory processes, and so forth. Howard, Galosy, Gaebelein, and Obrist's (1974) systematic review of these problems has led them to conclude that "none of the experimenters utilizing curare as a tool have controlled all the variables which might influence their results" (p. 360), pointing out that few investigators (1) have monitored the effectiveness of the neuromuscular block by measuring EMG, or (2) have measured the amount of ganglionic block produced by curare. Nor has there been any attempt to ascertain what effect the histamine-releasing properties might have on the results. Moreover, Howard, et al have pointed out that normal respiratory parameters have largely been ignored, as has the influence of ambient temperature, rate of infusion, and the like. The EEG arousal state of animals during conditioning under curare has not been investigated.

Hahn (1974) found that a variety of these factors associated with curarization procedures and the physiological changes which accompany curare injection have resulted in a regular increase or decrease in the heart rate. In summary, until these general problems are solved, any findings arising from the attempted conditioning of autonomic responses in the curarized animal must be regarded as suspect.

The Independence of Autonomic and Central Nervous System Activity

In addition to the various specific physiological problems which accompany the use of curare, we should like in this final section to mention a conceptual problem.

Implicit in the studies of those investigators who have used curare is the assumption that the conditioning of autonomic responses of animals injected with curare provides evidence of the independence of central and autonomic nervous system activities. Some experimenters, however, e.g., Obrist, Webb,

Sutterer, and Howard (1970) and Goesling and Brener (1972), have proposed that central and autonomic nervous system activities, rather than being independent, represent two components of a general response process. They have hypothesized that, since curare inhibits only the most peripheral manifestations of the somatomotor act, it is possible that somatic processes proximal to the myoneural junction retain an influence over autonomic activity even in the curarized animal.

A study by Goesling and Brener (1972) was designed to investigate the influence of the somatic response system on autonomic nervous system responding, and more specifically, the cardiovascular response in the curarized rat. Their basic procedure was to pretrain antagonistic somatomotor and cardiovascular responses in two groups of rats not under the influence of curare, and then compare the effects of heart rate conditioning under curare in these two groups of animals. If it is assumed that the two response systems are served in parallel by a common central process, the effects of different pretraining procedures should be noted in the curarized animals. On the other hand, if the two response systems are independently controlled, it would be anticipated that the experimental contingencies introduced under curare would serve as the primary determinants of heart change.

More specifically, these investigators, using shock as their aversive stimulus, trained animals to be active in a running wheel or to be immobile when placed in a small open field. Following ten days of training, all animals were curarized and punished either for the emission of high or low heart rates. Results revealed that those animals that had learned to be immobile in the pretraining procedure displayed the greatest *decrement* in heart rate under curare when punished for high heart rates, while those animals that had learned to be active in the pretraining procedure revealed the greatest *increments* in heart rate when punished for low heart rates. These findings, the authors point out, indicate that the effects of somatomotor training of animals not under curare is clearly in evidence when an autonomic nervous system response is conditioned in rats that had been placed under curare. Thus, the case for independent central control of somatomotor and cardiovascular activities become tenuous. Moreover, these experimenters have expressed the belief that the use of curare has had negative utility with respect to clarifying the relationship between cardiovascular and somatomotor activity, since some question must be raised concerning the independence of these response systems.

In summary, if Goesling and Brener's (1972) findings can be replicated, it would appear that animal studies (as well as human studies) have not been able, as yet, to clearly establish the instrumental conditioning of autonomic nervous system responses independent of somatic response system. Perhaps an answer will be forthcoming only when the relationship between the autonomic and somatic nervous systems have been worked out in detail.

In the interim, as a number of writers have suggested, the distinction should be made between conditioning and controlling the autonomic nervous system. We are aware that autonomic nervous responses can be placed under voluntary control. Where it appears that such control could be utilized in furthering the well-being of the individual, it would seem that appropriate training procedures should be developed.[7]

Summary

Early investigators were firmly convinced that autonomic responses could not be instrumentally conditioned. In the early sixties, Kimmel and his associates appeared to demonstrate that the instrumental conditioning of the human EDR was possible. These experimental findings have been responsible for generating considerable interest in this area, and a number of experiments have now indicated that not only the EDR, but heart rate, vasoconstriction, and salivation can also be instrumentally conditioned. In the reward paradigm, the general procedure consists of first obtaining an operant level of responding, then providing an experimental group with reinforcement, frequently in the form of the presentation of a light, for responses which markedly deviate from their operant response level. Control subjects, on the other hand, receive reinforcement which is not contingent on an appropriate response. Instrumental escape and avoidance paradigms have also been used in apparently successful demonstration of autonomic response conditioning.

Critics have called attention to the possibility that such instrumental responding may be mediated by either skeletal or cognitive responses. It is hypothesized that the reinforcing stimulus increases the probability of the occurrence of some voluntary muscular response (skeletal), or some thought or cognition (cognitive), either of which could have an autonomic response associated with it. Recent studies, however, have almost always monitored heart rate, respiration rate, and the movement of skeletal muscles in the hand and arm in order to control for skeletal mediation, and autonomic response conditioning has been obtained with such controls.

The control of cognitive mediators, however, represents another problem. One approach has been to ask the subjects for a report of what they were thinking about during the experiment, while a second approach has been to provide the subject with correct as well as erroneous instructions regarding the nature of the response-reinforcement contingency.

The experimental evidence that has been brought to bear on the problem of cognition and mediation is controversial and confusing. Some experimenters have reported that their subjects show little awareness of what was taking place during the experiment; others, however, have indicated that their subjects reported a conscious attempt to "figure out" the nature of the response-reinforcement contingency. Frequently, however, no relationship has been found between the level of conditioning and the subject's awareness of the relationship between the response and the reinforcement.

In an effort to control muscular responding and thus eliminate the possibility

---

[7] Applications of autonomic nervous system control have not been reported very frequently; Engel (1972) has reported a few patients who have successfully performed cardiac control for periods ranging from 6 months to 1 year. It is interesting to note that training sessions were not provided during this interval.

of skeletal mediators, some experimenters have injected their animal subjects with curare prior to the autonomic conditioning session. Although early experimental evidence has indicated that a variety of autonomic responses can be conditioned in drugged animals, many recent failures have been noted and concern has been expressed over artifacts arising from the use of curare. Some investigators have also called attention to the possibility that autonomic nervous system functioning may be independent of the skeletal system. If the experimental evidence by Goesling and Brener (1972), which appears to demonstrate some relationship between the autonomic and skeletal response systems, can be confirmed, the question of the independence of the two systems will be reopened.

References

Abbott, D. W. & Price, L. E. Stimulus generalization of the conditioned eyelid response to structurally similar nonsense syllables. *Journal of Experimental Psychology*, 1964, *68*, 368-371.

Adamec, R. & Melzack, R. The role of motivation and orientation in sensory preconditioning. *Canadian Journal of Psychology*, 1970, *24*, 230-239.

Adams, J. A. *Human memory*. New York: McGraw-Hill, 1967.

Albino, A. R. & Burnand, G. Conditioning of the *alpha* rhythm in man. *Journal of Experimental Psychology*, 1964, *67*, 539-544.

Allen, C. K. & Branum, A. R. Differential eyelid conditioning as a function of the probability of reinforcement of the conditioned stimuli. *Psychonomic Science*, 1971, *22*, 251-252.

Allen, J. A. Latent inhibition: Generalization during eyelid conditioning. Unpublished master's thesis, North Carolina State University, 1967.

Allison, J., Larson, D., & Jensen, D. D. Acquired fear, brightness preference, and one-way shuttlebox performance. *Psychonomic Science*, 1967, *8*, 269-270.

Amsel, A. The combination of a primary appetitional need with primary and secondary emotionally derived needs. *Journal of Experimental Psychology*, 1950, *40*, 1-14.

Amsel, A. The role of frustrative nonreward in noncontinuous reward situations. *Psychological Bulletin*, 1958, *55*, 102-119.

Amsel, A. Frustrative nonreward in partial reinforcement and discrimination learning: Some recent history and a theoretical extension. *Psychological Review*, 1962, *69*, 306-328.

Amsel, A. Partial reinforcement acquisition and extinction effects under within-subject and between-subject conditions. Paper presented at the meeting of the Psychonomic Society, Niagara Falls, 1964.

Amsel, A. Partial reinforcement effects on vigor and persistence: Advances in frustration theory derived from a variety of within-subjects experiments. In K. W. Spence & J. T. Spence (Eds.), *The psychology of learning and motivation*, Vol. 1. New York: Academic Press, 1967.

Amsel, A., Hug, J. J., & Surridge, C. T. Number of food pellets, goal approaches, and the partial reinforcement effect after minimal acquisition. *Journal of Experimental Psychology*, 1968, *77*, 530-534.

Amsel, A. & Penick, E. C. The influence of early experience on the frustration effect. *Journal of Experimental Psychology*, 1962, *63*, 167-176.

Amsel, A., Rashotte, M. E. & MacKinnon, J. R. Partial reinforcement effects within subject and between subjects. *Psychological Monographs*, 1966, *80*, No. 628.

Amsel, A. & Roussel, J. Motivational properties of frustration. I. Effect on a running response of the addition of frustration to the motivational complex. *Journal of Experimental Psychology*, 1952, *43*, 363-368.

Anderson, D. C., O'Farrell, T., Formica, R., & Caponigri, V. Preconditioning CS exposure: Variation in place of conditioning and presentation. *Psychonomic Science*, 1969, *15*, 54-55.

Anderson, D. C., Wolf, D. & Sullivan, P. Preconditioning exposure to the CS: Variation in place of testing. *Psychonomic Science*, 1969, *14*, 233-235.

Anderson, E. E. The externalization of drive: II. The effect of satiation and removal of reward at different stages in the learning process of the rat. *Journal of Genetic Psychology*, 1941a, *59*, 359-376.

Anderson, E. E. The externalization of drive: III. Maze learning by non-rewarded and by satiated rats. *Journal of Genetic Psychology*, 1941b, *59*, 397-426.

Anderson, N. H. Comparison of different populations: Resistance to extinction and transfer. *Psychological Review*, 1963, *70*, 162-179.

Andersson, B. The effect of injections of hypertonic NaCL solutions into different parts of the hypothalamus of goats. *Acta Physiologica Scandinavica*, 1953, *28*, 188-201.

Andersson, B. & Larsson, S. An attempt to condition hypothalamic polydipsia. *Acta Physiologica Scandinavica*, 1956, *36*, 377-382.

Annau, Z. & Kamin, L. J. The conditioned emotional response as a function of intensity of the US. *Journal of Comparative and Physiological Psychology*, 1961, *54*, 428-432.

Appel, J. B. Punishment and shock intensity. *Science*, 1963, *141*, 528-529.

Armus, H. L. Drive level and habit reversal. *Psychological Reports*, 1958, *4*, 31-34.

Armus, H. L. Effect of magnitude of reinforcement on acquisition and extinction of a running response. *Journal of Experimental Psychology*, 1959, *58*, 61-63.

Armus, H. L. & Garlich, M. M. Secondary reinforcement strength as a function of schedule of primary reinforcement. *Journal of Comparative and Physiological Psychology*, 1961, *54*, 56-58.

Ashida, S. & Birch, D. The effects of incentive shift as a function of training. *Psychonomic Science*, 1964, *1*, 201-202.

Ashton, A. B., Bitgood, S. C., & Moore, J. W. Auditory differential conditioning of the rabbit nictitating membrane response: III. Effects of US shock intensity and duration. *Psychonomic Science*, 1969, *15*, 127-128.

Ayres, J. J. B. & Quinsey, V. L. Between groups incentive effects on conditioned suppression. *Psychonomic Science*, 1970, *21*, 294-296.

Azrin, N. H. Some effects of two intermittent schedules of immediate and nonimmediate punishment. *Journal of Psychology*, 1956, *42*, 3-21.

Bacon, W. E. Partial-reinforcement extinction following different amounts of training. *Journal of Comparative and Physiological Psychology*, 1962, *55*, 998-1003.

Badia, P. & Defran, R. H. Orienting responses and GSR conditioning: A dilemma. *Psychological Review*, 1970, 77, 171–181.

Badia, P. & Harley, J. P. Habituation and temporal conditioning as related to shock intensity and its judgment. *Journal of Experimental Psychology*, 1970, *84*, 534–536.

Baer, P. E. & Fuhrer, M. J. Cognitive processes during differential trace and delayed conditioning of the GSR. *Journal of Experimental Psychology*, 1968, *78*, 81–88.

Bahrick, H. P. Sensory preconditioning under two degrees of deprivation. *Journal of Comparative and Physiological Psychology*, 1953, *46*, 39–42.

Baker, L. E. The pupillary response conditioned to subliminal auditory stimuli. *Psychological Monographs*, 1938, *50*, No. 223.

Baker, R. A. & Osgood, C. W. Discrimination transfer along a pitch continuum. *Journal of Experimental Psychology*, 1954, *48*, 241–246.

Baker, T. W. Properties of compound conditioned stimuli and their components. *Psychological Bulletin*, 1968, *70*, 611–625.

Barker, L. M. & Smith, J. C. A comparison of taste aversions induced by radiation and lithium chloride in CS-US and US-CS paradigms. *Journal of Experimental Psychology*, 1974, *87*, 644–654.

Barnes, G. W. Conditioned stimulus intensity and temporal factors in spaced-trial classical conditioning. *Journal of Experimental Psychology*, 1956, *51*, 192–198.

Barnes, G. W. & Kish, G. B. Reinforcing properties of the onset of auditory stimulation. *Journal of Experimental Psychology*, 1961, *62*, 164–170.

Baron, A. Delayed punishment of a runway response. *Journal of Comparative and Physiological Psychology*, 1965, *60*, 131–134.

Barrett, R. J., Peyser, C. S., & McHose, J. H. Effects of complete and incomplete reward reduction on a subsequent response. *Psychonomic Science*, 1965, *3*, 277–278.

Barry, H., III. Effects of strength of drive on learning and on extinction. *Journal of Experimental Psychology*, 1958, *55*, 473–481.

Bass, M. J. & Hull, C. L. The irradiation of a tactile conditioned reflex in man. *Journal of Comparative Psychology*, 1934, *17*, 47–65.

Batten, D. E. & Shoemaker, H. A. The effect of incentive palatability on a conditioned operant response. *Journal of Comparative and Physiological Psychology*, 1961, *54*, 577–579.

Bauermeister, J. J. & Schaeffer, R. W. Reinforcement relation: Reversibility within daily experimental sessions. *The Bulletin of the Psychonomic Society*, 1974, *3*, 206–208.

Bechterev, V. M. *General principles of human reflexology.* New York: International, 1928.

Beck, C. H., Warren, J. M. & Sterner, R. Overtraining and reversal learning by cats and rhesus monkeys. *Journal of Comparative and Physiological Psychology*, 1966, *62*, 332–335.

Beck, E. C. & Doty, R. W. Conditioned flexion responses acquired during combined catalepsy and de-efferentiation. *Journal of Comparative and Physiological Psychology*, 1957, *50*, 211–216.

Beck, R. C. On secondary reinforcement and shock termination. *Psychological Bulletin*, 1961, *58*, 24–45.

Beck, S. B. Eyelid conditioning as a function of CS intensity, UCS intensity, and manifest anxiety scale score. *Journal of Experimental Psychology*, 1963, *66*, 429–438.

Beecroft, R. S. *Classical conditioning.* Goleta, California: Psychonomic Press, 1966.

Beecroft, R. S. & Bouska, S. A. Acquisition of avoidance running in the rat. *Psychonomic Science,* 1967, *9,* 163-164.

Beeman, E. V., Hartman, T. F., & Grant, D. A. Influence of intertrial interval during extinction on spontaneous recovery of conditioned eyelid responses. *Journal of Experimental Psychology,* 1960, *59,* 279-280.

Benedict, J. O. & Ayres, J. J. B. Factors affecting conditioning in the truly random control procedure in the rat. *Journal of Comparative and Physiological Psychology,* 1972, *78,* 323-330.

Berger, B. D. Conditioning of food aversions by injections of psychoactive drugs. *Journal of Comparative and Physiological Psychology,* 1972, *81,* 21-26.

Berger, B. D., Yarczower, M., & Bitterman, M. E. Effect of partial reinforcement on the extinction of a classically conditioned response in the goldfish. *Journal of Comparative and Physiological Psychology,* 1965, *59,* 399-405.

Berger, D. F. Alternative interpretations of the frustration effect. *Journal of Experimental Psychology,* 1969, *81,* 475-483.

Berkson, G. Food motivation and delayed response in gibbons. *Journal of Comparative and Physiological Psychology,* 1962, *55,* 1040-1043.

Berkun, M. M., Kessen, M. L., & Miller, N. E. Hunger-reducing effects of food by stomach fistula versus food by mouth measured by a consummatory response. *Journal of Comparative and Physiological Psychology,* 1952, *45,* 550-554.

Berlyne, D. E. Novelty and curiosity as determinants of exploratory behavior. *British Journal of Psychology,* 1950, *41,* 68-80.

Berlyne, D. E. *Conflict, arousal, and curiosity.* New York: McGraw-Hill, 1960.

Bernstein, A. L. Temporal factors in the formation of conditioned eyelid reactions in human subjects. *Journal of General Psychology,* 1943, *10,* 173-197.

Bersh, P. J. The influence of two variables upon the establishment of a secondary reinforcer for operant responses. *Journal of Experimental Psychology,* 1951, *41,* 62-73.

Bevan, W. & Adamson, R. Reinforcers and reinforcement: Their relationship to maze performance. *Journal of Experimental Psychology,* 1960, *59,* 226-232.

Bevan, W. & Dukes, W. F. Effectiveness of delayed punishment on learning performance when preceded by premonitory cues. *Psychological Reports,* 1955, *1,* 441-448.

Biel, W. C. & Wickens, D. D. The effects of Vitamin B_1 deficiency on the conditioning of eyelid responses in the rat. *Journal of Comparative Psychology,* 1941, *32,* 329-340.

Bilbrey, J. & Winokur, S. Controls for and constraints on auto-shaping. *Journal of the Experimental Analysis of Behavior,* 1973, *20,* 323-332.

Birch, D. Discrimination learning as a function of the ratio of non-reinforced to reinforced trials. *Journal of Comparative and Physiological Psychology,* 1955, *48,* 371-374.

Birch D., Burnstein, E., & Clark, R. A. Response strength as a function of hours of food deprivation under a controlled maintenance schedule. *Journal of Comparative and Physiological Psychology,* 1958, *51,* 350-354.

Birch, H. G. The relation of previous experience to insightful problem solving. *Journal of Comparative and Physiological Psychology,* 1954, *38,* 367-383.

Birch, H. G. & Bitterman, M. E. Reinforcement and learning: The process of sensory integration. *Psychological Review,* 1949, *56,* 292-307.

Birk, L., Crider, A., Shapiro, D., & Tursky, B. Operant electrodermal conditioning under partial curarization. *Journal of Comparative and Physiological Psychology*, 1966, *62*, 165-166.

Birnbaum, I. M. Discrimination reversal, extinction, and acquisition after different amounts of overtraining. *American Journal of Psychology*, 1967, *80*, 363-369.

Bitterman, M. E. Techniques for the study of learning in animals: Analysis and classification. *Psychological Bulletin*, 1962. *59*, 81-92.

Bitterman, M. E. Classical conditioning in the goldfish as a function of the CS-US interval. *Journal of Comparative and Physiological Psychology*, 1964, *58*, 359-366.

Bitterman, M. E. Phyletic differences in learning. *American Psychologist*, 1965, *20*, 396-410.

Bitterman, M. E., Reed, P., & Krauskopf, J. Effect of duration of the unconditioned stimulus on conditioning and extinction. *American Journal of Psychology*, 1952, *65*, 257-262.

Bitterman, M. E., Reed, P. C., & Kubala, A. L. The strength of sensory preconditioning. *Journal of Experimental Psychology*, 1953, *46*, 178-182.

Black, A. H. Transfer following operant conditioning in the curarized dog. *Science*, 1967, *155*, 201-203.

Black R., Adamson, R., & Bevan, W. Runway behavior as a function of apparent intensity of shock. *Journal of Comparative and Physiological Psychology*, 1961, *54*, 270-274.

Black, R. W. Shifts in magnitude of reward and contrast effects in instrumental selective learning: A reinterpretation. *Psychological Review*, 1968, *75*, 114-126.

Black, R. W. & Black, P. E. Heart rate conditioning as a function of interstimulus interval in rats. *Psychonomic Science*, 1967, *8*, 219-220.

Black, R. W. & Spence, K. W. Effects of intertrial reinforcement on resistance to extinction following extended training. *Journal of Experimental Psychology*, 1965, *70*, 559-563.

Blazek, N. C. & Harlow, H. F. Persistence of performance differences on discriminations of varying difficulty. *Journal of Comparative and Physiological Psychology*, 1955, *48*, 86-89.

Blodgett, H. C. The effect of the introduction of reward upon the maze performance of rats. *University of California Publications in Psychology*, 1929, *4*, 113-134.

Bloomfield, T. M. Behavioral contrast and relative reinforcement frequency in two multiple schedules. *Journal of the Experimental Analysis of Behavior*, 1967, *10*, 151-158.

Boe, E. E. Bibliography on punishment. In B. A. Campbell & R. M. Church (Eds.), *Punishment and aversive behavior*. New York: Appleton-Century-Crofts, 1969.

Boe, E. E. & Church, R. M. Permanent effects of punishment during extinction. *Journal of Comparative and Physiological Psychology*, 1967, *63*, 486-492.

Boice, R. & Boice, C. An inverse effect of UCS intensity upon partially reinforced eyelid conditioning. *Psychonomic Science*, 1966, *5*, 69-70.

Bolles, R. C. *Theory of motivation*. New York: Harper & Row, 1967.

Bolles, R. C. Species-specific defense reactions and avoidance learning. *Psychological Review*, 1970, 77, 32-48.

Bolles, R. C. & Grossen, N. E. The noncontingent manipulation of incentive motivation. In J. H. Reynierse (Ed.), *Current issues in animal learning*. Lincoln: University of Nebraska Press, 1970.

Boneau, C. A. The interstimulus interval and the latency of the conditioned eye-lid response. *Journal of Experimental Psychology*, 1958, *56*, 464-472.

Boren, J. J., Sidman, M., & Herrnstein, R. J. Avoidance, escape, and extinction as functions of shock intensity. *Journal of Comparative and Physiological Psychology*, 1959, *52*, 420-425.

Bowen, J. & McCain, G. Occurrence of the partial reinforcement effect after only one NRNR sequence of trials. *Psychonomic Science*, 1967, *9*, 15-16.

Bower, G. H. A contrast effect in differential conditioning. *Journal of Experimental Psychology*, 1961, *62*, 196-199.

Bower, G. H. The influence of graded reductions in reward and prior frustrating events upon the magnitude of the frustration effect. *Journal of Comparative and Physiological Psychology*, 1962, *55*, 582-587.

Bower, G. H. & Miller, N. E. Rewarding and punishing effects from stimulating the same place in the rat's brain. *Journal of Comparative and Physiological Psychology*, 1958, *51*, 669-674.

Boyer, W. N. & Cross, H. A. Discrimination reversal learning in naive stump-tailed monkeys as a function of number of acquisition trials. *Psychonomic Science*, 1965, *2*, 139-140.

Brackbill, Y. & Koltsova, M. M. Conditioning and learning. In Y. Brackbill (Ed.), *Infancy and early childhood.* New York: Free Press, 1967.

Brackbill, Y., Lintz, L. M. & Fitzgerald, H. Differences in the autonomic and somatic conditioning of infants. *Psychosomatic Medicine.* 1968, *30*, 193-201.

Brady, J. V., Boren, J. J., Conrad, D. G., & Sidman, M. The effect of food and water deprivation upon intracranial self-stimulation. *Journal of Comparative and Physiological Psychology*, 1957, *50*, 134-137.

Brady, J. V. & Conrad, D. G. Some effects of limbic system self-stimulation upon conditioned emotional behavior. *Journal of Comparative and Physiological Psychology*, 1960, *53*, 128-137.

Brady, J. V. & Hunt, H. F. A further demonstration of the effects of electro-convulsive shock on a conditioned emotional response. *Journal of Comparative and Physiological Psychology*, 1951, *44*, 204-209.

Braud, W. G. Effectiveness of "neutral" habituated, shock-related and food related stimuli as CS for avoidance learning in goldfish. *Conditional Reflex*, 1971, *6*, 153-156.

Breland, K. & Breland, M. *Animal behavior.* New York: Macmillan, 1966.

Brener, J. & Hothersall, D. Heart rate control under conditions of augmented sensory feedback. *Psychophysiology*, 1966, *3*, 23-28.

Brener, J. & Hothersall, D. Paced respiration and heart rate control. *Psychophysiology*, 1967, *4*, 1-6.

Brimer, C. J. & Dockrill, F. J. Partial reinforcement and the CER. *Psychonomic Science*, 1966, *5*, 185-186.

Broadhurst, P. L. Emotionality and the Yerkes-Dodson law. *Journal of Experimental Psychology*, 1957, *54*, 345-352.

Brogden, W. J. Sensory pre-conditioning. *Journal of Experimental Psychology*, 1939, *25*, 323-332.

Brogden, W. J. Sensory pre-conditioning of human subjects. *Journal of Experimental Psychology*, 1947, *37*, 527-539.

Brogden, W. J. Acquisition and extinction of a conditioned avoidance response in dogs. *Journal of Comparative and Physiological Psychology*, 1949, *42*, 296-302.

Brogden, W. J. & Gantt, W. H. Intraneural conditioning: Cerebellar conditioned reflexes. *Archives of Neurology and Psychiatry*, 1942, *48*, 437–455.

Brogden, W. J., Lipman, E. A., & Culler, E. The role of incentive in conditioning and extinction. *American Journal of Psychology*, 1938, *51*, 109–117.

Brookshire, K. H., Warren, J. M., & Ball, G. G. Reversal and transfer learning following overtraining in rat and chicken. *Journal of Comparative and Physiological Psychology*, 1961, *54*, 98–102.

Brown, C. C. & Katz, R. A. Operant salivary conditioning in man. *Psychophysiology*, 1967, *4*, 156–160.

Brown, J. S. Generalization and discrimination. In D. Mostofsky (Ed.), *Stimulus generalization.* Stanford: Stanford University Press, 1965.

Brown, J. S., Bilodeau, E. A., & Baron, M. R. Bidirectional gradients in the strength of a generalized voluntary response to stimuli on a visual-spatial dimension. *Journal of Experimental Psychology*, 1951, *41*, 52–61.

Brown, J. S. & Farber, I. E. Emotions conceptualized as intervening variables— with suggestions toward a theory of frustration. *Psychological Bulletin*, 1951, *48*, 465–480.

Brown, J. S. & Jacobs, A. The role of fear in the motivation and acquisition of responses. *Journal of Experimental Psychology*, 1949, *39*, 747–759.

Brown, J. S., Kalish, H. I., & Farber, I. E. Conditioned fear as revealed by magnitude of startle response to an auditory stimulus. *Journal of Experimental Psychology*, 1951, *41*, 317–328.

Brown, P. L. & Jenkins, H. M. Auto-shaping of the pigeon's key-peck. *Journal of the Experimental Analysis of Behavior*, 1968, *11*, 1–8.

Brown, R. T. & Logan, F. A. Generalized partial reinforcement effect. *Journal of Comparative and Physiological Psychology*, 1965, *60*, 64–69.

Bruner, J. S., Mandler, J. M. O'Dowd, D. & Wallach, M. A. The role of overlearning and drive level in reversal learning. *Journal of Comparative and Physiological Psychology*, 1958, *51*, 607–613.

Brush, F. R., Brush, E. S., & Solomon, R. L. Traumatic avoidance learning: The effects of the CS-UCS interval with a delayed-conditioning procedure. *Journal of Comparative and Physiological Psychology*, 1955, *48*, 285–293.

Bryan, J. H. & Carlson, P. V. Spontaneous activity and food deprivation in human subjects. *Perceptual and Motor Skills*, 1962, *15*, 123–126.

Buchwald, A. M. & Yamaguchi, H. G. The effect of change in drive level on habit reversal. *Journal of Experimental Psychology*, 1955, *50*, 265–268.

Buerger, A. A. & Dawson, A. M. Spinal kittens: Long-term increases in electromyograms due to a conditioning routine. *Physiology and Behavior*, 1968, *3*, 99–103.

Buerger, A. A. & Dawson, A. M. Spinal kittens: Effect of clamping of the thoracic aorta on long-term increases in electromyograms due to a conditioning routine. *Experimental Neurology*, 1969, *23*, 457–464.

Bugelski, B. R. Extinction with and without sub-goal reinforcement. *Journal of Comparative Psychology*, 1938, *26*, 121–134.

Bunch, M. E. Experimental extinction in learning and memory. *Journal of General Psychology*, 1963, *69*, 275–291.

Burstein, K. R. The influence of UCS upon the acquisition of the conditioned eyelid response. *Psychonomic Science*, 1965, *2*, 303–304.

Burstein, K. R., Epstein, S., & Smith, B. Primary stimulus generalization of the GSR as a function of objective and subjective definition of the stimulus dimension. *Journal of Experimental Psychology*, 1967, *74*, 124–131.

Bursten, B. & Delgado, J. M. R. Positive reinforcement induced by intracerebral stimulation in the monkey. *Journal of Comparative and Physiological Psychology*, 1958, *51*, 6-10.

Butler, R. A. The effect of deprivation of visual incentives on visual exploration motivation in monkeys. *Journal of Comparative and Physiological Psychology*, 1957a, *50*, 177-179.

Butler, R. A. Discrimination learning by rhesus monkeys to auditory incentives. *Journal of Comparative and Physiological Psychology*, 1957b, *50*, 239-241.

Butter, C. M. & Thomas, D. R. Secondary reinforcement as a function of the amount of primary reinforcement. *Journal of Comparative and Physiological Psychology*, 1958, *51*, 346-348.

Calvin, J. S., Bicknell, E. A., & Sperling, D. S. Establishment of a conditioned drive based on the hunger drive. *Journal of Comparative and Physiological Psychology*, 1953, *46*, 173-175.

Camp, D. S., Raymond, G. A., & Church, R. M. Temporal relationship between response and punishment. *Journal of Experimental Psychology*, 1967, *74*, 114-123.

Campbell, A. A. The interrelations of two measures of conditioning in man. *Journal of Experimental Psychology*, 1938, *22*, 225-243.

Campbell, A. A. & Hilgard, E. R. Individual differences in ease of conditioning. *Journal of Experimental Psychology*, 1936, *19*, 561-571.

Campbell, B. A. & Kraeling, D. Response strength as a function of drive level and amount of drive reduction. *Journal of Experimental Psychology*, 1953, *45*, 97-101.

Campbell, B. A. & Masterson, F. A. Psychophysics of punishment. In B. A. Campbell & R. M. Church (Eds.), *Punishment and aversive behavior*. New York: Appleton-Century-Crofts, 1969.

Campbell, B. A. & Misanin, J. R. Basic drives. In P. H. Mussen & M. R. Rosenzweig (Eds.), *Annual Review of Psychology*, 1969.

Campbell, B. A., Smith N. F., Misanin, J. R., & Jaynes, J. Species differences in activity during hunger and thirst. *Journal of Comparative and Physiological Psychology*, 1966, *61*, 123-127.

Campbell, P. E., Crumbaugh, C. M., Knouse, S. B., & Snodgrass, M. E. A test of the "ceiling effect" hypothesis of positive contrast. *Psychonomic Science*, 1970, *20*, 17-18.

Campbell, P. E., Knouse, S. B., & Wroten, J. D. Resistance to extinction in the rat following regular and irregular schedules of partial reward. *Journal of Comparative and Physiological Psychology*, 1970, *72*, 210-215.

Cantor, G. N. & Spiker, C. C. Effects of nonreinforced trials on discrimination learning in preschool children. *Journal of Experimental Psychology*, 1954, *47*, 256-258.

Capaldi, E. J. The effect of different amounts of alternating partial reinforcement on resistance to extinction. *American Journal of Psychology*, 1957, *70*, 451-452.

Capaldi, E. J. The effect of different amounts of training on the resistance to extinction of different patterns of partially reinforced responses. *Journal of Comparative and Physiological Psychology*, 1958, *51*, 367-371.

Capaldi, E. J. Partial reinforcement: A hypothesis of sequential effects. *Psychological Review*, 1966, *73*, 459-477.

Capaldi, E. J. A sequential hypothesis of instrumental learning. In K. W. Spence & J. T. Spence (Eds.). *The psychology of learning and motivation*, Vol. 1. New York: Academic Press, 1967.

Capaldi, E. J. An analysis of the role of reward and reward magnitude in instrumental learning. In J. H. Reynierse (Ed.), *Current issues in animal learning.* Lincoln: University of Nebraska Press. 1970.

Capaldi, E. J. Memory and learning: A sequential viewpoint. In W. K. Honig & P. H. R. James (Eds.), *Animal memory.* New York: Academic Press, 1971.

Capaldi, E. J. & Deutsch, E. A. Effects of severely limited acquisition training and pretraining on the partial reinforcement effect. *Psychonomic Science,* 1967, *9,* 171-172.

Capaldi, E. J. & Hart, D. Influence of a small number of partial reinforcement training trials on resistance to extinction. *Journal of Experimental Psychology,* 1962, *64,* 166-171.

Capaldi, E. J., Hart, D., & Stanley, L. R. Influence of intertrial reinforcement on the aftereffect of nonreinforcement and resistance to extinction. *Journal of Experimental Psychology,* 1963, *65,* 70-74.

Capaldi, E. J., Lanier, A. T., & Godbout, R. C. Reward schedule effects following severely limited acquisition training. *Journal of Experimental Psychology,* 1968, *78,* 521-524.

Capaldi, E. J. & Spivey, J. E. Effect of goal-box similarity on the aftereffect of nonreinforcement and resistance to extinction. *Journal of Experimental Psychology,* 1963, *66,* 461-465.

Capaldi, E. J. & Stevenson, H. W. Response reversal following different amounts of training. *Journal of Comparative Physiological Psychology,* 1957, *50,* 195-198.

Capaldi, E. J. & Wargo, P. Effect of transitions from nonreinforced to reinforced trials under spaced-trial conditions. *Journal of Experimental Psychology,* 1963, *65,* 318-319.

Capaldi, E. J., Ziff, D. R., & Godbout, R. C. Extinction and the necessity or non-necessity of anticipating reward or nonrewarded trials. *Psychonomic Science, 1970, 18,* 61-63.

Carder, B. Rat's preference for earned in comparison with free liquid reinforcers. *Psychonomic Science,* 1972, *26,* 25-26.

Carder, B. & Berkowitz, K. Rat's preference for earned in comparison with free food. *Science,* 1970, *167,* 1273-1274.

Carlson, J. G. Frustrative nonreinforcement of operant responding: Magnitude of reinforcement and response force effects. *Psychonomic Science,* 1968, *11,* 307-308.

Carlton, P. L. & Vogel, J. R. Habituation and conditioning. *Journal of Comparative and Physiological Psychology,* 1967, *63,* 348-351.

Carter, L. F. Intensity of conditioned stimulus and rate of conditioning. *Journal of Experimental Psychology,* 1941, *28,* 481-490.

Cason, H. The conditioned pupillary reaction. *Journal of Experimental Psychology,* 1922, *5,* 108-146.

Cason, H. Backward conditioned eyelid reactions. *Journal of Experimental Psychology,* 1935, *18,* 599-611.

Cautela, J. R. The problem of backward conditioning. *Journal of Psychology,* 1965, *60,* 135-144.

Chacto, C. & Lubow, R. E. Classical conditioning and latent inhibition in the white rat. *Psychonomic Science,* 1967, *9,* 135-136.

Champion, R. A. Stimulus-intensity effects in response evocation. *Psychological Review,* 1962, *69,* 428-449.

Champion, R. A. & Jones, J. E. Forward, backward, and pseudoconditioning of the GSR. *Journal of Experimental Psychology,* 1961, *62,* 58-61.

Champion, R. A. & McBride, D. A. Activity during delay of reinforcement in human learning. *Journal of Experimental Psychology*, 1962, *63*, 589-592.

Charlesworth, W. R. & Thompson, W. R. Effect of lack of visual stimulus variation on exploratory behavior in the adult white rat. *Psychological Reports*, 1957, *3*, 509-512.

Chernikoff, R. & Brogden, W. J. The effect of different instructions upon the occurrence of sensory preconditioning. *Journal of Experimental Psychology*, 1949, *39*, 200-207.

Church, R. M. The varied effects of punishment on behavior. *Psychological Review*, 1963, *70*, 369-402.

Church, R. M. Response suppression. In B. A. Campbell & R. M. Church (Eds.), *Punishment and aversive behavior*. New York: Appleton-Century-Crofts, 1969.

Church, R. M. & Black, A. H. Latency of the conditioned heart rate as a function of the CS-US interval. *Journal of Comparative and Physiological Psychology*, 1958, *51*, 478-482.

Church, R. M., Brush, F. R., & Solomon, R. L. Traumatic avoidance learning: The effects of CS-UCS interval with a delayed conditioning procedure in a free-responding situation. *Journal of Comparative and Physiological Psychology*, 1956, *49*, 301-308.

Church, R. M., Raymond, G. A., & Beauchamp, R. D. Response suppression as a function of intensity and duration of a punishment. *Journal of Comparative and Physiological Psychology*, 1967, *63*, 30-44.

Cicala, G. A. & Kremer, E. The effects of shock intensity and d-amphetamine on avoidance learning. *Psychonomic Science*, 1969, *14*, 41-42.

Clark, F. C. The effect of deprivation and frequency of reinforcement on variable interval responding. *Journal of the Experimental Analysis of Behavior*, 1958, *1*, 221-228.

Clayton, K. N. Overlearning and reversal of a spatial discrimination by rats. *Perceptual and Motor Skills*, 1963a, *17*, 83-85.

Clayton, K. N. Reversal performance by rats following overlearning with and without irrelevant stimuli. *Journal of Experimental Psychology*. 1963b, *66*, 255-259.

Clayton, K. N. T-maze choice learning as a joint function of the reward magnitudes for the alternatives. *Journal of Comparative and Physiological Psychology*, 1964, *58*, 333-338.

Coate, W. B. Effect of deprivation on postdiscrimination stimulus generalization in the rat. *Journal of Comparative and Physiological Psychology*, 1964, *57*, 134-138.

Cofer, C. N. & Appley, M. H. *Motivation: Theory and research*. New York: Wiley, 1964.

Cohen, D. H. Effect of conditioned stimulus intensity on visually conditioned heart rate change in the pigeon: A sensitization mechanism. *Journal of Comparative and Physiological Psychology*, 1974, *87*, 495-499.

Cohen, D. H. & MacDonald, R. L. Some variables affecting orienting and conditioned heart-rate responses in the pigeon. *Journal of Comparative and Physiological Psychology*, 1971, *74*, 123-133.

Cohen, J. *Operant behavior and operant conditioning*. Chicago: Rand-McNally, 1969.

Cohen, M. J. & Johnson, H. J. Relationship between heart rate and muscular activity within a classical conditioning paradigm. *Journal of Experimental Psychology*, 1971, *90*, 222-226.

Cole, M., Gay, J., Glick, J. A., & Sharp, D. W. *The cultural context of learning and thinking.* New York: Basic Books, 1970.

Collier, G., Knarr, F. A., & Marx, M. H. Some relations between the intensive properties of the consummatory response and reinforcement. *Journal of Experimental Psychology,* 1961, *62,* 484–495.

Collier, G. & Marx, M. H. Changes in performance as a function of shifts in the magnitude of reinforcement. *Journal of Experimental Psychology,* 1959, *57,* 305–309.

Collier, G. & Rega, F. Two-bar sucrose preference. *Learning and Motivation,* 1971, *2,* 190–194.

Compione, J. C. & Beaton, V. L. Transfer of training: Some boundary conditions and initial theory. *Journal of Experimental Child Psychology,* 1972, *12,* 94–114.

Conrad, D. G. & Sidman, M. Sucrose concentration as reinforcement for lever pressing by monkeys. *Psychological Reports,* 1956, *2,* 381–384.

Cook, S. W. & Harris, R. E. The verbal conditioning of the galvanic skin reflex. *Journal of Experimental Psychology,* 1937, *21,* 202–210.

Coons, E. E., Levak, M., & Miller, N. E. Lateral hypothalamus: Learning of food-seeking response motivated by electrical stimulation. *Science,* 1965, *150,* 1320–1321.

Coons, E. E. & Miller, N. E. Conflict versus consolidation of memory traces to explain "retrograde amnesia" produced by ECS. *Journal of Comparative and Physiological Psychology,* 1960, *53,* 524–531.

Coppock, W. J. Pre-extinction in sensory pre-conditioning. *Journal of Experimental Psychology,* 1958, *55,* 213–219.

Corah, N. L. & Tomkiewicz, R. L. Classical conditioning of the electrodermal response with novel stimuli. *Psychophysiology,* 1971, *8,* 143–148.

Cotton, J. W. Running time as a function of amount of food deprivation. *Journal of Experimental Psychology,* 1953, *46,* 188–198.

Cotton, J. W. On making predictions from Hull's theory. *Psychological Review,* 1955, *62,* 303–314.

Coughlin, R. C. Frustration effect and resistance to extinction as a function of percentage of reinforcement. *Journal of Experimental Psychology,* 1970, *84,* 113–119.

Cousins, L. S., Zamble, E. D., Tait, R. W., & Suboski, M. D. Sensory preconditioning in curarized rats. *Journal of Comparative and Physiological Psychology,* 1971, *77,* 152–154.

Cowles, J. T. Food tokens as incentives for learning by chimpanzees. *Comparative Psychology Monographs,* 1937, *14,* No. 5.

Cowles, J. T. & Nissen, H. W. Reward expectancy in delayed responses of chimpanzees. *Journal of Comparative Psychology,* 1937, *24,* 345–358.

Crasilneck, H. B. & McCranie, E. J. On the conditioning of the pupillary reflex. *Journal of Psychology,* 1956, *42,* 23–27.

Cravens, R. W. & Renner, K. E. Conditioned hunger. *Journal of Experimental Psychology,* 1969, *81,* 312–316.

Cravens, R. W. & Renner, K. E. Conditioned appetitive drive states: Empirical evidence and theoretical status. *Psychological Bulletin,* 1970, *73,* 212–220.

Creelman, M. B. *The experimental investigation of meaning: A review of the literature.* New York: Springer, 1966.

Crespi, L. P. Quantitative variation of incentive and performance in the white rat. *American Journal of Psychology,* 1942, *55,* 467–517.

Cross, H. A. & Brown, L. T. Discrimination reversal learning in squirrel monkeys as a function of number of acquisition trials and prereversal experience. *Journal of Comparative and Physiological Psychology*, 1965, *59*, 429-431.

Crowell, C. R. & Anderson, D. C. Variations in intensity, interstimulus interval, and interval between preconditioning CS exposures and conditioning with rats. *Journal of Comparative and Physiological Psychology*, 1972, *79*, 291-298.

Culbertson, J. L., Kling, J. W., & Berkley, M. A. Extinction responding following ICS and food reinforcement. *Psychonomic Science*, 1966, *5*, 127-128.

Daly, H. B. Excitatory and inhibitory effects of complete and incomplete reward reduction in the double runway. *Journal of Experimental Psychology*, 1968, *76*, 430-438.

D'Amato, M. R. Secondary reinforcement and magnitude of primary reinforcement. *Journal of Comparative and Physiological Psychology*, 1955, *48*, 378-380.

D'Amato, M. R. Derived motives. *Annual Review of Psychology*, 1974, *25*, 83-106.

D'Amato, M. R. & Jagoda, H. Analysis of the role of overlearning in discrimination learning. *Journal of Experimental Psychology*, 1961, *61*, 45-50.

D'Amato, M. R. & Jagoda, H. Overlearning and position reversal. *Journal of Experimental Psychology*, 1962, *64*, 117-122.

D'Amato, M. R., Lachman, R., & Kivy, P. Secondary reinforcement as affected by reward schedule and the testing situation. *Journal of Comparative and Physiological Psychology*, 1958, *51*, 737-741.

D'Amato, M. R. & Schiff, D. Further studies of overlearning and position reversal learning. *Psychological Reports*, 1964, *14*, 380-382.

D'Amato, M. R. & Schiff, D. Overlearning and brightness discrimination reversal. *Journal of Experimental Psychology*, 1965, *69*, 375-381.

Davenport, J. W. Species generality of within-subjects reward magnitude effects. *Canadian Journal of Psychology*, 1970, *24*, 1-7.

Davenport, J. W. & Thompson, C. I. The Amsel frustration effect in monkeys. *Psychonomic Science*, 1965, *3*, 481-482,

Davis, J. D. & Keehn, J. D. Magnitude of reinforcement and consummatory behavior. *Science*, 1959, *130*, 269-271.

Davitz, J. R., Mason, D. J., Mowrer, O. H., & Viek, P. Conditioning of fear: A function of the delay of reinforcement. *American Journal of Psychology*, 1957, *70*, 69-74.

Dawson, M. E. Cognition and conditioning: Effects of masking the CS-UCS contingency on human GSR classical conditioning. *Journal of Experimental Psychology*, 1970, *85*, 389-396.

Dawson, M. E. Can classical conditioning occur without contingency learning? A review and evaluation of the evidence. *Psychophysiology*, 1973, *10*, 82-86.

Dawson, M. E. & Biferno, N. A. Concurrent measurement of awareness and electrodermal classical conditioning. *Journal of Experimental Psychology*, 1973, *101*, 55-62.

Dawson, M. E. & Grings, W. W. Comparison of classical conditioning and relational learning. *Journal of Experimental Psychology*, 1968, *76*, 227-231.

Dawson, M. E. & Reardon, P. Effects of facilitory and inhibitory sets on GSR conditioning and extinction. *Journal of Experimental Psychology*, 1969, *82*, 462-466.

Degtiar, E. N. Cited in Y. Brackbill & M. M. Koltsova, Conditioning and Learning. In Y. Brackbill (Ed.), *Infancy and early childhood*. New York: Free Press, 1967.

De Leon, G. Conditioning the human heart rate with noise as the unconditioned stimulus. *Journal of Experimental Psychology*, 1964, *68*, 518-520.

Delgado, J. M. R. Chronic implantation of intracerebral electrodes in animals. In D. E. Sheer (Ed.), *Electrical stimulation of the brain*. Austin: University of Texas Press, 1961.

Delgado, J. M. R. & Anand, B. K. Increase of food intake induced by electrical stimulation of the lateral hypothalamus. *American Journal of Physiology*, 1953, *172*, 162-168.

Delgado, J. M. R., Roberts, W. W., & Miller, N. E. Learning motivated by electrical stimulation of the brain. *American Journal of Physiology*, 1954, *179*, 587-593.

deLorge, J. & Bolles, R. C. The effect of food deprivation upon exploration in a novel environment. *Psychological Reports*, 1961, *9*, 599-606.

Denenberg, V. H. & Karas, G. C. Supplementary report: The Yerkes-Dodson law and shift in task difficulty. *Journal of Experimental Psychology*, 1960, *59*, 429-430.

Denny, M. R. & Dunham, M. D. The effect of differential nonreinforcement of the incorrect response on the learning of the correct response in the simple T-maze. *Journal of Experimental Psychology*, 1951, *41*, 382-389.

Denny, M. R. & King, G. F. Differential response learning on the basis of differential size of reward. *Journal of Genetic Psychology*, 1955, *87*, 317-320.

DeVito, J. L. & Smith, O. A., Jr. Effects of temperature and food deprivation on the random activity of macaca mulatta. *Journal of Comparative and Physiological Psychology*, 1959, *52*, 29-32.

Dews, P. Free-operant behavior under conditions of delayed reinforcement: I. CRF-type schedules. *Journal of the Experimental Analysis of Behavior*, 1960, *3*, 221-234.

DiCara, L. & Miller, N. E. Instrumental learning of vasomotor responses by rats: Learning to respond differentially in the two ears. *Science*, 1968a, *159*, 1485-1486.

DiCara, L. V. & Miller, N. E. Changes in heart rate instrumentally learned by curarized rats as avoidance responses. *Journal of Comparative and Physiological Psychology*, 1968b, *65*, 1-7.

Dietz, M. N. & Capretta, P. J. Modification of sugar and sugar-saccharin preference in rats as a function of electrical shock to the mouth. Proceedings of the 75th Annual Convention of the American Psychological Association, 1967, 161-162.

DiLollo, V. Runway performance in relation to runway goal-box similarity and changes in incentive amount. *Journal of Comparative and Physiological Psychology*, 1964, *58*, 327-329.

Dinsmoor, J. A. Punishment: I. The avoidance hypothesis. *Psychological Review*, 1954, *61*, 34-46.

Dinsmoor, J. A. Punishment: II. An interpretation of empirical findings. *Psychological Review*, 1955, *62*, 96-105.

Dinsmoor, J. A. Operant conditioning. In J. B. Sidowski (Ed.), *Experimental methods and instrumentation in psychology*. New York: McGraw-Hill, 1966.

Dinsmoor, J. A. *Operant conditioning: An experimental analysis of behavior*. Dubuque, Iowa: W. C. Brown Co., 1970.

Diven, K. Certain determinants in the conditioning of anxiety reactions. *Journal of Psychology*, 1936, *3*, 291-308.

Dmitriev, A. S. On methods of investigation of higher nervous activity in man.

Zhurnal Vysshei Nervnoi Deyatel'nosti, 1956, *6*, 905–912.

Dmitriev, A. S. & Kochigina, A. M. The importance of time as stimulus of conditioned reflex activity. *Psychological Bulletin*, 1959, *56*, 106–132.

Doty, R. W. Conditioned reflexes formed and evoked by brain stimulation. In D. E. Sheer (Ed.), *Electrical stimulation of the brain.* Austin: University of Texas Press, 1961.

Doty, R. W. & Giurgea, C. Conditioned reflexes established by coupling electrical excitation of two cortical areas. In A. Fessard, R. W. Gerard, & J. Konorski (Eds.), *Brain mechanisms and learning.* London: Blackwell Scientific Publications, Ltd., 1961.

Doty, R. W., Rutledge, L. T., Jr., & Larsen, R. M. Conditioned reflexes established to electrical stimulation of cat cerebral cortex. *Journal of Neurophysiology*, 1956, *19*, 401–415.

Dubin, W. J. & Levis, D. J. Generalization of extinction gradients: A systematic analysis. *Journal of Experimental Psychology*, 1973, *100*, 403–412.

Dufort, R. H. & Kimble, G. A. Changes in response strength with changes in the amount of reinforcement. *Journal of Experimental Psychology*, 1956, *51*, 185–191.

Dunham, P. J. Contrasted conditions of reinforcement. *Psychological Bulletin*, 1968, *69*, 295–315.

Dykman, R. A. & Gantt, W. H. The parasympathetic component of unlearned and acquired cardiac responses. *Journal of Comparative and Physiological Psychology*, 1959, *52*, 163–167.

Ebbinghaus, H. *Memory: A contribution to experimental psychology.* (Translated by H. A. Ruger & C. E. Bussenius.) New York: Teachers College, Columbia University, 1913.

Ebel, H. C. & Prokasy, W. F. Classical eyelid conditioning as a function of sustained and shifted interstimulus intervals. *Journal of Experimental Psychology.* 1963, *65*, 52–58.

Eckert, B. & Lewis, M. Competition between drives for intracranial stimulation and sodium chloride by adrenalectomized NACL-deprived rats. *Journal of Comparative and Physiological Psychology*, 1967, *64*, 349–352.

Edelberg, R. The electrodermal system. In N. S. Greenfield & R. A. Sternbach (Eds.), *Handbook of psychophysiology,* New York: Holt, 1972.

Edgington, E. S. Contradictory conclusions from two speed of performance measures. *Psychological Bulletin*, 1960, *57*, 315–317.

Egger, M. D. & Miller, N. E. When is a reward reinforcing?: An experimental study of the information hypothesis. *Journal of Comparative and Physiological Psychology*, 1963, *56*, 131–137.

Ehrenfreund, D. An experimental test of the continuity theory of discrimination learning with pattern vision. *Journal of Comparative and Physiological Psychology*, 1948, *41*, 408–422.

Ehrenfreund, D. & Badia, P. Response strength as a function of drive level and pre- and postshift incentive magnitude. *Journal of Experimental Psychology*, 1962, *63*, 468–471.

Eisenberger, R., Karpman, M. & Trattner, J. What is the necessary and sufficient condition for reinforcement in the contingency situation? *Journal of Experimental Psychology*, 1967, *74*, 342–350.

Eisman, E., Asimow, A, & Maltzman, I. Habit strength as a function of drive in a brightness discrimination problem. *Journal of Experimental Psychology*, 1956, *52*, 58–64.

Ellison, G. D. Differential salivary conditioning to traces. *Journal of Comparative and Physiological Psychology*, 1964, *57*, 373–380.

Ellison, G. D. & Konorski, J. Separation of the salivary and motor responses in instrumental conditioning. *Science*, 1964, *146*, 1071-1072.

Ellison, G. D. & Konorski, J. Salivation and instrumental responding to an instrumental CS pretrained using the classical conditioning paradigm. *Acta Biologiae Experimentalis*, 1966, *26*, 159-165.

Engel, B. T. Operant conditioning of cardiac function: A status report. *Psychophysiology*, 1972, *9*, 161-177.

Engel, B. T. & Chism, R. A. Operant conditioning of heart rate speeding. *Psychophysiology*, 1967, *3*, 418-426.

Engel, B. T. & Hansen, S. P. Operant conditioning of heart rate slowing. *Psychophysiology*, 1966, *3*, 176-187.

Eninger, M. U. Habit summation in a selective learning problem. *Journal of Comparative and Physiological Psychology*, 1952, *45*, 604-608.

Epstein, S. & Burstein, K. R. A replication of Hovland's study of stimulus generalization to frequencies of tone. *Journal of Experimental Psychology*, 1966, *72*, 782-784.

Erickson, M. T. & Lipsitt, L. P. Effects of delayed reward on simultaneous and successive discrimination learning in children. *Journal of Comparative and Physiological Psychology*, 1960, *53*, 256-260.

Erlebacher, A. Reversal learning in rats as a function of percentage of reinforcement and degree of learning. *Journal of Experimental Psychology*, 1963, *66*, 84-90.

Estes, B. W., Miller, L. B., & Curtin, M. E. Supplementary report: Monetary incentive and motivation in discrimination learning—sex differences. *Journal of Experimental Psychology*, 1962, *63*, 320.

Estes, W. K. An experimental study of punishment. *Psychological Monographs*, 1944, *57*, No. 263.

Estes, W. K. Comments on Dr. Bolles' paper. In M. R. Jones (Ed.), *Nebraska symposium on motivation*. Lincoln: University of Nebraska Press, 1958.

Estes, W. K. Learning theory and the new "mental chemistry." *Psychological Review*, 1960, *67*, 207-223.

Estes, W. K. Outline of a theory of punishment. In B. A. Campbell & R. M. Church (Eds.), *Punishment and aversive behavior*. New York: Appleton-Century-Crofts, 1969.

Estes, W. K. & Skinner, B. F. Some quantitative properies of anxiety. *Journal of Experimental Psychology*, 1941, *29*, 390-400.

Feather, B. W. Human salivary conditioning: A methodological study. In G. A. Kimble (Ed.), *Foundations of conditioning and learning*. New York: Appleton-Century-Crofts, 1967.

Fehrer, E. Effects of amount of reinforcement and of pre- and post-reinforcement delays on learning and extinction. *Journal of Experimental Psychology*, 1956, *52*, 167-176.

Ferster, C. B. The use of the free operant in the analysis of behavior. *Psychological Bulletin*, 1953a, *50*, 263-274.

Ferster, C. B. Sustained behavior under delayed reinforcement. *Journal of Experimental Psychology*, 1953b, *45*, 218-224.

Ferster, C. B. & Skinner, B. F. *Schedules of reinforcement*. New York: Appleton-Century-Crofts, 1957.

Fishbein, H. D. Effects of differential instructions, differential feedback, and UCS intensity on the conditioned eyelid response. *Journal of Experimental Psychology*, 1967, *75*, 56-63.

Fishbein, H. D. & Gormezano, I. Effects of differential instructions, differential payoffs, and the presence or absence of feedback on the percentage, latency, and amplitude of the conditioned eyelid response. *Journal of Experimental Psychology*, 1966, *71*, 535-538.

Fishbein, H. D., Jones, P. D., & Silverthorne, C. CS intensity and CS-UCS interval effects in human eyelid conditioning. *Journal of Experimental Psychology*, 1969, *81*, 109-114.

Fishbein, H. D. & LeBlanc, M. Human eyelid conditioning as a function of interstimulus interval. *Journal of Experimental Psychology*, 1967, 75, 130-133.

Fisher, A. E. & Coury, J. N. Cholinergic tracing of a central neural circuit underlying the thirst drive. *Science*, 1962, *138*, 691-693.

Fiske, D. W. & Maddi, S. R. *Functions of varied experience.* Homewood, Ill: Dorsey Press, 1961.

Fitzgerald, H. E., Lintz, L. M., Brackbill, Y., & Adams, G. Time perception and conditioning an autonomic response in human infants. *Perceptual & Motor Skills*, 1967, *24*, 479-486.

Fitzgerald, R. D. Effects of partial reinforcement with acid on the classically conditioned salivary response in dogs. *Journal of Comparative and Physiological Psychology*, 1963, *56*, 1056-1060.

Fitzgerald, R. D. Some effects of partial reinforcement with shock on classical conditioned heart rate in dogs. *Americal Journal of Psychology*, 1966, *79*, 242-249.

Fitzgerald, R. D. Vardaris, R. M., & Brown, J. S. Classical conditioning of heart rate deceleration with continuous and partial reinforcement. *Psychonomic Science*, 1966, *6*, 437-438.

Fitzgerald, R. D., Vardaris, R. M., & Teyler, T. L. Effects of partial reinforcement followed by continuous reinforcement on classically conditioned heart rate in the dog. *Journal of Comparative and Physiological Psychology*, 1966, *62*, 483-486.

Fitzwater, M. E. The relative effect of reinforcement and nonreinforcement in establishing a form discrimination. *Journal of Comparative and Physiological Psychology*, 1952, *45*, 476-481.

Fitzwater, M. E. & Reisman, M. N. Comparison of forward, simultaneous, backward, and pseudo-conditioning. *Journal of Experimental Psychology*, 1952, *44*, 211-214.

Fitzwater, M. E. & Thrush, R. S. Acquisition of a conditioned response as a function of forward temporal contiguity. *Journal of Experimental Psychology*, 1956, *51*, 59-61.

Fleming, R. A. Transfer of differentially conditioned eyelid responses as a function of the associative strength between the acquisition and transfer CSs and the associative strength between CS+ and CS- in the transfer task. Unpublished Ph. D. dissertation, University of Wisconsin, 1968.

Fletcher, H. J. A re-examination of conditioning to elements of a complex as a function of differential onset times. Unpublished Ph. D. dissertation, Ohio State University, 1960.

Forbes, A. & Mahan, C. Attempts to train the spinal cord. *Journal of Comparative and Physiological Psychology*, 1963, *56*, 36-40.

Foth, D. L. & Runquist, W. N. Effects of unconditioned stimulus intensity and schedules of 50% partial reinforcement in human classical eyelid conditioning. *Journal of Experimental Psychology*, 1970, *84*, 244-247.

Fowler, H. & Trapold, M. A. Escape performance as a function of delay of reinforcement. *Journal of Experimental Psychology*, 1962, *63*, 464-467.

Fowler, R. L. & Kimmel, H. D. Operant conditioning of the GSR. *Journal of Experimental Psychology*, 1962, *63*, 563-567.

Fox, R. E. & King, R. A. The effects of reinforcement scheduling on the strength of a secondary reinforcer. *Journal of Comparative and Physiological Psychology*, 1961, *54*, 266-269.

Franks, C. M. Pavlovian conditioning approaches. In D. J. Levis (Ed.), *Learning approaches to therapeutic behavior change.* Chicago: Aldine Publishing Co., 1970.

Freeman, G. L. The galvanic phenomenon and conditioned responses. *Journal of General Psychology*, 1930, *3*, 529-539.

Frey, P. W. Within- and between-session CS intensity performance effects in rabbit eyelid conditioning. *Psychonomic Science*, 1969, *17*, 1-2.

Frey, P. W. & Butler, C. S. Rabbit eyelid conditioning as a function of unconditioned stimulus duration. *Journal of Comparative and Physiological Psychology*, 1973, *85*, 289-294.

Frey, P. W. & Ross, L. E. Classical conditioning of the rabbit eyelid response as a function of interstimulus interval. *Journal of Comparative and Physiological Psychology*, 1968, *65*, 246-250.

Frezza, D. A. & Holland, J. G. Operant conditioning of the human salivary response. *Psychophysiology*, 1971, *8*, 581-587.

Fromer, R. The effect of several shock patterns on the acquisition of the secondary drive of fear. *Journal of Comparative and Physiological Psychology*, 1962, *55*, 142-144.

Fuhrer, M. J. & Baer, P. E. Differential classical conditioning: Verbalization of stimulus contingencies. *Science*, 1965, *150*, 1479-1481.

Fuhrer, M. J. & Baer, P. E. Cognitive processes in differential GSR conditioning: Effects of a masking task. *American Journal of Psychology*, 1969, *82*, 168-180.

Furchgott, E. & Rubin, R. D. The effect of magnitude of reward on maze learning in the white rat. *Journal of Comparative and Physiological Psychology*, 1953, *46*, 9-12.

Furedy, J. J. Classical appetitive conditioning of the GSR with cool air as UCS, and the roles of UCS onset and offset as reinforcers of the CR. *Journal of Experimental Psychology*, 1967, *75*, 73-80.

Furedy, J. J. Explicitly-unpaired and truly-random CS- controls in human classical differential autonomic conditioning. *Psychophysiology*, 1971a, *8*, 497-503.

Furedy, J. J. Cross-modal differentiation under identical reinforcement schedules, and UCS-intensity effects in human classical eyelid conditioning. *Canadian Journal of Psychology*, 1971b, *25*, 7-23.

Furedy, J. J. & Schiffmann, K. Test of the propriety of the traditional discriminative control procedure in Pavlovian electrodermal and plethysmographic conditioning. *Journal of Experimental Psychology*, 1971, *91*, 161-164.

Furedy, J. J. & Schiffmann, K. Concurrent measurement of autonomic and cognitive processes in a test of the traditional discriminative control procedure for Pavlovian electrodermal conditioning. *Journal of Experimental Psychology*, 1973, *100*, 210-217.

Galanter, E. & Bush, R. R. Some T-maze experiments. In R. R. Bush & W. K. Estes (Eds.), *Studies in mathematical learning theory.* Stanford: Stanford University Press, 1959.

Gallistel, C. R. Electrical self-stimulation and its theoretical implications. *Psychological Bulletin*, 1964, *61*, 23-34.

Gallup, G. G., Jr. Aggression in rats as a function of frustrative nonreward in a straight alley. *Psychonomic Science*, 1965, *3*, 99-100.

Gallup, G. G., Jr. & Altomari, T. S. Activity as a post-situation measure of frustrative nonreward. *Journal of Comparative and Physiological Psychology*, 1969, *68*, 382–384.

Gamzu, E. & Schwam, E. Autoshaping and automaintenance of a key-press response in squirrel monkeys. *Journal of the Experimental Analysis of Behavior*, 1974, *21*, 361–371.

Gantt, W. H. Cardiac conditioned reflexes to painful stimuli. *Federation Proceedings of American Societies for Experimental Biology*, 1942, No. 1, Part II, 28. (Abstract)

Gantt, W. H. & Loucks, R. B. Posterior nerve function as tested by the conditioned reflex method. *American Journal of Physiology*, 1938, *123*, 74–75.

Ganz, L. Hue generalization and hue discriminability in macaca mulatta. *Journal of Experimental Psychology*, 1962, *64*, 142–150.

Ganz, L. & Riessen, A. H. Stimulus generalization to hue in the dark-reared Macaque. *Journal of Comparative and Physiological Psychology*, 1962, *55*, 92–99.

Garcia, J. & Ervin, F. R. Gustatory-visceral and telereceptor-cutaneous conditioning—Adaptations in internal and external milieus. *Communications in Behavioral Biology*, 1968, *1*, 389–415.

Garcia, J., Ervin, F. R. & Koelling, R. A. Bait shyness: A test for toxicity with N=2. *Psychonomic Science*, 1967, 7, 245–246.

Garcia, J. & Kimeldorf, D. J. Temporal relationship within the conditioning of saccharin aversion through radiation exposure. *Journal of Comparative and Physiological Psychology*, 1957, *50*, 180–183.

Garcia, J., Kimeldorf, D. J., & Hunt, E. L. The use of ionizing radiation as a motivating stimulus. *Psychological Review*, 1961, *68*, 383–395.

Garcia, J., Kimeldorf, D. J., & Koelling, R. A. Conditioned aversion to saccharin resulting from exposure to gamma radiation. *Science*, 1968, *160*, 794–795.

Gardner, R. A. & Gardner, B. T. Teaching sign language to a chimpanzee. *Science*, 1969, *165*, 664–672.

Gardner, R. A. & Gardner, B. T. Early signs of language in child and chimpanzee. *Science*, 1975, *187*, 752–753.

Gardner, W. M. Auto-shaping in Bobwhite Quail. *Journal of the Experimental Analysis of Behavior*, 1969, *12*, 279–281.

Gatling, F. P. Study of the continuity of the learning process as measured by habit reversal in the rat. *Journal of Comparative and Physiological Psychology*, 1951, *44*, 78–83.

Gavalas, R. J. Operant reinforcement of an autonomic response: Two studies. *Journal of the Experimental Analysis of Behavior*, 1967, *10*, 119–130.

Gavalas, R. J. Operant reinforcement of a skeletally mediated autonomic response: Uncoupling of the two responses. *Psychonomic Science*, 1968, *11*, 195–196.

Geer, J. H. Measurement of the conditioned cardiac response. *Journal of Comparative and Physiological Psychology*, 1964, *57*, 426–433.

Geer, J. H. A test of the classical conditioning model of emotion: The use of nonpainful aversive stimuli as unconditioned stimuli in a conditioning procedure. *Journal of Personality & Social Psychology*, 1968, *10*, 148–156.

Geer, J. H. & Klein, K. Effects of two independent stresses upon autonomic responding. *Journal of Abnormal Psychology*, 1969, *74*, 237–241.

Gerall, A. A. & Obrist, P. A. Classical conditioning of the pupillary dilation response of normal and curarized cats. *Journal of Comparative and Physiological Psychology*, 1962, *55*, 486–491.

Gerall, A. A. & Woodward, J. K. Conditioning of the human pupillary dilation response as a function of the CS-UCS interval. *Journal of Experimental Psychology*, 1958, *55*, 501–507.

Gibson, J. J. The concept of the stimulus in psychology. *American Psychologist*, 1960, *15*, 694–703.

Gibson, J. J., Jack, E. G., & Raffel, G. Bilateral transfer of the conditioned response in the human subject. *Journal of Experimental Psychology*, 1932, *15*, 416–421.

Gibson, W. E., Reid, L. D., Sakai, M., & Porter, P. B. Intracranial reinforcement compared with sugar-water reinforcement. *Science*, 1965, *148*, 1357–1359.

Gleitman, H., Nachmias, J., & Neisser, U. The S-R reinforcement theory of extinction. *Psychological Review*, 1954, *61*, 23–33.

Gleitman, H. & Steinman, F. Depression effect as a function of retention interval before and after shift in reward magnitude. *Journal of Comparative and Physiological Psychology*, 1964, *57*, 158–160.

Godbout, R. C., Ziff, D. R., & Capaldi, E. J. Effect of several reward exposure procedures on the small trial PRE. *Psychonomic Science*, 1968, *13*, 153–154.

Goesling, W. J. & Brener, J. Effects of activity and immobility conditioning upon subsequent heart-rate conditioning in curarized rats. *Journal of Comparative and Physiological Psychology*, 1972, *81*, 311–317.

Goldstein, H. & Spence, K. W. Performance in differential conditioning as a function of variation in magnitude of reward. *Journal of Experimental Psychology*, 1963, *65*, 86–93.

Goldwater, B. C. Psychological significance of pupillary movements. *Psychological Bulletin*, 1972, *77*, 340–355.

Golla, F. L. Objective study of neurosis. *Lancet*, 1921, *201*, 215–221.

Gonzalez, R. C., Gleitman, H., & Bitterman, M. E. Some observations on the depression effect. *Journal of Comparative and Physiological Psychology*, 1962, *55*, 578–581.

Gonzalez, R. C., Longo, N., & Bitterman, M. E. Classical conditioning in the fish: Exploratory studies of partial reinforcement. *Journal of Comparative and Physiological Psychology*, 1961, *54*, 452–460.

Goodrich, K. P. Performance in different segments of an instrumental response chain as a function of reinforcement schedule. *Journal of Experimental Psychology*, 1959, *57*, 57–63.

Goodrich, K. P. Running speed and drinking rate as functions of sucrose concentration and amount of consummatory activity. *Journal of Comparative and Physiological Psychology*, 1960, *53*, 245–250.

Goodrich, K. P. & Zaretsky, H. Running speed as a function of concentration during pre-training. *Psychological Reports*, 1962, *11*, 463–468.

Goodson, F. F., Hermann, P. G., & Morgan, G. A. Water consumption of the rat as a function of drive level. *Journal of Comparative and Physiological Psychology*, 1962, *55*, 769–772.

Gormezano, I. Classical Conditioning. In J. B. Sidowski (Ed.), *Experimental methods of instrumentation in psychology*. New York: McGraw-Hill, 1969.

Gormezano, I. & Fernald, C. D. Human eyelid conditioning with paraorbital shock as the US. *Psychonomic Science*, 1971, *25*, 88–90.

Gormezano, I. & Moore, J. W. Effects of instructional set and UCS intensity on the latency, percentage, and form of the eyelid response. *Journal of Experimental Psychology*, 1962, *63*, 487–494.

Gormezano, I. & Moore, J. W. Classical conditioning. In M. H. Marx (Ed.),

Learning processes. New York: Macmillan, 1969.

Gormezano, I., Schneiderman, N., Deaux, D., & Fuentes, I. Nictitating membrane: Classical conditioning and extinction in the albino rat. *Science*, 1962, *133*, 33–34.

Grant, D. A. The pseudo-conditioning eyelid response. *Journal of Experimental Psychology*, 1943a, *32*, 139–149.

Grant, D. A. Sensitization and association in eyelid conditioning. *Journal of Experimental Psychology*, 1943b, *32*, 201–212.

Grant, D. A. A sensitized eyelid reaction related to the conditioned eyelid response. *Journal of Experimental Psychology*, 1945, *35*, 393–403.

Grant, D. A. Classical and operant conditioning. In A. W. Melton (Ed.), *Categories of human learning.* New York: Academic Press, 1964.

Grant, D. A. Cognitive factors in eyelid conditioning. *Psychophysiology*, 1973, *10*, 75–81.

Grant, D. A. & Adams, J. K. 'Alpha' conditioning in the eyelid. *Journal of Experimental Psychology*, 1944, *34*, 136–142.

Grant, D. A., Hake, H. W., Riopelle, A. J., & Kostlan, A. Effects of repeated pretesting with conditioned stimulus upon extinction of the conditioned eyelid response to light. *American Journal of Psychology*, 1951, *54*, 247–251.

Grant, D. A., Hake, H. W., & Schneider, D. E. Effects of repeated pre-testing with conditioned stimulus upon extinction of the conditioned eyelid response. *American Journal of Psychology*, 1948, *61*, 243–246.

Grant, D. A. & Hilgard, E. R. Sensitization as a supplement to association in eyelid conditioning. *Psychological Bulletin*, 1940, *37*, 478–479.

Grant, D. A., Hunter, H. G., & Patel, A. S. Spontaneous recovery of the conditioned eyelid response. *Journal of General Psychology*, 1958, *59*, 135–141.

Grant, D. A. & Meyer, H. I. The formation of generalized response sets during repeated electric shock stimulation. *Journal of General Psychology*, 1941, *24*, 21–38.

Grant, D. A. & Norris, E. B. Eyelid conditioning as influenced by the presence of sensitized beta-responses. *Journal of Experimental Psychology*, 1947, *37*, 434–440.

Grant, D. A., Riopelle, A. J., & Hake, H. W. Resistance to extinction and the pattern of reinforcement. I. Alternation of reinforcement and the conditioned eyelid response. *Journal of Experimental Psychology*, 1950, *40*, 53–60.

Grant, D. A. & Schiller, J. J. Generalization of the conditioned galvanic skin response to visual stimuli. *Journal of Experimental Psychology*, 1953, *46*, 309–313.

Grant, D. A. & Schipper, L. M. The acquisition and extinction of conditioned eyelid responses as a function of the percentage of fixed-ratio random reinforcement. *Journal of Experimental Psychology*, 1952, *43*, 313–320.

Grant, D. A. & Schneider, D. E. Intensity of the conditioned stimulus and strength of conditioning. I. The conditioned eyelid response to light. *Journal of Experimental Psychology*, 1948, *38*, 690–696.

Grant, D. A. & Schneider, D. E. The intensity of the conditioned stimulus and strength of conditioning. II. The conditioned galvanic skin response to an auditory stimulus. *Journal of Experimental Psychology*, 1949, *39*, 35–40.

Gray, J. A. Stimulus intensity dynamism. *Psychological Bulletin*, 1965, *63*, 180–196.

Green, K. F. & Garcia, J. Recuperation from illness: Flavor enhancement for rats. *Science*, 1971, *173*, 749–751.

Greenberg, I. The acquisition of a thirst drive. Unpublished Ph. D dissertation, University of Pennsylvania, 1954.

Greene, J. E. Magnitude of reward and acquisition of a black-white discrimination habit. *Journal of Experimental Psychology*, 1953, *46*, 113-119.

Grether, W. F. Pseudo-conditioning without paired stimulation encountered in attempted backward conditioning. *Journal of Comparative Psychology*, 1938, *25*, 91-96.

Grice, G. R. The relation of secondary reinforcement to delayed reward in visual discrimination learning. *Journal of Experimental Psychology*, 1948, *38*, 1-16.

Grice, G. R. Visual discrimination learning with simultaneous and successive presentation of stimuli. *Journal of Comparative and Physiological Psychology*, 1949, *42*, 365-373.

Grice, G. R. & Hunter, J. J. Stimulus intensity effects depend upon the type of experimental design. *Psychological Review*, 1964, *71*, 247-256.

Grice, G. R., Masters, L. & Kohfeld, D. L. Classical conditioning without discrimination training: A test of the generalization theory of CS intensity effects. *Journal of Experimental Psychology*, 1966, *72*, 510-513.

Grice, G. R. & Saltz, E. The generalization of an instrumental response to stimuli varying in the size dimension. *Journal of Experimental Psychology*, 1950, *40*, 702-708.

Grindley, G. C. Experiments on the influence of the amount of reward on learning in young chickens. *British Journal of Psychology*, 1929, *20*, 173-180.

Grings, W. W. Preparatory set variables related to classical conditioning of autonomic responses. *Psychological Review*, 1960, *67*, 242-252.

Grings, W. W. Verbal-perceptual factors in the conditioning of autonomic responses. In W. F. Prokasy (Ed.), *Classical conditioning: A symposium.*New York: Appleton-Century-Crofts, 1965.

Grings, W. W. Transfer of response from compound conditioned stimuli. *Psychonomic Science*, 1969, *15*, 187-188.

Grings, W. W. Compound stimulus transfer in human classical conditioning. In A. H. Black & W. F. Prokasy (Eds.), *Classical conditioning II. Current theory and research.* New York: Appleton-Century-Crofts, 1972.

Grings, W. W. & Kimmel, H. D. Compound stimulus transfer for different sense modalities. *Psychological Reports*, 1959, *5*, 253-260.

Grings, W. W. & Lockhart, R. A. Effects of "anxiety-lessening" instructions and differential set development on the extinction of GSR. *Journal of Experimental Psychology*, 1963, *66*, 292-299.

Grings, W. W. & O'Donnell, D. E. Magnitude of response to compounds of discriminated stimuli. *Journal of Experimental Psychology*, 1956, *52*, 354-359.

Grings, W. W. & Uno, T. Counterconditioning: Fear and relaxation. *Psychophysiology*, 1968, *4*, 479-485.

Grings, W. W., Uno, T., & Fiebiger, J. Component to compound stimulus transfer. *Psychonomic Science*, 1965, *3*, 29-34.

Grings, W. W. & Zeiner, A. Compound stimulus transfer. *Psychonomic Science*, 1969, *16*, 299-300.

Gross, C. G. Effect of deprivation on delayed response and delayed alternation performance by normal and brain operated monkeys. *Journal of Comparative and Physiological Psychology*, 1963, *56*, 48-51.

Grosslight, J. H., Hall, J. F., & Murnin, J. Patterning effect in partial reinforcement. *Journal of Experimental Psychology*, 1953, *46*, 103-106.

Grosslight, J. H. & Radlow, R. Patterning effect of the nonreinforcement-reinforcement sequence in a discrimination situation. *Journal of Comparative and Physiological Psychology*, 1956, *49*, 542-546.

Grosslight, J. H. & Radlow, R. Patterning effect of the nonreinforcement-reinforcement sequence involving a single nonreinforced trial. *Journal of Comparative and Physiological Psychology*, 1957, *50*, 23-25.

Grossman, S. P. *A textbook of physiological psychology*. New York: Wiley, 1967.

Guthrie, E. R. *The psychology of learning*. New York: Harper, 1935.

Guttman, N. Operant conditioning, extinction, and periodic reinforcement in relation to concentration of sucrose used as reinforcing agent. *Journal of Experimental Psychology*, 1953, *46*, 213-224.

Guttman, N. & Kalish, H. I. Discriminability and stimulus generalization. *Journal of Experimental Psychology*, 1956, *51*, 79-88.

Haber, A. & Kalish, H. I. Prediction of discrimination from generalization after variations in schedule of reinforcement. *Science*, 1963, *142*, 412-413.

Hahn, W. W. The learning of autonomic responses by curarized animals. In P. A. Obrist, A. H. Black, Jr., & L. V. DiCara (Eds.), *Cardiovascular psychophysiology: Current issues in response mechanisms, biofeedback, and methodology*. Chicago: Aldine, 1974.

Halgren, C. R. Latent inhibition in rats: Associative or nonassociative? *Journal of Comparative and Physiological Psychology*, 1974, *86*, 74-78.

Hall, J. F. Studies in secondary reinforcement: I. Secondary reinforcement as a function of the frequency of primary reinforcement. *Journal of Comparative and Physiological Psychology*, 1951a, *44*, 246-251.

Hall, J. F. Studies in secondary reinforcement: II. Secondary reinforcement as a function of the strength of drive during primary reinforcement. *Journal of Comparative and Physiological Psychology*, 1951b, *44*, 462-466.

Hall, J. F. The influence of learning in activity wheel behavior. *Journal of Genetic Psychology*, 1958, *92*, 121-125.

Hall, J. F. *Psychology of motivation*. Philadelphia: J. B. Lippincott, 1961.

Hall, J. F. *The psychology of learning*. Philadelphia: J. B. Lippincott, 1966.

Hall, J. F. *Verbal learning and retention*. Philadelphia: J. B. Lippincott, 1971.

Hall, J. F. & Kobrick, J. L. The relationship among three measures of response strength. *Journal of Comparative and Physiological Psychology*, 1952, *45*, 280-282.

Hall, J. F., Low, L., & Hanford, P. The activity of hungry, thirsty, and satiated rats in the Dashiell checkerboard maze. *Journal of Comparative and Physiological Psychology*, 1960, *53*, 155-158.

Hall, J. F. & Prokasy, W. F. Stimulus generalization to absolutely discriminable tones. *Perceptual and Motor Skills*, 1961, *12*, 175-178.

Hammes, J. A. Visual discrimination learning as a function of shock-fear and task difficulty. *Journal of Comparative and Physiological Psychology*, 1956, *49*, 481-484.

Hammond, L. J. Increased responding to CS- in differential CER. *Psychonomic Science*, 1966, *5*, 337-338.

Hammond, L. J. A traditional demonstration of the five properties of Pavlovian inhibition using differential CER. *Psychonomic Science*, 1967, *9*, 65-66.

Hammond, L. J. Retardation of fear acquisition by a previously inhibitory CS. *Journal of Comparative and Physiological Psychology*, 1968, *66*, 756-758.

Hanson, H. M. Effects of discrimination on stimulus generalization. *Journal of Experimental Psychology*, 1959, *58*, 321-334.

Hanson, H. M. Stimulus generalization following three-stimulus discrimination training. *Journal of Comparative and Physiological Psychology*, 1961, *54*, 181-185.

Hara, K. & Warren, J. M. Stimulus additivity and dominance in discrimination performance in cats. *Journal of Comparative and Physiological Psychology*, 1961, *54*, 86-90.

Harlow, H. F. Forward conditioning, backward conditioning and pseudo-conditioning in the goldfish. *Journal of Genetic Psychology*, 1939, *55*, 49-58.

Harlow, H. F. The effects of incomplete curare paralysis upon formation and elicitation of conditioned responses in cats. *Journal of Genetic Psychology*, 1940, *56*, 273-282.

Harlow, H. F. Studies in discrimination learning in monkeys: V. Initial performance by experimentally naive monkeys on stimulus-object and pattern discrimination. *Journal of General Psychology*, 1945, *33*, 3-10.

Harlow, H. F. The formation of learning sets. *Psychological Review*, 1949, *56*, 51-65.

Harlow, H. F. Motivation as a factor in the acquisition of new responses. In *Current theory and research in motivation: A symposium*. Lincoln: University of Nebraska Press, 1953.

Harlow, H. F. Learning set and error factor theory. In S. Koch (Ed.), *Psychology: A study of a science*, Vol. II. New York: McGraw-Hill, 1959.

Harlow, H. F., Gluck, J. P. & Suomi, S. J. Generalization of behavioral data between nonhuman and human animals. *American Psychologist*, 1972, *27*, 709-716.

Harlow, H. F., Harlow, M. K., & Meyer, D. R. Learning motivated by a manipulation drive. *Journal of Experimental Psychology*, 1950, *40*, 228-234.

Harlow, H. F., Harlow, M. K., Rueping, R. R., & Mason, W. A. Performance of infant rhesus monkeys on discrimination learning, delayed response, and discrimination learning set. *Journal of Comparative and Physiological Psychology*, 1960, *53*, 113-121.

Harlow, H. F. & Hicks, L. H. Discrimination learning theory: Uniprocess vs. duoprocess. *Psychological Review*, 1957, *64*, 104-109.

Harlow, H. F. & Stagner, R. Effect of complete striate muscle paralysis upon the learning process. *Journal of Experimental Psychology*, 1933, *16*, 283-294.

Harlow, H. F. & Toltzien, F. Formation of pseudo-conditioned responses in the cat. *Journal of General Psychology*, 1940, *23*, 367-375.

Harris, J. D. Forward conditioning, backward conditioning and pseudo-conditioning, and adaptation to the conditioned stimulus. *Journal of Experimental Psychology*, 1941, *28*, 491-502.

Hartman, T. F. Dynamic transmission, elective generalization, and semantic conditioning. In W. F. Prokasy (Ed.), *Classical conditioning: A symposium*. New York: Appleton-Century-Crofts, 1965.

Hartman, T. F. & Grant, D. A. Effect of intermittent reinforcement on acquisition, extinction, and spontaneous recovery of the conditioned eyelid response. *Journal of Experimental Psychology*, 1960, *60*, 89-96.

Hartman, T. F. & Grant, D. A. Differential eyelid conditioning as a function of the CS-UCS interval. *Journal of Experimental Psychology*, 1962, *64*, 131-136.

Hartman, T. F. & Ross, L. E. An alternative criterion for the elimination of "voluntary" responses in eyelid conditioning. *Journal of Experimental Psychology*, 1961, *61*, 334-338.

Harvey, B. & Wickens, D. D. Effect of instructions on responsiveness to the CS and to the UCS in GSR conditioning. *Journal of Experimental Psychology*, 1971, *87*, 137–140.

Harvey, C. B. & Wickens, D. D. Effects of cognitive control processes on the classically conditioned galvanic skin response. *Journal of Experimental Psychology*, 1973, *101*, 278–282.

Hastings, S. E. & Obrist, P. A. Heart rate during conditioning in humans: Effect of varying the inter-stimulus (CS-UCS) interval. *Journal of Experimental Psychology*, 1967, *74*, 431–442.

Hearst, E. & Koresko, M. B. Stimulus generalization and amount of prior training on variable interval reinforcement. *Journal of Comparative and Physiological Psychology*, 1968, *66*, 133–138.

Hebb, D. O. Drives and the C. N. S. (Conceptual nervous system). *Psychological Review*, 1955, *62*, 243–254.

Hebb, D. O. Alice in wonderland or psychology among the biological sciences. In H. F. Harlow & C. N. Woolsey (Eds.), *Biological and biochemical bases of behavior*. Madison: University of Wisconsin Press, 1958.

Heinemann, E. G. & Rudolph, R. L. The effect of discriminative training on the gradient of stimulus-generalization. *American Journal of Psychology*, 1963, *76*, 653–658.

Helson, H. *Adaptation-level theory: An experimental and systematic approach to behavior*. New York: Harper, 1964.

Hendricks, S. E. & Gerall, A. A. Acquisition and extinction of an instrumental response as a function of delay of intracranial stimulation reward and amount of training. *Psychonomic Science*, 1970, *19*, 187–188.

Hendry, D. P. (Ed.), *Conditioned reinforcement*. Homewood, Ill.: Dorsey Press, 1969.

Hess, W. R. Beitraege zur Physiologie des Hirnstammes. I: Die Methodik der lokalisierten Reizung und Ausschaltung subkortikaler Hirnabschnitte. Leipzig: Thieme, 1932.

Hetherington, E. M. & Ross, L. E. Discrimination learning by normal and retarded children under delay of reward and interpolated task conditions. *Child Development*, 1967, *38*, 639–647.

Hetherington, E. M., Ross, L. E., & Pick, H. L. Delay of reward and learning in mentally retarded and normal children. *Child Development*, 1964, *35*, 653–659.

Hilgard, E. R. Conditioned eyelid reactions to a light stimulus based on the reflex wink to sound. *Psychological Monographs*, 1931, *41*, No. 184.

Hilgard, E. R. & Campbell, A. A. The course of acquisition and retention of conditioned eyelid responses in man. *Journal of Experimental Psychology*, 1936, *21*, 310–319.

Hilgard, E. R., Campbell, A. A. & Sears, W. N. Conditioned discrimination: Development of discrimination with and without verbal report. *American Journal of Psychology*, 1937, *49*, 564–580.

Hilgard, E. R., Dutton, C. E. & Helmick, J. S. Attempted pupillary conditioning at four stimulus intervals. *Journal of Experimental Psychology*, 1949, *39*, 683–689.

Hilgard, E. R. & Humphreys, L. G. The retention of conditioned discrimination in man. *Journal of General Psychology*, 1938, *19*, 111–125.

Hilgard, E. R., Jones, L. V. & Kaplan, S. J. Conditioned discrimination as related to anxiety. *Journal of Experimental Psychology*, 1951, *42*, 94–99.

Hilgard, E. R. & Marquis, D. G. Acquisition, extinction, and retention of conditioned lid responses to light in dogs. *Journal of Comparative Psychology*, 1935, *19*, 29-58.

Hilgard, E. R. & Marquis, D. G. Conditioned eyelid responses in monkeys, with a comparison of dog, monkey, and man. *Psychological Monographs*, 1936, *47*, No. 212.

Hilgard, E. R. & Marquis, D. G. *Conditioning and learning.* New York: Appleton-Century-Crofts, 1940.

Hilgard, E. R., Miller, J., & Ohlson, J. A. Three attempts to secure pupillary conditioning to auditory stimuli near the absolute threshold. *Journal of Experimental Psychology*, 1941, *29*, 89-103.

Hilgard, E. R. & Ohlson, J. A. Pupillary conditioning to auditory stimuli near the absolute threshold. *Psychological Bulletin*, 1939, *36*, 577.

Hill, F. A. Effects of instructions and subject's need for approval on the conditioned galvanic skin response. *Journal of Experimental Psychology*, 1967, *73*, 461-467.

Hill, W. F. Activity as an autonomous drive. *Journal of Comparative and Physiological Psychology*, 1965, *49*, 15-19.

Hill, W. F. & Spear, N. E. Extinction in a runway as a function of acquisition level and reinforcement percentage. *Journal of Experimental Psychology*, 1963, *65*, 495-500.

Hill, W. F., Spear, N. E., & Clayton, K. N. T-maze reversal learning after several different overtraining procedures. *Journal of Experimental Psychology*, 1962, *64*, 533-540.

Hill, W. F. & Wallace, W. P. Effects of magnitude and percentage of reward on subsequent patterns of runway speed. *Journal of Experimental Psychology*, 1967, *73*, 544-548.

Hillman, B., Hunter, W. S., & Kimble, G. A. The effect of drive level on the maze performance of the white rat. *Journal of Comparative and Physiological Psychology*, 1953, *46*, 87-89.

Hitchcock, F. A. The total energy requirement of the albino rat for growth and activity. *American Journal of Psychology*, 1927, *83*, 28-36.

Hockman, C. H. & Lipsitt, L. P. Delay-of-reward gradients in discrimination learning with children for two levels of difficulty. *Journal of Comparative and Physiological Psychology*, 1961, *54*, 24-27.

Hoebel, B. G. & Teitelbaum, P. Hypothalamic control of feeding and self-stimulation. *Science*, 1962, *135*, 375-377.

Hoffeld, D. R., Kendall, S.B., Thompson, R. F., & Brogden, W. J. Effect of amount of preconditioning training upon the magnitude of sensory preconditioning. *Journal of Experimental Psychology*, 1960, *59*, 198-204.

Hoffeld, D. R., Thompson, R. F., & Brogden, W. J. Effect of stimuli time relations during preconditioning training upon the magnitude of sensory preconditioning. *Journal of Experimental Psychology*, 1958, *56*, 437-442.

Hoffman, H. S. & Fleshler, M. Stimulus factors in aversive controls: The generalization of conditioned suppression. *Journal of the Experimental Analysis of Behavior*, 1961, *4*, 371-378.

Holdstock, T. L. & Schwartzbaum, J. S. Classical conditioning of heart rate and galvanic skin responses in the cat. *Psychophysiology*, 1965, *2*, 25-28.

Holmes, J. D. & Gormezano, I. Classical appetitive conditioning of the rabbit's jaw movement response under partial and continuous reinforcement schedules. *Learning and Motivation*, 1970, *1*, 110-120.

Homme, L. E., DeBaca, P. C., Devine, J. V., Steinhorst, R., & Rickert, E. J. Use of the Premack principle in controlling the behavior of nursery school children. *Journal of the Experimental Analysis of Behavior*, 1963, *6*, 544.

Homzie, M. J. & Ross, L. E. Runway performance following a reduction in the concentration of a liquid reward. *Journal of Comparative and Physiological Psychology*, 1962, *55*, 1029-1033.

Honig, W. K. Generalization of extinction on the spectral continuum. *Psychological Record*, 1961, *11*, 269-278.

Hopkins, C. O. Effectiveness of secondary reinforcing stimuli as a function of the quantity and quality of food reinforcement. *Journal of Experimental Psychology*, 1955, *50*, 339-342.

Horenstein, B. R. Performance of conditioned responses as a function of strength of hunger drive. *Journal of Comparative and Physiological Psychology*, 1951, *44*, 210-224.

Hothersall, D. & Brener, J. Operant conditioning of changes in heart rate in curarized rats. *Journal of Comparative and Physiological Psychology*, 1969, *68*, 338-342.

House, B. J. & Zeaman, D. Transfer of a discrimination from objects to patterns. *Journal of Experimental Psychology*, 1960, *59*, 298-302.

Hovland, C. I. The generalization of conditioned responses. I. The sensory generalization of conditioned responses with varying frequencies of tone. *Journal of General Psychology*, 1937a, *17*, 125-148.

Hovland, C. I. The generalization of conditioned responses. II. The sensory generalization of conditioned responses with varying intensities of tone. *Journal of Genetic Psychology*, 1937b, *51*, 279-291.

Hovland, C. I. The generalization of conditioned responses. III. Extinction, spontaneous recovery, and disinhibition of conditioned and of generalized responses. *Journal of Experimental Psychology*, 1937c, *21*, 47-62.

Hovland, C. I. The generalization of conditioned responses. IV. The effects of varying amounts of reinforcement upon the degree of generalization of conditioned responses. *Journal of Experimental Psychology*, 1937d, *21*, 261-276.

Howard, J. L., Galosy, R. A., Gaebelein, C. J., & Obrist, P. A. Some problems in the use of neuromuscular blockade. In P. A. Obrist, A. H. Black, J. Brener, & L. V. DeCara (Eds.), *Cardiovascular psychophysiology: Current issues, response mechanisms, biofeedback, and methodology*. Chicago: Aldine, 1974.

Howard, T. C. & Young, F. A. Conditioned hunger and secondary rewards in monkeys. *Journal of Comparative and Physiological Psychology*, 1962, *55*, 392-397.

Howarth, C. I. & Deutsch, J. A. Dissipation of a drive process as the cause of apparently fast extinction in ESB habit. *Science*, 1962, *137*, 35-36.

Howat, H. G. & Grant, D. A. Influence of intertrial interval during extinction on spontaneous recovery of conditioned eyelid responses. *Journal of Experimental Psychology*, 1958, *56*, 11-15.

Hudgins, C. V. Conditioning and the voluntary control of the pupillary light reflex. *Journal of General Psychology*, 1933, *8*, 3-51.

Hughes, B. & Schlosberg, H. Conditioning in the white rat. IV. The conditioned lid reflex. *Journal of Experimental Psychology*, 1938, *23*, 641-650.

Hull, C. L. A functional interpretation of the conditioned reflex. *Psychological Review*, 1929, *36*, 498-511.

Hull, C. L. The mechanism of the assembly of behavior segments in novel combinations suitable for problem solving. *Psychological Review*, 1935, *42*, 210-245.

Hull, C. L. The problem of stimulus equivalence in behavior theory. *Psychological Review*, 1939, *46*, 9-30.

Hull, C. L. *Principles of behavior.* New York: Appleton-Century-Crofts, 1943.

Hull, C. L. Stimulus intensity dynamism (V) and stimulus generalization. *Psychological Review*, 1949, *56*, 67-76.

Hull, C. L. *Essentials of behavior.* New Haven: Yale University Press, 1951.

Hull, C. L., Livingston, J. R., Rouse, R. O., & Barker, A. N. True, sham, and esophageal feeding as reinforcements. *Journal of Comparative and Physiological Psychology*, 1951, *44*, 236-245.

Humphreys, L. G. Generalization as a function of method of reinforcement. *Journal of Experimental Psychology*, 1939a, *25*, 361-372.

Humphreys, L. G. The effect of random alternation of reinforcement on the acquisition and extinction of conditioned eyelid reactions. *Journal of Experimental Psychology*, 1939b, *25*, 141-158.

Hundt, A. G. Instrumental response rate and reinforcement density. Unpublished Ph. D. dissertation, University of Missouri, 1964.

Hunt, H. F. & Brady, J. V. Some effects of electro-convulsive shock on a conditioned emotional response ("anxiety"). *Journal of Comparative and Physiological Psychology*, 1951, *44*, 88-98.

Hunt, H. F. & Brady, J. V. Some effects of punishment and intercurrent "anxiety" on a simple operant. *Journal of Comparative and Physiological Psychology*, 1955, *48*, 305-310.

Hunter, W. S. Experimental studies in learning. In C. Murchison (Ed.), *Foundations of experimental psychology.* Worcester: Clark University, 1929.

Hutton, R. A., Woods, S. C., & Makous, W. L. Conditioned hypoglycemia: Pseudoconditioning controls. *Journal of Comparative and Physiological Psychology*, 1970, *71*, 198-201.

Ison, J. R. & Birch, D. T-maze reversal following differential endbox placement. *Journal of Experimental Psychology*, 1961, *62*, 200-202.

Ison, J. R. & Glass, D. H. "Classical" versus "instrumental" exposure to success rewards and later instrumental behavior following a shift in incentive value. *Journal of Experimental Psychology*, 1969, *79*, 582-583.

Ivanov-Smolensky, A. G. *Metodika issledovaniya uslovnykh refleksov u cheloveka.* (Method for investigating conditioned reflexes in man.) Moscow: State Medical Publishing House, 1933.

James, J. P. Latent inhibition and the preconditioning interval. *Psychonomic Science*, 1971, *24*, 97-98.

James, W. *Principles of psychology*, Vol. I. New York: Holt, 1890.

Jasper, H. & Shagass, C. Conditioning in the occipital alpha rhythm in man. *Journal of Experimental Psychology*, 1941, *28*, 373-387.

Jeffrey, W. E. & Cohen, L. B. Effect of spatial separation of stimulus, response, and reinforcement on selective learning in children. *Journal of Experimental Psychology*, 1964, *67*, 577-580.

Jenkins, H. M. & Harrison, R. H. Effect of discrimination training on auditory generalization. *Journal of Experimental Psychology*, 1960, *59*, 246-253.

Jenkins, H. M. & Sainsbury, R. S. Discrimination learning with the distinctive feature on positive or negative trials. In D. Mostofsky (Ed.), *Attention: Contemporary theory and analysis.* New York: Appleton-Century-Crofts, 1970.

Jenkins, W. O. A temporal gradient of derived reinforcement. *American Journal of Psychology*, 1950, *63*, 237-243.

Jenkins, W. O. & Clayton, F. L. Rate of responding and amount of reinforcement. *Journal of Comparative and Physiological Psychology*, 1949, *42*, 174-181.

Jenkins, W. O. & Stanley, J. C., Jr. Partial reinforcement: A review and critique. *Psychological Bulletin*, 1950, *47*, 193-234.

Jensen, A. R. On the reformulation of inhibition in Hull's system. *Psychological Bulletin*, 1961, *58*, 274-298.

Jensen, G. D. Learning and performance as functions of ration size, hours of deprivation, and effort requirement. *Journal of Experimental Psychology*, 1960, *59*, 261-268.

Jensen, G. D. Preference for bar pressing over "freeloading" as a function of number of rewarded presses. *Journal of Experimental Psychology*, 1963, *65*, 451-454.

Jernstedt, G. C. Joint effects of pattern of reinforcement, intertrial interval, and amount of reinforcement in the rat. *Journal of Comparative and Physiological Psychology*, 1971, *75*, 421-429.

Johnson, D. F. & Cumming, W. W. Some determiners of attention. *Journal of the Experimental Analysis of Behavior*, 1968, *11*, 157-166.

Johnson, H. J. & Schwartz, G. E. Suppression of GSR activity through operant reinforcement. *Journal of Experimental Psychology*. 1967, *75*, 307-312.

Johnson, J. L. & Church, R. M. Effects of shock intensity on non-discriminative avoidance learning of rats in a shuttlebox. *Psychonomic Science*, 1965, *3*, 497-498.

Jones, H. E. The retention of conditioned emotional reactions in infancy. *Journal of Genetic Psychology*, 1930, *37*, 485-497.

Jung, J. *Verbal learning.* New York: Holt, Rinehart and Winston, 1968.

Justensen, D. R., Braun, E. W., Garrison, R. G. & Pendleton, R. B. Pharmacological differentiation of allergic and classically conditioned asthma in the guinea pig. *Science*, 1970, *170*, 864-866.

Kagan, J. & Berkun, M. The reward value of running activity. *Journal of Comparative and Physiological Psychology*, 1954, *47*, 108.

Kalat, J. W. Taste salience depends on novelty, not concentration, in taste-aversion learning in the rat. *Journal of Comparative and Physiological Psychology*, 1974, *86*, 47-50.

Kalat, J. W. & Rozin, P. "Learned safety" as a mechanism in long-delay taste-aversion learning in rats. *Journal of Comparative and Physiological Psychology*, 1973, *83*, 198-207.

Kalish, H. I. The relationship between discriminability and generalization: A re-evaluation. *Journal of Experimental Psychology*, 1958, *55*, 637-644.

Kalish, H. I. & Haber, A. Prediction of discrimination from generalization following variations in deprivation level. *Journal of Comparative and Physiological Psychology*, 1965, *60*, 125-128.

Kamin, L. J. Traumatic avoidance learning: The effects of CS-UCS interval with a trace-conditioning procedure. *Journal of Comparative and Physiological Psychology*, 1954, *47*, 65-72.

Kamin, L. J. The delay-of-punishment gradient. *Journal of Comparative and Physiological Psychology*, 1959, *52*, 434-437.

Kamin, L. J. Backward conditioning and the conditioned emotional response. *Journal of Experimental Psychology*, 1963, *56*, 517-519.

Kamin, L. J. "Attention-like" processes in classical conditioning. In M. R. Jones (Ed.), *Miami symposium on the prediction of behavior, 1967: Aversive stimulation.* Coral Gables, Florida: University of Miami Press, 1968.

Kamin, L. J. & Schaub, R. E. Effects of conditioned stimulus intensity on the conditioned emotional response. *Journal of Comparative and Physiological Psychology*, 1963, *56*, 502-507.

Kappauf, W. E. & Schlosberg, H. Conditioned responses in the white rat. III. Conditioning as a function of the length of the period of delay. *Journal of Genetic Psychology*, 1937, *50*, 27-45.

Karn, H. W. Sensory preconditioning and incidental learning in human subjects. *Journal of Experimental Psychology*, 1947, *37*, 540-544.

Katkin, E. S. & Murray, E. N. Instrumental conditioning of autonomically mediated behavior: Theoretical and methodological issues. *Psychological Bulletin*, 1968, *70*, 52-68.

Kaufman, M. E. & Peterson, W. M. Acquisition of a learning set by normal and mentally retarded children. *Journal of Comparative and Physiological Psychology*, 1958, *51*, 619-621.

Kaye, H. The conditioned anticipatory sucking response. Unpublished manuscript, Brown University, 1966.

Kaye, H. Infant sucking behavior and its modification. In L. P. Lipsitt & C. C. Spiker (Eds.), *Advances in child development and behavior*, Vol. 3. New York: Academic Press, 1967.

Keeley, S. M. & Sprague, R. L. Effect of varying delay of reinforcement and postreinforcement intervals on learning of retardates. *Journal of Experimental Child Psychology*, 1969, *7*, 578-584.

Keesey, R. Intracranial reward delay and the acquisition rate of a brightness discrimination. *Science*, 1964, *143*, 702.

Keith-Lucas, T. & Guttman, N. Robust-single-trial delayed backward conditioning. *Journal of Comparative and Physiological Psychology*, 1975, *88*, 468-476.

Kelleher, R. T. & Gollub, L. R. A review of positive conditioned reinforcement. *Journal of the Experimental Analysis of Behavior*, 1962, Supplement to Vol. *5*, 543-597.

Kellogg, W. N., Deese, J., Pronko, N. H., & Feinberg, M. An attempt to condition the chronic spinal dog. *Journal of Experimental Psychology*, 1947, *37*, 99-117.

Kellogg, W. N., Pronko, N. H., & Deese, J. Spinal conditioning in dogs. *Science*, 1946, *103*, 49-50.

Kellogg, W. N. & Walker, E. L. An analysis of the bilateral transfer of conditioning in dogs, in terms of the frequency, amplitude, and latency of the responses. *Journal of General Psychology*, 1938, *18*, 253-265.

Kendall, S. B. & Thompson, R. F. Effects of stimulus similarity on sensory preconditioning within a single stimulus dimension. *Journal of Comparative and Physiological Psychology*, 1960, *53*, 439-442.

Kimble, G. A. Conditioning as a function of the time between conditioned and unconditioned stimuli. *Journal of Experimental Psychology*, 1947, *37*, 1-15.

Kimble, G. A. Behavior strength as a function of the intensity of the hunger drive. *Journal of Experimental Psychology*, 1951, *41*, 341-348.

Kimble, G. A. Shock intensity and avoidance learning. *Journal of Comparative and Physiological Psychology*, 1955, *48*, 341-348.

Kimble, G. A. *Hilgard and Marquis' conditioning and learning.* New York: Appleton-Century-Crofts, 1961.

Kimble, G. A., Mann, L. I., & Dufort, R. H. Classical and instrumental eyelid conditioning. *Journal of Experimental Psychology*, 1955, *49*, 407-417.

Kimmel, E. & Kimmel, H. D. A replication of operant conditioning of the GSR. *Journal of Experimental Psychology*, 1963, *65*, 212-213.

Kimmel, H. D. Amount of conditioning and intensity of conditioned stimulus. *Journal of Experimental Psychology*, 1959, *58*, 283-288.

Kimmel, H. D. Further analysis of GSR conditioning: A reply to Stewart, Stern, Winokur, & Fredman. *Psychological Review*, 1964, *71*, 160-166.

Kimmel, H. D. Instrumental conditioning of autonomically mediated responses in human beings. *American Psychologist*, 1974, *29*, 325-335.

Kimmel, H. D. & Baxter, R. Avoidance conditioning of the GSR. *Journal of Experimental Psychology*, 1964, *68*, 482-485.

Kimmel, H. D. & Hill, F. A. Operant conditioning of the GSR. *Psychological Reports*, 1960, 7, 555-562.

Kimmel, H. D. & Pennypacker, H. S. Differential GSR conditioning as a function of the CS-UCS interval. *Journal of Experimental Psychology*, 1963, *65*, 559-563.

Kimmel, H. D. & Sternthal, H. S. Replication of GSR avoidance conditioning with concomitant EMG measurement and subjects matched in responsivity and conditionability. *Journal of Experimental Psychology*, 1967, *74*, 144-146.

Kimmel, H. D., Sternthal, H. S., & Strub, H. Two replications of avoidance conditioning of the GSR. *Journal of Experimental Psychology*, 1966, *72*, 151-152.

Kimmel, H. D. & Yaremko, R. M. Effect of partial reinforcement on acquisition and extinction of classical conditioning in the Planarian. *Journal of Comparative and Physiological Psychology*, 1966, *61*, 299-301.

Kjerstad, C. L. The form of the learning curves for memory. *Psychological Monograph*, 1919, *26*, No. 116.

Klein, R. M. Intermittent primary reinforcement as a parameter of secondary reinforcement. *Journal of Experimental Psychology*, 1959, *58*, 423-427.

Kling, J. W. Generalization of extinction of an instrumental response to stimuli varying in the size dimension. *Journal of Experimental Psychology*, 1952, *44*, 339-346.

Kling, J. W. Learning: Introductory survey. In J. W. Kling and L. A. Riggs (Eds.), *Woodworth and Schlosberg's experimental psychology*. New York: Holt, Rinehart and Winston, 1971.

Kling, J. W. & Matsumiya, Y. Relative reinforcement values of food and intracranial stimulation. *Science*, 1962, *135*, 668-670.

Klinman, C. & Bitterman, M. E. Classical conditioning in fish: The CS-US interval. *Journal of Comparative and Physiological Psychology*, 1963, *56*, 578-583.

Koch, S. Clark L. Hull. In W. K. Estes, S. Koch, K. MacCorquodale, C. G. Mueller, Jr., W. N. Schoenfeld, & W. S. Verplanck (Eds.), *Modern learning theory*. New York: Appleton-Century-Crofts, 1945.

Koch, S. & Daniel, W. J. The effect of satiation on the behavior mediated by a habit of maximum strength. *Journal of Experimental Psychology*, 1945, *35*, 167-187.

Kohn, M. Satiation of hunger from food injected directly into the stomach versus food ingested by mouth. *Journal of Comparative and Physiological Psychology*, 1951, *44*, 412-422.

Konorski, J. & Miller, S. On two types of conditioned reflex. *Journal of General Psychology*, 1937, *16*, 264-272.

Koronakos, C. & Arnold, W. J. The formation of learning sets in rats. *Journal of Comparative and Physiological Psychology*, 1957, *50*, 11-14.

Kosupkin, J. M. & Olmstead, J. M. D. Slowing of the heart as a conditioned reflex in the rabbit. *American Journal of Physiology*, 1943, *139*, 550–555.

Koteskey, R. L. & Stettner, L. J. The role of nonreinforcement-reinforcement sequences in the partial-reinforcement effect. *Journal of Experimental Psychology*, 1968, *76*, 198–205.

Kraeling, D. Analysis of amount of reward as a variable in learning. *Journal of Comparative and Physiological Psychology*, 1961, *54*, 560–565.

Krasnagorsky, N. Die letzten fortschritte in der methodik der erforschung der bedingten reflexe an kindern. *Jahrbuch für Kinderheilkunde*, 1926, *114*, 255–267.

Krechevsky, I. "Hypothesis" versus "chance" in the pre-solution period in sensory discrimination-learning. *University of California Publications in Psychology*, 1932a, *6*, 27–44.

Krechevsky, I. Antagonistic visual discrimination habits in the white rat. *Journal of Comparative Psychology*, 1932b, *14*, 263–277.

Krechevsky, I. The docile nature of "hypotheses". *Journal of Comparative Psychology*, 1933, *15*, 429–443.

Krechevsky, I. A study of the continuity of the problem-solving process. *Psychological Review*, 1938, *45*, 107–133.

Kremer, E. F. Truly random and traditional control procedures in CER conditioning in the rat. *Journal of Comparative and Physiological Psychology*, 1971, *76*, 441–448.

Krippner, R. A., Endsley, R. C., & Tacker, R. S. Magnitude of G 1 reward and the frustration effect in a between-subjects design. *Psychonomic Science*, 1967, *9*, 385–386.

Kugelmass, S., Hakerem, G., & Mantgiaris, L. A paradoxical conditioning effect in the human pupil. *Journal of General Psychology*, 1969, *80*, 115–127.

Kurtz, K. H. & Pearl, J. The effects of prior fear experiences on acquired-drive learning. *Journal of Comparative and Physiological Psychology*, 1960, *53*, 201–206.

Lacey, J. I. Somatic response patterning and stress: Some revisions of activation theory. In M. H. Appley and R. Trumbull (Eds.), *Psychological stress: Issues in research.* New York: Appleton-Century-Crofts, 1967.

Lachman, R. The influence of thirst and schedules of reinforcement-nonreinforcement ratios upon brightness discrimination. *Journal of Experimental Psychology*, 1961, *62*, 80–87.

Lack, D. *The life of the robin.* London: H. F. and G. Witherby, 1943.

Laird, G. S. & Fenz, W. D. Effects of respiration on heart rate in an aversive classical conditioning situation. *Canadian Journal of Psychology*, 1971, *25*, 395–411.

Lang, P. J., Geer, J., & Hnatiow, M. Semantic generalization of conditioned autonomic responses. *Journal of Experimental Psychology*, 1963, *65*, 552–558.

Lang, P. J. & Melamed, B. G. Avoidance conditioning of an infant with chronic ruminative vomiting. *Journal of Abnormal Psychology*, 1969, *74*, 1–8.

Lashley, K. S. Reflex secretion of the human parotid gland. *Journal of Experimental Psychology*, 1916, *1*, 461–493.

Lashley, K. S. Learning: I. Nervous-mechanisms of learning. In C. Murchison (Ed.), *The foundations of experimental psychology.* Worcester: Clark University Press, 1929.

Lashley, K. S. An examination of the "continuity theory" as applied to discriminative learning. *Journal of General Psychology*, 1942, *26*, 241–265.

Lashley, K. S. & Wade, M. The Pavlovian theory of generalization. *Psychological Review*, 1946, *53*, 72–87.

Lawrence, D. H. Acquired distinctiveness of cues: I. Transfer between discriminations on the basis of familiarity with the stimulus. *Journal of Experimental Psychology*, 1949, *39*, 770–784.

Lawrence, D. H. The transfer of a discrimination along a continuum. *Journal of Comparative and Physiological Psychology*, 1952, *45*, 511–516.

Lawson, R. Amount of primary reward and strength of secondary reward. *Journal of Experimental Psychology*, 1953, *46*, 183–187.

Lawson, R. Brightness discrimination performance and secondary reward strength as a function of primary reward amount. *Journal of Comparative and Physiological Psychology*, 1957, *50*, 35–39.

Leaf, R. C. Avoidance response evocation as a function of prior discriminative fear conditioning under curare. *Journal of Comparative and Physiological Psychology*, 1964, *58*, 446–449.

Leaf, R. C., Kayser, R. J., Andrews, J. S., Jr., Adkins, J. W., & Leaf, S. R. P. Block of fear conditioning induced by habituation or extinction. *Psychonomic Science*, 1968, *10*, 189–190.

Leary, R. W. Homogeneous and heterogeneous reward of monkeys. *Journal of Comparative and Physiological Psychology*, 1958, *51*, 706–710.

Leonard, C. & Winokur, G. Conditioning versus sensitization in the galvanic skin response. *Journal of Comparative and Physiological Psychology*, 1963, *56*, 169–170.

Levey, A. B. & Martin, I. Sequence of response development in human eyelid conditioning. *Journal of Experimental Psychology*, 1974, *102*, 678–686.

Levine, M., Levinson, B., & Harlow, H. F. Trials per problem as a variable in the acquisition of discrimination learning set. *Journal of Comparative and Physiological Psychology*. 1959, *52*, 396–398.

Levine, S. UCS intensity and avoidance learning. *Journal of Experimental Psychology*, 1966, *71*, 163–164.

Levinthal, C. F. & Papsdorf, J. D. The classically conditioned nictitating membrane response: The CS-US interval function with one trial per day. *Psychonomic Science*, 1970, *21*, 296–297.

Levitt, R. A. & Fisher, A. E. Anticholinergic blockade of centrally induced thirst. *Science*, 1966, *154*, 520–521.

Levy, N. & Seward, J. P. Frustration and homogeneity of rewards in the double runway. *Journal of Experimental Psychology*, 1969, *81*, 460–463.

Lewis, D. J. Partial reinforcement in the gambling situation. *Journal of Experimental Psychology*, 1952, *43*, 447–450.

Lewis, D. J. Partial reinforcement: A selective review of the literature since 1950. *Psychological Bulletin*, 1960, *57*, 1–28.

Lewis, D. J., Butler, D., & Diamond, A. L. Direct manipulation of the fractional anticipatory goal response. *Psychological Reports*, 1958, *4*, 575–578.

Lewis, D. J. & Cotton, J. W. Learning and performance as a function of drive strength during acquisition and extinction. *Journal of Comparative and Physiological Psychology*, 1957, *50*, 189–194.

Lewis, D. J. & Cotton, J. W. Effect of runway size and drive strength on acquisition and extinction. *Journal of Experimental Psychology*, 1960, *59*, 402–408.

Lewis, D. J. & Duncan, C. P. Effect of different percentages of money reward on extinction of a lever pulling response. *Journal of Experimental Psychology*, 1956, *52*, 23–27.

Lewis, D. J. & Duncan, C. P. Expectation and resistance to extinction of a lever-pulling response as functions of percentage of reinforcement and amount of reward. *Journal of Experimental Psychology*, 1957, *54*, 115-120.

Lewis, D. J. & Duncan, C. P. Expectation and resistance to extinction of a lever-pulling response as a function of percentage of reinforcement and number of acquisition trials. *Journal of Experimental Psychology*, 1958, *55*, 121-128.

Lewis, D. J. & Kent, N. D. Attempted direct activation and deactivation of the fractional anticipatory goal response. *Psychological Reports*, 1961, *8*, 107-110.

Lewis, D. J. & McIntire, R. A. A control for direct manipulation of the fractional anticipatory goal response. *Psychological Reports*, 1959, *5*, 753-756.

Lichtenstein, P. E. Studies in anxiety: I. The production of a feeding inhibition in dogs. *Journal of Comparative and Physiological Psychology*, 1950, *43*, 16-29.

Liddell, H. S. The conditioned reflex. In F. A. Moss (Ed.), *Comparative psychology*. New York: Prentice-Hall, 1934.

Liddell, H. S. The nervous system as a whole: The conditioned reflex. In J. F. Fulton (Ed.), *Physiology of the nervous system (2nd Ed.)*. New York: Oxford University Press, 1943.

Lieberman, S. M. A study in secondary reinforcement. Unpublished master's thesis, University of Southern California, 1967.

Light, J.S. & Gantt, W. H. Essential part of reflex arc for establishment of conditioned reflex. Formation of conditioned reflex after exclusion of motor peripheral end. *Journal of Comparative Psychology*, 1936, *21*, 19-63.

Lindley, R. H. & Moyer, K. E. Effects of instructions on the extinction of a conditioned finger-withdrawal response. *Journal of Experimental Psychology*, 1961, *61*, 82-88.

Lipkin, S. G. & Moore, J. W. Eyelid trace conditioning, CS intensity, CS-UCS interval, and a correction for "spontaneous" blinking. *Journal of Experimental Psychology*, 1966, *72*, 216-220.

Lipsitt, L. P. & Castaneda, A. Effects of delayed reward on choice behavior and response speeds in children. *Journal of Comparative and Physiological Psychology*, 1958, *51*, 65-67.

Lipsitt, L. P. & Kaye, H. Conditioned sucking in the human newborn. *Psychonomic Science*, 1964, *1*, 29-30.

Lisina, M. I. The role of orientation in the transformation of involuntary reactions into voluntary ones. In J. G. Voronin, A. N. Leontiev, A. R. Luria, E. N. Sokolov, & O. S. Vinogradova (Eds.), *Orienting reflex and exploratory behavior*. Washington: American Institute of Biological Sciences, 1965.

Littman, R. A. Conditioned generalization of the galvanic skin reaction to tone. *Journal of Experimental Psychology*, 1949, *39*, 868-882.

Lloyd, A. J., Wilker, A., & Whitehouse, J. M. Nonconditionability of flexor reflex in the chronic spinal dog. *Journal of Comparative and Physiological Psychology*, 1969, *68*, 576-579.

Lockhard, R. B. Reflections on the fall of comparative psychology: Is there a message for us all? *American Psychologist*, 1971, *25*, 168-179.

Lockhart, R. A. Temporal conditioning of GSR. *Journal of Experimental Psychology*, 1966, *71*, 438-446.

Lockhart, R. A. & Grings, W. W. Interstimulus interval effects in GSR discrimination conditioning. *Journal of Experimental Psychology*, 1964, *67*, 209-214.

Logan, F. A. A note on stimulus intensity dynamism (V). *Psychological Review*, 1954, *61*, 77-80.

Logan, F. A. A micromolar approach to behavior. *Psychological Review*, 1956, *63*, 63-73.

Logan, F. A. *Incentive*. New Haven: Yale University Press, 1960.

Logan, F. A. *Fundamentals of learning and motivation*. Dubuque, Iowa: Wm. C. Brown Co., 1970.

Lolordo, V. M. Positive conditioned reinforcement from aversive situations. *Psychological Bulletin*, 1969, *72*, 193-203.

Longenecker, E. G., Krauskopf, J., & Bitterman, M. E. Extinction following alternating and random reinforcement. *American Journal of Psychology*, 1952, *65*, 580-587.

Longo, N., Milstein, S., & Bitterman, M. E. Classical conditioning in the pigeon: Effects of partial reinforcement. *Journal of Comparative and Physiological Psychology*, 1962, *55*, 983-986.

Longstreth, L. E. Incentive stimuli as determinants of instrumental response strength in children. *Journal of Comparative and Physiological Psychology*, 1962, *55*, 398-401.

Longstreth, L. E. A cognitive interpretation of secondary reinforcement. In J. K. Cole (Ed.), *Nebraska symposium on motivation*. Lincoln: University of Nebraska Press, 1971.

Lorenz, K. Der kumpan in der umwelt des vogels. *Journal für Ornithologie*, 1935, *83*, 137-213.

Lorenz, K. *Evolution and modification of behavior*. Chicago: University of Chicago Press, 1965.

Loucks, R. B. Preliminary report of a technique for stimulation or destruction of tissues beneath the integument and the establishing of conditioned reactions with faradization of the cerebral contex. *Journal of Comparative Psychology*, 1933, *16*, 439-444.

Loucks, R. B. The experimental delimitation of neural structures essential for learning: The attempt to condition striped muscle responses with faradization of the sigmoid gyri. *Journal of Psychology*, 1935, *1*, 5-44.

Loucks, R. B. Studies of neural structures essential for learning. II. The conditioning of salivary and striped muscle responses to faradization of cortical sensory elements and action of sleep upon such mechanisms. *Journal of Comparative Psychology*, 1938, *25*, 315-332.

Loucks, R. B. & Gantt, W. H. The conditioning of striped muscle responses based upon faradic stimulations of dorsal roots and dorsal columns of the spinal cord. *Journal of Comparative Psychology*, 1938, *25*, 415-426.

Lovejoy, E. *Attention in discrimination learning*. San Francisco: Holden-Day, 1968.

Lovibond, S. H. Sensory preconditioning: Central linkage or response mediation? *Journal of Experimental Psychology*, 1959, *58*, 469-475.

Lowes, G. & Bitterman, M. E. Reward and learning in the goldfish. *Science*, 1967, *157*, 455-457.

Lubow, R. E. Latent inhibition: Effects of frequency of non-reinforced pre-exposure to the CS. *Journal of Comparative and Physiological Psychology*, 1965, *60*, 454-455.

Lubow, R. E. Latent inhibition. *Psychological Bulletin*, 1973, *79*, 398-407.

Lubow, R. E., Markham, R. E., & Allen, J. Latent inhibition and classical conditioning of the rabbit pinna response. *Journal of Comparative and Physiological Psychology*, 1968, *66*, 688-694.

Lubow, R. E. & Moore, A. U. Latent inhibition: The effect of nonreinforced pre-exposure to the conditioned sitmulus. *Journal of Comparative and Physiological Psychology*, 1959, *52*, 415-419.

Lubow, R. E. & Siebert, L. Latent inhibition within the CER paradigm. *Journal of Comparative and Physiological Psychology*, 1969, *68*, 136-138.

Ludvigson, H. W. & Gay, R. A. Differential reward conditioning: S- contrast as a function of the magnitude of S+. *Psychonomic Science*, 1966, *5*, 289-290.

Ludvigson, H. W. & Gay, R. A. An investigation of conditions determining contrast effects in differential reward conditioning. *Journal of Experimental Psychology*, 1967, *75*, 37-42.

Lutz, R. E. & Perkins, C. C., Jr. A time variable in the acquisition of observing responses. *Journal of Comparative and Physiological Psychology*, 1960, *53*, 180-182.

MacDuff, M. M. The effect of retention of varying degrees of motivation during learning in rats. *Journal of Comparative and Physiological Psychology*, 1946, *39*, 207-240.

Mackintosh, N. J. The effects of overtraining on a reversal and a non-reversal shift. *Journal of Comparative and Physiological Psychology*, 1962, *55*, 555-559.

Mackintosh, N. J. Extinction of a discrimination habit as a function of overtraining. *Journal of Comparative and Physiological Psychology*, 1963, *56*, 842-847.

Mackintosh, N. J. Overtraining, extinction, and reversal in rats and chicks. *Journal of Comparative and Physiological Psychology*, 1965a, *59*, 31-36.

Mackintosh, N. J. Selective attention in animal discrimination learning. *Psychological Bulletin*, 1965b, *64*, 124-150.

Mackintosh, N. J. & Mackintosh, J. Reversal learning in octopus Vulgaris Lamarck with and without irrelevant cues. *Quarterly Journal of Experimental Psychology*. 1963, *15*, 236-242.

Maher, W. B. & Wickens, D. D. Effect of differential quality of reward on acquisition and performance of a maze habit. *Journal of Comparative and Physiological Psychology*, 1954, *47*, 44-46.

Malmo, R. B. Measurement of drive: An unsolved problem in psychology. In M. R. Jones (Ed.), *Nebraska symposium on motivation.* Lincoln: University of Nebraska Press, 1958.

Malmo, R. B. Heart rate reactions and locus of stimulation within the septal area of the rat. *Science*, 1964, *144*, 1029-1030.

Malmo, R. B. Classical and instrumental conditioning with septal stimulation as as reinforcement. *Journal of Comparative and Physiological Psychology*, 1965, *60*, 1-8.

Mandler, G., Preven, D. W., & Kuhlman, C. K. Effects of operant reinforcement on the GSR. *Journal of the Experimental Analysis of Behavior*, 1962, *5*, 317-321.

Mandler, J. M. The effect of overtraining on the use of positive and negative stimuli in reversal and transfer. *Journal of Comparative and Physiological Psychology*, 1968, *66*, 110-115.

Manning, A. A., Schneiderman, N., & Lordahl, D. S. Delay vs. trace heart rate classical discrimination conditioning in rabbits as a function of ISI. *Journal of Experimental Psychology*, 1969, *80*, 225-230.

Margolius, G. Stimulus generalization of an instrumental response as a function of the number of reinforced trials. *Journal of Experimental Psychology*, 1955, *49*, 105-111.

Margules, D. L. & Olds, J. Identical "feeding" and "rewarding" systems in the lateral hypothalamus of rats. *Science*, 1962, *135*, 374–375.

Marquis, D. P. Can conditioned responses be established in the newborn infant? *Journal of Genetic Psychology*, 1931, *39*, 479–492.

Marx, M. H. Some relations between frustration and drive. In M. R. Jones (Ed.), *Nebraska symposium on motivation*. Lincoln: University of Nebraska, 1958.

Marx, M. H. Resistance to extinction as a function of continuous or intermittent presentation of a training cue. *Journal of Experimental Psychology*, 1958, *56*, 251–255.

Marx, M. H. Resistance to extinction as a function of degree of reproduction of training conditions. *Journal of Experimental Psychology*, 1960, *59*, 337–342.

Marx, M. H. Learning processes. In M. H. Marx (Ed.), *Learning: Processes*. Toronto: Macmillan, 1969a.

Marx, M. H. Positive contrast in instrumental learning from qualitative shift in incentive. *Psychonomic Science*, 1969b, *16*, 254–255.

Marx, M. H., Henderson, R. L., & Roberts, C. L. Positive reinforcement of the bar-pressing response by a light stimulus following dark operant pretests with no aftereffect. *Journal of Comparative and Physiological Psychology*, 1955, *48*, 73–76.

Marx, M. H. & Murphy, W. W. Resistance to extinction as a function of a motivating cue in the startbox. *Journal of Comparative and Physiological Psychology*, 1961, *54*, 207–210.

Marzocco, F. M. Frustration effect as a function of drive level, habit strength and distribution of trials during extinction. Unpublished Ph. D. dissertation, State University of Iowa, 1951.

Mason, D. J. The relation of secondary reinforcement to partial reinforcement. *Journal of Comparative and Physiological Psychology*, 1957, *50*, 264–268.

Masserman, J. H. *Behavior and neurosis*. Chicago: University of Chicago Press, 1943.

Mattson, M. & Moore, J. W. Intertrial responding and CS intensity in classical eyelid conditioning. *Journal of Experimental Psychology*, 1964, *68*, 396–401.

May, M. A. Experimentally acquired drives. *Journal of Experimental Psychology*, 1948, *38*, 66–77.

May, R. B., Tolman, C. W., & Schoenfeldt, M. G. Effects of pretraining exposure to the CS on conditioned suppression. *Psychonomic Science*, 1967, *9*, 61–62.

McAllister, W. R. Eyelid conditioning as a function of the CS-UCS interval. *Journal of Experimental Psychology*, 1953a, *45*, 417–422.

McAllister, W. R. The effect on eyelid conditioning of shifting the CS-UCS interval. *Journal of Experimental Psychology*, 1953b, *45*, 423–428.

McAllister, W. R. & McAllister, D. E. Increase over time in the stimulus generalization of acquired fear. *Journal of Experimental Psychology*, 1963, *65*, 576–582.

McAllister, W. R., McAllister, D. E., & Douglass, W. K. The inverse relationship between shock intensity and shuttle-box avoidance learning in rats. *Journal of Comparative and Physiological Psychology*, 1971, *74*, 426–433.

McCain, G. Partial reinforcement effects following a small number of acquisition trials. *Psychonomic Monograph Supplement*, 1966, *1*, 251–270.

McCain, G. The partial reinforcement effect after minimal acquisition: Single pellet reward. *Psychonomic Science*, 1968, *13*, 151–152.

McCain, G. Different levels of performance with equivalent weights of reward. *Psychonomic Science*, 1969, *14*, 2-3.

McCain, G. & Brown, E. R. Partial reinforcement with a small number of trials: Two acquisition trials. *Psychonomic Science*, 1967, 7, 265-266.

McCain, G. & McVean, G. Effects of prior reinforcement or nonreinforcement on later performance in a double alley. *Journal of Experimental Psychology*, 1967, *73*, 620-627.

McClearn, G. E. & Harlow, H. F. The effect of spatial contiguity on discrimination learning by rhesus monkeys. *Journal of Comparative and Physiological Psychology*, 1954, *47*, 391-394.

McClelland, D. C. *Personality*. New York: Dryden, 1951.

McCulloch, T. L. & Pratt, J. G. A study of the presolution period in weight discrimination by white rats. *Journal of Comparative and Psychological Psychology*, 1934, *18*, 271-290.

McDonald, D. G. & Johnson, L. C. A re-analysis of GSR conditioning. *Psychophysiology*, 1965, *1*, 291-295.

McGeoch, J. A. *The psychology of human learning*. New York: David McKay, 1942.

McGonigle, B. Stimulus additivity and dominance in visual discrimination performance by rats. *Journal of Comparative and Physiological Psychology*, 1967, *64*, 110-113.

McHose, J. H. Effect of continued nonreinforcement on the frustration effect. *Journal of Experimental Psychology*, 1963, *65*, 444-450.

McHose, J. H. Relative reinforcement effects: S1/S2 and S1/S1 paradigms in instrumental conditioning. *Psychological Review*, 1970, 77, 135-146.

McHose, J. H. & Ludvigson, H. W. Role of reward magnitude and incomplete reduction of reward magnitude in the frustration effect. *Journal of Experimental Psychology*, 1965, *70*, 490-495.

McLaurin, W. A. Postirradiation saccharin avoidance in rats as a function of the interval between ingestion and exposure. *Journal of Comparative and Physiological Psychology*, 1964, *57*, 316-317.

Mednick, S. & Freedman, J. L. Stimulus generalization. *Psychological Bulletin*, 1960, *57*, 169-200.

Meehl, P. E. On the Circularity of the law of effect. *Psychological Bulletin*, 1950, *47*, 52-75.

Mellgren, R. L. Positive contrast in the rat as a function of number of preshift trials in runway. *Journal of Comparative and Physiological Psychology*, 1971, 77, 329-336.

Melton, A. W. The end-spurt in memorization curves as an artifact of the averaging of individual curves. *Psychological Monographs*, 1936, *47*, No. 212.

Melton, A. W. Implications of short-term memory for a general theory of memory. *Journal of Verbal Learning and Verbal Behavior*, 1963, *2*, 1-21.

Meltzer, D. & Brahlek, J. A. Quantity of reinforcement and fixed interval performance. *Psychonomic Science*, 1968, *12*, 207-208.

Mendelson, J. Role of hunger in T-maze learning for food by rats. *Journal of Comparative and Physiological Psychology*, 1966, *62*, 341-349.

Mendelson, J. & Chorover, S. L. Lateral hypothalamic stimulation in satiated rats: T-maze learning for food. *Science*, 1965, *149*, 559-561.

Menzies, R. Conditioned vasomotor responses in human subjects. *Journal of Psychology*, 1937, *4*, 75-120.

Metzger, R., Cotton, J. W., & Lewis, D. J. Effect of reinforcement magnitude and of order of presentation magnitudes on runway behavior. *Journal of Comparative and Physiological Psychology*, 1957, *50*, 184–188.

Meyer, D. R. Food deprivation and discrimination reversal learning of monkeys. *Journal of Experimental Psychology*, 1951a, *41*, 10–16.

Meyer, D. R. The effects of differential rewards on discrimination reversal learning by monkeys. *Journal of Experimental Psychology*, 1951b, *41*, 268–274.

Meyer, D. R., Polidora, J., & McConnell, D. G. Effects of spatial S-R contiguity and response delay upon discriminative performances by monkeys. *Journal of Comparative and Physiological Psychology*, 1961, *54*, 175–177.

Miles, R. C. The relative effectiveness of secondary reinforcers throughout deprivation and habit-strength parameters. *Journal of Comparative and Physiological Psychology*, 1956, *49*, 126–130.

Miles, R. C. Discrimination in the squirrel monkey as a function of deprivation and problem difficulty. *Journal of Experimental Psychology*, 1959, *57*, 15–19.

Miles, R. C. Effect of food deprivation on manipulatory reactions in cat. *Journal of Comparative and Physiological Psychology*, 1962, *55*, 358–362.

Miller, G. A. Some preliminaries to psycholinguistics. *American Psychologist*, 1965, *20*, 15–20.

Miller, J. The effect of facilitatory and inhibitory attitudes on eyelid conditioning. Unpublished Ph.D. dissertation. Yale University, 1939.

Miller, L. B. & Estes, B. W. Monetary reward and motivation in discrimination learning. *Journal of Experimental Psychology*, 1961, *61*, 501–504.

Miller, N. E. Studies of fear as an acquirable drive: I. Fear as motivation and fear-reduction as reinforcement in learning of new responses. *Journal of Experimental Psychology*, 1948, *38*, 89–101.

Miller N. E. Comments on multiple-process conceptions of learning. *Psychological Review*, 1951, *58*, 375–381.

Miller, N. E. Analytical studies of drive and reward. *American Psychologist*, 1961, *16*, 739–754.

Miller, N. E. Chemical coding of behavior in the brain. *Science*, 1965, *148*, 328–338.

Miller, N. E. & Banuazizi, A. Instrumental learning by curarized rats of a specific visceral response, intestinal or cardiac. *Journal of Comparative and Physiological Psychology*, 1968, *65*, 1–7.

Miller, N. E. & DeBold, R. C. Classically conditioned tongue-licking and operant bar pressing recorded simultaneously in the rat. *Journal of Comparative and Physiological Psychology*, 1965, *59*, 109–111.

Miller, N. E. & DiCara, L. Instrumental learning of heart-rate changes in curarized rats: Shaping, and specificity to discriminative stimulus. *Journal of Comparative and Physiological Psychology*, 1967, *63*, 12–19.

Miller, N. E. & DiCara, L. Instrumental learning of urine formation by rats: Changes in renal blood blow. *American Journal of Physiology*, 1968, *215*, 677–683.

Miller, N. E. & Dworkin, B. R. Visceral learning: Recent difficulties with curarized rats and significant problems for human research. In P. A. Obrist, A. H. Black, J. Brener, & L. V. DiCara (Eds.), *Cardiovascular psychophysiology: Current issues in response mechanisms, biofeedback, and methodology.* Chicago: Aldine, 1974.

Miller, N. E. & Kessen, M. L. Reward effects of food via stomach fistula compared with those of food via mouth. *Journal of Comparative and Physiological Psychology*, 1952, *45*, 555-564.

Miller, N. E., Richter, M. L., Bailey, C. J., & Southwick, J. B. "Thirst" induced or reduced, respectively, by minute injections of hypertonic NaCL or water into the ventricles of cats. Paper read at Eastern Psychological Association meeting, New York, 1955.

Mitchell, D. S. & Gormezano, I. Water deprivation effects in classical appetitive conditioning of the rabbit's jaw movement response. *Learning and Motivation*, 1970, *1*, 199-206.

Mitchell, K. M., Perkins, N. P., & Perkins, C. C., Jr. Conditions affecting acquisition of observing responses in the absence of differential reward. *Journal of Comparative and Physiological Psychology*, 1965, *60*, 435-437.

Moeller, G. The CS-UCS interval in GSR conditioning. *Journal of Experimental Psychology*, 1954, *48*, 162-166.

Mogenson, G. & Kaplinsky, M. Brain stimulation and mechanisms of reinforcement. *Learning and Motivation*, 1970, *1*, 186-198.

Mogenson, G. J. & Stevenson, J. A. F. Drinking and self-stimulation with electrical stimulation of the lateral hypothalamus. *Physiology and Behavior*, 1966, *1*, 251-254.

Moll, R. P. The effect of drive level on acquisition of the consummatory response. *Journal of Comparative and Physiological Psychology*, 1959, *52*, 116-119.

Montgomery, K. C. Spontaneous alternation as a function of time between trials and amount of work. *Journal of Experimental Psychology*, 1951, *42*, 82-93.

Montgomery, K. C. The effect of hunger and thirst drives upon exploratory behavior. *Journal of Comparative and Physiological Psychology*, 1953, *46*, 315-319.

Montgomery, K. C. & Segall, M. Discrimination learning based upon exploratory drive. *Journal of Comparative and Physiological Psychology*, 1955, *48*, 225-228.

Moore, A. U. & Marcuse, F. L. Salivary, cardiac and motor indices of conditioning in two sows. *Journal of Comparative Psychology*, 1945, *38*, 1-16.

Moore, B. R. The role of directed Pavlovian reactions in simple instrumental learning in the pigeon. In R. A. Hinde & J. Stevenson (Eds.), *Constraints on learning.* New York: Academic Press, 1973.

Moore, J. W. & Gormezano, I. Yoked comparisons of instrumental and classical eyelid conditioning. *Journal of Experimental Psychology*, 1961, *62*, 552-559.

Moore, J. W. & Gormezano, I. Effects of omitted versus delayed UCS on classical eyelid conditioning under partial reinforcement. *Journal of Experimental Psychology*, 1963, *65*, 248-257.

Moore, J. W. & Newman, F. L. Intertrial stimuli and generalization of the conditioned eyelid response. *Journal of Experimental Psychology.* 1966, *71*, 414-419.

Moss, E. & Harlow, H. F. The role of reward in discrimination learning in monkeys. *Journal of Comparative and Physiological Psychology*, 1947, *40*, 333-342.

Mowrer, O. H. Preparatory set (Expectancy): A determinant in motivation and learning. *Psychological Review*, 1938, *45*, 62-91.

Mowrer, O. H. On the dual nature of learning—A reinterpretation of "conditioning" and "problem solving." *Harvard Educational Review*, 1947, *17*, 102-148.

Mowrer, O. H. *Learning theory and behavior*. New York: Wiley, 1960.

Mowrer, O. H. & Jones, H. M. Habit strength as a function of the pattern of reinforcement. *Journal of Experimental Psychology*, 1945, *35*, 293-311.

Mowrer, O. H. & Solomon, L. N. Contiguity vs. drive-reduction in conditioned fear: the proximity and abruptness of drive-reduction. *American Journal of Psychology*, 1954, *67*, 15-25.

Moyer, K. E. & Korn, J. H. Effect of UCS intensity on the acquisition and extinction of an avoidance response. *Journal of Experimental Psychology*, 1964, *67*, 352-359.

Moyer, K. E. & Korn, J. H. Effect of UCS intensity on the acquisition and extinction of a one-way avoidance response. *Psychonomic Science*, 1966, *4*, 121-122.

Murdock, B. B., Jr. The immediate retention of unrelated words. *Journal of Experimental Psychology*, 1960, *60*, 222-234.

Murphy, J. V. & Miller, R. E. The effect of spatial contiguity of cue and reward in the object-quality learning of rhesus monkeys. *Journal of Comparative and Physiological Psychology*, 1955, *48*, 221-224.

Murphy, J. V. & Miller, R. E. Spatial contiguities of cue, reward, and response in discrimination learning by children. *Journal of Experimental Psychology*, 1959, *58*, 485-489.

Myer, J. S. & Ricci, D. Delay of punishment gradients for the goldfish. *Journal of Comparative and Physiological Psychology*, 1968, *66*, 417-421.

Myers, A. K. & Miller, N. E. Failure to find a learned drive based on hunger: Evidence for learning motivated by "exploration." *Journal of Comparative and Physiological Psychology*, 1954, *47*, 428-436.

Myers, J. L. Secondary reinforcement: A review of recent experimentation. *Psychological Bulletin*, 1958, *55*, 284-301.

Myers, N. A. Extinction following partial and continuous primary and secondary reinforcement. *Journal of Experimental Psychology*, 1960, *60*, 172-179.

Nelson, M. N. & Ross, L. E. Effects of masking tasks on differential eyelid conditioning: A distinction between knowledge of stimulus contingencies and attentional or cognitive activities involving them. *Journal of Experimental Psychology*, 1974, *102*, 1-9.

Neuringer, A. J. Animals respond for food in the presence of free food. *Science*, 1969, *166*, 399-401.

Nevin, J. A. The maintenance of behavior. In J. A. Nevin (Ed.), *The Study of Behavior*. Glenview, Illinois: Scott, Foresman, 1973a.

Nevin, J. A. Stimulus control. In J. A. Nevin (Ed.), *The Study of Behavior*. Glenview, Illinois: Scott, Foresman, 1973b.

Nevin, J. A. & Shettleworth, S. J. An analysis of contrast effects in multiple schedules. *Journal of the Experimental Analysis of Behavior*, 1966, *9*, 305-315.

Newman, F. L. Differential eyelid conditioning as a function of the probability of reinforcement. *Journal of Experimental Psychology*, 1967, *75*, 412-417.

Newman, F. L. & Woodhouse, J. Differential eyelid conditioning: Establishing differential responding prior to varying the probability of reinforcement. *Journal of Experimental Psychology*, 1969, *80*, 146-149.

Newman, J. R. & Grice, G. R. Stimulus generalization as a function of drive level, and the relation between two measures of response strength. *Journal of Experimental Psychology*, 1965, *69*, 357-362.

Nicholls, M. F. & Kimble, G. A. Effect of instructions upon eyelid conditioning. *Journal of Experimental Psychology*, 1964, *67*, 400–402.

Noble, M. & Adams, C. K. The effect of length of CS-US interval as a function of body temperature in a cold-blooded animal. *Journal of General Psychology*, 1963a, *69*, 197–201.

Noble, M. & Adams, C. K. Conditioning in pigs as a function of the interval between CS and US. *Journal of Comparative and Physiological Psychology*, 1963b, *56*, 215–219.

Noble, M., Gruender, A. & Meyer, D. R. Conditioning in goldfish (Mollienisia Sp.) as a function of the interval between CS and US. *Journal of Comparative and Physiological Psychology*, 1959, *52*, 236–239.

Noble, M. & Harding, G. E. Conditioning of rhesus monkeys as a function of the interval between CS and US. *Journal of Comparative and Physiological Psychology*, 1963, *56*, 220–224.

Norris, E. B. & Grant, D. A. Eyelid conditioning as affected by verbally induced inhibitory set and counter reinforcement. *American Journal of Psychology*, 1948, *61*, 37–49.

North, A. J. & Clayton, K. N. Irrelevant stimuli and degree of learning in discrimination learning and reversal. *Psychological Reports*, 1959, *5*, 405–408.

Notterman, J. M., Schoenfeld, W. N., & Bersh, P. J. Conditioned heart rate responses in human beings during experimental anxiety. *Journal of Comparative and Physiological Psychology*, 1952, *45*, 1–8.

Novin, D. & Miller, N. E. Failure to condition thirst induced by feeding dry food to hungry rats. *Journal of Comparative and Physiological Psychology*, 1962, *55*, 373–374.

Obrist, P. A., Webb, R. A., Sutterer, J. R. & Howard, J. L. The cardiac-somatic relationship: Some reformulations. *Psychophysiology*, 1970, *6*, 569–587.

Obrist, P. A., Wood, D. M., & Perez-Reyes, M. Heart rate during conditioning in humans: Effects of UCS intensity, vagal blockage, and adrenergic block of vasomotor activity. *Journal of Experimental Psychology*, 1965, *70*, 32–42.

O'Kelley, L. I. & Heyer, A. W., Jr. Studies in motivation and retention. V. The influence of need duration in retention of a maze habit. *Comparative Psychology Monographs*, 1951, *20*, 287–301.

Olds, J. Runway and maze behavior controlled by basemedial forebrain stimulation in the rat. *Journal of Comparative and Physiological Psychology*, 1956, *49*, 507–512.

Olds, J. Satiation effects in self-stimulation of the brain. *Journal of Comparative and Physiological Psychology*, 1958a, *51*, 675–678.

Olds, J. Effects of hunger and male sex hormone on self-stimulation of the brain. *Journal of Comparative and Physiological Psychology*, 1958b, *51*, 320–324.

Olds, J. & Milner, P. Positive reinforcement produced by electrical stimulation of septal area and other regions of the rat brain. *Journal of Comparative and Physiological Psychology*, 1954, *47*, 419–427.

Olton, D. S. Shock-motivated avoidance and the analysis of behavior. *Psychological Bulletin*, 1973, *79*, 243–251.

Orlebeke, J. F. & Van Olst, E. H. Learning and performance as a function of CS-intensity in a delayed GSR conditioning situation. *Journal of Experimental Psychology*, 1968, *77*, 483–487.

Osgood, C. E. *Method and theory in experimental psychology*. New York: Oxford University Press, 1953.

Ottenberg, P., Stein, M. Lewis, J., & Hamilton, C. Learned asthma in the guinea pig. *Psychosomatic Medicine*, 1958, *20*, 395–400.

Padilla, A. M. A few acquisition trials: Effects of magnitude and percent reward. *Psychonomic Science*, 1967, *9*, 241-242.

Parkinson, S. R. Sensory preconditioning of a conditioned emotional response. *Psychonomic Science*, 1968, *11*, 119.

Parks, E. R. The orientation reaction as a mediator of sensory preconditioning. *Psychonomic Science*, 1968, *11*, 11-12.

Passey, G. E. The influence of intensity of unconditioned stimulus upon acquisition of a conditioned response. *Journal of Experimental Psychology*, 1948, *38*, 420-428.

Passey, G. E. & Burns, T. C. Influence of variable reinforcement upon acquisition on the conditioned eyelid response. *Psychological Reports*, 1962, *11*, 547-552.

Passey, G. E. & Wood, D. L. Effect of pattern of reinforcement on the conditioned eyelid response. *Journal of Experimental Psychology*, 1963, *66*, 241-244.

Patten, R. L. & Deaux, E. B. Classical conditioning and extinction of the licking response in rats. *Psychonomic Science*, 1966, *4*, 21-22.

Patterson, M. M. Classical conditioning of the rabbit's (Oryctolagus Cuniculus) nictitating membrane response with fluctuating ISI and intracranial CS. *Journal of Comparative and Physiological Psychology*, 1970, *72*, 193-202.

Patterson, M. M., Cegavske, C. F., & Thompson, R. F. Effects of a classical conditioning paradigm on hind-limb flexor nerve response in immobilized spinal cats. *Journal of Comparative and Physiological Psychology*, 1973, *84*, 88-97.

Paul, C. & Kesner, R. Effects of overlearning trials upon habit reversal under conditions of aversive stimulation. *Psychological Reports*, 1963, *13*, 361-363.

Pavlov, I. P. *Conditioned reflexes*. (Translated by G. V. Anrep) New York: Dover Publications, 1927.

Peak, H. An evaluation of the concepts of reflex and voluntary action. *Psychological Review*, 1933, *40*, 71-89.

Peckham, R. H. & Amsel, A. Magnitude of reward and the frustration effect in a within-subject design. *Psychonomic Science*, 1964, *1*, 285-286.

Peckham, R. H. & Amsel, A. The within-S demonstration of a relationship between frustration and magnitude of reward in a differential magnitude of reward discrimination. *Journal of Experimental Psychology*, 1967, *73*, 187-195.

Penney, R. K. The effects of non-reinforcement on response strengths as a function of number of previous reinforcements. *Canadian Journal of Psychology*, 1960, *14*, 206-215.

Penneypacker, H. S. Measurement of the conditioned eyelid reflex. *Science*, 1964, *144*, 1248-1249.

Perin, C. T. Behavior potentiality as a joint function of the amount of training and the degree of hunger at the time of extinction. *Journal of Experimental Psychology*, 1942, *30*, 93-113.

Perin, C. T. A quantitative investigation of the delay-of-reinforcement gradient. *Journal of Experimental Psychology*, 1943, *32*, 37-51.

Perkins, C. C., Jr. The relation of secondary reward to gradients of reinforcement. *Journal of Experimental Psychology*, 1947, *37*, 377-392.

Perkins, C. C., Jr. The relation between conditioned stimulus intensity and response strength. *Journal of Experimental Psychology*, 1953, *46*, 225-231.

Perkins, C. C., Jr. & Weyant, R. G. The interval between training and test trials as a determiner of the slope of generalization gradients. *Journal of Comparative and Physiological Psychology*, 1958, *51*, 596-600.

Peterson, G. B., Ackill, J. E., Frommer, G. P., & Hearst, E. Conditioned approach and contact between signals for food or brain stimulation reinforcement. *Science*, 1972, *177*, 1009-1011.

Peterson, G. B. & Newman, F. L. Differential human eyelid conditioning as a function of the probability of reinforcement and CS intensity. *Journal of Experimental Psychology*, 1970, *85*, 318-320.

Peterson, N. Effect of monochromatic rearing on the control of responding by wavelength. *Science*, 1962, *136*, 774-775.

Pieper, W. & Marx, M. H. Conditioning of a previously neutral cue to the onset of a metabolic drive: Two instances of negative results. *Psychological Record*, 1963, *13*, 191-195.

Pliskoff, S. S., Wright, J. E., & Hawkins, T. D. Brain stimulation as a reinforcer: Intermittent schedules. *Journal of the Experimental Analysis of Behavior*, 1965, *8*, 75-88.

Porter, J. M. Extinction of an acquired response as a function of the interval between successive non-rewarded trials. *Journal of Comparative Psychology*, 1938, *26*, 261-270.

Postman, L. Association and performance in the analysis of verbal learning. In T. R. Dixon and D. L. Horton (Eds.), *Verbal Behavior and General Behavior Theory*. Englewood Cliffs, New Jersey: Prentice-Hall, 1968.

Powell, D. R., Jr. & Perkins, C. C., Jr. Strength of secondary reinforcement as a determiner of the effects of duration of goal response on learning. *Journal of Experimental Psychology*, 1957, *53*, 106-112.

Premack, D. Toward empirical behavioral laws: I. Positive reinforcement. *Psychological Review*, 1959, *66*, 219-233.

Premack, D. Rate of differential reinforcement in monkey manipulation. *Journal of the Experimental Analysis of Behavior*, 1963, *6*, 81-89.

Premack, D. Reinforcement theory. In D. Levine (Ed.), *Nebraska symposium on motivation*. Lincoln: University of Nebraska Press, 1965.

Premack, D. A functional analysis of language. *Journal of the Experimental Analysis of Behavior*, 1970, *14*, 107-125.

Premack, D. Catching up with common sense or two sides of a generalization: Reinforcement and punishment. In R. Glaser (Ed.), *The nature of reinforcement*. New York: Academic Press, 1971.

Premack, D. & Hillix, W. A. Evidence for shift effects in the consummatory response. *Journal of Experimental Psychology*, 1962, *63*, 284-288.

Premack, D., Schaeffer, R. W., & Hundt, A. Reinforcement of drinking by running: Effect of fixed ratio and reinforcement time. *Journal of the Experimental Analysis of Behavior*, 1964, *7*, 91-96.

Prewitt, E. P. Number of preconditioning trials in sensory preconditioning using CER training. *Journal of Comparative and Physiological Psychology*, 1967, *64*, 360-362.

Price, K. P. & Geer, J. H. Predictable and unpredictable aversive events: Evidence for the safety-signal hypothesis. *Psychonomic Science*, 1972, *26*, 215-216.

Prokasy, W. F. The acquisition of observing responses in the absence of differential external reinforcement. *Journal of Comparative and Physiological Psychology*, 1956, *49*, 131-134.

Prokasy, W. F. Developments with the two-phase model applied to human eyelid conditioning. In A. H. Black & W. F. Prokasy (Eds.), *Classical condi-*

tioning II: Current research and theory. New York: Appleton-Century-Crofts, 1972.

Prokasy, W. F. A two-phase model account of aversive classical conditioning performance in humans and rabbits. *Learning and Motivation,* 1973, *4,* 247–258.

Prokasy, W. F. & Ebel, H. C. Three components of the classically conditioned GSR in human subjects. *Journal of Experimental Psychology,* 1967, *73,* 247–256.

Prokasy, W. F., Ebel, H. C., & Thompson, D. D. Response shaping at long interstimulus intervals in classical conditioning. *Journal of Experimental Psychology,* 1963, *66,* 138–141.

Prokasy, W. F., Fawcett, J. T., & Hall, J. F. Recruitment, latency, magnitude, and amplitude of the GSR as a function of interstimulus interval. *Journal of Experimental Psychology,* 1962, *64,* 513–518.

Prokasy, W. F., Jr., Grant, D. A., & Myers, N. A. Eyelid conditioning as a function of unconditioned stimulus intensity and intertrial interval. *Journal of Experimental Psychology,* 1958, *55,* 242–246.

Prokasy, W. F. & Hall, J. F. Primary stimulus generalization. *Psychological Review,* 1963, *70,* 310–322.

Prokasy, W. F., Hall, J. F., & Fawcett, J. T. Adaptation, sensitization, forward and backward conditioning, and pseudo-conditioning of the GSR. *Psychological Reports,* 1962, *10,* 103–106.

Prokasy, W. F. & Harsanyi, M. A. Two-phase model for human classical conditioning. *Journal of Experimental Psychology,* 1968, *78,* 359–368.

Prokasy, W. F. & Kumpfer, K. One- and two-operator versions of the threshold model applied to the performances of Vs and Cs in human eyelid conditioning. *Journal of Experimental Psychology,* 1969, *80,* 231–236.

Prokasy, W. F. & Raskin, D. C. *Electrodermal activity in psychological research.* New York: Academic Press, 1973.

Prosser, C. L. & Hunter, W. S. The extinction of startle responses and spinal reflexes in the white rat. *American Journal of Physiology,* 1936, *117,* 609–618.

Pubols, B. H., Jr. The facilitation of visual and spatial discrimination reversal by overlearning. *Journal of Comparative and Physiological Psychology,* 1956, *49,* 243–248.

Purtle, R. B. Peak shift: A review. *Psychological Bulletin,* 1937, *80,* 408–421.

Putney, R. T., Erwin, T. J., & Smith, S. T., Jr. The facilitation of conditioned alpha blocking with an overt response. *Psychonomic Science,* 1972, *26,* 16–18.

Ramsay, D. A., Knapp, J. Z., & Zeiss, J. C. Transients in constant-current generators. *Behavior Research Methods Instrumentation,* 1970, *2,* 122–123.

Rashotte, M. E. & Amsel, A. The generalized PRE: Within-S PRF and CRF training in different runways, at different times of day, by different experimenters. *Psychonomic Science,* 1968, *11,* 315–316.

Raymond, B., Aderman, M., & Wolach, A. H. Incentive shifts in the goldfish. *Journal of Comparative and Physiological Psychology,* 1972, *78,* 10–13.

Razran, G. H. S. Conditioned responses in children. *Archives of Psychology,* 1933, *23,* No. 148.

Razran, G. H. S. A quantitative study of meaning by a conditioned salivary technique (semantic conditioning). *Science,* 1939, *90,* 89–90.

Razran, G. H. S. Stimulus generalization of conditioned responses. *Psychological Bulletin,* 1949, *46,* 337–365.

Razran, G. A note on second-order conditioning—and secondary reinforcement. *Psychological Review*, 1955, *62*, 327–332.

Razran, G. Backward conditioning. *Psychological Bulletin*, 1956, *53*, 55–69.

Razran, G. The dominance-contiguity theory of the acquisition of classical conditioning. *Psychological Bulletin*, 1957, *54*, 1–46.

Razran, G. The observable unconscious and the inferable conscious in current Soviet psychophysiology: Interceptive conditioning, and the orienting reflex. *Psychological Review.* 1961, *68*, 81–147.

Razran, G. Empirical codifications and specific theoretical implications of compound-stimulus conditioning: Perception. In W. F. Prokasy (Ed.), *Classical conditioning.* New York: Appleton-Century-Crofts, 1965.

Reese, H. W. & Lipsitt, L. P. *Experimental child psychology.* New York: Academic Press, 1970.

Reid, L. S. The development of noncontinuity behavior through continuity learning. *Journal of Experimental Psychology*, 1953, *46*, 107–112.

Reiss, S. & Wagner, A. R. CS habituation produces a "latent inhibition effect" but no active "conditioned inhibition." *Learning and Motivation*, 1972, *3*, 237–245.

Rescorla, R. A. Pavlovian conditioning and its proper control procedures. *Psychological Review*, 1967, *74*, 71–80.

Rescorla, R. A. Probability of shock in the presence and absence of CS in fear conditioning. *Journal of Comparative and Physiological Psychology*, 1968, *66*, 1–5.

Rescorla, R. A. Conditioned inhibition of fear resulting from negative CS-US contingencies. *Journal of Comparative and Physiological Psychology*, 1969, *67*, 504–509.

Restle, F. A theory of discrimination learning. *Psychological Review*, 1955, *62*, 11–19.

Revusky, S. H. Aversion to sucrose produced by contingent X-irradiation: Temporal and dosage parameters. *Journal of Comparative and Physiological Psychology*, 1968, *65*, 17–22.

Revusky, S. H. & Bedarf, E. W. Association of illness with prior ingestion of novel foods. *Science*, 1967, *155*, 219–220.

Revusky, S. H. & Garcia, J. Learned associations over long delays. In G. H. Bower (Ed.), *The psychology of learning and motivation: Advances in research and theory.* New York: Academic Press, 1970.

Reynolds, B. The acquisition of a trace conditioned response as a function of the magnitude of the stimulus trace. *Journal of Experimental Psychology*, 1945 *35*, 15–30.

Reynolds, B. The acquisition of black-white discrimination habit under two levels of reinforcement. *Journal of Experimental Psychology*, 1949, *39*, 760–769.

Reynolds, B. Resistance to extinction as a function of the amount of reinforcement present during acquisition. *Journal of Experimental Psychology*, 1950, *40*, 46–52.

Reynolds, G. S. Behavioral contrast. *Journal of the Experimental Analysis of Behavior*, 1961a, *4*, 57–71.

Reynolds, G. S. Attention in the pigeon. *Journal of the Experimental Analysis of Behavior*, 1961b, *4*, 203–208.

Reynolds, W. F. & Pavlik, W. B. Running speed as a function of deprivation period and reward magnitude. *Journal of Comparative and Physiological Psychology*, 1960, *53*, 615–618.

Rice, D. G. Operant conditioning and associated electromyogram responses. *Journal of Experimental Psychology*, 1966, *71*, 908-912.

Richter, C. P. Animal behavior and internal drives. *Quarterly Review of Biology*, 1927, *2*, 306-343.

Riess, D. Pavlovian phenomena in conditioned acceleration: Spontaneous recovery. *Psychonomic Science*, 1971, *23*, 351-353.

Ritchie, B. V., Ebeling, E., & Roth, W. Evidence for continuity in the discrimination of vertical and horizontal patterns. *Journal of Comparative and Physiological Psychology*, 1950, *43*, 168-180.

Robbins, D. Partial reinforcement: A selective review of the alleyway literature since 1960. *Psychological Bulletin*, 1971, *76*, 415-431.

Roberts, C. L., Marx, M. H., & Collier, G. Light onset and light offset as reinforcers for the albino rat. *Journal of Comparative and Physiological Psychology*, 1958, *51*, 575-579.

Roberts, W. A. Resistance to extinction following partial and consistent reinforcement with varying magnitudes of reward. *Journal of Comparative and Physiological Psychology*, 1969, *67*, 395-400.

Roberts, W. W. Both rewarding and punishing effects from stimulation of posterior hypothalamus of cat with same electrode at same intensity. *Journal of Comparative and Physiological Psychology*, 1958, *51*, 400-407.

Robinson, J. & Gantt, W. H. The cardiac component of the orienting reflex. *Federation Proceedings of American Societies for Experimental Biology*, 1946, *5*, No. 1, Part II, 87-88.

Robinson, J. S. Light onset and termination as reinforcers for rats living under normal light conditions. *Psychological Reports*, 1959, *5*, 793-796.

Rohrer, J. H. A motivational state resulting from nonreward. *Journal of Comparative and Physiological Psychology*, 1949, *42*, 476-485.

Rosen, A. J. Incentive-shift performance as a function of magnitude and number of sucrose rewards. *Journal of Comparative and Physiological Psychology*, 1966, *62*, 487-490.

Rosen, A. J. & Ison, J. R. Runway performance following changes in sucrose rewards. *Psychonomic Science*, 1965, *2*, 335-336.

Rosenzweig, M. R. Salivary conditioning before Pavlov. *American Journal of Psychology*, 1959, *72*, 628-633.

Ross, L. E. The decremental effects of partial reinforcement during acquisition of the conditioned eyelid response. *Journal of Comparative and Physiological Psychology*, 1959, *57*, 74-82.

Ross, L. E., Hetherington, M., & Wray, N. P. Delay of reward and the learning of a size problem by normal and retarded children. *Child Development*, 1965, *36*, 509-517.

Ross, L. E. & Spence, K. W. Eyelid conditioning performance under partial reinforcement as a function of UCS intensity. *Journal of Experimental Psychology*, 1960, *59*, 379-382.

Ross, S. M. & Ross, L. E. Comparison of trace and delay classical eyelid conditioning as a function of interstimulus interval. *Journal of Experimental Psychology*, 1971, *91*, 165-167.

Ross, S. M., Ross, L. E., & Werden, D. Trace and delay differential classical eyelid conditioning in human adults. *Bulletin of the Psychonomic Society*, 1974, *3*, 224-226.

Routtenberg, A. & Lindy, J. Effects of the availability of rewarding septal and hypothalamic stimulation on bar pressing for food under conditions of deprivation. *Journal of Comparative and Physiological Psychology*, 1965, *60*, 158–161.

Rozen, P. & Kalat, J. W. Specific hungers and poison avoidance as adaptive specializations of learning. *Psychological Review*, 1971, *78*, 459–486.

Rudolph, R. I., Honig, W. K., & Gerry, J. E. Effects of monochromatic rearing on the acquisition of stimulus control. *Journal of Comparative and Physiological Psychology*, 1969, *67*, 50–57.

Runquist, W. N. Performance in eyelid conditioning following changes in reinforcement schedule. *Journal of Experimental Psychology*, 1963, *65*, 617–618.

Runquist, W. N. & Spence, K. W. Performance in eyelid conditioning as a function of UCS duration. *Journal of Experimental Psychology*, 1959, *57*, 249–252.

Runquist, W. N., Spence, K. W., & Stubbs, D. W. Differential conditioning and intensity of the UCS. *Journal of Experimental Psychology*, 1958, *55*, 613–616.

Sainsbury, R. S. Effect of proximity of elements on the feature positive effect. *Journal of the Experimental Analysis of Behavior*, 1971a, *16*, 315–326.

Sainsbury, R. S. The "feature positive effect" and simultaneous discrimination learning. *Journal of Experimental Child Psychology*, 1971b, *11*, 347–356.

Sainsbury, R. Discrimination learning utilizing positive or negative cues. *Canadian Journal of Psychology*, 1973, *27*, 46–57.

Saltzman, I. J. Maze learning in the absence of primary reinforcement: A study of secondary reinforcement. *Journal of Comparative and Physiological Psychology*, 1949, *42*, 161–173.

Saltzman, I. J. & Koch, S. The effect of low intensities of hunger on the behavior mediated by a habit of maximum strength. *Journal of Experimental Psychology*, 1948, *38*, 347–370.

Sameroff, A. J. The components of sucking in the human newborn. *Journal of Experimental Child Psychology*, 1968, *6*, 607–623.

Scarborough, B. B. & Goodson, F. E. Properties of stimuli associated with strong and weak hunger drive in the rat. *Journal of Genetic Psychology*, 1957, *91*, 257–261.

Schaeffer, R. W. The reinforcement relation as a function of instrumental response base rate. *Journal of Experimental Psychology*, 1965, *69*, 419–425.

Schiffmann, K. & Furedy, J. J. Failures of contingency and cognitive factors to affect long-interval differential Pavlovian autonomic conditioning. *Journal of Experimental Psychology*, 1972, *96*, 215–218.

Schlosberg, H. & Solomon, R. L. Latency of response in a choice discrimination. *Journal of Experimental Psychology*, 1943, *33*, 22–39.

Schneiderman, N. Interstimulus interval functon of the nictitating membrane response of the rabbit under delay versus trace conditioning. *Journal of Comparative and Physiological Psychology*, 1966, *62*, 397–402.

Schneiderman, N. Determinants of heart rate classical conditioning. In J. H. Reynierse (Ed.), *Current issues in animal learning: A colloquium*. Lincoln: University of Nebraska Press, 1970.

Schneiderman, N. *Classical (Pavlovian) conditioning*. Morristown, New Jersey: General Learning Press, 1973.

Schneiderman, N. & Gormezano, I. Conditioning of the nictitating membrane of the rabbit as a function of the CS-UCS interval. *Journal of Comparative and Physiological Psychology*, 1964, *57*, 188–195.

Schneiderman, N., Smith, M. C., Smith, A. C., & Gormezano, I. Heart rate classical conditioning in rabbits. *Psychonomic Science*, 1966, *6*, 241–242.

Schneiderman, N., VanDercar, D. H., Yehle, A., Manning, A. A., Golden, T., & Schneiderman, E. Vagal compensatory adjustment: Relationship to heart rate classical conditioning in rabbits. *Journal of Comparative and Physiological Psychology*, 1969, *68*, 175–183.

Schnur, P. Latent inhibition: The effects of nonreinforced preexposure of the CS in differential eyelid conditioning. Unpublished master's thesis, North Carolina State University, 1967.

Schnur, P. & Ksir, C. J. Latent inhibition in human eyelid conditioning. *Journal of Experimental Psychology*, 1969, *80*, 388–389.

Schoelkopf, A. M. & Orlando, R. Delayed vs. immediate reinforcement in simultaneous discrimination problems with mentally retarded children. *Psychological Record*, 1965, *15*, 15–23.

Schoenfeld, W. N., Antonitis, J. J., & Bersh, P. J. A preliminary study of training conditions necessary for secondary reinforcement. *Journal of Experimental Psychology*, 1950, *40*, 40–45.

Schrier, A. M. Comparison of two methods of investigating the effect of amount of reward on performance. *Journal of Comparative and Physiological Psychology*, 1958, *51*, 725–731.

Schrier, A. M. & Harlow, H. F. Effect of amount of incentive on discrimination learning by monkeys. *Journal of Comparative and Physiological Psychology*, 1956, *49*, 117–125.

Schwartz, G. E. Cardiac responses to self-induced thoughts. *Psychophysiology*, 1971, *8*, 462–467.

Scull, J. W. The Amsel frustration effect: Interpretations and research. *Psychological Bulletin*, 1973, *79*, 352–361.

Segundo, J. P., Roig, J. A., & Sommer-Smith, J. A. Conditioning of reticular formation stimulation effects. *Electroencephalography and Clinical Neurophysiology*, 1959, *11*, 471–484.

Seidel, R. J. An investigation of the mediation process in preconditioning. *Journal of Experimental Psychology*, 1958, *56*, 220–225.

Seligman, M. E. P. Control group and conditioning: A comment on operationism. *Psychological Review*, 1969, *76*, 484–491.

Seligman, M. E. P. On the generality of the laws of learning. *Psychological Review*, 1970, *77*, 406–418.

Seligman, M. E. P., Bravman, S., & Radford, R. Drinking: Discriminative conditioning. *Psychonomic Science*, 1970, *20*, 63–64.

Seligman, M. E. P. & Campbell, B. A. Effect of intensity and duration of punishment on extinction of an avoidance response. *Journal of Comparative and Physiological Psychology*, 1965, *59*, 295–297.

Seligman, M. E. P., Ives, C. E., Ames, H., & Mineka, S. Conditioned drinking and its failure to extinguish: Avoidance, preparedness, or functional autonomy. *Journal of Comparative and Physiological Psychology*, 1970, *71*, 411–419.

Seligman, M. E. P., Mineka, S., & Fillit, H. Conditioned drinking produced by procaine, NaCL, and angiotensin. *Journal of Comparative and Physiological Psychology*, 1971, *77*, 110–121.

Senter, R. J. & Hummel, W. F. Suppression of an autonomic response through operant conditioning. *Psychological Record*, 1965, *15*, 1–5.

Seraganian, P. & Vom Saal, W. Blocking the development of stimulus control when stimuli indicate periods of nonreinforcement. *Journal of the Experimental Analysis of Behavior*, 1969, *12*, 767-772.

Seward, J. P., Pereboom, A. C., Butler, B., & Jones, R. B. The role of prefeeding in an apparent frustration effect. *Journal of Experimental Psychology*, 1957, *54*, 445-450.

Seward, J. P., Uyeda, A., & Olds, J. Resistance to extinction following cranial self-stimulation. *Journal of Comparative and Physiological Psychology*, 1959, *52*, 294-299.

Seward, J. P., Uyeda, A. A., & Olds, J. Reinforcing effect of brain stimulation on runway performance as a function of interval between trials. *Journal of Comparative and Physiological Psychology*, 1960, *53*, 224-228.

Shagass, C. Conditioning the human occipital rhythm to a voluntary stimulus: A quantitative study. *Journal of Experimental Psychology*, 1942, *31*, 367-379.

Shagass, C. & Johnson, E. P. The course of acquisition of a conditioned response of the occipital alpha rhythm. *Journal of Experimental Psychology*, 1943, *33*, 201-209.

Shanab, M. E. & Biller, J. D. Positive contrast in the runway obtained following a shift in both delay and magnitude of reward. *Learning and Motivation*, 1972, *3*, 179-184.

Shanab, M. E. & Cavallaro, G. Positive contrast obtained in rats following a shift in schedule, delay, and magnitude of reward. *Bulletin of the Psychonomic Society*, 1975, *5*, 109-112.

Shanab, M. E. & Ferrell, J. J. Positive contrast in the Lashley maze under different drive conditions. *Psychonomic Science*, 1970, *20*, 31-32.

Shanab, M. E., Sanders, R., & Premack, D. Positive contrast in the runway obtained with delay of reward. *Science*, 1969, *164*, 724-725.

Sheafor, P. J. & Gormezano, I. Conditioning the rabbit's (oryctolagus cuniculus) jaw-movement response: UR magnitude effects of URs, CRs, and pseudo-CRs. *Journal of Comparative and Physiological Psychology*, 1972, *81*, 449-456.

Shean, G. D. Instrumental modification of the galvanic skin response: Conditioning or control? *Journal of Psychosomatic Research*, 1970, *14*, 155-160.

Sheatz, G. C. Electrode holders in chronic preparations. In D. E. Sheer (Ed.), *Electrical stimulation of the brain*. Austin: University of Texas Press, 1961.

Sheffield, F. D. Hilgard's critique of Guthrie. *Psychological Review*, 1949, *56*, 284-291.

Sheffield, F. D. & Roby, T. B. Reward value of a non-nutritive sweet taste. *Journal of Comparative and Physiological Psychology*, 1950, *43*, 471-481.

Sheffield, F. D., Roby, T. B., & Campbell, B. A. Drive reduction versus consummatory behavior as determinants of reinforcement. *Journal of Comparative and Physiological Psychology*, 1954, *47*, 349-354.

Sheffield, F. D., Wulff, J. J., & Backer, R. Reward value of copulation without sex drive reduction. *Journal of Comparative and Physiological Psychology*, 1951, *44*, 3-8.

Sheffield, V. F. Extinction as a function of partial reinforcement and distribution of practice. *Journal of Experimental Psychology*, 1949, *39*, 511-526.

Shepard, W. O. Learning set in preschool children. *Journal of Comparative and Physiological Psychology*, 1957, *50*, 15-17.

Sherrington, C. S. Experiments on the value of vascular and visceral factors for the genesis of emotion. Philosophical *Transactions of the Royal Society in London*, 1900, *66*, 390–403.

Shurrager, P. S. & Culler, E. Conditioning in the spinal dog. *Journal of Experimental Psychology*, 1940, *26*, 133–159.

Sideroff, S., Schneiderman, N., & Powell, D. A. Motivational properties of septal stimulation as the US in classical conditioning of heart rate in rabbits. *Journal of Comparative and Physiological Psychology*, 1971, *74*, 1–10.

Sidman, M. Two temporal parameters of the maintenance of avoidance behavior in the white rat. *Journal of Comparative and Physiological Psychology*, 1953, *46*, 253–261.

Sidman, M. & Fletcher, F. G. A demonstration of auto-shaping with monkeys. *Journal of the Experimental Analysis of Behavior*, 1968, *11*, 307–309.

Sidman, M. & Stebbins, W. C. Satiation effects under fixed-ratio schedules of reinforcement, *Journal of Comparative and Physiological Psychology*, 1954, *47*, 114–116.

Siebert, L., Nicholson, L., Carr-Harris, E., & Lubow, R. E. Conditioning by the method of Ivanov-Smolenskii. *Journal of Experimental Psychology*, 1969, *79*, 93–96.

Siegel, P. S. Drive shift, a conceptual and experimental analysis. *Journal of Comparative and Physiological Psychology*, 1943, *35*, 139–148.

Siegel, P. S. & MacDonnell, M. F. A repetition of the Calvin-Bicknell-Sperling study of conditioned drive. *Journal of Comparative and Physiological Psychology*, 1954, *47*, 250–252.

Siegel, P. S. & Milby, J. B., Jr. Secondary reinforcement in relation to shock termination: Second chapter. *Psychological Bulletin*, 1969, *72*, 146–156.

Siegel, S. Overtraining and transfer processes. *Journal of Comparative and Physiological Psychology*, 1967, *64*, 471–477.

Siegel, S. Retention of latent inhibition. *Psychonomic Science*, 1970, *20*, 161–162.

Siegel, S. Flavor preexposure and "learned safety." *Journal of Comparative and Physiological Psychology*, 1974, *87*, 1073–1082.

Siegel, S. & Andrews, J. M. Magnitude of reinforcement and choice behavior in children. *Journal of Experimental Psychology*, 1962, *63*, 337–341.

Silver, C. A. & Meyer, D. R. Temporal factors in sensory preconditioning. *Journal of Comparative and Physiological Psychology*, 1954, *47*, 57–59.

Singh, D. Preference for bar pressing to obtain reward over freeloading in rats and children. *Journal of Comparative and Physiological Psychology*, 1970, *73*, 320–327.

Singh, D. & Query, W. T. Preference for work over "freeloading" in children. *Psychonomic Science*, 1971, *24*, 77–79.

Skinner, B. F. *The behavior of organisms: An experimental analysis.* New York: Appleton-Century-Crofts, 1938.

Slaughter, J., Hahn, W., & Rinaldi, P. Instrumental conditioning of heart rate in the curarized rat with varied amounts of pretraining. *Journal of Comparative and Physiological Psychology*, 1970, *72*, 356–359.

Slight, D. The conditioned psycho-galvanic response. In J. A. Lord (Ed.), *Contributions to psychiatry, neurology, and sociology.* London: Hoeber, 1929.

Slivinski, A. J. & Hall, J. F. The discriminability of tones used to test stimulus generalization. *American Journal of Psychology*, 1960, *73*, 581–586.

Slivka, R. M. & Bitterman, M. E. Classical appetitive conditioning in the pigeon: Partial reinforcement. *Psychonomic Science*, 1966, *4*, 181–182.

Small, W. S. Notes on the psychic development of the young white rat. *American Journal of Psychology*, 1899, *11*, 80–100.

Small, W. S. An experimental study of the mental processes of the rat. *American Journal of Psychology*, 1900, *11*, 133–165.

Smith, J. C. & Morris, D. D. The use of X rays as the unconditioned stimulus in five-hundred-day-old rats. *Journal of Comparative and Physiological Psychology*, 1963, *56*, 746–747.

Smith, J. C., Morris, D. D., & Hendricks, J. Conditioned aversion to saccharin solution using high exposure rates of X-rays as the unconditioned stimulus. *Radiation Research*, 1964, *22*, 507–510.

Smith, J. C. & Roll, D. L. Trace conditioning with x-rays as an aversive stimulus. *Psychonomic Science*, 1967, *9*, 11–12.

Smith, K. Conditioning as an artifact. *Psychological Review*, 1954, *61*, 217–225.

Smith M. C. CS-US interval and US intensity in classical conditioning of the rabbit's nictitating membrane response. *Journal of Comparative and Physiological Psychology*, 1968, *66*, 679–687.

Smith, M. C., Coleman, S. R., & Gormezano, I. Classical conditioning of the rabbit's nictitating membrane response at backward, simultaneous and forward CS-US intervals. *Journal of Comparative and Physiological Psychology*, 1969, *69*, 226–231.

Smith, M. C., DiLollo, V., & Gormezano, I. Conditioned jaw movement in the rabbit. *Journal of Comparative and Physiological Psychology*, 1966, *62*, 479–483.

Smith, M. P. The stimulus trace gradient in visual discrimination learning. *Journal of Comparative and Physiological Psychology*, 1951, *44*, 154–161.

Smith, O. A. Stimulation of lateral and medial hypothalamus and food intake in the rat. *Anatomical Record*, 1956, *124*, 363–364.

Smith, S. G. & Smith, W. M. A demonstration of autoshaping with dogs. *Psychological Record*, 1971, *21*, 377–379.

Snyder, C. & Noble, M. Operant conditioning of vasoconstriction. *Journal of Experimental Psychology*, 1968, *77*, 263–268.

Snyder, H. L. & Hulse, S. H. Effects of volume of reinforcement and number of consummatory responses on licking and running behavior. *Journal of Experimental Psychology*, 1961, *61*, 474–479.

Sokolov, E. N. Neuronal models and the orienting reflex. In M. A. B. Brazier (Ed.), *The central nervous system and behavior*. New York: Josiah Macy, Jr., Foundation, 1960.

Sokolov, E. N. *Perception and the conditioned reflex*. New York: Pergamon Press, 1963.

Solberg, K. B., Tyre, T. E., & Stinson, G. M. Ivan-Smolensky conditioning in adults and children using an electromyographic response measure. *Psychonomic Science*, 1970, *18*, 365–366.

Solomon, R. L. Punishment. *American Psychologist*, 1964, *19*, 239–253.

Solomon, R. L. & Corbit, J. D. An opponent-process theory of motivation: I. Temporal dynamics of affect. *Psychological Review*, 1974, *81*, 119–145.

Solomon, R. L. & Turner, L. H. Discriminative classical conditioning in dogs paralyzed by curare can later control discriminative avoidance responses in the normal state. *Psychological Review*, 1962, *69*, 202–219.

Spear, N. E. Choice between magnitude and percentage of reinforcement. *Journal of Experimental Psychology*, 1964, *68*, 44–52.

Spear, N. E. & Hill, W. F. Adjustment to new reward: Simultaneous and successive contrast effects. *Journal of Experimental Psychology*, 1965, *70*, 510–519.

Spear, N. E. & Pavlik, W. B. Percentage of reinforcement and reward magnitude effects in a T maze: Between- and within-subjects. *Journal of Experimental Psychology*, 1966, *71*, 521–528.

Spear, N. E. & Spitzner, J. H. Simultaneous and successive contrast effects of reward magnitude in selective learning. *Psychological Monographs*, 1966, *80*, No. 618.

Spear, N. E. & Spitzner, J. H. PRE in a T-maze brightness discrimination within and between Ss. *Journal of Experimental Psychology*, 1967, *73*, 320–322.

Spence, K. W. The nature of discrimination learning in animals. *Psychological Review*, 1936, *43*, 427–449.

Spence, K. W. Analysis of the formation of visual discrimination habits in the chimpanzee. *Journal of Comparative Psychology*, 1937a, *23*, 77–100.

Spence, K. W. The differential response in animals to stimuli within a single dimension. *Psychological Review*, 1937b, *44*, 430–444.

Spence, K. W. Continuous versus non-continuous interpretations of discrimination learning. *Psychological Review*, 1940, *47*, 271–288.

Spence, K. W. An experimental test of the continuity and non-continuity theories of discrimination learning. *Journal of Experimental Psychology*, 1945, *35*, 253–266.

Spence, K. W. Mathematical theories of learning. *Journal of General Psychology*, 1952, *49*, 283–291.

Spence, K. W. *Behavior theory and conditioning*. New Haven: Yale University Press, 1956.

Spence, K. W. Cognitive and drive factors in the extinction of the conditioned eye blink in human subjects. *Psychological Review*, 1966, *73*, 445–458.

Spence, K. W., Haggard, D. F., & Ross, L. E. UCS intensity and the associative (habit) strength of the eyelid CR. *Journal of Experimental Psychology*, 1958, *55*, 404–411.

Spence, K. W., Homzie, M. J., & Rutledge, E. F. Extinction of the human eyelid CR as a function of the discriminability of the change from acquisition to extinction. *Journal of Experimental Psychology*, 1964, *67*, 545–552.

Spence, K. W. & Platt, J. R. UCS intensity and performance in eyelid conditioning. *Psychological Bulletin*, 1966, *65*, 1–10.

Spence, K. W. & Ross, L. E. A methodological study of the form and latency of eyelid responses in conditioning. *Journal of Experimental Psychology*, 1959, *58*, 376–381.

Spence, K. W. & Tandler, B. F. Differential eyelid conditioning under equated drive as a function of the reinforcing UCS. *Journal of Experimental Psychology*, 1963, *65*, 35–38.

Sperling, S. E. The ORE in simultaneous and differential reversal: The acquisition task, the acquisition criterion and the reversal task. *Journal of Experimental Psychology*, 1970, *84*, 349–360.

Spiegel, E. A. & Wycis, H. T. Chronic implantation of intracerebral electrodes in humans. In D. E. Sheer (Ed.), *Electrical stimulation of the brain*. Austin: University of Texas Press, 1961.

Spies, G. Food versus intracranial self-stimulation reinforcement in food-deprived rats. *Journal of Comparative and Physiological Psychology*, 1965, *60*, 153–157.

Spooner, A. & Kellogg, W. N. The backward conditioning curve. *American Journal of Psychology*, 1947, *60*, 321–334.

Squier, L. H. Autoshaping key responses with fish. *Psychonomic Science*, 1969, *17*, 177–178.

Stanley, W. C., Cornwell, A. C., Poggiani, C., & Trattner, A. Conditioning in the neonatal puppy. *Journal of Comparative and Physiological Psychology*, 1963, *56*, 211–214.

Steckle, L. C. & Renshaw, S. An investigation of the conditioned iridic reflex. *Journal of General Psychology*, 1934, *11*, 3–23.

Stein, L., Sidman, M., & Brady, J. V. Some effects of two temporal variables on conditioned suppression. *Journal of the Experimental Analysis of Behavior*, 1958, *1*, 153–162.

Stern, J. A., Das, K. C., Anderson, J. M., Biddy, R. L., & Surphlis, W. "Conditioned" alpha desynchronization. *Science*, 1961, *134*, 388–389.

Stern, R. M. Operant conditioning of spontaneous GSRs: Negative results. *Journal of Experimental Psychology*, 1967, *75*, 128–130.

Stern, R. M. Operant modification of electrodermal responses and/or voluntary control of GSR. Paper presented to Society for Psycho-physiological Research, New Orleans, 1970.

Stevenson, H. W. *Children's learning.* New York: Appleton-Century-Crofts, 1972.

Stewart, M. A., Stern, J. A., Winokur, G., & Fredman, S. An analysis of GSR conditioning. *Psychological Review*, 1961, *68*, 60–67.

Stollnitz, F. Spatial variables, observing responses, and discrimination learning sets. *Psychological Review*, 1965, *72*, 247–261.

Stolz, S. B. & Lott, D. F. Establishment in rats of a persistent response producing a net loss of reinforcement. *Journal of Comparative and Physiological Psychology*, 1964, *57*, 147–149.

Storms, L. H., Boroczi, G., & Broen, W. E., Jr. Punishment inhibits an instrumental response in hooded rats. *Science*, 1962, *135*, 1133–1134.

Strassburger, R. C. Resistance to extinction of a conditioned operant as related to drive level at reinforcement. *Journal of Experimental Psychology*, 1950, *40*, 473–487.

Strong, T. N., Jr. Activity in the white rat as a function of apparatus and hunger. *Journal of Comparative and Physiological Psychology*, 1957, *50*, 596–600.

Suboski, M. D., DiLollo, V., & Gormezano, I. Effects of unpaired preacquisition exposure of CS and UCS on classical conditioning of the nictitating membrane response of the albino rabbit. *Psychological Reports*, 1964, *15*, 571–576.

Surridge, C. T. & Amsel, A. Acquisition and extinction under single alternation and random partial reinforcement conditions with a 24-hour intertrial interval. *Journal of Experimental Psychology*, 1966, *72*, 361–368.

Surridge, C. T., Rashotte, M. E., & Amsel, A. Resistance to extinction of a running response after a small number of partially rewarded trials. *Psychonomic Science*, 1967, *7*, 31–32.

Surwit, R. S. & Poser, E. G. Latent inhibition in the conditioned electrodermal response. *Journal of Comparative and Physiological Psychology*, 1974, *86*, 543–548.

Sutherland, N. S. & Holgate, V. Two-cue discrimination learning in rats. *Journal of Comparative and Physiological Psychology*, 1966, *61*, 198–207.

Sutherland, N. S. & Mackintosh, N. J. *Mechansims of animal discrimination learning*. New York: Academic Press, 1971.

Swenson, R. P. & Hill, F. A. Effects of instruction and interstimulus interval in human GSR conditioning. *Psychonomic Science*, 1970, *21*, 369–370.

Switalski, R. W., Lyons, J., & Thomas, D. R. Effects of interdimensional training on stimulus generalization. *Journal of Experimental Psychology*, 1966, *72*, 661–666.

Switzer, S. A. Backward conditioning of the lid reflex. *Journal of Experimental Psychology*, 1930, *13*, 76–97.

Tait, R. W., Marquis, H. A., Williams, R., Weinstein, L., & Suboski, M. D. Extinction of sensory preconditioning using CER training. *Journal of Comparative and Physiological Psychology*, 1969, *69*, 170–172.

Tait, R. W., Simon, E., & Suboski, M. D. "Partial reinforcement" in sensory preconditioning with rats. *Canadian Journal of Psychology*, 1971, *25*, 427–435.

Tait, R. W. & Suboski, M. D. Stimulus intensity of sensory preconditioning of rats. *Canadian Journal of Psychology*, 1972, *26*, 374–381.

Tarpy, R. M. *Basic principles of learning*. Glenview, Illinois: Scott, Foresman, 1975.

Tarte, R. D. & Snyder, R. L. Barpressing in the presence of free food as a function of food deprivation. *Psychonomic Science*, 1972, *26*, 169–170.

Tarte, R. D. & Snyder, R. L. Some sources of variation in the barpressing versus freeloading phenomenon in rats. *Journal of Comparative and Physiological Psychology*, 1973, *84*, 128–133.

Taylor, C. *The explanation of behaviour*. London: Routledge & Kegan Paul Ltd., 1964.

Taylor, G. T. A limitation of the contrafreeloading phenomenon. *Psychonomic Science*, 1972, *29*, 173–174.

Teel, K. S. Habit strength as a function of motivation during learning. *Journal of Comparative and Physiological Psychology*, 1952, *45*, 188–191.

Terrace, H. S. Discrimination learning with and without "errors." *Journal of the Experimental Analysis of Behavior*, 1963a, *6*, 1–27.

Terrace, H. S. Errorless transfer of a discrimination across two continua. *Journal of the Experimental Analysis of Behavior*, 1963b, *6*, 223–232.

Terrace, H. S. Behavioral contrast and the peak shift: Effects of extended discrimination training. *Journal of the Experimental Analysis of Behavior*, 1966, *9*, 613–617.

Terrell, G. & Ware, R. Role of delay of reward in speed of size and form discrimination learning in childhood. *Child Development*, 1961, *32*, 409–415.

Teyler, T. J. Effects of restraint on heart-rate conditioning in rats as a function of US location. *Journal of Comparative and Physiological Psychology*, 1971, *77*, 31–37.

Theios, J. & Blosser, D. The overlearning reversal effect and magnitude of reward. *Journal of Comparative and Physiological Psychology*, 1965, *59*, 252–256.

Theios, J., Lynch, A. D., & Lowe, W. F., Jr. Differential effects of shock intensity on one-way and shuttle avoidance conditioning. *Journal of Experimental Psychology*, 1966, *72*, 294–299.

Thomas, D. R. The effects of drive and discrimination training on stimulus generalization. *Journal of Experimental Psychology*, 1962, *64*, 24–28.

Thomas, D. R. Stimulus selection, attention, and related matters. In J. H. Reynierse, (Ed.), *Current issues in animal learning*. Lincoln: University of Nebraska Press, 1970.

Thomas, D. R., Freeman, F., Svinicki, J. G., Burr, D. E. S., & Lyons, J. The effects of extra-dimensional training on stimulus generalization. *Journal of Experimental Psychology*, 1970, *83*, Monograph 1.

Thomas, D. R. & King, R. A. Stimulus generalizaton as a function of level of motivation. *Journal of Experimental Psychology*, 1959, *57*, 323–328.

Thomas, D. R. & Lopez, L. J. The effects of delayed testing on generalization slope. *Journal of Comparative and Physiological Psychology*, 1962, *55*, 541–544.

Thomas, D. R. & Mitchell, K. The role of instructions and stimulus categorizing in a measure of stimulus generalization. *Journal of the Experimental Analysis of Behavior*, 1962, *5*, 375–381.

Thomas, D. R., Ost, J., & Thomas, D. H. Stimulus generalization as a function of the time between training and testing procedures. *Journal of the Experimental Analysis of Behavior*, 1960, *3*, 9–14.

Thomas, D. R., & Williams, J. L. A further study of stimulus generalization following three-stimuli discrimination training. *Journal of the Experimental Analysis of Behavior*, 1963, *6*, 171–176.

Thomas, E. Role of postural adjustments in conditioning of dogs with electrical stimulation of the motor cortex as the unconditioned stimulus. *Journal of Comparative and Physiological Psychology*, 1971, *76*, 187–198.

Thomas, E. & Wagner, A. R. Partial reinforcement of the classically conditioned eyelid response in the rabbit. *Journal of Comparative and Physiological Psychology*, 1964, *58*, 157–159.

Thompson, R. F. Sensory preconditioning. In R. F. Thompson & J. F. Voss (Eds.), *Topics in learning and performance*. New York: Academic Press, 1972.

Thorndike, E. L. Animal intelligence: An experimental study of the associative process in animals. *Psychological Review Monographs*, 1898, *2*, No. 8.

Thorndike, E. L. *Animal intelligence*. New York: Macmillan, 1911.

Thorndike, E. L. *Educational psychology, Vol. II. The psychology of learning.* New York: Teachers College, Columbia University, 1913.

Thorndike, E. L. Reward and punishment in animal learning. *Comparative Psychology Monographs*, 1932a, *8*, No. 39.

Thorndike, E. L. *The fundamentals of learning*. New York: Teachers College, Columbia University, 1932b.

Thorpe, W. H. *Learning and instinct in animals*. London: Methuen, 1956.

Tighe, T. J. Effect of overtraining on reversal and extra-dimensional shifts. *Journal of Experimental Psychology*, 1965, *70*, 13–17.

Timberlake, W. & Allison, J. Response deprivation: An empirical approach to instrumental performance. *Psychological Review*, 1974, *81*, 146–164.

Tinbergen, N. *The study of instinct*. Oxford, England: Clarendon Press, 1951.

Tolman, E. C. *Purposive behavior in animals and men*. New York: Appleton-Century-Crofts, 1932.

Tolman, E. C. Principles of performance. *Psychological Review*, 1955, *62*, 315–326.

Topping, J. S. & Parker, B. K. Constant and variable delay of reinforcement effects on probability learning by pigeons. *Journal of Comparative and Physiological Psychology*, 1970, *70*, 141–147.

Trabasso, T. & Bower, G. H. *Attention in learning: Theory and research*. New York: John Wiley, 1968.

Tracy, W. K. Wave length generalization and preference in monochromatically reared ducklings. *Journal of the Experimental Analysis of Behavior*, 1970, *13*, 163–178.

Trapold, M. A. & Doren, D. G. Effect of noncontingent partial reinforcement on the resistance to extinction of a runway response. *Journal of Experimental Psychology*, 1966, *71*, 429–431.

Trapold, M. A. & Fowler, H. Instrumental escape performance as a function of the intensity of noxious stimulation. *Journal of Experimental Psychology*, 1960, *60*, 323–326.

Trapold, M. A. & Holden, D. Noncontingent partial reinforcement of running: A replication. *Psychonomic Science*, 1966, *5*, 449–450.

Trapold, M. A., Homzie, M., & Rutledge, E. Backward conditioning and UCR latency. *Journal of Experimental Psychology*, 1964, *67*, 387–391.

Trapold, M. A. & Spence, K. W. Performance change in eyelid conditioning as related to the motivational and reinforcing properties of the UCS. *Journal of Experimental Psychology*, 1960, *59*, 209–213.

Traupmann, K. L. Acquisition and extinction of an instrumental running response with single- or multiple-pellet reward. *Psychonomic Science*, 1971, *22*, 61–63.

Treichler, F. R. & Hall, J. F. The relationship between deprivation weight loss and several measures of activity. *Journal of Comparative and Physiological Psychology*, 1962, *55*, 346–349.

Trost, R. C. & Homzie, M. J. A further investigation of conditioned hunger. *Psychonomic Science*, 1966, *5*, 355–356.

Trowill, J. A. Instrumental conditioning of the heart rate in the curarized rat. *Journal of Comparative and Physiological Psychology*, 1967, *63*, 7–11.

Tulving, E. Theoretical issues in free recall. In T. R. Dixon & D. L. Horton (Eds.), *Verbal behavior and general behavior theory*. Englewood Cliffs, N.J.: Prentice-Hall, 1968.

Tyler, D. W. Wortz, E. C., & Bitterman, M. E. The effect of random and alternating partial reinforcement on resistance to extinction in the rat. *American Journal of Psychology*, 1953, *66*, 57–65.

Uexküll, J. von. *Streifzüge durch die Umwelten von Tieren und Menschen.* Springer: Berlin, 1934.

Underwood, B. J. Stimulus selection in verbal learning. In C. N. Cofer & B. S. Musgrave (Eds.), *Verbal behavior and learning*. New York: McGraw-Hill, 1963.

Underwood, B. J. & Richardson, J. Verbal concept learning as a function of instructions and dominance level. *Journal of Experimental Psychology*, 1956, *51*, 229–238.

Valenstein, E. S., Cox, V. C., & Kakolewski, J. W. Modificaton of motivated behavior elicited by electrical stimulation of the hypothalamus. *Science*, 1968a, *159*, 1119–1121.

Valenstein, E. S., Cox, V. C., & Kakolewski, J. W. The motivation underlying eating elicited by lateral hypothalamic stimulation. *Physiology and Behavior*, 1968b, *3*, 969–972.

Valenstein, E. S., Cox, V. C., & Kakolewski, J. W. The hypothalamus and motivated behavior. In J. T. Tapp (Ed.), *Reinforcement and behavior*. New York: Academic Press, 1969.

Valenstein, E. S., Kakolewski, J. W., & Cox, V. C. A comparison of stimulus-bound drinking and drinking induced by water deprivation. *Communications in Behavioral Biology*, 1968, *2*, 227–233.

Vandament, W. E. & Price, L. E. Primary stimulus generalization under different percentages of reinforcement in eyelid conditioning. *Journal of Experimental Psychology*, 1964, *67*, 162–167.

VanDercar, D. H., Elster, A. J., & Schneiderman, N. Heart-rate classical conditioning in rabbits to hypothalmic or septal US stimulation. *Journal of Comparative and Physiological Psychology*, 1970, *72*, 145–152.

VanDercar, D. H. & Schneiderman, N. Interstimulus interval functions in different response systems during classical discrimination conditioning of rabbits. *Psychonomic Science*, 1967, *9*, 9–10.

Van Twyver, H. B. & Kimmel, H. D. Operant conditioning of the GSR with concomitant measurement of two somatic variables. *Journal of Experimental Psychology*, 1966, *72*, 841–846.

Vaughn, E. & Fisher, A. E. Male sexual behavior induced by intracranial electrical stimulation. *Science*, 1962, *137*, 758–760.

Vincent, S. B. The function of the vibrissae in the behavior of the white rat. *Behavior Monographs*, 1912, *1*, No. 5.

Voigt, W. H. Conditioning the human pupillary response. *Perceptual and Motor Skills*, 1968, *26*, 975–982.

Vom Saal, W. & Jenkins, H. M. Blocking the development of stimulus control. *Learning and Motivation*, 1970, *1*, 52–64.

Voronin, L. G. & Sokolov, E. N. Cortical mechanisms of the orienting reflex, and its relation to the conditioned reflex. *Electroencephalography and Clinical Neurology*, 1960, Supplement 13.

Wagner, A. R. The role of reinforcement and nonreinforcement in an "apparent frustration effect." *Journal of Experimental Psychology*, 1959, *57*, 130–136.

Wagner, A. R. Conditioned frustration as a learned drive. *Journal of Experimental Psychology*, 1963, *66*, 142–148.

Wagner, A. R. Frustration and punishment. In R. N. Haber (Ed.), *Current research in motivation.* New York: Holt, Rinehart & Winston, 1966.

Wagner, A. R. Stimulus-selection and a "modified continuity theory." In G. H. Bower & J. T. Spence (Eds.), *The psychology of learning and motivation.* New York: Academic Press, 1969.

Wagner, A. R., Siegel, L. S., & Fein, G. G. Extinction of conditioned fear as a function of percentage of reinforcement. *Journal of Comparative and Physiological Psychology*, 1967, *63*, 160–164.

Wagner, A. R., Siegel, S., Thomas, E., & Ellison, G. D. Reinforcement history and the extinction of a conditioned salivary response. *Journal of Comparative and Physiological Psychology*, 1964, *58*, 354–358.

Wagner, A. R., Thomas, E., & Norton, T. Conditioning with electrical stimulation of the motor cortex: Evidence of a possible source of motivation. *Journal of Comparative and Physiological Psychology*, 1967, *64*, 191–199.

Walker, E. Eyelid conditioning as a function of intensity of conditioned and unconditioned stimuli. *Journal of Experimental Psychology*, 1960, *59*, 303–311.

Walters, G. C. & Rogers, J. V. Aversive stimulation of the rat: Long term effects on subsequent behavior. *Science*, 1963, *142*, 70–71.

Warden, C. J. & Diamond, S. A preliminary study of the effect of delayed punishment on learning in the white rat. *Journal of Genetic Psychology*, 1931, *39*, 455–461.

Warren, J. M. Additivity of cues in visual pattern discriminations by monkeys. *Journal of Comparative and Physiological Psychology*, 1953, *46*, 484–486.

Warren, J. M. Perceptual dominance in discrimination learning by monkeys. *Journal of Comparative and Physiological Psychology*, 1954, *47*, 290–292.

Warren, J. M. Evolution, behavior and the prefrontal cortex. *Acta Neurobiologiae Experimentalis*, 1972, *32*, 581–593.

Warren, J. M. & Baron, A. The formation of learning sets by cats. *Journal of Comparative and Physiological Psychology*, 1956, *49*, 227-231.

Warren, J. M. & Hall, J. F. Discrimination of visual patterns as a function of motivation and frequency of reinforcement. *Journal of Genetic Psychology*, 1956, *88*, 245-250.

Watson, J. B. The place of the conditioned reflex in psychology. *Psychological Review*, 1916, *23*, 89-117.

Watson, J. B. *Behaviorism*. New York: W. W. Norton, 1924.

Watson, J. B. & Rayner, R. Conditioned emotional reactions. *Journal of Experimental Psychology*, 1920, *3*, 1-14.

Wedell, C. H., Taylor, F. V., & Skolnick, A. An attempt to condition the pupillary response. *Journal of Experimental Psychology*, 1940, *27*, 517-531.

Wegner, N. & Zeaman, D. Strength of cardiac CRs with varying unconditioned stimulus durations. *Psychological Review*, 1958, *65*, 238-241.

Wehling, H. E. & Prokasy, W. F. Role of food deprivation in the acquisition of the observing response. *Psychological Reports*, 1962, *10*, 399-407.

Weinstein, L. Negative incentive contrasts with sucrose. *Psychonomic Science*, 1970, *19*, 13-14.

Weinstock, R. B. Preacquisition exploration of the runway in the determination of contrast effects in the rat. *Journal of Comparative and Physiological Psychology*, 1971, *75*, 107-115.

Weinstock, S. Resistance to extinction of a running response following partial reinforcement under widely spaced trials. *Journal of Comparative and Physiological Psychology*, 1954, *47*, 318-322.

Weinstock, S. Acquisition and extinction of a partially reinforced running response at a 24-hour intertrial interval. *Journal of Experimental Psychology*, 1958, *56*, 151-158.

Weiss, R. F. Deprivation and reward magnitude effects on speed throughout the goal gradient. *Journal of Experimental Psychology*, 1960, *60*, 384-390.

Wendt, G. R. An interpretation of inhibition of conditioned reflexes as competition between reaction systems. *Psychological Review*, 1936, *43*, 258-281.

Wescott, M. R. & Huttenlocher, J. Cardiac conditioning: The effects and implications of controlled and uncontrolled respiration. *Journal of Experimental Psychology*, 1961, *61*, 353-359.

White, C. T. & Schlosberg, H. Degree of conditioning of the GSR as a function of the period of delay. *Journal of Experimental Psychology*, 1952, *43*, 357-362.

Wickens, D. D. A study of voluntary and involuntary finger conditioning. *Journal of Experimental Psychology*, 1939, *25*, 127-140.

Wickens, D. D. Studies in response generalization in conditioning. I. Stimulus generalization during response generalization. *Journal of Experimental Psychology*, 1943, *33*, 221-227.

Wickens, D. D. Compound conditioning in humans and cats. In W. F. Prokasy (Ed.), *Classical conditioning: A symposium*. New York: Appleton-Century-Crofts, 1965.

Wickens, D. D., Allen, C. K., & Hill, F. A. Effects of instructions and UCS strength on extinction of the conditioned GSR. *Journal of Experimental Psychology*, 1963, *66*, 235-240.

Wickens, D. D., Born, D. G., & Wickens, C. Response strength to a compound conditioned stimulus as a function of the element interstimulus interval. *Journal of Comparative and Physiological Psychology*, 1963, *56*, 727-731.

Wickens, D. D. & Briggs, G. E. Mediated stimulus generalization as a factor in sensory pre-conditioning. *Journal of Experimental Psychology*, 1951, *42*, 197–200.

Wickens, D. D. & Cross, H. A. Resistance to extinction as a function of temporal relations during sensory preconditioning. *Journal of Experimental Psychology*, 1963, *65*, 206–211.

Wickens, D. D., Cross, H. A., & Morgan, R. M. CS termination and the response strength acquired by elements of a stimulus complex. *Journal of Experimental Psychology*, 1959, *58*, 363–368.

Wickens, D. D. Gehman, R. S., & Sullivan, S. N. The effect of differential onset time on the conditioned response strength to elements of a stimulus complex. *Journal of Experimental Psychology*, 1959, *58*, 85–93.

Wickens, D. D. & Harding, G. B. Effect of UCS strength on GSR conditioning: A within-subject design. *Journal of Experimental Psychology*, 1965, *70*, 152–153.

Wickens, D. D., Meyer, P. M., & Sullivan, S. N. Classical GSR conditioning, conditioned discrimination, and interstimulus interval in cats. *Journal of Comparative and Physiological Psychology*, 1961, *54*, 572–576.

Wickens, D. D., Nield, A. F., Tuber, D. S., & Wickens, C. Strength, latency, and form of conditioned skeletal and autonomic responses as functions of CS-UCS intervals. *Journal of Experimental Psychology*, 1969, *80*, 165–170.

Wickens, D. D., Schroder, H. M., & Snide, J. D. Primary stimulus generalization of the GSR under two conditions. *Journal of Experimental Psychology*, 1954, *47*, 52–56.

Wickens, D. D. & Wickens, C. D. A study of conditioning in the neonate. *Journal of Experimental Psychology*, 1940, *26*, 94–102.

Wickens, D. D. & Wickens, C. D. Some factors related to pseudo-conditioning. *Journal of Experimental Psychology*, 1942, *31*, 518–526.

Wike, E. L. (Ed.), *Secondary reinforcement: Selected experiments*. New York: Harper and Row, 1966.

Wike, E. L. Secondary reinforcement: Some research and theoretical issues. In W. J. Arnold & D. Levine (Eds.), *Nebraska symposium on motivation*. Lincoln: University of Nebraska Press, 1970.

Wike, E. L. & Barrientos, G. Selective learning as a function of differential consummatory activity. *Psychological Reports*, 1957, *3*, 225–258.

Wike, E. L., Cour, C., & Mellgren, R. L. Establishment of a learned drive with hunger. *Psychological Reports*, 1967, *20*, 143–145.

Wike, E. L. & Knutson, D. L. Learned drives based on hunger. *Psychological Record*, 1966, *16*, 297–303.

Wilcove, W. G. & Miller, J. C. CS-UCS presentations and a lever: Human autoshaping. *Journal of Experimental Psychology*, 1974, *103*, 868–877.

Williams, D. I. The overtraining reversal effect in the pigeon. *Psychonomic Science*, 1967, *7*, 261–262.

Williams, D. R. Classical conditioning and incentive motivation. In W. F. Prokasy (Ed.), *Classical conditioning*. New York: Appleton-Century-Crofts, 1965.

Williams, D. R. & Williams, H. Auto-maintenance in the pigeon: Sustained pecking despite contingent non-reinforcement. *Journal of the Experimental Analysis of Behavior*, 1969, *12*, 511–520.

Wilson, R. S. Cardiac response: Determinants of conditioning. *Journal of Comparative and Physiological Psychology*, 1969, *68*, 1–23.

Wise, R. A. Hypothalamic motivational system: Fixed or plastic neural circuits? *Science*, 1968, *62*, 377–379.

Wittig, A. & Wickens, D. D. Latency and magnitude of GSR as a function of interstimulus interval. *Journal of Experimental Psychology*, 1966, *71*, 466-467.

Wittlin, W. A. & Brookshire, K. H. Apomorphine-induced conditioned aversion to a novel food. *Psychonomic Science*, 1968, *12*, 217-218.

Wolfe, J. B. & Kaplon, M. D. Effect of amount of reward and consummative activity on learning in chickens. *Journal of Comparative and Physiological Psychology*, 1941, *31*, 353-361.

Wolfle, H. M. Time factors in conditioning finger-withdrawal. *Journal of General Psychology*, 1930, *4*, 372-378.

Wolfle, H. M. Conditioning as a function of the interval between the conditioned and the original stimulus. *Journal of General Psychology*, 1932, *7*, 80-103.

Woodard, W. T. Classical respiratory conditioning in the fish: CS intensity. *American Journal of Psychology*, 1971, *84*, 549-554.

Woods, P. J. Signaled escape and signaled punishment: Additional instrumental conditioning paradigms. *Bulletin of the Psychonomic Society*, 1973, *1*, 310-312.

Woods, P. J. A taxonomy of instrumental conditioning. *American Psychologist*, 1974, *29*, 584-596.

Woods, P. J. & Feldman, G. B. Combination of magnitude and delay of reinforcement in instrumental escape conditioning. *Journal of Comparative and Physiological Psychology*, 1966, *62*, 149-151.

Woods, S. C., Makous, W., & Hutton, R. A. A new technique for conditioned hypoglycemia. *Psychonomic Science*, 1968, *10*, 389-390.

Woods, S. C., Makous, W., & Hutton, R. A. Temporal parameters of conditioned hypoglycemia. *Journal of Comparative and Physiological Psychology*, 1969, *69*, 301-307.

Woodworth, R. S. *Dynamics of Behavior.* New York: Holt, 1958.

Woodworth, R. S. & Schlosberg, H. *Experimental psychology.* New York: Holt, 1954.

Wright, J. H. Test for a learned drive based on the hunger drive. *Journal of Experimental Psychology*, 1965, *70*, 580-584.

Wyckoff, L. B., Jr. The role of observing responses in discrimination learning. *Psychological Review*, 1952, *59*, 431-442.

Wyckoff, L. B., Sidowski, J. & Chambliss, D. An experimental study of the relationship between secondary reinforcing and cue effects of a stimulus. *Journal of Comparative and Physiological Psychology*, 1958, *51*, 103-109.

Wyers, E. J., Peeke, H. V. S., & Herz, M. J. Partial reinforcement and resistance to extinction in the earthworm. *Journal of Comparative and Physiological Psychology*, 1964, *57*, 113-116.

Yehle, A. L. Divergencies among rabbit response systems during three-tone classical discrimination conditioning *Journal of Experimental Psychology*, 1968, *77*, 468-473.

Yehle, A., Dauth, G., & Schneiderman, N. Correlates of heart-rate classical conditioning in curarized rabbits. *Journal of Comparative and Physiological Psychology*, 1967, *64*, 98-104.

Yelen, D. Magnitude of the frustration effect and number of training trials. *Psychonomic Science*, 1969, *15*, 137-138.

Yerkes, R. M. *The dancing mouse.* New York: Macmillan, 1907.

Yerkes, R. M. & Dodson, J. D. The relation of strength of stimulus to rapidity of habit-formation. *Journal of Comparative Neurology and Psychology*, 1908, *18*, 459-482.

Young, F. A. An attempt to obtain pupillary conditioning with infrared photography. *Journal of Experimental Psychology*, 1954, *48*, 62-68.

Young, F. A. Studies of pupillary conditioning. *Journal of Experimental Psychology*, 1958, *55*, 97-110.

Young, F. A. Classical conditioning of autonomic functions. In W. F. Prokasy (Ed.), *Classical conditioning*: A symposium. New York: Appleton-Century-Crofts, 1965.

Zeaman, D. Response latency as a function of the amount of reinforcement. *Journal of Experimental Psychology*, 1949, *39*, 466-483.

Zeaman, D., Deane, G., & Wegner, N. Amplitude and latency characteristics of the conditioned heart response. *Journal of Psychology*, 1954, *38*, 235-250.

Zeaman, D. & House, B. J. The role of attention in retardate discrimination learning. In N. R. Ellis (Ed.), *Handbook of mental deficiency*. New York: McGraw-Hill, 1963.

Zeaman, D. & Wegner, N. The role of drive reduction in the classical conditioning of an autonomically mediated response. *Journal of Experimental Psychology*, 1954, *48*, 349-354.

Zeaman, D. & Wegner, N. A. A further test of the role of drive reduction in human cardiac conditioning. *Journal of Psychology*, 1957, *43*, 125-133.

Zeigler, H. P. Electrical stimulation of the brain and the psychophysiology of learning and motivation. *Psychological Bulletin*, 1957, *54*, 363-382.

Zeiler, M. D. & Price, A. E. Discrimination with variable interval and continuous reinforcement schedules. *Psychonomic Science*, 1965, *3*, 299-300.

Zener, K. The significance of behavior accompanying conditioned salivary secretion for theories of the conditioned response. *American Journal of Psychology*, 1937, *50*, 384-403.

Zimmerman, D. W. Durable secondary reinforcement: Method and theory. *Psychological Review*, 1957, *64*, 373-383.

Zimmerman, D. W. Sustained performance in rats based on secondary reinforcement. *Journal of Comparative and Physiological Psychology*, 1959, *52*, 353-358.

Subject Index

Acquired drives, 221-226; based on aversive vs. appetitive states, 221-222; summary of studies, 223.

Acquired thirst drive, experimental work, 224-226.

Active avoidance learning, one way vs. two way, 332-333; intensity of aversive stimulation, 331-335; types of, 331-332; versus passive, 191.

Activity, as measure of drive, 208.

Adaptation level theory, as explanation for stimulus intensity effects, 80.

Addiction, as an acquired motive, 226.

Additivity of cues and learning, 365-366.

Aftereffects hypothesis, and partial reinforcement, 292.

Air deprivation, as a drive and role in discrimination learning, 329-332.

Alpha response, 39.

Alpha rhythm, conditioning the blocking of, 71-72.

American sign language, 203.

Amount of reinforcement, and learning with summary of studies, 298-303; and strength of secondary reinforcing stimulus, 247; intrasubject variability, 303-304;

shifts in and contrast effects, 304-311.

Amplitude, as a response measure, 32.

Anticipation, of goal object, 215.

Arousal, as a drive state, 220-221; types of, 221.

Asthma, conditioning of, 62.

Attention, 352-359; as a mentalistic construct, 352; definition, 352; role of innate factors, 356-357; role of learning, 357-359.

Auditory stimulus, as a reinforcer, 238.

Autonomic nervous system (ANS), classical conditioning of ANS responses, 48-62; independence from central nervous system, 433-435; instrumental learning of ANS responses with summary of studies, 413-436.

Autoshaping, 170-172.

Aversive stimulation, delay, 335-341; escape task difficulty, 329-331; frequency of stimulation, 328; intensity of and learning, 328-329; separation of drive and reinforcing function, 102-104.

Avoidance learning, active avoidance and delay of aversive stimulation, 338-340; active vs. passive, 191; difficulty of obtaining in laboratory, 202.

Name Index

Abbott, D. W., 84
Ackill, J. E., 170
Adamec, R., 146
Adams, C. K., 110, 114, 131
Adams, G., 59
Adams, J. A., 12
Adams, J. K., 39, 67
Adamson, R., 307, 311
Aderman, M., 305, 309
Adkins, J. W., 157
Albino, A. R., 72
Allen, C. K., 98, 129, 162
Allen, J. A., 154, 156
Allison, J., 221, 244, 245
Altomari, T. S., 216
Ames, H., 222, 225
Amsel, A., 213, 214, 216, 219, 290,
    291, 294, 295, 297, 298, 311,
    328
Anand, B. K., 265
Anderson, D. C., 154, 155, 157
Anderson, E. E., 209, 222, 223
Anderson, J. M., 72
Anderson, N. H., 138, 285
Andersson, B., 223, 265
Andrews, J. M., 299
Andrews, J. S., Jr., 157
Annau, Z., 59, 99, 100
Antonitis, J. J., 252
Appel, J. B., 258
Appley, M. H., 213, 238
Armus, H. L., 250, 280, 300
Arnold, W. J., 369

Ashida, S., 309
Ashton, A. B., 106
Asimow, A., 280
Ayres, J. J. B., 42
Azrin, N. H., 262

Backer, R., 237
Bacon, W. E., 287
Badia, P., 24, 51, 305, 308
Baer, P. E., 165, 167, 169
Bahrick, H. P., 146
Bailey, C. J., 265
Baker, L. E., 59
Baker, R. A., 379
Baker, T. W., 88
Ball, G. G., 372
Banuazizi, A., 431, 433
Barker, A. N., 240
Barker, L. M., 344
Barnes, G. W., 76, 238
Baron, A., 336, 337, 343
Baron, M. R., 410
Barrett, R. J., 218
Barrientos, G., 298
Barry, H., III, 11, 278, 279, 281
Bass, M. J., 81, 83
Batten, D. E., 279
Bauermeister, J. J., 243
Baxter, R., 419, 420, 424
Beaton, V. L., 368, 373
Beauchamp, R. D., 262, 329, 331
Bechterev, V. M., 69, 81
Beck, C. H., 372